URBAN TRANSPORTATION PLANNING
A Decision-Oriented Approach

McGraw-Hill Series in Transportation

Consulting Editor
Edward K. Morlok, *University of Pennsylvania*

Dickey: *Metropolitan Transportation Planning*
Hennes and Ekse: *Fundamentals of Transportation Engineering*
Horonjeff and McKelvey: *Planning and Design of Airports*
Hutchinson: *Principles of Urban Transport Systems Planning*
Kanafani: *Transportation Demand Analysis*
Meyer and Miller: *Urban Transportation Planning: A Decision-Oriented Approach*
Morlok: *Introduction to Transportation Engineering and Planning*
Quinn: *Design and Construction of Ports and Marine Structures*

URBAN TRANSPORTATION PLANNING
A Decision-Oriented Approach

Michael D. Meyer
Professor of Civil Engineering
Massachusetts Institute of Technology

Eric J. Miller
Professor of Civil Engineering
University of Toronto

McGraw-Hill, Inc.
New York   St. Louis   San Francisco   Auckland   Bogotá
Caracas   Lisbon   London   Madrid   Mexico City   Milan
Montreal   New Delhi   San Juan   Singapore
Sydney   Tokyo   Toronto

This book was set in Times Roman by Better Graphics.
The editors were Kiran Verma and J. W. Maisel;
the production supervisor was Marietta Breitwieser.
The drawings were done by ECL Art.

URBAN TRANSPORTATION PLANNING
A Decision-Oriented Approach

Copyright © 1984 by McGraw-Hill, Inc. All rights reserved.
Printed in the United States of America. Except as permitted under the United States
Copyright Act of 1976, no part of this publication may be reproduced or distributed in any
form or by any means, or stored in a data base or retrieval system, without the prior written
permission of the publisher.

10 11 12 13 14 15   BRBBRB   95 9 8 7 6 5 4 3 2 1 0

ISBN 0-07-041752-0

Library of Congress Cataloging in Publication Data

Meyer, Michael D.
    Urban transportation planning.

    (McGraw-Hill series in transportation)
    Includes index.
    1. Urban transportation—Planning.   I. Miller, Eric J.
II. Title.   III. Series.
HE305.M49   1984   388.4'068   83-25573
ISBN 0-07-041752-0

CONTENTS

Foreword		xi
Preface		xiii

Chapter 1 Urban Transportation Planning: Context and Definition   1

- 1-0 Introduction   1
- 1-1 The Context of Urban Transportation Planning   2
- 1-2 A Definition of Urban Transportation Planning   6
- 1-3 A Framework for Urban Transportation Planning   9
- 1-4 Basic Principles of Urban Transportation Planning   12
  - 1-4-1 The Spatial Configuration of a Transportation System   12
  - 1-4-2 The Technology of Urban Transportation   13
  - 1-4-3 The Institutional Foundation of the Urban Transportation System   15
- 1-5 Chapter Summary   17
- References   18

Chapter 2 Transportation in an Urban Setting: Characteristics of Urban Travel and of the Transportation System   20

- 2-0 Introduction   20
- 2-1 Characteristics of Urban Travel   21
  - 2-1-1 Trip Purpose   21
  - 2-1-2 The Temporal Distribution of Trip Making   23
  - 2-1-3 The Spatial Distribution of Trip Making   27
  - 2-1-4 Modal Distribution of Trip Making   27
  - 2-1-5 Travel Cost   32
- 2-2 Characteristics of Urban Transportation Systems and Their Impacts   37

	2-2-1	Transportation System and Facility Performance	37
	2-2-2	Provision of Mobility	44
	2-2-3	Construction and Operational Impacts of Transportation Systems and Facilities on the Activity System	51
	2-2-4	Land Use–Transportation Interaction	62
2-3		Chapter Summary	69
		Questions	71
		References	72

Chapter 3 Transportation Planning and Decision Making 77

3-0 Introduction	77
3-1 An Evolving Perspective on the Planning and Decision-Making Process	77
3-2 Conceptual Models of Decision Making	87
3-2-1 The Rational Actor Approach	88
3-2-2 The Satisficing Approach	89
3-2-3 The Incrementalist Approach	90
3-2-4 The Organizational Process Approach	91
3-2-5 The Political Bargaining Approach	92
3-3 The Elements of Decision Making: Development of a Transportation Planning Process	96
3-4 Characteristics of a Decision-Oriented Planning Process	98
3-5 Steps in a Transportation Planning Process	102
3-6 Chapter Summary	105
Questions	106
References	107

Chapter 4 Data Management and Diagnosis 110

4-0 Introduction	110
4-1 The Transportation Planning Data Base	110
4-1-1 Classification Schemes for Data Collection	113
4-1-2 Sampling Methods in Data Collection	115
4-2 Data Collection Techniques	122
4-2-1 Household Travel Behavior Surveys	122
4-2-2 Origin-Destination Surveys	125
4-2-3 Inventories	126
4-2-4 Highway and Transit Counts	127
4-2-5 Special Data Collection Efforts	128
4-3 Developing a Data Collection and Management Plan	130
4-4 The Transportation Planning Sociopolitical Information Base	136
4-4-1 Planning Goals and Objectives	138
4-4-2 Market Research Information	141
4-5 Monitoring Transportation Performance: Identification of Problems and Opportunities for Improvement	145
4-5-1 Diagnostic and Performance Measures	145
4-5-2 Public Input into the Problem Identification Process	150

4-6		Chapter Summary	152
		Questions	155
		References	157

Chapter 5 An Introduction to Analysis and Evaluation — 159

- 5-0 Introduction — 159
- 5-1 Analysis and Evaluation in the Planning Process — 161
  - 5-1-1 Analysis — 161
  - 5-1-2 Evaluation — 166
- 5-2 Economic Concepts Underlying Transportation Analysis and Evaluation — 167
  - 5-2-1 Consumer Travel Behavior — 168
  - 5-2-2 The Supply Curve — 170
  - 5-2-3 Equilibrium — 171
  - 5-2-4 Welfare Measures — 172
- 5-3 Chapter Summary — 173
  - Questions — 174
  - References — 175

Chapter 6 Urban Activity System Analysis — 177

- 6-0 Introduction — 177
- 6-1 Basic Concepts and the Role of Urban Activity Analysis in Transportation Planning — 178
- 6-2 Alternative Approaches to Land-Use Forecasting — 184
  - 6-2-1 Econometric Models: EMPIRIC — 185
  - 6-2-2 Heuristic Models: Lowry-Type Models — 188
  - 6-2-3 Simulation Models: The NBER Model and CAM — 192
  - 6-2-4 Scenarios — 201
  - 6-2-5 Summary Comments — 203
- 6-3 Assessment of Transportation Impacts on the Urban Activity System — 210
  - Transportation Control Plan Impacts on CBD Retailing Activity: The Denver Case — 211
- 6-4 Chapter Summary — 217
  - Questions — 219
  - References — 222

Chapter 7 Demand Analysis — 225

- 7-0 Introduction — 225
- 7-1 Demand Analysis and the Planning Process — 225
- 7-2 Definitions and Basic Concepts — 228
- 7-3 Simplified Demand Estimation Techniques — 232
  - 7-3-1 Trend Analysis — 233
  - 7-3-2 Elasticity-Based Models — 235
  - 7-3-3 Manual Techniques — 242
- 7-4 The Urban Transportation Modeling System — 244
  - 7-4-1 Trip Generation — 246
  - 7-4-2 Trip Distribution — 250

		7-4-3	Modal Split	251
		7-4-4	Assignment	254
		7-4-5	Summary Comments	256
	7-5	Transportation Choice Models		257
		7-5-1	Overview of Choice Theory	257
		7-5-2	Choice Model Applications	269
	7-6	Analyzing Transportation Demand		273
		7-6-1	Problem Definition	274
		7-6-2	Choice of Analysis Technique	275
		7-6-3	Data Collection	276
		7-6-4	Calibration	277
		7-6-5	Validation	280
		7-6-6	Forecasting	283
	7-7	Chapter Summary		283
		Questions		284
		References		288

Chapter 8 Supply Analysis   293

8-0	Introduction		293
8-1	The Role of Supply Analysis in Transportation Planning		294
8-2	Analysis of Transportation System Performance		299
	8-2-1	Basic Concepts	300
	8-2-2	Performance Analysis Techniques	303
	8-2-3	Performance Analysis Applications	317
8-3	Impact Models		338
	8-3-1	Air Quality Impact	338
	8-3-2	Noise Impact	342
	8-3-3	Fuel Consumption Impact	348
8-4	Cost Models		351
	8-4-1	Basic Concepts	353
	8-4-2	Transit Cost Models	355
	8-4-3	Automobile User Costs	360
8-5	Chapter Summary		361
	Questions		363
	References		368

Chapter 9 Transportation System and Project Evaluation   372

9-0	Introduction	372
9-1	A Framework for Evaluation	373
9-2	Measures of Effectiveness in Evaluation	378
9-3	Technical Concepts Underlying Economic Evaluation Methods	383
	9-3-1 Impacts of System and Project Alternatives: Characteristics of Benefit and Cost Measurement	384
	9-3-2 Impacts of System and Project Alternatives: Measurement of Benefit and Cost	387

		9-3-3	Economic Concepts of Discounting and Capital Recovery	394
		9-3-4	Treatment of Uncertainty in Evaluation	398
	9-4	Comparative Assessment Methods		403
		9-4-1	Single Objective Assessment Methods	403
		9-4-2	Multiobjective Assessment Methods	406
	9-5	Evaluation of Alternative Transit System Configurations: The Southeastern Wisconsin Example		410
	9-6	Evaluation of Transportation Corridors: The Baltimore Example		419
	9-7	Evaluation of Implemented Programs and Projects (Ex Post Evaluation)		426
	9-8	Chapter Summary		432
		Questions		433
		References		434

Chapter 10 Program and Project Implementation 437

	10-0	Introduction		437
	10-1	Characteristics of a Programming Process		437
	10-2	The Two Basic Components of Programming		446
		10-2-1	Setting Priorities for Project Selection	446
		10-2-2	Determining Availability of Funding	450
	10-3	Design of the Transportation Program Document		455
	10-4	Examples of Scheduling, Budgeting, and Establishing Priorities		457
		10-4-1	A Proposed Method for Preparing a Regional Transportation Improvement Program: The Case of Southeastern Wisconsin	457
		10-4-2	Network Phasing: The MARTA Subway System	462
		10-4-3	The Portland Transit Agency Financial Programming Process	466
	10-5	Chapter Summary		469
		Questions		470
		References		471

Appendixes 473

A	Chronology of Selected Federal Actions Related to Urban Transportation Planning	473
B	Environmental Impact Statements	478
C	The Delphi Method of Consensus Building	512

Index 515

FOREWORD

"The world moves into the future as a result of decisions not as a result of plans" (Kenneth E. Boulding, "Reflections on Planning: The Value of Uncertainty").

Boulding's assertion neatly captures the essence of managing in a rapidly changing environment. Whether it be a transportation agency, a major corporation, a university, or a small business, decisions are the catalyst of managed change. Does this imply that planning no longer has any relevance? No it does not. Rather it implies that planning must satisy the information requirements of the decision-maker and of the decision-making process.

Until recently, many have thought of planning only in terms of program-level or project-level techniques—particularly in public sector organizations. But planning should equally be viewed as a process that is inextricably linked to organizational decision-making. The planning process in this sense becomes rooted to the premises of the organization. The process by which organizational objectives are determined, and, in turn, how resources are acquired, used, and disposed of to achieve the objectives is increasingly relevant to chief executive officers. The world does move into the future as a result of decisions and the organization unable to decide issues promptly and properly will become obsolete—and in a short period of time.

My philosphy about what makes for effective planning has undergone much refinement. As Secretary of the Pennsylvania Transporation Department, I have had ample opportunity to experiment with planning concepts. As a result of our probing, planning is viewed increasingly as a generic management function. It is moving in the direction of making useful information available to decision-makers (at all levels) in an organized and timely manner—enabling the organization to understand where it is and where it is going.

Organizational-level planning (as a process) is distinguishing itself apart from program-level planning and, in turn, project-level planning. A particular challenge has been the integration of decision-making between the respective levels—the highest level providing direction within which program-level planning occurs. The planning process that is evolving in the Pennsylvania Transportation Department represents a sharp departure from traditional transportation planning in favor of managing and directing what is essentially a very large and complex business enterprise.

It is noteworthy that in a major performance audit of the Pennsylvania Transportation Department in 1983–1984—an effort of unprecedented scope involving some ten national accounting firms—the "planning process" was a point of particular focus. What the auditors looked for—and found—did not exist as recently as four years ago in my own organization. I suspect it may not exist in most public organizations in any explicit and visible way. They found a planning process which has served to strengthen and develop the Transportation Department as an organization and effectively meet the service needs of the citizen. This is the bottom line in our business.

As already noted, the planning process in the Pennsylvania Transportation Department has continually evolved in terms of its supportive role for decision-making. In this light, I am particularly excited to see a textbook that encompasses what I consider to be essential based on my personal experience. The philosophies of Professors Meyer and Miller are strikingly in accord with my experience in managing one of the country's largest and most diversified transportation organizations. The transportation planner and engineer will increasingly have to integrate their technical skills within a larger transportation decision process—a strategic process if you will. This approach will strengthen the links between these professionals. More importantly, our transportation services will be made more responsive to the communities they serve.

Thomas D. Larson, P.E., Ph.D.
Secretary of Tranportation
The Pennsylvania Department of Transportation

PREFACE

On April 1, 1980, a transit labor strike in New York City left close to 6 million daily riders without public transit service. Although the severity of the impact of this strike on individual travelers and on the city as a whole was lessened because of the adoption of effective contingency measures by city government and private firms, the strike did significantly disrupt the normal functioning of the city. Transit system shutdowns over the past several years have caused economic and mobility problems in numerous other cities as well. In the case of automobile transportation, serious gasoline shortages in the United States during the 1970s twice created significant inconvenience and disruption to urban lifestyles based largely on extensive use of the automobile. In each of these instances, a disruption to the normal operation of an urban transportation system demonstrated how dependent urban areas are on the ability of such a system to move people and goods in an effective and efficient manner.

Although public awareness of transportation, and its importance in the functioning of cities, is increased dramatically when the systems do not operate properly or when they produce negative impacts on some segment of a community, urban transportation systems are basic elements of urban areas and have been so recognized by engineers and planners for millennia. Such systems not only provide basic mobility and accessibility in urban areas, but the policies and programs that guide system development have been used to meet a wide variety of public policy objectives as well (e.g., enhancement of air quality, reduction of petroleum consumption, more equitable distribution of government services). This book explores the characteristics of urban transportation planning and develops a framework for such planning that reflects the requirements and constraints of the current, and potential future, planning environment.

During the past 20 years, several urban transportation planning textbooks have been written, each contributing some useful insight into the planning process and the techniques used. We feel, however, that there are several problems with using these texts to teach transportation planning. First, few texts have outlined and developed in understandable terms an underlying concept of urban transportation planning. What is the purpose of such planning? What is it trying to accomplish? In this book, we argue that a major purpose of planning is to inform decision making. If one accepts this premise, many interesting characteristics of a planning process and the techniques used in this process can be identified.

Second, most urban transportation planning texts have focused exclusively on the technical analysis framework which comprises much of planning. In a decision-oriented planning approach, one cannot ignore the relationship between technique, process, and decision making. Indeed, in such an approach to planning, one must understand the basic characteristics of the decision-making process (or processes). In Chapter 3 we provide the basis for developing such an understanding. In addition, in the chapters on analysis and evaluation, we begin each chapter by discussing how the particular analysis approaches fit into a decision-oriented planning process. In addition, this book expands the traditional analytic framework of planning by including within the decision-oriented model the process of identifying problems and the project programming and system monitoring functions.

Third, most transportation planning textbooks have been written with either engineering students in mind (and thus fairly quantitative treatment is given to analysis techniques) or aimed at planning students (and thus primary emphasis is given to process and the environmental context). We are trying an experiment in this book in that we are aiming at both groups. We are strongly convinced that engineering students should be exposed to the issues of process and policy that often surround urban transportation planning. Likewise, planning students should understand, and be conversant in, the techniques that are used in the analysis process. Clearly, there are different levels of detail which instructors might want to present in these areas, with the analysis chapters perhaps providing the greatest range of possibilities. We have structured the analysis chapters (5 through 8) in such a way that those wishing to understand the basic concepts and the characteristics of the related techniques can read the beginning sections of the chapter. Those wishing more detail can continue reading the subsequent sections. It should also be noted that while basic concepts of microeconomic theory and their relationship to transportation planning are described in this book, it is assumed that the student has some prior knowledge of economics.

These observations, in themselves, are sufficient justification for a new text on urban transportation planning. However, there is a fourth, and possibly most important, motivation for our writing this book. The environment of planning (and this includes the political, fiscal, technological, social, economic, and institutional dimensions) has changed so dramatically over the past 10 years that a new text, and a new perception of urban transportation planning, is needed. Although discussed in more detail in Chapter 1, these changes include:

- Pressures of fiscal austerity which reduce the levels of resources to invest in, and plan for, transportation systems
- Greater awareness of natural resource limitations (e.g., oil availability)
- Changing demographics of urban populations in terms of household characteristics (e.g., age, number of workers, number of children)
- Inflationary spirals that have greatly increased the cost of providing and using transportation

- Changing structure and function of cities, including continued suburbanization in some cases, the return of economic activity and population to city centers in others, and, in most cases, increasing numbers of subcenters of economic activities
- Increasing attention to the rehabilitation and maintenance of the existing transportation infrastructure
- Greater variety of transportation options, including variable work hours, ride sharing, preferential treatment for high-occupancy vehicles, parking management, zoning, and marketing
- Increasing participation in urban transportation of groups not traditionally associated with such planning (e.g., private employers and other private sector groups, enforcement agencies, social service agencies, developers, community groups, and lobbyists)
- Advances in technology, not only of transportation vehicles and their control systems, but also in the use of computers especially microcomputers in planning

These ''environmental'' characteristics of planning have such an important influence on the substance and form of urban transportation planning that the planning approach of today is substantially different, along many dimensions, from that of 10 years ago. These differences are highlighted throughout the book.

In summary, the basic premise of this book is that urban transportation planning, to be effective, must be related to the types of decisions that will be made in a particular problem area and thus to the decision-making process that will produce these decisions. This simple premise leads to rather significant conclusions about the characteristics of the planning process and of the techniques used within this process. Most important, this premise requires that the planner understand the decision-making process and the characteristics of this process that often inhibit the adoption of a ''rational'' approach to planning. It is for this reason that we emphasize throughout this book the linkage between decision making and planning, the relationship between techniques and process, and the difference between planning aimed solely at quantitative analysis versus planning oriented toward influencing decisions.

This book is divided into four major parts, each designed to provide the reader with an understanding of some aspect of the urban transportation planning process shown in Fig. 1-1. The first part, consisting of Chapters 1 and 2, presents a general background on urban transportation. Chapter 2 describes in detail the major characteristics of urban travel and of the urban transportation system with which every transportation planner should be familiar. Such characteristics not only indicate the types of problems and opportunities that can exist in the urban transportation system, they can also provide directions for possible solutions.

The second part, consisting of Chapters 3 and 4, presents an overview of decision making in the urban transportation environment and discusses the first step of the proposed transportation planning process—data management and diagnosis. The discussion in Chapter 3 of decision making is a critical section in this book. As has been stated before, the underlying premise of this book is that planning, to be effective, must be related to decision making. As shown in Chapter 3, however, there are many different types of decision-making structures, each implying a different approach to planning. In this chapter, five major conceptual models of decision making are presented, with one ultimately being chosen as the model most relevant to the generalized transportation decision-making environment. The characteristics of a planning process corresponding to this decision-making model are then outlined.

In Chapter 4 the types of data used in transportation planning are presented. Because data availability is often a critical concern to planners, a great deal of the chapter is devoted to the techniques that can be used in collecting these data. A distinction is made between data collected on transportation system performance and information obtained from market research techniques. The role of goals and objectives and the important information they provide to the planning process are highlighted.

The third part, Chapters 5 through 9, examines the analysis techniques that can be used in transportation planning. In each case, the use of these tools and the information they provide to decision makers are discussed in detail. Chapter 5 introduces the role of analysis and evaluation in transportation planning. The key concepts in transportation analysis are outlined, with special attention given to the analytical framework for such analysis.

Chapter 6 introduces the theoretical and methodological approaches to land use modeling and discusses how this information is used in transportation planning. Special emphasis is placed not only on comparing analytical approaches to understanding urban growth, but also in understanding where land use modeling fits into the urban transportation planning process.

Chapter 7 discusses demand analysis, the area of transportation analysis that has received the most attention in the past 10 years. Because the planning framework developed in this book is designed for application at different problem scales, a range of demand analysis techniques is presented. The range extends from simple demand estimation techniques (e.g., trend analysis) to more complex computer models.

Chapter 8 presents the analysis approaches that can be used to assess the performance and impacts of the transportation system. This discussion of transportation system supply analysis, like the discussion of demand analysis in the preceding chapter, includes a range of techniques that can be used at different problem scales.

Chapter 9 provides an overall framework for evaluation, discussing both the techniques that can be used to assess the relative worth of alternatives and the approach for presenting this information to decision makers. Guidelines for project and plan evaluation are outlined, and the measurement of benefits and costs is discussed. Evaluation is viewed in this chapter as a critical link between technical analysis and decision making. As such, the concepts presented are important for a decision-oriented approach to planning.

The fourth and final part is Chapter 10, which focuses on the implementation aspects of urban transportation planning. This chapter examines the process of project programming, with special emphasis given to the political nature of such programming. Issues related to scheduling, budgeting, and priority setting are illustrated with case study examples. Because the transportation program document is viewed as an important program management tool, it is discussed in some detail.

ACKNOWLEDGMENTS

As many before us have noted, writing a book such as this requires the cooperation and support of many individuals. To mention everyone who contributed to this undertaking would fill several pages and lengthen an already voluminous text. We have thus decided to limit our acknowledgments to those who inspired much of what we say, those who went out of their way to help us in our endeavor, and those who encouraged us during those times when the completion of the task seemed so far away.

Although not directly involved with our effort, numerous individuals have significantly influenced our thinking on the planning approach proposed in this book. These persons include Professor Alan Altshuler, Secretary of Transportation for Pennsylvania Tom Larson, Professor Marvin Manheim, Secretary of Transportation for Massachusetts Fred Salvucci, Professor Joe Schofer, and Professor Richard Soberman. In his own way, each has provided intellectually challenging examples of what planning is and how it can become more effective.

Other individuals have played significant roles as sounding boards and as reviewers of numerous drafts. Professors Ralph Gakenheimer, Lester Hoel, Joel Horowitz, Kumares Sinha, Bob Stammer (and his students at Vanderbilt University), Gerry Steuart, and Nigel Wilson deserve special thanks in this regard. Professor Ed Morlok, consulting editor for the McGraw-Hill Transportation Engineering Series, provided excellent feedback and, in several cases, showed the errors in our ways.

Other individuals have also played a direct support role in helping us finish the book. Special thanks go to Lisa Magnano and Diana Ali for typing the many drafts of the book. Two others merit special attention for their contribution. Eric Schreffler spent considerable time obtaining background information critical for developing many of the book's arguments. And without Peter Belobaba, the logic and presentation of the material would have suffered considerably. Peter's contribution to this book has been immeasurable.

We would like to thank the MIT Class of 1922 Fellowship Program, the Natural Sciences and Engineering Research Council of Canada University Research Fellowship Program, and the University of Toronto–York University Joint Program in Transportation for their financial and material support during the course of writing this book.

Our wives have also shown great patience and understanding in allowing us to devote much of our time to this book. Without their support, we could never have completed it.

Finally, our parents, to whom this book is dedicated, deserve an expression of gratitude that can never be expressed adequately on paper. By providing us with opportunities throughout our lives to mature and learn, they are part of this book in a way that no one could ever measure.

Michael D. Meyer
Eric J. Miller

URBAN TRANSPORTATION PLANNING
A Decision-Oriented Approach

CHAPTER
ONE

URBAN TRANSPORTATION PLANNING: CONTEXT AND DEFINITION

1-0 INTRODUCTION

An urban transportation system is a basic component of an urban area's social, economic, and physical structure. Not only does the design and performance of a transportation system provide opportunities for mobility, but over the long term, it influences patterns of growth and the level of economic activity through the accessibility it provides to land. In recent years, changes to the urban transportation system have also been treated by many public officials as a means of meeting an assortment of national and community objectives. For example, such changes have been motivated in some cities by the desire to improve air quality, enhance the economic viability of downtown areas, provide government services to the elderly and handicapped, and reduce the dependence on petroleum-based energy. Planning for the development or maintenance of the urban transportation system is thus an important activity, both for promoting the efficient movement of people and goods in an urban area and for maintaining the strong supportive role that transportation can play in attaining other community objectives.

The approach toward urban transportation planning presented in this book is different from the traditional transportation planning process which envisioned a comprehensive and complete "plan" as the major product of the process. Rather, the approach recognizes that, to be effective, planning must be an integral part of the decision-making process. The *product* of planning can be any form of communication with decision makers that provides useful information in identifying alternative actions and selecting among them.

In the first section of this chapter, the context for this planning approach is presented, with special attention given to the trends over the past decade that have influenced its development. In the following two sections, a definition of urban transportation planning and the major characteristics of this approach are discussed. In the final section, several principles that are fundamental to urban transportation are introduced and discussed briefly.

1-1 THE CONTEXT OF URBAN TRANSPORTATION PLANNING

Urban transportation systems have been the focus of numerous planning efforts over the past 50 years. Before 1960, meeting the transportation needs of most urban areas was generally interpreted as providing the necessary highway capacity to accommodate an increasing demand for automotive mobility. The purpose of planning was defined as facilitating "rational" decision making by developing comprehensive plans for the urban area. These comprehensive plans outlined, in some detail, a pattern for urban development 20 to 25 years into the future. During the past 20 years, however, disenchantment with these comprehensive plans has grown. Such plans were perceived as inadequate for meeting the needs of decision makers and in general were considered unresponsive, myopic, and slow in meeting societal needs [Boyce et al., 1970; Hill, 1973; Greenburger et al., 1976; Altshuler, 1979].

By the late 1960s many urban areas began to experience citizen unrest over the disruption caused by the construction and operation of the large-scale facilities that resulted from these comprehensive plans. This dissatisfaction with the results of planning raised serious questions about the underlying attitudes of the professionals responsible for planning and generated debate over the implicit assumptions used in the analysis approach. In many cases, new planning studies were initiated to "open" the process to affected interests and other community groups [Gakenheimer, 1976; Pill, 1978]. Instead of developing plans primarily to accommodate auto use, the challenge for transportation planners became one of designing highway and transit facilities to provide desired levels of mobility in a fashion complementary to the surrounding urban area.

The image of comprehensive transportation planning that emerged in this decade was still one dominated by regionwide transportation plans. Further, these comprehensive planning efforts were based on many implicit assumptions about the future availability of gasoline, transportation technology, economic stability, and urban demographics that, by the end of the 1970s, had begun to change in significant ways. The important political, economic, and social trends that have evolved over the past 10 years, which have in turn affected transportation planning, include the following:

1. *Fiscal austerity as a theme of government policy.* The decade of the 1960s was an era of expanding public programs in many areas—housing, health care, social welfare, and transportation. During the 1970s, however, many of these programs were cut back because of increased pressure on government to reduce spending. Transportation investment did not escape this pressure for government austerity.

In response, many transportation officials began to examine more carefully transportation actions that could improve the transportation system in a less costly fashion than major capital investment. The result was the development in the 1970s of an increased emphasis on managing the existing transportation system more efficiently [Gakenheimer and Meyer, 1979].

2. *Increased awareness of an uncertain future.* The gasoline shortages in the United States during the last decade were a serious shock to many transportation planners who had assumed in their planning methodology and plans that gasoline would continue to be cheap and easily obtained. Whereas planners had once confidently forecasted future land use and then predicted the travel demand resulting from this spatial configuration, unexpected trends and developments in terms of energy availability, economic stability, and transportation technologies served to highlight how uncertain the future really is. This increased uncertainty influenced transportation planning in two major ways. First, new methods were developed to deal with the uncertainty of planning forecasts and the predicted impacts of alternative projects. These methods ranged from the multiple use of analysis tools with different assumed values of input parameters to extensive "futures" conferences where alternative scenarios of the future were developed. Second, project implementation began to be considered in stages, where only the first stage was fully detailed because of the greater certainty of the project characteristics. Later stages were designed with less detail to allow flexibility in responding to future circumstances.

3. *A changing perspective on the role of the automobile.* The automobile has dominated urban transportation in North America for the past several decades. It is likely that, given present trends, the automobile will continue to be the most significant mode of urban travel in the foreseeable future. However, the characteristics of automobile use, and of the automobile itself, will likely be quite different from previous years. From a technological perspective, the physical characteristics of the automobile already differ from previous models. There is a significant trend toward the use of smaller, more fuel-efficient automobiles. In 1970, for example, subcompacts represented only 2 percent of the total domestic United States automobile sales, and the standard model accounted for 37 percent, the largest percentage car type of United States sales. By 1981, the percentage of subcompacts sold had risen to 17 percent, while the sales of standard models had fallen to 10 percent of the market [*Automotive News*, 1982]. Recent studies have indicated that this popularity of smaller cars is likely to continue in future years [Secretary of Transportation, 1981; Meyer and Gomez-Ibanez, 1981].

Perhaps even more important than this evolution in technology is the change in patterns of automobile use. The major forces determining auto ownership and use include the income and demographic characteristics of consumers, government policy toward automobile use, and the cost of automobiles relative to other goods and to other forms of transportation. In responding to these forces, automobile commuters and organizations have, in some instances, resorted to new forms of automobile use, much different from those found 20 years ago. A good example of this is the increased importance of ride-sharing programs during the fuel shortages of the 1970s and in response to the subsequent increasing cost of gasoline.

With the changing automobile technology and increasing costs of auto ownership and operation, other forms of auto use could also evolve in future years. For example, with smaller, lighter, and more fuel-efficient cars, low-performance vehicles intended solely for local, intrametropolitan travel—the so-called urban cars—could become an important form of transportation. In addition, new forms of auto ownership (e.g., neighborhood-based auto rental agencies and joint auto ownership) could play an increasingly important role in dense urban areas [Wolfe and Miller, 1982].

This changing perspective on the role of the automobile could in turn have a significant impact on the analysis techniques used in transportation planning. Such techniques are currently based on generally common assumptions concerning auto ownership and auto use. These assumptions might have to be changed dramatically should the role of the automobile change.

4. *Changing household characteristics.* Much of the comprehensive transportation planning methodology developed and applied during the past two decades has been based on a specific set of assumptions concerning household travel behavior. Several characteristics of the household, however, have changed significantly over the past several years. Most important, the composition of the "household" has changed dramatically. Between 1970 and 1980, for example, 44 percent of the growth in United States households consisted of new single-person households. Single-parent households with children represented another 25.5 percent of the increase. The number of new households formed by single elderly individuals and by women as heads of households represented a significant portion of the total number of new households formed. The percentage of women in the labor force increased from 42.6 percent in 1970 to 51.1 percent in 1980, according to the latest United States census. The implication of these changes for transportation planning is that the variables once used to explain travel behavior might no longer be relevant. Travel models based on the assumption of a multiple-occupant household headed by a male could, in many cases, be outdated. Also, whereas transportation planners were once concerned with the ability of the transportation system to accommodate work trips, other types of trip making could become an important element of the planning process. For example, between 50 and 60 percent of the trip making in an average North American city during the day is nonwork-related.

5. *A broadening of the roles for transportation.* For many years, the only agencies directly involved with urban transportation planning were those responsible for the planning and implementation of transportation actions in the public sector. Not surprisingly, transportation investment was considered mainly with respect to its impact on the users of the transportation system and on private businesses, an important constituent group in the political process. During the 1970s, however, environmental groups, employers, public interest groups, and many others began to view transportation as a means of achieving a variety of objectives. Transportation policy began to play an important supportive role to other policy initiatives. Legislation and regulations formalized these supportive roles in the planning

process. In the United States, good examples of this supportive role include the use of transportation controls to improve air quality, investment in transportation to catalyze economic and urban revitalization, and improvements to the quality of life through transportation actions (e.g., auto restricted zones). Transportation planning today must therefore be viewed in a much broader context than it has in the past. Such planning must be closely tied to land use zoning regulations and financing mechanisms, with a greater sensitivity accorded to environmental effects and impacts on different groups in a community. Also, greater interest should be given to the role that nonpublic providers of transportation can plan in an urban area.

6. *Moving away from technological solutions.* During the 1960s technological innovation was considered by many to hold the key to solving many kinds of public problems. A 1968 study by the United States government, for example, evaluated future technologies for urban transportation and made several optimistic conclusions about the development and implementation of technologies such as automatic people movers, driverless cars and buses, and vehicle control mechanisms [U.S. Department of Housing and Urban Development, 1968]. Major advances in the use of such hardware have either not materialized or have been found ineffective. However, some innovations that represent new ways of using existing hardware (e.g., car pools and van pools) have been tried and found effective in many situations.

Also, new types of transportation service arrangements have been implemented, new institutional configurations have been formed, and new uses of existing technologies have been explored. For example, one of the more recent institutional developments is the formation of employer associations whose major purpose is to coordinate employee transportation [Schreffler and Meyer, 1983]. Public agencies often participate in association meetings, but most, if not all, of the service provision is arranged by the employers themselves. The importance of this trend away from technological solutions is that there is now a wide range of physical and institutional options that can be considered by transportation planners.

7. *Continuing suburbanization of urban areas.* One of the significant trends affecting the performance of the transportation system during the last 50 years has been the growth of suburban areas. Between 1910 and 1980, the percentage of the metropolitan area's population accounted for by the central city dropped from 68 percent to 39 percent in New York City, 85 percent to 36 percent in Cleveland, and 77 percent to 36 percent in Detroit. In the 1960s, New York City lost 9.7 percent of its jobs, while its suburbs gained 24.9 percent; in Los Angeles the respective figures were 10.8 and 16.2 percent; and in Chicago 13.9 and 64.4 percent [*Congressional Quarterly,* 1978]. A recent study estimated that the suburban population of the United States will be 39 percent of the urban population in 2000, an increase of 9 percent from 1975 [Harbridge House, 1980].

Not only have suburban areas grown in population, but in many suburban areas dense developments of retail, service, office, and residential activities have formed "mini downtowns" [Baerwald, 1982; Noguchi, 1982]. These activity centers create transportation problems relating not only to internal circulation but also to movements from one center to another. Thus, while the concern for suburban to central city travel will still exist, increasing interest in intrasuburban and intersuburban travel will present new challenges to transportation planners. New types of transportation services (e.g., demand-responsive minibus service) and new types of institutional arrangements (e.g., private employer transportation associations) could become important considerations.

8. *Increasing attention to system rehabilitation and maintenance.* For many years, highway and transit systems were constructed and expanded with little attention given to maintaining and rehabilitating highways and transit lines already in existence. Indeed, reducing the percentage of budgets used for transportation purposes and deferred maintenance created, by the late 1970s, a serious crisis in maintaining acceptable levels of service on many freeways and subway lines. For example, a 1981 report of the Secretary of Transportation to the U.S. Congress indicated that [U.S. Congress, 1981]:

The amount of interstate system pavement needing immediate replacement doubled from approximately 4 percent in 1975 to 9 percent in 1978.

Nearly 28 percent of all urban interstate mileage was heavily congested during daily peak-demand periods in 1981, compared to 23 percent in 1975.

One bridge in six on the federal-aid primary system in urban areas was considered deficient.

Over 95 percent of the existing mileage on the federal-aid urban system (consisting of 62 percent of all nonlocal urban highway and street mileage) will require repairing or pavement reconstruction by 1995.

The Congress did enact a law in 1982 that provided increased revenues (through an increase in the gasoline tax) to state transportation agencies for construction and rehabilitation. It will take some time, however, before the transportation system condition in many urban areas reaches acceptable levels. It seems likely, therefore, that maintenance and rehabilitation will be an important concern of transportation planners into the 1990s.

These trends indicate that the traditional image of transportation planning as a technical process focusing mainly on the transportation system is no longer appropriate. Many of the social and economic trends of the past decade also suggest that the underlying assumptions of the methodologies used in this technical process may no longer be valid. A new perspective on the transportation planning process, and how it responds to the new demands of the decision-making process, is needed.

1-2 A DEFINITION OF URBAN TRANSPORTATION PLANNING

There is not one, but many transportation planning processes under way in an urban area at any given time, each defined at a different level of complexity and purpose. For example, while transit planners examine alternative service configurations, traffic engineers might be identifying problems on the highway network, regional planners might be looking at urban development patterns and the provision of public services, individual employers might be considering alternative employee transportation programs, and social service agencies might be examining transportation options to improve delivery of their services to the general public.

With different groups and organizations concurrently conducting transportation planning activities in an urban area, the requirements of these planning efforts will vary from one group to the next. However, a primary purpose of each planning effort is the same in each case: to generate information useful to decision makers on the consequences of alternative transportation actions. The definition of urban transportation planning used in this book will focus on this basic purpose and on the following propositions suggested by Boulding [1974].

1. *The world moves into the future as a result of decisions, not as a result of plans.* Planning can only be effective if it provides useful information to those who must make decisions. It must not only provide information that is desired by decision makers, but also provide information that is needed to understand fully the short- and long-term consequences of alternative decision choices as well.
2. *All decisions involve the evaluation of alternative images of the future and the selection of the most highly valued feasible alternatives.* Decision making thus involves two major elements: an *agenda* consisting of alternative images of the future with some conception of the relationship between present action and future societal directions, and a *valuation scheme* which outlines preferences for the characteristics of likely decision outcomes. In the case of urban transportation, this valuation scheme is often intricately tied to societal values and goals as expressed in the political decision-making process.
3. *Evaluation and decision strategies, and the quality of decisions in general, depend on the degree of uncertainty associated with the items on the agenda.* Decisions regarding actions that will occur in the future are based on implicit and explicit assumptions about the likely consequences of alternative decision options and the future state of the urban area in which the decisions will be implemented. Thus, the greater degree of uncertainty associated with these assumptions, the higher the value that should be placed on decisions which leave future options open.
4. *The products of planning should be designed to increase the chance of making better decisions.* Planning should examine a wide range of agendas, the values and objectives underlying the decision, past decisions that were not considered to be effective, failures of past predictions, and early warning signals.
5. *The result of planning is some form of communication with decision makers.* The products of planning are only a small part of the information input to decision makers. To increase the usefulness of this planning information, some effort must be put into "adapting planning products and processes more precisely to the substantive and format requirements of those individuals who are potential users of these products." [de Bettencourt et al., 1981].

A decision-oriented approach to urban transportation planning should thus focus on the information needs of decision makers and should recognize the often limited capability of individuals not familiar with technical analysis to interpret the information that is produced. The underlying assumption of such an approach to planning is that the relevant decision makers can indeed be identified. In the context of urban transportation planning, decision makers are those individuals faced with the problem of allocating resources among competing needs to achieve certain ends. Decision makers can thus include elected officials who set general policies for resource allocation and who appropriate funds for the implementation of specific actions, transportation agency managers responsible for operating and maintaining components of the transportation system, private-sector managers who must determine the most efficient routing of urban commodity shipments, and corporate officials concerned with employee transportation.

Before transportation planning is defined, one statement made above should be reemphasized. The approach to urban transportation planning discussed above is based on the information needs of decision makers. It is important that planning provide not only the information *desired* by decision makers, but also information *needed* to provide a more complete understanding of the problem and of the implications of different solutions.

Given these considerations, urban transportation planning can be defined as the process of:

1. *Understanding* the types of decisions that need to be made.
2. *Assessing* opportunities and limitations of the future.
3. *Identifying* the short- and long-term consequences of alternative choices designed to take advantage of these opportunities or respond to these limitations.
4. *Relating* alternative decisions to the goals and objectives established for an urban area, agency, or firm.
5. *Presenting* this information to decision makers in a readily understandable and useful form.

Several concepts in this definition merit special attention. First, transportation planning is considered as a *process*. Such a process includes careful consideration of problem definition, incorporation of alternative viewpoints of analysis and evaluation, development of a goals and objectives statement, and completion of the technical analysis needed to determine impacts of alternative decisions. It should be emphasized that technical analysis, considered by many to be synonymous with planning, is just one component of the planning process.

Second, transportation planning should assess *opportunities* as well as limitations of the future. The traditional approach to planning focuses most attention on identifying where "problems" will occur in the transportation system. Clearly, such a focus is an important element of planning. However, there might be opportunities in the existing operation of the transportation system for significant improvements to be made. For example, even though bus routes in an urban transit network might be operating at acceptable performance levels, reorganizing the structure of the service might result in more efficient operations while maintaining, or even improving, service. Planning should thus include a proactive approach to issue definition.

Third, transportation planning should include a *long-range* and *short-range* perspective. The long-range planning component is a continuing activity that represents a statement of need and policy direction, thereby providing a context for periodic transportation decisions to be made in the near term. The long-range component of a transportation plan, to be relevant to decision makers, must be both flexible and responsive in scale (level of detail) and scope (alternatives and impacts considered) to the kinds of decisions likely to be made. The short-range component takes into account the more immediate needs of transportation system performance. The relationship between these two components is also a critical concern in the transportation planning process. That is, the extent to which short-term decisions might change the image of future system design and performance (and force or forgo future options), and how anticipated changes in an urban area might influence the effectiveness of shorter-term decisions, are important relationships that need to be addressed in transportation planning.

Fourth, the evaluation of alternative choices is directly related to the *goals and objectives* established for the planning process. As in Boulding's valuation scheme, goals and objectives form the basis of the measures of effectiveness used in evaluation. Because goals and objectives are intricately tied to values, careful consideration should be given to whose values are represented in a statement of goals and objectives, and efforts should be made to provide community input into the development of such a statement.

Finally, by far the most important *decision makers* for urban transportation planning are the elected and appointed government officials who must provide and maintain a transportation system that meets the mobility and accessibility needs of their constituents. At the same time, the officials must consider the equity implications of pursuing one program over another. The types of transportation decisions facing these officials include expanding or modifying the existing transportation infrastructure and changing the internal management structure of transportation agencies.

In summary, a decision-oriented approach to urban transportation planning focuses as much attention on the process of planning as it does on the techniques. In some ways, this approach requires the planner to reverse the traditional sequence of planning (i.e., proceeding from problem definition to a final decision) by first understanding the requirements of the final decision and then identifying the information and analysis needed to produce it. The information produced by the planning process can in this way be related to the needs of the decision-making process.

1-3 A FRAMEWORK FOR URBAN TRANSPORTATION PLANNING

A general framework for urban transportation planning that reflects the need for a decision-oriented approach is shown in Fig. 1-1. Although a more detailed explanation of this framework and of the characteristics of a decision-oriented planning process is included in subsequent chapters, several characteristics of this process merit special attention at this point. For example, perhaps the most significant difference between this framework and more traditional ones is that the planning process proposed in Fig. 1-1 encompasses a broad set of activities. To some, planning stops with the analysis and evaluation step, with program and/or project implementation and operations or monitoring (i.e., assessing how well the system is performing from a user's perspec-

10 URBAN TRANSPORTATION PLANNING

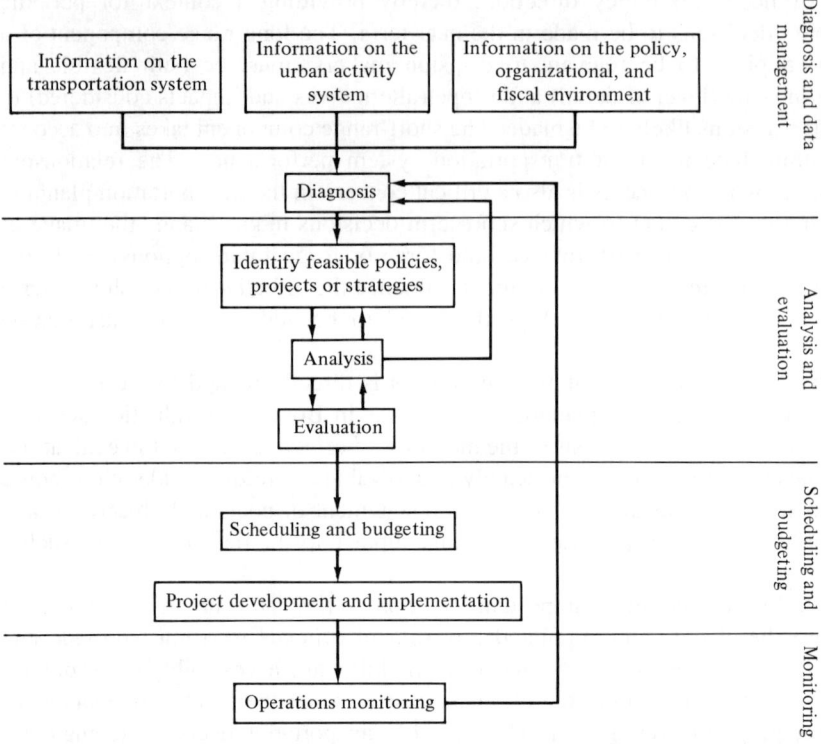

Figure 1-1 Steps in an urban transportation planning process.

tive) occurring outside the planner's purview. This structure has been adopted by most of the institutions established for transportation planning and/or operations in urban areas—there are *planning* agencies to develop plans and *implementing* agencies to build and operate facilities. One of the major problems with planning during the past decades, however, has been this separation of planning and implementation, resulting in a poor record of plan implementation. For planners, this implies the need to be aware of the requirements of the entire process, from initial data gathering activities to actual project operation.

A second characteristic of the suggested planning framework is the different types of data used for planning. Most urban areas already have a large (though generally outdated) data base of transportation system characteristics and an inventory of land use characteristics (generally even more outdated). As shown in Fig. 1-1, this type of information still provides important input into the transportation planning process. However, information relating to the policy, organizational, and fiscal environment of transportation decision making is also an important input. This information can provide planners with a better understanding of the problems and opportunities for improvement in the existing transportation system. Most important, information on the organizational and fiscal state of the transportation program can provide useful input for an assessment of the implementation feasibility of alternative projects, an understanding of the organizational requirements of other agencies, and an awareness of likely competition for investment funds.

A third characteristic of this transportation planning process relates to the sequential nature of the steps shown in Fig. 1-1. Frequently, there is overlap between the many tasks involved. For example, the scheduling and budgeting process may have to conform to deadlines established by local government requirements or process regulations from higher levels of government. Thus, the project budgeting activity may occur at specific times regardless of the stage at which the overall project development process may be. On the other hand, there are some activities, such as analysis and system monitoring, that should occur on a continuing basis. In any given planning agency, all of these steps will be occurring at one time or another. The overall flow of the process, however, must keep pace with decision making for the results of planning to be useful to decision makers. All too often, the planning process is delayed because of disagreements over the choice of analysis techniques or because of the need to collect a large amount of data. In such cases, decisions are made before the planning process is able to provide useful information.

A final characteristic of the planning framework proposed here is the feedback provided from the analysis and monitoring steps to the diagnosis step. The analysis task is thus undertaken not only to assess the consequences of a decision, but also to understand better the definition of the problem, which may require changing this definition based on preliminary analysis results. The monitoring step is really a function that should occur on a periodic basis. It serves as a major source of information on the performance of the transportation system, and thus is an important indicator of system deficiencies or opportunities for improvement [Meyer, 1980].

The planning process presented in Fig. 1-1 is offered to the reader as a general framework for transportation planning. This framework can be applied in establishing a more detailed process for specific problem areas or for different planning contexts, as a transportation system planning process, a subarea planning study, or a site-specific planning process. To be effective, however, this process must reflect the needs and characteristics of the relevant decision-making process. This implies an approach to planning that explores a wide variety of actions and is capable of responding quickly, and in some detail, to questions posed by decision makers.

The proposed framework makes new demands on the transportation planner. The role of the planner in this process ideally requires a mix of analytical and organizational skills. Such skills can include [Transportation Research Board, 1980]:

1. Feeling comfortable serving multiple objectives
2. Having the ability to cross the lines between the public and private sectors
3. Having the ability to operate in complex political environments or catalyze political coalitions to achieve implementation
4. Having the technical ability to identify and define problems and to assess alternative options
5. Providing expertise in a politically acceptable way
6. Operating at different scales and in response to different constituencies

7. Visualizing the need for, and ensuring the provision of, a variety of different services designed to meet different needs
8. Having the ability to accomplish all of this quickly and effectively

These characteristics represent a significant departure from the more traditional technical role assigned to planners. Yet such characteristics are necessary for planners to be effective in the rapidly changing environment of transportation decision making.

1-4 BASIC PRINCIPLES OF URBAN TRANSPORTATION PLANNING

In subsequent chapters, the characteristics of the planning process outlined in Fig. 1-1 will be described in more detail. The major steps in this process will serve as chapter topics, with special emphasis given to how these steps fit into an overall framework for decision-oriented planning. This relationship will receive particular attention in the chapters focusing on analysis and evaluation, topics that in the past have often been considered synonymous with planning. Before discussing the major steps in planning, however, it is first necessary to introduce the reader to the basic characteristics of urban transportation systems and of urban travel (which is done in the next chapter) and to the underlying concepts of decision making (which is done in Chap. 3).

There are several basic concepts about an urban transportation system that should be kept in mind when reading the following chapters. Although these concepts will be further discussed and developed in subsequent sections, it is useful to introduce them here to act as a point of departure for the rest of the book. Most important, a transportation system in an urban area is defined as consisting of the facilities and services that allow travel throughout the region, providing opportunities for: (1) *mobility* to residents of an urban area and movement of goods and (2) *accessibility* to land. Given this definition, an urban transportation system can be further characterized by three major components: the spatial configuration that permits travel from one location to another; the transportation technologies that provide the means of moving over these distances; and the institutional framework that provides for the planning, construction, operation, and maintenance of system facilities.

1-4-1 The Spatial Configuration of a Transportation System

One way to describe the spatial dimension of an urban transportation system is to consider the characteristics of individual trips from an origin to a destination. For example, a trip can consist of several types of movement undertaken to achieve different objectives. Travelers leaving home might use a local bus system to reach a suburban subway station (a trip collection process), proceed through the station to the subway platform (a transfer process), ride the subway to a downtown station (a line-haul process), and walk to a place of employment (a distribution process). Similarly, one can view a home-to-work trip by car as consisting of similar segments, with the local street system providing the trip collection process, a freeway providing the line-haul capability, a parking lot in the central business district serving as a transfer point, and walking, as before, serving the distribution function.

The facilities and services that provide these opportunities for travel, when interconnected to permit movement from one location to another, form a *network.* Thus, another way of representing the spatial dimension of an urban transportation system is as a set of road and transit networks. Even in the smallest urban areas, where mass transit is not available, the local street network provides the basic spatial characteristic of the transportation system.

The transportation system of a city can influence the way in which the city's social and economic structure, often called the *urban activity system,* develops. At the same time, changes in this structure can affect the ability of the transportation system to provide mobility and accessibility. Thus, the transportation system is closely related to the urban activity system and, historically, has been an important determinant of urban form [Owen, 1972; Moses and Williamson, 1972; Schaeffer and Sclar, 1975; Owen, 1976].

Because of the relation between transportation and urban activities, many of the methods used by transportation planners depend on estimates of trips generated by specific land uses. The relation also suggests that the *options* available to public officials dealing with transportation problems should include not only those related directly to the transportation system, but also actions such as zoning that affect the distribution of land use, and thus influence the performance of the transportation system.

The foregoing considerations point to two important principles for transportation planning: The transportation system should be

Considered as an integral part of the social and economic system in an urban area.

Viewed as a set of interconnected facilities and services designed to provide opportunities for travel from one location to another.

1-4-2 The Technology of Urban Transportation

The technology of urban transportation is closely related to the spatial configuration of the transportation system in that the design of transportation networks reflects the speed, operating, and cost characteristics of the vehicle or *mode* of transportation being used. Technology includes the means of propulsion, type of support (e.g., rubber tire on asphalt, steel wheel on steel rail, air cushion), means of guidance, and control technique (e.g., automatic spacing of rapid transit trains).

The development and widespread use of electric streetcars in urban areas during the late nineteenth century was a technological innovation that initiated the transformation of most North American cities. The advent of the electric streetcar permitted urban areas to expand beyond the boundaries that had been dictated by previous transportation technologies (e.g., walking, horse, horsecar), spawning "streetcar suburbs" with dramatically lower residential densities along streetcar lines radiating from the central city [Warner, 1962]. Whereas many industries had decentralized along railroad lines leading from the central city, and workers initially had to live near these factories, the introduction of streetcars now permitted more distant living.

Similarly, the introduction of trucks permitted industries to leave the narrow strips bordering railroad lines and to relocate throughout the urban area. This relocation of industry naturally caused substantial shifting of employment patterns and trip making.

The success of the streetcar in providing access from selected suburban areas to central business districts was followed by public acceptance of a second major technological innovation—the automobile, powered by the internal combustion engine. Increasing consumer preferences for lower-density living and for an ability to travel beyond established urban boundaries sparked a phenomenal growth in automobile ownership and usage, beginning in the 1920s. The automobile continued and accelerated the evolution of urban structure started by the electric streetcar. Its availability permitted further expansion of urban areas and, more important, provided access to land between the radial streetcar and railroad lines leading into the central city.

The technology of the internal-combustion engine, however, also led to the decline of other transportation modes used in urban areas by providing a less expensive and more flexible replacement for rail-based modes. While the automobile provided new opportunities for personal mobility and urban growth, motor buses rapidly replaced electric streetcars, to the extent that only five North American cities today still operate large-scale streetcar systems—Boston, Philadelphia, Pittsburgh, Toronto, and San Francisco (although this trend has reversed somewhat in recent years with new "light rail" systems in operation in Edmonton, Calgary, San Diego, and Buffalo). At the same time, the growth of private automobile use has dramatically reduced the use of public transportation in general, particularly since the end of World War II. According to the latest census figures, in 1980, 62.3 million Americans normally drove alone to work each day, another 19 million car-pooled, and 6 million used public transportation. The 6 million public transportation riders represented only 6.4 percent of the total daily work trips in the United States.

The low cost of automobile travel (for most trips) and the ease of a car's use for most types of trips that would be difficult if not impossible on transit—such as shopping for large quantities or recreational traveling with infants and pets—led to an explosion in the total amount of travel. Whereas some auto travel consists of travel that had formerly been done by transit, the bulk of auto travel simply did not exist before the auto-road system. It has been estimated that in 1910 the average urban dweller in the United States traveled 835 miles on transit and 65 miles by automobile. The transit value increased to 978 by 1920; but per capita urban automobile travel exceeded even this at 1322 miles. Per capita transit riding dropped thereafter to 878 in 1929 and 241 in 1974, whereas automobile use grew to 2822 and 6059 miles per capita in 1929 and 1974, respectively [Pushkarov and Zupan, 1977].

Although data on freight and truck movement in urban areas are very limited in comparison with person and automobile movements, some idea of the growth of such movement can be obtained from available data. Truck miles of travel in urban areas grew from an estimated 45 billion in 1960 to 172 billion in 1979 [U.S. Department of Commerce, 1980] —a 282 percent increase. In the period from 1960 to 1980—one year longer than that for which the truck data are available—the urban population grew by only 35.2 percent from 125 million to 169 million [U.S. Department of Commerce, 1981]. However, it must be remembered that these truck data include all types of trucks, not simply carriers of freight but also ones used in various service industries and for personal travel.

Automotive technology has thus been a major determinant of urban structure in North America, first by encouraging the development of low-density suburbs that are almost totally dependent on the private automobile for mobility, and then by making necessary the construction of urban freeways through established inner-city areas in order to give suburban dwellers easy access to central areas. Freight movement technology has also played a significant role in defining urban structure.

The technologies and the resulting modes available today for urban transportation are common to most cities but are often applied in different ways to serve different purposes. It should be noted that certain types of modes are more appropriate than others in serving different types of urban trips. Referring to the description of trip movements discussed in the previous section, some modes are more appropriate for serving collection movements, while others can provide more adequate line-haul capability.

The technological dimension of the urban transportation system suggests a third principle for urban transportation planning:

Transportation planners must consider the transportation system as consisting of different modes, each having different operational and cost characteristics.

1-4-3 The Institutional Foundation of the Urban Transportation System

The provision and maintenance of an urban road network and public transportation services have been, in most cases, considered the responsibility of government. Ever since "the urban transportation problem" emerged as a major public issue in the 1950s, the number of organizations established at all levels of government to deal with urban transportation has greatly increased. The proliferation of these organizations created the need for an institutional structure at the metropolitan and/or local level which would encourage coordinated transportation planning.

In the United States, this coordination has been carried out through the creation of formal organizational relationships and roles which rely on a bargaining and negotiating process to resolve conflicts and formulate policy. In many cities, memoranda of understanding exist which are agreements among representatives of the major transportation agencies in the region, defining the responsibilities of each agency and the formal mechanisms for adopting regional transportation policies. However, fragmentation of jurisdictional responsibilities, conflicting organizational mandates, the fact that those agencies responsible for project implementation are often not those doing the planning, and the inherently political nature of many transportation investment decisions have created a complex institutional structure at the metropolitan and/or local level which often hinders coordinated transportation action [Meyer, 1978].

In comparison to the United States context, numerous Canadian urban areas have metropolitan or regional governments with authority over regionwide services and facilities to coordinate the planning and implementation of transportation projects. The introduction of a metropolitan or regional "tier" of government has in many cases served to centralize transportation planning and decision-making activities and to increase the efficiency of transportation service provision. On the other hand, the retention of municipal jurisdictions with their own transportation-related functions has in some cases increased the amount of fragmentation and conflict over transportation policies between local and regional governments. Such conflicts, when combined with provincial government involvement in most urban transportation projects, have kept the debate over coordinated transportation planning alive in Canada as well as in the United States.

In both the United States and Canadian cases, the institutional structure for transportation has usually been considered from the public-sector perspective. That is, the major providers of transportation, and the most important actors in the planning process, were thought to be public agencies and officials. However, the opportunities for transportation in most urban areas include a variety of services, many of which are provided by private-sector groups. Many employers are actively involved with employee ride-sharing programs; land developers are concerned about transportation access to developed sites; private-sector groups such as taxi companies, bus firms, and school-bus operators can provide substantial transportation services; and business groups (such as chambers of commerce) can influence the policies and the planning process of government agencies [Gordon and Meyer, 1982].

Similarly, the institutional structure for transportation planning includes many public groups not associated with public transportation agencies. These groups can include community groups, special interests (such as transit rider associations), good government groups, etc. These groups, as well as individual citizens, can play an important role in the transportation planning process.

The institutional foundation of an urban transportation system is determined by the political, social, and historical characteristics of the locality. It is therefore difficult to describe, in general terms, the major transportation actors found in most urban areas. Not only do local agencies, public officials, private-sector groups, and the general public have a role to play, but in the United States context, federal and state agencies, through their control of funds and planning process requirements, can also influence metropolitan and/or local transportation decisions. In the Canadian case, while the federal government does not play a major role in urban transportation, the presence of a metropolitan and/or regional body between local and provincial governments in many cases makes the decision process just as complex.

The institutional dimension of the urban transportation system suggests two related principles underlying urban transportation planning:

> *The transportation system is usually planned, designed, built, operated, and maintained by organizations and individuals with different objectives, mandates, constituencies, and problem definitions.*

> *Changes to the urban transportation system can include a wide variety of infrastructure and service actions, applied at different geographic scales by the public and private sectors, to improve mobility and the urban environment.*

1-5 CHAPTER SUMMARY

1. Several political, economic, and social trends have influenced the substance and form of transportation planning during the past 10 years. These trends have included increasing pressures of fiscal austerity on government resources, an expanding awareness of future uncertainty, a changing perspective on the role of the automobile, changing characteristics of the average household, a broadening of roles for transportation, an increasing focus on management and service-oriented options, and the continuing suburbanization of urban areas.
2. There is not one, but many transportation planning processes under way in an urban area at any given time, each defined at a different level of complexity and purpose. In general, the focus of transportation planning has in recent years changed from large-scale infrastructure actions to managing the existing transportation system, resulting in a more "present-oriented" emphasis. The basic purpose of transportation planning, however, has not changed: to generate information useful to decision makers concerning the consequences of alternative transportation actions.
3. A decision-oriented approach to urban transportation planning should focus on the information needs of the decision makers. These decision makers can include publicly elected officials, transportation agency managers, private-sector managers, and corporate officials, although the elected or appointed government officials are likely to play the biggest role in determining the characteristics of urban transportation systems. Before the information is ultimately supplied to decision makers, however, the planning process should identify the consequences of decision alternatives and relate the various alternatives to established policy or performance objectives.
4. Urban transportation planning should include a long-range perspective, a short-range perspective, and a mechanism for linking the two. Long-range planning is a continuing activity that represents a statement of need and policy direction, thereby providing a foundation for short-range transportation decisions. Short-range planning should in turn consider the extent to which short-range decisions will change the future design and performance of the transportation system.
5. The urban transportation planning process model presented in this chapter encompasses a broad set of activities, starting with analysis and evaluation and, more important, continuing through project implementation and operations monitoring. To ensure effective implementation, planners have to be aware of the activities occurring throughout the entire process, ranging from initial data collection to project operations.
6. There are several basic principles or concepts that serve as the foundation of our perspective toward urban transportation planning:

The transportation system should be considered as an integral part of the social and economic system in an urban area.

The transportation system should be viewed as a set of interconnected facilities and services designed to provide opportunities for travel from one location to another.

Transportation planners must consider the transportation system as consisting of different modes, each having different operational and cost characteristics.

The transportation system is usually planned, designed, built, operated, and maintained by organizations and individuals with different objectives, mandates, constituencies, and problem definitions.

Changes to the urban transportation system can include a wide variety of infrastructure and service actions, applied at different geographic scales by the public and private sectors, to improve mobility and the urban environment.

REFERENCES

Altshuler, A.: "The Politics of Urban Transportation Innovation," *Technology Review*, May 1979.
Automotive News: *1982 Market Data Book*, Detroit, Apr. 28, 1982.
Baerwald, R.: "Land Use Change in Suburban Clusters and Corridors," *Transportation Research Record 861*, Transportation Research Board, Washington, D.C., 1982.
Boulding, K. E.: "Reflections on Planning: The Value of Uncertainty," *Technology Review*, October/November 1974.
Boyce, D. E., N. D. Day, and C. MacDonald: *Metropolitan Plan Making*, Regional Science Research Institute, Philadelphia, 1970.
Congressional Quarterly, Inc.: *Urban America, Policies and Problems*, Washington, D.C., August 1978.
de Bettencourt, J. S., M. B. Mandell, S. E. Polzin, V. L. Sauter, and J. L. Schofer: "Making Planning More Responsive to Its Users: The Concept of Metaplanning," *Environment and Planning A*, vol. 13, 1981.
Gakenheimer, R.: *Transportation Planning as Response to Controversy: The Boston Case*, MIT Press, Cambridge, 1976.
─────── and M. D. Meyer: "Urban Transportation Planning in Transition: The Sources and Prospects of Transportation System Management," *Journal of the American Planning Association*, January 1979.
Gordon, S., and M. Meyer: "Emerging Public-Private Partnership in Urban Transportation," *Transportation Research Record 877*, Transportation Research Board, Washington, D.C., 1982.
Greenburger, M., M. A. Crinson, and B. L. Crissey: *Models in the Policy Process*, Russell Sage Foundation, New York, 1976.
Harbridge House, Inc.: *The Future of the Auto in City Transportation*, Washington, D.C., May 1980.
Hill, M.: *Planning for Multiple Objectives*, Regional Science Research Institute Monograph Series, no. 5, Amherst, Mass., 1973.
Meyer, J., and J. Gomez-Ibanez: *Autos, Transit and Cities*, Harvard University Press, Cambridge, 1981.
Meyer, M. D.: "Organizational Response to a Federal Policy Initiative in the Public Transportation Sector: A Study of Implementation and Compliance," Unpublished Ph.D. dissertation, Department of Civil Engineering, MIT, Cambridge, 1978.
───────: "Monitoring System Performance: A Foundation for TSM Planning," *Special Report 190*, Transportation Research Board, Washington, D.C., 1980.
Moses, L., and H. F. Williamson, Jr.: "The Location of Economic Activity in Cities," in M. Edel and J. Rothenberg (eds.), *Readings in Urban Economics*, Macmillan, New York, 1972.
Noguchi, T.: "Shaping a Suburban Activity Center through Transit and Pedestrian Incentives: Bellevue CBD Planning Experience," *Transportation Research Record 861*, Transportation Research Board, Washington, D.C., 1982.
Owen, W.: *The Accessible City*, The Brookings Institute, Washington, D.C., 1972.

_____: *Transportation for Cities,* The Brookings Institute, Washington, D.C., 1976.
Pushkarev, B. S., and J. M. Zupan, *Public Transportation and Land Use,* Indiana University Press, Bloomington, 1977.
Pill, J.: *Planning and Politics, The Metro Toronto Transportation Plan Review,* MIT Press, Cambridge, 1978.
Schaeffer, K. H., and E. Sclar: *Access for All, Transportation and Urban Growth,* Penguin Books, Middlesex, England, 1975.
Schreffler, E., and M. Meyer: "Evolving Institutional Arrangements for Employer Involvement in Transportation: The Case of Employer Associations," *Transportation Research Record 914,* Transportation Research Board, Washington, D.C., 1983.
Secretary of Transportation: *The U.S. Automobile Industry 1980,* U.S. Department of Transportation Report DOT-P-10-81-02, Washington, D.C., January 1981.
Transportation Research Board: *Transportation System Management in 1980, State of the Art and Future Directions,* Special Report 190, Washington, D.C., 1980.
U.S. Congress: "The Status of the Nation's Highways: Conditions and Performance," *Report of the Secretary of Transportation to the U.S. Congress,* Committee on Public Works and Transportation, Committee Print 97-2, Washington, D.C., 1981.
U.S. Department of Housing and Urban Development: *Tomorrow's Transportation: New Systems for the Urban Future,* U.S. Government Printing Office, Washington, D.C., 1968.
Warner, S. B.: *Streetcar Suburbs, The Process of Growth in Boston 1870–1900,* Harvard University Press and MIT Press, Cambridge, 1962.
Wolfe, R. A., and E. J. Miller: *Transportation and Seniors in Ontario,* University of Toronto–York University Joint Program in Transportation, March 1982.

CHAPTER
TWO

TRANSPORTATION IN AN URBAN SETTING: CHARACTERISTICS OF URBAN TRAVEL AND OF THE TRANSPORTATION SYSTEM

2-0 INTRODUCTION

Urban transportation is the movement of people and goods between origins and destinations within an urban area. This movement can be carried out through a variety of modes, use different energy sources, and serve different needs. At the level of the individual traveler or goods movement, urban transportation is a *trip* from an origin to a destination to accomplish some activity at the destination. At the level of a metropolitan region, transportation is the aggregate of thousands or, in some cases, millions of individual trip-making decisions. These decisions result in vehicle and passenger trips over the transportation facilities provided in an urban area during specific time periods (travel *flows*). A transportation system thus consists of the facilities and services that allow these travel flows throughout an urban area.

The characteristics of urban travel flows and the facilities that permit such travel are basic to an understanding of transportation. In fact, it is the relationship between urban travel patterns (as determined by individual trip-making behavior) and urban transportation facilities (as shaped by the transportation planning and decision-making processes) that forms the basis of most urban transportation problems. This chapter presents an overview of the urban transportation system and of the travel flows it permits and discusses how the characteristics of this system relate to the urban transportation planning process. Transportation planners should be familiar with each of these characteristics as they relate to their metropolitan area because they not only define the substance and scope of transportation problems, but they can also provide useful indications of possible solutions.

2-1 CHARACTERISTICS OF URBAN TRAVEL

Every day, millions of trips are made in urban areas, satisfying a wide range of individual needs and using a variety of transportation means. There are five characteristics of this trip-making behavior that merit special attention—trip purpose, temporal distribution of trip making, spatial distribution of urban travel, selection of the mode used, and the cost of making the trip.

2-1-1 Trip Purpose

In transportation planning, individual passenger trips are often classified by the purpose of the trip and the trip origin. Common trip types include:

Work trips. Trips made to a person's place of employment such as a factory, a store, or an office.

Shopping trips. Trips made to a retail establishment regardless of the size or type of purchase. Trips made to a store "just to look" are shopping trips even though no purchase is made.

Social or recreation trips. Cultural trips made to recreational or entertainment facilities (e.g., church, civic meetings, concerts, sporting events). Travel to social activities (parties, visiting friends) would be included.

Business trips. Trips made in the course of performing a normal day's work. The origin of such trips is often the place of employment.

School trips. Trips made by students to an institution of learning.

Because trips are defined as one-way movements, another purpose, called "home" is often added to the list. For purposes of demand analysis, a further distinction is made which reflects the role the home plays in the trip. In large studies, five major purposes are usually considered: home-based work, home-based shop, home-based school, home-based other, and nonhome-based. For smaller urban areas, three categories have been successfully used: home-based work, home-based other, and nonhome-based. These definitions of trip purpose are discussed in greater detail in Chap. 7.

Table 2-1 demonstrates how daily urban passenger travel in Chicago is broken down. The home as a destination accounts for over 40 percent of urban trips, and if directional symmetry is assumed, it can be deduced that the home is either an origin or a destination for at least 80 percent of all urban trips made. This distribution of urban passenger trips by purpose in Chicago is fairly typical of most major urban areas.

Urban goods movement consists of all movement of goods in urban areas, including such things as fuel, food, waste, industrial supplies, and retail goods. The concept of trip purpose as related to goods movement thus reflects the type of activity being performed by the truck driver. A 1979 study which examined several characteristics of goods movement in major United States cities found that between 60 and 80

Table 2-1 Travel behavior by trip destination in Chicago

Purpose	Transit	Percent	Auto	Percent	Total	Percent	Mode split (transit)
Travel to:							
Home	787,571	46.8	5,985,165	42.1	6,772,736	42.6	11.6
Work	520,342	30.9	1,868,036	13.1	2,388,378	15.0	21.8
Business/work	11,981	0.7	491,577	3.4	503,558	3.2	2.4
Shop	82,354	4.9	2,010,521	14.1	2,092,875	13.1	3.9
School	93,313	5.5	299,500	2.1	392,813	2.4	23.7
Social/recreational	80,435	4.8	2,054,026	14.4	2,134,461	13.4	3.7
Personal business	96,435	5.7	1,004,940	7.0	1,101,375	6.9	8.7
Other	9,302	0.5	508,826	3.5	518,128	3.2	1.8
Total	1,681,733	100.0	14,222,591	100.0	15,904,324	100.0	10.6

Source: Chicago Area Transportation Study [1976].

percent of the truck trips in central business districts (CBDs) were for goods delivery, between 10 and 20 percent were for goods pickup, and between 10 and 20 percent were for service [Christiansen, 1979]. In this study, service included office machine repairs, plumbers, painters, building maintenance, telephone, etc. As the downtown areas of major cities continue to become more oriented to service industries, the characteristics of goods movement in these areas are likely to change as well.

Across entire metropolitan areas, truck trip purposes exhibit greater diversity, reflecting the wider variety of activities outside CBDs. In a sample of 11 areas, goods pick up and delivery (including mail) represented only 46.2 percent of the truck trips, whereas home-based and personal use was 28.4 percent, construction 4.9 percent, maintenance and repair 8.0 percent, and business use 7.2 percent, with the remaining 4.8 percent in other uses [Levinson, 1982].

An important aspect of trip purpose is that the length of urban trips, depending on the spatial location or origins and destinations, will vary by the purpose of the trip. Figure 2-1, for example, illustrates how the majority of trips in Toronto for all purposes take 30 minutes or less. When disaggregated by purpose, however, these trip durations differ considerably. The average duration of work trips in Toronto in 1966 was more than 6 minutes longer than that for nonwork trips. Shopping trips, more discretionary both in their timing and geographical destination than work trips, tend to be of shorter duration and length than the more mandatory daily trip to work. Recreational trips, on the other hand, are longer (see Table 2-2). For trucks, trip lengths are on the average shorter than those for autos. Average trip lengths for light and medium trucks are usually in the range of 2 to 3 miles, and 4 to 7 miles for heavy trucks [Levinson, 1976].

From a transportation planning perspective, an analysis of urban travel by trip purpose is important because it can be used to deduce demand patterns of urban travel. For example, information on the number of home-to-work trips originating in specific suburban areas and destined for the central business district can be used to derive levels

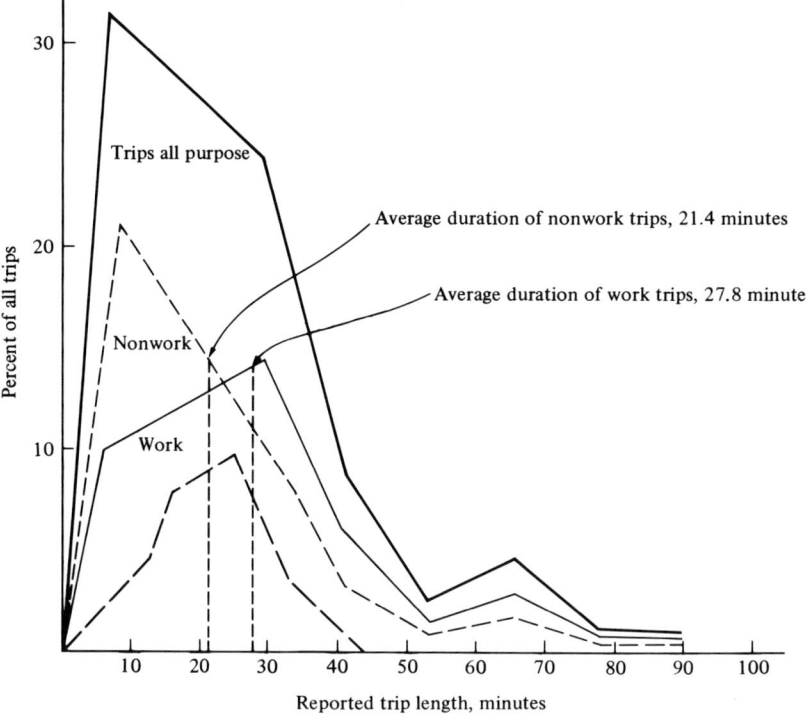

Figure 2-1 Temporal distribution of trip length, Toronto. (*Wagner* [*1980*].)

of demand on transportation facilities linking these two locations. Such information is also useful in determining the magnitude of problems that occur when the needs of two or more trip types conflict. For example, the allocation of limited downtown parking space between commuters who park all day and shoppers who park for only a few hours is an important policy issue in many urban areas [McShane and Meyer, 1981]. With regard to goods movement, information on trip purpose is important to assess major truck routes and analyze terminal or truck-stop congestion.

2-1-2 The Temporal Distribution of Trip Making

The concentration of trips at certain times of the day is a primary cause of problems associated wih congested transportation facilities. The peaking of travel between residential areas and places of employment is the most obvious example of how the temporal distribution of urban travel can affect the urban transportation system. Because most businesses require employees to be at their jobs beginning at 7 to 9 a.m. for shifts of 8 to 10 hours, travel to and from employment areas peaks each weekday morning, and again from 4 to 6 p.m. This "double peaking" of travel in urban areas is shown in Fig. 2-2. Note how work-related travel is far more peaked than total travel, which is distributed relatively more evenly throughout the day.

Table 2-2 Percent of vehicle trips, vehicle travel, and average trip length by trip purpose in the United States (1977)

Trip purpose	Percent of Trips	Percent of Travel	Trip length, miles
Earning a living			
Home to work	27.8	30.4	9.2
Work related	5.1	7.3	11.9
Subtotal	32.9	37.7	9.6
Family and personal business			
Shopping	17.0	10.0	4.9
Medical or dental	1.3	1.7	10.8
Other	14.0	11.2	6.7
Subtotal	32.3	22.9	5.9
Civic, educational, and religious	6.4	4.7	6.1
Social and recreational			
Visiting friends and relatives	8.4	11.3	11.2
Pleasure driving	0.4	0.8	15.7
Vacations	0.1	0.6	95.4
Other	10.4	11.3	9.1
Subtotal	19.3	24.0	10.2
Other and unknown	9.1	10.7	9.8
Total	100.0	100.0	8.3

Source: Roskin [1980].

In general, peak periods of truck traffic do not correspond with peak passenger traffic. Of course, a truck operating at a particular time is dependent upon the preference of those who receive the service or goods. Many retail stores, for example, prefer to receive shipments before 10 o'clock when most stores open. Thus, in many cities, truck activity is most intense right after the morning passenger peak and just before the evening rush hour (see Fig. 2-2). Again, hourly variations can differ from one part of an urban area to another. In many CBDs, trucking activity peaks before noon (for example, 45 percent of total delivery activity in downtown Brooklyn), while in others delivery activity peaks before noon, but the accumulation of service vehicles occurs between 12:00 and 3:00 p.m.

The peaking of travel demand in specific time periods results in congested highway facilities and transit services. *Congestion* is simply a condition of any transportation facility in which use of the facility is so great that there are delays for the users of that facility. Usually this happens when traffic approaches or exceeds facility capacity. Urban highway traffic demand during the peak hours is about double the average hourly demand, while for the public transit services, the peak-hour demand is three to four times the average [Wagner, 1980].

The solution to congestion in the 1960s often involved expanding the capacity of the highway and transit network to accommodate increased vehicular demand during

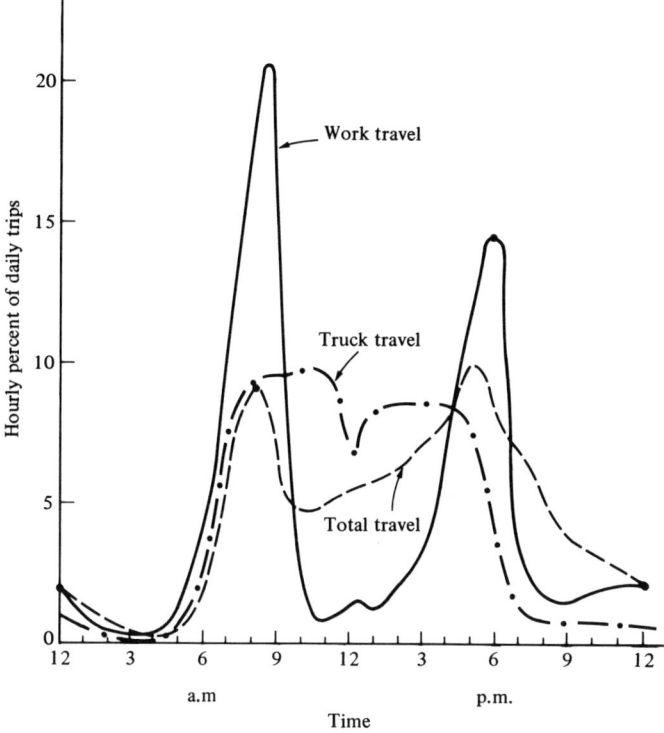

Figure 2-2 Typical hourly variation in travel.

peak hours. Today, however, such solutions are no longer feasible in many cities. Concern for the preservation of inner-city neighborhoods and citizen activism in local politics, when combined with cutbacks in government spending and political pressures to reduce taxes while maintaining urban services, have reduced investments in major urban highway projects.

An approach to handling the peaking of passenger travel demand that has been tried in some cities involves arranging work hours so that large groups of employees do not arrive and leave at the same times in order to make the periods of peak demand longer. As shown in Fig. 2-3, variable work-hour experiments have proved to be quite successful at spreading employee arrival times. In the case of the Yonge Street subway line in Toronto, the primary facility serving the central business district, the levels of congestion were reduced considerably. The implementation of variable work-hour programs is thus one option available for increasing the performance of facilities such as transit lines, parking facilities, tunnels, and bridges, without major capacity expansion [Wagner, 1980].

Although other objectives have begun to play an important role in transportation planning, relief of congestion still remains as one of the most important purposes of such planning. Congestion relief, however, does not necessarily imply expansion of facility capacity, as demonstrated by the variable work-hours experiment mentioned above. Other actions could include preferential treatment of high-occupancy vehicles,

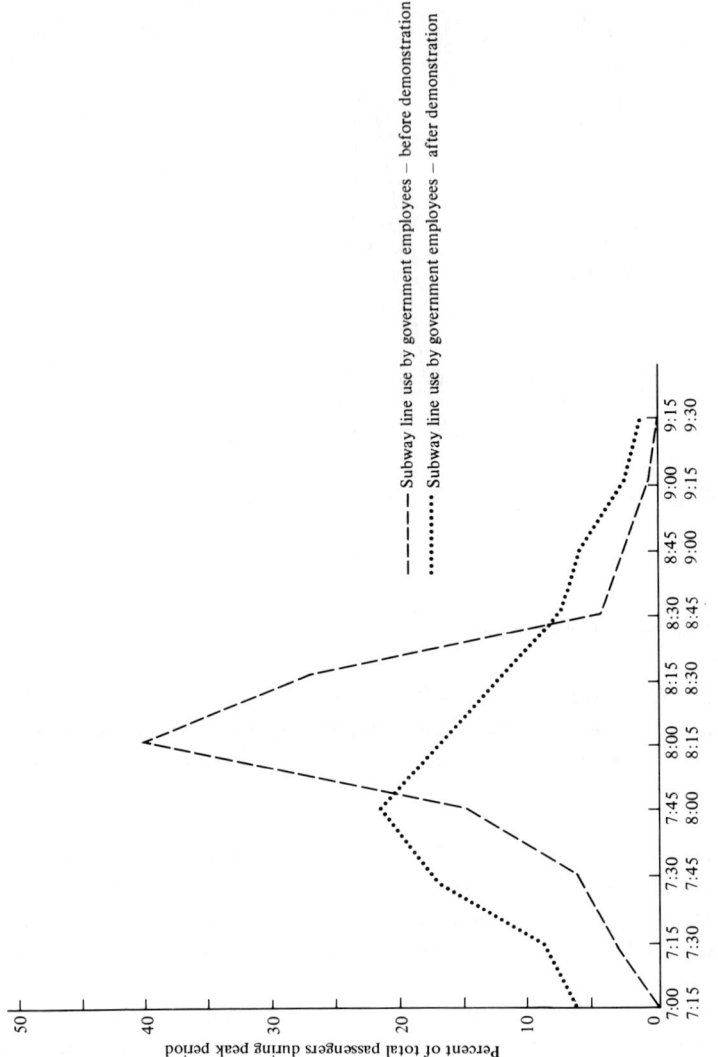

Figure 2-3 Impact of variable work hours on transit line congestion, Toronto. (*Wagner [1980]*.)

ride-sharing programs, alternative transit operating strategies, traffic engineering improvements, more efficient signalization schemes and traffic enforcement strategies, one-way streets, peak-hour parking prohibitions, and improvements to truck loading zones.

2-1-3 The Spatial Distribution of Trip Making

Not only are trips made over time, but they are also made over space. That is, each trip has an origin and a destination located at specific geographic points in an urban area. As noted in Sec. 1-4-1, the existence of transportation facilities that connect any particular origin and destination permits an individual to travel. Thus, the spatial distribution of travel in an urban area is directly related to the configuration of the transportation system. The road network connects all (or virtually all) places, but typically transit networks do not, so that transit travel tends to be more spatially restricted. In North America, it is largely CBD-oriented.

Figure 2-4a illustrates 1980 average daily traffic flows in San Diego. This figure is a common method used by planners to indicate urban travel patterns. It shows the increase in volume of traffic closer to the center of the city. This is partly owing to the orientation of many trips, especially work trips, to the CBD. However, many trips typically pass through CBDs; and travel in general is now very dispersed in orientation, owing to the growth of new outlying activity centers in the past 40 years. Figure 2-4b presents information on the spatial pattern of traffic and its variation with city size. Metropolitan areas are divided into CBDs and rings, with the higher numerical designation on rings indicating greater distance from the center.

The results of a 1977 nationwide personal transportation study provide some interesting data on the spatial nature of urban trip making in the United States [Roskin, 1980]. About 30 percent of all vehicle trips in the United States occurred within central city areas, and 36 percent occurred in suburban areas (the respective percentages for vehicle miles traveled were 27 percent and 39 percent). The average home-to-work length within central cities was 7.9 miles, and 10.4 miles in suburban areas. Trip lengths are typically longer the larger the city.

Understanding the spatial distribution of trip making becomes an important element of urban transportation planning when one considers that it indicates the need for mobility in an urban area, the level to which the existing transportation system satisfies this need, and those areas where action must be taken to improve system performance. As will be seen in later chapters, the spatial nature of urban travel is incorporated into every aspect of the planning approach.

2-1-4 Modal Distribution of Trip Making

The proportion of trips made in an urban area by different travel modes (e.g., transit, auto, van pool) varies markedly from city to city. One trend has clearly characterized this "mode split" over the past 30 years—the increasing dominance of the private automobile. This trend has been especially dramatic in the United States, where both the percentage of urban passenger trips made by transit and the absolute number of

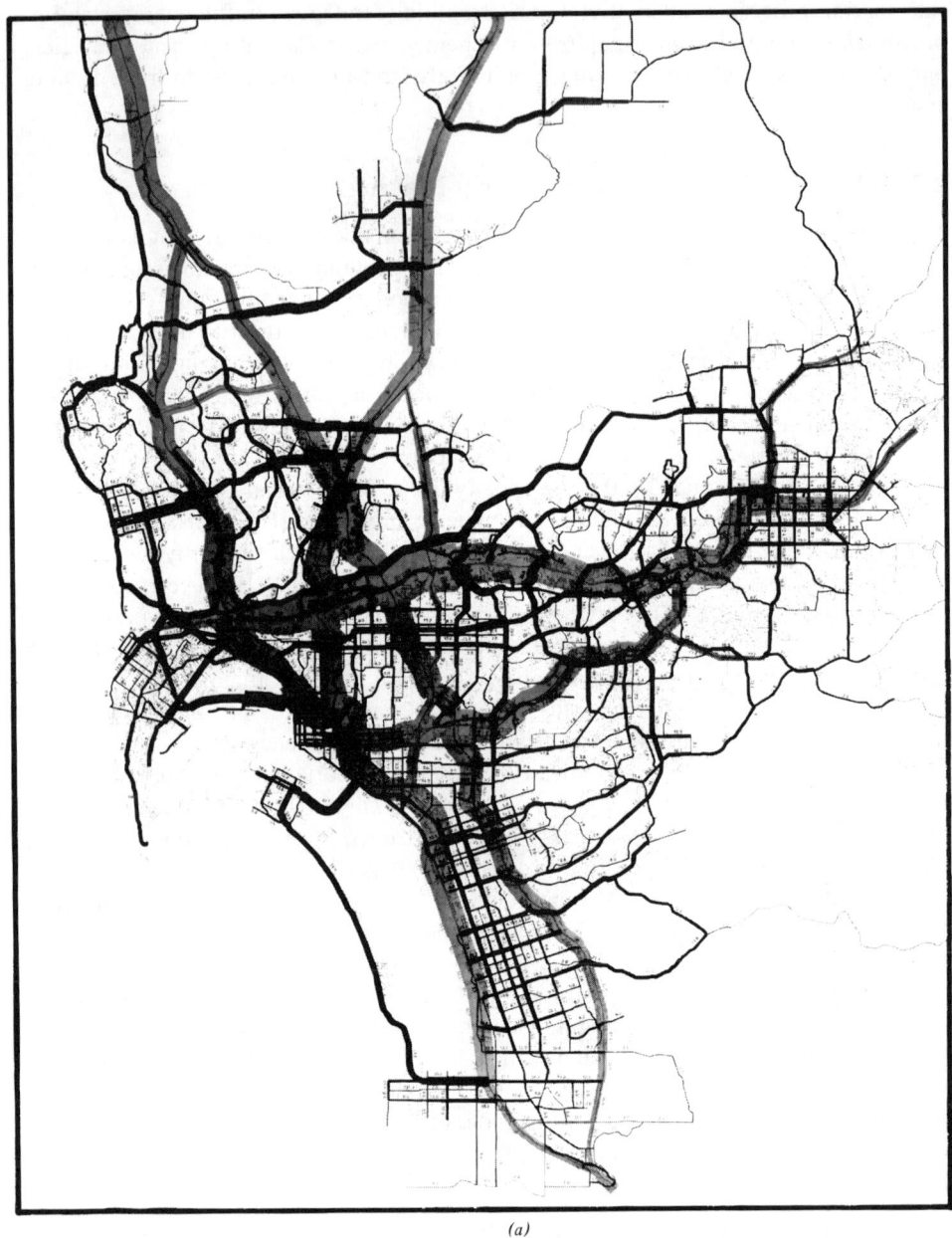

(a)

Figure 2-4(a) Average daily traffic volumes for San Diego.

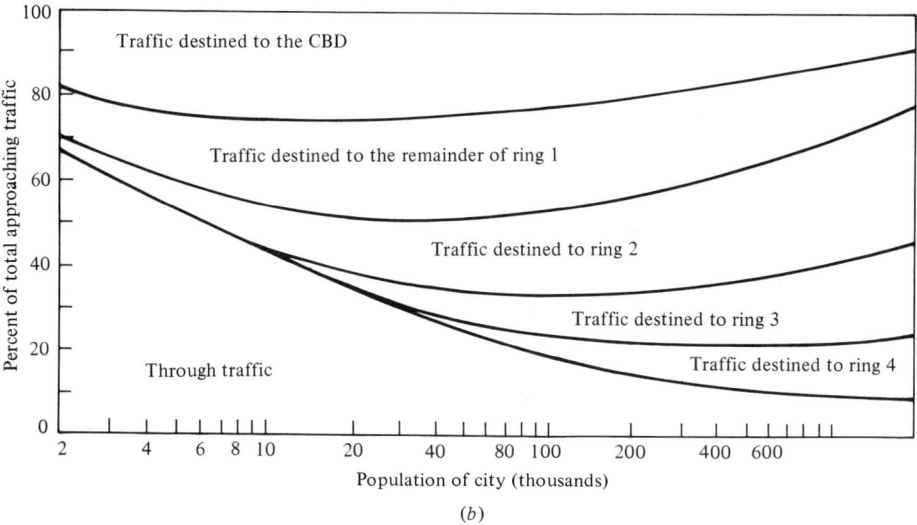

Figure 2-4(b) Spatial pattern of travel versus city size. (*Hansen [1961]*.)

trips has decreased significantly. Only recently, with the rising cost of motor fuels and increased governmental attention to public transit, has urban travel on public transit modes begun to stabilize [American Public Transit Association, 1981]. At the national level, the percentage of trip making made by public transit is very low, accounting for only 3 percent of total passenger miles and 6.4 percent of all work trips in 1980. The aggregate numbers can be misleading, however, because the transit share of the modal split in large metropolitan areas can be dramatically higher, especially to central business districts. For example, public transit accounted for 90 percent of the peak-hour trips entering or leaving the New York City central business district in 1974, 82 percent of such trips in Chicago, 49 percent in Boston, 44 percent in Ottawa, and 37 percent in Los Angeles. Similar statistics from 1970 counts include 68 percent in Toronto, 44 percent in Cleveland, and 40 percent in Vancouver [Transportation Research Board, 1980].

The technologies available today for urban passenger transportation are common to most cities but are often applied in different ways to serve different purposes. Table 2-3 shows some typical technologies, and the resultant travel modes, found in urban areas. It should be noted that certain modes are more appropriate than others in serving specific urban trips. For example, some modes are more appropriate for collection and distribution trips, while others can provide a better line-haul capability. This can be seen from Fig. 2-5, which focuses on service characteristics of these modes (grouped together for ease of presentation). Modes of very limited access such as rapid transit line with stations every mile often require the use of another mode (other than walking) for access—usually a local bus, streetcar, or automobile. Sometimes access and rapid-line haul speed are combined in the same vehicle, such as an express bus stopping

Table 2-3 Transportation technology and travel modes for North American cities

Guideway characteristics	Technology				
	Human powered	Highway— driver steered	Rubber tired— guided, partially guided	Rail	Other
Surface streets with mixed traffic	Bicycle	Automobile Truck Motorcycle Moped Paratransit Regular bus Express bus	Trolleybus	Streetcar Cable car	
Physical separation of traffic types, but traffic crossings permitted	Walking (on sidewalks) Bicycle (on lanes)	Bus, car or van pool on preferential lanes on arterial streets		Light rail transit	Ferry Hydrofoil Helicopter
Complete physical separation of traffic types	Walking (pedestrian bridges) Bicycle (paths)	Bus, car or van pool on busways	Rubber-tired rapid transit Automated guided transit Group rapid transit Personal rapid transit	Commuter rail Rail rapid transit	Tramway

Source: Adapted from Vuchic, [1981].

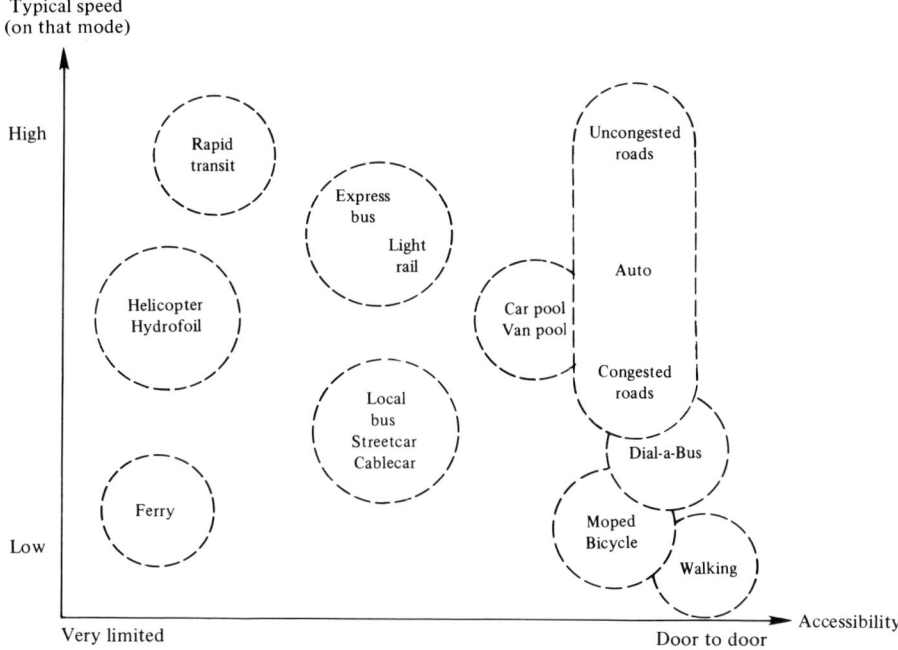

Figure 2-5 Service characteristics of most common urban passenger modes.

frequently in a residential area but then running nonstop (or perhaps stopping at only intersecting transit lines) to the downtown area.

Several factors influence an individual's choice of which mode to use in making a trip. One of the most important factors is the difference in trip time between modes for particular trips. For example, in those cases where an automobile is available, an actual or perceived transit trip time that is longer than that for driving would probably result in the trip being made by car (all else being equal). Other important factors include mode availability (e.g., auto ownership or accessibility to transit) and differences in actual costs, perceived costs, comfort, or convenience (e.g., availability of parking close to destination). Modal distribution can also be related to factors such as occupation, income, age, and other socioeconomic characteristics (see Fig. 2-6).

Much of public policy in the urban transportation sector during the past several years has focused on shifting the modal patterns of trip making. Preferential lanes on freeways for high-occupancy vehicles (i.e., car pools, vans, and buses) are designed to make these modes more attractive by reducing trip times [Levinson et al., 1973]. Parking policies that restrict access, increase parking prices, and reduce overall parking supply are meant to reduce the attractiveness of the automobile as a commuting mode [McShane and Meyer, 1981]. On the other hand, actions to improve transit service are undertaken to increase its attractiveness as a mode of travel. For example, although the direct causal relationship is not clear, actions taken by the Toronto transit authority shown in Fig. 2-7 seem to have contributed to increased ridership initially spurred by rising gasoline prices and parking costs.

32 URBAN TRANSPORTATION PLANNING

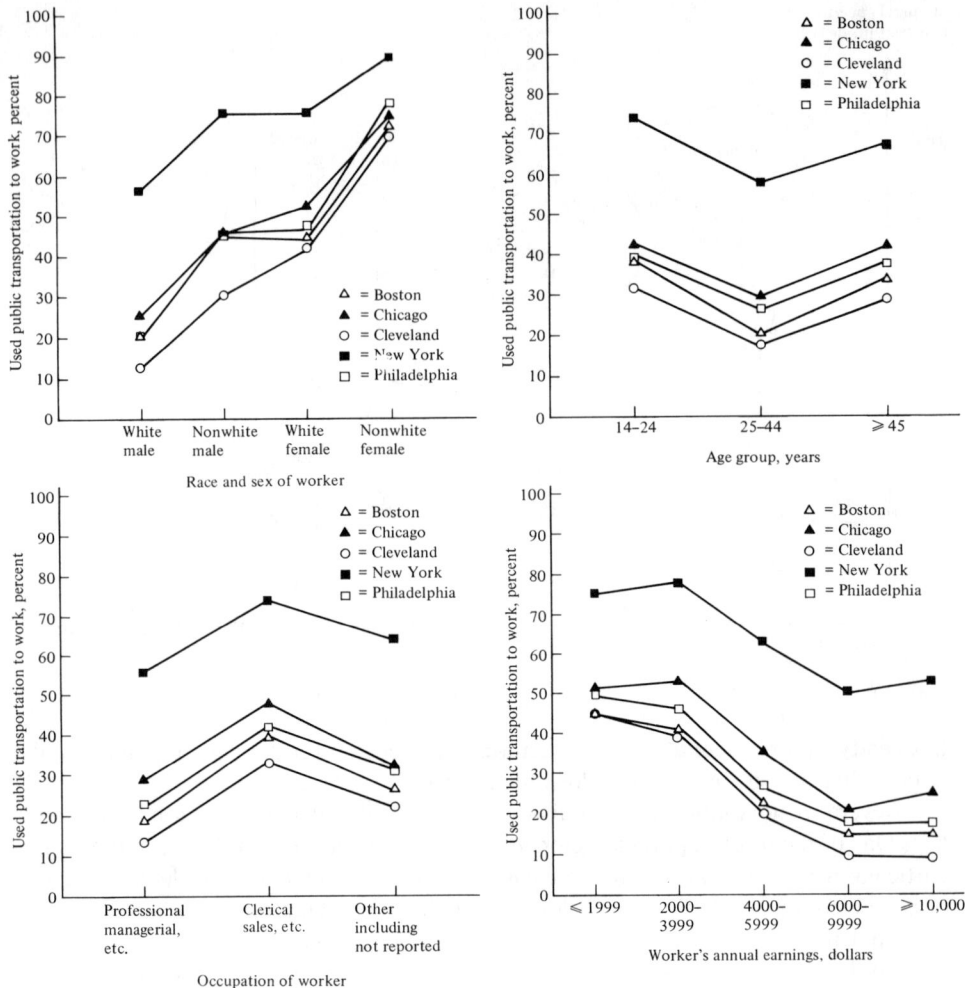

Figure 2-6 Mode distribution of urban tripmaking by income, occupation, age, and sex. (*Bock* [*1968*].)

2-1-5 Travel Cost

Travel has associated with it some *utility* or *disutility* which is a measure of the "desirability" of a travel option. This desirability depends on the attributes of the travel option, the user's tastes, and the characteristics of the activity to be performed at the destination. One of the most important attributes of a mode is the cost associated with its use. Indeed, the analysis of transportation demand, and the choice of mode, is often based on an assessment of the relative "costs" of one mode over another (including not only out-of-pocket expenditures but also time, discomfort, etc.).

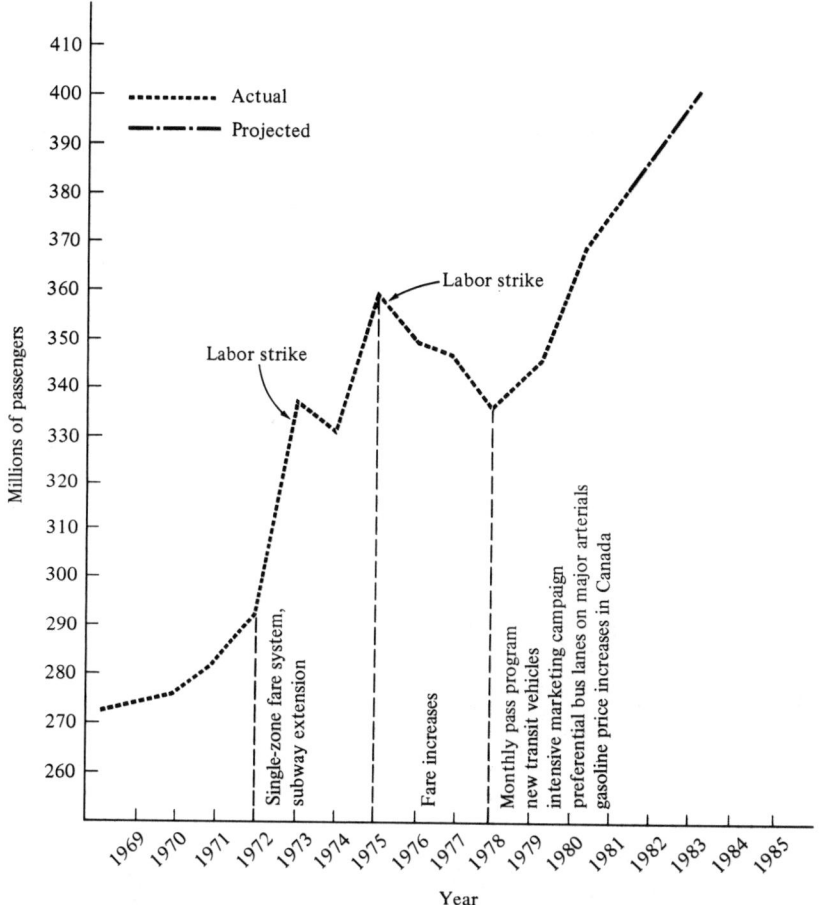

Figure 2-7 Transit ridership in Toronto, 1969–1982. (*Toronto Transit Commission* [*1982*].)

Turning first to the monetary expenditures, we find that statistics from the National Transportation Policy Study Commission provide a general picture. In 1975, the total United States expenditure for urban automobile travel (including that of light trucks) was $86.1 billion, of which users paid $82.7 billion. This purchased 77.6 billion person-miles of travel, for an average user cost of approximately 10.6 cents per person-mile and average total cost of 11.0 cents per person-mile. Transit expenditures were $4.2 billion, of which riders paid about half, $2.2 billion, for 33 billion person-miles of travel. The transit average cost to society was 12.7 cents per person-mile but to riders, only 6.7 cents, reflecting the subsidy [National Transportation Policy Study Commission, 1979]. Each of these averages masks great variations; for example, car and van pooling costs being much less per rider than single-occupant autos and driving and parking in downtown New York costing far above the average. Different transit

Sample calculation for a one-way, peak-hour auto work trip
(12-mile line-haul trip)

		Assumption regarding interest rate r, time, value v, and peak-hour traffic flow F	Auto costs (subcompact)	BART plus feeder bus	Integrated bus
Assumptions					
Interest rate	12%				
Time value per person per hour	$3 in vehicle				
Trip length					
Urban-suburban freeway	8 miles				
Central city freeway	4 miles				
Suburban arterial	2 miles				
Street in central business district	0.75 miles				
Persons per auto	1.5				
Auto type	Subcompact				
Cost categories (per vehicle trip)	Cost				
Residential collection		$r = 6\%, v = \$3.00$			
Public costs	0.023	$F = 1,000$	$4.54	$28.85	$6.34
Time costs	0.637	$= 5,000$	4.54	9.62	4.61
Direct operating costs	0.093	$= 10,000$	4.54	6.84	4.10
Auto capital costs	0.045	$= 20,000$	4.54	5.34	3.72
Accident costs	0.076	$= 30,000$	4.54	4.81	3.55
Line haul		$r = 6\%, v = \$1.50$			
Public costs	1.759	$F = 1,000$	3.47	25.60	3.64
Time costs	1.080	$= 5,000$	3.47	7.39	2.59
Direct operating costs	0.401	$= 10,000$	3.47	4.93	2.32
Auto capital costs	0.272	$= 20,000$	3.47	3.65	2.13
Accident costs	0.200	$= 30,000$	3.47	3.19	2.04
Downtown distribution		$r = 12\%, v = \$3.00$			
Public costs	0.335	$F = 1,000$	5.63	46.91	6.55
Time costs	1.295	$= 5,000$	5.63	13.43	4.73
Direct operating costs	0.035	$= 10,000$	5.63	8.88	4.20
Auto capital costs	0.017	$= 20,000$	5.63	6.51	3.82
Accident costs	0.028	$= 30,000$	5.63	5.68	3.65
Parking costs	2.145	$r = 12\%, v = \$1.50$			
		$F = 1,000$	4.97	43.45	3.78
		$= 5,000$	4.97	11.16	2.69
		$= 10,000$	4.97	6.96	2.42
Total cost per vehicle trip	8.44	$= 20,000$	4.97	4.81	2.23
Total cost per passenger trip	5.63	$= 30,000$	4.97	4.06	2.14

Figure 2-8 Calculation of travel costs (*Keeler, et al. [1975]*).

modes have different costs (and levels of service); and levels of usage affect costs dramatically.

Unfortunately, comprehensive data on the actual costs of alternative modes are simply unavailable. But some idea of the relative costs of selected modes can be obtained from estimated studies of the relative merits of one mode over another. Most studies of the relative costs of passenger travel modes have focused on one of two comparisons: bus transit vs. rail transit and auto vs. transit. The bus vs. rail transit comparison has been a controversial subject for many years, starting with the influential 1965 study by Meyer, Kain, and Wohl [1965]. Subsequent studies have used different assumptions on service design, travel time, volumes carried, and operating characteristics [Deen and James, 1969; Boyd, Asher, and Wetzler, 1973; Miller et al., 1973]. The major cost items in these studies have generally included capital and operating costs, maintenance costs, user fees, and a monetary value attached to travel time.

The second area of modal cost comparison, auto vs. transit, is best illustrated by a study conducted by Keeler et al. [1975]. This study examined the costs of auto, rapid transit (BART), and integrated bus travel in several work travel situations in the San Francisco area. The costs associated with transit and highway travel included all relevant capital and operating costs, time costs, and "public" costs relating to environmental impact, road maintenance, and administrative and/or overhead expenses. The cost calculation thus results in the "social cost" of each mode in that the cost to society of a modal trip is the basis of comparison. Figure 2-8 shows an example calculation of the social cost for the three modes. Note that the results were calculated with two alternative interest rates, two alternative time values, and at different traffic densities to assess the sensitivity of the findings to changes in these key variables.[1]

Even though these studies have focused on costs, the more careful authors have pointed out that minimum cost cannot be the sole basis for selecting a particular mode or combination of modes to serve an area. Meyer, Kain, and Wohl [1965] state:

> In sum, aspects of cost, price, service, and the specific demand characteristics of the traveling public are vitally important and must be integrated and synthesized to arrive at the most effective and economic choice or combination of choices in any particular application.

To this we could add considerations of energy, environmental impacts, and effects on area-land development.

The types of modal comparison studies represented by Meyer, Kain, and Wohl, and Keeler et al., have come under substantial criticism from some other researchers and practitioners. The major areas of criticism relate to alleged underlying assumptions of optimal domains for individual modes, using minimum cost per passenger trip as a sole criterion for determining the optimal mode and ignoring a number of important

---

[1] An interesting result of this comparison was that the bus mode dominated auto travel even at low densities. Given the dominance of the auto mode in San Francisco, this result did not seem to correspond with actual travel behavior. The authors of the report concluded that such a discrepancy could be caused by two factors: the value of travel time used was too low and bus service was not being provided and dispatched optimally. The general conclusion was that the "price" of travel on the expressways in San Francisco did not reflect the true opportunity cost of freeway space during rush hours.

characteristics which cannot be converted into dollars. One view of these studies is that of Vuchic [1979]:

> Because of these deficiencies, results of the economic studies have little realistic value. Since such important factors as reliability and high frequency of service, comfort, and safety enter the economic models only as cost items, while their major influence on passenger attraction is disregarded, these studies greatly distort the relationships among modes in favor of low investment/low performance systems.

Thus the controversy is intense, and many issues surround the interpretation (or misinterpretation) of cost comparisons.

One must therefore be careful when conducting comparative studies between modes in that more than just costs should be incorporated into the analysis. The analytical methods to be presented in Chaps. 4 to 9 overcome these limitations, incorporating costs along with other characteristics in the mode-investment decision. These are illustrated by an actual study reported in Sec. 9.5.

From the point of view of travel costs, there are two elements of modal cost comparisons that merit special attention because of their importance in travel demand analysis and project evaluation. First, from the perspective of the user, only those costs that occur in the short run, or *out-of-pocket costs,* are usually associated with a trip. These costs usually include gasoline, tolls, fares, parking costs, etc. Other costs—including vehicle ownership, maintenance and repair, and insurance costs—are indeed borne by the user but are not generally associated with a specific trip. This distinction is important when planners attempt to predict travel demand with models (see Chap. 7).[2] With reference to Fig. 2-8, a calculation which only considered perceived user cost (including time) would most likely enhance the desirability of the automobile mode.

From the perspective of society, urban travel has other "costs" which are often not monetary in nature. These can include environmental impacts, effects on government operations, and social impacts on both users and nonusers of the transportation system. These costs will be discussed in more detail in Chap. 9.

A second important element of modal cost comparisons is the *value of time* associated with travel. The underlying basis for assigning a monetary value to travel time relates to the fact that time not spent in travel can be used for productive purposes in other activities. In the case of travel to work, this assertion seems reasonable as long as a traveler is indifferent to traveling or working. Several studies have examined this "value" of time and have concluded that, in the case of the journey to work, the value of line-haul time ranges from 20 to 50 percent of the traveler's wage, while values for nonline-haul components of trip time (waiting time, transfer time, etc.) are about two to three times the value of line-haul time [Domencich and McFadden, 1975]. The use of value of time in project evaluation will be discussed in detail in Chap. 9.

---

[2] A 1977 study of commuter travel in Fort Worth used only those costs perceived by users of auto and bus, including time and discomfort costs, vehicle operating costs, fares, and parking fees. The results showed a user-perceived cost of $11.05 per passenger trip for bus and $7.03 for auto [Page, 1980].

In sum, although transportation systems and the patterns of travel on them exhibit different characteristics from one city to the next, there are similar trends present in most urban areas. The distribution of urban travel among available modes, its temporal and spatial distribution, the cost of travel, and the purpose of trips made are all important considerations in defining transportation problems and responding to them through the planning and decision-making processes.

2-2 CHARACTERISTICS OF URBAN TRANSPORTATION SYSTEMS AND THEIR IMPACTS

As defined earlier, an urban transportation system is comprised of both the infrastructure and the services provided in an urban area which permit an individual to leave one location and travel to another. There are several characteristics of this system and its operation that are important in understanding the role that transportation has in an urban area. These include system and facility performance, the provision of mobility, the construction and operational impacts of transportation facilities on the surrounding activity system, and the interrelationship between land use and transportation.

2-2-1 Transportation System and Facility Performance

As observed in Chap. 1, a trip can consist of several types of movement including collection, transfer, line-haul, and distribution processes. The transportation system providing this movement can be categorized as consisting of two components: vehicular movement on some form of guideway or right-of-way and terminal or transfer operations. This section introduces the concepts associated with the performance of both of these transportation facility types.

Guideways. Road networks and transit systems provide the basic infrastructure necessary for mobility in metropolitan areas. The operational performance (i.e., the ease of travel, the quality of service provided, and service reliability) of the facilities that permit travel is therefore an important consideration in maintaining acceptable levels of mobility. There are several performance characteristics fundamental to an understanding of the physical operations of transportation guideways. These characteristics include speed, volume, rate of flow, density, capacity, cost of operations, and level of service. Most of these characteristics are related to one another and to the particular transportation technology in use. In the *Highway Capacity Manual,* these terms are defined as follows [Transportation Research Board, 1980]:

Speed. A rate of motion expressed as distance per unit time, generally as miles per hour or kilometers per hour. In determining the *average running speed* of vehicles, the length of the facility under consideration is divided by the average time it takes vehicles to traverse the segment (i.e., by the summation of individual vehicle times divided by the total number of vehicles).

38 URBAN TRANSPORTATION PLANNING

Volume. The number of vehicles passing a point on a transportation facility during a 1-hour period.

Rate of flow. The number of vehicles passing a point on a facility during some period of time, expressed as an equivalent rate in vehicles per hour.

The distinction between volume and flow rate is an important one that warrants illustration. Suppose the following observations were made of the number of buses using a reserved freeway lane:

7:00–7:15	8 buses
7:15–7:30	10 buses
7:30–7:45	15 buses
7:45–8:00	13 buses

The bus volume during this hour is 46 buses, but the rate of flow for each 15-minute period is as follows:

7:00–7:15	8 buses/0.25 h = 32 buses/h
7:15–7:30	10 buses/0.25 h = 40 buses/h
7:30–7:45	15 buses/0.25 h = 60 buses/h
7:45–8:00	13 buses/0.25 h = 52 buses/h

These flow rates become important factors in determining facility capacity and flow control strategies (e.g., vehicle dispatching).

Density. The number of vehicles occupying a given length of facility, averaged over time.

Capacity. The maximum rate of flow that can be accommodated on a facility segment under prevailing conditions. As shown in Table 2-4, there are several factors that can influence facility and service capacity.

Cost of operations. The costs incurred by the agency responsible in the regular operation of the facility or service under consideration. In the highway sector, this can include maintenance and labor costs, while for transit this can include transportation (labor and fuel), maintenance, administration, marketing, taxes, licenses, and insurance. As shown in Fig. 2-9, these costs can vary among transportation modes.

Level of service. A qualitative measure of the effects of a number of factors (e.g., speed, travel time, traffic interruptions, safety, comfort, operating costs, volume-to-capacity ratios) on the performance of a facility. These qualitative measures have been grouped into different levels to represent different facility or service conditions. For example, levels of service for transit operations, pedestrian movements, and freeway performance are shown in Tables 2-5 through 2-7. In each case, level of service A indicates the best level (from a user's perspective) of facility performance, while level of service F represents the worst.

Table 2-4 Factors influencing transportation facilities and service capacity

Transit	Highway
1. Vehicle characteristics 　　number of available vehicles 　　allowable number of vehicles per transit unit 　　vehicle dimensions 　　seating configurations 　　number and location of doors 　　maximum speed 　　acceleration and deceleration 2. Facility characteristics 　　physical design 　　degree of separation from other traffic 　　intersection design (at same level or separated from cross traffic) 　　horizontal and vertical alignment 3. Stop characteristics 　　spacing of stops 　　whether on line or off line 　　method of fare collection 　　high-level or low-level loading 　　length of loading bays or platforms 　　turn-around facilities 4. Traffic characteristics 　　volume and nature of other traffic 　　cross traffic at intersections 5. Methods of controlling vehicle spacing, i.e., headways	1. Roadway characteristics 　　lane width 　　lateral clearance 　　roadway shoulders 　　auxiliary lanes 　　parking lanes 　　turning and storage lanes 　　surface conditions 　　alignment 　　grades 2. Traffic characteristics 　　proportion of trucks 　　proportion of buses 　　traffic interruptions 　　variations in traffic flow

Source: Adapted from Soberman and Hazard, [1980] and Transportation Research Board [1980].

40 URBAN TRANSPORTATION PLANNING

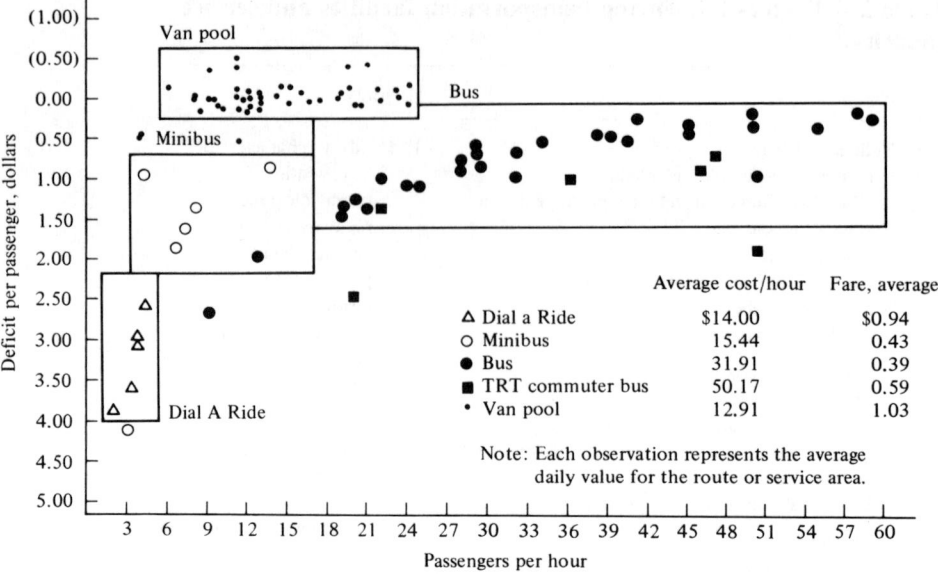

Figure 2-9 Cost characteristics of transit services, Norfolk, Virginia. (*Tidewater Transportation District* [*1982*].)

The relationship between three of these characteristics—rate of flow, average running speed, and density—is one of the fundamental relationships describing the conditions of vehicle flow. This relationship, expressed mathematically as

$$\text{Flow} = \text{speed} \times \text{density}$$

is the basis for determining the capacity of a facility and the level of service provided in its operation. There are additional relationships between flow and speed, flow and density, and speed and density which limit the range of combinations possible among the three variables. These relationships, shown in Fig. 2-10, also demonstrate the relationships between the maximum rate of flow (i.e., capacity), critical density, and critical speed. The operating conditions identified in Fig. 2-10 as "forced flow" are those often experienced during peak hours when congested conditions result in lower speeds and interrupted traffic flow.

Terminals. Terminals and transfer points are also an important component of the transportation system. In fact, given the importance that overall travel time has on travel behavior, the amount of time spent in accessing or leaving transportation modes can be a critical factor in the use of the transportation system.

Transportation terminals have several functions: (1) loading and unloading of passengers or freight onto vehicles, (2) storage of passengers or freight from the time of arrival to time of departure, (3) documentation of movement (e.g., ticketing or

Table 2-5 Level of service for basic freeway segments

Level of service	Density, passenger cars per mile per lane (passenger cars per kilometer per lane)	70 miles per hour (112 kilometers per hour)			60 miles per hour (96 kilometers per hour)			50 miles per hour (80 kilometers per hour)		
		Speed, miles per hour (kilometers per hour)	Volume to capacity	Maximum service flow rate per lane, ideal conditions, passenger cars per hour per lane	Speed, miles per hour (kilometers per hour)	Volume to capacity	Maximum service flow rate per lane, ideal conditions, passenger cars per hour per lane	Speed, miles per hour (kilometers per hour)	Volume to capacity	Maximum service flow rate per lane, ideal conditions, passenger cars per hour per lane
A	≤12(8)	≥60(96)	0.35	700	—	—	—	—	—	—
B	≤20(13)	≥57(91)	0.54	1100	≥50(80)	0.49	1000	—	—	—
C	≤30(19)	≥54(86)	0.77	1550	≥47(75)	0.69	1400	≥43(69)	0.67	1300
D	≤42(26)	≥46(74)	0.93	1850	≥42(67)	0.84	1700	≥40(64)	0.83	1600
E	≤67(42)	≥30(48)	1.00	2000	≥30(48)	1.00	2000	≥30(48)	1.00	1900
F	>67(42)	<30(48)	*	*	<30(48)	*	*	<30(48)	*	*

* Highly variable, unstable.
Source: Transportation Research Board [1980], as updated.

Table 2-6 Pedestrian levels of service on walkways

Level of service	Space, square foot per pedestrian	Average flow rate, pedestrians per minute per foot*	Mean speed, feet per minute†	Volume/capacity ratio‡
A	over 40	under 6	over 250	< .024
B	24–40	10–6	240–250	0.24–0.40
C	16–24	14–10	224–240	0.40–0.56
D	11–16	18–14	198–224	0.56–0.72
E	6–11	25–18	150–198	0.72–1.00
F	Under 6	0–25	0–150	0.00–1.00

* Flow rate relative to effective walkway width.
† Speeds are calculated based on space and flow rate variables.
‡ Assumed capacity = 25 pedestrians per minute per foot (1 foot = 0.305 meter).
Source: Transportation Research Board, [1980].

Table 2-7 Level of service for bus transit

Peak-hour level of service	Passengers/seat (approximate)	Approximate square feet per passenger
A	0.00–0.50	11.9 or more
B	0.51–0.75	11.8–8.0
C	0.76–1.00	7.9–6.1
D	1.01–1.25	6.0–4.8
E (scheduled load)	1.26–1.50	4.7–4.0
F (crush load)	1.51–1.60	< 4.0

(1 foot = 0.305 meter)

Source: Transportation Research Board [1980].

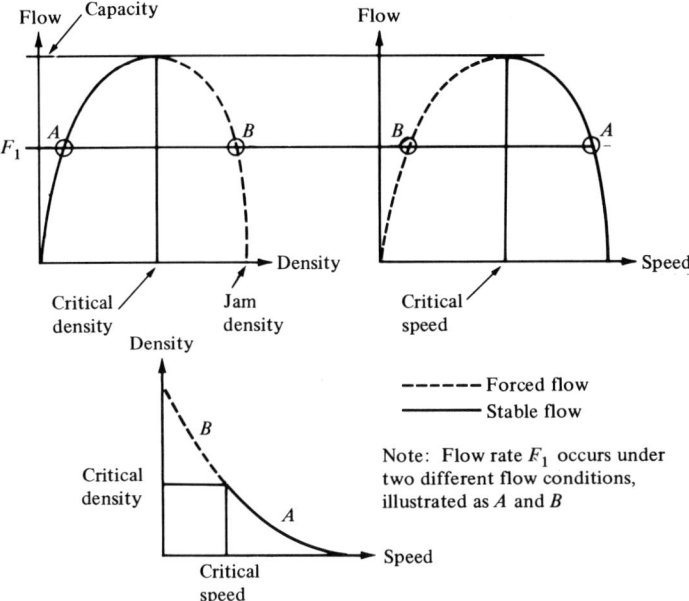

Figure 2-10 Relation between flow, density, and speed for vehicle movement. (*Transportation Research Board* [*1980*].)

billing), (4) vehicle storage and maintenance, and (5) concentration of passengers or freight into groups of economical size for movement [Morlok, 1978]. Like the performance of transportation facilities discussed above, the performance of terminals in fulfilling these functions can be measured in terms of capacity. In the case of passenger terminals, capacity can be defined as that volume which yields waiting times of an acceptable magnitude. As shown in Table 2-8, this capacity can be measured for the many different types of terminals that exist in an urban area. In the case of freight terminals, relationships can also be developed which determine terminal capacity based on the number of "servers" that exist to load or unload a shipment.

In recent years, increased attention has been given to the characteristics of passenger terminals that can make them more effective as transportation centers. This attention has not only included greater ease of access to the terminal, but has also improved passenger information mechanisms once the user is inside the terminal [Hoel, 1981]. Effective terminal design thus includes concern for much more than the traditional role of collection and distribution of passengers.

A more detailed discussion of transportation facility and system performance, and how performance characteristics are used in transportation planning, is included in Chap. 8. At this point, it is important to understand that many characteristics of vehicle flow are relevant to the users of transportation systems, including speed, level of service, and cost. These characteristics determine, in many ways, both the perceived and actual effectiveness and efficiency of urban transportation systems.

Table 2-8 Service times and capacities of urban passenger transport terminal processors

Processor	Mean time or capacity	Comments
Automobile parking service times		
Self park		
Get ticket at entrance	0.1 min/car	Gate
Pay at exit	0.2 min/car	Gate and variable fee
Attendant parking		
Pass. to leave car	0.5 min/car	
Attendant to park or deliver car	3.31 min/car	
Bus stop service times		
Exact fare local bus dwell times		
Simultaneous alighting and boarding		Standard 2-door buses
Morning peak	$y = 0.5 + 1.3A + 2.2B - 0.1AB$	y = dwell time, seconds
Midday	$y = 0.8 + 1.4A + 2.9B - 0.1AB$	A = no. of pass. alighting
Afternoon peak	$y = 2.4 + 1.1A + 2.1B$	B = no. of pass. boarding
Bus terminal capacity		
Street stops—downtown	160 buses/h	Max. observed with 3–5 berths/stop
Single-terminal berth		
Single-door loading and collect fare	$Q = 1000/B$	Theoretical: Q = buses/h
Double-door loading, prepaid fare	$Q = 2000/B$	B = boarding pass./bus approximate for $B \geq 20$
Rail transit service times		
Dwell times		
High-level platforms	$y = 1.1P$	y = dwell time, seconds
Low-level platforms	$y = 1.8P$	P = no. of pass/door (doors 2.4 ft wide)
Rail terminal capacity (per track)		
Electric rapid transit through station	30–40 trains/h	Lower values are maxima observed; higher values are theoretically achievable
Electric rapid transit stub station	15–20 trains/h	
Commuter railroad through station	15–20 trains/h	
Commuter railroad stub station	6–20 trains/h	
Automobile toll booth service time		
Pay flat toll at booth	0.1 min/car	
Passenger fare collector capacity		
Automatic	40–60 pass/min	
Manual barrier	25–50 pass/min	
Exit barrier	50–60 pass/min	Turnstile or revolving gate
Escalator-per 2-ft.-wide pass. lane	60 pass/min	

Source: Morlok [1978].

2-2-2 Provision of Mobility

Transportation systems in most urban areas provide unprecedented levels of mobility for urban residents. In most cases, this mobility is directly related to the ability of individuals to own and drive a car. From 1950 to 1980, the proportion of United States households owning at least one car rose from 52 percent to 86 percent; in Canada the respective percentage change was from 42 percent to 79 percent. During the same period, the proportion of adults with driving licenses went from 43 percent to 86 percent in the United States and from 35 percent to 75 percent in Canada.

However, in those situations where individuals are too old or infirm to drive a car, or too poor to own one, the high level of mobility provided by the automobile is of little use. Yet the spatial distribution of urban activities, having been heavily influenced by automobile use, generally requires some form of vehicle for transportation. Thus, although one of the most important characteristics of the urban transportation system is its provision of mobility, questions such as: "Mobility for whom?" and "At what cost?" have to be asked. In transportation, three groups have been identified as having some difficulty taking full advantage of the mobility provided by the auto-dominant urban transportation system—the elderly, the handicapped, and the poor.

One of the difficulties in examining the mobility problems of these groups is that there is a great deal of overlap in the classification schemes used. For example, a study in Portland, Oregon, found that 60 percent of the handicapped lived in households with family incomes less than $5000 [Crain and Courington, 1977]. Similarly, 40 percent of the nonhandicapped elderly were included in the same income category. Also, a nationwide survey in the United States found about 53 percent of the transportation handicapped to be elderly [Ellis et al., 1977].

Thus, in categorizing the mobility disadvantaged into these main groups, there is bound to be considerable overlap. Even with this overlap, however, many of the mobility problems for each group are the same. As noted by Revis, "the transportation disadvantaged (1) have no car or cannot drive because they are poor or physically unable to, (2) they often live in areas that are poorly served by public transportation, (3) for many, particularly the elderly and handicapped, the available transportation services do not meet their need for personalized door-to-door or door-through-door service, and (4) they may be confronted by serious physical design features of available transportation that create problems of orientation and maneuverability and that frequently discourage the transportation disadvantaged from making any trips" [Revis, 1976].

Mobility and the elderly. Mobility is an important factor in the physical, social, and psychological health of elderly people. Wachs [1979], in a recent study of the mobility needs of the elderly in Los Angeles, stated that:

> Physical health (of the elderly) depends upon access to medical facilities and other social services. The ability to maintain an active social life in old age depends upon accessibility to family and friends as well as recreational and cultural activities. Key ingredients of psychological health which are enhanced by mobility are freedom from isolation and the ability to choose one's range of activities.

Although mobility problems seem to afflict large numbers of elderly individuals, the degree of inconvenience experienced because of limited mobility opportunities is hard to measure. Trip making by the elderly is clearly much less frequent than that by other adults. As shown in Table 2-9, the total number of trips taken by an elderly person each year is less than half that for the average adult. This table also indicates that the elderly use public transit more often than the general public.

Table 2-9 Trips per capita and by mode

Mode	Percentage of all trips		Trips per capita	
	Persons 65 and over	All persons 16 and over	Persons 65 and over	All persons 16 and over
Auto driver	53.4	62.6	201	531
Auto passenger	35.9	25.7	135	218
Motorcycle		0.2		2
Truck (driver or passenger)	4.2	6.0	16	51
Subtotal: private vehicle	93.5	94.5	352	802
Transit bus	4.3	2.8	16	24
Rapid transit	0.5	0.9	2	8
Commuter rail	0.1	0.2		2
School bus	0.6	1.2	2	10
Taxi	0.6	0.3	2	2
Subtotal: public transportation	6.1	5.4	22	46
Other (airplanes, etc.)	0.4	0.1	1	1
Total	100.0	100.0	375	849

Source: Altshuler [1979].

Perhaps more significant measures of the mobility problems of the elderly are the degree to which they have automobiles available for trip making and the number of elderly persons licensed to drive. In a study of elderly travel behavior in the New York metropolitan region, Markovitz [1971] found that auto availability varied significantly with income (see Table 2-10). The elderly participants in this study averaged only 44 percent as many trips per capita as the general population. With respect to drivers'

Table 2-10 Automobile availability among the elderly in the New York metropolitan area

Household income	Percent of elderly households with no auto available
$0–$2999	83.7
$3000–$5999	58.2
$6000–$9999	29.6
over $10,000	20.6

Source: Markovitz [1971].

licenses, of those currently over 65, a significantly smaller percentage hold licenses than is the case for the general population. In Florida, for example, only 58 percent of those between 65 and 75 years of age, and 30 percent of those over 75, held licenses, as compared to 83 percent for those between 25 and 64 [U.S. Congress, 1974].

These measures indicate a relatively significant mobility disadvantage for those currently over 65. Two observations concerning these results, however, merit special attention. First, "life cycle" considerations must be included in these results. Thus, a 65-year-old and a 25-year-old having similar socioeconomic and auto-ownership levels would not generally be expected to have the same trip-making behavior. Second, the mobility problems for the future elderly might be different from those experienced by the elderly today. For example, studies in both the United States and Canada have shown that the makeup of the elderly is quite diverse, resulting in travel patterns and needs that differ significantly from one another [Wachs, 1979; Wolfe and Miller, 1982]. As shown in Fig. 2-11, this diversity, at least as predicted for Los Angeles, will require different approaches to serve the needs of each group. This seems to be a major challenge that will face transportation planning for elderly mobility in the coming decades.

Mobility and the handicapped. The mobility needs of physically handicapped individuals present challenges to transportation planners even more problematic than those of the elderly, because not only is general mobility an issue, accessibility to the vehicle is as well. The extent of the mobility problem for handicapped individuals in the United States, however, is a matter of contention because of uncertain estimates of the number of handicapped people living in urban areas. The U.S. Congressional Budget Office has estimated that there are about 13.4 million handicapped people, who, "because of medical problems or incapacities, experience more than average difficulty in using public transportation" [Lewis, 1981]. About 7.4 million of these individuals live in cities served by public transportation, a number that by the year 2010 is expected to grow by 70 percent. And of these 7.4 million, more than one-third live more than 0.5 mile from bus routes and subway stations, indicating a need for special types of transportation services that make line-haul facilities accessible or provide door-to-door service.

The characteristics of the services needed for this special market depend on the types of medical problems that limit mobility. One attempt to estimate the magnitude of these problems and their relationship to transportation requirements is summarized in Table 2-11. The data in this table come from studies conducted by the U.S. National Center for Health Statistics, adapted by Au and Baumann [Au and Baumann, 1981]. Although some of the assumptions reflected in this table are somewhat questionable (e.g., those requiring special aids need a vehicle with a lift), the data do provide a useful estimate of required vehicle mix and escort requirements. For example, 24 percent of the handicapped need, at the very least, some form of special access to a vehicle. Also, more than 50 percent of the handicapped are in no need of escort and can travel with the simple help of general aids (e.g., more negotiable steps on buses, weather protection at bus stops, and special seating arrangements on buses).

	Spanish American	New suburbanites	Black community	Central-city dwellers	Early suburbanites
Population forecast	Increase	Doubles, possibly triples	Decreases	Decreases	Increases
Travel forecast					
Auto driver	Doubles	Triples, possibly quadruples	Slight increases	Increases	Doubles
Auto passenger	Increases	Doubles	Little change	Little change	Increases
Bus passenger	Increases	Little change	Decreases	Decreases	Increases
Total trips	Doubles	Triples	Decreases	Little change	Doubles
Current inventory of services					
Bus	High	Low	High	High	Average
Taxi:					
fares	High	Varies	High	Varies	Varies
quality	High	Low	High	Average	Low
Specialized services	Average	Average	High	Low	High

Figure 2-11 Future transportation needs of the elderly in Los Angeles (*Wachs* [*1979*].)

Mobility and the poor. Much of the concern with equity issues in transportation during recent years has been related to the mobility opportunities and costs of travel to specific income groups. Such concerns are important because the poor often do not have access to automobiles and thus must rely on public transportation or other means for their mobility. As shown in Table 2-12, close to 25 percent of total transit ridership in the United States comes from households with incomes less than $6000. This income group also accounts for a large proportion of the taxi and pedestrian travel in urban areas.

To a large extent then, the mobility of lower income urban residents depends on the existence of government-provided transit service. And indeed, one of the key justifications of transit subsidization has been the premise that the poor are primary beneficiaries. Several studies of this premise, however, have concluded that in fact the

Table 2-11 Service requirements for the elderly and handicapped

Mobility status	Percent of transportation handicapped in population			Percent among E & H	Requirements	
	Age 0–64	Age 65 and over	Total		Reasons for escort	Vehicle
Confined to bed	0.10	0.12	0.22	3.3	Physical and psychological	Stretcher
Confined to house but not to bed	0.26	0.39	0.65	9.9	Psychological	Lift
Needs another person	0.11	0.17	0.28	4.3	Psychological	General aids
Needs a special aid	0.26	0.48	0.74	11.2	Physical	Lift
Has trouble getting around	0.72	0.56	1.28	19.5	Physical	General aids
Balance of the transportation handicapped	1.67	1.74	3.41	51.8	None	General aids
Total elderly and handicapped	3.12	3.46	6.58	100		

Source: Au and Baumann [1981].

Table 2-12 Mode use by household income
U.S. metropolitan areas, all trip purposes, 1977–78

	Income class					
	Less than $6,000, percent	$6,000–$10,000, percent	$10,000–$15,000, percent	$15,000–$20,000, percent	$20,000–$25,000, percent	$25,000 and over, percent
Auto drivers	8.9	11.6	21.1	20.2	15.0	23.2
Auto passengers	11.3	12.2	22.3	19.4	14.0	20.9
Transit (total)	24.9	17.8	19.1	14.1	10.0	14.1
Bus and streetcar	28.3	19.2	18.7	13.5	8.5	11.7
Subway	16.2	17.2	27.7	14.4	11.7	12.9
Commuter rail	9.3	6.0	7.9	18.9	20.1	37.8
Taxi	26.8	17.9	18.5	16.9	4.9	15.1
Bicycle	15.0	10.2	20.3	19.2	9.8	25.4
Walk	26.7	16.1	19.7	13.8	9.4	14.4
School bus	8.9	12.1	15.8	23.0	19.5	20.7
Other	13.7	22.3	18.9	19.3	12.3	13.4
All travelers	12.2	12.5	21.1	19.1	13.9	21.1
All people	16.1	13.9	21.4	17.7	13.1	17.8
All households	21.6	15.3	21.4	15.7	11.0	14.9

Source: Altshuler [1979].

Table 2-13 Incidence of transit funding burden in Boston

	Income group					
	0–6	6–10	10–15	15–20	20–25	25+
All modes						
Subsidy burden/income	0.0156	0.0174	0.0173	0.0168	0.0157	0.0128
(Fare and subsidy burden)/income	0.0312	0.0294	0.0244	0.0229	0.0202	0.0156
Local bus						
Subsidy burden/income	0.0108	0.0066	0.0065	0.0063	0.0058	0.0047
(Fare and subsidy burden)/income	0.0170	0.0126	0.0096	0.0079	0.0064	0.0053
Express bus						
Subsidy burden/income	0.0048	0.0107	0.0108	0.0105	0.0099	0.0080
(Fare and subsidy burden)/income	0.0094	0.0168	0.0148	0.0150	0.0132	0.0103

Note: The fare burden was allocated in proportion to ridership, while subsidy burden was estimated by the distribution of taxes supporting the transit authority.

Source: Palmere [1981].

contrary might be true[3] [Wohl, 1970; Altshuler, 1979; Cervero et al., 1980; Pucher and Hirschman, 1981]. For example, a recent study of the distribution of fare payments and tax support for transit service in the Boston metropolitan region revealed a regressive structure in allocating the funding burden (i.e., the poor pay a higher percentage of their income to support transit service than do higher income groups) [Palmere, 1981]. Table 2-13 shows the extent to which lower income groups in Boston bear a disproportionately high share of the fare and subsidy burden. The subsidy burden is calculated by estimating the incidence of taxes supporting the transit service by each household in each income group. The fare burden is determined by allocating costs to each income group in proportion to its ridership on the system. According to Table 2-13, individuals in the $0 to $6000 yearly income group spend over 3 percent of their income on transit service, while those over $25,000 per year spend about half that percentage.

[3] An interesting study of the distribution of fare payments by income class was undertaken by Pucher et al. [1981]. Their results of a national sample showed the following relationships:

Income class	Fare payments as % of total fare revenues	Fare payments as % of money income in each class
less than $6,000	22.8%	1.30%
$6,000–$10,000	17.0	0.63
$10,000–$15,000	19.4	0.38
$15,000–$20,000	14.4	0.20
$20,000–$25,000	10.8	0.20
over $25,000	15.5	0.08

The important lesson emerging from these experiences is that changes to the transportation system—and in particular, changes to the funding of services—can have substantial equity impacts that adversely affect those least able to afford such changes. In general then, the mobility problems of the poor, the elderly, and the handicapped merit special attention in the transportation planning process. As will be discussed in Chap. 9, the equitable distribution of costs and benefits is an issue which consistently surfaces in the decision-making process, and consequently in the evaluation phase of urban transportation planning.

2-2-3 Construction and Operational Impacts of Transportation Systems and Facilities on the Activity System

Every transportation facility and service has some impact on the urban activity system. These impacts range from direct physical effects on the natural environment to the more indirect social and economic effects on surrounding neighborhoods. Some impacts—such as changes in air quality, noise levels, energy consumption, and the displacement of residential and commercial buildings—can be quantified and effectively used in the project evaluation process. Other impacts, however, are not easily measured and are therefore difficult to incorporate into transportation planning methodology. These include project impacts on aesthetics, social impacts, and psychological impacts on those forced to move because of the project under consideration.

As shown in Table 2-14, three major impact categories are usually considered in project evaluation. Consideration of many of these impact categories has been mandated by federal, state, provincial, and local regulations. In the United States, for example, federal regulations have, for many years, required the preparation of an environmental impact statement (EIS) for major transportation projects supported by federal funds. The three categories of impacts shown in Table 2-14 are discussed separately below. Their incorporation into the evaluation and EIS process is discussed in greater detail in Chap. 9.

Physical impacts. During the 1970s, the physical impacts of the construction and operation of transportation facilities received increasing attention from public officials. In part, this attention was caused by a growing awareness of the significant contribution that the transportation sector makes to declining environmental quality. For example, automobile travel in many urban areas contributes between 40 and 80 percent of some air pollutants. In terms of energy consumption, total auto travel accounts for about 25 percent of United States oil consumption, with about two-thirds of this consumption occurring in urban areas [Altshuler, 1979]. It is therefore not surprising that public officials, when adopting policies designed to improve environmental quality, have repeatedly turned to changes in the transportation system as one method of achieving these objectives.

There are four major physical impacts that merit special attention—construction impacts on the ecology and the impacts on air quality, energy consumption, and noise levels of vehicles operating on the completed facility. Each of these impacts is briefly discussed below.

Table 2-14 Transportation facility impacts on the activity system

Physical impacts
   Aesthetics and historic value
   Infrastructure
   Terrestrial ecosystems
   Aquatic ecosystems
   Air quality
   Noise and vibration
   Disruption or damage to adjacent properties
   Traffic circulation and parking
   Public safety
   Energy

Economic impacts
   Employment, income, and business activity
   Residential activity
   Effects on property
   Regional and community plans
   Resource consumption

Social impacts
   Displacement of people
   Accessibility of facilities and services
   Effects of terminals on neighborhoods
   Special user groups

Source: Adapted from U.S. Department of Transportation [1979].

Ecology The construction of any transportation facility requires land which, in its natural state, determines the physical and biological characteristics of the region. Physical attributes include soil and topography and involve such physical processes as erosion and sedimentation. Biological attributes involve local plant and wildlife communities and the various interrelated processes which make up the biological system of the area.

The major focus of transportation planners in this impact category has been on the transportation-related impacts on biological systems in the vicinity of proposed transportation facilities. Plants and animals interact in complex ecosystems, even in urbanizing areas. Unfortunately, the construction of a transportation facility necessarily disrupts the equilibrium established between the components of these ecosystems. Consideration must therefore be given to the loss of, or injury to, important organisms both directly (e.g., through destruction of vegetation) or indirectly (e.g., through contamination of water supplies).

A set of guidelines developed by the United States government for environmental impact assessment identified the following questions as being crucial to any investigation of transportation-related impacts on the ecology [U.S. Department of Transportation, 1979]:

Are threatened or endangered organisms found in the project corridor?
Are organisms found in the corridor that are valuable for commercial, recreational, or ecological reasons?
Are nuisance organisms (such as rodents and insects) present that might mitigate or proliferate because of project-induced habitat changes?
Are organisms present that should be retained for aesthetic purposes?
Will ecosystem food webs be damaged, endangering important or protected organisms?
Will the diversity of important biological communities be lessened, promoting less ecosystem stability and ability to withstand stress?
Will ecosystem productivity be lessened, reducing the system's ability to support important or protected organisms?

In answering each of these questions, it is important to consider not only the impacts resulting from actual construction of the facility, but also those relating to its subsequent operation and maintenance (e.g., the runoffs of salts used to clear highways of snow).

Air quality The urban transportation system is a major source of air pollution in most metropolitan areas. In some cities, vehicle exhaust accounts for close to 90 percent of some pollutant categories (see Table 2-15). The most important pollutants emitted from highway vehicles include:

Carbon monoxide (CO) The most abundant of motor vehicle pollutants, CO emissions are caused by incomplete fuel combustion within the engine. Total motor vehicle CO emissions thus decrease as vehicle speeds increase, as the result of more complete combustion. Because carbon monoxide concentrations are found most often near congested roadway facilities in metropolitan areas, CO is considered to be more of a localized air pollution problem.

Hydrocarbons (HC) Hydrocarbon emissions are the result of unburned fuel and oil. Hydrocarbons are present in automobile exhaust and are also emitted as gasoline vapors from the fuel tank and carburetor. The most important impact of reactive HC emissions is that they play a dominant role in the formation of photochemical oxidants (smog). Like CO, the emission level of HC decreases with increases in vehicle speed.

Oxides of nitrogen Nitric oxide (NO) is produced in high temperature combustion processes. The toxic potential of NO lies in its ability to oxidize and produce nitrogen dioxide (NO_2), a major component in the formation of photochemical oxidants. By itself, NO_2 can irritate the eyes, nose, and lungs. Unlike CO and HC, emissions of nitrous oxides increase with increased vehicle speeds.

Table 2-15 Highway vehicle emissions as a percentage of total emissions in selected North American metropolitan areas

Area	NO_X	HC	CO
Atlanta	51	50	91
Baltimore	43	44	83
Boston	45	46	92
Chicago	27	31	74
Cincinnati	24	38	88
Cleveland	41	29	86
Dallas	27	37	89
Detroit	40	35	87
Houston	15	16	70
Los Angeles	55	43	91
Milwaukee	43	40	88
Minneapolis	45	38	90
New York	42	38	91
Philadelphia	38	31	86
Pittsburgh	22	37	67
St. Louis	20	39	77
San Diego	53	49	92
San Francisco	50	48	91
Seattle	58	54	87
Toronto	48	64	97
Washington	45	67	95

Source: Calculated from EPA, *1978 National Emissions Report,* Research Triangle Park, N.C., 1980; and Ontario Ministry of the Environment, *Air Quality Model for Toronto: 1979 Emissions,* Toronto, 1980.

Sulfur oxides Although generated primarily by nontransportation sources, sulfur is found in small amounts in gasoline. During combustion, this sulfur can be converted into sulfates which, when combined with other pollutants and moisture, can irritate the eyes, nose, throat, and lungs.

Particulates The automobile is not a major source of particulate matter in the atmosphere, although some unburned carbon can be emitted by engines. Particulates can cause breathing difficulties by themselves or can promote the toxic effects of other pollutants.

Public policy with regard to air quality and transportation has focused on two elements: control of engine pollutant emissions through nationally mandated emission standards and the implementation of controls on the use of automobiles in urban areas.

In the United States and Canada, the auto emission standards (expressed in grams per mile) are as follows:

	Grams per mile	
	United States	Canada
HC	1.5	2.0
CO	15.0	25.0
NO_x	2.0	3.1

The purpose of these standards is to control the air pollution problem at one of its major sources—the automobile engine. Automobile manufacturers are required to manufacture engines that meet these levels of pollutant emissions. Even with these controls, however, there can be such large concentrations of automobiles in urban areas that overall pollution levels can reach unhealthful proportions. In such instances, some form of control on automobile use may be considered.

One of the most dramatic examples of the potential impact of automobile restrictions on air quality occurred in the aftermath of a major snowstorm in Boston. In January 1978, a snowstorm that crippled the transportation system in the metropolitan area caused local officials to declare a week-long ban on automobile driving in the city. As shown in Fig. 2-12, the impact of this restriction on CO levels at three locations in the metropolitan area was dramatic. When the auto ban was lifted, CO levels at each location increased, in one case to a level considered unhealthful. Although the Boston ban on automobile use was a dramatic action, and not one likely to be replicated on a longer-term basis, it does illustrate the potential importance of transportation actions in improving air quality levels in urban areas.

Noise. The production of noise (and vibration) is one of the most apparent physical impacts of a transportation facility's operation. Exposure to high levels of noise over an extended period can have detrimental effects on the physical and mental health of human beings. In the case of urban transportation, however, noise levels are usually not high enough to actually cause physical harm. As shown in Table 2-16, noise levels vary for different types of transportation facilities and operations. As a rule of thumb, noise levels have to exceed 90 decibels on a fairly continual basis to cause hearing damage.

The most common unit of noise measurement is the decibel (dB), which is a logarithmic measure of sound pressure. A doubling of noise at its source produces a 3-dB increase in the sound pressure level, which is barely perceptible to the human ear (an increase of 10 dB in noise level will cause the noise to be perceived as being about twice as loud). For example, if a highway carrying 500 vehicles per hour produces a noise level of 50 dB for an observer a specific distance away, an increase in traffic

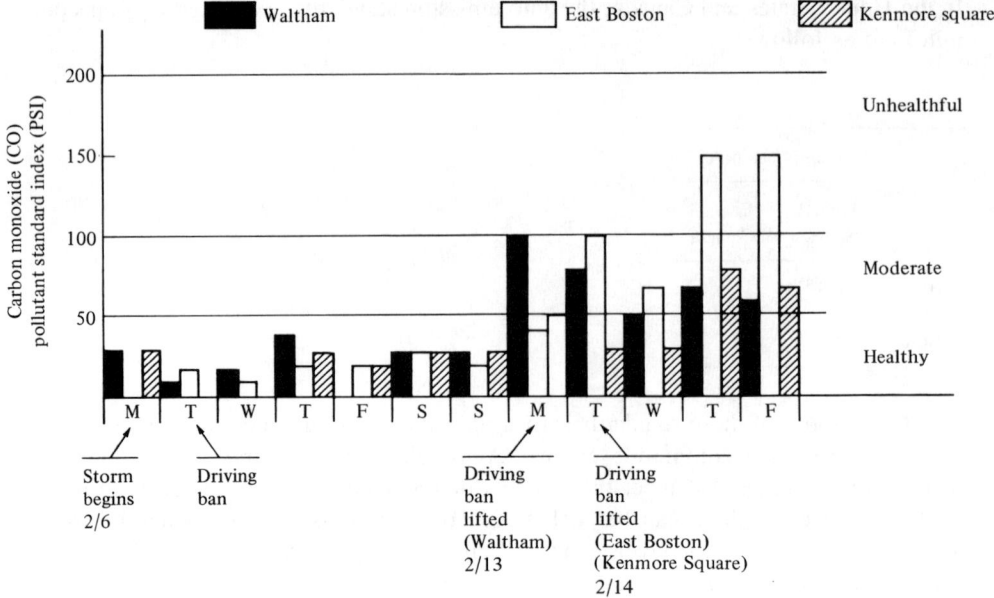

Figure 2-12 Air quality impacts of automobile use ban in Boston. (*U.S. Environmental Protection Agency, Information Booklet, 1980.*)

volume to 1000 vehicles per hour (under identical operating conditions) would produce a noise level of 53 dB, a change barely perceptible to the human ear. A volume increase to 5000 vehicles per hour, a tenfold increase in traffic volume, would increase noise level to about 60 dB, a doubling of the sound level for the observer.

Another important characteristic of noise in terms of human hearing is that sound intensity decreases with the square of the distance from a point source. In the case of a transportation facility, the noise level will decrease from 3 to 4.5 dB each time the distance from the facility is doubled.

In general then, the production of noise by a transportation facility can be one of the most perceptible impacts of its operation. Transportation-related noise becomes of special concern in those instances where adjacent land uses are particularly sensitive to noise disruption, for example hospitals and schools. Measures that can be taken to reduce this impact range from changes in traffic operation (e.g., reduced speed limits) to noise shielding (e.g., constructed barriers or vegetation).

Energy Highway vehicles are the largest single consumers of petroleum in the United States and Canada and are consequently a significant element of total energy consumption. Beginning in the mid-1970s with gasoline shortages caused by foreign embargoes on petroleum exports to the United States, a concern for the energy consumption of the transportation sector has grown in recent years. As an approximation, auto travel accounts directly for about one-quarter of the United States petroleum consumption and a similar percentage of the oil consumption in Canada.

Table 2-16 Transportation noise in urban areas

Type and location	Noise level, dBA	Individual reaction
Jet takeoff at 2000 ft	100	
		Vocal effort
Freight train at 50 ft	95	
Philadelphia rail car (below ground)		
Station platform	93–98	
Inside cars	82–95	
Heavy truck at 50 ft	90	Very annoying
Busy city street		
Toronto subway car		
Station platform	84	
Inside cars	78	Annoying
Philadelphia trolley car (above ground)		
Station platform	80–85	
Inside cars	65–75	
Highway traffic at 50 ft	70	Telephone use difficult
Light car traffic at 50 ft	60	Intrusive

Sources: James H. Botsford, "Damage Risk," *Transportation Noises—A Symposium on Acceptability Criteria*, pp. 103–113; *Road and Rail Noise Effects on Housing*, Central Mortgage and Housing Corporation, Ottawa, 1977.

The energy requirements for the various modes of travel in an urban area have been estimated in a large number of studies [U.S. Department of Transportation, 1976; Federal Energy Administration, 1976; Congressional Budget Office, 1977; Transportation Research Board, 1977; System Design Concepts, 1979]. The major problem with most of these estimates is that they are often highly dependent on vehicle technology, actual operating conditions, service strategies used (in the case of mass transit), and vehicle occupancy. Thus, consistent estimates of modal energy use are difficult to obtain. Table 2-17 gives an example of the range of such energy usage. It is important to note that this estimate has been based on typical United States conditions in travel markets generally appropriate for each mode. In other situations, the energy requirements could be very different.

The purpose of Table 2-17 is not to present the "true" energy efficiencies of each mode. Rather, Table 2-17 illustrates what many studies have concluded with respect to the energy consumption transportation linkage—the automobile is the least efficient mode of transportation in terms of energy consumption. Ride-sharing programs (i.e., car pools and van pools) along with conventional transit services provide a much more

Table 2-17 Energy requirements for various modes

Mode	Modal energy per pass.; Btu
Van pool	2,400– 2,430
Conventional bus	3,000– 4,100
Express bus	3,800– 3,830
Heavy rail (old)	3,990– 4,020
Commuter rail	5,000– 5,020
Light rail	5,050– 5,070
Car pool	5,420– 5,450
Heavy rail (new)	5,500– 6,580
Average auto	10,140–10,160
Single-occupant auto	14,190–14,225
Dial-a-ride	17,230–17,240

Source: Taken from several studies on energy requirements of urban transportation modes including System Design Concepts, *Urban Public Transportation and Energy,* Final Report, October 1979; U.S. Congressional Budget Office, *Urban Transportation and Energy: The Potential Savings of Different Modes,* a study prepared for the Committee on Environment and Public Works, U.S. Senate, No. 95-8, Washington, D.C., September 1977; and H. Levinson and R. Weant (eds.), *Urban Transportation: Perspectives and Prospects,* Eno Foundation, Westport, Conn., 1982.

efficient operation from the point of view of people carried per unit of energy consumed. This especially becomes the case when the energy used for constructing transportation facilities is considered in the overall energy efficiency analysis.

As in the case of air quality, national policy with regard to energy consumption in the transportation sector has focused both on the consumption of fuel by automobile engines and on encouraging local transportation actions that reduce gasoline consumption. In the former case, fuel economy standards for engine gasoline consumption have been established by Congress and the U.S. Department of Transportation. Over time, as the vehicle fleet mix changes, these standards should improve the fuel efficiency level of automobile travel. In the second case, many of the transportation actions that can be taken to improve air quality will also benefit energy conservation. Public transit policies such as fare reductions and the provision of express bus services in congested corridors, along with car pooling and van pooling, appear to be most effective from an energy standpoint.

Three other aspects of the energy impact merit attention as they relate to urban transportation planning. First, because of the heavy dependence of the urban transportation system on petroleum fuels, a significant decrease in fuel availability could seriously disrupt the normal functioning of an urban area. To handle such a situation, transportation planners must consider a wide variety of actions, and different "packages" of actions, that could be implemented to minimize the effects of the disruption on urban travel. Such contingency planning has received increasing attention since the OPEC oil embargo in the winter of 1974 [Humphrey, Salvucci, and Meyer, 1980; Meyer and Belobaba, 1982]. Second, land use impacts of large-scale transportation investment, in the long run, could influence regional energy consumption by concentrating activities in certain areas. Third, consistent progress is being made on improving the energy efficiency of automobiles and in developing alternative energy sources for them, such as fuels from coal and plants, and electric motors.

Economic impacts. The maintenance of a healthy economic climate and a business community able to provide a local employment base has generally been a major factor in determining transportation investment and policy decisions. As discussed in Sec. 2-2-1, changes in transportation systems can affect the level of accessibility provided to certain areas of the metropolitan region. Over the longer term, this increased accessibility can influence the type and extent of economic development in urbanized and urbanizing areas.

In older urban areas, changes to the transportation system can serve to influence industry and business decisions to remain in central cities, affect the level of retail sales, and alter the characteristics of the municipal revenue base (e.g., through changes in parking fees). In the first case, highway and/or transit access for employees and clients—as well as highway, rail, airport, or seaport access for goods—is an important factor in locational decisions for firms. Several types of transportation-related actions that can be successfully used in downtown economic programs include the rebuilding of transportation terminals, the provision of new highway and transit access to economically depressed areas of the region, joint development activities around new transit stations, the development use of air rights over transportation facilities, environmental improvements such as pedestrianization schemes, and improved urban goods movements, [Meyer et al., 1979].

A recent indication of the importance of transportation-related actions in encouraging economic development was the level of funds devoted to transportation investment in the Urban Development Action Grant (UDAG) program of the United States government [Meyer and McShane, 1983]. Established in 1977, the purpose of the program was to "leverage significant private investments" by providing public funding of project components desired by developers [U.S. Department of Housing and Urban Development, 1978]. Between April 1978 and October 1980, out of 889 projects supported by UDAG funds, close to 30 percent used UDAG moneys to construct parking facilities or make street improvements. This finding does not suggest that the existence of the UDAG program or the funding of transportation programs in any way caused private development to occur. However, the level of funding made available and the interest of private developers in the program support the notion that improvements to the transportation system could be influential factors in proposals for urban development.

Transportation system changes can also affect the level of retail sales in an urban area, once again because of the accessibility provided to shoppers. In a study of the changing pattern of downtown department-store patronage in three cities, Sternlieb

[1962] concluded that the early success of such stores could be attributed to the extensive mass transit systems in existence during the 1920s and 1930s. Their later decline came about when urban highway programs encouraged suburbanization and provided easy access to suburban retail locations.

Another component of perceived success of downtown retail activities is the existence of ample parking. Downtown businessmen have argued for many years that parking is essential in stimulating retail sales. A study conducted in 1965 estimated that a single parking space could generate up to $10,000 in annual retail sales [Smith et al., 1965]. In 1972, a 3-day parking strike in Pittsburgh closed virtually all the parking spaces in the downtown area. Downtown retailers estimated that sales declined by 6 to 7 percent during the strike, with substantially greater losses incurred by stores heavily patronized by auto drivers[4] [Hoel and Roszner, 1972].

Although the above examples indicate a relationship between retail sales and transportation accessibility, the impacts of transportation system changes will be heavily influenced by such factors as the density of the urban area and the type and level of mode use. In Boston, for example, where there is a high concentration of retail activity in the downtown area, the implementation of an auto-restricted zone and improved transit service have positively influenced sales levels in the retail district [Weisbrod, 1982]. In the case of a transit mall in Minneapolis, however, there has been little evidence of an overall increase in retail sales since the mall was constructed [Heaton and Goodman, 1980].

The final economic impact discussed in this section is the effect on municipal finances and personal incomes of transportation-related changes. Perhaps the most extensive analysis of such issues was undertaken as part of the BART impact study [Grefe and McDonald, 1979]. This study found that the total value of goods and services purchased in the San Francisco region between 1964 and 1976 as a result of BART construction was $3.1 billion. Operating expenditures will contribute an estimated $149 million per year to the regional economy, including an increase of nearly $52 million annually in personal income. These income and sales changes will in turn contribute to local government revenues in the form of taxes.[5]

These positive effects, however, must be weighed against the increased burden on municipal budgets and individual incomes of constructing and funding the BART system. In this regard, the BART study found that the construction and operation of the system placed the heaviest burden on low-income households. The study also concluded that, despite early statements about BART's boon to the economic welfare of the region, the majority of the tax burden for the BART system will be placed on households, not on business and commercial establishments. Over the life of the bonds

---

[4] The relatively low sales decline in nonauto patronized stores indicates the large percentage of patrons using transit to the downtown area. Recent surveys have shown that in many large city downtown stores, between 50 percent and 75 percent of the customers arrive by transit [American Public Transit Association, 1981].

[5] Another example of the impact of transportation-related actions on municipal revenues is the collection of parking fines in an urban area. In Washington, D.C., a vigorous enforcement campaign has provided the city close to $10 million in annual revenues. In Boston, a similar enforcement campaign begun in 1982 produced $200,000 in revenues each week.

used to fund BART, approximately 64 percent of the property taxes in the region will be paid by home owners.

Social impacts. The social impacts associated with the construction and operation of transportation facilities primarily involve the physical displacement of people and social institutions during the facility construction and the effects on neighborhood cohesion once the facility is in operation (see Table 2-18). The social impacts of displacement of people can be generally categorized as follows:

Family and social ties. May be weakened or broken by geographic separation or relocation.
Attitudes and behavior. May change as part of a psychological response to separation from neighbors or familiar surroundings.
Disruption of neighborhood patterns. Relocation of large numbers of households may weaken or dissolve "community cohesion" in both the abandoned and new neighborhoods involved.
Business people's reactions. Along with financial losses, business owners may lose steady customers and goodwill associated with their businesses when forced to relocate.
Relocation housing availability. Replacement housing that is both livable and matches the needs of the relocated households has to be found.

Table 2-18 Attributes directly measured for the assessment of social impact

Land use—community and neighborhood form
    Proximity to city center
    Proportion of mixed land usage
    Proportion of undeveloped land area
    Density of population
    Age of dwellings in area
    Location of social institutions
    Location of neighborhood boundaries

Human ecological—modal characteristics of area residents
    Stability of area and housing tenure
    Ethnicity of residents
    Socioeconomic status of residents
    Age distribution of residents
    Transportation characteristics of residents

Sociopsychological—individual-level attributes
    Use of local facilities
    Neighboring—ties to friends and relatives in area
    Participation in area associations
    Identification and evaluation of area
    Individual values in regard to residential area
    Highway issue involvement

Source: Guseman et al. [1975].

Of special concern in the assessment of social impacts are those groups that can be particularly affected by changes to the community structure, including the elderly, lower-income families, ethnic groups, and longtime residents. These groups have been found to experience the most negative and long-term effects of displacement [Fried, 1966].

Completion of facility construction does not imply that the major social impacts of the facility have ended. A recent highway design manual noted that [U.S. Department of Transportation, 1980]:

> A new transportation facility may induce extensive business or industrial development and population growth, straining local services and facilities. Moreover, if the needs, desires, and social values of the incoming residents are at variance with the current residents, conflicts may arise and a new social structure may evolve.

Several guidelines for assessing the social impact of transportation facilities have been produced in recent years [Guseman et al., 1975; Kaplan et al., 1972; Manheim et al., 1975; U.S. Department of Transportation, 1979]. These guidelines have identified several attributes of community character and structure that can be directly measured in the assessment of social impact (see Table 2-18). In those cases where transportation investment in urban areas significantly affects selected community groups, a detailed assessment of social impacts and of the actions needed to mitigate negative effects usually becomes an important task in the planning process.

2-2-4 Land Use–Transportation Interaction

One of the fundamental relationships in the study of transportation is the linkage between land use and transportation. Put simply, trip-making patterns, volumes, and modal distributions are largely a function of the spatial distribution of land use. Likewise, the pattern of land use is influenced by the level of accessibility provided by the transportation system from one activity area to another. In most books, the interaction between land use and transportation is not discussed in the same section as transportation system characteristics. We feel, however, that this interaction is so important and fundamental to the overall understanding of system performance that introductory remarks are warranted in this section.

This land use–transportation relationship is represented by the diagram in Fig. 2-13. The development of land for a particular use results either in the generation of new trips originating from that area or new trips attracted to that area, or both. The development of land in an urban area thus creates new travel demands and, consequently, a need for transportation facilities, whether in the form of new infrastructure or more efficient operation of existing facilities. Such improvements to the transportation system make the land more accessible to existing activity centers, thereby making it more desirable and affecting its monetary value. Increased accessibility and improved land values in turn influence the locational decisions of individuals and firms, once again spurring new land development and starting this cycle again, until an equilibrium is reached or until some other external factor intervenes.

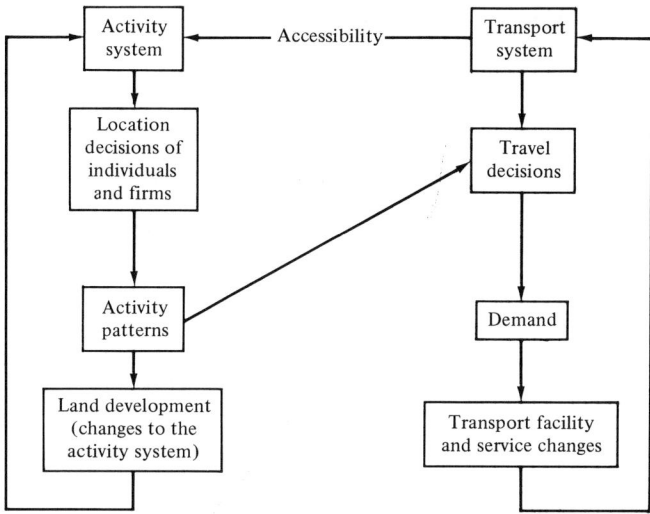

Figure 2-13 Land use–transportation interaction.

An important dimension of the relationships shown in Fig. 2-13 is the time it takes for the cycle to complete itself. In the short run, the predominant influence is that of land use on the performance of the transportation system. For example, the impact of a new suburban shopping mall on the surrounding street system is likely to be severe, to the point of requiring major street and/or transit improvements. Similarly, the opening of a large office building in the center city could significantly tax the ability of a nearby subway station to handle the peak-hour rush.

In the long run, the provision of transportation infrastructure and the introduction of new technologies will influence urban form because of the improved accessibility that results. This impact is obvious in the historical development of United States cities. In the 1800s, when urban travel was mainly by foot and on horseback, city structures were highly centralized with dense concentrations of commerce and industry located in the urban core. As noted in Sec. 1-4-2, the introduction of more advanced transportation technology (for both passenger and goods movement) allowed the urban area to expand and decentralize. This rapid decentralization became known as urban sprawl and, in some cases, led to public efforts to promote higher land use densities and to reverse the trend toward suburbanization [Real Estate Research Corporation, 1974].

Research on the exact relationship between the provision of transportation and the development of land has taken many forms. As shown in Table 2-19, this research has ranged from site-specific studies of the impact of a transportation facility (e.g., a subway station or road) on property values to regional studies of the impact of changes in transportation accessibility on the density of land development. One of the interesting characteristics of this research record is that the evidence is not at all clear whether, given the high level of access currently provided by urban transportation systems,

Table 2-19 Sample of land use–transportation studies

Author	Date	Type of transportation facility	Conclusions
Adkins	1959	Expressway	Value of land closest to expressway increased on the order of 300–600%. Land farther from expressway experienced smaller value increases.
Allen and Mudge	1974	Fixed heavy rail	Major transportation investment impact is to transfer land development from one part of the region to another.
Ashley and Bernard	1965	Highway interchanges	Major development at interchanges caused by many factors including market condition and financing arrangements.
Davies	1976	Subway	Increased population density occurred near subway stations as compared to rest of region.
Donnelly	1982	Rail transit	Land use planning in affected communities responded to new rail transit and will likely shape future growth. Development focused within 0.25 mile of transit station.
Downing	1973	Bus routes	Property values highly dependent upon accessibility.
Gauthier	1970	Railroads	Improvement in transportation may help some parts of the region while harming others.
Knight and Trygg	1977	Rapid transit system	No evidence that any rapid transit improvements have led to net new urban economic or population growth.
Lerman et al.	1977	Rapid transit system	Land closer to subway station experienced greater increase in property value.
Metropolitan Transportation Commission	1979	Rapid transit system	Development within transit corridors was measurably different than without system. System may have prevented further central city decentralization.
Mohring	1961	Highway	Increase of land value near highway balanced by relative decreases elsewhere.
Spengler	1930	Subway	New transit lines tend to shift value, not create new value. Areas already developed do not show marked increase in land value when new transit lines are opened.

Table 2-19 (*continued*)

Author	Date	Type of transportation facility	Conclusions
U.S. Environmental Protection Agency	1975	Highway	Value of land near new or improved highways increased substantially. Value of land for single-family dwelling is, on the average, not affected significantly by highways.
U.S. Department of Transportation	1980	Beltways	No strong evidence exists to suggest that beltways improve a metropolitan area's competitive advantage. Differences in housing patterns between beltway and nonbeltway cities not statistically significant.

Source: Adapted from Lerman et al. [1977].

incremental improvements in this access can alone affect metropolitan patterns of urban development.

At the site-specific level, several studies have shown the importance of transportation accessibility on property values and on household and/or firm location decisions. For example, a study of a sample of real estate transactions in Washington, D.C. from 1969 to 1976 concluded that: (1) the distance of a parcel from a subway station appeared to be a determinant of the variation in values of properties, (2) the value of a parcel tended to increase as a nearby station's opening date approached, and (3) the availability of parking positively influenced retail property values [Lerman et al., 1977].

With respect to location decisions, Cheslow and Olsson [1975] concluded that, apart from house and neighborhood-related attributes such as lot size, quality of schools, extent of crime, and housing cost, household location decisions are also influenced by accessibility to workplaces, shopping and business centers, recreation opportunities, and health facilities. In essence then, each household must make a trade-off between housing price, transportation costs, and these other attributes when deciding upon a housing location.

At the regional level, the impact of transportation investment on metropolitan development is less clear. In Toronto, increased land values and development activities along the Yonge Street and Bloor Street subway corridors have been attributed to the existence of the rapid transit lines [Heenan, 1968; Bower, 1979]. Although property values undeniably increased during the initial decade of subway operations, these and similar attempts to quantify the impact of the subway on land values have found it difficult to totally separate the effects of rapid transit on land development from all the other elements affecting the land development process. More recent studies of the entire subway system have found this task even more difficult, given the rapid rise of all land values. The Toronto subway system, however, does seem to have been a major factor in clustering development near subway stations, rather than a force in attracting new development to the region.[6]

An extensive impact evaluation of San Francisco's BART system has come to serve as the point of departure for critiques on the land use impact of rapid transit investment. In general, BART's impact on regional land use configurations has been quite limited. As noted in one evaluation report [Metropolitan Transportation Commission, 1979]:

> Population and employment have not increased in the BART district at the expense of the other Bay Area counties. Nor has the system caused a redistribution of office space on a regional level. However, within the greater BART service area employment has increased most rapidly in the relatively narrow corridors along the BART lines . . .

This report also points out, however, that some decisions by local developers have indeed been influenced by the existence of the BART system, and that development around some suburban stations has actually been constrained by local zoning changes designed to maintain a low-density area profile.

In summary, land use development and the provision of transportation services and infrastructure are, in large part, functions of one another. In the past, when urban areas were experiencing demand for rapid expansion and growth, the location of transportation facilities (and the accessibility they afforded) provided a strong means to influence the direction of this growth. In more recent times, it has become apparent that, although the overall regional impact of new investments in transportation facilities on urban structure is often negligible, the *distributional* impact on new development *within* a region can be substantial, given the right circumstances. With a high level of accessibility already available through existing transportation systems, the use of transportation investment *by itself* to influence land use is likely to produce minimal results.

---

[6] Other factors which made the environment in Toronto conducive to such a land use impact for the subway include:

1. The entire region, and particularly the CBD, was experiencing rapid growth and economic expansion, and there was little central area deterioration.
2. The original subway lines followed already heavily used surface streetcar routes. The subway thus increased accessibility to areas where demand for additional residential and commercial floor space was high.
3. The metropolitan government was able to provide capital support for both land acquisition and construction. This resulted in a great deal of publicly owned surplus land available for sale back to developers.
4. The policy-making powers of the metropolitan government gave it substantial control over both its own and other properties adjacent to subway lines. Metropolitan Toronto was able to coordinate the land use policies of the different municipalities through which the subway runs.
5. The transit commission sold air rights (i.e., over bus and subway terminals and over switching yards) to developers.
6. There was a great deal of cooperation between public and private sectors in terms of development adjacent to subway stations, particularly in the form of direct access to the subway stations.

Given the nature of past experiences with using transportation investments to influence urban development, some additional conclusions seem appropriate:

1. Transportation is only one factor that influences development decisions and hence land use impacts (see Fig. 2-14). In general, land development impacts near transportation facilities are caused by many economic, governmental, and social factors including:

   Regional demand for new development
   Availability of developable land
   Complementary local government actions, e.g., zoning and land use plans
   Appropriate adjacent land uses
   Attractive sites for development

   More recently, government officials have used tax incentives, financial aid, and technical assistance programs to influence developers' decisions as to the location of proposed projects. Although few detailed studies have been made on the effectiveness of these programs, the evidence that does exist seems to suggest that such use of government power can indeed affect the land use configuration in an urban area, when applied consistently [Lyall, 1975; U.S. Department of Commerce, 1980].

2. Because direct governmental action over land development through land use plans and zoning is often more effective than the use of transportation investment strategies, transportation planning and investment should be coordinated with land use planning. In Canada and in many other countries, transportation is regarded as a land use and is fully integrated with general urban planning [Holmes, 1974]. Although this is generally not the case in the United States, such coordination is essential for the development of a transportation investment program that meets the development needs of an urban area.

3. The development of land in market-oriented economies is mainly the responsibility of private entrepreneurs and developers. Thus, the feasibility of new development, and the use of transportation investment to encourage such development, needs to be evaluated at least in part from a private investment perspective, with an understanding of the factors that can influence development decisions [Witherspoon, 1979; U.S. Department of Housing and Urban Development, 1979; U.S. Conference of Mayors, 1980]. Coordinated transportation and private investment planning characterizes the many "joint development" projects found throughout North America [U.S. DOT, 1979; Paaswell et al., 1979]. Although at one time primarily associated with highway investments, joint development now includes "real estate development that is closely linked to public transportation services and station facilities" [Urban Land Institute, 1979]. In joint development projects, private sector interests play key roles in the implementation of the development proposal and in defining the desirable characteristics of the complementary transportation investment.

4. The land use impact of transportation investment tends to involve changes in the spatial distribution of activities within a metropolitan area, both in terms of the

68 URBAN TRANSPORTATION PLANNING

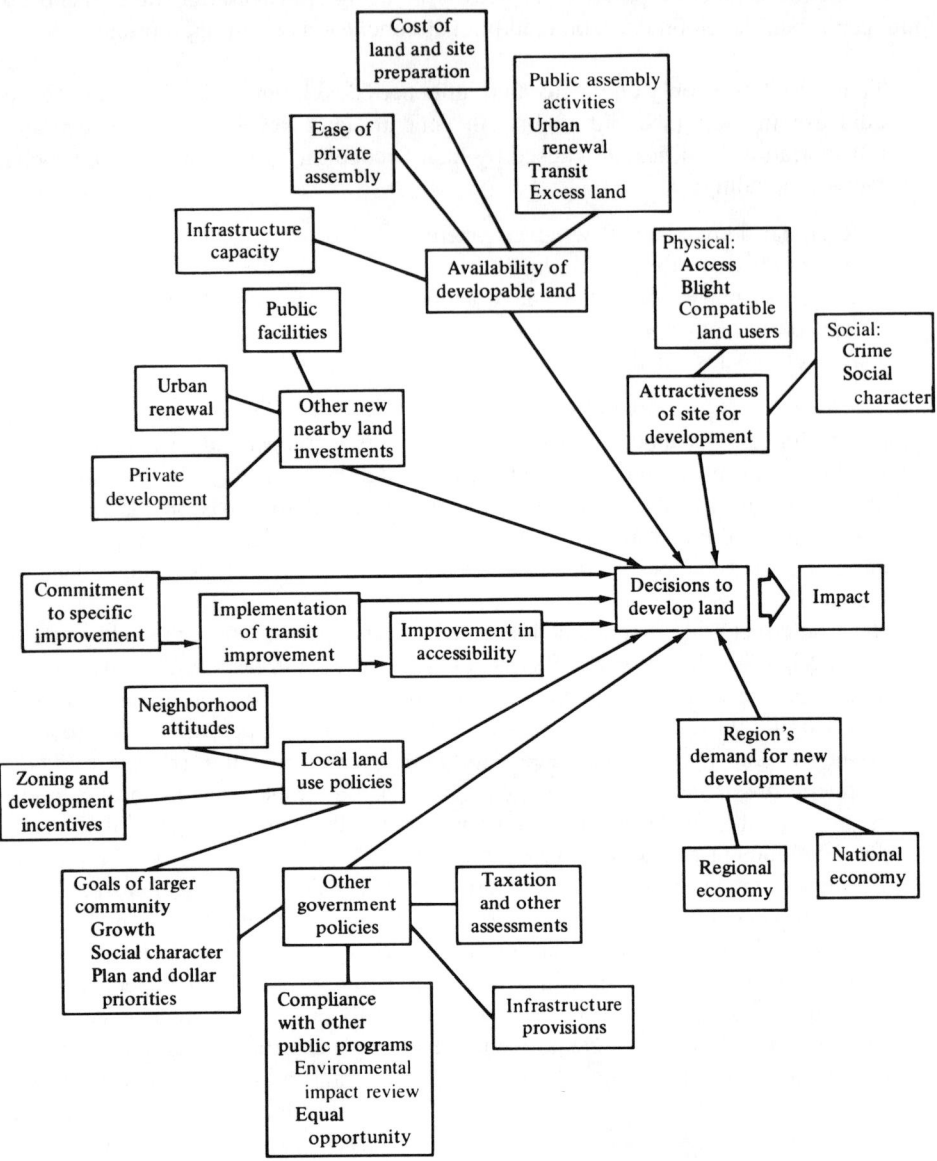

Figure 2-14 Factors influencing land use impact. (*Knight and Trygg* [*1977*].)

location of new development and changing property values. A major investment in transportation infrastructure seldom creates a net increase of development within a metropolitan area. Recent rapid transit investments seem not to have had major effects on urban structure, but impacts involving increases in the intensity of land use near stations and in downtown areas have occurred [U.S. Congress, 1979].

2-3 CHAPTER SUMMARY

1. A knowledge of the characteristics of urban travel patterns is required by transportation planners so that the needs for transportation facilities can be matched to actual planning and decision-making activities. *Trip purpose* determines the origins and destinations involved and, consequently, the length of urban trips. The *temporal distribution* of urban travel is the primary cause of congestion on transportation facilities at certain times of the day. The *spatial distribution* of urban travel is directly related to the configuration of the transportation system. The *modal distribution* of urban trips is related to both the trip purpose and the temporal distribution of travel, and is generally determined by the costs (actual and perceived) of using different modes for a given trip. These characteristics of urban travel can differ substantially from one city to the next, but there are nevertheless similar trends exhibited in most urban areas.
2. The operational performance of transportation facilities is a transportation system characteristic of importance to planners. Speed, volume, rate of flow, density, capacity, operating costs, and level of service are related to each other and are a function of the particular transportation technology being considered. The relationship between rate of flow, average running speed, and density (Flow = Speed × Density) is the basis for determining a facility's capacity and the level of service it provides under specific operating conditions. It is these operational characteristics that determine a user's perception of the performance or effectiveness of a transportation facility.
3. A second major characteristic of the urban transportation system is the *mobility* it provides to individuals. Although the automobile orientation of most North American cities is such that personal mobility is now at unprecedented levels, not everyone is able to enjoy the mobility an automobile provides. The *elderly*, for example, are a group that tends to be heavily dependent on public transit for urban travel. *Physically handicapped* individuals are not only dependent on public transportation, they may also require either special devices for accessibility to public transit vehicles or specialized transportation services. Finally, *low-income households* often do not have access to automobiles and therefore rely on government-subsidized transit services. Along with the mobility issues these groups present to transportation planners, the issue of the equitable distribution of costs and benefits of transportation facilities among income groups also emerges regularly in the decision-making process.
4. Transportation facilities and their operation can have both direct and indirect impacts on the urban activity system, and these impacts can therefore be classified as another characteristic of the urban transportation system. The *physical impacts* of a transportation facility begin when the facility is under construction—as land is consumed, natural ecosystems are disturbed, and topographical patterns are altered. Guidelines for environmental impact assessment established by governments attempt to mitigate some of the physical impacts of transportation facility construction.

5. Once constructed, the operation of a transportation facility can have adverse impacts on the *air quality* in an urban area. Vehicle emissions of carbon monoxide, hydrocarbons, nitrogen oxides, sulfur oxides, and assorted particulates are a major source of air pollution in most metropolitan areas. Automobile emission standards have been an attempt by federal governments to control the air pollution problem at one of its major sources.

   An operational transportation facility can also produce significant levels of *noise and vibration,* to the point of causing physical harm to the hearing of those nearby. Distance from the transportation facility, operational changes, and noise barriers are all possible remedies to noise impacts.
6. An impact of the transportation system that has become a concern in the recent past involves the consumption of *petroleum energy* by highway vehicles. The single-occupant automobile is the least energy-efficient mode of urban travel, with public transit vehicles providing a far higher level of passenger miles per unit of energy consumed. Public policy in the area of transportation and energy has focused both on fuel economy standards for automobile engines and on encouraging local transportation programs designed to reduce gasoline consumption.
7. *Economic impacts* of new transportation facilities can also play a large role in determining transportation investment and policy decisions. The increased accessibility provided by transportation system improvements can affect industrial location decisions, the level of retail sales either downtown or at suburban shopping centers, and both municipal tax revenues and levels of personal income in an urban area.
8. A final impact of the construction and operation of transportation facilities involves the physical displacement of households and the disruption of neighborhoods. *Social impacts* of transportation facilities tend to affect elderly, low-income, and ethnic groups to a greater extent than most other groups in urban areas. Guidelines for assessing the social impacts of transportation facilities have been developed to help ensure that the actions required to reduce the negative social effects of a new facility are taken in the planning stages.
9. The characteristics of the infrastructure and services that comprise the urban transportation system reflect past transportation policy and investment decisions and define the overall role played by the transportation system in a given urban area. The relationship between *land use* and *transportation* is an important consideration, in that travel patterns are influenced by changes to the transportation system. The land development and transportation facility relationship is thus a circular one, and it can take years to complete a single cycle. Studies of the land-development impacts of transportation investments have generally found that these impacts tend to be distributive in terms of the location of new development in a metropolitan area, and that public investments in transportation facilities designed to influence land use patterns *by themselves* tend to produce minimal results. Financial incentives and technical assistance to developers, coordination of transportation planning with land use planning, and public and private joint development efforts are all methods available to governments to use transportation investment funds more effectively in influencing land development.

QUESTIONS

1. Summarize the interrelationships between trip purpose, temporal distribution, mode choice, and cost in urban travel. How do these interrelationships contribute to the "problems" associated with urban transportation?
2. From a transportation planning/policy standpoint, what are the relative merits of dealing with urban transportation problems through:
   (a) Expansion of transportation facility capacity
   (b) Intervention in land use and transportation system development
   (c) Policies designed to encourage changes in individuals' travel behavior
   What are the issues and constraints that would apply to each of these approaches (e.g., economic cost, political feasibility, etc.)?
3. Find the latest available travel data for *your* urban area (or one with which you are familiar) from census statistics or from a recent transportation planning study. Analyze the data on urban travel by trip purpose and/or modal split. Use your familiarity with the characteristics of the particular urban area under consideration to explain any significant patterns or any differences from the patterns outlined in this chapter.
4. The percentage of work trips made by some means of public or mass transit in many North American cities ranges from 22 percent to over 55 percent. Assume that, in some unspecified urban area, public transit service is suddenly shut down because of a labor strike. What transportation actions could be considered by local government agencies to help those stranded by the shutdown to get to work, while at the same time avoiding serious congestion on the road network?
5. In the land use–transportation interaction process conceptualized in Fig. 2-13, at what point is it possible for public agencies to intervene and influence the process? Specifically, what policies do you think would be most effective in guiding the process, given the economic, institutional, and political realities in North American urban areas, and given the results of the transportation and land use studies outlined in Table 2-19?
6. Over the past decade, United States federal legislation requiring public transit systems to provide access for handicapped persons to their facilities has been introduced and modified several times. How can such legislation affect the design and operation of urban transit services? What are the alternatives to making all transit facilities accessible to the handicapped? What considerations arise in making decisions about transportation services for the handicapped (as well as for the elderly)? To what extent is urban mobility a "right" for *all* groups in society?
7. Many urban transportation planners accept the premise that, in general, lower-income persons tend to live in inner-city areas and tend to make shorter trips on public transit, more often, during all periods of the day. Conversely, it is assumed that middle- and upper-income persons live in suburban areas and tend to use transit less frequently, for longer suburb-to-CBD commute trips during the morning and evening rush hours.
   (a) In terms of equity and income distribution, what implications does this premise have for *(i)* distance-based transit fares and *(ii)* peak and off-peak

transit fares? Use the data provided in Tables 2-9 to 2-13 to support your arguments.

(b) How accurate is this premise? What trends and considerations might reduce its validity?

8. Consider a 6-mile-long urban expressway, consisting of two lanes of vehicle flow in each direction. The expressway currently carries 1400 vehicles per hour *per lane* during peak periods. The time (in minutes) needed to travel the length of the expressway is given by this simple service function:

$$t = 0.009V - 4.7$$

where V = vehicle flow per lane of traffic.

(a) Under existing conditions, find the travel time on the expressway, the average speed of vehicles, and density of traffic (vehicles per mile).
(b) How will time, speed, and density be affected by an increase in vehicle flow of 500 vehicles per hour per direction (250 per lane)?
(c) What volume of flow (per lane) can be accommodated on the expressway before average speeds drop below 30 miles per hour?
(d) Assume that, when vehicle volumes reach 3900 vehicles per hour per direction, a third lane is added in each direction. What happens to travel time, speeds, and vehicle density after the lanes are added?
(e) Summarize in tabular form the vehicle volumes, travel times, average speeds, and vehicle densities for the results (a) through (d) above.

9. For the transportation facility impacts listed in Table 2-14, discuss:

(a) Possible techniques (quantitative and qualitative) that could be used to assess each type of impact
(b) The extent to which the evaluation of each impact and control of its effects should be required by federal or state or provincial regulations
(c) How you feel each impact category has been handled in the past by transportation planners and decision makers

REFERENCES

Adkins, W. G.: "Land Value Impacts of Expressways in Dallas, Houston, and San Antonio, Texas, "*Highway Research Bulletin 227,* Highway Research Board, 1959.

Allen, B., and R. Mudge: *The Impact of Rapid Transit on Urban Development: The Case of the Philadelphia–Lindenwold High Speed Line,* Rand Corporation Paper P-5246, 1974.

Altshuler, A. A.: *The Urban Transportation System: Politics and Policy Innovation,* MIT Press, Cambridge, 1979.

American Public Transit Association: *Transit Fact Book, 1980,* Washington, D.C., 1981.

Ashley, R. N., and W. F. Bernard: "Interchange Development Along 180 Miles of I-94," *Highway Research Record 96,* Highway Research Board, 1965.

Au, T., and D. M. B. Baumann: "Strategies for Providing Transportation to the Elderly and Handicapped," in Transportation Systems Center, *Transportation for the Elderly and Handicapped: Programs and Problems 2,* February 1981.

Banfield, E. C.: *The Unheavenly City Revisited*, Little, Brown, Boston, 1974.

Bock, F. C.: *Factors Influencing Modal Trip Assignment*, National Cooperative Highway Research Program Report 57, Transportation Research Board, 1968.

Bower, R. J.: "The Influence of the Subway System on the Growth of Metropolitan Toronto," in U.S. Congress, *New Urban Rail: How Can Its Development and Growth-Shaping Potential Be Realized?* Committee on Banking, Finance, and Urban Affairs, Committee Print 96-7, December 1979.

Boyd, J. N. A., and E. Wetzler: *Evaluation of Rail Rapid Transit and Express Bus Service in the Urban Commuter Market*, Institute for Defense Analysis, Washington, D.C., October 1973.

Cerverco, R. B., et al.: *Efficiency and Equity Implications of Alternative Transit Fare Policies*, Final Report, U.S. Department of Transportation Report Number DOT-1-80-32, September 1980.

Cheslow, M. D., and M. L. Olsson: *Transportation and Metropolitan Development*, The Urban Institute, October 1975.

Chicago Area Transportation Study, *Transportation Improvement Program FY76–FY80*, Chicago, June 1976.

Christiansen, D.: *Urban Transportation Planning for Goods and Services*, U.S. Department of Transportation, Washington, D.C., June 1979.

Congressional Budget Office: *Urban Transportation and Energy: The Potential Savings of Different Modes*, a study prepared for the Committee on Environment and Public Works, U.S. Senate, No. 95-8, U.S. Government Printing Office, Washington, D.C., September 1977.

Crain, J., and W. Courington: *Incidence Rates and Travel Characteristics of the Transportation Handicapped in Portland, Oregon*, Transportation Systems Center Report No. UMTA-OR-06-004-77-1, April 1977.

Davies, G. W.: "The Effect of a Subway on the Spatial Distribution of Population," *Journal of Transport Economics and Policy*, vol. 10, no. 2, May 1976, pp. 126–136.

Deen, T. B., and D. H. James: "Relative Costs of Bus and Rail Transit Systems," *Highway Research Record 293*, Highway Research Board, Washington, D.C., 1969.

DeLeuw, Cather, et al.: *Land Use Impacts of Rapid Transit: Implications of Recent Experience*, U.S. Department of Transportation, August 1977.

Domencich, T., and D. McFadden: *Urban Travel Demand: A Behavioral Analysis*, North Holland, Amsterdam, 1975.

Donnelly, P.: *Rail Transit Impact Studies: Atlanta, Washington, San Diego*, U.S. Department of Transportation Report DOT-I-82-3, March 1982.

Downing, P.: "Factors Affecting Commercial Land Values: An Empirical Study of Milwaukee, Wisconsin," *Land Economics*, February 1973.

Ellis, R. H., et al.: *Potential Approaches for Improving the Mobility of Different Market Segments of the Transportation Handicapped*, Peat, Marwick, Mitchell and Co., 1977.

Federal Energy Administration: "Energy Conservation Potential of Urban Mass Transit," *Conservation Paper 34*, 1976.

Fried, M.: "Grieving for a Lost Home: Psychological Costs of Relocation," *Urban Renewal*, James Wilson (ed.), MIT Press, Cambridge, 1966.

Gauthier, H. L.: "Geography, Transportation, and Regional Development," *Economic Geography*, October 1970.

Grefe, R., and A. McDonald: *Economic and Financial Impacts of Bay Area Rapid Transit*, Report No. HUD 000164/DOT/P-30/79/04, 1979.

Gusman, P., et al.: *Social Impacts: Evaluation of Highway Project Development in Urban Residential Areas*, Texas State Department of Highways and Public Transportation Report TT1-2-8-75-190-1, August 1975.

Hansen, W. G.: "Traffic Approaching Cities," *Public Roads*, vol. 31, no. 7, April 1961.

Heaton, C., and J. Goodman: "Automobile-Restrictive Measures in Central Business Districts: Some Recent Findings and Views," *Transportation Research Record 747*, Transportation Research Board, 1980.

Heenan, G. W.: "The Economic Effect of Rapid Transit on Real Estate Development," *Appraisal Journal*, April 1968.

Hoel, L. A.: "Guidelines for Planning Public Transportation Terminals," *Transportation Research Record 817*, Transportation Research Board, Washington, D.C., 1981.

―――― and E. Roszner: *The Pittsburgh Parking Strike,* Report to the Urban Mass Transportation Administration, 1972.

Holmes, E. H.: *Coordination of Urban Development and the Planning and Development of Transportation Facilities,* U.S. Department of Transportation, March 1974.

Humphrey, T., F. Salvucci, and M. D. Meyer: *Transportation and Energy Contingency Planning: The Case of the Yourtown Urbanized Area,* Report prepared for the U.S. Department of Transportation, Center for Transportation Studies, MIT, Cambridge, 1980.

Kaplan, Marshall, Gans, and Kahn: *Social Characteristics of Neighborhoods as Indicators of the Effects of Highway Improvements,* Report No. DOT/FH 11-7789, 1972.

Keeler, T., K. Small, and Associates: *Automobile Costs and Final Intermodal Cost Comparisons,* Part III, Monograph no. 21, Institute of Urban and Regional Development, University of California, Berkeley, July 1975.

Knight, R. L., and L. L. Trygg: "Evidence of Land Use Impacts of Rapid Transit Systems," *Transportation,* vol. 6, 1977, pp. 231–247.

Kuhn, T.: *Public Enterprise Economics and Transport Problems,* University of California Press, Berkeley, 1962.

Lerman, S. R., et al.: *The Effect of the Washington Metro on Urban Property Values,* Center for Transportation Studies Report 77-18, MIT, November 1977.

Levinson, H. S.: "Truck Priorities and Restrictions—A Planning Perspective," in G. Fisher (ed.), *Goods Transportation in Urban Areas,* U.S. Department of Transportation Report DOT-OS-60099, Washington, D.C., May 1976.

Levinson, H. S., et al.: *Bus Use of Highways, State of the Art,* National Cooperative Highway Research Program Report 143, Transportation Research Board, 1973.

Levinson, H. S.: "Urban Travel Characteristics," in W. S. Homburger, (ed.), *Transportation and Traffic Engineering Handbook,* 2d ed., Prentice-Hall, Englewood Cliffs, N.J., 1982.

Lewis, D. L.: "Providing Private Cars to Severely Disabled People," in Transportation Systems Center, *Transportation for the Elderly and Handicapped: Programs and Problems 2,* February 1981.

Lyall, K.: "Tax Base Sharing: A Fiscal Aid Toward More Rational Land Use Planning," *Journal of the American Institute for Planners,* March 1975, pp. 90–100.

Manheim, M. L., et al.: "Transportation Decision Making: A Guide to Social and Environmental Considerations," *National Cooperative Highway Research Program Report 156,* Transportation Research Board, 1975.

Markovitz, J. K.: "Transportation Needs of the Elderly," *Traffic Quarterly,* vol. 25, 1971.

McShane, M., and M. D. Meyer: *The Relationships between Parking Policy and Urban Goals,* U.S. Department of Transportation Report No. MA-06-0094, January 1981.

Metropolitan Transportation Commission: *Land Use and Urban Development Impacts of BART,* Report HUD 0001682 and DOT/P-30/79/09, April 1979.

――――: *BART in the San Francisco Bay Area—Final Report for the BART Impact Program,* U.S. Department of Transportation Report Number DOT-P-30-79-17, September 1979.

Meyer, J., J. Kain, and M. Wohl: *The Urban Transportation Problem,* Harvard University Press, Cambridge, 1965.

Meyer, M. D., and P. Belobaba: "Contingency Planning for Response to Urban Transportation System Disruptions," *Journal of the American Planning Association,* September 1982.

Meyer, M. D., and M. McShane: "Parking Policy and Downtown Economic Development," *Journal of the Urban Planning and Development Division,* American Society of Civil Engineers, vol. 109, no. 1, May 1983.

Meyer, M. D., et al.: *Urban Development and Revitalization: The Role of Federal and State Transportation Agencies,* Final Report, Report No. MA-11-0033, September 1979.

Miller, D. R., et al.: "Cost Comparison of Busway and Rail Rapid Transit," *Highway Research Record* 459, Highway Research Board, Washington, D.C., 1973.

Mitric, S.: *Comparison of Modes in Urban Transit,* Technical Report, Department of Civil Engineering, Ohio State University, Columbus, July 1976.

Mohring, H.: "Land Values and the Measurement of Highway Benefits," *Journal of Political Economy,* vol. 79, 1961, pp. 236–49.

Morlok, E. K.: "The Comparison of Transport Technologies," *Highway Research Record 238,* Highway Research Board, Washington, D.C., 1968.

———: *Introduction to Transportation Engineering and Planning,* McGraw-Hill, New York, 1978.

National Transportation Policy Study Commission, *National Transportation Policies through the Year 2000,* Washington, D.C., 1979.

Paaswell, R., et al.: *An Analysis of Joint Development Projects,* U.S. Department of Transportation Report Number NY-11-0020, May 1979.

Page, J. C.: "Speed Is the Name of the Game," *Technology Review,* vol. 82, no. 8, August/September 1980, pp. 42–52.

Palmere, A. J.: *"Alternatives for Financing the MBTA,"* Unpublished masters thesis, Kennedy School of Government, Harvard University, April 1981.

Pucher, J., and I. Hirschman: "Distribution of the Tax Burden of Transit Subsidies in the United States," *Public Policy,* vol. 29, no. 3, Summer 1981.

Pucher, J., et al.: "Socioeconomic Characteristics of Transit Riders: Some Recent Evidence," *Traffic Quarterly,* vol. 35, no. 3, July 1981.

Real Estate Research Corporation: *The Costs of Sprawl,* U.S. Government Printing Office, Washington, D.C., 1974.

Revis, J. S.: *Transportation Requirements for the Handicapped, Elderly, and Economically Disadvantaged,* National Cooperative Highway Research Program Synthesis 39, Transportation Research Board, 1976.

Roskin, M.: *Purposes of Vehicle Trips and Travel: Report 3, 1977, NPTS,* Federal Highway Administration Report FHWA/PL/81/001, U.S. Department of Transportation, December 1980.

Smith, Wilbur, and Associates: *Parking in the City Center,* May 1965.

Soberman, R., and H. Hazard: *Canadian Transit Handbook,* University of Toronto-York University Joint Program in Transportation, January 1980.

Spengler, E. H.: *Land Values in New York in Relation to Transit Facilities,* Columbia University Press, New York, 1930.

Sternlieb, G.: *The Future of the Downtown Department Store,* Harvard University Press, Cambridge, 1962.

System Design Concepts, Inc.: *Urban Public Transportation and Energy,* Final report, Prepared for the Urban Mass Transportation Administration, October 1979.

Tidewater Transportation District, Paper presented at the summer conference of the Transportation Research Board, Charlottesville, Va., 1982.

Toronto Transit Commission, *Transit in Toronto,* Toronto, Ont., 1982.

Transportation Research Board: *Energy Effects, Efficiencies, and Prospects for Various Modes of Transportation,* Synthesis of Highway Practice 43, National Cooperative Highway Research Program, Washington, D.C., 1977.

———: *Interim Materials on Highway Capacity,* Transportation Research Circular, January 1980.

Urban Land Institute: *Joint Development: Making the Real Estate–Transit Connection,* U.S. Department of Transportation Report Number UMTA-DC-06-0183-79-1, June 1979.

U.S. Conference of Mayors: *Transportation and Urban Development, A Review of Federal Programs and Strategies That Promote the Coordination of Public Transportation and Private Investment,* U.S. Department of Transportation Report Number DOT-P-30-80-33, October 1980.

U.S. Congress, Senate, Special Committee on Aging: *Transportation and the Elderly: Problems and Progress,* Report No. 34-273, 93rd Congress, 2nd Session, 1974.

U.S. Congress: *New Urban Rail Transit: How Can Its Development and Growth-Shaping Potential Be Realized?* Subcommittee on The City, Committee on Banking, Finance and Urban Affairs, U.S. House of Representatives, December 1979.

U.S. Department of Commerce: *The Impact of Local Tax Policy on Urban Economic Development,* Economic Development Administration, September 1980.

———: *Statistical Abstract of the United States,* U.S. Government Printing Office, Washington, D.C., 1980, 1981.

U.S. Department of Housing and Urban Development: *The Private Development Process, A Guidebook for Local Government,* Report Number HUD-PDR-352-2, February 1979.

U.S. Department of Transportation: *Energy Primer: Selected Transportation Topics,* Transportation Systems Center, Cambridge, Mass., 1976.

———: *Guidelines for Assessing the Environmental Impact of Public Mass Transportation Projects,* Report No. DOT-P-79-00-001, April 1979.
———: *Joint Development Report,* Report Number TX-11-0006, June 1979.
———: *Design of Urban Streets,* Federal Highway Administration Technology Sharing Report 80-204, January 1980.
———: *The Land Use and Urban Development Impacts of Beltways,* Report DOT-P-30-80-40, October 1980.
U.S. Environmental Protection Agency: *Secondary Impacts of Transportation and Wastewater Investments: Review and Bibliography,* Office of Research and Development, January 1975.
Vuchic, V.: "Comparative Analysis and Selection of Transit Modes," in G. Gray and L. Hoel (eds.), *Public Transportation: Planning, Operations and Management,* Prentice-Hall, Englewood Cliffs, N.J., 1979.
———: *Urban Public Transportation, Systems and Technology,* Prentice-Hall, Englewood Cliffs, N.J., 1981.
——— and R. Stanger: Lindenwold Rail Line and Shirley Busway: A Comparison," *Highway Research Record 459,* Highway Research Board, Washington, D.C., 1973.
Wachs, M.: *Transportation for the Elderly: Changing Lifestyles, Changing Needs,* University of California Press, Berkeley, 1979.
Wagner, F. A.: *Alternative Work Schedules: The Impacts on Transportation,* National Cooperative Highway Research Program Synthesis of Highway Practice 73, Transportation Research Board, Washington, D.C., November 1980.
Weisbrod, G. E.: "Business and Travel Impacts of Boston's Downtown Crossing Automobile-Restricted Zone," *Transportation Research Record 887,* Transportation Research Board, Washington, D.C., 1982.
Witherspoon, R.: "Transit and Urban Economic Development: How Cities Could Use Transit as a Development Tool; Why They Don't; What To Do about it," *Transit Journal,* Spring 1979.
Wohl, M.: "Transit Subsidies: By Whom, For Whom?" *Journal of the American Institute of Planners,* January 1970.
Wolfe, R. A. and E. J. Miller: *Transportation and Seniors in Ontario,* University of Toronto–York University Joint Program in Transportation, March 1982.

CHAPTER
THREE

TRANSPORTATION PLANNING AND DECISION MAKING

3-0 INTRODUCTION

The underlying premise of this book is that planning methodology and the analysis tools used within the planning process should be consistent with the substance and form of the transportation decision-making process. There are, however, many different ways of viewing the decision-making process. Understanding the nature of alternative decision-making processes, and the needs and capabilities of those who are responsible for them, is thus a prerequisite for the development of an effective transportation planning process. This chapter examines the characteristics of different decision-making models and identifies a framework for planning that reflects the requirements of a decision process related to transportation planning.

3-1 AN EVOLVING PERSPECTIVE ON THE PLANNING AND DECISION-MAKING PROCESS

The transportation planning process that evolved out of early experiences with large-scale urban transportation studies in the mid-1950s and early 1960s, and which was then formalized in governmental directives on comprehensive transportation planning in the mid-sixties, was based on the premise of rational choice. That is, the appropriate decision on the adoption of transportation programs and projects would be determined through a sequence of choices arrived at in a rational manner with significant technical assistance from systems analysis, operations research, and computer model building. The set of procedural steps followed by a decision maker in this rational model included [Dror, 1968]:

1. Understanding the context for decision making by identifying and weighing societal values and goals
2. Establishing operational objectives for the specific problem area under consideration
3. Identifying all possible alternatives
4. Evaluating all the consequences of each alternative
5. Selecting the alternative whose probable consequences maximize the likelihood of achieving the specified goals

This view of decision making was reflected in the structure of the community planning processes that began to evolve during the 1950s in response to United States federal requirements for the development of comprehensive community plans. These planning efforts were designed to first identify the community goals and objectives, then examine in a comprehensive way (i.e., by considering all geographic parts of the community and all functional elements which influenced physical development) the alternatives for community development. The recommended alternative was the one which maximized some performance measure. The rapid spread of this comprehensive planning approach is demonstrated by the fact that in 1954 only 11 United States cities had comprehensive planning agencies, a number which mushroomed to 319 by 1967 [Mogulof, 1971].

Within the context of this general trend toward comprehensive planning, transportation planners began to undertake large-scale urban transportation studies that closely reflected the characteristics of the community development planning process. These studies incorporated the assumption of a rational decision-making process into the overall purpose and methodology of transportation planning. The structure of this transportation planning process began with an articulation of policy or community goals, which led to an identification of transportation system problems. Once these problems were identified, alternative transportation solutions were identified and evaluated, and a set of actions was recommended based on a determination that the chosen set returned the most benefit for the costs incurred. This process (shown in Fig. 3-1), with minor variations, has served as the basis of most transportation planning efforts during the past 25 years.

A good example of this process is provided by the 1962 transportation plan for Chicago [Chicago Area Transportation Study, 1962]. The transportation planning process was described as consisting of "fact gathering, forecasting and plan making" (see Fig. 3-2). The overall objective of planning was to secure a transportation system for the Chicago area which reduced "travel frictions" within the constraints of safety, economy, and the desirable development of land use. As stated in the plan, "it does not matter, basically, whether people in urban areas move by bus, automobile, suburban railroad, or elevated-subway train, as long as the main purpose is achieved."

TRANSPORTATION PLANNING AND DECISION MAKING **79**

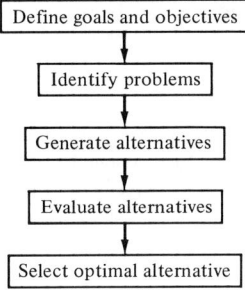

Figure 3-1 The "rational" transportation planning model.

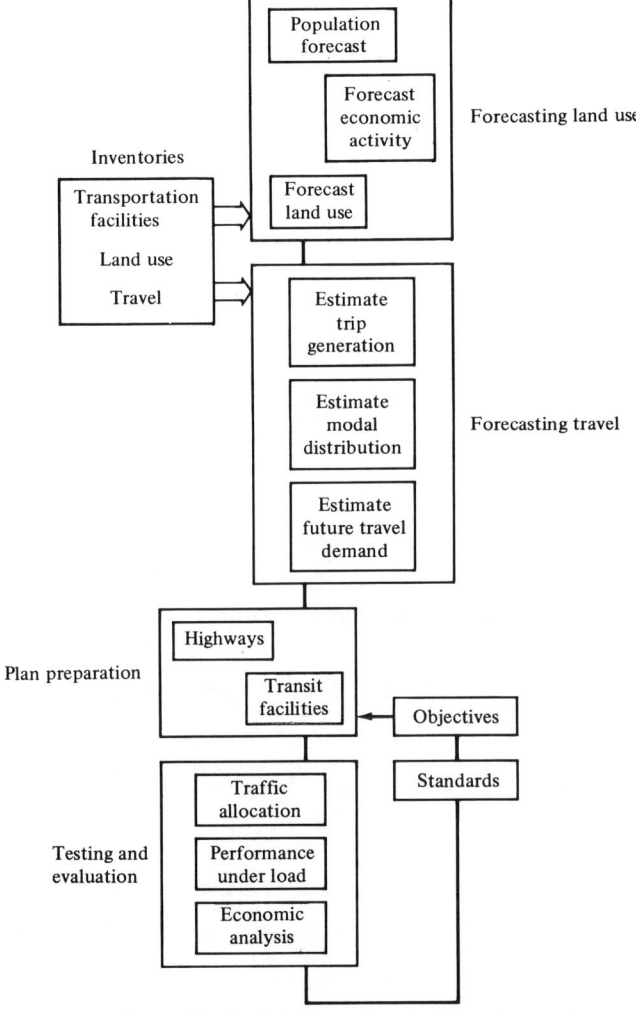

Figure 3-2 The planning process for Chicago's 1962 transportation plan. (*Chicago Area Transportation Study [1962].*)

Perhaps the most important characteristic of the Chicago plan which reflected the rational planning approach was the selection of a single criterion of choice—lowest transportation cost. As described in the plan,

> The single objective chosen is to provide that transportation system for the region which will cost least to build and use over a period of thirty years. In other words, the target is to plan a system the sum of whose measurable costs for all travelers and taxpayers in the region will be at a minimum. . . . Total costs are defined here as construction and travel costs, the latter including time, accident, and other user costs.

Table 3-1 shows the recommended Chicago transportation plan in comparison to other alternatives. Note that, as mentioned above, the index of choice was the dollar cost per vehicle mile of each alternative.

Table 3-1 Evaluation matrix for the transportation alternatives in the 1962 Chicago plan

Characteristics	Plan					
	A	B	K	L-3*	I	J
Miles of proposed routes	288	327	466	520	681	968
Cost of completion in millions (after 1960 and including arterial street improvements)	$907	$1,274	$1,797	$2,007	$2,457	$3,180
Average weekday vehicle miles of assigned travel to arterial and express facilities for 1980 (in thousands)						
Arterials	45,036	41,963	34,380	33,149	31,531	24,245
Express facilities	22,878	25,191	33,320	34,414	35,061	41,574
Total	67,914	67,054	67,700	67,563	66,592	65,819
Daily vehicle equivalent hours of travel (in thousands)	2,420	2,283	2,049	1,990	1,937	1,990
Estimated annual traffic fatalities	781	698	638	626	606	638
Estimated daily traffic accidents	504	450	378	359	346	416
Costs converted to cents per vehicle mile						
Travel (accident, time, and operating costs)	9.10	8.71	8.11	7.96	7.90	8.04
Interest and principal (on construction costs)	.43	.62	.86	.96	1.20	1.57
Total	9.53	9.33	8.97	8.92	9.10	9.61

*Recommended Plan.
Source: Chicago Area Transportation Study, [1962].

Much of the early effort by engineers and planners to structure the planning process thus focused on analysis and evaluation techniques which could provide quantitative estimates of the benefits and costs of alternative transportation projects and system configurations. A large-scale transportation network and land use modeling methodology was developed to provide transportation planners with a means of determining transportation system impacts. In the minds of many engineers and planners, the transportation planning process soon became synonymous with this modeling methodology.[1]

Early research efforts aimed at "improving the transportation planning or decision-making process" focused almost exclusively on the development of quantitative evaluation methodology, often ignoring the question of what type of decision-making process really existed and what type of information was needed for making decisions within this context [Bureau of Public Roads, 1966; Federal Highway Administration, 1967, 1973; Jessiman et al., 1967; Highway Research Board, 1970; Smith, 1971].

In an examination of the professional and societal context of transportation planning during this period, Altshuler argued that the "rational" nature of such a planning process could be found in the transportation profession's main assumptions, its self-image, its procedures, and its orientation toward key societal values [Altshuler, 1974]. Further, transportation planning was an activity "whose theories and preoccupations at any moment in time closely reflected the government programs and political moods which were dominant or which had been in the recent past." The characteristics of the rational transportation planning process, many of which created severe problems for it when political moods began to change, were identified by Altshuler [1974] as the following:

1. Transportation planners assumed that there was a general public consensus that the mission of transportation planning was to provide the most cost-effective means of expanding the highway network. Because of this consensus, little attention needed to be paid to those who opposed the transportation policies and programs designed to achieve this objective.

---

[1] In the United States, federal guidelines to local transportation planners on an appropriate structure for the transportation planning process encouraged this technical approach to planning. *Policy and Procedure Memorandum 50-9*, issued by the Federal Highway Administration in 1969, is a good example of such guidelines [Federal Highway Administration, 1969]. According to this memorandum, the urban transportation planning process was to be based on

> . . . the collection, analysis, and interpretation of pertinent data concerning existing conditions and historical growth; the establishment of community goals and objectives; and the forecasting of future urban development and future travel demands. . . .

The comprehensive character of the planning process was found in the requirement

> . . . that the economic, population, and land use element be included; that estimates be made of the future demands for all modes of transportation both public and private for both persons and goods; that terminal and transfer facilities and traffic control systems be included in the inventories and analyses; and, that the entire area, within which the forces of development are interrelated and which is expected to be urbanized within the forecast period, be included.

2. This consensus on the purpose of transportation planning was expected to last a long time because it was based on long-term economic and cultural trends (e.g., the steady growth of motor vehicle travel) that were becoming permanent elements of society. The vision of a future heavily dependent upon the automobile for mobility was firmly engrained into the professional attitudes of most planners and engineers.
3. Transportation planners were confident that they could plan for the public without ever dealing directly with elected officials or affected citizens. The assumed public consensus discussed above gave planners a clear mandate for their activities, which when combined with their expertise, left little doubt that the planners were the critical actors in providing the "best" solutions to the problems facing the community.
4. The collective concern of the transportation profession was to perfect techniques that would demonstrate the "one best way" to solve given problems. As stated previously, much of the planning research undertaken at this time focused on improving travel-demand forecasting techniques so that planners could better estimate the impacts of alternative project specifications.
5. Transportation planning was comprehensive in its regional scope and was structured to produce comprehensive network plans to accommodate long-term forecasts of travel demand. The planning focus was "calibrated to the regional scale."

These characteristics of rational transportation planning present an image of a process centralized in a few agencies, dominated by technical procedures, and placing a high value on the provision of personal mobility. By the late 1960s, however, this image of transportation planning was being severely questioned in several cities by large numbers of people who protested the large-scale expansion of the highway network and the local disruption it created. A new image of planning, one based on public participation and development of consensus and focusing on the amelioration of project impacts rather than accommodating demands for increased personal mobility, started to replace the previous style of planning. The test of good planning was not the ability to produce comprehensive plans consisting of large-scale projects, but rather the ability to produce modest plans focused on site-specific problems.[2] Legislation and

---

[2] In the United States, federal transportation planning guidelines were changing to reflect these new characteristics of planning. An interesting illustration of this evolution was the changing definition of who was responsible for transportation investment decisions. Originally, state governments were considered the major party responsible for such decisions. The 1962 Federal-Aid Highway Act, however, stated that,

> The Secretary shall not approve . . . any program for projects in any urban area of more than 50,000 population unless he finds that such projects are based on a continuing, comprehensive transportation planning process *carried on cooperatively by States and local communities*. . . .[emphasis added]

This responsibility was redefined in the 1970 Federal-Aid Highway Act which specified that,

> No highway project may be constructed in any urban area of fifty thousand population or more *unless the responsible public officials of such urban area* in which the project is located *have been consulted*

governmental guidelines began to reflect these new characteristics of the planning process (see Appendix A).

In some situations, local planners adopted a more aggressive role in the planning process and became resources to local opposition groups, helping to transform their often vaguely stated aspirations to well-defined projects and programs. This style of planning, called advocacy planning, represented a complete break from the rationalist planning tradition and reinforced the participatory planning process described above [Goodman, 1971; Lupo et al., 1971; Kaplan, 1973; Catanese, 1974; National Wildlife Federation, 1977; Smith, 1979].

This evolving professional image of the planning process was being reinforced throughout this period by studies and research which examined the link between the rational planning model and decision making. Perhaps the best known critique of the rational planning model was made by Braybrooke and Lindblom [1963], who argued that comprehensive planning was doomed to fail because of the practical limits on rationality (i.e., man's limited problem-solving capabilities, the lack of truly comprehensive information, the high cost of comprehensive analysis, and the difficulty in evaluating values or goals). The decision-making process was defined by these authors as being:

1. Incremental or tending toward relatively small changes
2. Remedial, in that decisions are made to move away from ills rather than toward goals
3. Serial, in that problems are not solved at one stroke but are successively attacked
4. Exploratory, in that goals are continually being redefined or newly discovered
5. Fragmented or limited, in that problems are attacked by considering a limited number of alternatives rather than all possible alternatives
6. Disjointed, in that there are many dispersed "decision-points"

Other studies of planning and its relationship to the political decision-making process generated further questions about the validity of the planning structure and the

---

and their views considered with respect to the corridor, the location and the design of the project. [emphasis added]

This act also established a new federal-aid urban highway system and required that the system components be

. . . selected so as to best serve the goals and objectives of the community as determined by the *responsible local officials* of such urbanized areas [and the routes were to be] . . . *selected by the appropriate local officials and the State highway departments, in cooperation with each other.* . . . [emphasis added]

The Federal-Aid Highway Act of 1973, however, amended this section and required that urban system projects be *selected* by appropriate local officials with the *concurrence* of the state highway department. This act also allowed local officials, for the first time, to substitute nonhighway transit projects for highway projects. By 1973, then, the role of local officials in some major federal transportation programs had gone from consulting to shared authority [U.S. Congress, 1977].

applicability of its technical rationality [Meyerson and Banfield, 1955; Altshuler, 1965; Perin, 1967; Rabinovitz, 1969; Friedman, 1971; Rondinelli, 1973; Greenberger et al., 1976].

Within the urban transportation sector, only a few studies have been made of the process by which decisions are made. An even smaller number have examined how the information generated from the evaluation stage of the planning process is used by decision makers in making their final choice. A 1974 study of the urban political and planning contexts of 12 North American and European cities concluded that the institutional fragmentation of decision-making responsibility and influence had created a structure of decision making unresponsive to the transportation needs of urban areas [Colcord, 1974]. A subsequent study by the Office of Technology Assessment (OTA) of the U.S. Congress examined the process by which United States metropolitan areas made decisions about the development and modernization of rail transit systems and reached similar conclusions [OTA, 1976]:

> Responsibility for transit planning and decision making is divided among many governmental agencies, particularly at the local and regional levels of government. The fragmentation of decision-making power has led to three major problems.
> Because no single lead agency has the authority to set priorities among transit improvement projects, plans are developed to offer something for everyone. . . .
> The division of responsibilities for implementing transit and highway plans makes it difficult to utilize traffic management strategies. . . .
> Because regional organizations lack the power to control land use, transit cannot be used effectively as a tool for shaping regional development.

More recent studies of the politics of transportation have reemphasized the importance attributed to political factors in transportation decision making by these earlier research efforts. Hamer, for example, examined the decision-making and planning processes for investments in rapid-rail transit in five United States cities [Hamer, 1976]. In general, he found that the planning which supported the decision to construct a rail-rapid transit system was based on faulty projections of key variables and a premature imposition of constraints. Although not the focus of the study, Hamer also suggested that "an interesting hypothesis links the advocacy of rail rapid transit to an unhealthy relationship between regional decision makers and various pressure groups. These include downtown property owners, contractors, and consultants who might be called on to build the recommended systems."

Pill, in his study of the Metropolitan Toronto Transportation Plan Review, examined the relationship between planning and decision making [Pill, 1979]. Several of the study's recommendations illustrate the importance of political factors in transportation planning:

1. A study to review a long-range plan must become involved in major immediate issues during its tenure if it is to be credible to political decision makers.
2. If an independent agency is to conduct such a study, the director must play a political role.

3. To be credible, and thus to have impact, such an agency must have a direct line to top decision makers.
4. Recommendations which have no possibility of acceptance should be avoided, at least in the early stages.
5. A transportation study should venture into areas of marginal political acceptability only after it has established solid credibility on both technical and political levels.

Altshuler has also examined the political factors associated with transportation decision making [Altshuler, 1979]. He found that political acceptability of transportation innovations will vary with the degree to which they inconvenience powerful institutions and large or well-organized blocks of voters. Altshuler ranked innovative options in order of acceptability as follows:

1. The ideal innovation is one that consumers will buy voluntarily in the marketplace at a price high enough to cover its cost (e.g., car pooling and van pooling).
2. Among measures that entail some compulsion, the most attractive are those that alleviate widely perceived problems at little or no cost, and that either operate on corporate enterprises rather than individual travelers (e.g., new-car performance standards) or entail the exercise of traditional government powers in relatively unobtrusive ways (such as traffic management improvements).
3. In the next broad category of acceptability are measures that entail significant public or private cost for the benefits they confer, but in a manner that permits substantial diffusion and deferment of the blame.
4. The least acceptable innovations are those that entail substantial costs or interference with established patterns of behavior, imposed in such a manner that the blame will fall clearly and inescapably upon the public officials who adopt the innovation.

In addition to these studies, several others have examined the importance of political conflict in transportation decision making and planning [Gakenheimer, 1976; Banks, 1977; Steiner, 1978]. The general conclusion that can be drawn from all of these studies is that the planning and design of transportation systems are as much a political process as they are a technical one.

Beginning in the early 1970s, serious questions also began to be raised about the relevance and use of the information generated by transportation planners. These questions were first raised with respect to the large-scale models used to predict land use and transportation variables [Lee, 1973] and then later extended to the entire methodological approach [Barker and Roark, 1979; de Bettencourt et al., 1979; Schulz et al., 1979]. These critiques focused on the weak linkage between the results of planning and how they were used by decision makers. The conventional transportation planning process "had not involved the relevant decision makers nor had it adequately informed them on policy issues" [Lee, 1977]. Thus, part of the solution was to understand better the decision-making process and to tailor the planning methodology and analysis style to the information needs of the decision-making body.

To some, understanding the decision-making process meant understanding politics [Cherington, 1971]:

> Perhaps most important, the design and implementation system inevitably involves a large measure of politics—not party politics, but politics all the same. In short there are a good many items of transportation irrationality in the process. I am not sure that these problems can ever be handled within the framework of systems analysis, but I am sure that they rarely are. Yet at times these political questions bulk so large in the decisionmaking process as to far outweigh some of the niceties of intermodal choice. . . .

The politics of transportation decision making included those who had influence in the decision-making process, the formation and composition of coalition groups, the important role played by key elected officials in the final choice, and the importance of funding and who could control it.

To others, understanding the decision-making process meant undertaking a detailed examination of the institutional environment in which it occurred. A good opportunity for examining this environment arose in 1975 when the U.S. Department of Transportation (DOT) issued new planning regulations designed to change the focus of local transportation planning and decision making from a long-range perspective to one more concerned with operational improvements to the existing transportation system. Several studies of the response to this regulation were nearly unanimous in concluding that the institutional relationships existing at the local level were not conducive to the type of planning process envisioned in the regulations [System Design Concepts, Inc., 1977; Meyer, 1978; Jones and Sullivan, 1978]. Specifically, these studies identified the gap between planning agencies and those responsible for project implementation as a critical barrier for successfully implementing the planning process outlined in the regulations [Jones, 1976].

> The planning style embodied in the regulations does not match the negotiated character of implementation planning. Modal agencies—as opposed to metropolitan planning organizations—are staffed and organized to implement projects, not policy. Project outcomes are structured by funding availability, eligibility criteria, design standards, rules-of-thumb, and political give-and-take. They rarely reflect explicit policy objectives or policy trade-offs at a regional or systemwide scale. They more typically reflect ad hoc responses to local pressures than the pursuit of system efficiencies.

No matter which aspect of decision making one considers most important, it is clear that transportation planners should better understand how decisions are made, how planning information is used in the decision-making process, and how their work could be an important element of the political process itself. Such an understanding becomes a crucial prerequisite for developing a planning process that reflects the participatory and consensual nature of our systems of government and that provides the type of information useful to all actors in the planning process. An effective transportation planning process can be defined as one which provides opportunities for a wide-ranging examination of the many alternatives that can be considered in solving specific problems, and which generates information on the consequences and implementation characteristics of these alternatives that is useful and understandable to those who must make the final decision. The role of the planner thus becomes one of planning *with* the interested public groups and officials, rather than planning *for* a unitary general public, as in the rationalist tradition. As will be seen in the next section, however, the role and characteristics of a planning process depend very much on the type of decision-making approach that is assumed; and there is no clear consensus on what type of approach really exists in urban government.

3-2 CONCEPTUAL MODELS OF DECISION MAKING

One of the first difficulties in relating decision-making characteristics to the development of a transportation planning process is that there exist in all organizations and governments different levels of decision making, involving a wide variety of participants and often requiring different forms of information support. There are many differences involved, including (1) type, frequency, structure, and complexity of the decisions; (2) the characteristics, capabilities, and "needs" of the decision makers; and (3) the organizational and political context [Keen and Morton, 1978]. These differences make it very difficult to identify a single model of decision making that can be used to guide the development of a planning process. For the purpose of this discussion, we will focus exclusively on the characteristics of the decision-making process that occurs at higher managerial and political levels, as most transportation planning activity is focused on influencing these decisions.

There are five major conceptual models of decision making which emerge from past studies of the decision-making process. These models can be classified as (1) the rational actor approach, (2) the satisficing approach, (3) the incrementalist approach, (4) the organizational process approach, and (5) the political bargaining approach. Before these models are discussed, it is important to deal first with how they are interrelated and how they can be used.

The five decision-making models are based on the principles and concepts of two major disciplines—political science and management science. Because of their separate backgrounds, one must be careful in comparing the different models. For example, the incremental, rational, and satisficing models were developed on the basis of single-decision processes, while the organizational process and political bargaining models were developed to reflect the organizational and political settings within which decisions occurred. Even with these different backgrounds, however, there are several similarities between the models and their underlying assumptions. These similarities will be discussed in the following pages. It is important for the reader to understand that these models cannot be considered mutually exclusive from one another. Each model, however, should also be understood as a conceptualization of the decision-making process in a specific institutional environment. Thus, the models can be distinguished from one another based on the way in which the decision process is perceived.

The importance of these models to planners lies in their representation of common ways of understanding decision making. As will be shown later, different characteristics of the decision-making process imply different strategies for providing information as input to that process. In some cases, such models might allow planners to introduce proposals into the planning process in terms tolerable to the participants whose underlying concerns are described by these different decision models. These models can thus provide a useful way to identify the important linkages between planning and decision making. More will be said about the use of these models in the concluding part of this section.

3-2-1 The Rational Actor Approach

As described in the preceding section, this model traditionally assumes a rational, completely informed set of decision makers whose decision process is based on maximizing the attainment of a set of goals and objectives. Modified versions of the rational model have relaxed some of the more rigid requirements of complete information and have developed a model of rational decision making that recognizes the limitations of decision maker's capability to digest information [March and Simon, 1958]. The rational model has most often been used in a normative sense (i.e., as a model of what decision making should be). Indeed, much of the effort in operations research, management science, decision analysis, and systems analysis during the past several years has adopted the "rational" logic of decision making. Thus, although there is very little evidence to support the validity of the rational model as a descriptive tool, it might still prove valuable as a means of formulating an analysis framework and of forcing "rationality" onto the political process [Keen and Morton, 1978].

> The rational concept defines the logic of optimal choice; this remains theoretically true, even where it is descriptively unrealistic. Without the precision and formalism of rationalist theory, we would almost certainly have made less progress in developing descriptive insights. . . . For example, the concept of consistent, absolute utility functions has been invaluable in all theories of decision making, especially those that argue such functions are nonexistent.

A transportation example of the rational actor model is the decision-making structure established by Governor Francis W. Sargent of Massachusetts in 1970 to determine the future directions of transportation policy in the Boston metropolitan region. After a long and controversial public debate about the highway construction program in the region, Governor Sargent established a working group of transportation and community experts to analyze the options available to him in setting the direction of transportation policy in Boston. The study design document for this working group described the process in the following manner [Commonwealth of Massachusetts, 1970]:

> Its aim is to advise the Governor and his Secretary of Transportation on whether and how to seek implementation on these projects, taking into account their feasibility and all their relevant impacts, together with those of alternative proposals that command substantial support within the region.
> Where disagreement among the participants persists at the conclusion of the Planning Review, a well-developed set of alternatives will be presented to the Governor and Secretary, accompanied by a thorough analysis of the advantages and disadvantages of each.

This approach reflects quite closely the characteristics of rational decision making: the existence of clearly defined decision makers, a rigorous examination of alternatives, and a final decision dependent upon the goals and objectives of the decision maker.

With respect to the characteristics of a planning process designed to support rational decision making, this model probably requires the most structured and data-intensive planning effort of the five models discussed here. The planning process would be structured to identify all feasible alternatives, to compare these alternatives along some set of evaluation criteria, and to rank them in order of preference with respect to defined goals and objectives. These tasks would, of course, require the development of analysis techniques to obtain the impact measures necessary for alternatives comparison.

3-2-2 The Satisficing Approach

Critiques of the rational actor approach have focused on its requirement for comprehensive knowledge and the selection of the "optimal" alternative. For most observers of decision making, these requirements are rarely satisfied. In this model of decision making, decision makers choose alternatives that satisfy some minimum level of acceptability or which induce the least harm or disturbance while conveying some benefit. The search process in decision making is thus best described as satisficing [Simon, 1969]:

> We cannot, within practicable computational limits, generate all the admissible alternatives and compare their relative merits. Nor can we recognize the best alternative, even if we are fortunate enough to generate it early, until we have seen all of them. We satisfice by looking for alternatives in such a way that we can generally find an acceptable one after only moderate search.

Even in this model, however, the underlying basis for decision making is rational choice, although rationality is limited by the resources and ability of the decision maker to acquire and process information. This model of decision making has several important characteristics besides that of a satisficing search process [Simon, 1957; March and Simon, 1958]. These include (1) alternatives and consequences of action are discovered sequentially through the search process, (2) each action deals with a restricted range of situations and consequences, (3) decision making is goal-oriented and adaptive, and (4) decision makers will define a set of actions that can be implemented in recurrent situations.

A transportation example of the satisficing model is the selection of one particular alignment for an urban expressway, which, while assumed to follow the rational actor approach, is in fact a satisficing approach to transportation decision making. The number of alignments which could be considered is theoretically infinite, meaning that only a select few are even considered in the planning process. The alternatives considered and ultimately selected have to meet explicit or implicit levels of performance in terms of cost, travel times, traffic capacity, and environmental impact. The final decision on an alignment, then, is a choice among relatively few alternatives based on the consideration of relatively few consequences of each. The first alternative alignment meeting the required levels of performance and surviving the process of public scrutiny will usually be the one selected, whether it is in fact the "optimal" alternative or not.

The type of planning process that would be effective in this mode of decision making is one where acceptable levels of performance are identified and used to develop a feasible set of decision alternatives. Because the satisficing model is still based on rational choice, information on the impacts of alternatives must still be obtained, although the evaluation criteria can be limited to a small set that are most relevant to the decision makers. Attainment of specific goals and objectives still drives the planning process.

3-2-3 The Incrementalist Approach

This model of decision making argues that decisions are made on the basis of marginal or incremental differences in their consequences [Lindblom, 1959; Braybrooke and Lindblom, 1970]. This approach is different from the rational model in that it presents a limited strategic approach (in both the total number of alternatives considered and in the estimation of their consequences), has a "means" orientation, is remedial in that it moves away from problems rather than toward predetermined objectives, and assumes limited coordination and communication among key decision makers. The characteristics of the incrementalist model are the following [Lindblom, 1968]:

1. Rather than attempting a comprehensive survey and evaluation of all alternatives, the decision maker focuses on only those policies which differ incrementally from existing policies.
2. Only a relatively small number of policy alternatives are considered.
3. For each policy alternative, only a restricted number of "important" consequences are evaluated.
4. The problem confronting the decision maker is continually redefined. Incrementalism allows for countless "ends-means" and "means-ends" adjustments which, in effect, make the problem more manageable.
5. Thus, there is no one decision or "right" solution, but a "never ending series of attacks" on the issues at hand through serial analyses and evaluation.
6. As such, incremental decision making is described as remedial, geared more to the alleviation of present, concrete, social imperfections than to the promotion of future social goals.

The incremental approach to transportation policy-making is evident in many situations where specific problems require the implementation of some form of traffic management strategy. For example, as a major artery in a downtown area begins to experience increased demand for transit service along with increased levels of vehicle congestion, it is common for traffic management policies to be implemented as reactions to the perceived problem. Parking and stopping regulations may be implemented first to smooth traffic flow, followed by exclusive bus lanes, which may eventually be replaced by an exclusive transit mall. This evolution of traffic management policies for a single artery reflects the tendency of decision makers to react to an existing problem with policies differing only marginally from policies in effect.

The incrementalist approach raises serious questions about the appropriate role for planning given that, according to the model, decisions are made with limited information, time, and expertise; problem definitions usually vary between different levels of government; and the alternatives selected differ only slightly from existing policies and programs. At most, the purpose of planning in this decision-making model is to define those alternatives that differ marginally from the status quo and then provide information on the marginal differences between them.

3-2-4 The Organizational Process Approach

This model recognizes the fact that most individuals belong to organizations and that decision making is therefore influenced by the formal and informal structures of the organization, channels of communication, and standard operating procedures. Early work on this model of decision making focused on the importance of organizational goals in the choice process and on the bargaining among organizational members to satisfy their goals first [Cyert and March, 1963].

Decision making in the context of this model is consequently affected by the organizational setting within which it occurs. The importance of this context is found in three areas [Allison, 1971]. First, governmental action, whether it be in foreign or domestic policy, is the output of organizations. Decisions made by government leaders trigger organizational routines within the bureaucracy to implement them. Second, these organizational routines often define the "range of effective choice" open to government leaders. The alternatives considered by decision makers many times come from agencies or organizational units whose own perception of the scope and severity of the problem heavily influences the set of alternatives presented to decision makers. Finally, policies and programs can be successful only to the extent that the organizations responsible for their implementation have the capability of carrying out their responsibility. For example, the physical resources available to a department of public works can be considered a constraint against which proposals for public works action can be measured.

The organizational process model is particularly well suited to the transportation field because the actions of many of the organizations involved in transportation planning and implementation are guided by design standards (i.e., standard operating procedures). Highway construction, for example, must usually meet standards of lane width, clearance, sight distance, geometrics, and land acquisition. In fact, much of the public opposition to expressway construction that developed in the late 1960s can be related to highway design standards that required massive land acquisition and thus major disruption. The standards which had been developed for construction of intercity highways were not appropriate in an urban setting and led to significant conflict between the agencies trying to apply the standards and the citizens affected by the projects.

The role of planning in this model of decision making is to provide the necessary information on the alternatives being considered to organization decision makers. Perhaps the most important impact on planning of this decision-making model is the significance that implementation has in the overall program and/or project development process. Because organizations are critical for program implementation, understanding the capabilities, skills, and resources of implementing organizations is important information for decision makers when choosing among program alternatives [Elmore, 1978; Meyer, 1982].

3-2-5 The Political Bargaining Approach

This view of decision making argues that the decision process is pluralistic and that the large number of actors involved in a decision often have diverse goals, values, and interests, creating conflict and a subsequent need for bargaining [Allison, 1971].

> Policymaking is therefore a process of conflict and consensus building. The advocate of a particular policy must build a consensus to support his policy. Where there are rival advocates or rival policies, there is competition for support, and all the techniques of alliance appear—persuasion, accommodation, and bargaining.

The important difference of this model from the rational actor approach is that the outcomes of this bargaining process are seldom "optimal" in any objective sense. The outcomes represent those aspects of the problem solution that the decision makers can agree on, with the more controversial aspects potentially ignored or left for future discussion.

Some have argued that the bargaining nature of the decision-making process represents a degree of power sharing among diverse interests that often leads to stalemate [Altshuler and Curry, 1976]. Others, however, have argued that the search for consensus (and thus the need for bargaining) is necessary for realizing the objectives of most political leaders and is the only effective strategy to follow given the existing form of government [Schlesinger, 1973].

The events surrounding a financial crisis experienced by Boston's transit system in the fall of 1980 are a classic example of decision making as political conflict and bargaining. With the transit system on the verge of a shutdown because of insufficient operating funds, transit management, the unions, local governments, the state legislature, and the governor all blamed each other for the problems of the Massachusetts Bay Transportation Authority (MBTA). As a shutdown became imminent, representatives of localities refused to allocate any more property tax revenues to the system, while both the legislature and the governor were reluctant to use more state tax revenues for Boston's transportation. Only after the transit system actually shut down for a day was a temporary solution formulated and a compromise reached, one which allowed the system to operate with emergency funds through the end of the year. A temporary solution was the only kind of response decision makers could agree on, while the more controversial issue of completely restructuring the MBTA or its financing was not debated.

The role of planning in such a decision process is much broader than that for the four decision-making concepts discussed previously. The planning process should be designed to provide as much information as possible on the alternatives being proposed by the interest groups, which means that the analysis approach should be flexible enough to respond quickly to requests for information on alternatives that surface during negotiations. Also, the analysis should be sensitive to the issues likely to be raised by competing interests and incorporate as much information as possible in the evaluation results to clarify these issues.

As was illustrated by the five perspectives on decision making discussed above, there are several ways to look at the decision process. All of these decision-making models relate in some respects to one another. For example, in each model, some form of rational behavior is assumed to exist, although the rational actor, satisficing, and incremental models are clearly more dependent upon such an assumption than the other two. The organizational process model adds a sociological dimension to the perspective on decision making in that it argues that the results of decision making are really a product of the organizational context in which they occur. Finally, the political bargaining model introduces the political nature of decision making and the importance of power distribution.

The rational nature of decision making, as described in each model, is very much determined by whose goals and objectives are being considered. An important distinction needs to be made between "normative rationality," where societal goals and objectives are the focus of decision making, and "descriptive rationality," which recognizes personal goals and objectives and focuses on individual behavior. For example, the incremental model can still be understood as a rational model if one views the individual decision maker's objectives as the criterion of analysis. It might be perfectly rational to not spend much time on the decision or to feel that policy means are important as ends. Even in the case of the organizational process model, where the organization is viewed as a constraint on the "search" for alternatives, there could conceivably be individual decision makers trying to rationalize decisions within a set of organizational constraints.

The importance of these alternative perspectives is that they define, in many ways, the type and purpose of planning activities that would be most effective in each decision-making context (i.e., the matching of capabilities with decision-making conditions). The challenge to the planner or analyst is to determine which defining characteristics of a decision-making process make one conceptual model or a combination of models (and the consequent planning process thereby implied) the most relevant description of the decision process to be followed (see Table 3-2).

It is also important to realize that decision making is dynamic and not rigidly structured over time. Thus, in the same city but under different circumstances, alternative views of the decision-making approach might be appropriate. Once understood, these decision-making characteristics provide strong guidance on the type of planning information that is most useful and on the most appropriate structure for a planning process.

Table 3-2 Summary of decision-making models

Model of decision making	Rational actor	Satisficing	Incremental	Organizational process	Political bargaining
Decision-making behavior assumed	Alternatives are selected to attain some set of predetermined goals and objectives in a utility-maximizing manner.	The first alternative to meet some minimal level of acceptability is inevitably selected.	Decision making is geared toward moving away from problems rather than toward the attainment of objectives. Decisions are made on the basis of the marginal differences in their consequences.	Decisions are highly influenced by organizational structures, channels of communication, and standard operating procedures (SOPs).	The decision process is pluralistic and is characterized by conflicts and bargaining.
Characteristics of the decision-making process assumed	All relevant alternatives are considered. Decision makers can attain a comprehensive knowledge of the impacts of each before making a decision. The evaluation criteria used can differentiate accurately among the choices considered. Alternatives can be ranked, and an "optimal" alternative can be selected.	It is impossible to generate *all* feasible alternatives and to compare them. Alternatives are sequentially discovered. Decision making is goal oriented but adaptive in nature. The underlying choice is rational, but is constrained by available resources and the ability to acquire and process information.	Both the number of alternatives and consequences which can be identified are limited, meaning only a small number can be considered. There is only limited coordination and communcation among decision makers. Decision makers tend to focus efforts on policies differing marginally from those existing. There is no "right" solution, but a continual series of responses to problems. Problems are continually redefined to make them fit solutions.	Government action is the output of organizations. Organizational goals are important in the choice process, as members bargain to satisfy their own goals. Operating routines define the range of alternatives open to decision makers. Alternatives are initially proposed by organizational units with their own perceptions of problems. Selected policies can only be successful when the units chosen to implement them have the capacity to carry out the policy.	The large number of actors involved in decision making, with diverse goals, values, and interests creates conflict and a need for bargaining. Outcomes of the process are not "optimal" but represent those aspects of a problem on which decision makers can agree. Controversial problems or issues tend to be ignored or put off for future discussion.

	Actions are remedial in nature, addressing present problems not future objectives.		
Implications for the planning process	The planning process is highly structured and data intensive. The process consists of the following steps: (1) identify all feasible alternatives; (2) compare them according to evaluation criteria selected; (3) rank order the alternatives with respect to defined goals; and (4) select the "optimal" alternative.	Because rational choice is still involved, provision of information on the impacts of each alternative is still crucial, but the set of evaluative criteria is limited to those relevant to decision makers. Planners should identify and employ the defined acceptable levels of policy performance to develop a feasible set of alternatives.	Because the alternatives selected differ only slightly from existing policies, planners have to define those alternatives that differ marginally from the status quo and provide decision makers with information on the marginal differences. Little if any information on the impacts of other alternatives is required.	Planners should understand the goals and objectives of the organizations involved so that specific types of information can be incorporated into any analysis. Understanding limits to implementation is important to both planners and decision makers when proposing and choosing among alternative projects or programs.	Planners should have a broader role. An analysis approach flexible enough to respond to the information needs related to alternatives presented by different interests and alternatives arising from negotiation is needed. Issues likely to be raised by competing interests should be anticipated. Evaluation results must include as much information as possible to clarify these issues.

3-3 THE ELEMENTS OF DECISION MAKING: DEVELOPMENT OF A TRANSPORTATION PLANNING PROCESS

Given the argument from the previous section that alternative forms of decision making imply different approaches to planning, developing one single analysis framework for urban transportation planning becomes problematic. Not only do approaches of governmental decision making differ from one city to the next, but as noted in the opening section, there is not one transportation planning process in an urban area; rather, a larger number of planning efforts are simultaneously undertaken by different agencies and groups throughout the metropolitan region.

The relationship of these planning efforts to one another will vary with government structure. For example, in the United States, many different agencies and jurisdictions have responsibility for some portion of the transportation infrastructure, whereas in Canada a greater acceptance of metropolitan government has provided a mechanism for greater coordination of transportation planning activities. Even with these considerations, however, it is possible to identify some key characteristics of decision making in the urban transportation sector that can be found in most cities throughout North America, which in turn can lead to an identification of the characteristics of an effective planning process. Further, no matter what perspective of the nature of the decision-making process one adopts, each approach still includes some common elements or stages of the process itself (e.g., problem identification, debate, and implementation), which can be related to the way the planning process is structured to support each stage of the decision process. By examining both the characteristics of the decision-making process and the elements of the process, we seek to develop a general framework for transportation planning that can serve as the basis for guiding transportation planning efforts at any level.

Although our view of the decision-making process most resembles that described by the political bargaining model, several characteristics from the other models are also present. The major characteristics of our perspective of the decision-making process, some of which follow logically from the others, include its being pluralistic, resource-allocative, consensus-seeking, problem-simplifying, and uncertainty-avoiding.

1. *Pluralistic*. A basic tenet of the rational model of comprehensive planning is that there exists an identifiable public interest, most often defined through goals and objectives, that guide planning efforts. What has become increasingly clear over the past 20 years, however, is that there are many agencies and groups that have interest in public issues and that, through legislation and court interpretation, now have access to the decision-making process. Thus, there is not one, but many publics involved in the decision-making process, a reality which inevitably highlights conflicting objectives and leads to unquantifiable value judgments. Viewed from a slightly different perspective, centralized decision making and planning become most difficult in an urban area that is politically and institutionally fragmented. One consequence of the pluralistic nature of decision making is that the number of public issues and problems brought before decision makers is so great and diverse that the time spent on one particular topic is often quite limited.

2. *Resource-allocative.* Decision makers face several fundamental types of problems, one of the most important being the equitable allocation of resources, both financial and organizational. Whereas this allocation process during the heyday of federal social programs was primarily concerned with how new funds would be expended, the current trend toward austerity in local government programs and a reassessment of funding from higher levels of government will create new pressures on local decision makers. More specifically, redistribution of existing resources (i.e., one group will gain only at another group's expense) will replace the distribution of new funds as the major item on the decision makers' agenda [Levine and Rubin, 1980]. A longtime observer of urban policy-making has noted that, in this new context of decision making, "resource problems impose strong constraints and political costs on urban policy-makers rather than providing opportunities and political benefits" [Yates, 1978].

   The resource-allocation purpose of decision making and the constraints imposed by a shrinking level of available resources focus much of the attention of decision makers (and those who would influence them) on the budget process. Programs and projects will not be implemented unless funding can be provided either from local sources (which automatically places them in competition with other community "needs") or from sources external to the local government body, such as the private sector or higher levels of government.

3. *Consensus-seeking.* The large number of groups involved in and trying to influence the decision-making process, combined with the limited amount of resources available to satisfy their respective demands, inevitably leads to conflict. Resolution of conflict thus becomes one of the political necessities underlying the decision-making process, resulting in negotiated compromises, bargaining, and the formation of coalitions. The importance of resolving this conflict is underscored by the fact that elected officials (and those appointed by them) hold office for a set period, after which they must again win reelection. One way to avoid alienating any constituency powerful enough to create problems in a reelection effort is to seek a consensus on the major decisions made during the term in office. This is not to say that every actor in the decision process must agree to a decision, or that a decision will not be made if significant opposition arises; the search for consensus is simply a decision maker's attempt to satisfy as many constituent groups as possible.

4. *Problem-simplifying.* Urban problems, by their very nature, are often extremely complex. Transportation problems can be especially complex, as the urban transportation system is a subsystem of the social, economic, political, and other forces often referred to as the "urban activity system" [Manheim, 1979]. An urban transportation problem can be linked to physical patterns of development, land use, and property values; can carry with it significant environmental impacts such as neighborhood disruption, noise, and air pollution; and can ultimately serve to alter human activities by changing levels of mobility or accessibility. Decision makers facing so complex a problem can be hard-pressed to develop a coherent and effective policy response.

   To deal with this complexity, decision makers often try to develop separable well-defined issues which can be handled much more easily, and for which clearer assignments can be made, leading to results which are more easily monitored. Reducing the dimensionality of a problem, however, runs a risk of oversimplifying a problem area to such an extent that the action adopted for its solution might at most address some of the symptoms, without solving the root cause of the problem. Indeed, such a solution could actually exacerbate the original problem (through factors not taken into account) or even create new problems.

5. *Uncertainty-avoiding.* Most decision making is concerned with the future or, more specifically, with the future outcomes and implications of decisions made today. Once again, because of the political nature of decision making and the need to show effective leadership, decision makers tend to shy away from options with uncertain results. One consequence of this aversion to risk is that the time horizon for most decisions is quite short, at most 2 to 3 years. Beyond this time frame, political and economic forces can drastically change the context of the problem and the likely success of actions taken. The degree of uncertainty related to these external forces has increased greatly in recent decades with the higher rate of change of key variables outside the control of local decision makers, such as the availability and price of gasoline and the level of interest rates. One consequence of this short time frame for decision-maker interest has been a great difficulty in obtaining decision-maker involvement in long-range planning efforts.

Another consequence of avoiding uncertainty is the nature of alternatives considered in the decision process. Except in situations where an individual or a group of individuals has initiated and strongly pushed a new concept, innovation or dramatic changes from previously accepted practice are rare. The uncertainty associated with the "newness" of innovative approaches tends to be sufficient to limit their chances for support, advocacy, or adoption.

These postulated characteristics of decision making—pluralistic, resource-allocative, consensus-seeking, problem-simplifying, and uncertainty-avoiding—suggest a decision process that is based on compromise, negotiation, and bargaining; a process influenced by powerful interest groups; a process where decision makers necessarily contend with many different issues; and a process oriented more toward perceived short-term issues of importance and crisis response than toward problems of uncertain dimensions likely to face a city 10 years hence. This is not to say that in some situations decision makers do not actively participate in longer-range policy decisions or that some decision makers do not adopt a strong leadership stance and make a decision with little or no compromise. There are many examples in which such actions have occurred. However, the political nature of decision making, the limited time available for decision makers on a specific issue, and their tendency to avoid making choices in the face of uncertainty often lead to the type of decision process described above.

3-4 CHARACTERISTICS OF A DECISION-ORIENTED PLANNING PROCESS

The implications of the style of decision making described above for the most appropriate structure for transportation planning are significant. Their significance lies not only in helping to identify the type of information that decision makers want, but also in identifying the type of information needed to overcome what some might consider deficiencies of the decision process (e.g., a myopic focus on short-run problems and issues). Within this context, a transportation planning process should have the following characteristics:

1. *Establish the future context.* Given the political tendency of decision makers to focus on the short term, it is essential that planners provide a good understanding of the future implications of decisions made today. This understanding might involve an examination of the opportunities forgone by making the decision, an identification of the degree to which the program and/or project selected diverges from long-range directions set by previous plans, and an analysis of the program and/or project impact on those aspects of community development which can only occur over a longer time frame, such as changes in land use patterns. A long-range component of the planning process should provide a "framework whose role is constant but whose dimensions may shift; as a distant early-warning mechanism that seeks out both the opportunities and the limitations of the future and offers them as a background for the decisions that must be made today" [Shulz et al., 1979].
2. *Respond to different scales of analysis.* Many of the classical transportation planning efforts of the mid-1960s focused almost exclusively on large-scale, regional transportation system configurations. At this level of analysis, it was very difficult for political decision makers to obtain the information of most interest to them (i.e., the benefits of specific improvements and an identification of those who will gain or lose). This, along with the fact that there are decision makers responsible for transportation actions at different jurisdictional levels, implies that the transportation planning process should have a capability to undertake analysis at several scales. A classification of these different analysis levels was recently developed based on the concept of an "operating environment" [Roark, 1981]. An operating environment was defined as a subsystem within the transportation network related to major transportation facilities (e.g., freeway corridors, arterial corridors, and modal transfer points), major urban concentrations (e.g., employment sites, activity centers, and outlying commercial centers), and geographical settings (e.g., neighborhoods, central business districts, and regional environments) (see Fig. 3-3). The advantages of reducing the scale of analysis were defined as follows: identification of a lead agency, specific goals and measurable objectives could be more easily obtained, constituencies are more readily identifiable at this level, and specific project impacts are more easily estimated.
3. *Expand scope of the problem definition.* As pointed out earlier, transportation affects many aspects of community life and can itself be affected by political, social, and economic factors. Transportation problems, and their solutions, are not as simple as some might define them. One purpose of planning is therefore to explore beyond the simply defined problem and examine the total system in which it occurs to identify secondary and tertiary impacts of project implementation, as well as to identify alternative means of solution. For example, the shipment of goods in an urban area consists of many interrelated movements and decisions.

Freeway corridors

Freeway construction
Freeway access control through ramp closure and metering
Separate reversible lanes for high-occupancy vehicles (HOVs)
Freeway lanes for exclusive use by HOVs during peak hours
Contraflow lanes for HOVs during peak hours
Preferential access for HOVs
Surveillance and freeway monitoring
Express bus services

Arterial corridors

Turning lanes and prohibitions
Intersection widening and signal improvements
Bus-loading strategies
Traffic signalization
Parking restrictions
Access control
One-way street pairs
Truck loading and unloading areas
Preferential treatment for HOVs
Exclusive bus lanes
Express bus services
Expansion of road capacity

Central business district

All actions listed for arterial corridor plus:
Auto restricted zones
Transit malls
Fare-free transit zones
Parking management programs
Alternative work hours
Express buses and shuttle buses
Street maintenance
Pedestrian amenities
Street construction

Regional operating environments

Ride-sharing programs
Coordinated transit services
Highway construction programs
Computerized traffic signal control
Specialized transportation programs (e.g., elderly and handicapped)
Rapid-transit construction
Light rail and commuter services
Parking management programs
Alternative work schedules
Transit fare programs

Neighborhoods

Parking restrictions and permits
Traffic diversion actions (stop signs, barriers, mazes)
Ride-sharing programs
Bikeways
Street construction
Demand-responsive transit
Sidewalks
Noise barriers
Transit shelters

Outlying commercial centers

Direct transit service
Shoppers' shuttle
Dial-a-ride service
Parking management programs
Specialized transportation services
Traffic management actions
Pedestrian amenities

Modal transfer points

Timed transfers
Fare collection policies
Transit centers
Joint fares
Information strategies
Passenger amenities
Parking management actions

Major outlying employment centers

Ride-sharing programs
Preferential parking for HOVs
Parking management programs
Express buses to work sites
Brokerage and coordination programs
Alternative work schedules
Subscription bus services
Traffic management actions

Major activity centers

Parking restrictions or fees
Fringe parking
Alternative work schedules
Brokerage
Ride-sharing programs
Subscription bus services
Event scheduling
Direct transit service
Traffic management actions

Figure 3-3 Operating environments for transportation actions. *(Roark [1981].)*

Problems in urban goods movement could be caused by congestion at terminals; travel delays resulting from inefficient vehicle routing; loading delays caused by management, labor, or contractual work rules; and unloading delays because of congestion on the streets. In this particular case, one must look at the physical and organizational characteristics of the entire trip-making behavior and service delivery and use pattern to understand fully the range of potential problems (and solutions) related to urban goods movement.

This particular example of urban goods movement pinpoints an especially difficult problem in transportation planning that once again illustrates the need for a broadened scope of the problem definition. Because goods movement is an essentially private-sector activity, planning for its improvement runs into problems of organizational responsibilities, inadequate information, conflict between different planning approaches for the public and private sectors, and disagreement over appropriate solutions. Dealing with urban goods movement solely from the perspective of the public sector can result in proposals that are unimplementable.

4. *Maintain flexibility in analysis.* Because of the dynamic nature of the political process, an effective planning process must possess a capability for a relatively quick analysis of the program and project alternatives that surface from political debate. The process should be capable of responding with credible information that permits a comparative evaluation between the new alternative and those originally considered. Given the large number of possible alternatives that could be considered, this analysis procedure should also be used to screen initial alternatives so as to focus debate on those whose benefit and cost considerations clearly dominate the others.

5. *Provide continuity over time.* The economic, political, fiscal, and social environment in which we live is constantly changing. With this change, new problems arise, and old problems reappear as old solutions are rendered ineffective by changed circumstances. An important attribute of a planning process is thus that it be continuous, that is, that it continually monitor environmental conditions and the effectiveness of the transportation system in responding to them. This monitoring should then be used to update existing plans and programs so as to reflect evolving or changed economic, political, social, and fiscal realities. The short interest span of political decision makers on any one topic implies that planners could, in some ways, serve as the "memory" of the community as transportation issues continually resurface on the public agenda.

6. *Relate to the programming and budgeting process.* With limited resources available for improvements to the transportation network, much of the interest of decision makers is focused on the programming and budgeting process. The specifics of this process vary from one city or governmental structure to another. In some cases, political decison makers may be interested in the progress of specific projects because these projects are important politically. In other cases, decision makers may not be interested in specific projects, but rather in the overall policy they represent. For example, many officials are most interested in the overall level of project construction because this represents government action; the specifics of which projects are being implemented are of little concern.

To provide this focus on implementation, one of the products of the planning process should include a continually updated plan which consists of a program of action staged over a multiyear period [Manheim, 1979]. Those actions programmed for implementation in the near term (i.e., within 1 to 3 years) should be outlined in detail, whereas those actions considered for implementation beyond this time frame can be less detailed. By relating planning activities to a transportation program, it becomes much easier to see the impact of choosing one project over another or to see how desired results are often contingent upon alternative outcomes of earlier actions. Relating the planning process to programming and

budgeting can thus result in the development of an agenda for project implementation which appeals to the action orientation of decision makers.
7. *Provide opportunities for public involvement.* Given the pluralistic nature of decision making, it is important that opportunities are provided to all interested groups to become informed on the objectives and framework of the planning process, to exchange ideas and information with planners and decision makers, and to influence the final outcome of the planning process. As noted earlier, the definition of "public" includes local and regional decision makers, professionals and technical staff who advise officials, organized interests such as business and civic groups, and the general public. It is important, however, to distinguish between those individuals who want to become involved in the planning process because they are a project advocate or are adversely impacted, and those that should become involved because of the mutual benefit gained from such involvement. Private developers, for example, are often not actively involved in transportation planning even though their actions tremendously affect the performance of the existing and future transportation system.

The objectives of a public involvement program are many, including:

Promote and exchange information between planners and the public

Allow an opportunity for each public group to interact with the planners during each step of the planning process

Permit an identification of social and/or neighborhood impacts

Provide a flexible framework for maximum public involvement

Contribute to planning agency visibility and credibility

Conform to governmental requirements

Operate within the existing political and organization framework

Utilize resources only commensurate with the value and potential benefit of the involvement mechanism being used

The type of planning process described here is one that is very sensitive to alternative viewpoints on problem definitions and solutions and recognizes that valuable information for planning can be obtained from actors not directly involved in the process.

3-5 STEPS IN A TRANSPORTATION PLANNING PROCESS

An attempt to simplify in conceptual terms any process as complex and as dependent on situational circumstances as transportation decision making runs the risk of underemphasizing the important differences in characteristics of the process from one decision to the next. It is also almost impossible to construct a theoretical framework to fit all situations; however, given our objective of developing a planning process that reflects the decision-making characteristics of the transportation planning sector specifically, some simplifying assumptions are possible and appropriate.

Although the decision-making process has been described by several authors in many different ways, there seem to be four stages that are important in the eventual outcome of the decision and that are common to most descriptions: problem identification and/or definition, debate and choice, implementation, and evaluation and feedback.

1. *Problem identification and/or definition.* Decisions are made, and policies formulated, in response to perceived differences between desired states of affairs and the decision maker's perception and/or interpretation of the actual situation. The political process is generally effective in identifying these differences, with the media, lobbyists, elected officials, and constituent groups all playing a role in identifying the problems that should be solved through government action. At other times, however, the political process can lag behind in understanding what the actual problems are. For example, the public opposition to highway projects in many cities during the late 1960s reached violent proportions because the political decision process had not yet understood the degree to which the highway program was opposed. There was little recourse left for opponents except to create confrontations to put their issues on the public agenda. Also within the political process, different levels of awareness and varied abilities to participate effectively can prevent timely identification of problems.

    A critical issue in problem identification is the way in which the problem is perceived and thus defined. For many years, the urban transportation problem was perceived almost exclusively as one of highway congestion, and the response to this problem definition was straightforward—planning new or expanded highway systems. This definition has changed during the past decade so that problems associated with urban transportation now include, at the very least, the relationship between transportation and energy consumption, air quality, equity, safety, congestion, land use impact, noise, and more efficient utilization of fiscal resources [Altshuler, 1979]. The solutions to these problems are by no means obvious and often require policy action outside of the transportation sector. Cutbacks in government funding programs are also likely to create new types of problems for decision makers, such as how to maintain existing infrastructure and transportation services given a decreasing level of funds. Indeed, one of the major transportation problems during the next decade is sure to be the maintenance of the existing transportation infrastructure.

2. *Debate and choice.* A decision is a choice between alternatives. Because of limited resources and the need to set priorities, the selection of one alternative over another might occur in an atmosphere of conflict. As stated previously, this decision process is often characterized by bargaining, consideration of a limited number of alternatives, incremental adjustment to existing situations, and search for consensus. The specific characteristics of the debate and choice process,

however, are dependent upon many of the factors identified previously in the discussion on alternative conceptual models of decision making. For the purposes of formulating a planning process responsive to decision-making characteristics, we will assume that individual decision makers act rationally within political and resource constraints. However, collective decision making (i.e., in which several decision makers must agree to a course of action) places greater emphasis on the political nature of decision making, and thus increases the possibility of choices being characterized more by compromise and incremental adjustments and less by optimality.
3. *Implementation.* Traditionally, the most interesting aspect of political decision making to observers of the process was the way in which the decision was reached. To many, this is the key element in understanding the outcome of the decision process. Recent studies of several government programs, however, have concluded that the decision to adopt one policy, program, or project over others is just the beginning of understanding the outcome of a decision [Murphy, 1971; Derthik, 1972; Pressman and Wildavsky, 1979; Lloyd and Meyer, 1984]. Implementing the final decision often implies a new type of politics and a new set of actors. Within the transportation area, the implementation of plans and programs cannot occur until specific projects are scheduled for implementation, a process requiring a determination of which projects should receive funding. Thus, the process of programming and budgeting transportation projects becomes a critical step in project implementation and in achieving the final objectives of the decision.
4. *Evaluation and feedback.* Because actions taken by governments do not always solve the problems for which they were designed, and given the problems of implementation discussed above, monitoring is needed to correct any distortions that might occur during implementation. It also provides information for management decisions to be made at each stage of implementation, allowing for a flexible approach to program and/or project implementation and permitting understanding not only of what occurred, but why. Monitoring can involve informal feedback mechanisms (e.g., constituent reactions and complaints, media reporting, or unofficial agency reports) or more formal ones (e.g., official progress reports from implementing agencies).

A transportation planning process designed to support this decision-making structure should provide the information *desired* and *needed* by decision makers in each stage of the decision process. The purpose of the planning process is not only to provide that information which is of most interest to decision makers (e.g., cost, immediate impacts, benefits), but also to provide information which gives decision makers a more complete understanding of the important implications of their decision (e.g., opportunities forgone, long-run impacts, equity issues).

The relationship between the planning process (originally outlined in Chap. 1) and the decision-making process described above is shown in Fig. 3-4. The major points of interaction between the decision-making process and planning (shown with heavy arrows in Fig. 3-4) are assumed to occur in the diagnosis, analysis and evaluation,

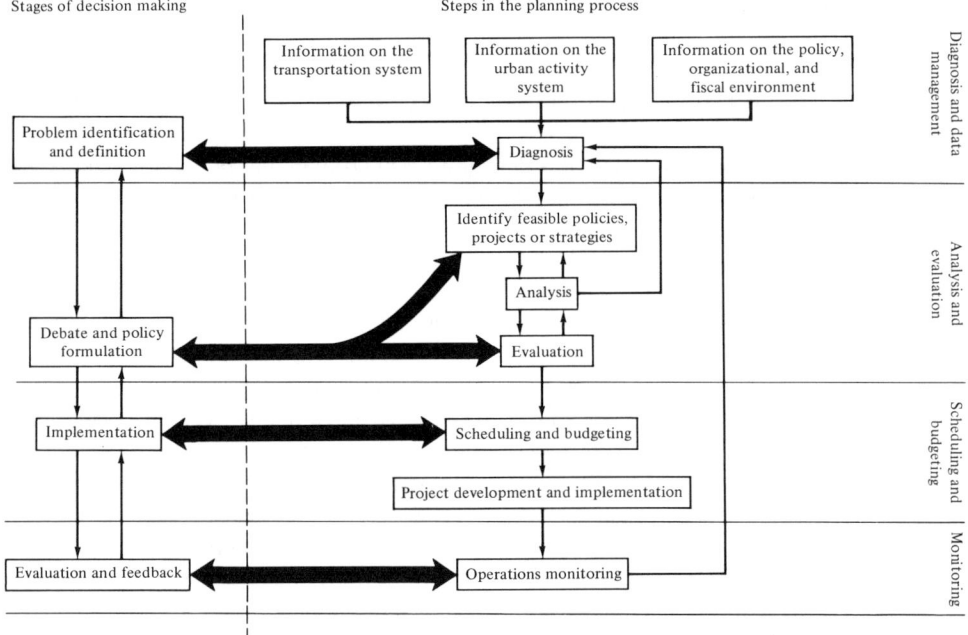

Figure 3-4 Steps in a decision-oriented transportation planning process

scheduling and budgeting, and operations and monitoring tasks. It is from these tasks that the most useful information to decision makers and the most active decision-maker participation in the planning process result. In the remainder of this book, the major steps in the transportation planning process, and their relationship to decision making, will be discussed in detail.

3-6 CHAPTER SUMMARY

1. During the late 1950s and 1960s, much of the urban transportation planning for North American cities was based on the concept of rational choice. The comprehensive plans that resulted from such planning often recommended system alternatives based on a single criterion of choice, usually lowest transportation cost. The characteristics of this type of transportation planning presented an image of a process centralized in a few agencies, dominated by technical procedures, and placing a high value on the provision of personal mobility.
2. In the late 1960s and early 1970s, a new image of planning, based on public participation and development of consensus and focusing on the amelioration of project impacts, began to replace the previous style of planning in many cities. In some cases, planners provided support to community groups in their involvement in transportation planning, a concept called advocacy planning.

3. Also beginning in the early 1970s, several studies of the politics of transportation decision making highlighted the political factors that characterized such a decision-making process, the formation and composition of coalition groups, the role played by elected officials in the final choice, and the importance of funding and who controlled it.
4. The role and characteristics of a decision-oriented planning process depend very much on the type of decision-making approach assumed. There are five major conceptual models which have been used to explain the decision-making process —the rational actor approach, the satisficing approach, the incrementalist approach, the organizational process approach, and the political bargaining approach. The importance of these models to planners lies in their representation of decision making and in the strategies for providing information that each implies.
5. The *rational actor* approach assumes a rational, completely informed set of decision makers whose criterion of decision is maximizing the attainment of an explicit set of goals and objectives.
6. The *satisficing* approach, although still based on the concept of rational choice, suggests that decision makers choose alternatives which satisfy some minimum level of acceptability or which induce the least harm or disturbance.
7. The *incrementalist* approach argues that decision makers focus only on those policies which differ incrementally from existing policies.
8. The *organizational process* approach places decision making within an organizational context and identifies the organizational characteristics which limit or constrain decision-maker choice.
9. The *political bargaining* approach states that decisions result from bargaining and search for consensus among the many participants in a decision process.
10. The major characteristics of the decision-making process assumed in this book include its being pluralistic, resource-allocative, consensus-seeking, problem-simplifying, and uncertainty-avoiding. In response to these characteristics, a decision-oriented transportation planning process should perform the following tasks: establish the future context, respond to different scales of analysis, expand the scope of the problem definition, maintain flexibility in analysis, provide continuity over time, relate planning to programming and budgeting, and provide opportunities for public involvement.
11. The transportation planning process can be viewed as consisting of four major stages: (1) diagnosis and data management, (2) analysis and evaluation, (3) scheduling and budgeting, and (4) system monitoring.

QUESTIONS

1. How did changing political moods and other historical events alter the five steps of the rational transportation planning process shown in Fig. 3-1?
2. For your urban area, review a transportation plan that was produced more than 10 years ago and compare it with a recent plan. What are the major differences between the two plans? What factors do you think contributed to these differences?

3. The different conceptual models of decision making suggest that there may be different roles appropriate for transportation planners under different circumstances.
   (a) Given your knowledge of decision making in your locality, what, in your opinion, is the most appropriate role for transportation planners in responding to the political process?
   (b) With recent trends toward austerity and other government initiatives to alter local government decision making, how would you expect decision making to change in the near future? How can transportation planners adapt to this change?
   (c) Advocacy planning was a big issue in the 1970s. Do you see a future for greater advocacy on the part of planners and "technocrats?" Is there any way that transportation planners can themselves influence the decision-making approach used in their situation?
4. For a transportation project or program with which you are familiar, analyze the decision making approach used with the help of the models discussed. Which model(s) best explains the process used? What factors make the application of any one model difficult? Develop a conceptual framework of the process undertaken.
5. The conceptual models of decision making discussed in this chapter assume an underlying basis of stability in the process. Assume that an urban area suddenly faces a crisis (e.g., a shutdown of transit service, a fuel shortage). How will the decision-making process likely change in this situation? What impact will this change have on the role of the planner?
6. For each of the characteristics of decision making (pages 96 to 98), identify a political action that you are familiar with which illustrates the response of the political process to that characteristic (e.g., what recent political activity would support the notion that the political process is "pluralistic"?). How did each of these political actions, in your opinion, help or hinder the eventual outcome in terms of a policy or a project?
7. Figure 3-3 shows the types of transportation actions that can be considered at different scales of analysis or operating environments. For one of these operating environments, identify the major actors likely to play an important role in transportation planning at this level.
8. In Fig. 3-4, the broad arrows represent links between the planning and decision-making processes. For each of the links shown:
   (a) Discuss the physical means by which these links could be made (e.g., meetings, reports).
   (b) Identify the barriers to effective communication in each case.
   (c) Which of the link stages do you think is/are most important to the selection of the most appropriate solution to a transportation problem?

REFERENCES

Allison, G.: *Essence of Decision*, Little, Brown, Boston, 1971.
Altshuler, A.: *The City Planning Process*, Cornell University Press, Ithaca, New York, 1965.

——: "A Decade of Change in Urban Transportation Planning," Speech made at the Harvard Graduate School of Design, May 2, 1974.

——: *The Urban Transportation System, Politics and Policy Innovation,* MIT Press, Cambridge, 1979.

Altshuler, A., and R. Curry: "The Changing Environment of Urban Development Policy—Shared Power or Shared Impotence?" *Urban Law Annual,* Winter 1976.

Banks, J.: *Political Influence in Transportation Planning: The San Francisco Bay Area Metropolitan Transportation Commission's Regional Transportation Plan,* Report UCB-ITS-DS-77-1, University of California, January 1977.

Barker, W., and J. Roark: *The Role of the Urban Transportation Planner in Public Policy,* Informal paper series 11, North Central Texas Council of Governments, Arlington, Texas, 1979.

Braybrooke, D., and C. Lindblom: *A Strategy of Decision,* Free Press, New York, 1970.

Bureau of Public Roads: *Modal Split,* U.S. Department of Commerce, Washington, D.C., 1966.

Catanese, P.: *Planners and Local Politics, Impossible Dreams,* Sage, Beverly Hills, Calif., 1974.

Chicago Area Transportation Study: *The 1962 Transportation Plan,* Chicago, 1962.

Colcord, F.: *Urban Transportation Decisionmaking, Summary,* U.S. Department of Transportation, Report OST-TPI-76-02, I, Washington, D.C., September 1974.

Commonwealth of Massachusetts: *Study Design for a Balanced Transportation Development Program for the Boston Metropolitan Region,* Prepared by the Steering Group on the Boston Transportation Planning Review, Boston, November 1970.

Cyert, R., and J. March: *A Behavioral Theory of the Firm,* Prentice-Hall, Englewood Cliffs, N.J., 1963.

de Bettencourt, J., M. Mandell, S. Polzin, V. Sauter, and J. Schofer: "Making Planning More Responsive to Its Users: The Concept of Metaplanning," *Environment and Planning A,* vol. 13. 1981.

Derthik, M.: *New Towns In-Town,* Urban Institute, Washington, D.C., 1972.

Dror, Y.: *Public Policymaking Reexamined,* Chandler, San Francisco, 1968.

Elmore, R.: "Organizational Models of Social Program Implementation," *Public Policy,* no. 2, Spring 1979.

Federal Highway Administration: *Guidelines for Trip Generation Analysis,* U.S. Department of Transportation, Washington, D.C., 1967.

——: "Guidance on the Transportation Planning Process," *Policy and Procedure Memorandum 50-9,* 1969.

Friedmann, J.: "The Future of Comprehensive Planning: A Critique," *Public Administration Review* 31, May/June 1971.

Gakenheimer, R.: *Transportation Planning As a Response to Controversy: The Boston Case,* MIT Press, Cambridge, 1976.

Goodman, R.: *After the Planners,* Simon and Schuster, New York, 1971.

Greenberger, M., M. Chenson, and B. Crissey: *Models in the Policy Process,* Russell Sage, New York, 1976.

Hamer, A.: *The Selling of Rail Rapid Transit,* D.C. Heath, Lexington, Mass., 1976.

Highway Research Board: "Transportation Analysis: Past and Prospects," *Highway Research Record 309,* Highway Research Board, Washington, D.C., 1970.

Jessiman, W., D. Brand, A. Tumminia, and C. R. Brussee: "A Rational Decision-Making Technique for Transportation Planning," *Highway Research Record 180,* Highway Research Board, Washington, D.C., 1967.

Jones, D.: *The Politics of Metropolitan Transportation Planning and Programming—Implications for Transportation System Management,* Report UCB-ITS-SR-76-11, University of California, November 1976.

—— and E. Sullivan: "TSM: Tinkering Superficially at the Margin?" *Transportation Engineering Journal of ASCE,* vol. 10, no. TE6, November 1978.

Kaplan, M.: *Urban Planning in the 1960s, A Design for Irrelevancy,* MIT Press, Cambridge, 1973.

Keen, P., and M. Morton: *Decision Support Systems, An Organizational Perspective,* Addison-Wesley, Reading, Mass., 1978.

Lee, D.: "Requiem for Large-Scale Models," *Journal of the American Institute of Planners,* vol. 39, no. 3, May 1973.

——: *Improving Communication among Researchers, Professionals and Policy Makers in Land Use and*

Transportation Planning, U.S. Department of Transportation, Report DOT-TPI-77-10-12, Washington, D.C., 1977.

Levine, C., and I. Rubin (eds.): *Fiscal Stress and Public Policy,* Sage, Beverly Hills, Calif., 1980.

Lindblom, C.: "The Science of Muddling Through," *Public Administration Review,* vol. 19, Spring 1959.

_____: *The Policy-Making Process,* Prentice-Hall, Englewood Cliffs, N.J., 1968.

Lloyd, E., and M. Meyer: "Strategies for Overcoming Opposition to Project Implementation," *Transportation Policy and Decisionmaking,* 1984.

Lupo, A., F. Colcord, and E. Fowler: *Rites of Way, the Politics of Transportation in Boston and the U.S. City,* Little, Brown, Boston, 1971.

Manheim, M.: *Fundamentals of Transportation System Analysis,* MIT Press, Cambridge, 1979.

March, J., and H. Simon: *Organizations,* John Wiley, New York, 1958.

Meyer, M.: "Organizational Response to a Federal Policy Initiative in the Public Transportation Sector: A Study of Implementation and Compliance," Unpublished Ph.D. thesis, Department of Civil Engineering, MIT, June 1978.

_____: "Public Policy Development Process," *Transportation Research Record 837,* Transportation Research Board, 1982.

Meyerson, M., and E. Banfield: *Politics, Planning and the Public Interest,* Free Press, New York, 1970.

Mogulof, M. B.: *Governing Metropolitan Areas,* Urban Institute, Washington, D.C., 1971.

Murphy, J.: "Title I of ESEA: The Politics of Implementing Federal Education Reform," *Harvard Educational Review* 41, 1971.

National Wildlife Federation: *The End of the Road, A Citizen's Guide to Transportation Problemsolving,* Washington, D.C., 1977.

Office of Technology Assessment: *An Assessment of Community Planning for Mass Transit,* United States Congress, February 1976.

Perin, C.: "The Noiseless Secession from the Comprehensive Plan," *Journal of the American Institute of Planners,* September 1967.

Pill, J.: *Planning and Politics, The Metro Toronto Transportation Plan Review,* MIT Press, Cambridge, 1979.

Pressman, J., and A. Wildavsky: *Implementation,* University of California Press, Berkeley, 1979.

Rabinovitz, F.: *City Politics and Planning,* Atherton, Chicago, 1969.

Roark, J.: "Experiences in Transportation System Management," *National Cooperative Highway Research Program Synthesis of Highway Practice 81,* Transportation Research Board, November 1981.

Rondinelli, D.: "Urban Planning as Policy Analysis," *Journal of the American Institute of Planners,* vol. 39, January 1973.

Schlesinger, J.: *Systems Analysis and the Political Process,* RAND Corporation, 1973.

Schulz, D., J. Schofer, and N. Pedersen: "An Evolving Image of Long-Range Transportation Planning," *Traffic Quarterly,* vol. 3B, no. 3, July 1979.

Simon, H.: "A Behavioral Model of Rational Choice," in H. Simon, *Models of Man,* John Wiley, New York, 1957.

_____: *Sciences of the Artificial,* MIT Press, Cambridge, 1969.

Smith, H.: *The Citizen's Guide to Planning,* American Planning Association, Washington, D.C., 1979.

Smith, W.: "Rational Location of a Highway Corridor: A Probabilistic Approach," *Highway Research Record 348,* Highway Research Board, Washington, D.C., 1971.

Steiner, H.: *Conflict in Urban Transportation,* D.C. Heath, Lexington, Mass., 1978.

System Design Concepts, Inc.: *Operating Multi-Modal Urban Transportation Systems,* U.S. Department of Transportation, Washington, D.C., 1977.

U.S. Congress: *Urban System Study,* Report of the U.S. Secretary of Transportation to the U.S. Congress, Committee on Public Works and Transportation, 1977.

Yates, D.: *The Ungovernable City,* MIT Press, Cambridge, 1978.

CHAPTER
FOUR

DATA MANAGEMENT AND DIAGNOSIS

4-0 INTRODUCTION

The foundation of effective transportation planning, at any level of analysis, is a good data base. Transportation planners have long placed great emphasis on the importance of collecting data for use in determining the existing condition of the transportation network. In addition, data have proved to be necessary for the calibration and application of travel forecasting models, for evaluating the overall performance of system operations, and for gauging the degree to which planning goals and objectives are achieved.

In this chapter, we will examine the types of data needs transportation planners usually face and the techniques used to gather this information. Two major types of information are identified—quantifiable data, which can be used in technical analysis, and the more subjective information (e.g., the identification of goals and objectives) that often comes from the political or decision-making process.

4-1 THE TRANSPORTATION PLANNING DATA BASE

In the early years of transportation planning, there were two basic reasons for gathering travel data: to determine the origin and destination of highway users entering urban areas and to estimate the total number of vehicles using urban highways. In the first case, the origin and destination information was used to solve site-specific problems, such as the location of a new bridge or a highway route to bypass a city. In the second case, automatic or manual traffic counters were used to determine vehicle volumes on congested highways so that the need for highway expansion or highway control could be clearly established. Today, most state, provincial, and local transportation agencies still conduct a systematic program of vehicle counting on selected highway segments [Federal Highway Administration, 1970; Smith et al., 1975; Sharma and Werner, 1981].

Beginning in 1944, when the U.S. Congress first made funds available for highway projects in urban areas, several state highway departments, in cooperation with the U.S. Bureau of the Census, developed a new data collection procedure that was based on home interviews in a sample of households in an urban area. This procedure was tested in several medium-sized United States cities and was found to provide an adequate estimate of the total travel occurring within an urban area [Highway Research Board, 1944]. The information collected in these home interviews usually included the type of housing structure occupied by those being interviewed, the number of vehicles available, the number of persons in the household, the household income category, and a description of the trips (i.e., origin, destination, trip purpose, trip times, and travel modes) made by household members 5 years or older.

These early transportation studies also collected a large amount of data on land use in the urban area, such as the type of land use, the area of land devoted to each activity, and the location of individual parcels of land. In addition, transportation network inventories were conducted as part of each study. These inventories identified roadway locations, roadway length, pavement width, speeds, parking restrictions, and (in the case of transit) vehicle headways, number of seats per vehicle, and overall line capacity. Collecting and processing these data consumed a substantial percentage of the planning study budget, in some cases more than 50 to 60 percent of the total funds available.

Today, because of the variety of actions considered by transportation planners and the diverse objectives that transportation planning often strives to achieve, the data base in most urban areas consists of a large number of data items, collected by numerous agencies and serving a wide variety of purposes. These data are used to calibrate and update travel behavior models, to design roads and transit facilities, to monitor the performance of individual facilities or services and of the overall system, to identify potential problem sites in the transportation network, to ascertain the degree to which specific planning objectives are being met, and to determine the financial contributions of local governments in relation to the services being received, such as a city's contribution to the transit deficit based on the number of trips originating in that city (for an excellent discussion of the uses of traffic data in project planning and design, see Pedersen and Samdahl [1982]).

Table 4-1 shows some of the transportation-related data items usually collected in urban areas. These data can be used to provide many forms of information useful to planners and decision makers on the performance of transportation systems. For example, the primary data collected on transit system operations can be used to compute performance measures (on a route-by-route basis or systemwide). Such measures might include ridership per mile of service, ridership per vehicle-mile, ridership per vehicle hour, ridership per dollar of cost, and ridership per capita. On the highway side, data on travel behavior can be used to estimate the total vehicle miles of travel in an urban area, a measure which is often the basis for determining energy consumption and air quality impacts of automobile emissions.

Table 4-1 Example of data often collected for urban transportation planning

Highway data
  Road miles
    By functional classification
    By geographic area
  Lane miles of arterials during peak period
    By functional classification of arterials
    By number of lanes
    By geographic area
    By one-way or two-way direction
  Miles of reversible lanes
  Vehicle miles of travel
    By functional classification
    By geographic area
    By vehicle type
  Passenger occupancy
    By vehicle type
    By geographic area
  CBD cordon measurement
    Passenger occupancy
    Vehicle type
  Traffic volume and congestion

Public transit data
  Land area within 0.25 mile of weekday transit service (population within band can be determined by census data)
    By number of boardable vehicles per 24-hour period
    By geographic area
  Transit user survey
    Number of linked passenger trips
    Average linked trip distance
    Average linked trip time
    Trip purpose
    Rider characteristics
      Age
      Sex
      Income
      Whether handicapped
      Automobile availability
  Limited transit user survey
    Unlinked passenger trips
    Unlinked passenger miles or average
    Unlinked trip distance
    Average unlinked trip time

Public transit data
  Rider characteristics
    Age
    Sex
    Race
    Handicapped
  Selected data from transit operators (classified by mode)
    Annual unlinked passenger trips
    Annual revenue passengers
    Annual vehicle-miles
    Annual revenue vehicle-miles
    Number of revenue vehicles
    Age distribution of revenue vehicles
    Average age of revenue vehicles

Demographic data
  Population
    By geographic area
  Dwelling units
    By geographic area
  Employment
    By geographic area
    By CBD
  Passenger vehicle registrations
    By county located in or containing urbanized area
    By vehicle type
  Land areas
    By urbanized area
    By central city
    By central business district
    By federal-aid system boundaries

Measurement of system performance
  Highway system: land area and dwelling units within travel time contours
    From CBD
    From airport
    From major non-CBD employment center
    From major non-CBD shopping center
  Transit system: land area and dwelling units within travel time contours from CBD

Source: Transportation Research Board [1976].

Before discussing the specific techniques used in collecting the types of transportation data shown in Table 4-1, it is necessary to examine two important aspects of data collection: (1) classification schemes for data collection and (2) the use of sampling procedures in data collection efforts.

4-1-1 Classification Schemes for Data Collection

Transportation planners often group data for collection and processing by geographic location or type of transportation facility. For example, one of the first steps in many past transportation studies has involved dividing the urban area into analysis units, sometimes called traffic zones, which form the basis for analysis of travel movements within, into, and out of the urban area (see Fig. 4-1). The selection of these zones can be based on several criteria including [Baass, 1981]:

1. Achieving homogeneous socioeconomic characteristics for each zone's population
2. Minimizing the number of intrazonal trips
3. Recognizing physical, political, and historical boundaries
4. Generating only connected zones and avoiding zones that are completely contained within another zone
5. Devising a zonal system in which the number of households, population, area, or trips generated and attracted are nearly equal in each zone
6. Basing zonal boundaries on census zones

This last criterion is especially important because both the United States and Canadian agencies responsible for census data conduct a census every 10 years, meaning their information can be used to update the socioeconomic data for the transportation planners' own zonal systems (for a discussion of transportation planning uses of the 1980 U.S. Census, see Sosslau, [1983]).

As shown in Fig. 4-1, the traffic analysis zones of an urban area can also be grouped into larger analysis units reflecting corridors of travel or sectors of the urban area defined by rings surrounding the central business district. Data collected at the individual zone level can be aggregated to these larger geographical units for analyses undertaken at this level.

Another scheme important for data collection is the functional classification of urban streets and highways. Most United States highway data are classified according to the character of service they are intended to provide and use the following functional classifications [Federal Highway Administration, 1978; American Association of State Highway and Transportation Officials, 1984]:

Interstate. Fully controlled access facilities that are part of the interstate system. The major purpose of these highways is to provide access to and through urban areas.
Freeway and expressway. Fully controlled access facilities that are not part of the interstate system, but whose purpose is similar.

114 URBAN TRANSPORTATION PLANNING

Figure 4-1 Example layout of analysis units.

Principal arterial. Streets and highways having high traffic volumes, serving the longest urban trips, and providing access to major activity centers. Service to abutting land is subordinate to the movement of traffic.

Minor arterial. Streets and highways interconnecting with the principal arterial system. More emphasis is placed on land access and providing service to trips of moderate length.

Collector. Streets penetrating neighborhoods, collecting traffic from local streets, and channeling it to the arterial system. The collector system primarily provides land access.

Local. Streets providing direct access to abutting land. Through traffic is usually discouraged.

In sum, the transportation data-collection activities in urban areas are usually structured on the basis of analysis units and facility classification schemes. Because these schemes have been used for many years, periodic updates of the data provide an opportunity to monitor changes in socioeconomic and system characteristics over time.

4-1-2 Sampling Methods in Data Collection

The collection and processing of data can be a complex and costly activity. Because the basic unit of data collected for transportation planning is usually an individual household or a single-vehicle movement, it is economically infeasible to develop a data base consisting of every household or vehicle movement in an urban area. In response to this problem, methods have been developed to allow planners to make reliable inferences about the characteristics of an entire population based on the characteristics found in a carefully selected, statistically significant sample. The critical issue in undertaking such sampling, of course, is how to select a sample representative of the characteristics of the entire population.

Cochran, in a classic text on survey methodology, outlined the steps to be followed in planning and executing a survey [Cochran, 1977]:

1. Establish a clear statement of the survey objectives.
2. Define the population to be sampled and the target groups to be focused on.
3. Identify the specific data that are relevant for the purpose of the survey.
4. Specify the degree of precision required from the survey results (i.e., how much error can be tolerated in the results).
5. Determine the methods to be used in obtaining survey results.
6. Divide the population into sampling units and list the units from which the sample will be drawn.
7. Select the sampling procedure and the sample size.
8. Pretest the survey and field methods to ensure that the procedures are workable and the survey is understandable.
9. Establish a good supervisory structure for managing the survey.
10. Determine the procedures for analyzing and summarizing the data.
11. Store the data and analysis results for future reference.

Two tasks in step 7 of the survey methodology merit special attention—selecting the sampling procedures to be used and determining the size of the sample to be taken. In the former case, four major types of sampling procedures are commonly used in data collection efforts: simple random sampling, sequential sampling, stratified random sampling, and cluster sampling [Soberman and Hazard, 1980].

Simple random sampling is a procedure for selecting units out of a population such that each population unit has an equal chance of being drawn. The units in the population are assigned numbers from 1 to N, and numbers between 1 and N are drawn from a random number table or from a computer program especially designed to produce such numbers. The specific units in the population which correspond to these random numbers become the randomly drawn sample.

Sequential sampling draws a sample from every *n*th element in the population. This procedure is based on the assumption that the target population has been listed in random order.

Stratified random sampling divides the population of N units into subpopulations of $N_1, N_2, \ldots, N_L$ units, according to differences in some defining characteristic. Random samples are then taken within each strata.

Cluster sampling involves grouping sampling units, usually on a spatial or geographical basis (e.g., grouping households on the basis of neighborhood blocks). Clusters are then selected at random for the sample. Although cluster sampling is cheaper to undertake than other procedures, the statistical analysis associated with such sampling tends to be more difficult.

Each of these sampling procedures is an attempt to reduce the bias in the results that might come from measurement error, unrepresentative sample selection, or varying question interpretations. In each case, the cost of survey sampling is different and must be balanced against the degree of accuracy required.

The second important component of the surveying strategy is selecting sample size. Although the accuracy of population estimates will increase with the size of the sample, there is always a point at which the additional accuracy is not worth the associated costs of data collection and analysis. In transportation planning, determining an appropriate sample size can be very difficult because data are seldom collected for strictly one purpose. For example, the same data base could be used both to validate existing planning statistics (e.g., trip generation rates) and to calibrate travel forecasting models. Different levels of accuracy (and different sample size) may thus be required, depending upon the purposes for which the data will be used. The challenge to the transportation planner becomes one of first deciding how the collected data will (or could) be used and then determining the size of sample needed to provide the required level of accuracy for the most sensitive of the data uses.

The determination of sample size involves two major steps:

1. Because the purpose of sampling is to gain information about the nature or distribution of elements in a particular population, one must make assumptions about the form of the underlying distribution of these elements when selecting a sample size. One common assumption is that the population is normally distributed (see Fig. 4-2a). An important characteristic of the normal distribution is that, no matter what the mean μ or standard deviation σ of a particular normal distribution, the same proportion of observations will always lie between the mean and a specified number of standard deviations. Thus, as shown in Fig. 4-2a, 68.26 percent of the area under the distribution will always be within one standard deviation of the mean, and 95.46 percent, within two standard deviations for any normally distributed variable.
2. Some decision must be made about the acceptable limits of error for the sample. This is usually done by specifying that a sample mean for a data item should be within some value d of the true average value for a certain percentage of samples. This latter percentage (i.e., the percentage of samples falling within the desired limit of error) is called the *level of confidence*. This level of confidence is denoted

DATA MANAGEMENT AND DIAGNOSIS 117

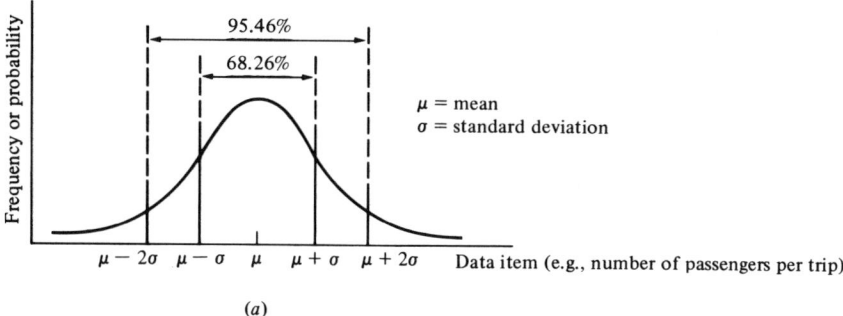

(a)

Normal distribution with a $(1 - \alpha)$ percent confidence interval

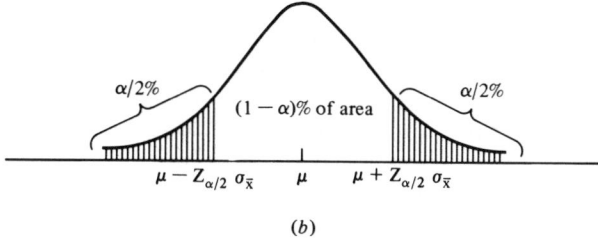

(b)

Figure 4-2 The normal distribution.

as $100(1 - \alpha)$, where α is the fraction of the area under the normal distribution falling outside the confidence limits (see Fig. 4-2b). For example, one could specify that the accuracy of a particular normally distributed variable should be within plus or minus two units of the true mean at a 95 percent confidence level. That is, plus or minus two units around the true value will include the estimated value 95 percent of the time (note in this case that $d = 2$ and $\alpha = 0.05$)

Once an assumption about the distribution of the elements of a population has been made and the desired sample precision has been chosen, the required sample size can be determined. For example, if one assumes that the elements of a particular population are normally distributed, it can be shown that the sample size required to achieve a precision of d units with $100(1 - \alpha)$ percent confidence is

$$n = \left[\frac{Z_{1-(1/2)\alpha}\sigma}{d}\right]^2 \tag{4-1}$$

where
- n = sample size
- d = tolerable margin of error of mean value
- σ = standard deviation of population distribution
- α = fraction of area under normal curve representing events *not* within confidence level (thus, $1 - \alpha$ is desired level of confidence)
- $Z_{1-(1/2)\alpha}$ = standard normal statistic corresponding to the $1 - \alpha$ confidence level (found in tables in any statistics book)

For example, assume an agency wanted to estimate the required proportion of some vehicle type (e.g., trucks) within a tolerance of ±0.025 with a 95 percent level of confidence. Also assume that a previous survey has shown the standard deviation of the underlying vehicle type distribution to be 0.04. The sample size can thus be calculated as

$$n = \left[\frac{Z_{1-0.05/2}(0.04)}{0.025}\right]^2 = 9.8 \text{ or } 10$$

Thus, vehicle classification data should be collected on 10 randomly selected days to meet the required precision.

One of the problems with using Eq. (4-1) is that σ is often unknown. Existing records or preliminary samples can be used to estimate σ and thus determine the appropriate sample size. Another distribution, the t distribution, allows the sample mean and standard deviation to be used, instead of the population mean and standard deviation. As sample size increases, the t distribution approaches the shape of the normal curve. The t distribution is used, for example, in transit sampling efforts where the data item examined is number of bus trips per route per hour and where the sample size is small (e.g., less than 30 trips) [Attanucci et al., 1981].

Another approach, based on an estimate of the proportion of the data item in the population, is also used by planners. The equation for this sample size determination is

$$n = \frac{[Z_{1-(1/2)\alpha}]^2(p)(1-p)}{d^2} \qquad (4\text{-}2)$$

where p is the observed value of the proportion of the data item in the population (e.g., percentage of trip types of all trips made in an area), and the remaining symbols are the same as in Eq. (4-1).

One modification of Eq. (4-2) can occur when planners are interested in the relative error r from the true mean value instead of the absolute error d. For example, planners might want to estimate a variable with an error not exceeding 5 percent of the true mean value. In order to make this estimation, Eq. (4-2) is modified by substituting $r \cdot p$ for d. The resulting formula is

$$n = \frac{[Z_{1-(1/2)\alpha}]^2(p)(1-p)}{(rp)^2} = \frac{[Z_{1-(1/2)\alpha}]^2(1-p)}{r^2 p} \qquad (4\text{-}3)$$

where r is the margin of error or precision, expressed as a fraction of the mean value, and the remaining symbols are the same as above. Instead of using Eq. (4-3), planners can use tables or figures which show the relationship between proportions (frequencies), confidence intervals, margins of error (precision), and sample sizes. Table 4-2 and Fig. 4-3 are examples of such aids.

For instance, suppose one wished to estimate the total number of trips for one trip type within an urban area, and it was estimated that 50 percent of all trips in the area ($p = 0.50$) were indeed of this trip type. Assume that planners require an estimate of this number within ±5 percent ($r = 0.05$) of the real value 95 percent of the time ($\alpha = 0.05$). Using Table 4-2, one can see that the level of precision for a value of p of 0.50 is 8.85 percent at a sample size of 500, 6.26 percent for n equal to 1000, and 4.43

percent for n equal to 2000. Thus, for the required level of precision, a sample size of between 1000 and 2000 would be necessary. To determine the exact value, Eq. (4-3) can be used; that is

$$n = \frac{(1.96)^2(0.50)}{(0.05)^2(0.50)} = 1537$$

Thus, 1537 observations are needed to achieve the specified level of precision.

Because some survey methods rely on voluntary questionnaire return, and given that many individuals contacted will not respond, the sample size in such cases must be adjusted by the expected response rate. Incorporating this change, Eq. (4-3) becomes

$$n = \frac{[Z_{1-(1/2)\alpha}]^2(1-p)}{r^2(p)(s)} \tag{4-4}$$

where s is the expected response rate from the survey. Suppose in the previous example the sampling method used was a mail-back survey in which planners expected to have a 60 percent response rate. The required sample size would be

$$n = \frac{(1.96)^2(0.50)}{(0.05)^2(0.50)(0.60)} = 2561$$

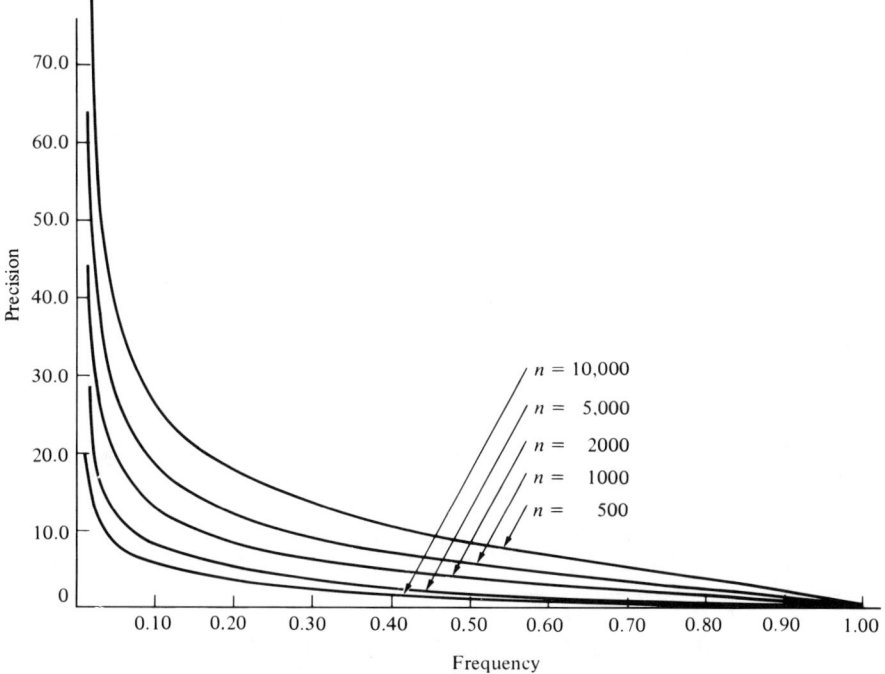

Figure 4-3 Precision versus frequency for 95 percent confidence level sampling. (*Adapted from lecture notes of Professor A. Ceder.*)

Table 4-2 Sample size related to frequency, precision, and confidence interval

	Sample size														
	90% confidence interval					95% confidence interval					99% confidence interval				
Frequency	500	1000	2000	5000	10,000	500	1000	2000	5000	10,000	500	1000	2000	5000	10,000
0.10	22.14	15.65	11.07	7.00	4.95	26.56	18.78	13.28	8.40	5.94	34.35	24.29	17.17	10.86	7.68
0.11	20.99	14.84	10.49	6.64	4.69	25.19	17.81	12.59	7.96	5.63	32.57	23.03	16.28	10.30	7.28
0.12	19.98	14.13	9.99	6.32	4.47	23.98	16.96	11.99	7.58	5.35	31.00	21.92	15.50	9.80	6.93
0.13	19.89	13.50	9.54	6.14	4.27	22.91	16.20	11.05	7.24	5.12	29.62	20.94	14.81	9.37	6.62
0.14	18.29	12.93	9.14	5.78	4.09	21.95	15.52	10.97	6.94	4.91	28.38	20.06	14.19	8.97	6.34
0.15	17.57	12.42	8.78	5.55	3.93	21.18	14.90	10.54	6.67	4.71	27.25	19.27	13.63	8.62	6.09
0.16	16.91	11.96	8.45	5.35	3.78	20.29	14.35	10.14	6.42	4.54	26.23	18.55	13.12	8.30	5.87
0.17	16.30	11.53	8.15	5.15	3.65	19.57	13.84	9.78	6.19	4.38	25.30	17.89	12.65	8.00	5.66
0.18	15.75	11.14	7.87	4.98	3.52	18.90	13.36	9.45	5.98	4.23	24.44	17.28	12.22	7.73	5.46
0.19	15.24	10.77	7.62	4.82	3.41	18.28	12.93	9.14	5.78	4.09	23.64	16.71	11.82	7.48	5.29
0.20	14.76	10.44	7.38	4.67	3.30	17.71	12.52	8.85	5.60	3.96	22.90	16.19	11.45	7.24	5.12
0.21	14.31	10.12	7.16	4.53	3.20	17.17	12.14	8.59	5.43	3.84	22.21	15.78	11.10	7.02	4.97
0.22	13.89	9.82	6.95	4.39	3.11	16.67	11.79	8.34	5.27	3.73	21.56	15.24	10.78	6.82	4.82
0.23	13.50	9.55	6.75	4.27	3.02	16.20	11.46	8.11	5.12	3.62	20.95	14.81	10.47	6.62	4.68
0.24	13.13	9.29	6.57	4.15	2.94	15.75	11.14	7.88	4.98	3.52	20.37	14.41	10.19	6.44	4.56
0.25	12.78	9.04	6.39	4.04	2.86	15.34	10.84	7.67	4.85	3.43	19.83	14.02	9.91	6.27	4.43
0.26	12.45	8.80	6.22	3.94	2.78	14.94	10.56	7.47	4.72	3.34	19.31	13.66	9.66	6.11	4.32
0.27	12.13	8.58	6.07	3.84	2.71	14.56	10.30	7.28	4.60	3.26	18.82	13.31	9.41	5.95	4.21
0.28	11.83	8.37	5.92	3.74	2.65	14.20	10.04	7.10	4.49	3.18	18.36	12.98	9.18	5.81	4.11
0.29	11.55	8.16	5.77	3.65	2.58	13.85	9.80	6.93	4.38	3.10	17.91	12.67	8.96	5.66	4.01
0.30	11.27	7.97	5.54	3.56	2.52	13.53	9.56	6.76	4.28	3.02	17.49	12.37	8.74	5.53	3.91
0.31	11.01	7.78	5.50	3.48	2.46	13.21	9.34	6.51	4.18	2.95	17.08	12.08	8.54	5.40	3.82
0.32	10.76	7.61	5.38	3.40	2.41	12.91	9.13	6.45	4.08	2.89	16.69	11.80	8.34	5.28	3.73
0.33	10.51	7.43	5.26	3.32	2.35	12.62	8.92	6.31	3.99	2.82	16.31	11.54	8.16	5.16	3.65
0.34	10.28	7.27	5.14	3.25	2.30	12.34	8.72	6.17	3.90	2.76	15.95	11.28	7.98	5.04	3.57
0.35	10.06	7.11	5.03	3.18	2.25	12.07	8.53	6.03	3.82	2.70	15.60	11.03	7.80	4.93	3.49
0.36	9.84	6.95	4.92	3.11	2.20	11.81	8.35	5.93	3.73	2.64	15.26	10.79	7.63	4.83	3.41

0.37	9.63	6.81	4.81	3.04	2.15	11.55	8.17	5.78	3.65	2.58	14.94	10.56	7.47	4.72	3.34
0.38	9.43	6.66	4.71	2.98	2.11	11.31	8.00	5.66	3.58	2.53	14.62	10.34	7.31	4.62	3.27
0.39	9.23	6.53	4.61	2.92	2.06	11.07	7.83	5.54	3.50	2.48	14.32	10.12	7.16	4.53	3.20
0.40	9.04	6.39	4.52	2.86	2.02	10.84	7.67	5.42	3.43	2.42	14.02	9.91	7.01	4.43	3.14
0.41	8.85	6.26	4.43	2.80	1.98	10.62	7.51	5.31	3.36	2.38	13.73	9.71	6.87	4.34	3.07
0.42	8.67	6.13	4.34	2.74	1.94	10.41	7.36	5.20	3.29	2.33	13.45	9.51	6.73	4.25	3.01
0.43	8.50	6.01	4.25	2.68	1.90	10.19	7.21	5.10	3.22	2.28	13.18	9.32	6.59	4.17	2.95
0.44	8.32	5.89	4.16	2.63	1.86	9.99	7.06	4.99	3.16	2.23	12.92	9.13	6.46	4.08	2.89
0.45	8.16	5.77	4.08	2.58	1.82	9.79	6.92	4.89	3.10	2.19	12.66	8.95	6.33	4.00	2.83
0.46	7.99	5.65	4.03	2.53	1.79	9.59	6.78	4.80	3.03	2.15	12.48	8.77	6.20	3.92	2.77
0.47	7.84	5.54	3.92	2.48	1.75	9.40	6.65	4.70	2.97	2.10	12.16	8.60	6.08	3.84	2.72
0.48	7.66	5.43	3.84	2.43	1.72	9.22	6.52	4.61	2.91	2.06	11.92	8.43	5.96	3.77	2.66
0.49	7.53	5.32	3.76	2.38	1.68	9.03	6.39	4.52	2.86	2.02	11.68	8.26	5.84	3.69	2.61
0.50	7.38	5.22	3.69	2.33	1.65	8.85	6.26	4.43	2.80	1.98	11.45	8.10	5.72	3.62	2.56
0.51	7.23	5.11	3.62	2.29	1.62	8.63	6.14	4.34	2.74	1.94	11.22	7.94	5.61	3.55	2.51
0.52	7.09	5.01	3.54	2.24	1.59	8.51	6.02	4.25	2.69	1.90	11.00	7.78	5.50	3.48	2.46
0.53	6.95	4.91	3.47	2.20	1.55	8.34	5.90	4.17	2.64	1.86	10.78	7.62	5.39	3.41	2.41
0.54	6.81	4.82	3.41	2.15	1.52	8.17	5.78	4.09	2.58	1.83	10.57	7.47	5.28	3.34	2.36
0.55	6.67	4.72	3.34	2.11	1.49	8.01	5.66	4.00	2.53	1.79	10.36	7.32	5.18	3.27	2.32
0.56	6.54	4.63	3.27	2.07	1.46	7.85	5.55	3.92	2.48	1.76	10.15	7.18	5.07	3.21	2.27
0.57	6.41	4.53	3.20	2.03	1.43	7.69	5.44	3.85	2.43	1.72	9.94	7.03	4.97	3.14	2.22
0.58	6.28	4.44	3.14	1.99	1.40	7.54	5.33	3.77	2.38	1.68	9.74	6.89	4.87	3.08	2.18
0.59	6.15	4.35	3.08	1.95	1.38	7.38	5.22	3.69	2.33	1.65	9.54	6.75	4.77	3.02	2.13
0.60	6.02	4.26	3.01	1.91	1.35	7.23	5.11	3.61	2.29	1.62	9.35	6.61	4.67	2.96	2.09

Source: Adapted from lecture notes, Professor A. Ceder, Department of Civil Engineering, Massachusetts Institute of Technology.

The use of Eqs. (4-2) through (4-4) assumes that the sample n is small relative to the total population size. However, in those cases where the estimated sample size is a substantial percentage of the total population (that is, n/N is greater than some standard, usually set at 0.10), the following formula should be used to modify the sample size estimate:

$$n_1 = \frac{n_0}{1 + n_0/N} \qquad (4\text{-}5)$$

where n_0 = number of sample observations originally estimated

n_1 = adjusted number of observations

N = total population

For example, assume that an original estimate of the size of a household sample to estimate mode of travel was 2561 households. Further assume that these 2561 households were part of a district containing 8537 households. Because $2561/8537 = 0.30$ exceeds our standard of 0.10, Eq. (4-5) should be used. Thus,

$$n_1 = \frac{2561}{1 + 2561/8537} = 1970$$

In this case, 1970 instead of 2561 households need to be surveyed for the requisite level of precision.

For those interested in further reading on sample size determination as it relates to transportation data collection, the U.S. DOT has prepared several useful guides (see, for example, Ferlis [1980]; Ferlis et al. [1981]; and Attanucci et al. [1981]).

4-2 DATA COLLECTION TECHNIQUES

A study conducted in 1971 identified eight types of data collection activity commonly undertaken in the United States metropolitan areas: (1) home interview origin-destination surveys, (2) truck-taxi origin-destination surveys, (3) roadside origin-destination surveys, (4) arterial link inventories, (5) transit route inventories, (6) speed runs, (7) traffic counts, and (8) land area measurements [Creighton Hamburg, 1971]. In addition to these data collection activities, which are still common today in most urban areas, transportation planners are also making greater use of transit on-board surveys and other surveys focusing on special groups (e.g., car poolers, elderly, handicapped, or employees at a specific employment center). Because each data collection technique presents its own set of limitations and uses, the following sections discuss in some detail the characteristics of the major techniques in use today.

4-2-1 Household Travel Behavior Surveys

Of all the data collection efforts undertaken in urban transportation planning, household travel behavior surveys are probably the most expensive and detailed. As shown in Table 4-3, numerous person, household, and trip characteristics can be obtained in a household survey. Three basic techniques can be used to collect these data—a personal home interview, a telephone interview, and a mail survey.

The personal home interview was the technique most often used in early transportation studies when new data bases were being formed. The ability of the interviewer to explain questions, a longer time per interview (compared to other techniques), and higher response rates because of personal interaction made the home interview a valuable technique in developing an extensive data base. However, the home interview is a particularly time-consuming and expensive technique which, given financial constraints on planning budgets, becomes very difficult to undertake. From a methodological perspective, the possibility of biased results because of certain interviewer actions and statements is also a cause of concern. Even with these limitations, the

Table 4-3 Home interview household and trip data

Household record	Person trip record
Structure type	Sex
Type of living quarters	Race
Interview address	Age
Number of passengers	Occupation
Number of persons	Industry
Persons age 5 and up	Origin location
Overnight visitors	Destination location
Time at present address	Purpose "from"
Previous address	Purpose "to"
Time at previous address	Land use at origin
Sex	Land use at destination
Race	Starting time of trip
Age 5 and up making trips	Arrival time of trip
Age 5 and up not making trips	Mode of travel
Total trips made	Blocks walked to origin
Persons age 16 and up	Blocks walked at destination
Driver status (age 16 and up)	Number of persons in car
Number of walking trips	Kind of parking
Income	Screen line control points
Occupation	Expressway used
Industry	Principal route of travel
Age	First work trip
Worked on travel day	Expressway entrance
Year-round resident	Expressway exit
Part-time resident; months lived at address	Automobile available
Persons employed	Income
Auto driver trips	Structure
	Density
	Car pool
	Park and shop

Source: Creighton Hamburg, Inc. [1971].

home interview is often the best way of getting the most complete information (see, for example, Parvatanani et al. [1982]).

Given the generally prohibitive costs of personal home interviews, telephone surveys have been used in their place. The advantages of such an approach over personal household visits include (1) a shorter length of time required to complete each interview, (2) fewer people required to administer a survey, (3) the ability to closely supervise telephone interviews, and (4) the ability to easily recontact those interviewed. The disadvantages, of course, relate to the ability of those being called to easily refuse to answer the questions. Also, to maintain the validity of the random sample, ideally, personal interviews should be undertaken at households that could not be reached by telephone.

To reduce the potential for bias in telephone surveys, several steps can be taken [U.S. Department of Transportation, 1973]:

1. The samples should not be selected from the telephone book because this would eliminate those not having a telephone (between 10 and 20 percent of the households in an urban area) and those having unlisted numbers. Other means are therefore required to choose household samples. For example, a semirandom dialing technique has been used in some instances. In this technique, telephone numbers are sampled randomly from a telephone book, and then one is added to the number (e.g., 924-3521 becomes 924-3522). This increases the chance of reaching valid numbers over a random dialing technique and assures that unlisted numbers will be reached in the study area.
2. As mentioned above, those households for which no telephone number is available could be visited in person. A common way of choosing households is to use a document called a "reversed listing," which lists *all* households by street address (regardless of having a telephone) and provides telephone numbers for those listed in the telephone directory. Such a listing is available through most real estate agencies.
3. Each household to be contacted should be sent a preinterview letter explaining the purpose and procedure of the survey.
4. In those cases where a household has a large number of trips to report, it might be necessary to send an interviewer to ensure that all the information is obtained.

A third technique that can be used for household surveys is the mail-back questionnaire approach. The trade-off in this case is between the much reduced cost of data collection and the potentially low response rate. Several special actions, however, have been shown to increase response rates, including mailing a second questionnaire or reminder to those households not responding to the initial request within a specified time period (e.g., 1 or 2 weeks), pretesting the questionnaire to avoid misleading or confusing questions, and using a personally signed cover letter (see, for example, Dilman [1978]; Sheskin and Stopher [1982]).

Regardless of which technique is used, the household travel survey should be supplemented with a small stratified in-person home interview survey. The purpose of this stratified sample survey is to estimate the validity of the results from the larger random sample. This survey can also be used to obtain additional information for specific household types (e.g., low income) or trip purposes which may be poorly represented in the random sample survey. The size of this stratified sample depends on the resources available, the needs of the planners, and the degree to which the initial random sample is considered representative of the population. In general, the stratified sample survey should be at least 5 percent of the random sample survey size.

In summary, the household travel behavior survey can be a useful data collection technique in the urban transportation planning process. Such surveys provide timely data on socioeconomic characteristics and travel behavior in an urban area, data which are extremely important for calibrating and using travel forecasting models. However, the collection of these data tends to be both time-consuming and expensive.

4-2-2 Origin-Destination Surveys

Origin-destination (O-D) surveys can also provide useful transportation data because they highlight the patterns of movement of persons and goods in a particular area of interest. Such data can help planners and engineers estimate the demand on existing transportation facilities, calibrate or verify travel forecasting models, determine the feasibility of new routes or facilities, identify travel characteristics from specific types of land use, and determine the adequacy of parking or other terminal facilities.

For transportation planning purposes, there are several types of trips that can be of interest. These trips include those internal to a planning study area, those that are made between such areas, or those that pass through the study area. Several types of boundaries and trips merit special attention.

Cordon. The perimeter established as the boundary of the planning study area
Screenline. An imaginary line established to divide the study area into parts to check the accuracy of survey data
Internal trip. A trip having either its origin or destination in the study area but which crosses a cordon line
Through trip. A trip having both its origin and destination outside of the study area

Apart from the home interview survey method discussed in the last section, there are three major techniques for collecting O-D data: a roadside interview, a postcard survey, and a license-plate survey. The roadside interview involves stopping cars and commercial vehicles at specific interview stations (e.g., cordon or screenline points) and asking the driver questions on origin, destination, trip purpose, route used, and intermediate stops made. Because it is impractical to stop all traffic at interview stations, a sampling procedure must be employed.

The postcard survey can consist of distributing mail-back postcards at roadside stations or sending postcards to a sample of vehicle owners. In both cases, the origins and destinations of trips made on a specific date are obtained.

The license-plate survey requires roadside observers to note the last four digits of license plates as cars pass their station. The route of a vehicle can thus be traced by its successive appearance at a series of recording stations [Crabtree and Krause, 1982].

The results of O-D surveys are often expanded to represent a 100 percent sample (it is therefore important to know what percentage of trips is included in the survey sample) and checked with other O-D data and traffic counts. When validated, the O-D data can be used to construct origin and destination tables that show the number of trips made between zones in the urban area.

4-2-3 Inventories

Transportation planners should not only be aware of the characteristics of travel demand in an urban area (collected through home interview and O-D surveys), they must also have data on the physical characteristics of the land use and transportation systems which handle this demand. These inventories of system capability and use have become an important source of information in the transportation planning process. The highway network inventory usually consists of road section (link) capacities, average travel times or speeds for each link, parking conditions, the percentage of commercial vehicles, and total traffic volumes. In some cases, planners and engineers have included measures of roadway surface quality, right-of-way widths, highway gradients, and accident rates.

A transit network inventory often includes the number of vehicles in the fleet, number of seats available, measures of route utilization, speeds, and, in some cases on-off passenger counts at specific transit stops (see Table 4-4). Finally, a land use inventory can include a wide variety of data on the characteristics of land use in an urban area (see Table 4-5). Much of these data can be collected through the use of aerial photographs, while other data items require special surveys.

In most urban areas, a land use and network inventory has been in existence for many years. Transportation planners are therefore becoming increasingly concerned

Table 4-4 Typical data items in a transit inventory

List of transit companies and/or operating agencies
Total number and type of transit vehicles
Transit routes by type of service
Total number of miles of routes by type and company
Route number, description, and terminal-to-terminal mileage
Location of transfer points, terminals, and parking facilities
Location of stops
Hours of operation
Headway by hour of day
Running time by route segment by hour of day
Average turn-around time by time period
Total annual and weekday vehicle miles and hours
Fare structure
Total annual and average weekday costs
Accidents by type and location
Franchise limitations and other regulatory constraints

Source: Creighton Hamburg, Inc. [1971].

Table 4-5 Typical data items in a land use inventory

Address—location
Type of land use
Vacant unusable
Vacant zoned by type
Secondary land use code
Secondary land use of parcels in 100s acres
Number owner-occupied dwelling units
Number renter-occupied dwelling units
Number nonwhite occupied dwelling units
Nonconformng land use code
Number persons dwelling on parcel
Number of uses
Number of secondary uses
Watershed
Dwellings

Source: Creighton Hamburg, Inc. [1971].

with updating the inventory where such data are useful for transportation planning activities. For the land use inventory, the disaggregate results of the national census should provide a good basis for updating much of the existing land use data. The transportation network inventory can be updated as changes occur in the system or as new data are collected by government agencies as part of a continuing system monitoring program. This latter data source becomes particularly important given the operations orientation of recent transportation planning activities.

In some instances, special inventory surveys might be needed to obtain information on specific transportation-related activities. For example, inventories of urban parking capacity (supply, cost, and utilization data) have been undertaken in many urban areas. Such inventory data are important not only for use in travel forecasting models, but also for use in policy discussions on the types of transportation facilities to be provided in the downtown area.

4-2-4 Highway and Transit Counts

As mentioned earlier, most urban areas have been involved in an extensive program of manual and automatic traffic counting for many years. Such counts are used for a variety of purposes—validating survey data, establishing traffic flow trends, assessing the transportation impact of large traffic generators, and determining the environmental impact of transportation facility operations. The major types of traffic count efforts include the following:

Cordon counts. These counts are undertaken to obtain estimates of the total number of vehicle movements occurring within the area defined by the cordon and the number of vehicles entering or leaving. Automatic traffic recorders can be used to determine the total number of vehicles crossing the cordon line, while manual counts can supplement this information with data on vehicle classifications. When conducting these cordon counts, it is important to carefully note the time period in which the traffic movements occurred, especially if the cordon counts are taken in conjunction with a comprehensive travel behavior survey.

Screenline counts. The purpose of screenline counts is to evaluate the completeness and accuracy of the reported trip data within a cordon study area. Because the validity of a screenline analysis depends on identifying as many of the vehicles that cross the screenline as possible, the screenline itself should be chosen very carefully. Often, natural barriers to traffic flow (e.g., rivers or railroad tracks) are used because they involve a minimum number of crossing points. The screenline should extend across the study area from one cordon boundary to another. Generally, hourly traffic counts and classification counts are taken at every crossing point along the screenline for each of the 5 workdays of the week. Although the number of counts taken at each screenline crossing will vary depending on travel characteristics in the study area and the length of the given travel survey, at least five counts should be taken at each location for each of the 5 workdays [U.S. Department of Transportation, 1973].

Other traffic counts. Traffic counts are taken in an urban area for a variety of other reasons. Areas of employment concentration often experience high levels of congestion during peak hours, and traffic counts can be taken to monitor these congestion levels to determine whether some action is necessary. Traffic counts are also taken on major highway facilities (usually by functional classification) for determining the levels of pollutant emissions and energy consumption, for comparing actual counts with those estimated by travel forecasting models, and for monitoring the effectiveness of actions taken to reduce vehicle volumes on transportation facilities.

Just as planning and highway agencies collect traffic data, transit properties also collect a variety of information relating to transit operations. These data have been used for vehicle scheduling, route planning, marketing, deficit allocation, and external reporting requirements. A recent guide to transit data collection argues that the data collection procedure in a transit agency should consist of two phases: (1) a determination of the "base" conditions of each route in the system and (2) periodic monitoring to detect changes which may have occurred [Attanucci et al., 1981]. Table 4-6 shows the type of data that should be collected in this data collection program, while the major types of data collection techniques are outlined in Table 4-7.

4-2-5 Special Data Collection Efforts

Transportation planners can become involved with projects that require special data for assessing project feasibility or evaluating a recently implemented project. Site surveys are undertaken to obtain information from employees (at their places of employment) and from shoppers and users of recreational facilities. The purpose of these surveys can range from identifying the characteristics of specific trip types to determining the

Table 4-6 Data items in sample comprehensive route profile

General effectiveness data
  1. Boardings per trip, per day
  2. Revenue per trip, per day
  3. Maximum load per trip
  4. Running time by route segment
  5. Difference between scheduled and actual arrival times

Data for specialized analyses
  6. Distribution of boardings, revenue by fare category
  7. Transfer rates per day
  8. Passengers boarding and alighting by stop per trip
  9. Average unlinked trip length per passenger
  10. Average unlinked trip travel time per passenger
  11. Passenger miles per day
  12. Passenger characteristics and attitudes
  13. Passenger travel patterns

Data collection design items
  14. Relationship between boardings and revenue per trip
  15. Relationship between boardings and maximum load per trip

Data needs in monitoring phase
  16. Bus arrival time
  17. Load at peak load point
  18. One or more of the following:
      Total boardings
      Boardings by fare category
      Revenue

Source: Attanucci, Burns, and Wilson [1981].

Table 4-7 Seven principal transit data collection techniques

Technique	Description
Ride check	Check taken on board vehicle, recording the number of passengers boarding and alighting at each stop and the bus arrival time at selected points
Point check	Check taken on street, estimating passengers on board vehicle and recording vehicle arrival time. *Peak* load count taken at peak load point. *Multiple* point checks include several points along a route
Boarding count	On-board count of total number of passengers boarding, most often broken down by fare category
Fare box reading	Recording of fare box register reading at selected points. Requires registering fare boxes
Revenue count	Count of revenue in fare box vault, by bus
Transfer count	Count of transfer tickets collected on each bus, which may involve specially issued transfer tickets
Survey	Variety of techniques in which passengers are asked to provide information

Source: Attanucci, Burns, and Wilson [1981].

feasibility of new services to these sites. This type of survey, which can be conducted in person or by distributing questionnaires, has been particularly effective in surveying target groups such as the elderly. In these cases, natural gathering points such as elderly housing complexes, social centers, church groups, and medical centers provide efficient survey distribution locations [Billheimer and Trexler, 1980].

In recent years, many transportation planners have become involved with surveys that attempt to assess the potential of ride-sharing programs at specific employment centers. In those cases where direct surveys of employees were used, transportation planners had to work very closely with top management officials of the targeted firms to develop an effective strategy for approaching the employees and for providing incentives for them to participate in the survey. Another technique used in such situations involves distributing mail-back surveys by leaving them on the windshields of parked cars.

Perhaps one of the most challenging data collection efforts for transportation planners is the collection of evaluation data needed to assess the performance of newly implemented services or facilities. Not only is it necessary in such cases to identify the outcome or impact of a new program or project, it is also important to ascertain the reasons behind the outcome. Thus, the data collection efforts of many evaluation studies include activities to gather data on the physical changes caused by the new project, as well as on individuals' attitudes and behavior, which might help to explain the results of new service implementation or facility construction (see Fig. 4-4). In such evaluation studies, it is extremely important to have an experimental design which specifies the type of information to be collected, identifies the techniques to be used, and outlines where and when such data are to be collected. Most important, this design should carefully determine the data which should be collected *before* a project is implemented so that useful comparisons can be made before and after project implementation.

4-3 DEVELOPING A DATA COLLECTION AND MANAGEMENT PLAN

Because the effectiveness of planning depends very much upon the existence of a good data base, designing a data collection and management plan for an urban area becomes an important task in transportation planning. This plan should not only outline the method for data collection in terms of the data to be collected and the collection intervals, but it should also identify agency responsibilities for data collection activities [Meyer, 1980]. Such a plan will become especially important in the coming decade as significant portions of the existing data base become outdated. Faced with cutbacks in funds, transportation planners will need to look very carefully at new and innovative ways to use existing data sources and to minimize the number of expensive data collection efforts. More specifically, planners must look at a multitude of ways to combine the data collection activities discussed previously into alternative packages that can be carried out under differing levels of funding.

The data collection and management plan should provide a schedule of data collection activities over a specified period, identify likely unmet data needs, establish

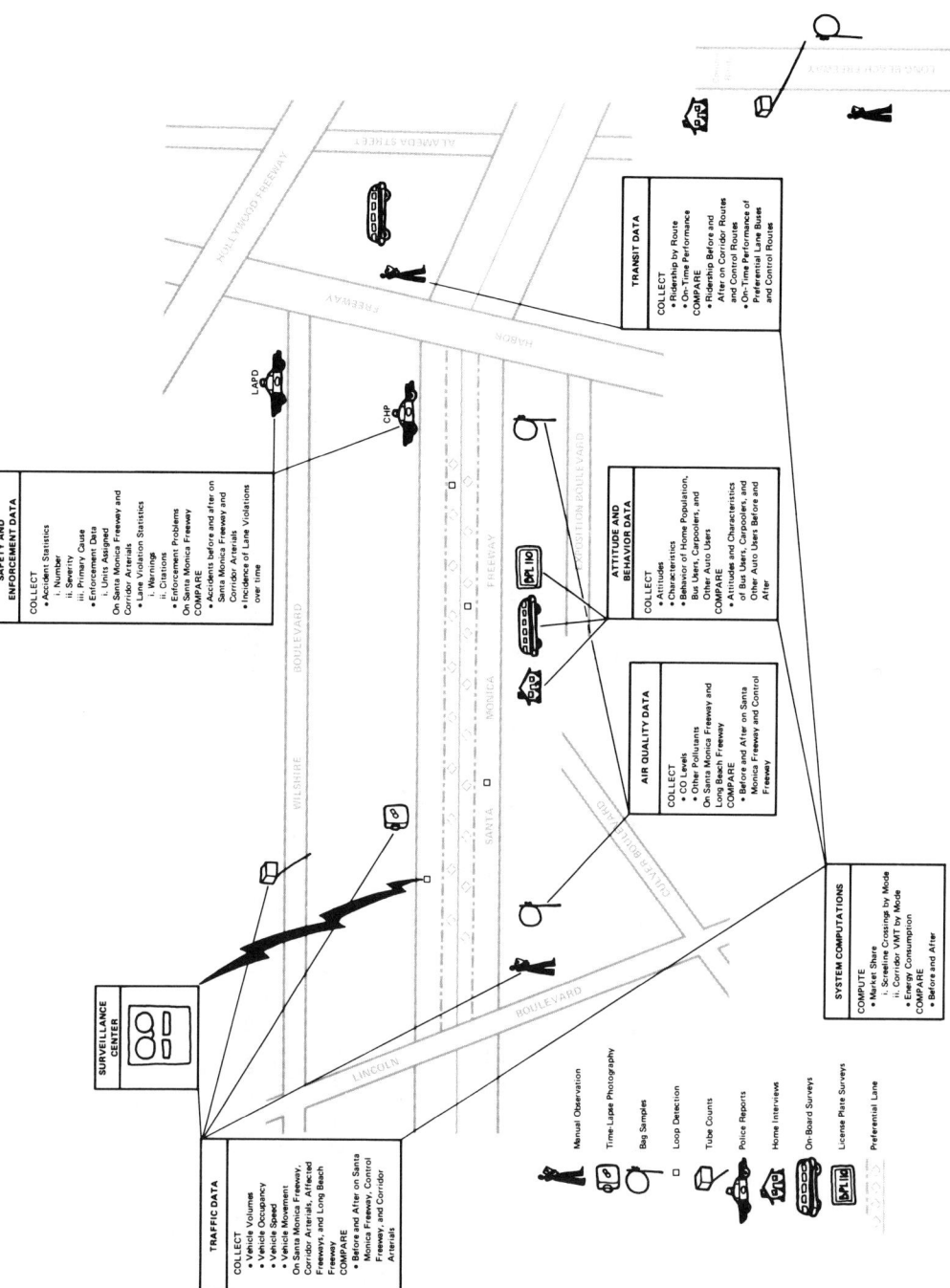

Figure 4-4 Data collection plan for the Santa Monica diamond lane project. *(Billheimer and Trexler, 1980.)*

Table 4-8 Characteristics of different data collection techniques

Survey type	Reported response rates	Cost per completed survey, 1979 dollars	Advantages	Disadvantages
Home interviews Face to face (20–30 minutes)	85%	$15–$50	Flexibility; can accommodate long or complicated questionnaires; high response rate; well-defined population	High cost; difficult to survey in undesirable neighborhoods; interviewer-dependent
Drop off/pick up	75%	$2–$5	Well-defined population; interviewer available to clear up questions	Difficult to reach undesirable neighborhoods
Drop off/mail back	50%	$2–$5		
Telephone interviews	50% (one call) 97%–100% (follow-up)	$3–$16	Flexibility; high response rate; low cost; encourages frankness; easy to screen for undesired subpopulation	Unlisted numbers may add sampling bias; inability to use visual aids; necessarily short
Mail surveys	20%–40%	$2–$5	Low cost; large number of samples in small time; wide distribution; well-defined population	Nonrespondent bias; can be costly to screen for desired subpopulations if not identified beforehand

On-board surveys			
Face to face (1–2 minutes)	85%–95%	$2–$4	Transit user population clearly defined; low cost
Pick up	55%–97%	$2–$4	
Mail back	20%–40%	$2–$4	Population limited to users and biased toward frequent users; limited number of questions
Roadside surveys			
Stop and interview (1–2 minutes)	20%–40%	$2–$5	Automobile user population clearly defined; low cost
Stop and issue mail-back survey	20%–40%	$2–$4	
Mail surveys from license samples	20%–40%	$2–$4	Traffic disruption problems when vehicles are stopped, interview necessarily short; recall problems when surveys are mailed from license samples
Site surveys			
Face to face (20–30 minutes)		$10–$50	Flexibility; transit users and nonusers in single locale
			High costs; sampling frame ill-defined; interviewer-dependent

Source: Billheimer and Trexler [1980].

Table 4-9 Data collection options for Minneapolis–St. Paul under three budget scenarios*

Data collection activities	1981	1982	1983	1984	1985	1986	1987	1988	1989	1990	Total
Household travel surveys	(250) [175] 62.5										(250) [175] 62.5
Parking supply surveys		(5) [5] 5		(5) [5] 5		(5) [5] 5		(5) [5] 5		(5) [5] 5	(25) [25] 25
Transit counts		(10) [8] 6		(10) [8] 6		(10) [8] 6		(10) [8] 6		(10) [8] 6	(50) [40] 30
Highway counts		(20) [14] 6		(20) [14] 6		(20) [14] 6		(20) [14] 6		(20) [14] 6	(100) [70] 30
Transit on-board surveys		(15) [7.5] 3.8					(15) [7.5] 3.8				(30) [15] 7.6

Attraction-based surveys			(67.5)[33.8]0							(67.5)[33.8]0
Business surveys		(15)[10]5					(4)[2]0			(8)[4]0
Special needs surveys			(15)[10]5	(15)[10]5	(15)[10]5	(15)[10]5	(15)[10]5	(15)[10]5	(15)[10]5	(150)[100]5
Total costs {high / medium / low}	(265)[135]67.5	(65)[44.5]25.8	(96.5)[45.8]5	(50)[37]22	(15)[10]5	(50)[37]22	(30)[17.5]8.8	(54)[39]22	(15)[10]5	(50)[37]22	(680.5)[412.8]205.1

* All figures shown are in thousands of 1981 dollars. ( ) High budget; [ ] Medium budget; Low budget

Source: Cambridge Systematics, Inc. [1980].

priorities among these needs, determine the level of resources to be devoted to each of these needs, and estimate the cost of the data collection efforts on an annual basis. With respect to annual cost estimates, the level of resources needed will depend on the type of data collected, the techniques used, and the sample size required. As shown in Table 4-8, the cost of different types of data collection techniques varies tremendously from one technique to another. However, the usefulness of these techniques also varies, with the most costly data collection techniques tending to provide much higher response rates.

Data collection and management alternatives developed for the Minneapolis–St. Paul region are shown in Table 4-9. Three budgets, representing different combinations of high-, medium-, and low-cost component levels, were identified. This was done on the basis of an assessment of essential data needs as well as those needs considered nonessential but potentially useful. The budget level recommended was the most costly one because planners considered it essential to conduct the household surveys as soon as possible to take advantage of complementary data from the 1980 census. A large "front-end" cost for these surveys was common for each budget scenario. Other data collection efforts were needed to update planning models, monitor system operation, and determine achievement of performance objectives.

Although it is certainly preferable to have a comprehensive data collection plan that includes all types of transportation data, it is often difficult within the institutional framework of most cities to coordinate such activities. Agencies collect data for their own use, with little concern for what other agencies are doing. In such a context, it becomes important to at least develop a data management strategy for similar types of data collected by different agencies. Such a strategy is illustrated in Fig. 4-5, where different objectives for collecting traffic counts are matched with agency responsibilities and characteristics of the data collection approach.

The technical data base is thus a critically important component of an effective transportation planning process. These data are collected by a large number of agencies in an urban area and reflect a variety of decisions made by agency and political officials. Such officials are not only concerned about the impact of new services and facilities, they are also interested in the transportation problems likely to occur in the future, the performance of the existing system, and the degree to which policy objectives are attained. A careful examination of how the existing data base is providing the needed information for these issues is thus an important task in any transportation planning process. The types of techniques used, the level of accuracy desired, and the scheduling of data collection activities over time thus become important concerns for planners.

4-4 THE TRANSPORTATION PLANNING SOCIOPOLITICAL INFORMATION BASE

The transportation planning data base discussed up to this point has focused exclusively on the needs of planning methodology (i.e., the data needed to analyze,

Objective	Type of application	Responsible agency	Sample population	Precision
1. Regional VMT estimate by highway functional class and geographic subarea	Regional	Metropolitan Planning Agency (MPO)	All streets; January–December; 24 hours; weekdays	± 25% local streets ± 5% arterial streets ± 5% freeways
2. Screenline counts for forecast model validation and update	Screenline	MPO	Selected streets on screenlines; same months as original household survey; 24 hours; weekdays	10%
3. Coverage count of one-quarter of nonlocal city street network	Single location	City Traffic Engineering (TE) Department	Selected streets; January–December; 24 hours; weekdays	Count for 1 day
4. CBD cordon count	Cordon line	City TE Department	Same situations as used in previous years; May; 7:00 A.M.–7:00 P.M.; weekdays	Count for 1 day. Calculate precision
5. VMT estimate for a specific transportation improvement corridor	Corridor	MPO City TE Department State DOT	Street segments in corridor; May; peak periods (A.M. and P.M.); weekdays	2%
6. Volume counts at specific locations	Single location	City TE Department	January–December; varied times; weekdays	Count for 1 day

Figure 4-5 Example traffic counting program. (*Ferlis, Bowman, and Cima,* [*1981*].)

evaluate, and monitor the existing transportation system and changes made to it). As discussed in Chap. 3, however, the role of the planner is one of planning *with* interested public groups and officials rather than planning *for* a perceived unitary general public. If planners are to adopt this more "open" process of planning, they must have information on the desires and attitudes of the community with respect to both general directions for the planning process and specific reactions for or against plan and project proposals.

Because transportation system and service changes can affect a great number of people, the amount of discussion between transportation planners and public officials and/or community groups is usually quite high. Thus, much of the information on community attitudes and desires needed by planners can be discovered through ad hoc meetings and conversations. It is also important, however, for planners to establish a formal, systematic approach for obtaining community input. There are two types of information that are especially important for planning purposes: community goals and objectives and attitudinal data obtained through market research techniques.

4-4-1 Planning Goals and Objectives

Traditionally, one of the first steps in the transportation planning process has been the identification of a set of *goals and objectives* to "guide" planners in their analysis and evaluation of transportation proposals. Significant financial and organization resources were often spent conducting a public involvement program to solicit information on community goals and objectives. The importance of such community goals and objectives lies in the fact that the attitudes and desires of the community with respect to transportation and the type of community wanted could be different from the image of the community held by planners. Also, attitudes and desires can change over time, potentially invalidating many of the explicit and implicit assumptions inherent in previous planning studies. As stated before, much of the unrest in urban areas during the late 1960s and early 1970s over transportation investment can be attributed to an incompatibility between transportation agency mandates and planning objectives and the desires of the local population.

The development of a set of goals and objectives, however, can be hindered by difficulties in defining what exactly is meant by values, goals, objectives, measures of effectiveness (or criteria), and standards; and in understanding the interrelationship between them. For the purpose of this discussion, these terms will be defined as follows [Wachs and Schofer, 1969; Thomas and Schofer, 1970]:

Values. Basic social drives that govern human behavior. They include the desire to survive, the need to belong, the need for order, and the need for security. Because values are assumed to be shared by most groups in a culture, one can speak of societal values.

Goals. Generalized statements which broadly relate the physical environment to values, but for which no test for fulfillment can be readily applied.

Objectives. Specific, measurable statements related to the attainment of goals.

Measures of effectiveness. Measures or tests which reflect the degree of attainment of particular objectives.

Standards. Minimum acceptable level for the criterion measure (i.e., a fixed level of attainment of an objective).

An example of how these terms could be used might be:

Value. Need for order.
Goal. Maintain and/or improve the quality of transportation.
Objective. Improve the reliability of the movement of persons and goods on the existing transportation system.

Measure of effectiveness. Degree of schedule adherence of bus trips.

Standard. The number of bus trips arriving more than 5 minutes late at any bus stop on a particular route should not exceed 10 percent of the total bus trips on that route during an 8-hour period.

As can be seen from this example, the degree of specificity increases as one proceeds from values to standards. One value can also lead to more than one goal, each goal can lead to one or more objective, and the attainment of each objective can be judged with one or more measures of effectiveness. One objective could also satisfy different goals. For example, an objective of reducing travel costs for elderly and low-income persons could satisfy the achievement of two goals: (1) improve the quality of transportation services and (2) provide for equitable distribution of public funds (see Fig. 4-6).

In order for a goals and objectives statement to be useful for transportation planning and decision making, several criteria have to be met [JHK & Associates and Peat, Marwick, Mitchell & Co., 1977]:

1. Goals and objectives must be clear, concise, unambiguous, and understandable to all actor groups.
2. Objectives must logically follow from applicable goals.
3. Goals and objectives must reflect the views, perceptions, and aspirations of the community.
4. Each objective must be measurable by at least one measure of effectiveness (MOE).
5. The MOEs must be measurable with reasonable effort.
6. Goals and objectives must be developed independent of specific transportation plans and not be mode-specific.

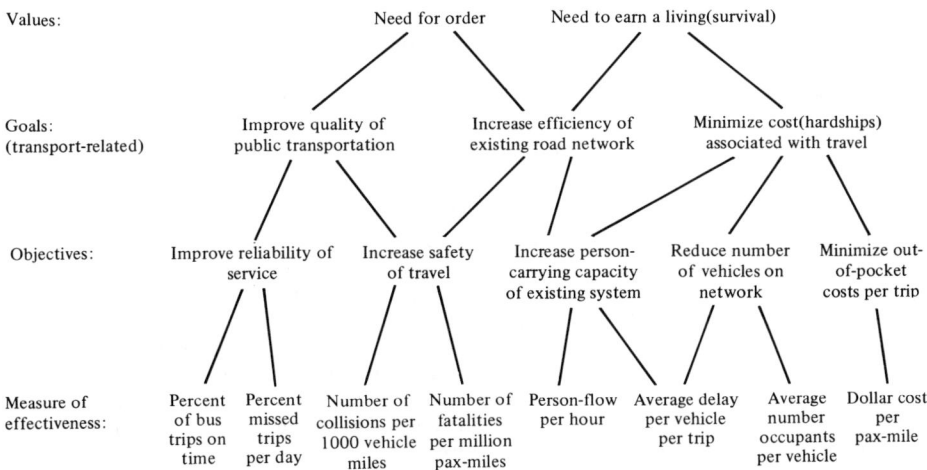

Figure 4-6 Values, goals, objectives, and measures of effectiveness in transportation planning.

A typical list of goals and objectives for short-range transportation planning is shown in Table 4-10. Clearly, new goals and objectives could be added to reflect the attitudes and desires of local communities that might not be captured in the list shown here.

Table 4-10 Recommended goals and objectives for TSM

Goal	Objective
1. To maintain and/or improve the quality of transportation services on the existing transportation system	1. To reduce the travel time required for the movement of persons and goods on the existing transportation system 2. To reduce the travel costs required for the movement of persons and goods on the existing transportation system 3. To improve the safety of the existing transportation system 4. To improve the security of the movement of persons and goods on the existing transportation system 5. To improve the comfort and convenience of the existing transportation system 6. To improve the reliability of the movement of persons and goods on the existing transportation system
2. To increase the efficiency of the existing transportation system	7. To reduce automobile usage in the immediate future 8. To increase transit patronage in the immediate future 9. To increase pedestrian and bicycle travel in the immediate future 10. To increase the person movement capacity of the existing transportation system to adequately serve demand 11. To increase transportation system productivity
3. To minimize the cost to improve the quality of service on, and efficiency of, the existing transportation system	12. To minimize the capital costs of improving the existing transportation system 13. To minimize the operating costs and deficits of the existing transportation system
4. To minimize the undesirable environmental impacts of existing transportation facilities and services	14. To reduce existing transportation system noise and vibration impacts 15. To reduce existing undesirable transportation system air quality impacts 16. To reduce existing transportation system energy consumption
5. To promote desirable and minimize undesirable social and economic impacts of existing transportation facilities and services	17. To provide adequate service to the transportation disadvantaged and transit-dependent 18. To promote desirable and minimize adverse economic impacts resulting from improvements in the existing transportation system 19. To equitably distribute transportation service and costs 20. To minimize the displacement of residences, businesses, and community facilities caused by improvements to the existing transportation system

Source: Abrams and DiRenzo [1979].

The effort transportation planners put into developing goals and objectives can vary according to the political, social, and demographic changes occurring in the urban area. In cases where little or no change is occurring along these dimensions, verifying that previous goals and objectives statements for the community represent its true desires could be a simple task. In other cases, however, where rapid growth and in-migration are affecting the basic characteristics of a community, a major effort might be needed to develop a new statement of goals and objectives. In either case, the effort of thinking about and defining such a statement provides useful information to the planning process.

The literature on the types of techniques that can be used to obtain this kind of information is extensive. The techniques include citizen advisory committees, newspaper mail-back coupons, public hearings, and referenda [Arnstein, 1969; Weiss, 1974; Jordan et al., 1976]. Through the use of these techniques, a consensus should develop among those involved in the process on the appropriate goals for the planning process, on whether a goal should be regarded as a means or an end, and on the relative value of the goals [Young, 1966]. A more extensive discussion of how goals, objectives, and measures of effectiveness can be used in the evaluation of alternative projects or systems is found in Chap. 9.

4-4-2 Market Research Information

With many transportation planners becoming increasingly interested in the provision and utilization of alternative transportation services, information about consumer preferences and the characteristics of consumer demand is becoming an important data requirement. *Market analysis* is one method of obtaining this information. This approach involves the identification of *market segments* and the attributes of transportation services that reflect the desires of these different groups.

For the purpose of this discussion, a market segment will be defined as a subset of the population having specific characteristics that distinguish it from other population groups. Criteria for selecting market segments can include demographic and socioeconomic characteristics (e.g., age, income, sex, race, occupation, and life-cycle stage), attitudes (e.g., lifestyle and personality), use of existing services (e.g., auto versus transit), and perceptions of different services and preferences (e.g., sensitivity to price and importance of service attributes). In defining market segments, it is important to determine those characteristics which affect both the ability and willingness of individuals within selected population groups to use transportation services [Woodruff et al., 1981].

Market research data on perceptions and preferences for different services are often gathered through the use of questionnaires that are based on psychological scales (see Fig. 4-7). The most common form of scaling is the Likert scale, which requires the respondent to react to a strongly worded statement about a service attribute or policy goal by indicating his or her level of agreement or disagreement on a five- or seven-point scale. Although easily administered and readily understood by respondents, the Likert scale only measures attributes on an ordinal, rather than a cardinal, scale. That is, the planner cannot infer from the results of this type of question the relative

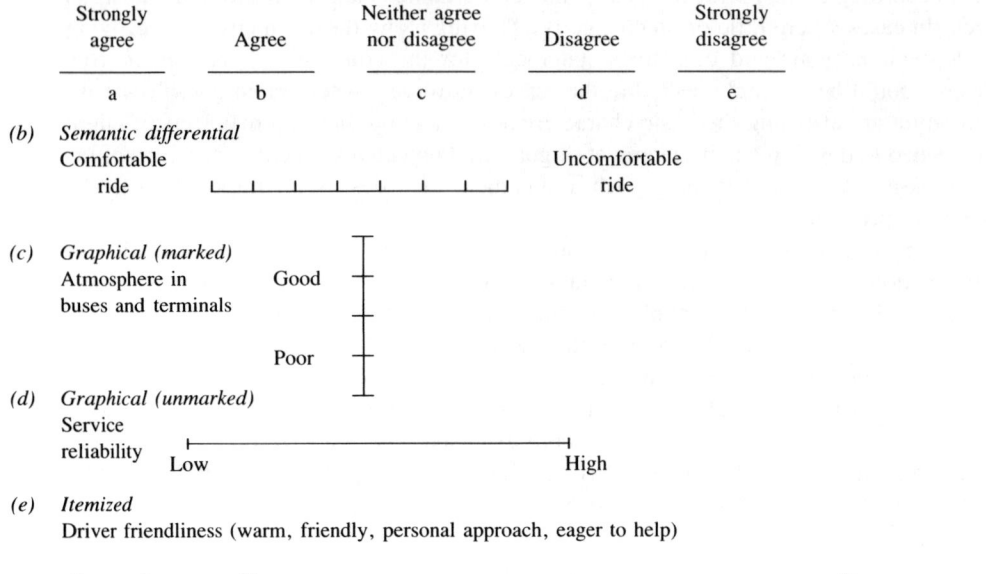

Figure 4-7 Example interview rating scales. (*Urban and Hauser* [*1980*].)

importance of service attributes as identified by the respondents. For example, planners noticing a movement from "extremely poor" to "very poor" on item e in Fig. 4-7 could conclude that driver friendliness is increasing, but one could not conclude that a movement from "extremely poor" to "poor" meant twice the improvement in friendliness as the movement from "extremely poor" to "very poor" [Urban and Hauser, 1980].

Rating scale results can provide useful information to decision makers on how well existing and new services perform with respect to specific attributes, or how specific locations compare to one another based on perception. In Fig. 4-8, for example, the ratings of seven different shopping locations are shown in the continuous lines that connect all 16 service attributes. The importance of the 16 attributes based on importance rating data could be shown in the figure by averaging the total score for each

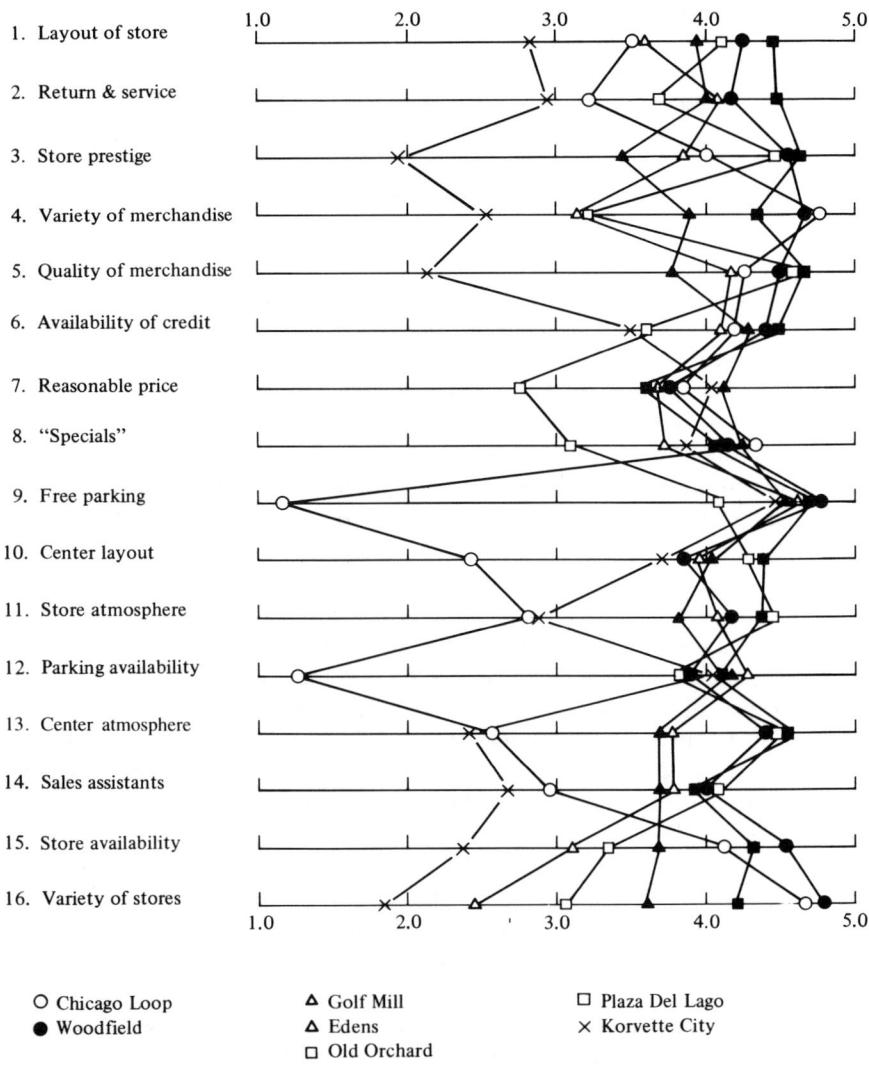

Figure 4-8 Perceptual ratings of service characteristics. (*F. Koppelman and J. Hauser* [*1975*].)

attribute, indicating which service characteristics are considered to be most important from the consumer's perspective. A similar rating scheme could be used to identify the important attributes of transportation services.

The process of turning scale measures into numerical values is called *scaling*. Analytical approaches to scaling attitude measures range from relatively complicated methods, such as factor analysis or linear regession, to the development of a scoring function. For the scoring function method to be used, the respondents must specify not only their perceptions of service attributes, but also the weight or importance attached to each attribute.[1] Such information can be obtained for a sample of individuals and can be used to derive an initial indication of the importance of various attributes and the feasibility of the different alternatives. (In Chap. 9, we will see how the Delphi process can be used to identify weights for evaluation criteria that are the product of group interaction.)

It is important for transportation planners to understand that market research differs from traditional transportation data gathering in that it seeks opinion, attitudes, and preferences from consumers, along with the more customary behavioral and socioeconomic data. The market research approach represents a rather significant departure from the "revealed preferences" approach used by most transportation planners. In this latter approach, travel and consumer behavior is estimated by looking at past behavior and developing models based on the relationship between this behavior and physical and/or socioeconomic characteristics underlying the behavior (more will be said about this in Chap. 7). Perhaps most important, market research provides useful diagnostic information on consumer perceptions. This type of information is important when transportation improvements are designed to achieve objectives other than those related to mobility (e.g., the use of transportation investment to enhance the retail "climate" of downtown areas). Also, the market research approach is the only approach applicable when one desires to predict behavior in response to something new, where existing options do not include the new feature.

In summary, market analysis techniques could become useful tools for transportation planners, especially given the service-oriented transportation actions now being considered in many urban areas. Service-oriented actions, the focus of much of transportation planning, can only be effective when efforts have been made to understand consumer behavior and preferences. Market research can provide transportation planners and managers with (1) a model of how consumers *process information* to form perceptions of transportation alternatives; (2) explicit measures of *consumer perceptions* of each transportation alternative; (3) identification and measures of *consumer feelings* such as biases toward specific modes, personal expectations, and perception of societal norms; (4) measures of the *relative importance* of perceptions and feelings as they influence consumer preferences twoard transportation alternatives; and (5) an understanding and measurement of how situational constraints, such as availability, combine with preference to *influence behavior*, such as choice of transportation mode [Hauser, Tybout, and Koppelman, 1981]. Because the validity of the information obtained from market research methods is dependent upon the effectiveness of the tools used, transportation planners should be extremely careful in the design and use of techniques such as mail and telephone surveys.

---

[1] The scoring function is of the form

$$P_{ij} = w_{i1}y_{ij1} + w_{i2}y_{ij2} + \ldots + w_{in}y_{ijn}$$

where P_{ij} = preference that individual i has for alternative j
w_{ik} = importance that individual i places on service attribute k
y_{ijk} = individual i's perception of alternative j relative to attribute k

4-5 MONITORING TRANSPORTATION PERFORMANCE: IDENTIFICATION OF PROBLEMS AND OPPORTUNITIES FOR IMPROVEMENT

Most of the data and information discussed previously are collected by transportation planners for use in the analysis and evaluation of alternative actions. Some of these data, however, when augmented by the collection of additional data items, can serve as a basis for a monitoring program designed to identify (1) where *problems* occur (or are likely to occur) in the transportation system and (2) where *opportunities* exist for improving the effectiveness and efficiency of current services even though they might not be related to identifiable problems. Because the transportation system affects the activities of individuals, the identification (and definition) of problems cannot realistically rely solely on technical criteria. Clearly, whether a situation or condition is regarded as a problem depends not only on its more objective dimensions, but also on the way it is perceived by people. Many transportation problems thus reach the agenda of public officials because of public perceptions (often catalyzed by local media) that the existing services or infrastructure are inadequate in some way.

Two aspects of the problem or opportunity identification process merit special attention—the use of diagnostic and performance measures for identifying problems and opportunities for system improvement, and public input into problem identification. Each of these aspects is discussed below.

4-5-1 Diagnostic and Performance Measures

One of the most effective methods for identifying problems in system operations involves defining a set of measures that can (1) locate areas of deficiency in a transportation system (diagnostic measures) and (2) provide an indication of the overall performance of the transportation system (performance measures). In most cases, such measures should relate to the goals and objectives established previously for the planning process or service operation.

By making use of diagnostic measures, the planner searches for road segments, intersections, bus routes, or terminals where identifiable problems exist with respect to existing or future facility operations. For example, a transit agency concerned with providing the most cost-efficient service might adopt a measure of net cost per revenue passenger for monitoring the economic performance of individual routes. Those routes which do not meet a certain *performance standard* could be considered "problem" routes and thus candidates for more detailed analysis (see Fig. 4-9).

One problem with this approach is that such standards are often developed in relationship to one objective. This unidimensional problem identification thus does not reflect the many objectives served by transportation. For example, one explanation for a low revenue/cost ratio of some transit routes might be a high percentage of elderly riders who usually pay lower fares. Performance standards should therefore only be used to identify candidate routes that merit further analysis. Another approach to overcoming this problem is to develop a multi-dimensional ranking scheme that identifies problem routes along several different dimensions (see Fig. 4-10).

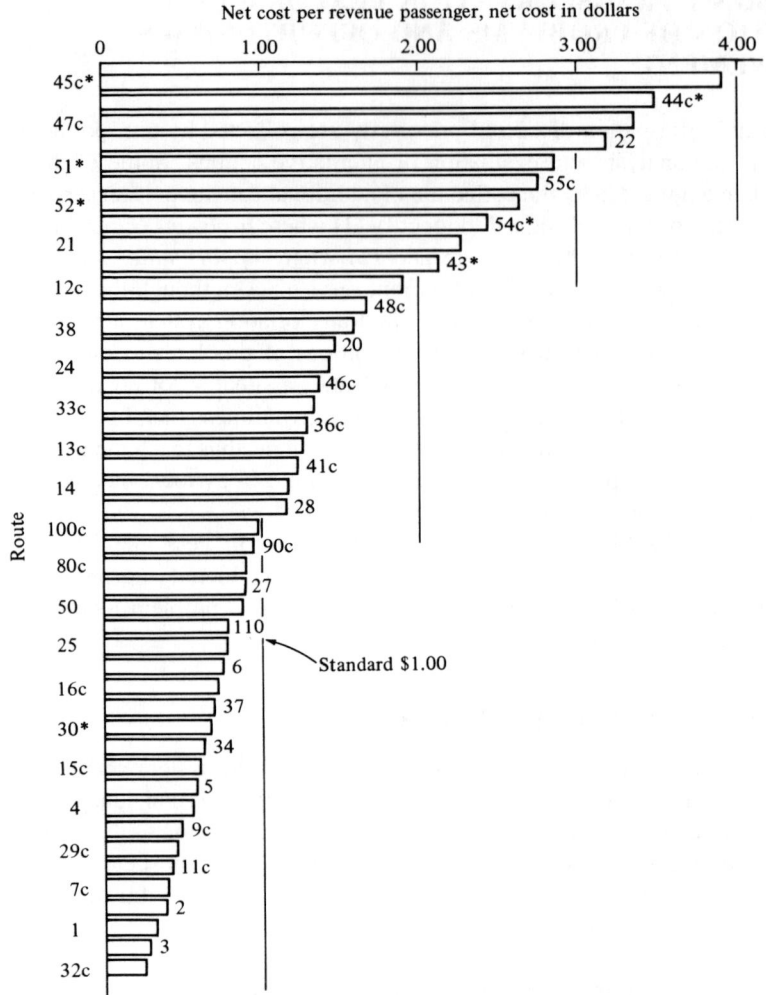

Figure 4-9 Performance measurement of bus routes.

Similarly, highway agencies concerned with traffic congestion or safety might use a series of diagnostic measures to identify problem sites. For example, many agencies use a simple measure of volume-to-capacity to indicate the amount of traffic on specific segments of the highway network relative to the theoretical capacity of these segments. Likewise, the number of accidents at specific intersections or on specific road segments could be used to isolate problem sites. Color-coded network maps can be used to indicate the locations of problem areas (e.g., the average speed of each highway segment, the volume-to-capacity ratio of each segment, high accident locations, or areas of high pollutant emissions).

Route	Daily scheduled trips	Revenue Avg.	Revenue Rank	Total passengers Avg.	Total passengers Rank	Regular Avg.	Regular Rank	Transfer Avg.	Transfer Rank	Student Avg.	Student Rank	Elderly Avg.	Elderly Rank	Handicap Avg.	Handicap Rank	Children Avg.	Children Rank	No. of categories in top 15%	No. of categories in bottom 15%
				Note: the routes that follow are in the top 15% for at least one category without being in the bottom 15% of any category															
1	104	$15.26	2	52.72	1	26.36	1	13.18	1	2.11	2	5.27	2	0.53	3	5.27	1	7	0
2	54	$15.53	1	49.54	2	26.25	2	11.89	2	0.99	6	7.43	1	0.99	1	1.98	3	6	0
3	78	$6.95	6	23.97	4	10.55	7	5.99	3	2.40	1	3.59	7	0.24	10	1.20	5	1	0
4	30	$6.84	7	19.83	7	9.72	9	1.98	8	1.98	3	4.96	3	0.59	2	0.59	8	1	0
13	26	$7.27	5	22.60	6	11.52	6	3.39	6	1.81	4	3.39	8	0.45	5	2.03	2	1	0
				Note: the routes that follow are neither in the top or bottom 15% of any category															
5	68	$8.91	3	24.00	3	15.60	3	3.60	5	0.48	10	3.60	6	0.24	9	0.48	10	0	0
8	66	$7.75	4	23.86	5	12.17	5	4.77	4	1.19	5	4.77	4	0.48	4	0.48	11	0	0
9	24	$6.79	8	16.82	10	12.45	4	1.68	10	0.34	12	1.68	10	0.17	12	0.50	9	0	0
10	24	$5.98	9	16.90	9	9.47	10	1.69	9	0.34	11	4.23	5	0.34	7	0.85	6	0	0
12	42	$5.93	10	17.17	8	10.30	8	2.58	7	0.86	7	1.72	9	0.34	6	1.37	4	0	0
				Note: the routes that follow are in the bottom 15% for at least one category without being in the top 15% of any category															
6	46	$4.76	11	12.18	11	8.28	11	1.22	12	0.85	8	1.22	11	0.24	8	0.37	13	0	1
7	26	$3.87	12	9.48	12	7.40	12	1.04	13	0.19	13	0.38	14	0.09	13	0.38	12	0	4
11	26	$3.22	14	8.74	14	6.03	14	1.31	11	0.17	14	0.44	13	0.17	11	0.61	7	0	5

Figure 4-10 Multiple objective transit performance analysis, Bridgeport, Connecticut. (*Wilson and Gonzalez* [1982].)

Regardless of which diagnostic measures are chosen for problem identification, several factors should be kept in mind:

1. The required data must be collected periodically to allow updating of the problem identification process.
2. Many measures are related to one another, meaning surrogates can be used to identify closely related problems.
3. Standards used to identify the level of system or facility performance above (or below) which the performance is considered problematic must be carefully defined to relate to the problems being faced by the organization or community.
4. Diagnostic measures should be related to planning and agency objectives.
5. Diagnostic measures only identify where problem areas exist; they do not indicate what types of corrective actions might be required.

The diagnostic measures discussed above can be used in service- or site-specific planning. Transportation officials, however, are most often concerned with the overall performance of the transportation system, and specifically with the degree of attainment of goals and objectives. In such instances, data on system performance and trends in travel behavior can be collected as part of a regional monitoring program [Meyer, 1980]. The foundation of such a program would be a set of performance measures that relate characteristics of system operation to specified planning goals and objectives. As in the evaluation criteria (or measures of effectiveness) used in the analysis and evaluation of selected transportation actions, performance measures can range from those directed toward measuring volume of travel by mode in a region to those which estimate regional energy consumption and air pollution emissions.

The usefulness of performance measures depends on several characteristics of the measures themselves, including [Cambridge Systematics, 1980]:

1. *Measurability* requires that the data be available and that the tools exist to perform any required calculations.
2. *Pertinence* relates to the degree to which performance measures reflect the policies or objectives for which they were developed.
3. *Clarity* implies that the measure should be easily understood by planners and decision makers.
4. *Sensitivity and responsiveness* indicate the level of change that can occur in the transportation or activity systems and still be detected by the performance measure.
5. *Appropriate level of detail* addresses the issue of whether the measure is specified at a level of detail applicable to its intended use.
6. *Insensitivity to exogeneous factors* requires that the performance measure not be influenced by nontransportation events that could distort a true indication of performance.
7. *Comprehensiveness* means the degree to which the performance measure can indeed measure across all the market segments and locations for which it is intended to be used.

8. *Discrimination between influences* assesses the degree to which one can differentiate among individual components affecting the performance of a system.

In some cases, performance measures cannot totally satisfy these characteristics. For example, it is often difficult to separate the effect of changes in the transportation system from the general impacts of the state of the economy. However, the above characteristics do provide a useful checklist for the development of an effective set of performance measures. An illustrative list of performance measures is shown in Table 4-11.

Although not as thoroughly researched as methods for problem identification, the process of identifying *opportunities* for system improvement is likely to receive increased attention in future years as budget constraints make increasing the efficiency of existing public services an attractive alternative to large capital expenditures on new services. Increasing the efficiency of such services will require implementation of innovative service characteristics, restructuring management control systems, or using different funding arrangements. The impetus for taking such actions is not an objective or perceived need to overcome some serious deficiency in the system, but rather a perception that, by taking such actions, some improvements can be made in the system operation. In some sense, identifying opportunities for improvement reflects the adoption of a proactive perspective on planning, rather than a reliance on the reactive process of responding to problems.

A recently developed approach to transit service planning is a good example of a planning process that systematically examines the opportunities for improving service characteristics [Wilson and Gonzalez, 1982]. In this process, general actions which can be applied to any part of the transit network during any time period are identified. These generic actions, along with the conditions of bus routes that might suggest their applicability, are shown in Table 4-12. The task of the planner is to identify the operating conditions of transit routes and pinpoint those routes where there is potential for implementing a generic action.

There are two principal advantages of this process over the problem-centered approach. First, a wider set of actions than those directed toward resolving specific problems can be considered by transit planners. Second, some routes which are not classified as problems will still be the subject of planners' attention. Any improve-

Table 4-11 Examples of performance measures

Percent of population with access to transit
Passenger and vehicle miles traveled
Annualized investment of public dollars for designated existing transportation investment per capita
Contribution to ambient air quality
Contribution to energy conservation
Transit subsidy per capita
Number of accidents
Population within a specified travel time of designated economic areas

Table 4-12 Generic actions and appropriate route conditions

Generic action	Route conditions
A. Holding strategy	Schedule adherence problem Long route Point on route with low through ridership
B. Increase running layover time	Schedule adherence problem Low loads
C. Increase frequency	Unacceptable crowding Moderate rather than high ridership Even load profile
D. Decrease frequency	Low productivity and loads Time between arrivals below policy levels
E. Split route	Low productivity Uneven load profile Long route
F. Short turns	Tapering load profile Long route High ridership
G. Express or zonal service	High ridership Tapering load profile Long route Large time differentials local and express zone
H. Partial returning of bus empty	Large imbalance in flows Large time differential in service and empty running time High frequencies
I. Eliminate route segment	Low ridership generation on segment Vehicle savings possible from elimination Higher frequency possible from elimination
J. Eliminate trips	Low ridership on trips High cost savings from elimination

Source: Wilson and Gonzalez [1982].

ments made to these routes will potentially increase system efficiency and effectiveness.

In sum, the process of identifying problems and opportunities in system operation depends on the careful selection of measures that can be used by planners to identify areas of deficiency and opportunity. Although such measures are useful for planning purposes, planners should not place so much weight on these measures that they ignore more general community goals in their pursuit of objective measures of success.

4-5-2 Public Input into the Problem Identification Process

Because many of the "problems" with the transportation system occur at the local level and are sometimes more closely related to public perceptions than to actual fact, opportunities should be provided for public participation in the problem identification process. Many of the techniques discussed in Sec. 4-4-1 for obtaining public input into the identification of goals and objectives can be used in the problem identification process, and hence will not be repeated here. The following example illustrates how one urban area undertook an extensive public involvement program to identify major problems in the region. Although conducted at the metropolitan scale, similar types of programs could be used at the corridor, subarea, or neighborhood level.

In 1973, the Lake-Porter County Regional Transportation and Planning Commission initiated a regional public involvement program to identify the most important problems in the region, which is located immediately southeast of Chicago and consists of the two most northwestern counties of Indiana. The commission wanted to incorporate the views of public officials, representatives of civic organizations and the business community, professionals with talents related to planning, and the general public into the formal planning process. Ten public meetings were held throughout the region, at which participants initially voiced their perceptions of the most critical problems and

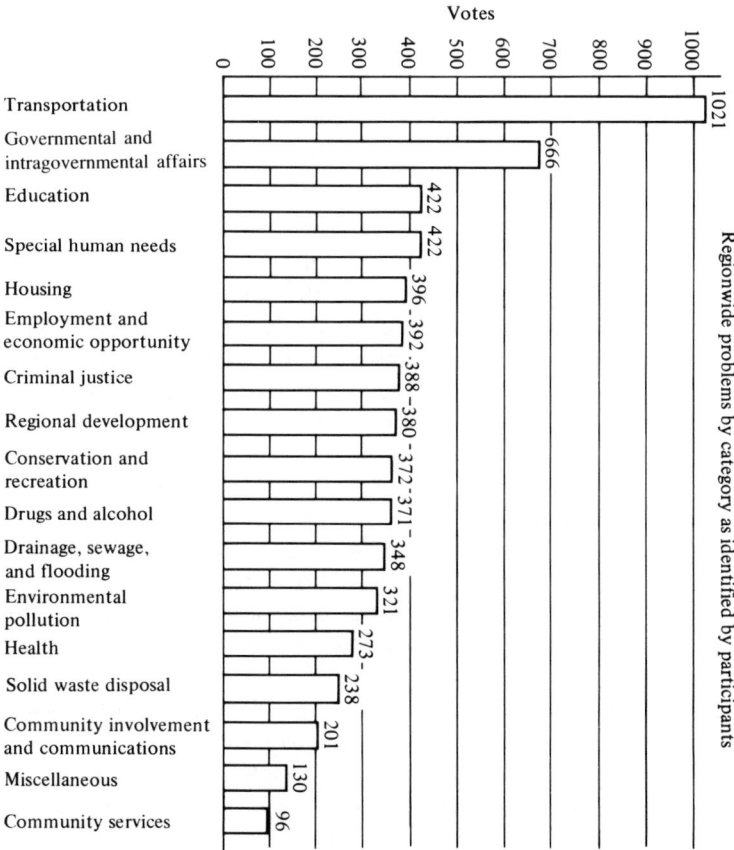

Figure 4-11 Example of public problem identification. (*Lake-Porter County Regional Transportation and Planning Commission, 1973.*)

then discussed the characteristics of each problem. At the end of each meeting, a vote was taken to determine a priority ranking of the identified problems. At the conclusion of the public meeting program, commission planners conducted a community attitudes survey based on a sample of 2000 households to check the validity of the public meeting results.

Specific problem statements (e.g., the need for free transportation for the elderly, the lack of intercommunity mass transit, and poor maintenance of roads) were combined by commission planners into problem categories and compared with respect to their importance, as determined by votes at the public meetings (see Fig. 4-11). The more specific information was used by local planners to improve transportation services, while the more general information on problem priorities was used by the commission in allocating its own resources and as a major input into the identification of regional goals and objectives [Lake-Porter County Regional Transportation and Planning Commission, 1973].

Although every urban area need not undertake as extensive a problem identification process as the one described above, opportunities for public involvement should be provided. Such opportunities will not only improve a planning agency's ability to assess and respond to community needs, they will also provide a mechanism for increasing cooperation and understanding among citizens, local officials, and planners.

4-6 CHAPTER SUMMARY

1. The relatively simple origin-destination surveys and traffic volume counts used for years by highway planners were supplemented in the 1960s by more extensive data collection efforts, notably home interview surveys and transportation–land use inventories. As a result, the data base in most urban areas today includes many different data items collected by numerous agencies and serving diverse purposes. This data base is useful in the application of travel behavior models and in monitoring the performance of the transportation system so that problems can be identified and the degree of attainment of objectives can be assessed.
2. The collection and processing of data in urban areas are often done on the basis of spatial units of analysis. Traffic zones are delineated according to one or more criteria, and can in turn be aggregated into corridors of travel or sectors of the urban area. Also of importance is the functional classification scheme used for urban streets and highways which groups roadways according to their purpose in handling urban traffic.
3. The use of *sampling methods* in data collection enables planners to select a small percentage of the entire population or available data base for closer examination. Procedures designed to help the planner select a sample representative of the characteristics of the targeted population include *simple random* sampling, *sequential* sampling, *stratified random* sampling, and *cluster* sampling. No matter which technique is employed, the cost of survey sampling must be weighed against the degree of accuracy required in the data collected.

Closely related is the concept of *sample size* which also influences the accuracy of the survey. Choosing an appropriate sample size involves making assumptions about how the elements to be surveyed are actually distributed, as well as determining the desired limits of error for the sample. Based on the specifics of a given situation, one of the equations described in this chapter can then be used to calculate the necessary sample size.

4. Of the many data collection techniques in use, *household travel behavior surveys* are the most detailed and most costly. Personal in-home interviews, telephone interviews, and mail-back questionnaires can all be used to collect data on the demographic characteristics and trip-making behavior of individual households. Each instrument has both advantages and disadvantages with respect to cost, complexity, survey bias, and response rate; thus planners should use a strategy which maximizes the usefulness of the data collected.

    Origin-destination surveys are used to identify the movement of persons and vehicles in an urban area, helping planners to estimate travel demand on existing and planned transportation facilities. Apart from home interview surveys, roadside interviews, postcard surveys, and license-plate surveys can also be used to collect O-D data.

5. The physical characteristics of land use and transportation systems can be catalogued by undertaking *inventories* of highway or transit system capability and the patterns of land use. Because such inventories have in many cases become outdated, the attention of transportation planners is shifting to updating and maintaining the data base in the inventories.

    Highway and transit counts can supplement the data collected in regional inventories and can be done through either manual or automatic methods. *Cordon counts* estimate the total number of vehicle movements within a specific geographical area, while *screenline counts* validate the accuracy of the cordon counts by accounting for every vehicle crossing a specified boundary over a given time period. Traffic counts may also be used for more specific purposes, such as determining the level of congestion at a particular intersection or the number of passengers making use of a particular transit route.

6. The importance of a good data base for effective urban transportation planning indicates the need for the development of a data collection and management plan which details the data to be collected and the collection methods, as well as agency responsibilities for data collection. Such a plan should schedule data collection activities over a 5- to 10-year period, identify any unmet data needs and establish priorities among them, determine the level of resources to be devoted to each of the needs, and estimate the annual costs to be incurred.

7. Because the planner's role is to work *with* interested officials and representatives of the public, information is required concerning the desires and attitudes of the community in general. Although much of this information can be obtained through formal and informal public meetings, the establishment of *goals and objectives* for transportation planning can help to "guide" planners in analyzing and evaluating proposals. Clear statements of the goals and objectives for transportation planning are especially important in situations where community attitudes toward transpor-

tation tend to change rapidly, thereby invalidating many of the assumptions inherent in the planning approach taken. In any situation, the effort of defining such statements can ensure that the type of community envisioned by the public coincides with the objectives pursued by transportation planners.
8. The attitudes and preferences of consumers can be measured through the use of *market analysis* techniques which identify distinct *market segments* and the transportation service attributes that reflect the preferences of each segment. Questionnaires containing attitudinal questions are a common method of gathering market research data. These questions can involve the use of a *psychological scale* which requires the respondent to specify the strength of a particular attitude or perception.

    Scaling is the process of transforming these scale measures into numerical values. It can involve complex statistical techniques, such as factor analysis or linear regression, or more simple approaches, such as the development of a weighted scoring function to relate responses to different service attributes. These methods can derive an indication of the relative importance of different attributes from the responses of a sample of individuals. Market analysis techniques are therefore important in understanding consumer preferences and behavior, particularly with the focus of transportation planning shifting to service-oriented transportation actions.
9. The data collected by transportation planners can also be used as a basis for a monitoring program that identifies *problems* in the transportation system and *opportunities* for making improvements. *Diagnostic and performance measures* can be used to locate areas of deficiency and to provide an indication of the overall performance of the transportation system. Diagnostic measures help the planner identify the specific services or facilities that do not meet some minimum *performance standard*.

    In situations where transportation officials are more concerned about the overall performance of the transportation system and the degree of attainment of goals and objectives, performance measures that relate system characteristics to specified planning goals can be developed. For such measures to be useful to planners, they should possess several characteristics, including measurability, clarity, sensitivity and responsiveness, and comprehensiveness.

    The identification of opportunities for system improvement is likely to grow in importance as planners strive to increase the efficiency of existing services in the face of budgetary constraints. The development of a framework that matches observed conditions in the transportation system with possible improvement strategies is one approach to making opportunity identification more systematic.
10. Because transportation "problems" are closely related to public perceptions of transportation system performance, public involvement should be an integral part of the problem identification process. A program of public participation can incorporate the views of diverse interests into the formal planning process. Public meetings and surveys of community attitudes can give planners an indication of problem priorities, to be used for allocating planning resources and as input into the definition of community goals and objectives. Public involvement, then, is an

important source of information that can be used to complement the data collected by planners.

QUESTIONS

1. For an urban transportation plan with which you are familiar, identify the major data items likely used in developing the plan. What data collection techniques were likely used in obtaining this information?
2. Summarize how the types of data collected in urban transportation planning changed with the transition in such planning discussed in Chap. 3. What general social and political trends have directly affected the type of data collected?
3. Obtain a copy of the latest census information for your urban area. What data found in the census results are directly useful for urban transportation planning? How does the scale of analysis affect the usefulness of this census information?
4. Given three origins and destinations a, b, and c, and the estimated frequency of trips shown in the table below, determine the required sample size with a precision for all matrix cells of ± 10 percent and a 95 percent confidence interval. Use both Table 4-2 and Eq. (4-3) to make these estimates.

	From		
To	a	b	c
a		0.05	0.20
b	0.15		0.10
c	0.15	0.05	

5. When using the equation for determining sample size, the standard deviation term is often replaced with a composite standard deviation term which incorporates other variability factors into the equation. Thus, for example, the composite standard deviation for a determination of average passenger vehicle occupancy could include (see Ferlis [1980])

$$SO = (SOL^2 + SOS^2 + SOW^2)^{1/2}$$

where SO = composite standard deviation
SOL = standard deviation of average occupancy across link days (specific measurement location) within a season
SOS = standard deviation of average occupancy across seasons
SOW = standard deviation of average occupancy across time periods during a day as a result of short counts

Assume an agency wants to estimate the annual average vehicle occupancy for a region with ± 0.01 with a 95 percent level of confidence. Assuming the planners have determined the values of SOL to be 0.05, SOS to be 0.015, and SOW to be 0.017, how many sample link days are necessary to meet the required precision?

What happens to the sample size when the tolerance is reduced to ± 0.02? ± 0.03? ± 0.04? and ± 0.05?

6. For the types of trips shown in Fig. P4-6, identify the techniques that could be used to collect relevant trip data. For those trips internal to, or entering or leaving, the "tight cordon," identify the techniques that could be used to collect data on transit trips.

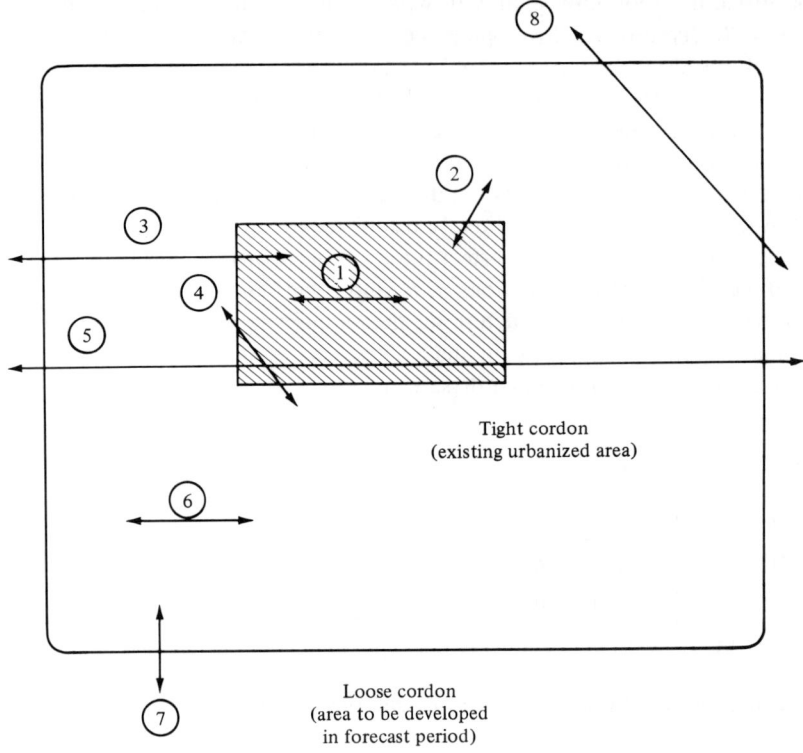

Figure P4-6

7. Assume that a new shared-ride taxicab service is to be implemented in your urban area. You have been asked by the city planning director to outline a detailed data collection effort to identify what impact such service will have on urban travel, especially with respect to trips by elderly persons. Further, your budget for data collection has been limited to $20,000. Describe a before and after data collection plan that meets both the needs of the study and the specified resource constraints. How would your plan change if the budget was doubled?

8. Develop a goals and objectives statement for a particular transportation planning process in your urban area. What measures of effectiveness can be used to measure attainment of the goals and objectives you identified?

9. Detail the techniques or approaches that can be used to identify community goals and objectives. What level of effort do you think is necessary to obtain this type of information?

10. Develop a questionnaire that can be applied for a specific transportation issue in your community. What types of information do you want to collect? Why? How many questionnaires do you want to send out?
11. Identify diagnostic measures that can be used in your community to pinpoint transportation problem spots. What effort would be needed to collect the required data to use these measures? How important do you think such information is in the everyday activities of transportation agencies?

REFERENCES

Abrams, C., and J. DiRenzo: *Measures of Effectiveness for Multimodal Urban Traffic Management*, vol. 2, U.S. Department of Transportation Report FHWA-RD-79-113, December, 1979.

American Association of State Highway and Transportation officials, *A Policy on Geometric Design of Highways and Streets*, Washington D.C., 1984.

Arnstein, S. R.: "A Ladder of Citizen Participation," *Journal of the American Institute of Planners*, July 1969.

Attanucci, J., I. Burns, and N. H. M. Wilson: *Bus Transit Monitoring Manual*, vol. 1, U.S. Department of Transportation Report UMTA-IT-09-9008-81-1, August 1981.

Baass, K. G.: "Design of Zonal Systems for Aggregate Transportation Models," *Transportation Research Record 807*, Transportation Research Board, 1981.

Billheimer, J. W., and R. R. Trexler: *Evaluation Handbook for Transportation Impact Assessment*, U.S. Department of Transportation Report No. UMTA-IT-06-0203-81-1, December 1980.

Cambridge Systematics Inc.: *Performance Measures and Travel Behavior Inventory Study, Final Report, Phase 1—Development of Performance Measurements*, Prepared for Metropolitan Council, St. Paul, Minn., Dec. 31, 1980.

Cochran, W. G.: *Sampling Techniques*, 3d edition, John Wiley, New York, 1977.

Crabtree, L., and G. Krause: "Vehicle Origin Survey," *Transportation Research Record 886*, Transportation Research Board, Washington, D.C., 1982.

Creighton Hamburg, Inc.: "Data Requirements for Metropolitan Transportation Planning," *National Cooperative Highway Research Program Report 120*, Highway Research Board, Washington, D.C., 1971.

Dilman, D. A.: *Mail and Telephone Surveys—The Total Design Method*, John Wiley, New York, 1978.

Federal Highway Administration: *Guide for Traffic Volume Counting Manual*, Transmittal 96, March 1970.

Federal Highway Administration: *Highway Functional Classification*, Transmittal 155, volume 20, Appendix 12, U.S. Department of Transportation, December 1978.

Ferlis, R.: *Guide for Estimating Urban Vehicle Classification and Occupancy*, U.S. Department of Transportation Report DOT-FH-11-9249, Washington, D.C., March 1980.

Ferlis, R., L. Bowman, and B. Cima: *Guide to Urban Traffic Volume Counting*, U.S. Department of Transportation Report FWHA-PL-81-091, September 1981.

Hauser, J. R., A. M. Tybout, and F. S. Koppelman: "Consumer-Oriented Transportation Service Planning: Consumer Analysis and Strategies," *Applications of Management Science*, vol. 1, 1981, pp. 91–138.

Highway Research Board: *Proceedings of the Twenty-Fourth Annual Meeting of the Highway Research Board*, Washington, D.C., 1944.

JHK & Associates and Peat, Marwick, Mitchell & Co.: *Basic TSM Goals and Objectives—Working Paper No. 3*, Prepared for Federal Highway Administration, June 1977.

Jordan, D., et al.: *Effective Citizen Participation in Transportation Planning*, vols. 1 and 2, U.S. Department of Transportation Report No. FHWA/SES-76-10, 1976.

Koppelman, F., and J. Hauser: "Destination Choice Behavior for Non-grocery Shopping Trips," *Transportation Research Record 673*, Transportation Research Board, 1975.

Lake-Porter County Regional Transportation and Planning Commission: *Problem Identification—A Phase in the Development of the Regional Plan*, Hammond, Ind., June 1973.

Meyer, M. D.:"Monitoring System Performance: A Foundation for TSM Planning," *Special Report 190,* Transportation Research Board, Washington, D.C., 1980.

Parvatanani, R., P. Stopher, and C. Brown: "Origin-Destination Travel Survey for Southeast Michigan," *Transportation Research Record 886,* Transportation Research Board, Washington, D.C., 1982.

Pedersen, N., and D. Samdahl: "Highway Traffic Data for Urbanized Area Project Planning and Design," *National Cooperative Highway Research Program Report 255,* Transportation Research Board, Washington, D.C., December 1982.

Sharma, C., and A. Werner: "Improved Method of Grouping Province-Wide Permanent Traffic Counters," *Transportation Research Record 815,* Transportation Research Board, 1981.

Sheskin, I., and P. Stopher: "Pilot Testing of Alternative Administration Procedures and Survey Instruments," *Transportation Research Record 886,* Transportation Research Board, Washington, D.C., 1982.

Smith, Wilbur, and Associates: *Guide to Urban Traffic Volume Counting,* Report to the Federal Highway Administration, October 1975.

Soberman, R. M., and H. A. Hazard (eds.): *Canadian Transit Handbook,* University of Toronto–York University Joint Program in Transportation, Toronto, January 1980.

Sosslau, A. B.: *Transportation Planners Guide to Using the 1980 Census,* U.S. Department of Transportation Report DTFH61-80-C-00070, January 1983.

Thomas, E. N., and J. L. Schofer: "Strategies for the Evaluation of Alternative Transportation Plans," *National Cooperative Highway Research Program Report 96,* Highway Research Board, 1970.

Transportation Research Board: *Proposed Urban Transportation Data Reporting Requirements for States and Metropolitan Planning Organizations,* National Academy of Sciences, Washington D.C., 1976.

U.S. Department of Transportation: *Urban Origin-Destination Surveys,* Transmittal 143, vol. 20, Appendix 34, Federal Highway Administration, 1973.

Urban, G. L., and J. R. Hauser: *Design and Marketing of New Products,* Prentice-Hall, Englewood Cliffs, N.J., 1980.

Wachs, M., and J. L. Schofer: "Abstract Values and Concrete Highways," *Traffic Quarterly,* January 1969.

Weiss, M.: *A Study of Public Participation in Highway Planning and Decision-Making,* Texas Transportation Institute Research Report 148-5, August 1974.

Wilson, N. H. M., and S. Gonzalez: *Methods for Service Design,* Paper prepared for a Workshop on Short-Range Transit Operations, Planning, and Management, Atlanta, Ga., Mar. 7–10, 1982.

Woodruff, R. B., et al.: "Market Opportunity Analysis for Short-Range Public Transportation Planning," *National Cooperative Highway Research Program 212,* Transportation Research Board, September 1981.

Young, R. C.: "Goals and Goal-Setting," *Journal of the American Institute of Planners,* vol. 32, no. 2, March 1966.

CHAPTER
FIVE

AN INTRODUCTION TO ANALYSIS AND EVALUATION

5-0 INTRODUCTION

The second major step in the planning process illustrated in Fig. 1-1 is the analysis and evaluation of the alternative projects or programs under consideration. An important distinction needs to be made between *analysis* and *evaluation*. Analysis is a means for achieving an understanding of how the transportation system and its components work, and hence of how changes to that system will alter its performance. Evaluation involves a synthesis of all the benefits, costs, and impacts generated by the analysis phase of the planning process so that judgments can be made concerning the relative merits of alternative actions. Thus, the needs of the evaluation phase have a direct impact on the information that must be produced by the analysis process.

The following three chapters discuss the techniques and overall approaches used to analyze the impacts of alternative projects and programs. These chapters reflect the three areas of analysis most often found in transportation planning. The first area of analysis, determining the socioeconomic and land use characteristics of an urban area, is discussed in Chap. 6. As mentioned in Sec. 2-2, the land use–transportation relationship is a fundamental paradigm on which much of transportation planning is based. Most of the analysis of the demand for transportation is based on assumptions concerning the trip-generating characteristics of land use and households in a study area. Chapter 6 is thus an important starting point for a discussion of analysis in transportation planning.

An understanding of the demand for the use of current and proposed transportation services and facilities is fundamental to transportation planning. Indeed, one of the most common definitions of a transportation "problem" involves situations in which the demand exceeds or comes close to the capability of the service or facility to provide acceptable levels of service. Chapter 7 presents a detailed discussion of demand analysis, both the techniques in use today and the overall role for such analysis in transportation planning.

The provision of opportunities for travel, and the overall performance of these services or facilities, is considered the "supply" side of transportation. The characteristics of transportation supply are important not only because they influence demand (e.g., a congested facility will be avoided if alternative routes are available), but also because they relate to the cost of providing the facility or service. Chapter 8 discusses the techniques used to examine the supply-side characteristics of transportation as well as how such analysis is used in transportation planning.

The results of the analysis process presented in the following chapters are then incorporated into evaluation, the process of assessing the advantages and disadvantages of each alternative. Chapter 9 presents a conceptual framework of evaluation and discusses how evaluation techniques such as benefit and cost methods fit into this framework. Because the information produced during the evaluation process is critically important to decision makers, Chap. 9 also examines methods of presenting such information to decision makers in a readily understandable form.

This chapter serves as an introduction to the four chapters that follow. A basic premise of this chapter is that the technical analysis and evaluation process involves the interaction of theory, data, and technique. *Theory* consists of our knowledge of, and assumptions about, the system being analyzed. *Data* provide the empirical, objective information against which we test and modify our theories. *Techniques* provide the tools with which we analyze our data and operationalize our theories. An important point to consider is that the validity of the techniques used (and, hence, the results of the analysis) depends on the quality of the data and the underlying theories describing the system.

Another basic premise of this chapter is that analysis and evaluation, just like the much broader transportation planning process, must be related to the decision-making process. Analysis and evaluation should be sensitive to the needs of decision makers and to information on the distributional consequences of alternative options. This sensitivity is important not only to make the results of analysis and evaluation relevant to decision makers, but also to make it credible in the eyes of all involved parties.

This chapter is divided into two major sections. Section 5-1 discusses the characteristics of effective analysis and evaluation, with special attention given to the overall analysis and evaluation *process* rather than to the techniques used within the process. Section 5-2 then presents an overview of the microeconomic concepts which provide the theoretical basis for much of the technical analysis and evaluation. The basic approach used in analysis is to characterize the system under study along physical and behavioral dimensions and then to use these characterizations to better understand the consequences of changes to the system. For many years, the underlying concept in transportation analysis has been to characterize the transportation system as a transportation market and then to assess the direct and indirect impacts of market transactions.

Economic concepts of the demand for transportation service and the supply of such service thus play an important role in analysis.

5-1 ANALYSIS AND EVALUATION IN THE PLANNING PROCESS

5-1-1 Analysis

There are three major characteristics of analysis which have significant impact on the effectiveness of planning and which, therefore, deserve special attention. The first characteristic relates to the linkage between analysis and decision making. Although previous chapters have outlined the importance of goals and objectives in establishing this linkage, no predetermined set of goals and objectives is likely to exist to define and bound each problem for the analyst. Analysis, however, cannot exist in such a vacuum. The result is that, explicitly or implicitly, analysts adopt a set of goals and objectives—usually their own and/or their organization's—upon which to base their work. Without a linkage between analysis and decision making, the analyst is less able to integrate all relevant aspects of the problem into the analysis, especially qualitative (typically political) concerns. As a result, analysis can easily become largely irrelevant to the decision-making process if it fails to address the "real" issues as they are perceived by the decision maker. Thus, to be useful, the analysis must, among other things, be:

1. Responsive to policy variables and contexts
2. Responsive to the timetable established for decision making (e.g., an analysis that becomes available 6 months after a decision has been made can contribute very little to that decision)
3. Sensitive to the scale of impacts involved (a large-scale "macro" model is hardly required to analyze a minor bus route extension; whereas a "back-of-the-envelope" hand calculation is unlikely to answer adequately the questions associated with the proposal to build a major new urban freeway)
4. Perceived as being cost-effective
5. Credible to the decision maker

Credibility, in addition to requiring all of the other points listed above, involves making the analysis process understandable to the decision maker, ensuring that the analysis is based on a set of mutually acceptable assumptions, and arriving at "believable" results. This is not to say that the planner should "give the decision maker the numbers desired." Rather, analysis should ideally provide an opportunity for the planner and the decision maker to learn from each other so that both can arrive at a better understanding of the transportation system and its interactions. Unfortunately, the decision maker is often all too willing to treat analysis as a "black box" whose results are either to be uncritically accepted or unconditionally rejected; while at the same time the planner-as-analyst is often unwilling or unable to explain the process to the decision maker, to open the black box and establish a dialogue between himself and the decision maker that could lead to improved analysis and, hopefully, to better decisions.

A second characteristic of analysis, and one which is often overlooked in discussions of the planning process, is that analysis often includes the initial task of identifying a set of feasible alternatives, which then becomes the focus of subsequent analysis. Most descriptions of the transportation planning process assume that either the alternatives are a "given," and that the planner need only conduct an analysis and evaluation, or that the planner has complete freedom to identify alternatives for analysis. In some cases, the alternatives under consideration might have indeed come from previous studies or been identified by public officials. In other cases, however, planners need to develop and to analyze a wide range of alternatives that have not been previously identified.

A 1979 Department of Transportation study of alternatives generation for major transit investments was one of the few efforts to examine the process of identifying alternatives [Herald, 1980]. The author of the study initially hypothesized that several factors would influence the identification of alternatives, ranging from goals and objectives to "carryover" alternatives from previous studies. Thirteen alternatives analysis studies were examined to identify the major inputs into the identification of alternatives (see Table 5-1). The study found that, at least in the instances examined, the relationship between goals and objectives and the development of alternatives was weak, that alternatives selection was significantly influenced by prior analysis results, and that the most common technique for generating alternatives was a loosely structured trial-and-error method.

There are two aspects of alternatives identification that can have a significant impact on transportation planning. First, no matter where the alternatives originate, transportation planners should explore a wide range of alternatives, giving special attention to developing alternatives which highlight the trade-offs among objectives. This diversity in alternatives can be achieved by considering different project scales, system designs, operating characteristics, vehicle technologies, and relationships to existing system operations. In the case of corridor or large-scale regional transportation studies, it is especially important for planners to consider minor alternatives along with any major alternatives. Minor alternatives include operational changes or a modest investment in changing the physical design of a facility (see Table 5-2). Major actions involve high levels of investment and produce significant impacts on the socioeconomic system.

The need to examine a wide range of alternatives must be considered within the analysis capability and resource limitations of the planning organization. For example, the use of a large-scale computer simulation model to analyze a large number of network designs is generally prohibitively expensive and time-consuming. In most planning applications, a more appropriate analysis approach involves the use of *sketch planning* techniques—explicitly designed to analyze a large set of alternatives in a quick and broad-based manner—to examine the full set of alternatives under consideration with the objective of identifying a small set of the most promising alternatives, which can then be analyzed in greater detail. The recent development of micro-

Table 5-1 Use of potential inputs to the identification of alternatives in past studies

Study	National goals and objectives	Local goals and objectives	Assessment of needs	Forecasts of future conditions	Local opportunities constraints	External requirements constraints	Carryover alternatives	Catalog of technologies	Operational feasibility	Public involvement
				Potential inputs to alternatives identification process						
Buffalo	●	●	—	—	○	○	●	○	—	●
Denver 1975	●	●	●	—	●	○	—	●	●	○
Denver 1976	●	●	—	—	●	○	●	●	—	●
Honolulu 1975	○	○	●	●	●	○	●	●	—	○
Honolulu 1976	●	●	●	●	●	—	●	●	●	○
Los Angeles	○	○	○	○	●	○	●	○	—	○
Miami	●	○	○	—	●	○	—	●	—	●
Pittsburgh	—	●	—	—	○	—	●	●	●	○
San Juan (Draft)	●	●	●	●	●	○	●	●	—	—
Washington F	●	○	—	—	●	○	●	●	—	○
Washington J-H	●	○	—	—	○	○	●	—	—	●
Washington K	●	○	—	—	○	○	●	—	—	●
West Shore (Draft)	○	—	—	—	●	○	●	●	●	●

● Documented presence
○ Implied presence
— No apparent involvement

Source: Herald [1980].

Table 5-2 Components for minor alternatives

Policy	General description	Examples
	Policies to increase supply	
Operational modifications	Highway capacity management	Preferential lanes, traffic controls, channelization, ramp metering
	Transit operations improvements	Route and schedule changes, modal integration
Construction	Small-scale projects	Upgrade of existing facilities (e.g., selective land additions and intersection upgrade)
	Policies to modify demand	
Peak-period travel reduction	Change in activity scheduling	Staggered work hours, shorter work week
Reduction in trip making	Land use development policies	Coordinated residential development policy and industrial and commercial location policy
Pricing	Incentives and disincentives	Parking pricing, road pricing, transit pricing
Vehicle controls	Restrictions and incentives	Ride sharing, auto restricted zones

Source: Lane et al. [1979].

computer hardware and software applications in transportation planning has greatly expanded the capability of planners to undertake sketch planning.

A second important aspect of alternatives identification is the definition of a no-action or do-nothing alternative. Comparison of a proposed transportation action to the no-action alternative should result in one of three determinations [Lane et al., 1979]:

1. That the consequences of the proposed action are clearly preferable to the consequences of no action, and therefore the action should be taken
2. That the consequences of the proposed action are clearly worse than the consequences of no action, and therefore the action should not be taken
3. That the consequences of the proposed action are not substantially better or worse than the consequences of no action, and therefore the action should be reevaluated or redesigned

If more than one transportation action is being considered (as is usually the case), then those actions which have consequences preferable to no action are retained for further evaluation, while those which are inferior to no action are eliminated from further consideration. The no-action alternative, defined as the maintenance of existing facilities and services and the continuation of existing transportation policies, thus serves as a benchmark against which decision makers can assess the value of available options.

The third characteristic of analysis to be discussed in this chapter is that planners often use *models* of the transportation system and its relationship to socioeconomic activities to analyze the consequences of changes to the system. A model is an abstraction and a simplification of a "real world" system. As such, it can be used to "experiment" with the system, to make conditional forecasts about what might occur within the system if certain changes to that system are introduced.

In general, there are three basic assumptions made in models of the transportation system that have significant impact on the validity of the model. These are:

1. The key characteristics of the system may be specified or described in terms of a set of observable variables.
2. There is an assumed explicit functional relationship between these observed variables and the observed behavior of the individuals. In other words, it is assumed that direct "cause and effect" relationships exist and that they may be at least approximately represented within the theory or model. It is this assumption that often prompts modelers to speak of "behavioral" models in that they believe that the model truly "explains" behavior, that it captures the essence of the cause and effect interaction. It is more correct to say, however, that most models "explain" only in a statistical, correlative sense.
3. It is assumed that the functional structure or nature of this relationship is the same for all individuals and is constant over time (or, if it does vary with time or across individuals, it does so in some specifiable way).

The important characteristics of a decision-oriented transportation planning process were defined in Chap. 3 as establishing the future context, responding in scale of analysis to decision-maker concerns, expanding the scope of the problem definition, maintaining flexibility in analysis, providing continuity over time, relating to the programming and budgeting process, and providing opportunities for public involvement. "Good" analysis can play an important role in virtually every aspect of this planning process. By forecasting future states and identifying potential future problems and opportunities, it can help establish the future context for planning. By seeking to establish causal relationships within the system, it can help expand the scope of the problem definition, both by seeking out root causes underlying the "symptoms" that are often initially perceived as "the problem" and by identifying previously unforeseen impacts of a proposed policy. Often the technical staff is among the "longest lived" within a planning organization, helping to provide the "institutional memory" essential if continuity over time is to be maintained within the organization. Further, the data collection, maintenance, and analysis functions are central to the monitoring of the transportation system that is required by a continuing planning process. Finally, the more the analysis process is open to public involvement, the more likely it is that the results of that analysis will be understood by and acceptable to the public and will perhaps lead to implementable decisions.

Whenever a particular analysis technique or process is perceived to have failed in adequately informing the planning and decision-making processes, it is inevitably because it has failed to adhere to some of the characteristics described above. It might not have responded adequately to the problem scale involved, or it might have been inflexible and inadequate in its choice of variables and impacts analyzed, or it could have responded too narrowly in terms of its problem definition, and so on. These are easy pitfalls to stumble into, for the characteristics listed above for good analysis are not easily met. This is particularly the case given the fact that analysis techniques tend to be rigid in their assumptions and limited in their applicability; that data are often limited, typically outdated, expensive to gather, and seldom precisely suited to the issue at hand; and that we are all too often woefully ignorant about the complex causal interactions which drive our urban activity and transportation systems. The challenge of transportation analysis is to strive, within these many limitations—using analytical rigor complemented by professional judgment—to produce analysis that is timely, cost-effective, and credible.

5-1-2 Evaluation

Many of the characteristics of "good" analysis discussed above are important guidelines for "good" evaluation as well. As already mentioned, evaluation is the process of determining the desirability of different courses of action and presenting this information to decision makers in a comprehensible and useful form. There are several characteristics of an effective evaluation process that merit special attention.

1. *Evaluation should focus on the decisions to be made and the key issues to be faced by decision makers.* The selection of the evaluation criteria, the planning time horizon, the scope of the analysis (i.e., the factors to be included), and the scale of analysis will all depend on the nature of the decision(s) at hand [Schofer, 1978].
2. *Evaluation should relate the consequences of alternatives to goals and objectives.* Similar to the first point above, the information provided by the evaluation process, to be relevant to decision making, must be directly tied to stated objectives of the decision-making and planning processes. Because these objectives can relate to a wide-ranging set of issues, the evaluation process must be able to deal with quantitative and qualitative information and to potentially give as much importance to social, economic, and environmental impacts as it does to transportation impacts [Manheim et al., 1975].
3. *Evaluation should determine how particular interests are affected by transportation proposals.* Changes to the transportation system can affect different groups in a wide variety of ways. A classic example of this is an improvement to a transportation facility which provides benefits to users of the facility but which, at the same time, creates "costs" to nearby residents in terms of higher noise levels, decreased air quality, and increased congestion on local streets. Opportunities should thus be provided for interaction between planners and the public so that these localized impacts can be identified.

4. *Evaluation should be sensitive to the time frame in which project impacts are likely to occur.* By its very nature, transportation capital investment involves trading present expenditures for future net benefits. Evaluation should identify the time stream of benefits and costs as they are expected to occur over the useful life of the project. Because it is often difficult to predict future benefits and costs, any uncertainty associated with such predictions should be clearly documented.
5. *Evaluation should, in the case of regional transportation planning, produce information on the likely impacts of alternatives at a level of aggregation that permits both system and subarea impact assessment.* Because many of the significant impacts of transportation actions occur at the local level, the evaluation process must be able to assess impacts at this level. A subarea impact assessment is especially important in determining the distributional consequences of transportation investments.
6. *Evaluation should analyze the implementation requirements of each alternative.* The implementation of alternatives can require the use of many different resources—funding, labor, construction capability, engineering and design expertise, and the commitment of significant professional resources. The evaluation process must explicitly consider these factors so that the projects emerging from the planning process are indeed feasible.
7. *Evaluation should provide information to decision makers on the value of alternatives in a readily understandable and useful form and in a timely fashion.* Because most decision makers are not experts in the field of transportation planning, the information produced by evaluation should be presented in a format which is easily understood and which highlights the trade-offs that have to be made between alternatives. Evaluation should also occur throughout the planning process to structure the information flow that takes place among participants.

The evaluation process thus provides important guidance for establishing the rest of the planning process. Not only does evaluation identify the type of information that must be produced by the analysis process (and, hence, the data that must be collected), it also establishes the procedures to be used and the schedule that must be followed to produce timely input into decision making. Because an important aspect of evaluation is an assessment of the distributional consequences of the alternatives under consideration, evaluation also provides an important opportunity for public input into the planning process.

5-2 ECONOMIC CONCEPTS UNDERLYING TRANSPORTATION ANALYSIS AND EVALUATION[1]

As stated at the beginning of this chapter, a technical analysis and evaluation process involves the interaction of theory, data, and technique. Some of the most important

---

[1] Professor Cliff Winston, MIT Dept. of Civil Engineering, contributed significantly to this section.

theoretical concepts that form the basis of analysis and evaluation come from economic theory. In this section, four economic concepts that are especially important for transportation analysis and evaluation—the theory of consumer behavior, the supply curve, equilibrium, and welfare measures—are reviewed. More detailed discussion of the derivation and further use of these concepts can be found elsewhere [Wohl, 1972; Mohring, 1976; Nicholson, 1978; Layard and Walters, 1978].

5-2-1 Consumer Travel Behavior

The basic premise of the theory of consumer behavior is that an individual will select a bundle of goods that he desires over all other bundles that he can afford. Generally, a particular bundle will be preferred to another bundle if it yields the greatest utility (i.e., satisfaction). Formally, the individual's problem consists of maximizing a utility function U subject to a budget constraint, namely,

$$\max U = U(X_1, \ldots, X_n) \quad \text{subject to} \quad Y = P_1 X_1 + \ldots + P_n X_n \quad (5\text{-}1)$$

where $X_1, X_2, \ldots, X_n$ = goods that are consumed
$P_1, P_2, \ldots, P_n$ = prices of goods
Y = income

The solution to this problem can be illustrated graphically by using an indifference curve and a budget line. An indifference curve represents the various combinations of particular goods that will enable the individual to maintain a given level of utility. Thus, for the case of two goods, Fig. 5-1 characterizes the consumer's utility maximizing consumption of X_1 and X_2 given his income Y.

The utility maximizing values of X can, in general, be expressed in a functional relationship as

$$\begin{aligned} X_1^* &= f(P_1, \ldots, P_n, Y) \\ X_2^* &= f(P_1, \ldots, P_n, Y) \\ &\quad \vdots \\ X_n^* &= f(P_1, \ldots, P_n, Y) \end{aligned} \quad (5\text{-}2)$$

These functions are known as *demand functions,* and they denote the utility maximizing quantity of a good that an individual will purchase, given the prices of all goods that he consumes and his income.

The equilibrium level of consumption that was obtained for the goods in Fig. 5-1[2] (denoted by E) has an important economic interpretation. A consumer has reached equilibrium in consumption when his valuation of the goods is the same as the market's valuation. The consumer's valuation of the goods is represented by a trade-off among

---

[2] This can be generalized to n goods.

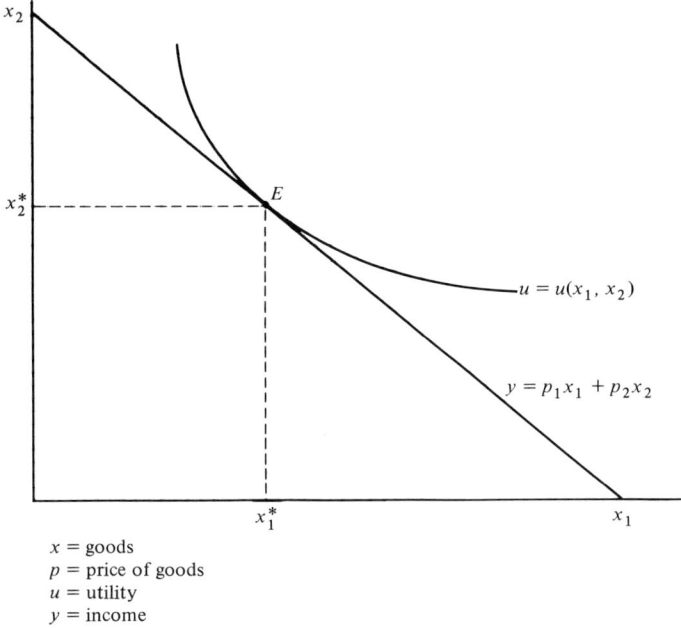

x = goods
p = price of goods
u = utility
y = income

Figure 5-1 Consumer utility maximizing behavior.

the commodities that he or she is willing to make along his or her indifference curve,[3] while the market's valuation of the commodities is represented by their price.[4]

Thus far it has been assumed that utility is simply a function of the quantity of the good(s) consumed. However, many if not most goods (including transportation services) are not consumed for their sheer quantity, but rather for their attributes [Lancaster, 1966]. That is, food is consumed for its nourishment and its taste; clothes for their comfort, aesthetic value, and durability; and so on. In other words, it is the attributes of goods which generate their utility, not the quantity of the goods per se. This implies that, in general, the demand for a good depends on its price,[5] its characteristics, and the characteristics of the consumer that purchases the good.

In the case of transportation, the "good" being demanded is transportation services by various modes between points in space for particular purposes. The "price" of this good is generally taken to be not simply the monetary cost of the trip,[6] but other costs perceived by the user as well, including the time spent traveling. If the

---

[3] This trade-off is technically referred to as the marginal rate of substitution.

[4] In technical terms, consumer equilibrium occurs in the two-good case when the marginal rate of substitution on the goods is equal to their relative prices.

[5] More precisely, the price and characteristics of the good relative to all other goods.

[6] Generally this cost is defined as the short-run or out-of-pocket or perceived cost of the trip rather than the long-run or "true" cost, on the assumption that tripmakers rarely, if ever, use long-run costs in evaluating their travel options.

monetary *value of time* is known, then time and price can be combined to yield a *generalized cost* of travel (other factors may be included also). This, however, is not a prerequisite for most transportation demand analyses, and it is very common for price to be represented by a vector of service measures, such as times and costs. As discussed further in Chap. 7, the utility of a trip (and hence the demand for such a trip) depends upon a wide range of trip characteristics, characteristics of the available modes, and characteristics of the individuals making the trips.

5-2-2 The Supply Curve

The supply curve expresses the quantity of a given good (Q_S) which will be supplied or produced as a function of the price of the good, expressed mathematically as $Q_S = Q_S(P)$. The supply function is usually upward-sloping (or at least nondecreasing) to the right, indicating that, all else being equal, greater quantities of goods will only be produced, in the short run, if the price of the good rises. This is because increased production is achieved in the short run through a more intensive use of existing capital (i.e., existing plant and equipment) and labor (e.g., production bonuses and overtime), meaning higher marginal operating costs must be incurred. In the long run, capital, labor, and production techniques can all change in order to reduce these marginal costs. Such a change in production will result in a change in the short-run supply function Q_S to a new curve Q_S' (which will generally lie below and to the right of Q_S, representing the producer's ability to supply a greater quantity of the good at any given price) rather than a movement along the existing supply curve Q_S. On the other hand, a long-run supply curve, representing optimal adjustment of capital and labor at each level of production, is often found to be decreasing over a substantial range of output.

Thus, as is the case with the demand function, the supply function ultimately depends on a range of factors other than just the good's market price, including the prices of the "input factors" (labor, materials, plant, and equipment) and the technology used to produce the good.

In the analysis of transportation services, "supply" is defined along at least three dimensions. The first of these is the concept of system *performance*, that is, the travel times, headways, and capacities that the transportation system provides for a given capital investment (representing the infrastructure and vehicles comprising the system), operating strategy, and demand level. As such, a performance function in an inverse supply function of the form $P_S = P_S(Q)$, where "price" P_S is interpreted in a very generalized way (e.g., travel times and costs). The classic example of a performance function is the volume-delay curve for a section of roadway (discussed in Chaps. 2 and 8), in which the performance of the roadway—as measured by the travel time required to traverse it—is a function of the volume of flow (i.e., the demand for the transportation service provided by the roadway).

Performance measures generally relate to factors which influence the demand for transportation, such as times and costs; that is, they are perceived by and relate to the *users* of the transportation service. The second dimension of supply consists of the closely related concept of system *impacts*; that is, the nontransportation effects that operation of the transportation system has on energy consumption, air pollution, noise levels, and the environment and the community as a whole. While they are also, in a sense, "performance" measures, impacts relate to factors which are generally perceived by and affect *nonusers* of the system. As is clear from Chaps. 1 through 3, transportation impacts are quite typically as important to transportation planners and decision makers as transportation performance per se.

The third important transportation supply dimension consists of the *costs* faced by the *operators* of the transportation system attempting to provide a particular quantity of service (i.e., to meet a particular demand level). Just as performance functions define the costs faced by transportation system users and impact functions define nonusers' costs, so do cost functions define the monetary costs of operating the system. These costs depend upon traditional economic factors such as the cost of labor, materials and capital, available technology, scale of operation, and management efficiency.

5-2-3 Equilibrium

The point of intersection between the demand and supply curves is known as the *equilibrium point* (see Fig. 5-2). At this point, the price of the good is such that $Q_D = Q_S = Q_E$; that is, the quantity demanded is equal to the quantity supplied. At equilibrium there is no "pressure" within the system for demand or supply to move to another price-quantity "operating point."

Under most conditions, markets can be expected to move toward the equilibrium point, provided that shifts in the demand and supply curves do not occur. Note that if excess demand were to exist (that is, $Q_D > Q_S$), then prices would likely rise as consumers "bid up" the price of the available goods. This in turn would stimulate both an increase in Q_S (since more producers would enter the market or those in the market would produce more intensively) and a decrease in Q_D (as fewer people would be willing to purchase the good at the higher prices), thus driving the market

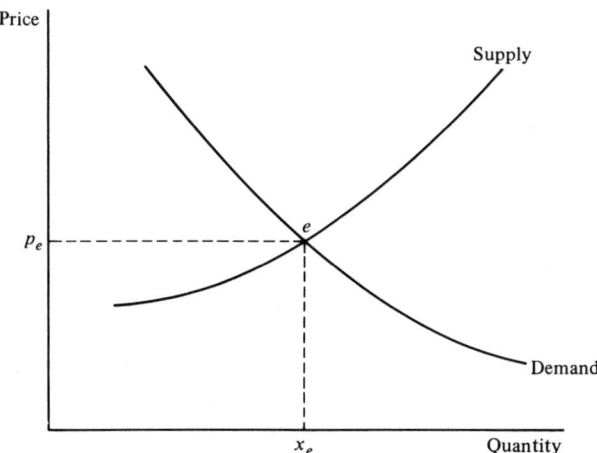

Figure 5-2 Equilibrium of supply and demand.

172 URBAN TRANSPORTATION PLANNING

toward the equilibrium point. A similar argument can be developed for the excess supply case $Q_S > Q_D$.

Equilibrium is an absolutely fundamental concept in transportation systems analysis in that it is what links the supply side and the demand side. The equilibrium level of traffic Q_E must give rise to a level of performance P_S on the supply side which in turn gives rise to a level of demand Q_D on the demand side (which itself equals Q_E). That is, while it is often convenient to take demand as fixed and exogenously given within an analysis of transportation supply (and vice versa within a demand analysis), ultimately this assumption is relaxed, and an equilibrium is established between demand and supply in order to achieve a description of the expected system state under a given set of operating conditions. This, of course, presupposes that transportation systems tend to be in a state of equilibrium (or, at least, would arrive at such a state if left undisturbed for a sufficient period of time). Transient disequilibria clearly exist: a freeway traffic jam caused by an accident or a stalled vehicle is but one example of such a phenomenon. Nevertheless, the assumption that travel markets tend toward equilibrium positions has proved to be a very workable and useful hypothesis and forms the basis upon which all of the demand and supply analysis techniques of Chaps. 7 and 8 are built.

5-2-4 Welfare Measures

Welfare measures are used to analyze the change in a consumer's welfare from a change in the price of one of the goods he consumes.[7] A well-known measure that is used to approximate this change in welfare is called *consumer surplus*. Specifically, it uses an individual's demand curve to measure the difference between what an individual is willing to pay for a good (which reflects the benefits he receives from the good) and the amount he actually pays. For instance, the amount of consumer surplus an individual receives from the consumption of quantity X_1 is shown in Fig. 5-3a, while the change in his consumer surplus resulting from a change in the price of that good is shown in Fig. 5-3b.

The major drawback of consumer surplus as a measure of net welfare is that it assumes a constant marginal utility of income, an assumption which is often not valid. Two other means have been developed by economists to measure more precisely the change in welfare. These measures are:

1. *Compensating variation (CT)*. The amount of money that can be taken from an individual after a price change, while leaving him as well-off as he was before.
2. *Equivalent variation (EV)*. The amount of money needed to give an individual to make him as well-off as he was before the price change.

These measures are based on a compensated demand curve, a demand curve which holds real income or utility constant. Compensating and equivalent variation measures bound the measure of consumer surplus; that is, the consumer surplus measure falls

---

[7] The analysis can also be carried out for multiple price changes and quality changes.

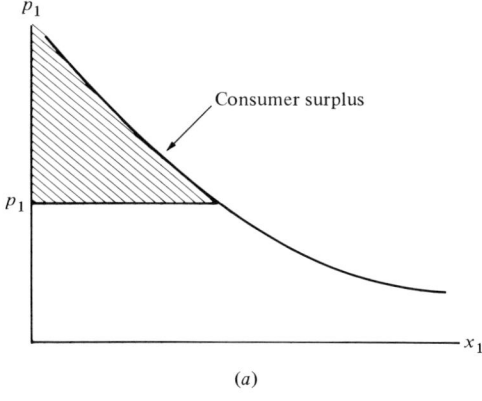

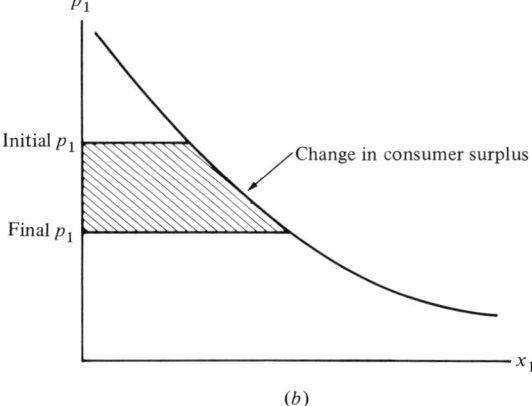

Figure 5-3 Consumer surplus as a measure of net welfare.

between both the CT and EV measures. Methods have been developed to estimate these measures, including a recent method based on disaggregate travel demand models (such models will be discussed in Chap. 7) [Small and Rosen, 1981]. These methods, however, will not be discussed in this text because of the lengthy discussion necessary to explain the underlying concepts and the mechanics of undertaking each method. Interested readers are referred to Willig [1976]; Hausman [1981]; and Small and Rosen [1981].

5-3 CHAPTER SUMMARY

1. Technical analysis and evaluation involve the interaction of *theory, data,* and *technique.*
2. *Analysis* is a means of understanding how the transportation system and its components work and how changes in that system will alter its performance.

Evaluation synthesizes all the benefits, costs, and impacts generated by the analysis phase in order to provide input into judgments on the relative merit of alternative actions.
3. To be useful, analysis must be responsive to policy variables and contexts, responsive to the decision-making timetable, sensitive to the scale of impacts, perceived as being cost-effective, and credible in the eyes of the decision maker.
4. There are several characteristics of effective evaluation; it should

   Focus on the decisions to be made and the key issues to be faced by decision makers.

   Relate the consequences of alternatives to goals and objectives.

   Determine how particular interests are affected by transportation proposals.

   Be sensitive to the time frame in which project impacts are likely to occur.

   Produce information on the likely impacts of alternatives at a level of aggregation that permits both system and subarea impact assessment.

   Analyze the implementation requirements of each alternative.

   Provide information to decision makers on the value of alternatives in a readily understandable and useful form and in a timely fashion.

5. Four major economic concepts serve as the basis for transportation analysis and evaluation—the theory of consumer travel behavior, the supply curve, equilibrium, and welfare measures.

QUESTIONS

1. A medium-sized urban area (population 500,000) is experiencing increasing congestion on its downtown streets during the morning and afternoon peak periods. The city's transit service consists of a radially oriented bus system. A circumferential freeway around the city's periphery was built during the 1960s as part of an interregional freeway system, but auto access to the downtown depends on a system of four- and six-lane arterial roads. The amount of white-collar, office-based employment in the downtown area is increasing at a somewhat greater rate than the rate at which blue-collar, industrially based employment is decentralizing to locations nearer to the freeway.

   Given this brief description of the urban area:
   (*a*) What would you define as the transportation problem(s) facing this urban area?
   (*b*) Generate a set of short-run alternatives to address the problem(s).
   (*c*) Generate a set of long-run alternatives to address the problem(s).
   (*d*) What is the "do-nothing" alternative?

2. Given two goods (1 and 2) and the following utility and budget functions:

$$U = (x_1)(x_2)$$
$$Y = P_1 x_1 + P_2 x_2$$

where U = utility
  Y = household income
  x_i = amount consumed of good i
  P_i = price per unit of good i

show that the demand function for good x_1 is given by

$$x_1 = \frac{Y}{2p_1}$$

3. The demand for transportation services on a given roadway is denoted by the equation

$$D = 2000 - 10t$$

where D = number of trips per hour using roadway
  t = "price" of travel, defined as time (in minutes) required to travel roadway

The performance curve for this roadway is given by

$$t = 10 + 0.001D$$

What are the equilibrium demand level and travel time for this roadway? If the roadway is improved so that the performance curve is changed to

$$t' = 5 + 0.001D$$

what is the change in consumer surplus which results?

4. Consider an urban freeway. Define the users, nonusers, and operators of this system. Define what you consider to be important performance measures, nonuser impacts, and costs associated with this system.

REFERENCES

Hausman, J. A.: "Exact Consumer's Surplus and Dead Weight Loss," *The American Economic Review*, vol. 71, no. 4, September 1981, pp. 662–676.

Herald, W.: "Generating Alternatives for Alternatives Analysis," Presented at the 59th annual meeting of the Transportation Research Board, Washington, D.C., January 1980.

Lancaster, K. J.: "A New Approach to Consumer Theory," *Journal of Political Economy*, vol. lxxxiv, 1966, pp. 132–157.

Lane, J. S., et al.: "The No-Action Alternative, Impact Assessment Guidelines," *National Cooperative Highway Research Program Report 217*, Transportation Research Board, December 1979.

Layard, P. R. G., and A. A. Walters: *Microeconomics Theory*, McGraw-Hill, New York, 1978.

Manheim, M. L., et al.: "Transportation Decision Making: A Guide to Social and Environmental Considerations," *National Cooperative Highway Research Program Report 156,* Transportation Research Board, 1975.

Mohring, H.: *Transportation Economics,* Ballinger, Cambridge, Mass., 1976.

Nicholson, W.: *Microeconomic Theory: Basic Principles and Extensions,* 2d ed., Dryden, Hinsdale, Ill., 1978.

Schofer, J. L.: "Emerging Methods in Transportation Evaluation," in W. F. Brown, R. B. Dial, D. S. Gerdall, and E. Weiner (eds.), *Emerging Transportation Planning Methods,* Office of University Research, U.S. Dept. of Transportation, Washington, D.C., 1978, pp. 53–96.

Small, K. A., and H. S. Rosen: "Applied Welfare Economics with Discrete Choice Models," *Econometrica,* vol. 49, no. 1, January 1981, pp 105–130.

Willig, R.: "Consumer's Surplus without Apology," *The American Economic Review,* vol. 66, September 1976, pp. 589–97.

Wohl, M.: *Transportation Investment Planning,* D.C. Heath, Lexington, Mass., 1972.

CHAPTER
SIX
URBAN ACTIVITY SYSTEM ANALYSIS

6-0 INTRODUCTION

As discussed in Chap. 2, the need for passenger transportation services is derived from people's needs to participate in activities of various types (work, shop, visit friends and relatives, etc.), located in a variety of places dispersed over the urban region. Similarly, freight transportation services are required to move goods from point to point within the urban region, as well as into and out of the region, so that economic activities can take place. In order to estimate the demand for transportation services, one must first understand the *urban activity system* which generates this demand. A definition of land use activities in an urban area and their relationship to the generation of trips is thus an important prerequisite of demand analysis, which is discussed in detail in Chap. 7.

Since it takes a considerable amount of time to develop land and construct buildings, for employment and other activities to grow, decline, or change radically in nature, and for large numbers of people to change where they live or work, transportation planners can usually take the current activity system as being "fixed and given" for short-term analyses. In such cases, an inventory of the current activity system for the study area is required (see Chap. 4), but the analyst generally does not need to predict how this activity system will change over time. In the longer run, however (where the "long run" is probably anything greater than 5 years in the future), the urban activity system clearly does change: neighborhoods gain or lose population or employment of various types; new areas on the urban fringe may be developed, while older, developed areas may decline in quality, be renovated, or undergo redevelopments; and so on. As a result of these changes, travel demand patterns (and transportation system requirements) will also change. Hence, any longer-term transportation planning analysis must explicitly consider expected changes in the urban activity system in order to predict future travel demand adequately.

Further, proposed transportation system improvements can potentially influence future activity patterns by altering the accessibility levels of various locations and activities. As discussed in Chap. 2, the impact of the transportation system on activity patterns is complex and is contingent on a host of other factors. Nevertheless, concern over the "nontransportation" impacts of transportation policies—including the explicit use of transportation to achieve nontransportation objectives (e.g., enhance the commercial viability of the downtown)—necessitates a capability to analyze and predict transportation impacts on urban activity, in both the short and the long term.

Transportation planners can thus potentially face two major analytical tasks with respect to the urban activity system: (1) forecasting future states of this activity system as a first step in forecasting the future demand for transportation and (2) predicting the impacts that proposed transportation system changes are likely to have (in either the short or the long run) on urban activities. Sections 6-2 and 6-3 discuss a range of analytical techniques and issues associated with each of these two tasks. For a more detailed discussion of urban activity system models, see, among others, Highway Research Board [1969]; Brown et al. [1972]; Wilson [1974]; Franklin [1974]; Federal Highway Administration [1975]; and Batty [1976]. Section 6-1 provides some background to these discussions of technique by presenting some basic concepts and issues associated with the analysis of the urban activity system. This section also discusses some issues concerning the role of urban activity analysis within the transportation planning process.

6-1 BASIC CONCEPTS AND THE ROLE OF URBAN ACTIVITY ANALYSIS IN TRANSPORTATION PLANNING

In speaking of the urban activity system (or of urban *land use*—the two terms will be used virtually interchangeably within this chapter), transportation planners are actually referring to the spatial distribution of people and activities within an urban region. In particular, transportation planners are concerned with the spatial distributions of population and employment, which, given the current modeling state of the art, constitute a primary input into transportation demand models (see Chap. 7). Implicit in this concept of spatial distribution are several other concepts which are important in characterizing an urban activity system. One of these is the *building stock* which physically occupies the land. People occupy and use buildings of specific sizes, types, and qualities, located on specific sites within a given topography. These buildings are costly to construct, maintain, or demolish. Thus, where people live and where firms locate not only depends on their preferences or *demand* for certain locations, but also upon the availability or *supply* of suitable building stock at these locations. Hence, a land use *market* exists in which people and activities compete for the locations and buildings available within an urban area and in which the supply of these locations and buildings presumably adjusts over time to meet these demands.

A major factor linking the demand and supply sides of this market together is the *price* or *rent* associated with the buildings and the land being bought and sold. Developers, builders, and landlords will presumably wish to maximize the prices they charge so as to maximize their profits. They are constrained (in principle at least) by the existence of other suppliers who will underprice them if they charge too much. Similarly, home owners and renters will wish to minimize the prices they pay for accommodation. Because land and buildings are scarce commodities, however, other home owners and renters will "bid up" the price in an effort to obtain a particular location, with the location presumably going to the person or activity to whom it is most valuable (and, hence, to the person who is willing to pay the most for it). The end result of this bidding process is an "equilibrium bid rent surface" which defines the equilibrium price or rent of land (or building stock) at each point in the urban region and which represents both the profit-maximizing result for the suppliers of the land and the utility-maximizing result for the purchasers of the land [Alonso, 1964].

In general, it is expected that these rents will decline as one moves farther from the city center, which has generally been assumed to be the most attractive or desirable location for most activities. The concept of declining rents with distance is also applicable in urban subcenters, in which the densest economic activity is not necessarily at the center of the city. Figure 6-1 depicts a typical rent surface, in which the central peak represents the downtown area, ridges of high rent represent major commercial streets, and local peaks along these ridges represent major intersections.

It is not clear whether most urban systems ever reach a state of equilibrium. Exogenous "shocks" to the urban activity system happen continuously: in- and out-migration of people and jobs, changes in interest rates and capital availability, changes in the transportation system, changes in zoning and other controls and guidelines for

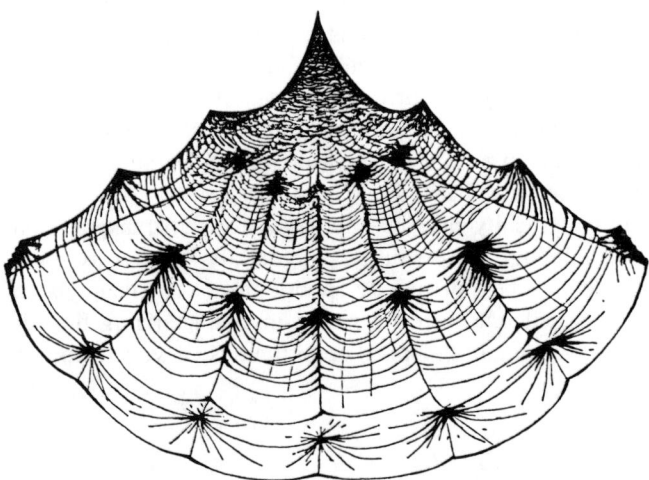

Figure 6-1 Example of an urban bid rent surface. (*Berry, Tennant, Garner, and Simmons [1963].*)

development—these and other factors will all alter the status quo and cause the urban activity system to adapt and evolve over time. Further, considerable inertia and durability exist in the system, which may prevent it from adjusting quickly to changing conditions. While not invalidating the notion of an urban market and its interaction between demand and supply, mediated by price, these observations do highlight the need to recognize that this interaction is, in fact, a dynamic one and hence one which cannot be adequately modeled or analyzed from a static perspective.

As is explicit in its name, the urban activity system consists of people participating in a range of activities at different locations and times. People do not occupy space (or buildings) for the sake of mere occupation; they do so for some purpose—to live in a home, to produce goods or services (and in so doing, to provide employment opportunities to the resident population), and so on. In general, people and activities will choose among locations based on a location's *attractiveness* for a particular type and scale of activity and on the location's *accessibility* to other activities.

The attractiveness of a location for a given activity potentially depends upon a wide variety of factors. For example, the attractiveness of a neighborhood as a residential location depends on such characteristics as the price, size, type, age, and quality of the available housing; the quality and proximity of schools (if the household contains school-age children); the availability of parks and other recreational facilities; the extent to which the neighborhood is "hazard-free" (where hazards might include busy, noisy streets; noxious factories; etc.); and the social-ethnic-racial composition of the neighborhood (and perceived trends in this composition). Similarly, the attractiveness of a location for a retail store depends upon such factors as the availability of a suitable building for the store; the location of the building relative to the street, pedestrian flows, and parking; the rent to be paid for the building; the expected market at the location for the goods being sold; and the mix of retail stores currently located in the neighborhood.

In principle, therefore, attractiveness (and, hence, location choice) depends upon a relatively complex set of attributes which are perceived by the decision maker and which enter into his preference or choice considerations. In modeling practice, however, the analyst is limited in terms of the number of attraction attributes which can be specified and observed. The result is that gross surrogates, generally "size" variables (e.g., total retail floor space in a zone as a measure of retail attractiveness or total number of single-family housing units in a zone as a measure of residential attractiveness), are used in place of more specific "behavioral" variables.

The concept of accessibility typically provides the basis for the transportation component of urban activity modeling. Accessibility is generally defined as some aggregate measure of the size and closeness of activity opportunities of a given type to a particular location. For example, if one were interested in characterizing the accessibility of a residential zone i to retail shopping opportunities, a very common measure used is

$$A_i = \sum_{j=1}^{n} F_j(t_{ij})^{-b} \qquad (6\text{-}1)$$

where A_i = accessibility of zone i to shopping opportunities
F_j = amount of retail floor space in zone j
t_{ij} = travel time from zone i to zone j
n = number of zones with retail stores
b = parameter indicating the sensitivity of trip making to travel time (i.e., the larger b is in magnitude, the less likely people are to travel long distances to shop)

In general, it is assumed that location choice is positively correlated with accessibility. That is, it is assumed that people would like to have more accessibility than less to shopping and employment opportunities, that retail stores would like to be highly accessible to high-income households, and so on. For a more detailed discussion of the concept of accessibility, and particularly of its definition through the use of individual choice models, see Ben-Akiva and Lerman [1979].

The above discussion of the basic concepts of urban activity system analysis suggests that there is an important linkage between the urban activity system and the transportation system. One would expect, therefore, that characteristics of both would be fully integrated in urban transportation planning. However, the role of urban activity system analysis within the urban transportation planning process as a whole is a rather ambiguous and, at times, even contradictory one. In principle (i.e., as presented in transportation planning texts—including this one), the transportation–land use interaction is of fundamental importance to planning and should represent the starting point for the analysis of many transportation policies and issues. In practice, however, the planning and analysis of the urban transportation and activity systems proceed essentially independently of one another. Further, even when land use considerations are incorporated within transportation planning analyses, the results have been very mixed, to say the least.

The large amount of independence which has existed between urban transportation and activity system analysis and planning stems primarily from the simple fact that, institutionally and professionally, different agencies and people are responsible for and trained to do transportation planning and analysis on the one hand and land use (or "urban") planning and analysis on the other. To be sure, an urban planning department may well be concerned with both transportation and land use issues, but typically, even in such cases, a relatively autonomous "transportation group" will exist within the planning department to deal with transportation issues.

This institutional dichotomy encourages planners and analysts to think of "transportation problems" or "land use problems" as independent entities. Thus, for example, alternatives for addressing the issue of improving transportation energy efficiency typically involve encouraging the use of more energy-efficient energy modes (transit or car pool) and improving the technical efficiency of the vehicles and systems in operation (e.g., improved automobile fuel economy), but they rarely include specific policies for encouraging an urban land use structure which facilitates improved transportation energy efficiency (i.e., which facilitates shorter trip lengths, encourages the use of high-efficiency modes, reduces the need to travel, etc.).

This focus on "one side of the problem" is further manifested in analytical techniques, which typically model the transportation system given the land use system (or vice versa) rather than the dynamic interaction between the two. This not only leads to a potentially "myopic" or partial analysis of the problem of interest, but can also result in the development of models which contain serious internal inconsistencies. The classic example of this is the urban transportation modeling system (or UTMS and often called UTPS, see Chap. 7) which, among other things, predicts the distribution or flow of work trips from residential zones to employment zones, given the zonal population and employment levels as generated separately by a land use forecasting model. The usual land use forecasting model used to generate these numbers distributes residential population among zones based on place of employment. In other words, a zone-to-zone work-trip flow pattern is implicit in the land use forecasts but is ignored by UTMS, which forecasts its own flow pattern—one which might bear little resemblance to the original pattern implicit in the land use forecasts. At the same time, these land use forecasts are generated based on an assumed future transportation system that might bear little relationship to any of the actual transportation system alternatives under consideration. It is thus often unclear whether the land use or the transportation forecasts are in any way compatible with one another or with the system alternatives under consideration.

The near total abandonment of large-scale land use models in current planning practice is clearly representative of the general trend in urban transportation planning during the 1970s away from long-range planning in favor of short-range planning. Indeed, the disenchantment with the results of most large-scale land use modeling exercises played an important part in encouraging this trend (i.e., if one cannot predict the future adequately, long-range planning becomes a difficult, and quite possibly fruitless, thing to do). It is interesting to note, however, that this shift in emphasis from the long range to the short range and from the comprehensive to the problem-specific has not substantively altered many of the "technical" issues faced by the analyst. These include:

1. *The dynamic nature of the urban area.* Whether one is looking at the short run or the long, the urban area remains a dynamic place in which multiple actors react and interact over time in response to a wide variety of stimuli. This implies that even "simple" models typically need to be dynamic in nature and typically need to simulate the activities of a range of actors.
2. *The complexity of urban behavior.* In his critique of large-scale models, Lee observed that "the sum of knowledge of urban structure is large, but the density is thin" [Lee, 1973]. By and large, this comment holds true today and is equally applicable to large- and small-scale models. A crude representation of retailers' decisions and decision making discussed in Sec. 6-3 will serve to illustrate the limited state of our knowledge concerning many key actors and interactions within the urban area, as well as the extent to which such limitations can seriously jeopardize the validity of our analyses.
3. *The need for good quality, detailed data.* Without good information about the phenomena under study, theories cannot be tested and improved and models

cannot be developed and used. The never-ending lament of analysts and modelers is for more and better data. Again, a short-run, focused analysis framework may reduce the quantity of data required relative to a long-run, comprehensive approach, but it may well require more detailed data than the latter.

The shift from long-range, comprehensive models to short-range, problem-specific models thus does not eliminate many of the problems inherent in urban activity system modeling. As we learn more about "bits and pieces" of the urban activity system, about present trends and how these trends can be appropriately projected into the near term, the potential for combining these "bits and pieces" into a more comprehensive, longer-range forecasting capability will presumably be enhanced. Whether such a capability does, in fact, emerge would appear to depend on the evolution of the planning process (i.e., will longer-range planning again emerge as a dominant concern?), the formulation of integrated land use–transportation models that produce valid and useful results, and the development of time-series data bases of appropriate size and quality to support such an activity. The development of such data bases in turn depends on the continuing evolution of computing capabilities and costs, and the willingness of public agencies to implement and support (financially and otherwise) such systems.

The difficulty that analysts face in compiling a good data base on the current activity system and its trends, let alone in forecasting how this system is apt to change over time, has serious implications for the design and analysis of transportation alternatives and, in short, for the transportation planning process as a whole. That is, since it is the urban activity system which drives the demand for transportation and hence which motivates the provision of transportation services, if great uncertainty exists in our understanding of how that activity system is changing over time, then clearly great uncertainty is going to exist in our forecasts of transportation demand and in our ability to generate, evaluate, and choose alternative courses of action. For example, if we are only capable of generating very crude forecasts of aggregate population and employment totals, then analytical techniques which depend upon precise data disaggregated along a number of socioeconomic dimensions are of little use to us, since we will be unable to forecast the data inputs required.

The existence of uncertainty about future activity system states reinforces the need for a cyclical planning process of the sort outlined in Fig. 1-1, in which continuous monitoring of the system permits new trends and issues to be identified and diagnosed as they emerge and new policies to be formulated as required in response to these emerging trends. Even more fundamental, it argues for the need for flexibility within the transportation system itself. That is, one would ideally like to have a transportation system which is suitable for a range of likely future activity system states or which can adapt appropriately over time to the urban activity system as it evolves.

At the most general level, the challenge to planners is to understand the dynamics of the urban activity system and its relationship to the transportation system. To return to a theme that was introduced in the first chapter, it is most important for planners in a decision-oriented planning process to understand the decision-making process and the types of decisions that need to be made. Understanding the dynamics of the urban activity system requires an awareness of the key decision makers and the factors that influence their decisions. A number of actors can play critical roles: developers (who develop land, construct buildings, and sell or lease these buildings); firms (who build, buy, or lease buildings and provide employment); residents (who buy, sell, and maintain houses or rent apartments); and governments (who regulate construction and land uses, set taxes, provide services, provide the transportation infrastructure, etc.).

In short, the above observations simply return us to the opening statement of this chapter: the transportation–land use interaction is of fundamental importance to planning, and if it is not well understood and analyzed, then our understanding and our analyses in subsequent stages of the planning process will suffer or be limited accordingly.

6-2 ALTERNATIVE APPROACHES TO LAND USE FORECASTING

A wide range of analytical techniques has emerged over the years for predicting future urban activity patterns. These include:

1. "Econometric" models in which a set of simultaneous, "structural" equations describing the urban activity system is specified a priori and then econometrically calibrated, usually using standard regression techniques
2. "Heuristic" models which use a set of ad hoc rules for allocating activities to zones
3. Simulation models in which decisions by key actors (e.g., decisions to construct, renovate, or demolish buildings; decisions to change job or residential locations) are explicitly simulated over time
4. Scenarios or other judgmental techniques

Each of these approaches is discussed in the following subsections. Some of the models discussed are no longer in general use. It is important, however, in understanding the evolution of land use modeling that the contributions of these modeling efforts be discussed.

The above models generally assume that regional population and employment totals are exogenously determined; that is, that they are forecasted separately, outside of the land use model itself (which concerns itself with distributing these totals spatially over the urban region). Procedures for forecasting population over time include [Steuart, 1977]:

1. The "ratio-trend" method, which relates the population of a study area to the rising or falling ratio of that area's population to the population of a larger area, for which an accepted population forecast exists
2. The "cohort-survival" method, which adds the effects of net natural increase and net-migration to the existing population
3. The "economic-base" method, which gears population growth to a forecast of employment growth

4. The application of a constant or gradually declining compounded annual rate or percentage increase in population
5. A constant absolute rate of population increase per annum or per 5- or 10-year period

Employment forecasts typically tend to be more difficult to perform. Techniques used include trend extrapolation, input-output analysis and judgmental estimations. For more detailed discussions of population and employment forecasting see, among others, Isard [1960]; Wrigley [1967]; Wilson [1974].

6-2-1 Econometric Models: EMPIRIC

Undoubtedly the archetypal econometric model is EMPIRIC, which was originally developed in the early 1960s for use in the Boston Regional Planning Project. Over the subsequent decade, it was applied in several other North American cities, including Atlanta, Denver, Minneapolis, St. Paul, Seattle, Toronto, Washington, D.C., and Winnipeg [Federal Highway Administration, 1975]. EMPIRIC consists of a set of simultaneous linear equations which predict the *change* in a zone's *share* of the regional population (disaggregated by income group) and employment (disaggregated by industry type) which is expected to occur between two points in time, as a function of a range of exogenous and endogenous variables [Hill, 1965; Hill, Brand and Hansen, 1965; Brand, Barber, and Jacobs, 1967]. Table 6-1 presents the Boston version of the model, in which four income groups and five industry types are used, resulting in a system of nine equations. Noteworthy features of this model are as follows:

1. Exogenous variables in the model include measures of the availability of water and sewage and of the "developability" of the land for each zone (based on past development within the zone). Thus, the model is sensitive to nontransportation services as well as to historical development trends.
2. The transportation system is represented by a set of accessibility measures for various modes, activities, and population groups.
3. The model is dynamic in that not only does it predict population and employment changes between time periods, but these changes depend upon both current period conditions and the conditions which existed in the previous time period. That is, "lagged" variables are used to capture the impacts which prior conditions have on current activities.
4. Interdependencies exist between population and employment groups. For instance, the growth of low-income households in a zone in one time period may lead to a decline of higher-income households in subsequent time periods.

At a fairly abstract level, EMPIRIC possesses considerable conceptual appeal. As an explicitly dynamic model, it avoids the difficulties to which static models are prone when they try to model an obviously dynamic process based on one "snapshot" of the system. In particular, EMPIRIC does not attempt to recreate the existing urban area in

Table 6-1 The EMPIRIC model equations

$$\Delta F_{<5k} = 0.637\Delta F_{5-10k} - 0.295\Delta F_{10-15k} + 0.018\Delta SVC + 0.133(t-1)F_{<5k} \quad (6\text{-}2a)$$
$$- 0.109(t-1)F_{10-15k} + 0.044(t-1)WATER - 0.298\Delta VACCTE(0.05)$$
$$- 0.068(t-1)VACCTE(0.15)$$

$$\Delta F_{5-10k} = 0.530\Delta F_{<5k} + 0.337\Delta F_{10-15k} + 0.022\Delta RET + 0.060\Delta SVC \quad (6\text{-}2b)$$
$$- 0.101(t-1)F_{5-10k} + 0.036(t-1)SVC + 0.044(t)SEWER$$
$$+ 0.025(t-1)CIPOP + 0.302\Delta VACCTE(0.05) + 0.114\Delta QACCTE(0.005)$$

$$\Delta F_{10-15k} = -0.125\Delta F_{<5k} + 0.637\Delta F_{5-10k} + 0.294\Delta F_{\geq 15k} \quad (6\text{-}2c)$$
$$- 0.224(t-1)F_{10-15k} + 0.196(t-1)SEWER + 0.145\Delta SEWER$$

$$\Delta F_{\geq 15k} = -0.282\Delta F_{5-10k} + 0.603\Delta F_{10-15k} - 0.278(t-1)F_{\geq 15k} \quad (6\text{-}2d)$$
$$+ 0.145(t-1)WATER + 0.118(t-1)SEWER + 0.046(t-1)CIPOP$$
$$- 0.384\Delta VACCF_{\geq 10}(0.15) + 0.093\Delta QACCTE(0.05)$$

$$\Delta M\&C = 0.220\Delta OTHER - 0.302(t-1)M\&C - 0.015(t-1)FIR \quad (6\text{-}2e)$$
$$+ 0.138(t-1)CIMFG + 0.278\Delta QACCF_{<10}(0.05)$$
$$+ 0.121(t-1)VACCTF(0.05)$$

$$\Delta OTHER = 0.456\Delta M\&C + 0.081\Delta RET - 0.132\Delta FIR + 0.106(t-1)M\&C \quad (6\text{-}2f)$$
$$- 0.194(t-1)OTHER - 0.414\Delta VACCTE(0.15) + 0.095(t-1)QACCTF(0.05)$$

$$\Delta RET = 0.440\Delta OTHER - 0.117(t-1)F_{\geq 15k} + 0.126(t-1)OTHER \quad (6\text{-}2g)$$
$$- 0.363(t-1)RET + 0.165(t-1)CIRET + 0.213\Delta VACCTF(0.15)$$
$$- 0.064(t-1)QACCTF(0.05)$$

$$\Delta SVC = -0.252\Delta OTHER - 0.510(t-1)SVC + 0.022(t-1)FIR \quad (6\text{-}2h)$$
$$+ 0.620\Delta WATER + 0.240\Delta SEWER + 0.564\Delta QACCTF(0.05)$$
$$+ 0.390(t-1)VACCTF(0.05)$$

$$\Delta FIR = 0.614\Delta OTHER + 0.020(t-1)SVC - 0.159(t-1)FIR \quad (6\text{-}2i)$$
$$+ 0.110(t-1)QACCTF(0.05)$$

where: population variables (expressed in 1959 dollars) are

$F_{<5k}$ = number of families with annual income less than $5000
F_{5-10k} = number of families with annual income between $5000 and $9999
F_{10-15k} = number of families with annual income between $10,000 and $14,999
$F_{\geq 15k}$ = number of families with annual income equal to or greater than $15,000

Employment variables are

M&C = manufacturing and construction (SIC codes 15–39)
OTHER = wholesale, transportation, communication, utilities, government, and other (SIC codes 1–14, 40–50, 91–99)
RET = retail (SIC codes 52–59)
SVC = service (SIC codes 70–89)
FIR = finance, insurance, and real estate (SIC codes 60–67)

Land developability variables are

CIPOP = capacity (land developability index) for population
= (NAP/GA)(GA−UA)
CIMFG = capacity (land developability index) for manufacturing
= (NAM/GA)(GA−UA)
CIRET = capacity (land developability index) for retail
= (NAR/GA)(GA−UA)

where NAP = net residential area
NAM = net manufacturing area
NAR = net retail area
UA = total used area
GA = gross area

Table 6-1 (*continued*)

Utility service variables are

WATER = index, from 1 to 7, of water supply service, multiplied by *UA*
SEWER = index, from 1 to 5, of sewage disposal service, multiplied by *UA*

Accessibility variables are

$$\text{Accessibility of zone } g \text{ to activity } i = \sum_{h=1}^{n} R_{ih} e^{-bt_{gh}} \quad (6\text{-}2j)$$

where R_{ih} = quantity of activity i in zone h
H = total number of zones
t_{gh} = travel time between zones g and h
b = empirically derived parameter
VACCTF = vehicle accessibility of zone to total families
QACCTF = transit accessibility of zone to total families
$\text{VACCF}_{\geq 10}$ = vehicle accessibility of a zone to families with annual income equal to or greater than $10,000
$\text{QACCF}_{<10}$ = transit accessibility of zone to families with annual income less than $10,000
VACCTE = vehicle accessibility of zone to total employment
QACCTE = transit accessibility of zone to total employment
VACCM&C = vehicle accessibility of zone to manufacturing and construction employment
VACCR&S = vehicle accessibility of zone to retail and service employment

Notes: 1. Variables measured in the forecast year are preceded by t, while variables measured in the previous time period are preceded by $t - 1$.
2. Variables representing changes between the base year and the forecast year are preceded by Δ.
3. Numbers in parentheses following accessibility variables indicate the value of the b parameter used in Eq. (6-2j).
4. All equations relate to zonal variables, changes in variables, etc. For simplicity of presentation, however, a zonal identification subscript has not been shown.

Source: Brand, Barber, and Jacobs [1967].

---

its entirety; rather, it attempts the somewhat simpler task of predicting incremental changes over time to this existing system. Similarly, the simultaneous structure of the model directly addresses the "social dynamic" which exists within urban areas, as people and activities of different types compete for available land, attract and repel one another, and so on. Finally, the sensitivity of the model to both transportation and nontransportation services widens the range of public policies directly addressable within the model.

The central task associated with the development of a model such as EMPIRIC involves the specification of the system of structural equations which constitute the model. Ideally this system of equations should embody the causal interactions which exist among the endogenous and exogenous variables within the system. In practice, this task is often complicated by the lack of a strong theoretical understanding of these causal interactions, by a lack of appropriate data (which results in ignoring certain interactions or in using "proxy" or "instrumental" variables to approximate the preferred but unavailable "causal" variables), and by technical requirements associated with the econometric estimation of the model parameters. In particular, care must be taken that the system of equations is *identified*, that is, that the model parameters are, in fact, statistically estimable.

EMPIRIC in many respects typifies these difficulties in that a lack of reliable price data (for either housing or land) precluded the inclusion of price variables in the model; while the rudimentary state of operational (i.e., implementable within a practical planning model) theory concerning the dynamics of urban location and change led, as is made explicit in the model's name, to the adoption of a primarily empirical specification of the model's functional form.

6-2-2 Heuristic Models: Lowry-Type Models

The term "heuristic models" is used here in reference to a set of models that are based on a range of procedures for allocating activities over urban regions. These models do not attempt to simulate the actual decision making which underlies this allocation process. (For reviews of such models, see, for instance, Brown et al. [1972], or Lowry [1968].) By far the most universally employed of these models is the *Lowry model*, first developed in 1964 for application in Pittsburgh [Lowry, 1964] and later modified and further developed for applications throughout North America and Great Britain [Goldner, 1971; Batty, 1972]. The key concept underlying the model involves defining two classes of employment: "retail" and "basic." Retail employment arises from all activities which [Goldner, 1971]

> are implicitly related to population and purchasing power. All activities for which a local market or service area can be identified for final products or services are in the category of "retail." The criterion is locational, flowing from the existence of a *local market or service area*.

Basic employment is composed of "everything else," that is, of all those activities which are "site-oriented" in that their locations are dependent upon factors other than the size and location of "residence-oriented" local market areas. The model assumes that the basic employment in each zone of the urban area E_b is exogenously determined. Given E_b, the model allocates these workers to residential areas in the urban area using a work-to-residence distribution function. Given this residential distribution, the distribution of retail employment serving this population E_r is similarly allocated using a resident-to-shop distribution function. These workers, in turn, must be allocated to residences, which then generate additional retail activity (employment), and so on. Thus the model incorporates a multiplier effect in which each new employee (basic or retail) generates further retail employment, until the entire process converges to an equilibrium state. In particular, if each worker requires m additional retail workers ($m < 1$), then for each initial basic worker there will exist at equilibrium $(1 + m + m^2 + m^n + \cdots) = 1/(1 - m)$ total workers. Figure 6-2 presents a flowchart for this basic Lowry model, while Table 6-2 summarizes the equations involved.

Garin [1966] reformulated Lowry's model using matrix notation and was able to demonstrate that the Lowry model converged to a unique equilibrium employment distribution. This is a comforting piece of information to possess whenever one

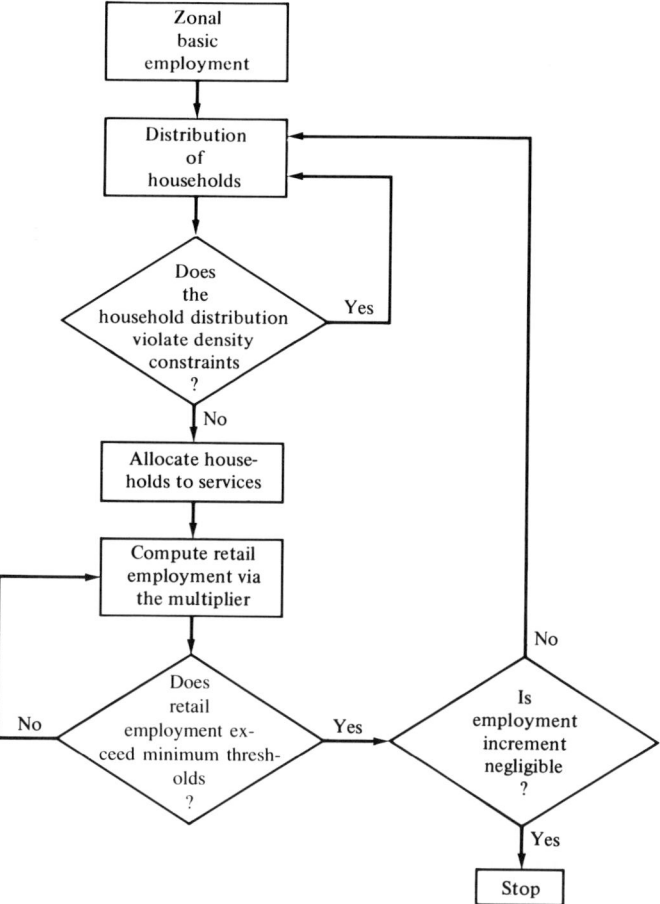

Figure 6-2 Lowry model flowchart.

engages in an iterative solution procedure such as the one shown in Fig. 6-2. Garin also developed an equation to directly solve for the final total employment distribution (and hence the final residential population distribution as well), thus obviating the need for an iterative procedure. Implicit in these findings is a demonstration that the Lowry model is a static model whose predictions are entirely determined by the assumed basic employment distribution, the allocation functions, and a few key system parameters. That is, the way in which the iterative procedure shown in Fig. 6-2 appears to dynamically "grow" the city is entirely illusory and in no way truly dynamic or causal. Rather, it simply represents a mechanical, iterative procedure for computing the static "equilibrium" solution.

The Lowry model can be made "quasi-dynamic" by adding increments of basic employment over time to the existing distributions, thereby "building" the city over the forecast period rather than simply using the horizon year totals to generate a "one-

Table 6-2 The Lowry model equations

Land use

$$A_j = A_j^U + A_j^B + A_j^R + A_j^H \quad (6\text{-}3a)$$

Retail sector

$$E^k = a^k N \quad (6\text{-}3b)$$

$$E_j^k = b^k \left(\sum_{i=1}^{n} \frac{c^k N_i}{T_{ij}^k} + d^k E_j \right) \quad (6\text{-}3c)$$

$$E^k = \sum_{j=1}^{n} E_j^k \quad (6\text{-}3d)$$

$$E_j = E_j^B + \sum_{k=1}^{m} E_j^k \quad (6\text{-}3e)$$

$$A_j^R = \sum_{k=1}^{m} e^k E_j^k \quad (6\text{-}3f)$$

Household sector

$$N = f \sum_{j=1}^{n} E_j \quad (6\text{-}3g)$$

$$N_j = g \sum_{i=1}^{n} \frac{E_i}{T_{ij}} \quad (6\text{-}3h)$$

$$N = \sum_{j=1}^{n} N_j \quad (6\text{-}3i)$$

Constraints

$$E_j^k \geq Z^k \quad \text{or} \quad E_j^k = 0 \quad \text{for all } j, k \quad (6\text{-}3j)$$

$$N_j \leq Z_j^H A_j^H \quad (6\text{-}3k)$$

$$A_j^R \leq A_j - A_j^U - A_j^B \quad (6\text{-}3l)$$

Variables

A = area of land (thousands of square feet)
E = employment (number of persons)
N = population (number of households)
T = index of trip distribution
Z = constraints

Superscripts and subscripts

U = unusable land
B = basic sector
R = retail sector
H = household sector
k = class of establishments within retail sector ($k = 1, \ldots, m$)
i,j = tracts or zones within region ($i,j = 1, \ldots, n$)

Unspecified functions and coefficients are represented by lowercase letters (a, b, c, d, e, f, g).

Source: Lowry [1964].

shot" forecast. It should be noted, however, that unless the model contains other factors (such as density constraints) which might be sensitive to the sequencing of these employment increments (and thus yield different horizon year forecasts depending on the order and magnitude of the increments), the incremental approach will yield the same horizon year forecast as the one-shot approach. Also note that the incremental approach implicitly assumes that all previously allocated employment and residential population remains fixed in place—clearly an important assumption given that a significant percentage of the North American urban population move their residences and/or their place of employment each year.

Aside from the very important consideration of the static nature of the model, at least three other major issues exist with respect to the Lowry model. First, the division of employment into basic and retail is conceptually interesting and important in that it permits prediction of at least some of the employment distribution to be "endogenized" within the model. In practical terms, however, it creates two major difficulties: the modeler must explicitly define what types of employment belong to each of the two groups, and the modeler must be able to predict—by zone—the basic employment distribution for the forecast year (or the zonal increments in basic employment if the incremental approach is adopted). This latter problem is not unique to the Lowry model. Virtually all land use forecasting models assume exogenously supplied employment forecasts of one form or another, although the Lowry model is perhaps more demanding in its requirements than many (recall that EMPIRIC, for instance, only requires a forecast of the total employment for each category considered for the urban region as a whole, rather than for each zone within that region).

Second, the Lowry model is clearly only as good as the allocation submodels used to distribute workers to residences and residences to shopping areas. The original Lowry model used an extremely crude allocation formula (i.e., Eq. 6-3c). Considerable work has been done in Great Britain [Batty, 1972; Wilson, 1974] and, more recently, in the United States [Putman, 1978] on the application of entropy models (see Sec. 7-4-2 for a description of entropy models) to the Lowry modeling framework, with the objective of providing a theoretically sounder, statistically estimable allocation procedure. Despite these advances, problems remain in that, as will be discussed in Sec. 7-4-2, these types of models are inherently *descriptive* in nature, while their *predictive* capabilities (which is what is required within the Lowry model) are uncertain at best.

Third, the Lowry model ignores the entire issue of the market for land and buildings; that is, the demand, supply, and price of land and buildings, which are central to the allocation of people and firms over space. Aside from some simple (and typically nonbinding) constraints, people and firms are allowed by the model to locate "at will" over a flat, featureless plain. Thus, the model implicitly assumes that the supply of buildings perfectly adjusts to demand and that price is irrelevant to the process.

Even with these problems, many of the spatial distribution models in use today are based on the overall approach outlined in the Lowry model. One of the more recent models used to distribute residential population is called the disaggregated residential allocation model (DRAM) [Putman, 1978, 1981]. The equation that DRAM uses as the basis for distributing households among individual zones is

$$N_i = \sum_j E_j \frac{W_i C_{ij} \exp(\beta C_{ij})}{\sum_i W_i C_{ij} \exp(\beta C_{ij})} \qquad (6\text{-}4)$$

where N_i = number of households (by type) in zone i
E_j = employment in zone j
C_{ij} = travel time (or cost) between zones i and j
W_i = attractiveness of zone i

The attractiveness of a zone is related to land availability and income characteristics and is of the form

$$W_i = V_i^a \times P_i^b \times R_i^d \times N_{1,i}^q \times N_{2,i}^r \times N_{3,i}^s \times N_{4,i}^t \qquad (6\text{-}5)$$

where
V_i = vacant, buildable land in zone i
P_i = one plus the fraction of buildable land in zone i which has already been built upon
R_i = residential land in zone i
$N_{k,i}$ = one plus the fraction of employed residents of zone i in the kth income quartile
a,b,d,q,r,s,t = empirically derived parameters

This model was developed to improve upon earlier Lowry-type models. Specifically, DRAM provides a more sophisticated calibration procedure, allows the analyst to disaggregate by income group, and permits the full integration of this model with transportation system models [Turner and Putman, 1981].

6-2-3 Simulation Models: The NBER Model and CAM

Simulation models are characterized by their explicitly dynamic nature and their attempt to replicate (albeit in a simplified and abstract way) key events which occur over time. That is, simulation models attempt to replicate the evolution of an urban area over several time periods as the outcome of a series of interrelated actions by the people and firms which constitute that urban area. By their very definition, such models are extremely complicated, large, and data-hungry. They typically consist of a relatively large number of submodels, each of which deals with one aspect or actor within the system, interconnected by the information about the urban system which they share.

The typical structure of a simulation model can be characterized as consisting of a set of information (current population, employment and building stock characteristics, etc.) at some basic time period stored in a central data bank. Submodels characterizing the actors and their interrelationships draw upon this information as a basis for their actions (residential location shifts, employment changes by zone, building stock adjustments, etc.). Given these actions, the data base is updated so that at the end of the time period, there exists a new system state which serves as the basis for the decisions to be made in the next simulation time period. Finally, from time to time exogenous changes may be imposed on the system (changes in migration rates into and out of the region, changes in total regional employment levels, or changes in interest rates).

The best known urban system simulation model is probably the National Bureau of Economic Research (NBER) model. A lesser-known but relatively successful model is the community analysis model (CAM) developed by the MIT–Harvard University Center for Urban Studies in association with the U.S. Department of Housing and Urban Development. Each of these models is discussed briefly below.

The NBER model[1]. A major criticism of the models discussed thus far has been their lack of economic content. Noting that the theoretical and behavioral foundation of most urban simulation models was quite weak, NBER set out to develop a simulation model that was explicitly based on microeconomic concepts of the utility-maximizing household and the profit-maximizing firm. The model was originally developed by using the city of Detroit as a test site, but has undergone further developmental work with data from Pittsburgh, San Francisco, Minneapolis, and Washington, D.C. The NBER model identifies three main actors: *employers* who locate their industries in given zones within the region and who employ given numbers of employees; *households* who supply labor to the employers and who buy (or rent), maintain, and sell (or vacate) housing; and *suppliers of housing* who build (renovate, maintain, etc.) and sell (or rent out) housing. Households can only locate in a zone if vacant housing of a suitable type is available. The price of housing depends upon the competition for the available housing. In turn, the demand for and supply of housing over time depend, among other factors, on price.

Figure 6-3 displays the major submodels in the NBER system. Briefly, these are:

1. *Employment location submodel.* Employment changes for each of nine industrial groups for each zone in the region are specified for each time period. In the Detroit prototype, all employment data were exogenously supplied. In later versions of the model, the "retail" components were endogenously determined in a Lowry-like procedure. This employment by occupation types is then transformed into household types[2] (in the Detroit model, 72 household types—characterized by their size, income, and age and education of the household head—were used).
2. *Movers submodel.* "Movers" consist of in- and out-migrants for the region, newly formed households (resulting from children moving out, divorce, etc.), dissolved households (because of death, reconsolidation of families, etc.), and intraregional movement of households from one location to another. In general, simple "moving rates" are used to generate the various classes of movers.
3. *Demand allocation submodel.* This submodel predicts the probability that a household of a certain type with a worker employed in a given zone will wish to

---

[1] For a detailed description of this model, see Ingram et al. [1972].
[2] The model assumes that only one-worker households exist and that all households have an employed person; that is, no "unemployed household" or multiworker households exist.

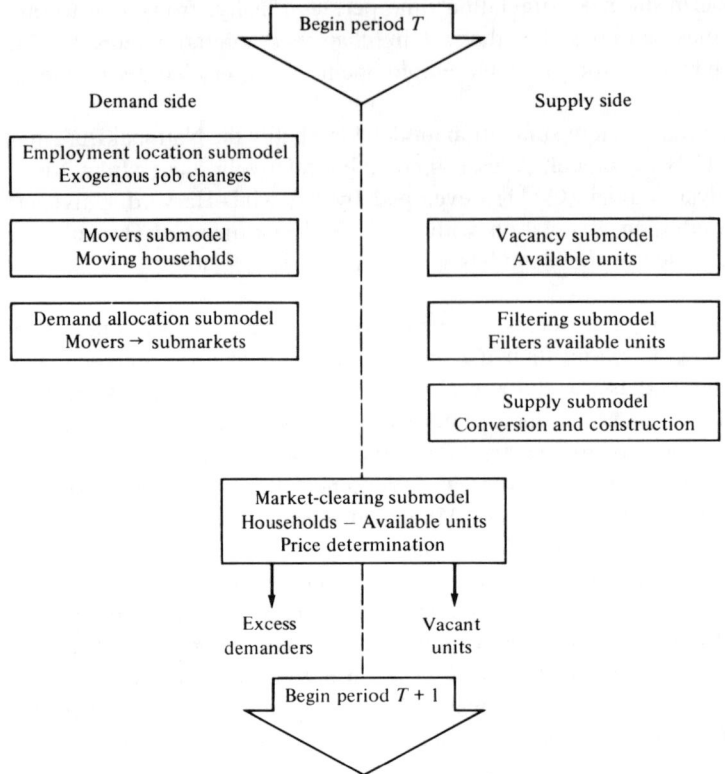

Figure 6-3 The National Bureau of Economic Research (NBER) model. *(Ingram, Kain, and Ginn [1972].)*

live in a housing unit of a given type (in Detroit, 27 housing types were used). The model builders had considerable difficulty in developing this submodel for two major reasons. First, they had difficulty finding a suitable functional form for the submodel. Initially, they tried to use a linear probability model, but the results failed to adequately fit the observed data. Later, a disaggregate logit model (for a description of logit models, see Sec. 7-5) was employed, with somewhat greater success [Quigley, 1976]. Second, and ultimately more troublesome, the decision to predict choice of housing type independent of and prior to choice of location made it very difficult to associate a price with that housing type. That is, it is in principle simple to define a "generalized price" GP_{ijkh} for a housing unit of type k, located in a residential zone i, for a household of type h, whose worker is employed in zone j as

$$GP_{ijkh} = P_{ik} + C_{ij} + V_h \times T_{ij} \tag{6-6}$$

where P_{ik} = price of housing type k in zone i
C_{ij} = dollar cost of commuting from zone i to zone j
T_{ij} = travel time between zone i and zone j
V_h = value of time for a worker in household type h

However, what is required in the demand allocation model is GP_{jkh}, the generalized price which is *not* conditional on the location i of the housing unit. This implies some sort of "average" or "typical" generalized price. Several such variables were tried, with mixed success. Finally, the generalized prices for all zones were ranked, and the 5th percentile generalized price (for a given household type) was used as a measure of GP_{jkh}.

4. *Vacancies submodel.* This is essentially a "bookkeeping" procedure which simply keeps track of the vacant units by type and zone that were left over from previous time periods or were vacated by movers during the current time period being simulated.
5. *Filtering submodel.* "Filtering" consists of upgrading (through maintenance or renovation) or downgrading (through a lack thereof) the quality of the housing stock, and hence shifting the existing housing stock from one category to another. At any point in time, the owners know the prices which they can receive for their housing if they upgrade, downgrade, or maintain the status quo, as well as the costs associated with each of these actions, and thus they can choose the action which maximizes their profits. In order to reduce the amount of bookkeeping involved, as well as to attenuate the large fluctuations in the quality of the housing stock which would otherwise result, the model only allows vacant units to be filtered in any given time period.
6. *Supply submodel.* This submodel generates the construction of new housing and the conversion of existing housing (conversion consists of changing the housing *type,* for example from a single-family to a multiple-family dwelling, as opposed to filtering, which consists of changing the housing *quality*) during each time period. Given that the prices and costs for all construction and conversion options in all zones are known, a linear program could be written and solved to determine the profit-maximizing level of activity, subject to zoning and other constraints (for example, that only a portion of vacant land in any given zone can be developed in any one time period and that the total amount supplied cannot exceed the total forecasted demand plus a normal vacancy rate). In practice, the size and cost of the linear program involved proved to be prohibitive. The program was "approximated" by a procedure in which activities were ranked according to their profit-to-cost ratio, and then activity levels consistent with the system constraints were chosen, beginning with the ones with the highest profit-to-cost ratios.
7. *Market clearing submodel.* This submodel links the demand and supply sides of the housing market by assigning households demanding housing of given types (as determined by the demand allocation submodel) to available units in specific zones (as determined by the vacancy, filtering, and supply submodels). This assignment is accomplished through the use of a linear program for each housing market (i.e., each housing category) which allocates households to locations so as to minimize the systemwide average cost of commuting, subject to the constraints that the number of households allocated to each zone does not exceed the number of vacancies available in that zone and that all households are allocated to a location. (In order to ensure that this constraint is satisfied in the case of excess demand, a dummy location "HOTEL" is included with very high travel costs; households assigned to HOTEL in one time period show up as unlocated people in the next

iteration.) Prices in the next time period are computed as a weighted average of the current time period's prices and the "shadow prices" defined by the linear program's dual variables.

The NBER model can be criticized on many counts. Its data requirements are enormous, and it is a very expensive model to run. Like the Lowry model, it makes strong assumptions about the ability to exogenously estimate detailed employment characteristics. Furthermore, the basis of some individual submodels is suspect, most notably the structuring of the whole demand side of the model, in which it is assumed that households choose the type of housing they want and then search for a neighborhood in which to locate. Considerable empirical evidence suggests that, if anything, the process is the reverse: people identify a neighborhood (or small set of neighborhoods) within which they wish to live and then evaluate the housing stock available within this neighborhood [Hall, 1980]. Alternatively, a simultaneous search over housing type and location certainly is not implausible [Lerman, 1976]. In addition, the assumption that households choose their residential location so as to minimize the average commuting costs for the urban region as a whole simply does not appear to be credible.

Despite these criticisms, the model has been discussed in some detail here in order to illustrate the complexity and the difficulties inherent in attempting to simulate an urban region's housing market in a reasonably comprehensive fashion. In Sec. 6-1 we raised the issues of the dynamic nature of urban areas; the need to address the demand, supply, and market-clearing processes in order to understand the evolution of urban land-use patterns; and the need to explicitly consider the major actors at work within urban regions. The NBER model's major contribution to the field is its comprehensive attempt to address these issues in a pragmatic yet relatively theoretically rich way.

The community analysis model (CAM)[3]. Figure 6-4 compares the major submodels of CAM with the NBER submodels discussed above. At this level of abstraction, the differences between the two models appear to be rather small, the addition of a few extra submodels and the reordering of some submodels in CAM aside. The major differences between the two models lie in what is "inside the boxes" and in the theoretical constructs used to generate the submodels.

In contrast to the explicitly "disciplinary" approach adopted by the NBER in which a model was formulated based on economic theory and then calibrated with observed data, the builders of CAM adopted a far more inductive approach in that they first started with as comprehensive a time-series data base as they could obtain (in this case, for New Haven, Connecticut) and then experimented with a wide range of models in an attempt to understand and explain the trends and the interactions which they observed. Central to achieving this understanding was the identification of a set of *actors* responsible for the major decisions affecting the urban area, their *roles* (i.e., what decisions or actions were available to them), what *information* they used in

---

[3] For a detailed discussion of this modeling approach, see Birch et al. [1974]; Birch [1976].

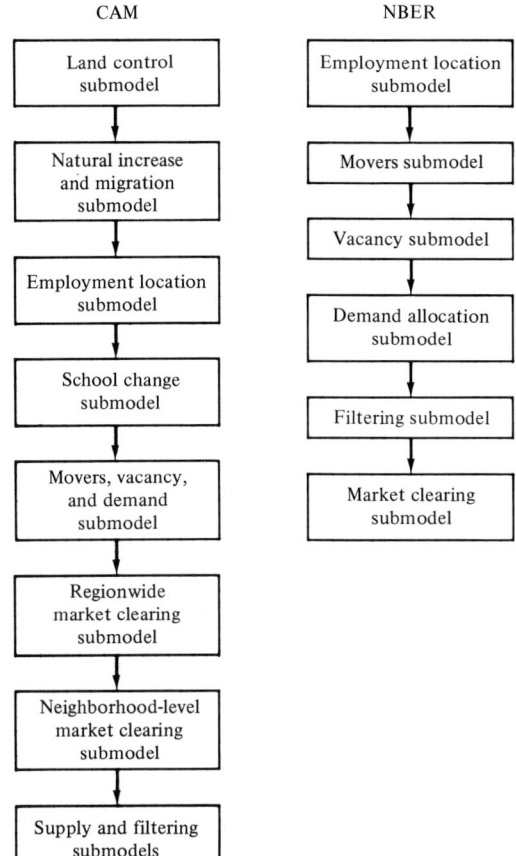

Figure 6-4 Comparison of CAM and NBER models. (*Birch [1976].*)

making these decisions, and how to best *characterize* these actors. Table 6-3 presents the 11 actors ultimately chosen, the decisions for which they are responsible, the variables used to characterize them, and the major variables or determinants influencing their decision making. Points to note from this table include:

1. Both *households* and *individuals* enter the model, reflecting the fact that some decisions (e.g., where and in what type of house to live) are made by the household as a whole, whereas others are more properly considered as being made by the individual concerned (e.g., whether to go to school or get a job). This implies the need to be able to relate households and individuals to one another (or to "map" them onto one another) in order to keep track of how individual decisions affect the households in which the individuals live and vice versa.
2. Any one individual in an urban area may well play several roles (i.e., represent several different actors) simultaneously. For example, in addition to being a

Table 6-3 Actors within the community analysis model

Actor	Decision	Stratification	Major determinants
Household	To move within region	Age By ethnic or racial background By education	Life cycle Race Educational level Racial change Forced moves
	Choice of neighborhood		Life cycle Race Educational level Available units Social class of neighborhood Job accessibility of neighborhood Location of neighborhood Racial transition of neighborhood
	Choice of unit		Housing preferences Financial capability Availability of mortgage credit
	Migrate in and out of region		Employment opportunities Unemployment Income levels in region Educational mix in region City size Proximity to other areas
Individual	Have children	Age By ethnic or racial background By education	Life cycle Race Level of education
	Obtain education		Ethnic/racial background
	Join workforce		Age Ethnic/racial background Educational level Growth rate of local economy
Homeowner	Setting selling price of home	Age By education By price of home By ethnicity	Potential demand relative to available vacancies
	Investing in home maintenance		Characteristics of homeowner (e.g., housing preferences) Characteristics of housing unit (e.g., age of unit) Characteristics of neighborhood (e.g., average housing condition)

Table 6-3 (*continued*)

Actor	Decision	Stratification	Major determinants
Landlord	Setting rent levels on apartments	Rent level of apartments	Potential demand relative to available vacancies
	Investing or disinvesting in maintenance for apartments (including abandoning apartments)		Characteristics of tenants (e.g., age, education, ethnicity) Characteristics of apartment (e.g., age of unit) Characteristics of neighborhood (e.g., ethnic composition)
Builder	Constructing single-family homes under contract	Contract vs. speculative Type of unit (tenure and price)	Vacancy rate in submarket and region Availability of suitable vacant land Availability of credit
	Constructing apartments under contract		Absorption rate in submarket Excess demand in submarket Vacancy rate in submarket and region Zoning restrictions Availability of suitable vacant land Availability of credit
	Constructing single-family homes and apartments speculatively		Assessment of prospects for future demand in the neighborhood according to demand in nearby areas, rate of growth in nearby areas Availability of suitable land Availability of credit
Lender	Lending for new construction and home mortgages	None	Security of loans: depends on characteristics of loan applicant (e.g., age, ethnicity, education), characteristics of housing unit (e.g., condition), and characteristics of neighborhood (e.g., ethnic composition, average housing condition) Availability of funds
	Refusing to grant loans in certain neighborhoods		Risk attached to loans: depends on characteristics of neighborhood (e.g., ethnic composition, average housing condition)

Table 6-3 (*continued*)

Actor	Decision	Stratification	Major determinants
Insurer	Insuring homes and apartments	None	Expected profit (excess of premium revenue over insurance payments): depends on characteristics of insurance applicant (e.g., age, ethnicity, education), characteristics of housing unit (e.g., condition), and characteristics of neighborhood (e.g., ethnic composition, average housing condition)
	Refusing to write insurance in certain neighborhoods		Expected loss (excess of insurance payments over premium revenue): depends on characteristics of neighborhood (e.g., ethnic composition, average housing condition)
Zoning board member	Determining permissible land uses, granting variances	None	Density preferences of existing residents of neighborhood Extent of commercial activity in a neighborhood
Employer	Location of a new firm Expansion of employment Relocation Contraction of employment Closing a firm's operations	Major SIC code divisions	Vacant land in a neighborhood Characteristics of the population of a neighborhood Population density Proportion of jobs in a given industry located in a given area, called job concentration Proportion of jobs in a given area which are in a given industry, called job specialization The tenure and value of occupied housing units
School superintendent	Modify school characteristics	None	Residents' reactions to school characteristics Court decisions
Resident	Support (or not) existing school policies	Age By ethnic or racial background By education	Percent minority in school Teachers' qualifications in school Public image of school Curriculum in school Class size in school Resident's attitude toward education Social class of resident

Source: Birch, [1976].

member of a household, the individual may also be a home owner, a resident, an employer, or a landlord.
3. While several of its actors are the same as those in the NBER model (e.g., households and builders), CAM possesses a far richer "cast of characters" than any other model discussed to this point. These additional actors are considered necessary in order to adequately represent the key roles which factors such as school quality, insurance rates, and availability of capital play in urban development.

Figure 6-5 shows how the various actors interact within the model. Boxes indicate the various submodels in which the actors' decisions are actually simulated, ovals represent key pieces of information used and/or generated by these submodels, and circles represent the key descriptors of the "system state" (distributions of jobs, households, housing, etc.) as they exist at any point in time. As is illustrated by Table 6-3 and Fig. 6-5, the key strength of CAM lies in its detailed representation of the actors and their interrelationships. The actual decision models tend, in general, to be relatively simple (simple interaction rates, simple probability models, etc.).

The hypothesis which underlies this modeling approach is that behavior is complex because of the multitude of actors, motives, and interactions involved. Once one has sorted out this "tangled web" of actors and their interactions and has done a reasonably good job of accurately identifying and characterizing these actors and interactions, the behavior of any given actor is relatively straightforward to represent and relatively constant over time. This modeling approach can be contrasted to that of the NBER model (and most other models discussed in this book) in which essentially the opposite approach is taken: a limited number of actors are considered but a relatively complicated decision function is assumed in order to try to explain the complex set of observed actions.

After its initial development in New Haven, CAM was applied to Houston, Texas, and then subsequently to Dayton, Ohio; Worcester, Massachusetts; Rochester, New York; and Charlotte, North Carolina. Although not explicitly developed for use in transportation studies, CAM was used in all six cities in a wide range of policy applications.

6-2-4 Scenarios

An alternative to the use of mathematical forecasting techniques such as the ones discussed in the previous subsections is the use of future *scenarios* constructed on the basis of professional judgment, current or expected trends, and so on. If this approach is adopted, it is typical to construct several scenarios, representing the expected range in likely future states.

Although not heavily based on analytical technique, scenario analysis can still be a complex process. The first task is to identify the key dimensions that are likely to affect future land use. This requires the planner to develop a conceptual model of the land development process and of its interaction with physical, economic, sociological, and political forces. For example, it could be hypothesized that future land development could be significantly impacted by the state of the economy (e.g., availability of

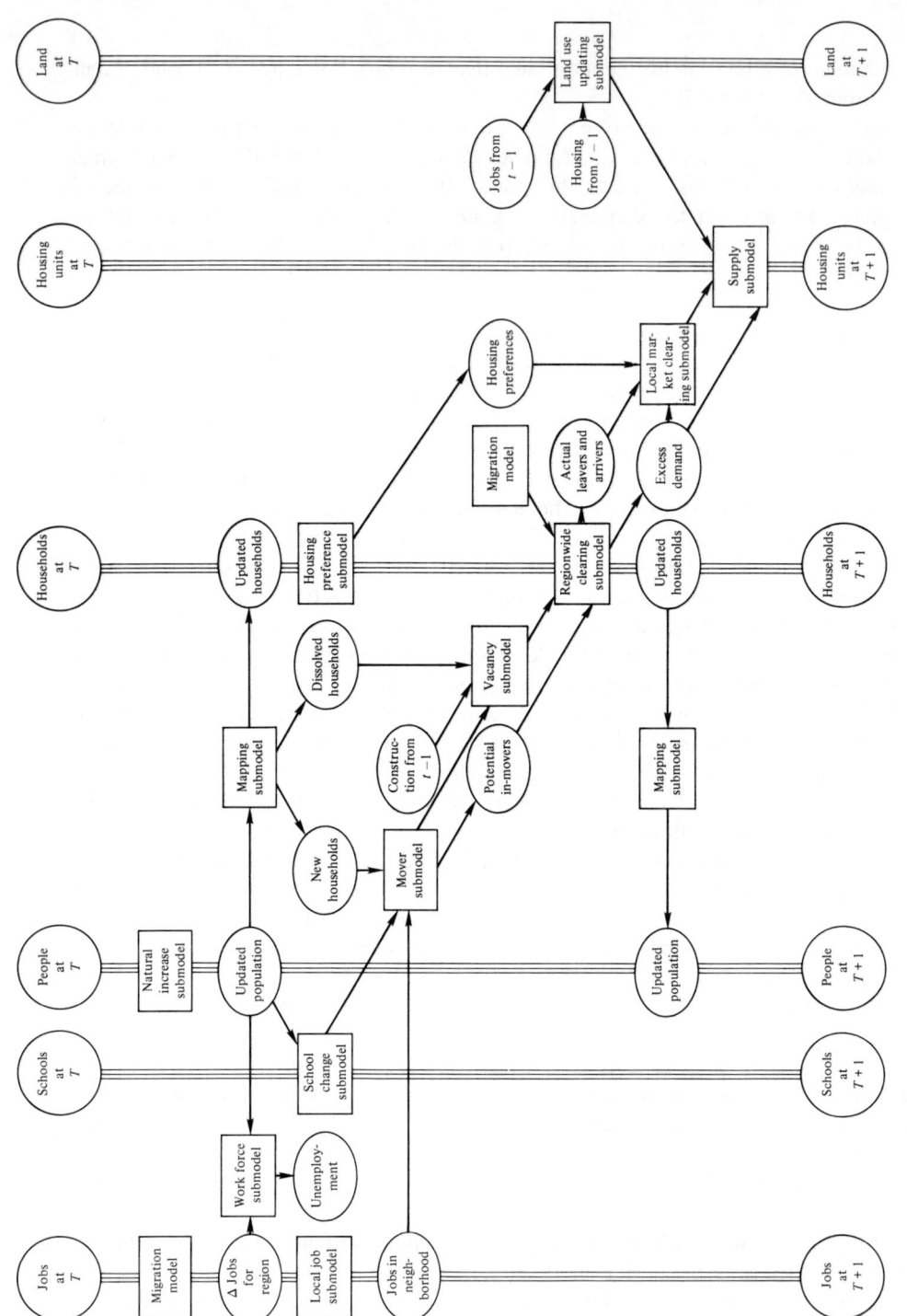

Figure 6-5 Information flow in CAM. (*Birch [1976]*.)

capital), the types of transportation technologies likely to exist, the socioeconomic characteristics of urban residents, the availability and price of energy, etc. Once the key variables have been identified, the next task is to determine how to predict the range in their future values. One of the most common approaches is to convene a conference of "experts" or "futurists" having some knowledge of past trends and future prospects. The purpose of this conference is to describe likely value ranges for the dimensions identified earlier. These ranges can then be used to identify land use patterns given the different values of the dimensions, with the resulting land use scenarios serving as alternative sources of land use information that can be input into subsequent analysis and evaluation. Because one does not know which scenario will occur, the components of the analyzed changes to the transportation system which work well under all or most of the scenarios become the best candidates for adoption, all else being equal.

Advantages of the use of scenarios include:

1. They are inexpensive and quick to construct relative to model forecasts.
2. Because they are less costly, a wider range of future states can typically be examined than in the case of model forecasts.
3. They often represent the only technique available when lack of data and/or theory renders model forecasting impossible.
4. They may encourage the analyst to think deeply and imaginatively about future system states and interactions in a way which the more mechanistic process of model forecasting may not.

On the other hand, scenario-based analyses are often viewed as being more hypothetical or conjectural in nature (and hence somewhat more suspect) than model-based forecasts. Furthermore, they may not be able to achieve the internal consistency and level of quantitative detail typically achievable by model forecasts.

A good example of the use of scenarios in urban activity system analysis is provided by a transit system planning process used in southeastern Wisconsin (Milwaukee) [Southeastern Wisconsin Regional Planning Commission, 1981]. As shown in Fig. 6-6, planners developed scenarios of alternative "futures," relating the growth of the urban area in each scenario to four external factors: energy cost and availability, energy-related technology, population lifestyles, and national economic activity. Two alternative future scenarios were developed for each factor, resulting in a range of regional growth estimates. Centralized and decentralized land use plans were then developed for each scenario. Table 6-4 illustrates the different assumptions that were made with regard to the key external factors and their impact on the land use plans.

6-2-5 Summary Comments

Of all the steps in transportation systems analysis, the representation of the urban activity system is perhaps the most important and yet the most complex. The four types of urban activity models discussed above illustrate the major approaches that have been

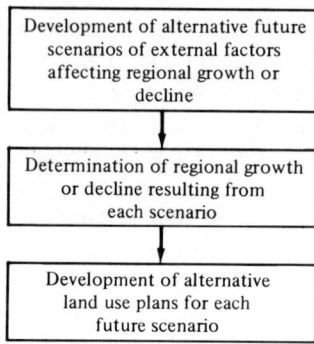

Figure 6-6 Scenario analysis for transit system planning in Milwaukee. (*Southeastern Wisconsin Regional Planning Commission, [1981]*.)

used by transportation and land use planners to represent the land use activities in an urban area, a prerequisite to the analysis of the demand for transportation. It is important to note that not only are the results of urban activity modeling used in transportation analysis, but that transportation is an important input variable in most urban activity models. The transportation component of the models relates to the influence of accessibility on the location decisions of households and other actors in an urban area, with the level of complexity in the representation of accessibility differing from one model to the next.

Although an important component of transportation analysis, urban activity modeling has often been viewed with skepticism by many transportation planners. Such modeling has usually required large amounts of data, extensive use of computers, and the expenditure of significant planning resources [Lee, 1973]. The result of this disenchantment with large-scale models, in combination with generalized trends within the planning process toward short-range planning (and hence, shorter-run, more limited analyses) was an abandonment, by and large, of large-scale land use modeling efforts during the 1970s.

Despite this rather gloomy history, the large-scale modeling era is not without its contributions. Many models were operationalized and provided input into comprehensive transportation studies, particularly in Great Britain [Batty, 1972] where relatively simple versions of the Lowry model were used quite successfully in a number of regional and subregional transportation studies (where "successfully" means that the models generated population and employment forecasts which were deemed to be acceptable and usable by the planners and decision makers concerned). Recent research on the theoretical foundations of land use modeling, and on the techniques themselves, has produced some models that can be more easily incorporated into the transportation planning process. Models such as DRAM have been used with some success in several cities (e.g., Seattle and Kansas City) and have provided planners with important estimates of urban growth and the location of this growth in an urban area. The challenge to transportation planners is to develop and use an analysis approach that better integrates land use and transportation planning (see Fig. 6-7).

Table 6-4 Alternative futures: Key external factors, attendant regional change, and land use plans

Key external factor	Moderate growth scenario	Stable or declining growth scenario
Energy		
The future cost and availability of energy, particularly of petroleum	Oil price to converge with world oil price, which will increase at 5 percent annual rate to $72 per barrel in the year 2000 (1979 dollars)	Oil price to converge with world oil price, which will increase at 2 percent annual rate to $39 per barrel in the year 2000 (1979 dollars)
	Petroleum-based motor fuel to increase to $2.30 per gallon by the year 2000 (1979 dollars)	Petroleum-based motor fuel to increase to $1.50 per gallon by the year 2000 (1979 dollars)
	Assumes some potential for major and continuing disruptions in oil supply	Assumes no major or continued disruptions in oil supply
The degree to which energy conservation measures are implemented, particularly with respect to the automobile	Low degree of conservation in all sectors, resulting in increase in energy use of 3 percent	High degree of conservation in all sectors, resulting in increase in energy use of 2 percent or less
	Automobile fuel efficiency of 27.5 miles per gallon	Automobile fuel efficiency of 32 miles per gallon

Table 6-4 (*continued*)

Key external factor	Moderate growth scenario	Stable or declining growth scenario
Population lifestyles		
The degree to which the changing role of women affects the composition of the labor force	Female labor force increases to 50 to 55 percent, and total labor force participation is 60 to 65 percent.	Female labor force increases to 65 to 70 percent, and total labor force participation is 70 to 75 percent.
The future change in fertility rates	A continuation of below-replacement-level fertility rates during the next decade, followed by an increase to replacement level by the year 2000	A continuation of below-replacement-level fertility rates to the year 2000
The future change in household sizes	Average household size stabilizes	Average household size continues to decline
Economic conditions		
The degree to which the region will be able to compete with other areas of the nation for the preservation and expansion of its economic base	Region is considered to have relatively high attractiveness and competitiveness.	Region is considered to have relatively low attractiveness and competitiveness.
The future change of real income	Per capita and household income increase envisioned as a result of the attractiveness and competitiveness of region, an increased proportion of the population being of work force age, and increased population labor force participation.	Per capita increase likely but no household income increase envisioned as a result of the lack of attractiveness and competitiveness of region, but increased proportion of the population is of work force age, and there is increased population labor force participation.

Attendant regional change	Moderate growth scenario	Stable or declining growth scenario
Population of the region in year 2000		
Size	2,219,300 persons	1,688,400 persons
Age distribution	29.2 percent—0–19 years of age 58.5 percent—20-64 years of age 12.3 percent—65 years of age or older	26.8 percent—0–19 years of age 60.6 percent—20-64 years of age 12.6 percent—65 years of age or older
Number of households	681,100 to 739,400	673,600 to 750,600
Household sizes	Average of 2.9 to 3.1 persons	Average of 2.2 to 2.5 persons
Economic activity of region in year 2000		
Employment	1,016,000 jobs	887,000 jobs
Structure	Manufacturing 32 percent Services 40 percent Other 28 percent	Manufacturing 30 percent Services 41 percent Other 29 percent
Personal income	$29,600 to $32,000 per household in 1979 dollars (38 to 50 percent increase over 1970, or a 1.1 to 1.4 percent annual rate of increase) $10,000 per capita in 1979 dollars (54 percent increase over 1970, or a 1.4 percent annual rate of increase)	$21,400 to $23,700 per household in 1979 dollars (0 to 11 percent increase over 1970, or a 0.0 to 0.3 percent annual rate of increase) $9,500 per capita in 1979 dollars (46 percent increase over 1970, or a 1.3 percent annual rate of increase)

Table 6-4 (continued)

Land use plan characteristics	Moderate growth scenario		Stable or declining growth scenario	
	Centralized plan	Decentralized plan	Centralized plan	Decentralized plan
Urban growth and density				
New urban residential land	Occurs primarily at medium residential densities along the periphery of, and outward from, existing urban centers	Occurs primarily at suburban residential densities in a diffused pattern in areas proximate to, and removed from, existing urban centers	Occurs primarily at medium residential densities along the periphery of and outward from, existing urban centers	Occurs primarily at suburban residential densities in a diffused pattern in areas proximate to, and removed from, existing urban centers
Urban density	Existing developed portions of Milwaukee County generally maintain residential density existing in 1970	Existing developed portions of Milwaukee may decrease in residential density between 1970 and 2000	Existing developed portions of Milwaukee County generally maintain residential density existing in 1970	Existing developed portions of Milwaukee may decrease in residential density between 1970 and 2000

Population distribution				
Milwaukee County	1,049,600 persons	898,500 persons	830,000 persons	700,000 persons
Percent change from 1970	− 0.4	−14.8	−21.3	−33.6
Percent change from 1978	10.0	− 5.8	−13.0	−26.6
Outlying counties (Ozaukee, Washington, Waukesha)	677,600 persons	786,700 persons	480,000 persons	605,000 persons
Percent change from 1970	93.8	125.0	37.2	73.1
Percent change from 1978	52.8	77.4	8.2	36.4
Employment distribution				
Milwaukee County	593,600 jobs	523,400 jobs	552,300 jobs	525,300 jobs
Percent change from 1970	16.2	2.4	8.1	2.8
Percent change from 1978	5.6	− 6.9	− 1.8	− 6.6
Outlying counties (Ozaukee, Washington, Waukesha)	231,400 jobs	274,800 jobs	181,900 jobs	206,900 jobs
Percent change from 1970	119.5	160.7	72.6	96.3
Percent change from 1978	63.6	94.3	28.6	46.3

Source: Southeastern Wisconsin Regional Planning Commission [1981].

210 URBAN TRANSPORTATION PLANNING

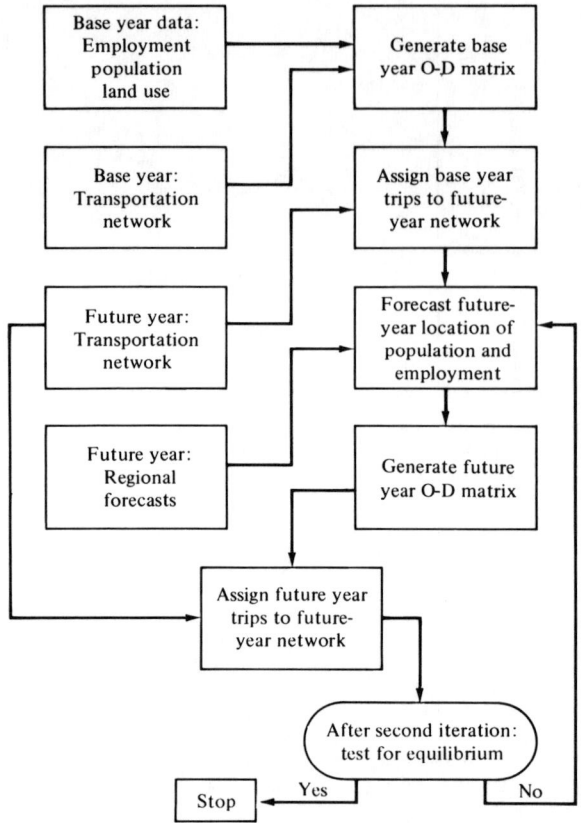

Figure 6-7 An integrated land use and transportation planning model. (*Putman* [*1978*].)

6-3 ASSESSMENT OF TRANSPORTATION IMPACTS ON THE URBAN ACTIVITY SYSTEM

Two major approaches exist for the assessment of transportation impacts on the urban activity system. One is the ex post evaluation of the impacts which implemented transportation policies and actions have had on the urban activity system. Section 2-2-4 presented several examples of such ex post assessments in its discussion of transportation–land use interactions, while Sec. 9-7 will discuss issues associated with ex post project evaluation in general. Perhaps the only further observation required here is that in all ex post evaluations, one is primarily interested in a *with* and *without* comparison (i.e., what has occurred which would not have occurred if the transportation system change had not been implemented, and vice versa), whereas what one almost inevitably observes is a *before* and *after* comparison (i.e., what existed before and after the system change), which need not be the same thing. While this is potentially troublesome in any ex post evaluation, it is perhaps particularly so in the assessment of urban activity system impacts, given the wide range of other factors (typically uncontrollable, in either a policy or an experimental design sense, and possibly even unobservable) which may be simultaneously changing and affecting the urban activity system. This problem would appear to represent the major reason why the record is still so unclear and why debate still goes on as to just what the impacts of even major transportation system improvements (e.g., subways and freeways) *really* are on urban activity systems.

The second form of impact assessment involves an attempt to predict impacts prior to project implementation as one part of the analysis phase of the planning process. Such a priori assessments generally involve the development of a model of the urban activity system (or the portion of that system which is of immediate interest within the analysis) which is sensitive to the proposed transportation system changes, and the use of this model to predict and compare expected future activity system states with and without implementation of each of the proposed transportation alternatives. Thus, a priori assessment is focused directly at the with and without level of analysis, although it can only estimate impacts by using forecasted (rather than "real") data.

The large-scale, "comprehensive" land use models discussed in the previous section are rarely used in impact assessment analyses because of their scale of analysis (which is generally too gross), their high cost and large data requirements, and, often, their insensitivity to the transportation policies of interest (for an example of how a large-scale model system was used in such a manner, see Putman, [1980]). Typically, smaller-scale models, specially developed for the specific problem of interest, are employed. It is therefore difficult to discuss impact assessment models in general terms. Rather than attempting to do so, the next subsection presents a case study of a specific impact assessment model which provides a good illustration of the state of the art, as well as highlights some of the issues and problems associated with this state of the art.

6-3-1 Transportation Control Plan Impacts on CBD Retailing Activity: The Denver Case[4]

The U.S. Clean Air Act of 1970 required metropolitan areas falling short of specified air quality standards to adopt transportation control plans (TCPs) to limit automobile emissions. Central business districts (CBDs) typically are among the areas targeted for such TCPs because of high concentrations of traffic, the inefficiency of traffic operations on congested streets, and the general availability of transit alternatives to the private automobile. TCP options for CBDs generally include policies that restrict automobile use (e.g., reduce available parking) and promote transit use (e.g., increase route frequencies). Such policies can potentially affect the accessibility of the CBD for retail shopping relative to other shopping areas in the metropolitan region (e.g., suburban shopping malls) and possibly endanger the viability of the CBD for retail activities.

---

[4] The discussion in this subsection is based on Kern and Lerman [1978].

In order to assess the potential impacts of TCP alternatives on CBD retail activity in Denver, two models for predicting CBD retail sales were developed: an "aggregate" model (which predicts aggregate zonal retail sales as a function of zonal characteristics) and a "disaggregate" model (which uses disaggregate or individual choice travel demand models to help predict zonal retail employment levels). The purpose of developing two models was to provide at least a partial check on the sensitivity of the analysis results to the choice of modeling method. That is, if the results obtained from the two models were substantially the same, then the analysts could feel reasonably confident that their predictions were not particularly dependent upon the assumptions and limitations inherent in their choice of technique (although other theoretical or data-related assumptions common to both models could, of course, still limit the validity of the results). Each of these models is summarized below, and then the results and implications of the overall analysis are discussed.

The aggregate model. Time and budget limitations necessitated the use of readily available data in the development of the impact assessment models. A time-series (1960 to 1970) data base, originally developed for the Denver version of the EMPIRIC model, was available to the model builders, and it was selected as the data base for the aggregate model. Thus, the definition of the variables available for use in the model and the zone system characterizing the study area were determined by this existing EMPIRIC data base.

The final version of the model, a simple linearized equation calibrated using ordinary least-squares regression, was

$$\log S_i^t = 3.238 + 0.271 \log \frac{C_i}{\overline{C}_j} + 0.585 \log S_i^{t-1} - 0.351 \log Y_i + 0.200 \log W_i \tag{6-7}$$

where S_i^t = retail sales in zone i during time period t

C_i = accessibility of zone i to households by auto

$$= \sum_{k=1}^{n} H_k f(t_{ik})$$

H_k = number of households in zone k

t_{ik} = travel time by auto to zone k from zone i

$\overline{C}_j$ = average accessibility of all shopping zones other than zone i to households

$$= \frac{1}{n-1} \sum_{\substack{k=1 \\ k \neq i}}^{n} C_k$$

$\dfrac{C_i}{\overline{C}_j}$ = "competitive accessibility" of zone i relative to all competing zones

Y_i = proportion of households in zone i with incomes in lowest 15 percent of regional income distribution

W_i = number of white-collar workers per acre in zone i

The model predicts the retail sales per acre in any zone i during a given time period t as a function of the zone's competitive accessibility, its sales per acre in the previous time period, and a pair of "control variables" (the proportion of low-income households living in the zone and the number of white-collar workers per acre employed within the zone). The model can be used to predict the impact of transportation system changes[5] (where these changes are represented in terms of changes in the competitive accessibility term) on a given zone's retail activity (where this activity is measured in terms of the zone's annual retail sales per acre).

The disaggregate model. Figure 6-8 presents the overall structure of the disaggregate model, which actually consists of a system of interconnected submodels. In the words of the model developers [Kern and Lerman, 1978]:

> The disaggregate model system treats retail employment activity as simultaneously determined with peoples' shopping choices. It is derived from some of the basic Lowry model concepts, but involves a much more sophisticated set of models than has been used previously. There are two relatively intuitive features of the model system. First, where retailers choose to locate and/or expand their activities depends on how many people will shop there; second, the decisions of individuals about where to shop are influenced by the level of service provided by the transportation system to various centers and the scale of retail activity at each center.

[5] In the original calibration of the model, two accessibility terms were included: the car term shown and a similar term for transit accessibility. The transit accessibility term, however, proved to be incorrectly signed (i.e., negative, indicating that an increase in accessibility by transit would cause a decrease in retail sales) and statistically insignificant. Given this result, the transit accessibility term was dropped from the final version of the model. Thus, the model is sensitive to auto system changes only.

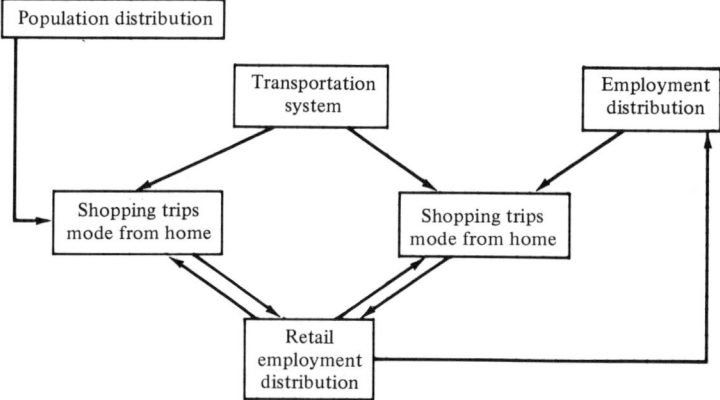

Figure 6-8 A disaggregate retail sales model system. (*Kern and Lerman [1978].*)

Note from Fig. 6-8 that shopping trips both from home and work were explicitly modeled within the system. The model is labeled "disaggregate" because disaggregate or individual choice models, which predict the choice probabilities associated with the trip-making alternatives faced by individuals living and working within the study area, are used to predict both the home-based and work-based shopping trip making (for a discussion of individual choice models, see Sec. 7-5). An appealing property of individual choice models is that, theoretically, a well-specified model should be transferable from one urban area to another. That is, a model calibrated in one city should be usable in another city, if properly applied. Because appropriate home-based and work-based shopping trip choice models did not exist in the Denver case and the time, budget, and data were not available to develop such models, existing models developed elsewhere were "borrowed" and, with only minor updating, were applied to Denver. Trip frequency, destination, and mode choice models for home-based shopping trips developed for San Francisco and for noon-hour, work-based shopping trips developed for Los Angeles were used. The detailed specifications of these models are not of immediate importance and have been reported elsewhere [Kern and Lerman, 1978]. The key point to note is that both models are sensitive to transportation service variables (for both transit and auto) and to the scale of retail activity in the competing destination zones (as measured by the zonal retail employment levels).

The third submodel in Fig. 6-8 represents retailers' responses (as measured by changes in zonal retail employment levels) to changes in the level of shopping trip making to each zone. Defining R_i as the retail employment in zone i and T_i as the total number of shopping trips (i.e., home-based plus work-based) to zone i, the model assumes that the change in retail employment ΔR_i from a base value R_i^0 is *directly proportional* to the change in shopping trips ΔT_i from the corresponding base value T_i^0 as given by

$$\frac{\Delta R_i}{R_i^0} = \frac{\Delta T_i}{T_i^0} \tag{6-8}$$

Since the shopping trip models depend on zonal retail employment as attraction variables, the changes in retail employment implied by Eq. (6-8) will generate further changes in the distribution of shopping trips, which in turn will cause further retail employment changes, and so on. The model iterates in a Lowry-like fashion until it finally converges (i.e., until the changes between iterations are arbitrarily small).

Analysis results and discussion of the model. Table 6-5 presents the aggregate and disaggregate models' predictions of the impacts of three possible transportation control measures:

1. Elimination of convenient parking spaces, forcing auto users to walk from their parking place to their shopping location an extra 2.5 minutes on average
2. The same policy as in (1), but with a 5-minute extra walk
3. A 5-minute reduction in transit waiting time for trips to or from the CBD (2.5-minute reduction for within-CBD trips, which already had a noon-time average waiting time of 5 minutes)

Table 6-5a Denver aggregate model results

One-way change in driver time	Long-run change in retail sales, full adjustment	Proportion of full adjustment taking place in first decade after change in level of service
+2.5 minutes	−17.5%	41.5%
+5.0 minutes	−32.7%	41.5%

Table 6-5b Denver disaggregate model results

Policy	Original number of trips	Response to change in level of service	% of original trips	Response to change in size of retail center	% of original trips	New number of trips	% of original trips
+2.5 minutes one-way walk time for parkers	53,000	−2917	−5.5	−12,869	−24.3	37,214	70.2
+5.0 minutes one-way walk time for parkers	53,000	−5259	−9.9	−17,355	−32.7	30,386	57.3
−5.0 minutes one-way wait time for transit riders	53,000	+425	+0.8	+2,271	+4.3	55,696	105.1

Source: Kern and Lerman [1978].

Table 6-5a shows that the aggregate model predicted a 17.5 percent and a 32.7 percent decline in downtown retail sales in response to the 2.5- and 5-minute increases in auto drivers' walk times, respectively, while the model predicted no change in retail sales for any type of transit improvement, for the simple reason that the model is insensitive to transit system changes. The aggregate model also predicted that 41.5 percent of these total changes would occur in the first decade after implementation of increased walk times. The disaggregate model's predictions (Table 6-5b) were even more extreme: 29.8 percent and 42.7 percent decreases in shopping trips to the downtown in response to the increases in auto drivers' walk times, while the improved transit wait times were predicted to generate only a 5.1 percent increase in trips. The disaggregate model results are further broken down into the response to the actual level of service change (as measured by the change generated in the first iteration of the model) and the response to subsequent changes in retail center size (as measured by subsequent iteration of the model). As can be seen from the table, the bulk of the change in trips results from the cumulative effect of the changing attractiveness of the retail center rather than from the transportation system change per se. Despite differences in methodology, therefore, the two techniques both indicated that the downtown retail sector appears to be highly sensitive to auto restriction measures, while at the same time it is at best marginally sensitive to transit system improvements.

Considerable space has been devoted to presenting this case study because it demonstrates the strengths and weaknesses of the state of the art. Strengths of the approach include:

1. A well-defined, limited problem is identified; that is, no attempt to "model the world" is made.
2. Appropriate modeling techniques are employed in that they are responsive to the policy issues being investigated, they make good use of available data and models, and they represent the technical state of the art.
3. Through the use of available data and transferable, "precalibrated" models, the modelers were able to focus the bulk of the analysis on the assessment of alternatives, rather than on data collection and model development.
4. The use of two techniques to analyze the problem provides a consistency check on the analysis results and provides extra freedom to the analyst to think imaginatively about the problem and to represent it in somewhat different ways.

Several weaknesses of the modeling state of the art are also apparent from this case study, however. One weakness relates to the concept of attractiveness. In the disaggregate model in particular, cumulative changes in shopping center attractiveness dominate the overall predictions of changes in retail activity. The model only incorporates attraction measures relating to center size (measured in terms of retail employees). Clearly, other factors also influence the attractiveness of locations for shopping activities, such as the type, quality, and price of goods being offered for sale; the quality of the neighborhood within which the stores are located; the safety, ease of movement, and quality of environment for pedestrians; and so on. There potentially exists a wide range of options for improving the attractiveness of an urban downtown that might well counterbalance the negative impact of loss of accessibility resulting from auto restrictions. Empirical evidence indicates, for instance, that under appropriate conditions a well-planned and implemented downtown "auto-restricted zone" can be of net benefit to the downtown in that the improved attractiveness and quality of experience in the area more than compensate for the access restrictions imposed [Weisbrod, 1982]. The analysis presented in this case study could not address such considerations, however, because the relationships involved are not well understood and are difficult to quantify and to express in mathematical functional form.

A second major difficulty lies in a lack of understanding of a key actor's decision-making process and of how to operationalize this process in model form. The actor referred to is the retailer, who decides whether or not to open a store or to go out of business, whether to grow or shrink in store size, whether to move to a new location, etc. In both models in the case study (including the disaggregate model), the retailer is treated in a very aggregate, ad hoc fashion. In the disaggregate model, for instance, the retail sector adjusts its employment level (and hence presumably its scale of operations, sales, etc.) directly in response to the number of shoppers—presumably through staff reductions, store closings, and stores moving to more profitable locations. While these responses are all possible, others are also conceivable, such as increasing advertising to try to enhance the shopping center's image and visibility, taking reduced profit margins (either through the higher inventory costs implicit in lower sales or through marking down prices in order to try to maintain sales levels), and cutting costs through reducing inventory levels, improving employee efficiency, etc. In all of the above examples, the retailer can respond in ways which may or may not result in changes in employment and, more important, which may or may not result in a net gain of customers and/or sales levels.

Because of practical and theoretical limitations, the model oversimplifies both the retailer's decision process and the factors which attract shoppers to particular retail locations. Moreover, it links these two simplified concepts together into a "vicious circle" in which a decrease in accessibility must lead to a decrease in retail employment, which, in turn, must lead to a decrease in attractiveness and a further decrease in shopping trips, and so on, ad infinitum. Thus, the results presented in Table 6-5 are essentially imbedded in the model through the adoption of these crucial assumptions. The validity of these assumptions is untestable unless one is able to include a more complex representation of attraction and retailer decision making into the model (so as to ascertain which factors tend to dominate under what range of conditions) and/or test the model against historical data in order to verify the extent to which it is able to replicate a real world response.

6-4 CHAPTER SUMMARY

1. An understanding of the urban activity system and its interaction with the urban transportation system is of importance to transportation planning because it is

required to predict the effects which changes in the urban activity system will have on future transportation demand, as well as to assess the impacts which proposed transportation system changes are likely to have on the activity system.
2. Activities occupy both land and buildings. Thus, the location of activities depends on both people's preferences or *demand* for certain locations and on the *supply* of suitable building stock at these locations. The interaction between demand and supply within the land use market results in a *bid rent* surface over the urban area which reflects the competition between activities for given locations.
3. In addition to price, factors affecting location choice include the *attractiveness* of the location for a given activity (as measured by a wide range of variables or characteristics) and the location's *accessibility* to other activities or groups of people.
4. Alternative approaches to forecasting future activity system states include:

   "Econometric" models in which a set of simultaneous, "structural" equations describing the urban activity system is specified a priori and then econometrically calibrated, usually using standard regression techniques
   "Heuristic" models which use a set of ad hoc, a priori reasonable rules for allocating activities to zones
   Simulation models in which decisions by key actors (e.g., decisions to construct, renovate, or demolish buildings; decisions to change job or residential locations) are explicitly simulated over time
   Scenarios or other judgmental techniques

5. An example of an econometric land use model is EMPIRIC, which was originally developed for Boston and subsequently applied to several other North American cities. EMPIRIC consists of a set of simultaneous linear equations which predict the change in a zone's share of the regional population (disaggregated by income group) and employment (disaggregated by industry type) which is expected to occur between two points in time, as a function of a range of exogenous and endogenous variables. The dynamic, simultaneous structure of EMPIRIC is conceptually appealing, but limitations in available data and operational theory somewhat restricted the choice of variables actually used in the model.
6. The Lowry model is a heuristic model which iteratively allocates households to residential locations and "retail" or "population-serving" workers to employment locations, based on an exogenously supplied distribution of "basic" employment. Lowry models in various forms and of varying levels of complexity have also been widely applied, although they too are subject to a number of criticisms, including lack of a dynamic structure, lack of a representation of urban land markets, and overdependence on inadequate activity allocation models.
7. Simulation models include the National Bureau of Economic Research (NBER) model and the community analysis model (CAM). Simulation models attempt to replicate the evolution of an urban area over several time periods as the outcome of a series of interrelated actions by the people and firms which comprise the urban

area. By their very definition, such models are extremely complicated, large, and data-hungry. They typically consist of a relatively large number of submodels, each of which deals with one aspect or actor within the system, interconnected by the information about the urban system which they share.
8. Most large-scale land use forecasting models have suffered from a number of problems relating to data intensiveness and cost of operation. Given these problems, in combination with the general trend in the field away from long-range planning in favor of short-range planning, large-scale, long-range forecasting models have largely been abandoned over the past decade in favor of smaller-scale, problem-specific models and analyses.
9. An example of a small-scale, problem-specific analysis is the assessment of the impact of transportation control plan policies on downtown retail activity in Denver. Two simple models were developed to analyze the problem, both of which made use of readily available data and/or previously calibrated models. Both models indicated that policies restricting auto access to the downtown would severely reduce retail activity in the downtown, while policies improving transit access would have, at best, marginal impact. The validity of these results can be questioned, however, because of several strong assumptions embedded within the analysis concerning retailers' and shoppers' responses to system changes that may overemphasize the sensitivity of retail activity to transportation system changes.
10. Despite their interconnection, transportation planning and land use planning are typically performed separately, usually by separate agencies and professionals. It can thus be institutionally cumbersome to perform integrated analyses and planning studies. Separation of the two functions, however, can result in "myopic" definitions of problems and their possible solutions and in potentially serious misspecifications in both transportation and land use models.
11. Regardless of whether one is doing long-range or short-range forecasting, urban activity system analysis is complicated by three major factors: the dynamic nature of the urban area; the complexity of urban behavior; and the need for good quality, detailed data.

QUESTIONS

1. Figure P6-1 presents a simple three-zone system. Using the basic Lowry model as given in Table 6-2 and the data provided in Table P6-1, compute the total employment for each of these zones after three iterations of the model. What were the changes in total employment for each zone between iterations 2 and 3? Are further iterations required to achieve convergence? Do not compute land area totals (you have insufficient data to do so), and do not worry about the residential density constraint. The retail employment threshold constraint, however, must be maintained.
2. In most land use models, the *supply* of building stock (residential buildings, store floor space, etc.) is ignored or otherwise assumed away. A notable exception to

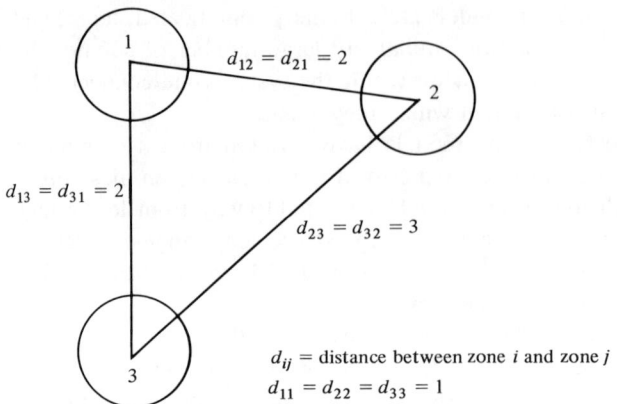

d_{ij} = distance between zone i and zone j
$d_{11} = d_{22} = d_{33} = 1$

Figure P6-1 Three-zone system.

Table P6-1 Data describing three-zone system

Basic employment data:	Impedance function:	Model parameters:
$E^B_1 = 100$	$T^k_{ij} = T_{ij} = d^2_{ij}$	$f = 1.0$ households/worker
$E^B_2 = 200$		
$E^B_3 = 100$		

	Two retail sectors: $k = 1$	2
	$a^k = 0.1$	0.05
	$c^k = 1$	1
	$d^k = 0.1$	0.5
	$Z^k = 10$	10

this generalization is the NBER model [Ingram et al., 1972]. Describe the modeling procedure used by NBER to represent the supply side of the housing market. In particular discuss:
(a) Model methodologies used
(b) "Information flow" within the models
(c) Treatment of time
(d) "Market clearing" (i.e., how the supply and demand sides are "brought together")
(e) Any other aspects of the procedure which you feel are relevant to its description or critique

3. Evaluate a large-scale land use forecasting model of your choice in terms of:
(a) Data requirements
(b) Likely development costs
(c) Theoretical assumptions
(d) Usefulness in practical planning applications
(e) Any other strengths or weaknesses of the model which are noteworthy

4. For an urban area with which you are familiar, trace its history of land use modeling. Was a large-scale modeling system developed and used? Is it still in use? If not, what techniques, if any, are being used? What is the current state of the data base? What are the implications of these findings for transportation planning in this urban area?
5. Figure P6-5 presents a three-zone region. Table P6-5 provides a travel time matrix for this system, the current distribution of retail floor space in the region, as well as retail floor space estimates for three future distributions, and the retail expenditures per residential zone for the current and future scenarios. A simple model for estimating the impact on retail sales of proposed shopping center development is given by Lakshmanan and Hansen [1965]:

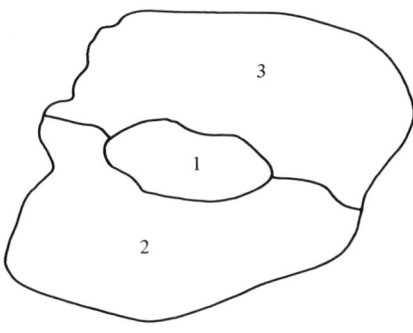

Figure P6-5 Three-zone system.

Table P6-5 Data for three-zone region

From	Travel times, min To			Zone	Retail floor space, ft² (1000s) Alt			
	1	2	3		0	1	2	3
1	10	20	25	1	3	3	3	3.25
2	20	15	30	2	0.5	1	1.75	1.75
3	25	30	20	3	0.5	1	1.25	1

Retail expenditure, $/year, (1000s)

Zone	Current, 0	Future, 1–3
1	100	100
2	50	100
3	100	150
Total	250	350

$$S_j = \sum_{i=1}^{n} \frac{C_i(F_j)^a(t_{ij})^{-b}}{\sum_{k=1}^{n}(F_k)^a(t_{ik})^{-b}}$$

where S_j = total expenditure at retail stores in zone j
C_i = total retail expenditures generated by residential zone i
F_j = retail floor space in zone j
t_{ij} = travel time between zones i and j
n = number of zones
a,b = model parameters

Using the Lakshmanan and Hansen model and the data provided, do the following:
 (a) Compute total retail expenditure at each retail center (i.e., in each zone) and the retail expenditure to floor space ratio at each center for the current and three future scenarios. Assume a travel time exponent of 2.0 and a floor space exponent of 1.0.
 (b) Assuming that the number of shopping trips made is directly proportional to retail expenditure, compute average shopping trip lengths for the four retail systems.
 (c) Determine which of the three alternative future systems you would recommend. Make explicit your criteria for this evaluation and the reasoning underlying your choice.
6. Transportation access is usually assumed to play a significant role in determining the viability of a given location for retail activity. The Kern and Lerman model discussed in Sec. 6-3-1 represents one attempt to model this interaction. If you were going to analyze the impacts of transportation policies (e.g., parking control, energy prices, transit incentives, downtown auto-restricted zones) on the commercial viability of the downtown area, how would you go about doing so? Write your answer in the form of a research proposal. This proposal should include:
 (a) Problem definition
 (b) Theoretical framework and hypotheses
 (c) Method of analysis
 (d) Data requirements
In your answer do not worry about time and budget constraints. Likely data problems (acquisition of data, quality of data, etc.), however, should be discussed if and when they are relevant.

REFERENCES

Alonso, W.: *Location and Land Use*, Harvard University Press, Cambridge, Mass., 1964.
Atherton, T. J., and E. S. Eder: "Impacts of CBD Fare-Free Transit on Retail Sales," Presented at the 61st annual meeting of the Transportation Research Board, Washington, D.C., January 1982.
Batty, M.: "Recent Developments in Land-Use Modelling: A Review of British Research," *Urban Studies*, vol. 9, no. 2, June 1972.
———: *Urban Modelling*, Cambridge University Press, London, 1976.

Ben-Akiva, M., and S. R. Lerman: "Disaggregate Travel Mobility Choice Models and Measures of Accessibility," in D. A. Hensher and P. R. Stopher (eds.), *Behavioural Travel Modelling*, Croom-Helm, London, 1979.

Berry, B., R. Tennant, B. Garner, and J. Simmons: *Commercial Structure and Commercial Blight*, Research paper 85, Dept. of Geography, University of Chicago, Chicago, Ill., 1963.

Birch, D.: "Overview of the Model," MIT, Dept. of Urban Studies, Cambridge, Mass., 1976.

―――, R. Atkinson, S. Sandstrom, and L. Stack: *The New Haven Laboratory: A Test-Bed for Planning*, Lexington Books, D.C. Heath, Lexington, Mass., 1974.

Brand, D., B. Barber, and M. Jacobs: "Technique for Relating Transportation Improvements and Urban Development Patterns," *Highway Research Record 207*, 1967, pp. 53-67.

Brown, H. J., J. R. Ginn, F. J. James, J. F. Kain, and M. R. Straszheim: *Empirical Models of Urban Land Use: Suggestions on Research Objectives and Organization*, National Bureau of Economic Research Exploratory Report 6, Columbia University Press, New York, 1972.

Federal Highway Administration: *An Introduction to Urban Development Models and Guidelines for Their Use in Urban Transportation Planning*, U.S. Dept. of Transportation, Washington, D.C., 1975.

Franklin, J. (ed.): *Models of Employment and Residential Location*, Rutgers University, Center for Urban Policy Research, New Brunswick, N.J., 1974.

Garin, R. A.: "A Matrix Formulation of the Lowry Model for Intrametropolitan Activity Allocation," *Journal of the American Institute of Planners*, vol. 32, 1966, pp. 361-364.

Goldner, W.: "The Lowry Model Heritage," *Journal of the American Institute of Planners*, vol. 37, no. 2, 1971, pp. 100-110.

Hall, P. D.: "Search Behavior in Urban Housing Markets," Unpublished Ph.D. thesis, MIT, Dept. of Civil Engineering, Cambridge, Mass., 1980.

Highway Research Board: *Urban Development Models*, Special Report No. 97, Washington, D.C., 1969.

Hill, D. M.: "A Growth Allocation Model for the Boston Region," *Journal of the American Institute of Planners*, vol. 31, May 1965, pp. 111-120.

Hill, D. M., D. Brand, and W. B. Hansen: "Prototype Development of Statistical Land-Use Prediction Model for Greater Boston Region," *Highway Research Record 114*, Washington, D.C., 1965, pp. 51-70.

Ingram, G. K., J. F. Kain, and J. R. Ginn: *The Detroit Prototype of the NBER Urban Simulation Model*, National Bureau of Economic Research, New York, 1972.

Isard, W.: *Method of Regional Analysis: An Introduction to Regional Science*, MIT Press, Cambridge, Mass., 1960.

Kern, C., and S. R. Lerman: "Models for Predicting the Impact of Transportation Policies on Retail Activity," Presented at the 57th annual meeting of the Transportation Research Board, Washington, D.C., 1978.

Lakshmanan, T. R. and W. G. Hansen: "A Retail Market Potential Model," *Journal of the American Institute of Planners*, vol. 31, May, pp. 134-143, 1965.

Lee, D. A.: "Requiem for Large-Scale Models," *Journal of the American Institute of Planners*, vol. 39, no. 3, May 1973, pp. 163-178.

Lerman, S. R.: "Location, Housing, Car Ownership and Mode to Work: A Joint Choice Model," *Transportation Research Record*, no. 610, 1976, pp. 6-11.

Lowry, I. S.: *A Model of Metropolis*, RM-4035-RC, Rand Corp., Santa Monica, Calif., 1964.

―――: "Seven Models of Urban Development: A Structural Comparison," in *Urban Development Models*, Highway Research Board Special Report 97, Washington, D.C., 1968, pp. 151-174.

Putman, S. H.: "The Integrated Forecasting of Transportation and Land Use," in W. F. Brown, R. B. Dial, D. S. Gendall, E. Weiner (eds.), *Emerging Transportation Planning Methods*, U.S. Dept. of Transportation, Office of University Research, 1978, pp. 119-148.

―――: "Calibrating Urban Residential Location Models No. 3: Empirical Results for Non-U.S. Cities," *Environment and Planning A*, vol. 12, 1980, pp. 813-827.

―――: "Theory and Practice in Urban Modelling: The Art of Application," Presented at the 13th annual conference of the Regional Science Association—British Section, University of Durham, September 1981.

Quigley, J. M.: "Housing Demand in the Short Run: An Analysis of Polytomous Choice," *Explorations in Economic Research*, vol. 3, no. 1, 1976.
Southeastern Wisconsin Regional Planning Commission: *Alternative Futures for Southeastern Wisconsin,* Technical Report No. 25, 1981.
Steuart, G. N. (ed.): *Urban Transportation Planning Guide,* University of Toronto Press, 1977.
Turner, C. G., and S. H. Putman: *Kansas City Metropolitan Region Development Forecasting Model Project Final Report,* Prepared for the Mid America Regional Council, Kansas City, April 1981.
Weisbrod, G. E.: "Business and Travel Impacts of Boston's Downtown Crossing Automobile-Restricted Zone," *Transportation Research Record 887,* Transportation Research Board, Washington D.C., 1982.
Wilson, A. G.: *Urban and Regional Models in Geography and Planning,* Wiley, New York, 1974.
Wrigley, E. A.: "Demographic Models and Geography," Chapter 6 of R. J. Corley and P. Haggett (eds.), *Socio-Economic Models in Geography,* Methuen, University Paperbacks, London, pp. 189–216.

CHAPTER SEVEN
DEMAND ANALYSIS

7-0 INTRODUCTION

One of the most important areas of analysis in urban transportation planning is the estimation of traveler demand for transportation facilities and services. Indeed, much of the past research on planning techniques has focused on demand model formulation and use. In this chapter, an overview of transportation demand analysis concepts, techniques, and issues is presented. Because the appropriate demand analysis approach for any particular problem context depends on the characteristics and scope of the problem, special attention is given to identifying the types of situations each approach is suited for.

Section 7-1 briefly discusses the relationship between demand analysis and the planning process. Section 7-2 then defines some basic terms and concepts which underlie demand analysis. Sections 7-3, 7-4, and 7-5 present and briefly discuss a range of currently available demand analysis techniques. Finally, Sec. 7-6 discusses the major tasks involved in a demand analysis, regardless of the technique employed.

7-1 DEMAND ANALYSIS AND THE PLANNING PROCESS

Dealing as it does with predicting how many people of what type will use a given transportation facility for what purpose under a given set of circumstances, demand analysis is clearly of central importance in addressing a wide range of planning issues. Indeed, the urban transportation modeling system (UTMS), the large-scale, computer-based system of demand models that has dominated transportation planning for many years (see Sec. 7-4), is often referred to as the urban transportation *planning* system, (UTPS), presumably as a reflection of this central role. In this book, the latter terminology has not been used since it seems to imply that this modeling system *is* the planning process. As should be clear from the discussion in Chap. 3, this is certainly not the case. Analysis is only one component of the planning process, and, in fact, demand estimation is only one component of analysis. Analysis provides input into the planning and decision-making process. As such, it is only of use to the extent that it aids in that process. In order to do so, as discussed in Chap. 5, analysis must be timely, cost-effective, responsive to the policy variables of interest, sensitive to the scale of the impacts involved, and presented in a way that is understandable and useful to decision makers. Further, it is important to note that as the planning environment changes over time, so must the analysis techniques employed if they are to remain useful within that planning environment.

Large-scale, comprehensive, aggregate models such as UTMS were developed in an era of long-range, multiyear, big budget planning studies which focused on major regional transportation facility developments. Beginning with the highway revolt of the late 1960s and early 1970s and continuing throughout the 1970s, the focus within transportation planning switched from the long range to the short and medium range, from large-scale capital projects to transportation system management (TSM) strategies and low-capital operational improvements, and from a "pro-highway bias" to an emphasis on promotion of pro-transit alternatives and imposition of controls on the use of the automobile. All of these shifts in the planning environment imply a need for smaller-scale, cheaper, more responsive, and more clearly focused analytical techniques. Individual choice models, sketch-planning techniques, and the development of a range of simplified manual pocket calculator and microcomputer analysis techniques, discussed in the following sections, all represent important responses to shifting needs. Indeed, the ongoing revolution in computer technology—resulting in the development of inexpensive, easily used, and ever-more-powerful programmable calculators, microcomputers, and minicomputers—further reinforces this trend by providing a range of computing capabilities, environments, and costs which the planner can match against his analysis needs and budget constraints.

Not only is the nature of transportation system issues and responses changing over time, but the environment within which the transportation system operates is changing as well [Wachs, 1982; Miller, 1982]. The assumption of a stereotypical household with one worker who lives in the suburbs and commutes to work in the downtown core, upon which so much of our demand analyses—past and present—are based, is simply no longer tenable. Employment decentralization in all North American cities (including those which have retained a healthy and growing core area) makes for multicentered travel flows that are typically more difficult to analyze than the simpler, traditional radial flow pattern. Multiple-worker households are the norm for most of North America, again significantly complicating our representation of travel behavior. Demographic shifts also appear to be occurring within most cities. Traditionally the suburbs have been the preserve of white-collar workers and the relatively well-to-do, while the central cities have tended to be occupied by the working class and the poor. "Gentrification" (i.e., the return of the white-collar middle class to the central city) and simultaneous shifts of the poor and the working class to the suburbs are tending to reverse this trend at least somewhat.

The cumulative implications of these observations are twofold. First, old correlations, aggregate rates and responses, and behavioral assumptions may no longer be valid. In order to assess their validity, to establish new relationships as required, and to achieve a better understanding of how these relationships in turn might evolve over time implies the need to adopt a more explicitly behavioral approach to transportation demand analysis. Trends in this direction are apparent. These include the development of new techniques such as individual choice models which, while not behavioral techniques per se, do facilitate investigations of behavioral relationships; an increasing interest in the use of "attitudinal" data and methods in transportation demand analysis; and a gradual recognition among many researchers that transportation demand analysis may have as much to do with the social sciences as it does with engineering or applied econometrics.

The second implication is that new data (and, quite probably, new data collection procedures) are required if we are to investigate these new demand relationships. As with many of our analysis techniques, much of the data currently available to planners were originally collected during the comprehensive planning studies of the 1950s and 1960s. The demise of the big budget planning studies in the 1970s also resulted in the demise, by and large, of major data collection projects. For some time now analysts have been making do with increasingly old data which, at best, have been updated from time to time through small-sample surveys, etc. Analysts find themselves in the uncomfortable position of trying to analyze new problems with old data—data which, furthermore, were collected in response to different planning problems, for use in different analysis techniques.

The availability of good quality, relevant data is absolutely crucial to any demand analysis. It may well be that one of the biggest challenges facing the demand analyst in the 1980s will be the identification of data requirements and the articulation of these needs in a way which planners and decision makers can understand and react to. A premium will clearly be placed on techniques which make maximum use of available data; however, it is also clear that new data must be collected in the coming years as well if demand analysis techniques and their ability to address current and emerging planning needs are to improve.

In the following sections, the overall approach to demand analysis and the techniques used to estimate demand are discussed in some technical detail. In order to explain the techniques, and the assumptions on which they are based, inclusion of such technical information was necessary. The reader is encouraged to think carefully about how each technique discussed in this chapter fits into the model of decision-oriented planning outlined in previous chapters. For what types of decisions is each technique most useful? How does the use of each technique relate to the characteristics of decision-oriented planning presented in Chap. 3? These questions are critically important to planners responsible for any form of analysis in transportation planning.

7-2 DEFINITIONS AND BASIC CONCEPTS

The starting point for all analyses of the demand for transportation services is the fact that this demand is a *derived* one. That is, people do not travel for the sake of the traveling experience itself (the occasional "Sunday drive," bicycle ride, or walk in the park aside). Rather, they travel so that they can participate in various activities located at the destinations of their journeys. Homes, workplaces, stores, and schools all occupy finite amounts of space and are located at separate, discrete points in the urban landscape. It is the transportation system which "mediates" between these locations of activity, that is, which physically connects them and which enables people to move from point to point and from activity to activity.

Two major implications can be drawn from the derived nature of transportation demand. First, no transportation demand analysis can be performed without explicitly considering the socioeconomic *activity system*—consisting of people and activities of various types and quantities distributed over space—which is served by the transportation system and which "generates" travel demand. This interaction between the activity and transportation systems was discussed at some length in Chaps. 2 and 6. In this chapter, we will focus on the analysis of transportation demand, given a particular activity system.

Second, since one does not travel for the sake of traveling but rather for the sake of "getting there," one can speak of the *disutility* or *generalized cost* of travel, measured in terms of the time, monetary cost, inconvenience, discomfort, etc. associated with the trip. That is, all else being equal, one would always presumably prefer to spend less time traveling from here to there, spend less money, and be more comfortable. Further, one can speak of the *utility* associated with participation in the activity which generates the trip. Thus, it is reasonable to assume that travel decisions are based on the potential trip maker's assessment of the "pros and cons" or net utilities associated with the various travel options with which he is presented. This concept of the utility of travel is an extremely powerful one which, as discussed at length in this chapter, provides the starting point for a number of transportation demand modeling techniques.

Given a particular socioeconomic activity system which defines people's residential locations, workplaces, shopping opportunities, and so on, the demand for travel manifests itself in terms of *trips* made at given times by individuals from point to point within the urban area. These trips made by individuals can be characterized in terms of a number of attributes or dimensions, including:

1. The *purpose* of the trip (work, shop, social, etc.)
2. The *time of day* of the trip
3. The *origin* of the trip
4. The *destination* of the trip
5. The *mode(s)* of travel (auto, bus, bicycle, etc.) used to make the trip
6. The *route* from origin to destination through the chosen mode's network taken for this trip
7. The *frequency* (i.e., number of trips per unit time) with which such trips are made

In speaking of "the" origin and destination of a trip, one is implicitly defining a trip as consisting of movement between a single origin and a single destination for a single purpose. A *trip end* is, therefore, simply defined as one end (i.e., an origin or a destination) of a trip. In addition to their purposes, modes, etc., trips are usually also defined as being *home-based* (if they either begin or end at home) or *nonhome-based* (if they neither begin nor end at home). This latter distinction is maintained because home-based trips typically constitute a majority of trips and are, in addition, conceptually easier to analyze and model.

A *trip chain* is defined as a connected sequence of trips wherein the chain's origin and destination are the same point in space. Thus, a morning trip from home to work, combined with the afternoon's return trip from work to home, constitutes a home to work to home trip chain. Similarly, if the worker stopped at a shopping plaza on the way home, the trip chain would be home–work–shop–home and would consist of three trips (home to work, work to shop, and shop to home). Travel demand is typically analyzed at the level of the trip rather than the trip chain, either because in practice little difference exists between the two concepts (e.g., whether one models a home–work–home trip chain or two home-based work trips is essentially an arbitrary decision) or because trip modeling is typically "easier" to do (although theoretically less elegant) than trip-chain modeling. Recognition of the need for trip-chain models to analyze certain policy issues (e.g., the impact of rising energy prices on the consolidation of simple trips into trip chains) has grown over the last few years, leading to a variety of experimental models of trip chaining or "activity patterns" [Adler and Ben-Akiva, 1979; Damm, 1979; Horowitz, 1980].

In addition to identifying the attributes of travel demand itself, one can characterize individual trip makers in terms of various social, physical, and economic descriptors (e.g., the person's age, sex, income, occupation, and education). Each such characteristic can be thought of as a dimension along which each individual can be measured or identified (e.g., 30 to 39 years old, male, more than 1 year post-secondary education). The number of these dimensions determines the extent to which individuals can be differentiated from one another; that is, they define the extent of our knowledge about people acting within the system under study. Unlike the previously mentioned dimensions of demand, the trip-maker characteristics of potential relevance to the description of a traveler's behavior are not necessarily clearly defined and are potentially large in number. The criteria for choosing these characteristics are first, assumed relevance in meaningfully categorizing the individual in question, and second, observability (and, implicitly, measurability).

Similarly, one can observe various physical and economic descriptors of both the transportation system and the socioeconomic activity system (e.g., the physical characteristics and level of service of the transportation system; the number, type, and size of stores at a given location). As is the case with the descriptors of trip makers, system characteristics are chosen based on an assessment of their impact on people's decision making and on their measurability.

One can observe the number and types of trips being made within an urban area, the characteristics of the people making these trips, and the characteristics of the activity and transportation systems which generate and serve these trips. One cannot, however, observe the *process* by which people decide to make a given trip or set of trips. This process is a mental one involving the perception of one's needs and opportunities for travel, evaluation of these needs and opportunities given one's preferences or attitudes, and choice of a course of action or pattern of behavior based upon this evaluation. This choice of travel behavior may be constrained to a greater or lesser extent by physical, temporal, social, or economic factors. It may also vary in terms of temporal stability (e.g., the journey to work is not a trip choice that is reevaluated on a day-to-day or even necessarily a month-to-month basis, whereas an individual's recreational trip making over time can show considerable variation). Nevertheless, the concept of *choice* as a mechanism for analyzing travel behavior has proved to be extremely useful and will be discussed in greater detail below.

This discussion of the "dimensions" of travel demand (that is, the characteristics of travel demand and of the people and systems which determine that demand) illustrates the enormous, and potentially overwhelming, complexity and level of detail inherent in travel demand analysis. The demand for travel in an urban region is the result of the decisions of thousands or even millions of individuals—based upon a variety of motives, perceptions, and preferences—made within a complex physical, social, and economic environment. It is improbable that planners could ever possess the theoretical understanding, the empirical data, or the analytical and computational capabilities that would be required to faithfully replicate (let alone predict) travel demand at this most fundamental level of detail.

In order to achieve a conceptually and analytically tractable formulation of the travel demand problem, it is necessary to work at a more *aggregate* level of system representation than that of the individual trip maker. Individuals are, in principle and in fact, exactly that: individual, unique, and for all practical purposes unpredictable with respect to the intricacies of their behavior. Aggregates of people, however, will tend to exhibit common tendencies and behave in similar ways. In other words, in the aggregate, statistical regularities emerge which are sufficiently strong, stable, and theoretically reasonable to be useful in the analysis and prediction of travel demand. Further, it is typically aggregate values that are required in planning (e.g., peak-hour link volumes, total vehicle miles traveled, average fleet fuel consumption, average peak-period link speed) as opposed to predictions of individual activities or experiences.

Aggregation is performed in at least three dimensions: the spatial, the temporal, and the socioeconomic. Spatial aggregation is performed by dividing the urban region into a set of *zones* and then treating these zones as the basic units of analysis. Thus, rather than dealing with *trips* made by individuals from point to point, the analysis is concerned with total *flows* of people from zone to zone. Zonal characteristics used to "explain" these flows typically take the form of zonal totals (e.g., total number of workers living in the zone) or zonal averages (e.g., average zonal household income). The transportation system is also spatially aggregated into a network of *links* and *nodes* which may or may not (but usually not) constitute a one-to-one correspondence to the actual transportation network.

Temporal aggregation is performed by grouping travel flows (which will tend to occur at varying levels over time) into discrete time periods. Typical time periods include the weekday peak period (e.g., 7 to 9 a.m. and/or 4 to 6 p.m.), the weekday off-peak period, the weekday, and the year. Thus, one might analyze total weekday peak-period flows between zones in order to identify deficiencies in network capacity. Alternatively, total yearly transit ridership might be analyzed in order to estimate transit revenues. In all cases, the temporal distribution of flows within the time period is not of interest. Temporal aggregation reduces the complexity of the analysis by converting a continuous variable (time of trip) to a discrete, nominal variable (i.e., the trip occurs during a given time period or it does not).

Finally, socioeconomic aggregation occurs whenever one categorizes individuals into "homogeneous" groups. It is common, for instance, to group households according to their income level, auto-ownership level, and family size for the purpose of trip generation analysis (see Sec. 7-4-1). In such cases, the explicit assumption is that all members of a given group (e.g., two-car, four-person, middle-income households) behave in the same way (e.g., generate the same number of daily trips), or at least the variance in their behavior is small relative to the differences in behavior observed between their group and other groups.

In principle, the choice of aggregation level for a given analysis should depend on the identification of an appropriate "behavioral unit" of analysis (the individual, the household, the firm, the urban area, etc.), based on the analyst's understanding of the functional relationships which exist within the system under study and on the scale and complexity of the particular problem application. In practice, the level of aggregation employed typically depends as much (or more) on the quality and level of detail of the available data, on the time and monetary constraints imposed on the analysis, and on the analytical techniques available for use as it does upon strict behavioral or theoretical arguments.

A wide range of techniques exists for analyzing transportation demand. In this chapter, three broad classes of analysis methods are considered:

1. Simplified techniques
2. The urban transportation modeling system
3. Individual choice models

Simplified techniques include trend analysis, elasticity-based and pivot-point techniques, and various types of manual techniques (e.g., nomographs, work sheets). In general such techniques employ a number of limiting assumptions which simplify the problem under consideration to the point where it can be analyzed by using simple calculations which are typically performed by hand (or on a pocket calculator) rather than on a computer. Section 7-3 discusses how these techniques can be used, as well as their strengths and weaknesses.

A second major approach to the analysis of transportation demand involves the use of a relatively standardized set of models which have evolved over the last 30 years of transportation planning—the so-called urban transportation modeling system (UTMS).

Although originally developed, and probably best suited, for long-range, comprehensive planning, this system of models has been used in one form or another in a wide range of planning applications. The terminology and structuring of the travel demand question employed by UTMS (that is the "paradigm" of demand analysis which it represents) permeate the entire field of urban transportation demand analysis, regardless of specific problem contexts or actual analysis methods employed. For both of these reasons, no discussion of travel demand analysis would be complete without a description of UTMS, and such a description is presented in Sec. 7-4.

While UTMS has been extensively employed within the transportation planning field for nearly 30 years, it has also been seriously criticized from many points of view for almost the same length of time. Most fundamentally, UTMS is not behavioral in nature; that is, it is not based in any real sense on a coherent theory of travel behavior. This characteristic in turn results in certain inconsistencies within the modeling system (e.g., zone-to-zone travel times assumed by one component of the system may not be the same as those assumed by a subsequent system component); highly abstract and/or unrealistic representations of travel behavior (e.g., the prediction of "trip ends"—that is, flows into and out of zones—independent of where these flows are coming from or going to); and, ultimately, an inability to significantly improve either the system as a whole or its constituent components.

In order to improve upon some or all of these deficiencies it would appear necessary to adopt a more explicitly behavioral approach toward conceptualizing and modeling travel demand. This is, indeed, the direction which research in the field has taken, especially since the late 1960s. In particular, a major stream of research activity emerged during the 1970s, focusing on the concept of travel behavior as the outcome of individual decision makers choosing a particular action from a range or set of potential actions. Section 7-5 briefly discusses these models and their current planning applications.

7-3 SIMPLIFIED DEMAND ESTIMATION TECHNIQUES

Simplified demand analysis techniques are applicable in any analysis situation in which more detailed techniques (and/or the data required by these techniques) cannot be used because of budget or time constraints, are inappropriate for the level of detail required, or are simply not available for use. Examples of such situations include:

1. Analysis of simple (typically small-area, short-range) planning issues, such as transit route extensions and site-specific land use development impacts on transportation (e.g., impacts of a new shopping center on the local street system).
2. Severe data deficiencies which make the application of more complex techniques impossible and which cannot be remedied by collecting new data, typically because of budget or time constraints. This is a very common problem facing urban transportation planners in developing countries. It is also becoming increasingly the case in many North American cities which possess relatively old

data bases and which may not be willing to commit the financial resources required to update and upgrade these bases.
3. "Screening" of a wide range of alternatives in order to select a short list of alternatives for more detailed analysis. This type of analysis is known as *sketch planning,* and its objective is to allow the analyst to examine a large number of alternatives quickly and cheaply, thus permitting [McCoomb, 1982]

> . . . a two-step planning sequence in which the first step uses simplified, macro-transportation planning techniques (sketch planning) to carry out broad strategic-level planning on the land-use and transportation system options, and the second step uses conventional, urban transportation planning models to perform the detailed tactical-level planning leading to final alternative choice and functional design.

In this section, a range of simple demand analysis techniques is briefly discussed. In increasing order of complexity it includes trend analysis, elasticity-based models, and graphical and/or manual methods for computing transportation demand. Each of these technique types is discussed in turn in the following three subsections.

7-3-1 Trend Analysis

The simplest sort of demand model is estimated by plotting historical demand levels vs. time and then extrapolating the plotted trend into the future. Trend analysis is extremely common both within and outside of transportation planning. Whenever growth rates are used to project future growth or whenever past and current experiences are extrapolated into the future, one is either explicitly or implicitly engaging in a trend analysis.

The pitfalls inherent in trend analysis can be great, as is illustrated in Fig. 7-1. In this example, several trend projections made during the mid-1960s for United States airline patronage are plotted along with the actual patronage achieved during the period 1967–1982. Two key points can be observed from this figure. First, the functional form (or shape) of the trend curve being extrapolated is ultimately arbitrary. In Fig. 7-1, four different analysts, using essentially the same data, projected four markedly different curves yielding significantly different projections, particularly for time periods further into the future.

A range of functional forms can be assumed in trend analysis, from a simple linear trend curve (implying a constant increment of growth per unit time) through the so-called S curve or logistic curve (an example of which is the U.S. Federal Aviation Administration curve in Fig. 7-1), which projects accelerated growth over a certain time period, followed by a period of decreasing growth rates, ultimately leading to a "steady state" of little or no growth. The choice among these and other functional forms obviously depends upon which one appears to "best fit" the historical data. This choice is inevitably arbitrary, given a lack of additional information about the system being analyzed. This observation leads to the second key point to be drawn from Fig. 7-1: since trend analyses only attempt to establish a relationship between system

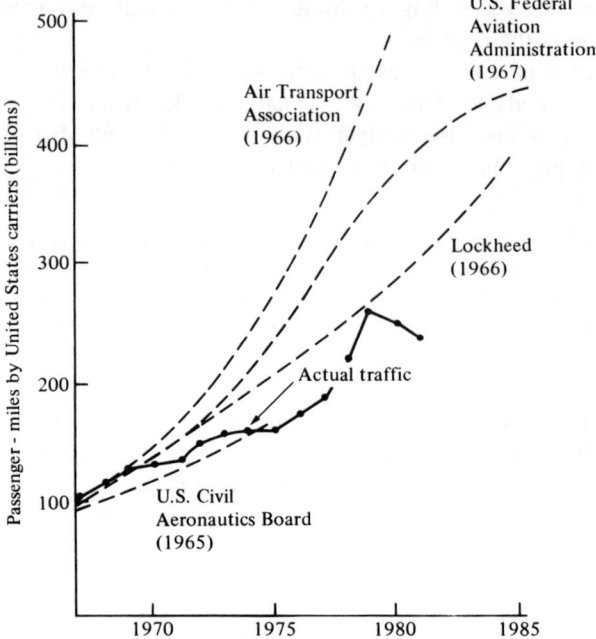

Figure 7-1 Predicted and actual air traffic in the United States. (*de Neufville* [*1976*].)

demand and time, they implicitly assume that all other factors and/or relationships affecting demand are constant over time. Hence, if key factors or relationships do vary significantly over time, then actual demand will "leave the trend curve," and the trend projection can, as a result, be seriously in error.

This is precisely what occurred in the case of airline traffic in the 1970s. Air travel is highly dependent on economic conditions. Recession, inflation, and—perhaps most critically—skyrocketing energy prices all combined to significantly alter the structure of airline demand. None of these events was captured in the trend projections of the 1960s. Indeed, these projections implicitly assumed a growing economy, rising real incomes, and effectively infinite supplies of cheap fossil fuels.

Despite these very serious problems, trend analysis can play at least two important roles in transportation demand analysis. First, in the absence of better information, an examination of past trends and a careful judgmental assessment of how these trends might continue (or change) over time are probably the best that an analyst can do. The key in such instances, however, is clearly not simply to extrapolate past trends but rather to think carefully about what the likely causal factors underlying these trends are and how they might change over time.

Second, trend analysis, while an unreliable *predictive* tool, is a very useful *diagnostic* tool for characterizing what has historically occurred within the system and what is likely to happen if changes do not occur. It can be used to help identify likely future problem areas (e.g., increasingly congested roadways) and/or future opportunities for system change (e.g., rising gasoline prices which may make public transit increasingly attractive to choice riders). It should not, however, be further used to examine the impacts which alternative strategies for addressing these problems or exploiting these opportunities might have on the system. Pursuit of such a predictive task requires more elaborate models and techniques (such as those described in the sections below).

7-3-2 Elasticity-Based Models

In order to progress beyond simple trend extrapolations of demand the analyst must possess or assume some knowledge of the demand function. As a minimum, the analyst should know what some of the key variables within the demand function are, whether they have a positive or negative impact on demand, and the sensitivity of demand to changes in these variables. These three issues are all captured within the concept of *demand elasticity*.

The elasticity of demand with respect to a certain variable (such as fare or headway) is defined as the rate of change of demand with respect to that variable, normalized by the current levels of demand and the variable in question. Mathematically, if D_0 is the current demand level and x_0 the current value of the system variable of interest, then the elasticity of demand with respect to x, e_{Dx} is defined as

$$e_{Dx} = \frac{\partial D/\partial x}{D_0/x_0} = \frac{\partial D/D_0}{\partial x/x_0} \tag{7-1}$$

where $\partial D/\partial x$ is the partial derivative of D with respect to x.

A demand elasticity is thus a measure of the sensitivity of demand to changes in system conditions. Equation (7-1) expresses elasticity as a point estimate, since it is defined for a given "operating point" (D_0, x_0) and uses the derivative at this point to measure rate of change. It should be noted that elasticity will generally vary from one operating point to another. In other words, it is not a constant but a variable which characterizes how the sensitivity of demand to system conditions varies with these conditions.

The concept of elasticity, as defined above, is of little use to planners unless the demand function D is a known and differentiable function of x so that the partial derivative $\partial D/\partial x$ can be evaluated. This requirement is met when models assuming explicit demand functions are employed (such as those discussed in Secs. 7-4 and 7-5). However, planners often encounter situations in which such models are either inappropriate or unavailable. In such cases, if some information about how demand has changed in response to a specific change in the system is available, then the *arc elasticity*, defined as the percentage change in demand given a percentage change in an explanatory variable, can be of use. The arc elasticity of demand with respect to the variable x, $\bar{e}_{Dx}$ is defined as

$$\bar{e}_{Dx} = \frac{\text{percent change in } D}{\text{percent change in } x}$$

$$= \frac{\Delta D/D_0}{\Delta x/x_0} \qquad (7\text{-}2)$$

$$= \frac{\Delta D/\Delta x}{D_0/x_0}$$

where ΔD is the change in demand level from the original value of D_0 which occurs when x varies from x_0 by the amount Δx. The point elasticity e_{Dx} and the arc elasticity $\bar{e}_{Dx}$ are not equal, except in the very special case when D is represented as a linear function of x.

D is said to be *elastic* with respect to x if the absolute value of the elasticity is greater than 1, that is, in the case where a 1 percent change in x results in a greater than 1 percent change in D. Similarly, D is *inelastic* with respect to x if a 1 percent change in x results in less than a 1 percent change in D. In the event that the absolute value of e_{Dx} is exactly 1, then D possesses *unit elasticity* with respect to x.

Direct demand elasticities are those that involve variables relating "directly" to the demand in question. The elasticity of transit demand with respect to transit fare, transit travel time, transit service headway, etc. would all be direct elasticities. Similarly, an *indirect* or *cross* elasticity typically relates to variables characterizing other modes of travel. For example, if travel times by auto between two points increase, all else being equal, one might expect transit ridership to increase somewhat. The relationship between these two changes could be measured in terms of the cross elasticity of transit demand with respect to auto travel time.

Demand elasticity models can be computed in three ways [U.S. Department of Transportation, 1980]:

1. Quasi-experimental approaches, which include demonstration projects or practical experiments in which fares or services are altered under relatively controlled conditions, and monitoring patronage changes which occur in response to actual changes in fares or services
2. Time-series analyses of demand levels that are not related to a specific fare or service change, usually involving some form of regression analysis of the time-series data (e.g., Gaudry [1975])
3. Derivation of elasticities from cross-sectional demand models

Of these three methods, the quasi-experimental approach is probably the one which is most readily usable by planners under most circumstances. Given data from such a study of demand changes, demand elasticities are generally constructed in one of two ways. The first assumes that elasticity is constant over the range of the service variable that is of interest. This is equivalent to specifying a demand function of the form

$$D = ax^b \qquad (7\text{-}3)$$

where it can be shown that if the system can be observed at two "operating points," (D_0, x_0) and (D_1, x_1), then

$$e_{Dx} = b = \frac{\log D_1 - \log D_0}{\log x_1 - \log x_0} \quad (7\text{-}4)$$

and the expected demand level D_2, given a change in the service variable to a new value of x_2, is given by

$$D_2 = D_0 \left(\frac{x_2}{x_0}\right)^b \quad (7\text{-}5)$$

here D_0, x_0, and x_2 are all known quantities, and b is given by Eq. (7-4).

Alternatively, one can assume that the demand function is approximately linear over the range of interest. In this case, the arc elasticity can be computed directly from Eq. (7-2), given the observation of the two operating points (D_0, x_0) and (D_1, x_1). Note that since elasticities are not constant along a linear demand curve, the value of the arc elasticity will vary depending on whether it is computed with the point (D_0, x_0) or the point (D_1, x_1) as its base. Either point can be used in the calculation as the base point, *providing that all subsequent calculations retain this point as the base*. That is, the new expected demand level D_2, given a new service variable value of x_2, can be obtained by replacing D_1 and x_1 in Eq. (7-2) with D_2 and x_2 and rearranging to yield

$$D_2 = D_0 \left[1 + \bar{e}_{Dx}(x_2 - x_0)/x_0\right] \quad (7\text{-}6)$$

If D_1 and x_1 had been used as the base point in Eq. (7-2), then they would replace D_0 and x_0 in Eq. (7-6). This is illustrated in Fig. 7-2, in which a new demand level D_2 is computed using both point 0 (1000 riders/day, 25-cent fare) and point 1 (950 riders/day, 30-cent fare) as the base point. Analysis based on Eq. (7-6) is often referred to within the literature as *pivot-point analysis* and represents the most common approach to the use of elasticities in transportation demand analysis.

Note that if a constant elasticity assumption had been made for the system shown in Fig. 7-2, then from Eq. (7-4) the estimated elasticity would have been -0.28, and the estimated new demand level for the 35-cent fare, as calculated by Eq. (7-5), would have been 906. As illustrated by this example, the constant elasticity assumption generally will not generate the same result as the linear demand assumption. Further, it will generate a more conservative (i.e., smaller) estimate of the expected system change (in Fig. 7-2, a 44-passenger-per-day decrease rather than a 50-passenger-per-day decrease) than will the linear demand assumption.

Elasticity-based models are extremely useful in analyzing incremental system changes, particularly when limited data and time are available for the analysis. Changes in a mode's ridership due to price increases or frequency changes, for instance, are often predicted using some form of elasticity calculation. If the data needed to calculate a local elasticity are not available, elasticities are often "borrowed" from other locations and applied to the local problem context.

A number of issues exist in the use of elasticity-based models, which the analyst should keep in mind. These include:

238 URBAN TRANSPORTATION PLANNING

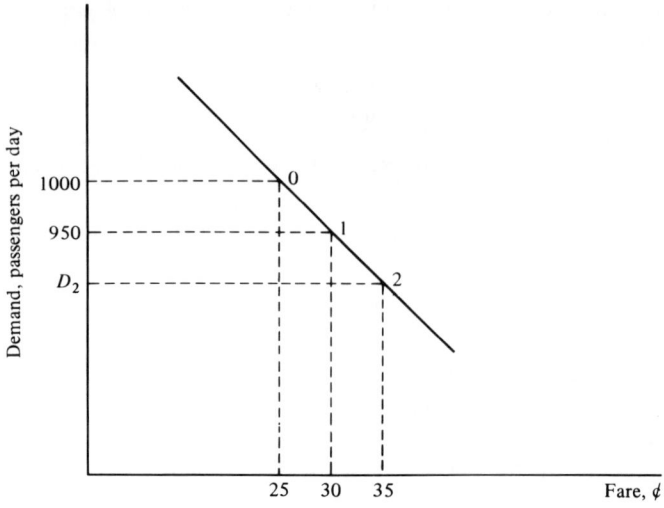

Elasticity at point 0: $e_0 = \dfrac{(950 - 1000)}{(30 - 25)} \dfrac{25}{1000} = -0.25$

Estimate of D_2 using point 0 as base: $D_{2,0} = e_0 \left(\dfrac{1000}{25}\right)(35 - 25) + 1000 = 900$

Elasticity at point 1: $e_1 = \dfrac{(1000 - 950)}{(25 - 30)} \left(\dfrac{30}{950}\right) = -0.315$

Estimate of D_2 using point 1 as base: $D_{2,1} = e_1 \dfrac{950}{30} (35 - 30) + 950 = 900$

Figure 7-2 Example of an elasticity analysis.

1. An individual's travel elasticity will in general depend upon a host of factors including income, trip purpose, time of day of the trip, availability and level of service of competing modes, and service characteristics other than the one being measured in the elasticity calculation. Elasticities are often computed from fairly aggregate statistics with little or no market segmentation. Thus, considerable potential for "aggregation bias" exists in most elasticity calculations. Application of an elasticity computed for another system or city obviously compounds this potential problem.
2. Since elasticities assume that all factors other than the one in question are being held constant, they are useful only for short-run predictions, since in the long run many of these factors are apt to change.
3. Most elasticity analyses implicitly or explicitly assume either the constant elasticity case or the linear demand case as the basis for their calculations. Either assumption is most tenable for small changes in the system. The larger the projected system change, the more likely it will be that the demand response will be a nonlinear, nonconstant-elasticity response, which is poorly predicted by the elasticity analysis.

4. Considerable confusion exists over the correct use of pivot-point techniques. As discussed above, pivot-point analysis assumes a linear demand function that permits a new demand to be estimated based on an elasticity which has been computed at a particular base or pivot point. Correct usage of this technique requires consistency in the definition of the pivot point. That is, the same point must be used to estimate the elasticity and to predict new demand levels. Pivot-point analysis does *not* assume a constant elasticity. If an assumption of constant elasticity is preferred, then Eq. (7-5) should be used rather than Eq. (7-6). In particular, if the elasticity has not been computed locally but has instead been "borrowed" from elsewhere (and, hence, the appropriate pivot point is not known), then it is probably preferable to make the constant elasticity assumption (which is typically the assumption implicit within this approach) and to use Eq. (7-5).

Tables 7-1 and 7-2 present summaries of transit fare and service elasticities, respectively, derived from a review of a large number of United States, British, and Canadian studies [U.S. Department of Transportation, 1980]. Points to note from these tables include:

1. Transit demand is inelastic. For instance, a 1 percent reduction in fare will result, on average, in only a 0.28 percent increase in aggregate patronage (assuming the mean quasi-experimental aggregate fare elasticity shown in Table 7-1).
2. As has been noted above, elasticities depend on a wide range of factors. The "disaggregate" fare elasticities of Table 7-1 illustrate this point, as the elasticities presented vary with trip length, type, time of day and purpose, as well as by the

Table 7-1 Summary of transit fare elasticities

	Aggregate fare elasticities	
Estimation method:		
Quasi-experimental	-0.28 ± 0.16	(67 cases)
Time-series	-0.42 ± 0.24	(28 cases)
Cross-sectional	-0.53 ± 0.35	(28 cases)
Type of fare change:		
Fare increase	-0.34 ± 0.11	(14 cases)
Fare decrease	-0.37 ± 0.11	(9 cases)
Fare change to fare-free:		
Within CBD only	-0.52 ± 0.11	(4 cases)
Systemwide	-0.30 ± 0.17	(6 cases)
City size:		
Populations greater than 1 million	-0.24 ± 0.10	(19 cases)
Populations 500,000 to 1 million	-0.30 ± 0.12	(11 cases)
Populations less than 500,000	-0.35 ± 0.12	(14 cases)

Table 7-1 (*continued*)

	Disaggregate fare elasticities	
Transit mode:		
Bus	−0.35 ± 0.14	(12 cases)
Rapid rail	−0.17 ± 0.05	(10 cases)
Commuter rail	−0.31	(1 case)
Trip length:		
London: bus		
Trips less than 1 mile	−0.55	(1 case)
Trips between 1 and 3 miles	−0.29	(1 case)
London: rapid rail		
Trips between 1 and 3 miles	−0.25	(1 case)
Trips greater than 3 miles	−0.60	(1 case)
Route type:		
Radial-arterial	−0.09 ± 0.02	(3 cases)
Intrasuburban	−0.31 ± 0.05	(3 cases)
Systemwide	−0.24 ± 0.08	(3 cases)
CBD-oriented	−0.40 ± 0.04	(3 cases)
Non-CBD-oriented	−0.62 ± 0.09	(3 cases)
Systemwide	−0.55 ± 0.08	(3 cases)
Intra-CBD	−0.52 ± 0.11	(4 cases)
Systemwide	−0.43 ± 0.08	(3 cases)
Time period:		
Peak	−0.17 ± 0.09	(5 cases)
Off-peak	−0.40 ± 0.26	(5 cases)
All hours	−0.29 ± 0.19	(5 cases)
Trip purpose:		
Work	−0.10 ± 0.04	(6 cases)
School	−0.19 to −0.44	(3 cases)
Shop	−0.23 ± 0.06	(5 cases)
Income group:		
Less than $5,000	−0.19 ± 0.10	(2 cases)
$5,000 to $14,999	−0.25 ± 0.11	(4 cases)
More than $15,000	−0.28 ± 0.13	(4 cases)
Age group:		
1–16 years	−0.32 ± 0.01	(2 cases)
17–24 years	−0.27 ± 0.03	(2 cases)
25–44 years	−0.18 ± 0.10	(2 cases)
45–64 years	−0.15 ± 0.03	(2 cases)
More than 65 years	−0.14 ± 0.02	(2 cases)

Source: (Mayworm, Lago, and McEnroe [1980].)

Table 7-2 Summary of transit service elasticities

	Headway elasticities	
Bus (quasi-experimental):		
Peak	-0.37 ± 0.19	(3 cases)
Off peak	-0.46 ± 0.26	(9 cases)
All hours	-0.47 ± 0.21	(7 cases)
Commuter rail (quasi-experimental):		
Peak	-0.38 ± 0.16	(5 cases)
Off-peak	-0.65 ± 0.19	(5 cases)
All hours	-0.47 ± 0.14	(5 cases)
Commuter rail (nonexperimental):		
All hours	-0.47 ± 0.11	(4 cases)
	Vehicle-miles elasticities	
Bus (quasi-experimental):		
All hours	$+0.63 \pm 0.24$	(3 cases)
Bus (nonexperimental):		
Peak	$+0.33 \pm 0.18$	(3 cases)
Off-peak	$+0.63 \pm 0.11$	(3 cases)
All hours	$+0.69 \pm 0.31$	(17 cases)
Rapid rail (nonexperimental):		
Peak	$+0.10$	(1 case)
Off-peak	$+0.25$	(1 case)
All hours	$+0.55$	(1 case)
	Total travel-time elasticities	
Bus (nonexperimental):		
Peak	-1.03 ± 0.13	(2 cases)
All hours	-0.92 ± 0.37	(2 cases)
Bus and rapid rail (nonexperimental):		
Off-peak	-0.59	(1 case)
	In-vehicle-time elasticities	
Bus (quasi-experimental):		
Peak	-0.29 ± 0.13	(9 cases)
Off-peak	-0.83	(1 case)
Bus (nonexperimental):		
Peak	-0.68 ± 0.32	(7 cases)
Off-peak	-0.12	(1 case)
Rapid rail (nonexperimental):		
Peak	-0.70 ± 0.10	(2 cases)
Bus and rapid rail (nonexperimental):		
Peak	-0.30 ± 0.10	(2 cases)
All hours	-0.27	(1 case)
Commuter rail (nonexperimental):		
All hours	-0.59 ± 0.28	(9 cases)

Table 7-2 (*continued*)

	Total out-of-vehicle-time elasticities	
Bus and rapid rail (nonexperimental):		
All hours	-0.59 ± 0.15	(3 cases)
	Walk-time elasticities	
Bus (nonexperimental):		
Peak	-0.26	(1 case)
Off-peak	-0.14	(1 case)
	Wait-time elasticities	
Bus and rapid rail (nonexperimental):		
Peak	-0.20 ± 0.07	(4 cases)
Off-peak	-0.21	(1 case)
All hours	-0.54	(1 case)
	Transfer-time elasticities	
Bus and rapid rail (nonexperimental):		
Peak	-0.40 ± 0.18	(3 cases)
	Number-of-transfers elasticities	
Bus (nonexperimental):		
Off-peak	-0.59	(1 case)

Source: (Mayworm, Lago, and McEnroe [1980].)

trip maker's income and age. In general, the more discretionary the trip (in terms of whether to make the trip or not, the destinations and modes available for the trip, etc.), the higher the magnitude of the fare elasticity. Thus, shopping trips are more fare elastic than work trips, and high-income people have higher elasticities than poorer people.

3. While still inelastic, service elasticities tend to be larger in magnitude than fare elasticities. A 1 percent improvement in service frequency is likely to result in a bigger patronage increase than a 1 percent decrease in fares.

7-3-3 Manual Techniques

Manual techniques generally represent simplified versions of more complex, comprehensive (and, often, computer-based) techniques such as UTMS or individual choice models (discussed in Secs. 7-4 and 7-5, respectively). They typically achieve this simplification by:

1. Working at a very aggregate spatial scale
2. Focusing on the impacts of a limited number of key variables
3. Eliminating or at least greatly reducing the data collection phase of the analysis through the use of "typical" data gathered from other cities and studies, which is presented in tabulated, graphical, or nomographical form
4. Eliminating the model calibration phase of the analysis through the use of a "typical" or "precalibrated" model
5. Presenting the technique to the user in the form of detailed (but simply stated) step-by-step instructions, often in the form of a work sheet

Manual techniques possess several major strengths. First, virtually all of the analysis effort is spent in actually analyzing alternatives rather than in collecting data and developing models, as is often the case with more complicated techniques. Second, while the techniques are admittedly aggregate and abstract, they are hopefully based on a sound understanding of key relationships and factors influencing transportation demand. Finally, "nontechnical" planners can readily use the techniques, which not only enables "the analyst" and "the planner" to be one and the same person, but also encourages a greater understanding on the planner's part of the assumptions, techniques, and difficulties involved in performing a demand analysis.

The major weaknesses of these techniques are essentially the opposites of their strengths. Cities vary in structure and composition and hence in trip-making characteristics; thus "typical" data and models may prove to be very untypical of local conditions and relationships. Aggregation and abstraction always have implicit within them the danger of oversimplification, of ignoring or obscuring important interactions and relationships. And, perhaps most important, considerable judgment and experience are often required in order to evaluate issues such as the ones just raised, implying that potential exists for these techniques to be seriously misused by people who do not fully understand their underlying assumptions and limitations.

Despite these caveats, manual techniques have emerged over the past decade as important analysis tools for a wide variety of planning applications, ranging from the analysis of route-level TSM alternatives to use in regionwide sketch-planning exercises. Figures 7-3 and 7-4 provide a very simple example of one such technique used to predict changes in transit mode split resulting from changes in travel time components (access, wait, ride), fares, etc. Figure 7-3 illustrates the use of the work-sheet format to guide the user through the calculations, while Fig. 7-4 is an example of a "precalibrated" model presented in a graphical form for easy use. Note that this analysis procedure is, in fact, a form of elasticity analysis in which the transit mode split arc elasticity (percent change in mode split relative to the percent change in the service variable of interest) has been redefined in terms of the curves of Fig. 7-4 in order to simplify both the presentation of the required data and the calculations which the user must perform.

Many manual techniques, although "simplified," still require many pages of text to explain. Further, they consist to a large extent of detailed modifications of conventional aggregate, UTMS-like models or individual choice models. For both of these reasons, these techniques are not discussed further here, and the reader is referred to a

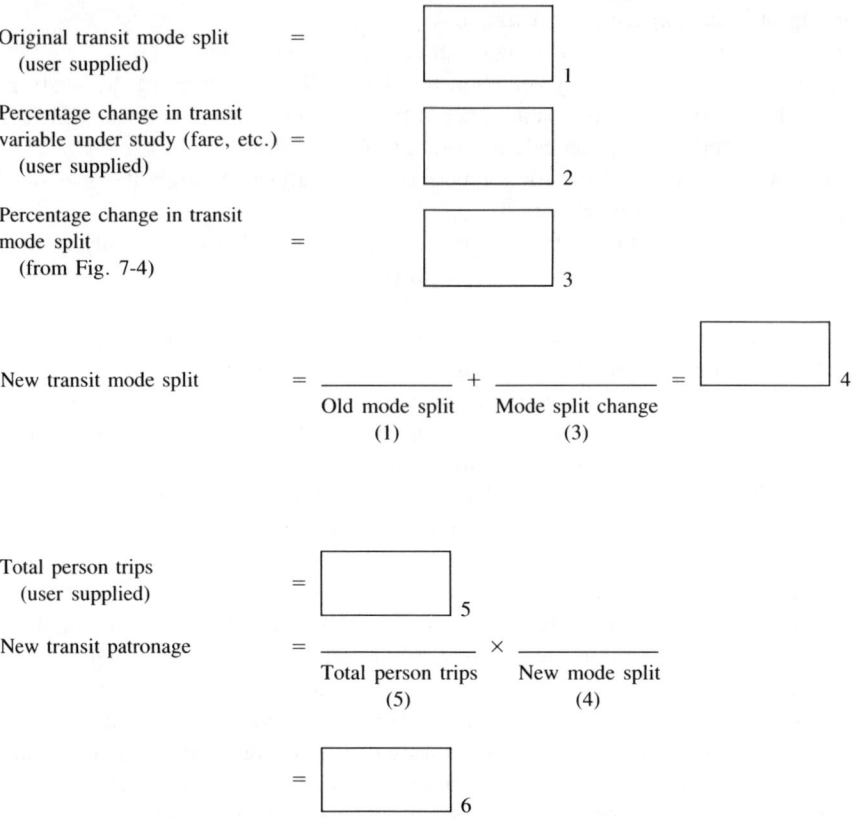

Figure 7-3 Work sheet for calculating new transit patronage based on transit service changes. (*Adapt. from Voorhees and Associates [1977].*)

number of references which deal with them in detail [Hinkle et al., 1976; Voorhees, 1977; Sosslau et al., 1978; Cambridge Systematics, 1979; McCoomb, 1982].

7-4 THE URBAN TRANSPORTATION MODELING SYSTEM

The standard approach to urban travel demand modeling commonly employed by the transportation planning profession is embodied in a system of models generally known as the urban transportation modeling system (UTMS). UTMS is used to predict the number of trips made within an urban area by type (work, nonwork, etc.), time of day (peak-period, daily, etc.) and zonal origin-destination (O-D) pair, the mode of travel used to make these trips, and the routes taken through the transportation network by these trips. The final product of UTMS is a predicted set of modal flows on links in a network. As such, it represents an "equilibrium" procedure in which the demand for transportation (represented by zonal O-D flows by mode) is assigned to the modal networks constituting the transportation system as a function of these networks'

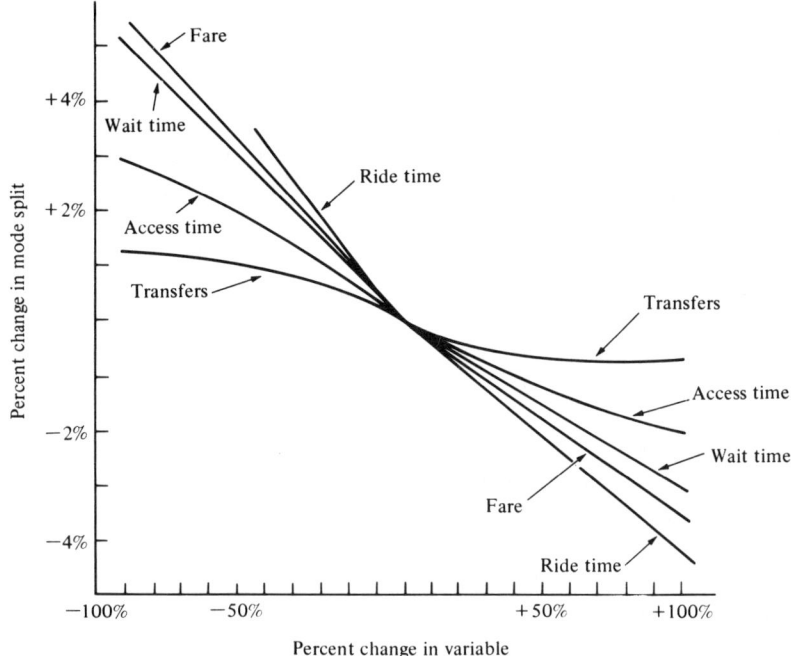

Figure 7-4 Transit mode split changes as a function of transit service changes. (*Adapted from Voorhees and Associates* [1977].)

performance (supply) characteristics. The major inputs to UTMS are a specification of the activity system generating these flows and the characteristics of the transportation system which is to serve these flows.

UTMS consists of four major stages (and hence is often referred to as the four-stage model), as shown by Fig. 7-5:

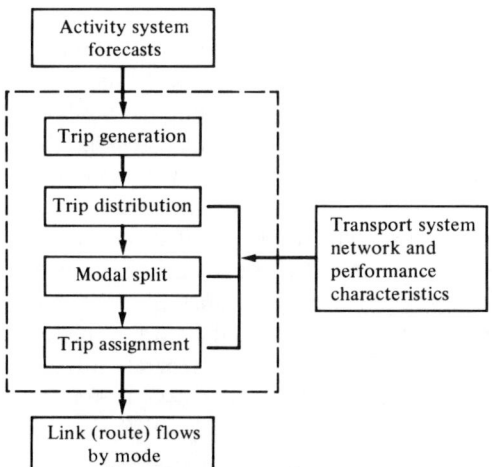

Figure 7-5 The urban transportation modeling system.

1. *Trip generation* is the prediction of the number of trips produced by and attracted to each zone, that is, the number of trip ends "generated" within the urban area. In other words, the trip generation phase of the analysis predicts total flows into and out of each zone in the study area, but it does not predict where these flows are coming from or going to.
2. *Trip distribution* is the prediction of origin-destination (O-D) flows, that is, the linking of the trip ends predicted by the trip generation model together to form trip interchanges or flows.
3. *Modal split* models predict the percentages of flow which will use each of the modes (auto, transit, walk, etc.) that are available for travel between each origin-destination pair.
4. *Trip assignment* places the O-D flows for each mode on specific routes of travel through the respective model networks.

The four stages of UTMS thus correspond to a sequential decision process (see Fig. 7-6), in which people decide to make a trip (generation), decide where to go (distribution), decide what mode to take (modal split), and decide what route to use (assignment). For most trips, this is undoubtedly a highly unrealistic representation of travelers' decision making. UTMS, however, makes no claims of being a behavioral representation of trip making. Rather, it represents a pragmatic approach to reducing the extremely complex phenomenon of travel behavior into analytically manageable components that can be dealt with using relatively simple techniques and reasonable amounts of data.

Given the major role which UTMS has played in transportation demand analysis, it is well documented in the literature [Hutchinson, 1974; Stopher and Meyburg, 1975; Dickey, 1975; Steuart, 1977; Morlok, 1978; Kanafani, 1983]. In this section, only a limited description of each component is presented in order to provide a brief overview of UTMS.

7-4-1 Trip Generation

Trip generation models are used to predict the trip ends generated by a household or a zone, usually on a daily or a peak-period basis. Trip ends are classed as being either a *production* (defined as the home end of a home-based trip or the origin of a nonhome-based trip) or an *attraction* (the nonhome end of a home-based trip or the destination of a nonhome-based trip). Separate models are used to predict productions and attractions. Variables used as predictors of trip productions include household income, auto ownership and size, number of workers per household, residential density, and distance of the zone from the central business district (CBD). Trip attraction predictors include zonal employment levels (possibly disaggregated by occupation type), zonal floor space (disaggregated by business type), and accessibility to the work force (i.e., some weighted accessibility measure). Two general classes of trip generation models have traditionally been employed: linear regression models and cross-classification models [Federal Highway Administration, 1975].

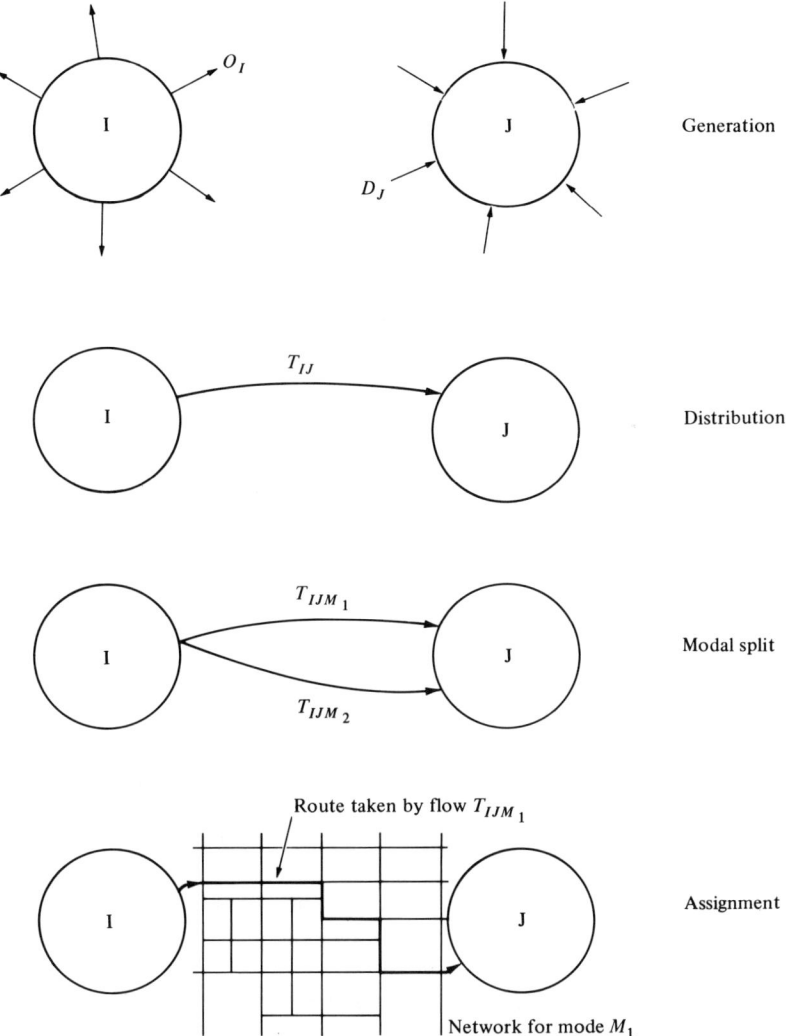

Figure 7-6 Steps in the sequential modeling of transportation demand.

Regression models Given the high correlations which typically exist between trip generation and the variables listed above, ordinary least-squares regression is often used to estimate models that predict trip generation as a linear function of one or more of these variables. Three examples of typical trip generation regression models are

$$T = 1.229 + 1.379V \tag{7-7}$$

$$T_w = 0.135P + 0.145 \, DU - 0.253C \tag{7-8}$$

$$A = 61.4 + 0.93E \tag{7-9}$$

where T = number of person trips per day per household
 V = number of vehicles per household
 T_w = work-trip productions per zone
 P = zonal population
 DU = number of dwelling units per zone
 C = total number of automobiles owned in the zone
 A = peak-hour work trip attractions per zone
 E = total employment in the zone

Equation (7-7) predicts total daily trip productions per household, while Eq. (7-8) predicts daily work trip productions for an entire zone. Finally, Eq. (7-9) is a trip attraction model, which predicts the total number of work trips attracted to a given zone as a function of the number of employees working in that zone.

Regression models are very easy and inexpensive to construct from data that are typically available in planning studies. Problems with the use of such models, however, include:

1. Correlation among explanatory variables (particularly income and auto ownership) may create estimation problems.
2. The assumption that the explanatory variables have linear, additive impacts on trip generation may be wrong.
3. The model's parameters may not be stable over time.
4. "Best fit" equations may yield counter-intuitive results [e.g., the negative auto-ownership coefficient in Eq. (7-8) implies that as auto-ownership levels increase, trip productions decrease—something which one would not normally expect].
5. By using zonal averages, important socioeconomic variations within the zone may be obscured or may yield spurious results.

Category analysis Rather than grouping households spatially (i.e., by zones) as in regression models, cross-classification analysis groups individual households together according to common socioeconomic characteristics (auto-ownership level, income, household size, etc.) so as to create relatively homogeneous groups. Average trip production rates are then computed for each group from observed data. Figure 7-7 provides an example of a cross-classification trip production model in which total daily home-based trip rates are predicted as a function of household size and auto ownership. Figure 7-7a presents the data required to *construct* the cross-classification trip rates: total number of trips and total number of households for the study area for each household-size–auto-ownership category. Figure 7-7b shows the daily trip rates which result from dividing daily trips by the number of households for each category. Figure 7-7c presents an example of the data required to *forecast* trip productions for a given zone, that is, the number of households in each size–auto-ownership category expected to be living in the zone in the forecast year. Finally, Fig. 7-7d shows the forecasted number of daily home-based trips generated by this zone, which is obtained by multiplying the number of households in each category (Fig. 7-7c) by the corresponding trip rate for the category (Fig. 7-7b). The trips generated by each household

(a) Number of households and total trips made, categorized by household size and auto-ownership level

Family size	Automobile ownership					
	0		1		2 or more	
	No. of households	No. of trips	No. of households	No. of trips	No. of households	No. of trips
1	925	1,098	1,872	4,821	121	206
2	1,471	2,105	1,934	6,129	692	1,501
3	1,268	1,850	3,071	13,989	4,178	19,782
4 or more	745	1,509	4,181	18,411	4,967	25,106

(b) Household trip rates

Family size	Automobile ownership		
	0	1	2 or more
1	1.19	2.57	1.70
2	1.43	3.16	2.17
3	1.45	4.55	4.74
4 or more	2.02	4.40	5.05

(c) Forecasted number of households in one zone, categorized by household size and auto-ownership level

Family size	Automobile ownership		
	0	1	2 or more
1	24	42	8
2	10	51	107
3	11	31	158
4 or more	3	17	309

(d) Forecasted number of trips from this zone

Family size	Automobile ownership			
	0	1	2 or more	Total
1	29	106	14	151
2	14	161	232	407
3	16	141	749	906
4 or more	6	75	1564	1645
Total	65	485	2559	3109

Figure 7-7 A cross-classification trip generation analysis. (*Morlok* [1978].)

category are then summed to yield the total number of trips generated by the zone (3109 trips in this example).

Cross-classification analysis can be similarly performed for trip attraction calculations. In such cases, classification is generally done with respect to employment type (e.g., manufacturing, retail, office) and possibly employment density (i.e., number of employees per acre). Since trip productions and attractions are calculated separately, one must ensure that the areawide production and attraction totals are the same. In general they will not be. This can be corrected by multiplying each zone's trip attractions by the ratio of total productions to total attractions. This approach to the problem is based on the expectation that trip production models are better predictors of trip rates than the somewhat cruder trip attraction models.

Category analysis avoids the regression model's assumption of a linear, additive relationship between trip generation and its explanatory variables, as well as the pitfalls inherent in spatially aggregated models. It does, on the other hand, require considerably more detailed data than do typical regression models, both to initially construct and, more critically, to use in predicting future trip generations. As with regression models, the stability of the estimated rates over time may also be a concern.

7-4-2 Trip Distribution

The task of a trip distribution model is to "distribute" or "link up" the zonal trip ends (i.e., the productions and attractions for each zone as predicted by the trip generation model) in order to predict the *flow* of trips T_{ij} from each production zone i to each attraction zone j.

Many types of trip distribution models exist. These include *growth factor* techniques such as the Fratar method, which were used in early transportation studies but which are now used mostly for short-term updating of trip tables and estimation of "through trips" for urban areas [Fratar, 1954; Brokke, 1958; Hutchinson, 1974]; *intervening opportunities* models, which have seen limited use over the years, are cumbersome to calibrate, and have never enjoyed generalized acceptance [Stouffer, 1940; Schneider, 1960; Golding and Davidson, 1970]; *disaggregate destination choice* models (discussed in Sec. 7-5); and, finally, the virtually universally used *gravity model*.

The gravity model, in one form or another, has been in existence for over 100 years. It received its name from its earliest derivation as an analogy drawn between the "spatial interaction" of trip making and the gravitational interaction of physical bodies distributed over space. The most typical version of the gravity model used in transportation planning applications is

$$T_{ij} = \frac{O_i D_j f_{ij}}{\sum_{j=1}^{n} D_j f_{ij}} \tag{7-10}$$

where O_i = total number of trips produced in zone i
D_j = total number of trips attracted to zone j
f_{ij} = "friction factor"

The friction factor is an inverse function of the "cost" of travel (travel time, distance, monetary out-of-pocket cost, "generalized cost," etc.) between zones i and j, denoted here as c_{ij}. Common functional forms for the friction factor f_{ij} include

$$f_{ij} = c_{ij}^{-b} \tag{7-11a}$$

$$f_{ij} = e^{-bc_{ij}} \tag{7-11b}$$

$$f_{ij} = \text{graphical function of } c_{ij}.$$

In all cases, the function f_{ij} must be empirically calibrated for any given urban area in order to derive the value of the parameter b [if either Eqs. (7-11a) or (7-11b) are used] or the locus of the graphical function (if this latter method is used) which enables the model to "best fit" observed data for the area under analysis.

Equation (7-10) automatically satisfies the logical constraint that the total number of trips predicted to leave any zone i is equal to the observed productions O_i. It does not, in general, satisfy the converse logical constraint that the total number of trips predicted to enter zone j is equal to the observed attractions D_j. The latter requirement is accomplished through an iterative "balancing" procedure in which the trip attractions used in Eq. (7-10) are systematically adjusted until predicted and observed attractions are equal for all zones in the system [Bureau of Public Roads, 1965; Hutchinson, 1974; see also Question 4 at the end of this chapter].

Equation (7-10), in combination with the balancing procedure mentioned above, represents the standard gravity model formulation which has been used throughout North America for more than two decades. Despite its widespread use, the gravity model suffers from a number of shortcomings, perhaps most notably its lack of a credible theoretical basis. This shortcoming can be partially remedied by deriving essentially the same mathematical form as a so-called entropy model, either through an analogy with statistical mechanics [Wilson, 1967] or through the use of information theory [Webber, 1977]. The latter approach, in particular, serves to make clear the theoretical underpinnings of the model, which in essence consist of two main points. The first is that the model is derivable from an explicit set of constraints (those already discussed—that predicted and observed trip ends for each zone must match—plus any other "information" that one might have about the system being modeled). Second, the model is no more and no less than a logical, self-consistent procedure for *describing* an observed set of flows. Its *predictive* capabilities are unclear, especially in light of its explicit lack of behavioral assumptions (aside from the recognition that travel distance or time is an important determinant of spatial interaction). Indeed, the amount of error involved in gravity model predictions has been shown to be large, even in "good fitting" models [Smith and Hutchinson, 1979].

7-4-3 Modal Split

Modal split models are used to predict the percentage of trips using each of the modes available to the given trip makers. Figure 7-6 shows modal split as occurring after trip distribution in the UTMS structure, in which case the model is known as a *trip-interchange* modal split model. In some versions of UTMS, however, modal split is performed prior to distribution. In this latter case, the model is known as a *trip-end* model, since it "splits" trip ends (i.e., productions and attractions) rather than flows. Both types of models are discussed briefly below.

Trip-end models Trip-end modal split modeling is based on the assumption that transit ridership is primarily a function of socioeconomic variables; that is, virtually all transit riders are assumed to be "captive" riders—people who have no other choice but to ride transit. This assumption is most valid in areas which possess relatively low transit service levels.

The major advantage of such models is that they are simple to apply and require relatively little data for calibration or prediction. In particular, since the trips have not yet been distributed (and hence the modal service characteristics associated with the trips are not yet known), the only variables that can be used in these models are those that were used in the trip generation stage: auto ownership, income, distance from the CBD, household size, zonal population density, etc. The major disadvantage of these models is that they are generally insensitive to transportation policy changes.

Figure 7-8 displays a typical trip-end modal split model, in which the percentage of trips from a given zone made by transit is expressed as a function of auto-ownership level and zonal population density. Thus, for example, if a given zone has a population density of 50 persons per acre and an auto-ownership distribution of zero-, one-, and two-car households of 20 percent, 50 percent, and 30 percent, respectively, then reading values off the curves of Fig. 7-8, one finds that the estimated percentage of transit trips for this zone is

$$(85)(0.20) + (43)(0.50) + (34)(0.30) = 49\%$$

Trip-interchange models Since trip-interchange models are used after trip distribution, they can utilize the service characteristics (travel times, costs, etc.) of the alternative modes available for the given trip (along with any relevant socioeconomic

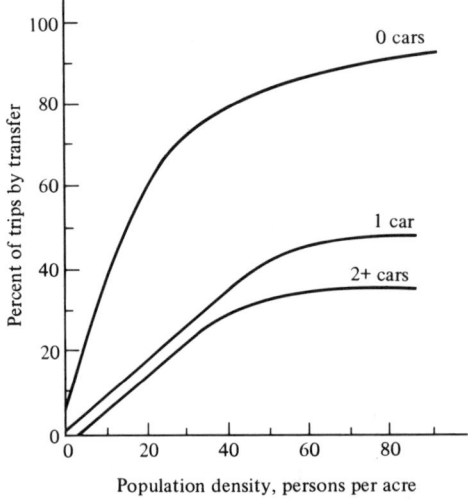

Figure 7-8 A trip-end modal split model. (*Ontario, Ministry of Transportation and Communications [1970].*)

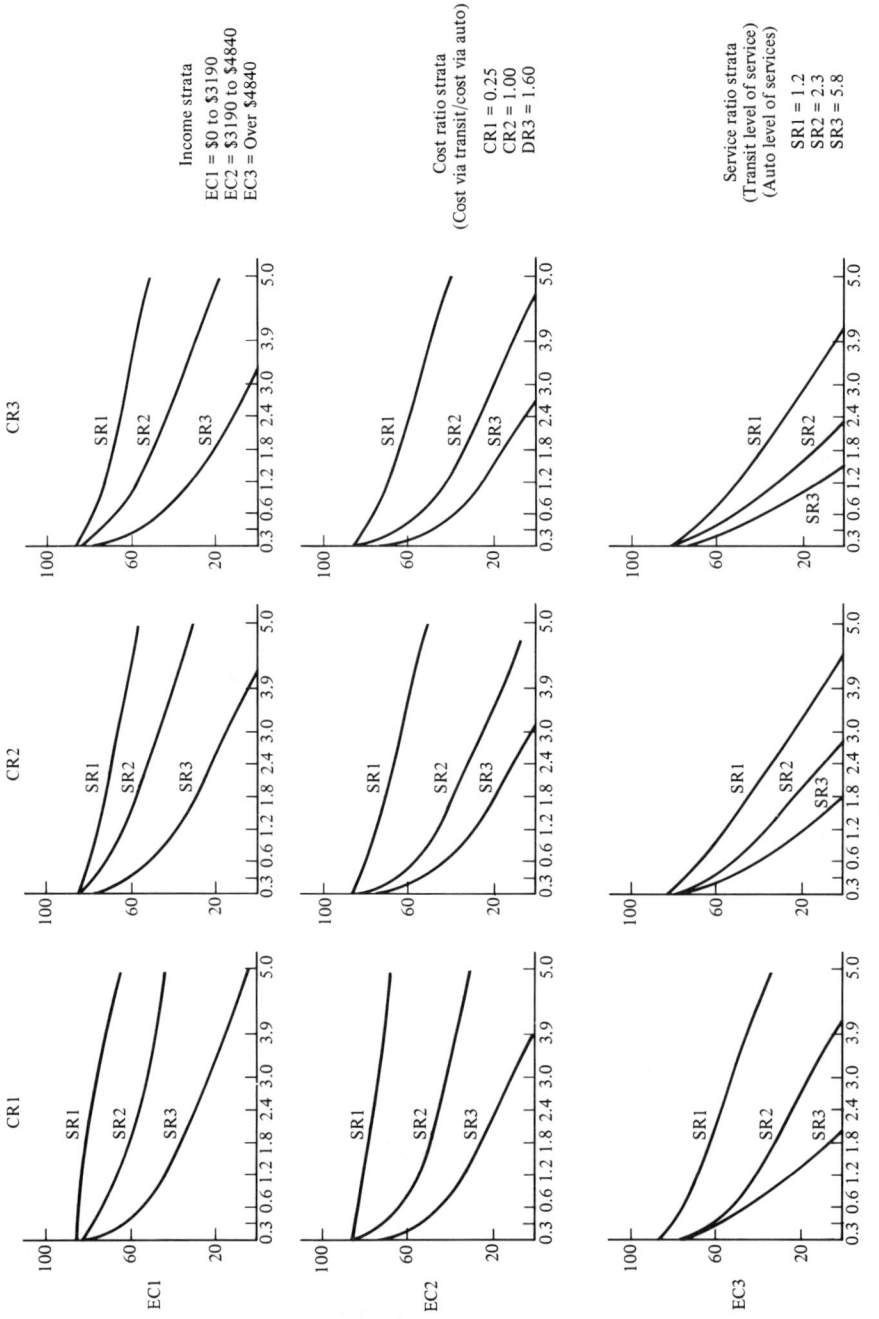

Figure 7-9 A trip interchange modal split model using diversion curves. (*Kates, Peat, Marwick & Co.* [1967].)

characteristics such as income or auto ownership) to determine the modal splits. Typically this has been accomplished through the use of diversion curves, which express the percentage of transit trips as a function of one or more service ratios and socioeconomic categories, as illustrated by Fig. 7-9.

Diversion curves require a considerable amount of data to construct, are difficult to update over time, and are restricted to simple binary modal choice situations (typically auto vs. transit). In recent years disaggregate modal choice models, in particular the multinomial logit model, have proved to be a very powerful approach to modal split modeling. These models are discussed separately in Sec. 7-5.

7-4-4 Assignment

The last step in the UTMS sequence is the assignment of the predicted modal flows between each origin-destination pair to actual routes through the given mode's network. Although manual assignment techniques are possible for very small networks, the networks involved in practical-sized problems usually require the use of digital computers for solution. All such computerized approaches are based on the assumption that the underlying principle determining route selection is what has been labeled *user equilibrium:* in a user-equilibrated network no user can improve his travel time (cost) by unilaterally changing routes [Wardrop, 1952]. Thus, assignment procedures are based on the assumption that each individual chooses the route which he perceives as being the best for himself, that is, that each individual minimizes or "optimizes" his own travel time or cost. This approach can be contrasted with the concept of *system optimization,* in which the system users would be assigned to routes so as to minimize the systemwide average cost of travel. User equilibrium does not, in general, yield the same route assignments as system optimization, meaning a system in user equilibrium will typically not have the lowest possible average system cost. The need to generate user equilibrium rather than system optimal solutions has important ramifications in that the former generally involve far more cumbersome and costly techniques to solve than do the latter.

Traffic assignment techniques include:

1. Minimum path (all-or-nothing) assignment
2. Equilibrium assignment
3. Stochastic assignment

Each of these techniques is discussed briefly in turn.

Minimum path (all-or-nothing) assignment In this approach, "ideal" (i.e., uncongested) minimum travel time paths (routes) are computed for each O-D pair, and all flows between these pairs are loaded onto these routes (Chap. 8 discusses procedures for calculating minimum paths). A given route receives "all or nothing" of a given O-D pair's flow. Advantages of this approach are that it is simple and inexpensive to use, it depicts the routes most travelers would be expected to use in the absence of capacity and/or congestion effects, and the results are easy to understand and interpret. The major disadvantage of the approach is that it clearly generates unrealistic flow patterns in situations where capacity constraints and congestion effects do exist.

Equilibrium assignment Equilibrium assignment techniques explicitly recognize that transportation network link costs generally depend on link flow levels. Hence, these techniques search for a user-equilibrium solution in which link flows and costs are simultaneously solved for. Early approaches to this problem involved the use of approximate *capacity restraint* methods (one example of which is shown in Fig. 7-10) in which flow is incrementally loaded onto the network, thus allowing congestion to gradually "build up" and travel-time estimates to adjust in response to this. Advantages of the capacity restraint approach relative to all-or-nothing assignment are that it more realistically approximates peak-hour flow characteristics than all-or-nothing assignment, it achieves a distribution of trips over a number of routes for any given origin-destination pair, and it is guaranteed to converge to a solution. The major disadvantage of the approach is that there is no guarantee as to the nature of this solution. That is, there is no guarantee that the flow pattern obtained is optimal in user-equilibrium terms, or in any other terms.

In the 1970s, however, true user-equilibrium algorithms were developed, based on mathematical programming formulations of the problem, which do guarantee convergence to the user-equilibrium solution [Bruynooghe et al., 1968; Dafermos, 1971; LeBlanc et al., 1975; Leventhal et al., 1973; Murchland, 1969; Nguyen, 1974a, 1974b]. Such algorithms are available within the U.S. Department of Transportation UTPS computer modeling package. They are also used in the University of Montreal's EMME bimodal (auto and transit) traffic assignment model [Florian et al., 1979], which has been operationally applied to Winnipeg and Vancouver.

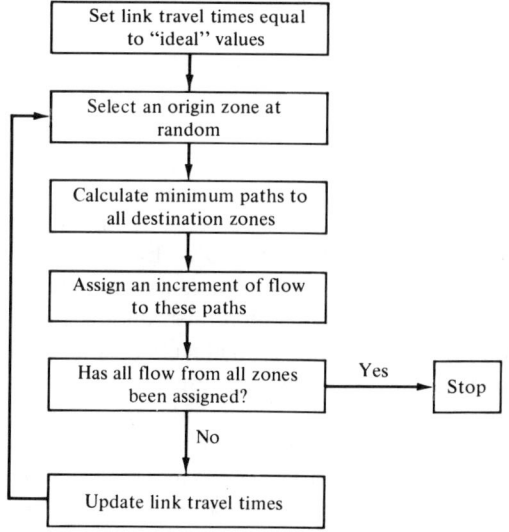

Figure 7-10 Capacity restraint trip assignment.

While the detailed description of these algorithms is beyond the scope of this text (for such a description, see, for example, Kanafani [1983]), the importance of the development of true equilibrium assignment techniques cannot be overemphasized. Such techniques provide a very strong theoretical framework for the assignment process and hence greatly enhance the validity and practical usefulness of the predictions which are generated.

Stochastic assignment Various stochastic approaches to traffic assignment have been proposed and used since the late 1960s. These procedures recognize that several routes between an origin and a destination might be perceived to have equal travel times or otherwise be equally attractive to a traveler and, as a result, might be equally likely to be used by that traveler. Or, in other words, these procedures treat link costs as random variables that can vary among individuals (given their individual preferences, experiences, and perceptions) rather than deterministically (as is done by the other assignment techniques discussed in this section). Suggested procedures include use of an incremental assignment in a stochastic simulation procedure [Burrell, 1968], use of a multinomial logit model to predict route choice probabilities [Dial, 1971], and the use of a multinomial probit model within a "stochastic user-equilibrium" framework [Daganzo and Sheffi, 1977]. Of these, the last is conceptually the most promising, although it has not yet been applied outside of an experimental context. An introduction to the concepts underlying the logit and probit models mentioned here is provided in Sec. 7-5.

7-4-5 Summary Comments

UTMS was originally developed during the 1950s and 1960s to provide input into the comprehensive, long-range transportation planning studies performed in most North American cities during that time period. The primary purpose of these studies was to plan the major transport facilities (principally highways) required by urban regions to cope with postwar urban growth. With the decline of long-range planning studies during the 1970s, the large-scale comprehensive UTMS computer models have decreased in importance and use, primarily because they have been found to be too data-hungry, overly aggregate, and too expensive to address most current planning issues.

This does not mean, however, that UTMS as an *approach* to urban transportation demand analysis is not still of great importance. A considerable amount of the terminology and the worldview adopted by most demand analysts is drawn directly from UTMS. In the next section, for instance, the discussion of individual choice models is presented within the four-stage framework of generation, distribution, mode split, and assignment (although generation, distribution, and assignment are spoken of in terms of trip frequency, destination choice, and route choice, respectively). Such consistency is useful in terms of ensuring a common language and understanding among demand analysts. It does, however, also pose potential problems in terms of limiting one's ability to think imaginatively about transportation demand, particularly in terms of achieving a better behavioral understanding of some of the processes involved.

The component models of UTMS are still very much part of the transportation analyst's standard tools. Trip generation models, gravity models, and simple assignment techniques are continuously being used to analyze the traffic impacts of new shopping centers, residential developments, etc. Standardized computer packages exist for use by planning departments, including UTPS (provided by the Urban Mass Transportation Administration and the Federal Highway Administration), PLANPAC (provided by the Federal Highway Administration), and System 33 (provided by the Ontario Ministry of Transportation and Communications). A majority of demand analyses, if they progress beyond simple trend or elasticity calculations, almost inevitably employ some variation on the UTMS theme for their analysis technique, including many manual and sketch-planning techniques. For example, the U.S. Department of Transportation has developed a microcomputer-based demand analysis package which corresponds closely to the UTMS framework. Thus, while new techniques and analysis needs are emerging (as discussed in the following sections), aggregate, four-stage, UTMS-based models still by and large constitute the most common approach employed by "in the field" transportation planners.

7-5 TRANSPORTATION CHOICE MODELS

7-5-1 Overview of Choice Theory

As discussed in Sec. 7-2, transportation demand can be characterized as the sum or aggregation of the decisions of all individual trip makers within an urban region. In Secs. 7-3 and 7-4 a number of techniques for predicting demand directly at the aggregate level were discussed. An alternative approach which has emerged over the past decade as a viable analysis technique is to model directly the decision process of individual trip makers and then explicitly sum over all trip makers in order to obtain the aggregate demand predictions typically required by the evaluation process.

By far the most common starting point for quantitative choice models is the notion of utility maximization. That is, it is assumed that the decision maker is able to assign at least an ordinal ranking to the alternatives available in terms of their relative desirability (i.e., the alternative's utility). Being a rational person, the decision maker will then choose the alternative with the maximum utility (i.e., the one which maximizes the benefits). As discussed in Chap. 5, utility maximization is central to microeconomic theory but is not restricted to it in its applications. In particular, as observed in Sec. 7-2, given the derived nature of transportation demand, it seems reasonable that people will want to minimize their travel time and cost, maximize their comfort and convenience, and so on, whenever possible. In this context, utility simply represents a convenient generalized function which accounts for the "goods" and the "bads" involved in trip making and which forms the basis for the traveler's decision making.

Conventional microeconomics makes extremely strong assumptions concerning the decision maker's ability to use perfectly all information available and relevant to the decision and to make a completely rational, consistent decision given this information. A major relaxation of some of these assumptions is possible through the introduction of the concept of *random utility*. Primarily originating in the field of psychology [Thurstone, 1927; Luce and Suppes, 1965], such models represent an attempt to retain the analytical tractability provided by the economic assumption of a human being as a rational utility maximizer within a more flexible or realistic worldview. These models recognize that, in practice, people do not always choose the "objectively best" course of action, nor do they necessarily exhibit consistent choices over time. That is, random utility theory still assumes that an individual will choose that alternative which *appears* to maximize his or her utility at the time at which the choice is being made. However, utility is assumed to consist of two components: the systematic, observable utility which is identical to the conventional microeconomic utility function; and a random term which is intended to capture such effects as variations in perceptions and tastes of individual trip makers, misspecification of the utility function by the analyst, and "measurement errors" on the part of the analyst [Manski, 1973].

If one can assume that this random term enters the utility function additively, then the utility of some course of action i for an individual t can be expressed as

$$U_{it} = V_{it} + \epsilon_{it} \tag{7-12}$$

where U_{it} = random utility of alternative i for individual t
V_{it} = systematic (observable) portion of utility
ϵ_{it} = random portion of utility

Further, the systematic utility V_{it} is assumed to be a function of the attributes of the alternative X_i and the characteristics of the individual S_t. In particular, it is typically assumed (for reasons of analytical tractability) that V_{it} is given by

$$V_{it} = b_1 Z_{it1} + b_2 Z_{it2} + \ldots + b_n Z_{itn}$$
$$= bZ_{it} \tag{7-13}$$

where b = row vector of parameters
$Z_{it} = f(X_i, S_t)$ \hfill (7-14)

Since the modeler cannot observe the value of the random terms for any given decision maker (if that were possible, then these values would be incorporated within the systematic or observable portion of the utility function and would no longer need to be treated as random), the modeler cannot say with certainty which alternative will have the maximum utility for the decision maker and will thus be chosen. What can be assessed is the *probability* that a given alternative i from a set of alternatives available to individual t will be the maximum utility alternative for that individual and hence be chosen. That is, given Eq. (7-12) and given a set of alternatives C_t, the probability of individual t choosing alternative i from this set of alternatives (P_{it}) is

$$P_{it} = P(U_{it} \geq U_{jt} \ \forall \ j \in C_t) \tag{7-15}$$

Or, substituting Eq. (7-12) into (7-15),

$$P_{it} = P(V_{it} + \epsilon_{it} \geq V_{jt} + \epsilon_{jt} \quad \forall j \in C_t)$$
$$= P(\epsilon_{jt} - \epsilon_{it} \leq V_{it} - V_{jt} \quad \forall j \in C_t) \tag{7-16}$$

Equation (7-16) is an expression for the joint cumulative distribution function of the random variables $\epsilon_{jt} - \epsilon_{it}$ evaluated at the points $V_{it} - V_{jt}$. Thus, if one knows or assumes the distribution of the ϵ's, one can use this equation to compute the probability of an individual making a given choice. Perhaps the most obvious assumption to make is that the ϵ's are distributed multinomially normal. This assumption generates what is known as a *probit* model. Unfortunately, multinomial probit models cannot be expressed easily in an analytically closed form [Daganzo, 1979] and hence are computationally cumbersome and expensive to use. Indeed, until the late 1970s practical calibration procedures for generalized multinomial probit models did not exist. While such techniques do exist now [Daganzo, 1979; Hausman and Wise, 1978], they are still largely experimental in nature and have not yet been accepted into common planning practice.

An alternative assumption concerning the distribution of the ϵ's is that they are each independently and identically distributed (*iid*) with a Gumbel Type I distribution whose cumulative distribution function is given by

$$F(w) = e^{-e^{-w}} \tag{7-17}$$

Choice of this particular distribution is motivated entirely by considerations of analytical convenience, since when Eq. (7-17) is integrated in order to evaluate Eq. (7-16), it can be shown [Domencich and McFadden, 1975; Hensher and Johnson, 1981] that the final expression for P_{it} is the multinomial *logit* model given by

$$P_{it} = \frac{e^{V_{it}}}{\sum_{j \in C_t} e^{V_{jt}}} \tag{7-18}$$

As an example of a multinomial logit model, consider a three-mode choice situation in which a worker must choose between auto, bus, and walking for his journey to work. The systematic utility functions associated with these alternatives might take the form

$$V_{\text{auto}} = 1.0 - 0.1(TT_{\text{auto}}) - 0.05(TC_{\text{auto}}) \tag{7-19a}$$

$$V_{\text{bus}} = \quad\quad - 0.1(TT_{\text{bus}}) - 0.05(TC_{\text{bus}}) \tag{7-19b}$$

$$V_{\text{walk}} = -0.5 - 0.1(TT_{\text{walk}}) \tag{7-19c}$$

where TT_i = travel time by mode i, minutes
TC_i = travel cost by mode i, dollars

Assume that a given individual is faced with travel times of 5, 15, and 20 minutes for the auto, bus, and walk modes, respectively, for his journey to work. Similarly, his out-of-pocket travel costs by auto and bus are $0.60 and $0.50, respectively. In this case, the values of the systematic utility functions given by Eq. (7-19) are

$$V_{\text{auto}} = 0.47 \quad V_{\text{bus}} = -1.525 \quad V_{\text{walk}} = -2.5$$

Substituting these values into Eq. (7-18), the probability of this worker choosing the auto mode is

$$P_{auto} = \frac{e^{0.47}}{e^{0.47} + e^{-1.525} + e^{-2.5}}$$

$$= \frac{1.6 + 0.2172 + 0.0821}{1.6}$$

$$= \frac{1.6}{1.8993}$$

$$= 0.842$$

Similarly $P_{bus} = \frac{0.2172}{1.8993} = 0.114$

and $P_{walk} = \frac{0.0821}{1.8993} = 0.043$

The logit model has a tractable, convenient functional form. In particular, it can be calibrated relatively easily and efficiently using fairly standardized maximum likelihood techniques. Major characteristics and issues associated with the use of this model include:

1. The independence of irrelevant alternatives assumption
2. Representation of the individual's decision-making structure
3. Specification of the utility function
4. Aggregation of predictions
5. Data requirements
6. Model transferability

Each of these topics is discussed briefly below. For a more detailed discussion of these and other issues concerning individual choice models, the reader is referred to several texts and review articles which deal exclusively with individual choice models [Domencich and McFadden, 1975; Daganzo, 1979; Hensher and Johnson, 1981; Manski and McFadden, 1981; Manski, 1981; Amemiya, 1981; Kanafani, 1983].

Independence of irrelevant alternatives The logit model belongs to a class of models which possesses the so-called independence of irrelevant alternatives (IIA) property. This property can perhaps be illustrated most easily by observing from Eq. (7-18) that the relative probability of an individual t choosing alternative i rather than k, another alternative in the choice set, is

$$\frac{P_{it}}{P_{kt}} = \frac{e^{V_{it}}}{e^{V_{kt}}} \tag{7-20}$$

The key point to note about Eq. (7-20) is that the relative probability of choosing i rather than k depends only on the characteristics (utility) of the alternatives i and k. That is, it is independent of any other alternatives which may be available. Further, as long as the values of V_{it} and V_{kt} do not change, this relative probability will not change, regardless of whether other alternatives are added to or deleted from the choice set.

The IIA property is both one of the strengths of the logit model and its major weakness. The property is advantageous in that it means that the model can be calibrated based on one choice set and then used to predict choices from a modified choice set. Thus, for example, a mode split model can be calibrated based on currently available modes and then used to examine the impact of the introduction of a new mode into the system. The property can also be exploited in cases where the choice set is potentially very large (e.g., shopping destination choice, residential location choice, etc.) to eliminate the need for explicitly including the entire choice set in the calculations. That is, a subset randomly selected from the overall choice set can be used to generate statistically consistent estimation and prediction results [McFadden, 1977].

The problem with the IIA property is that care must be taken that the alternatives included in the choice set are, indeed, independent of each other. Figure 7-11 provides a simple example of a case in which the independence assumption is violated, with disastrous results [Daganzo and Sheffi, 1977]. Figure 7-11a presents a simple route choice problem in which two routes with equal travel times are available and in which the probability of either route being chosen is clearly 0.5. Figure 7-11b presents a modification of the first problem in which one route has been split into two subroutes which are identical except for an arbitrarily small link at one point. Travel times on all three routes remain equal. Obviously, this arbitrarily small change in the network should have no practical effect on the system state: there are still essentially two "real" routes available, and the traffic should split evenly between them. As shown by Fig. 7-11b, however, a simple-minded application of the logit model to the second case results in a prediction of 0.33, 0.33, 0.33 for the three routes, or a ⅓ to ⅔ split between the two "real" routes. This is a direct result of the IIA property (note that the ratio P_1/P_2 equals 1.0 in both cases; that is, it is independent of what other alternatives are

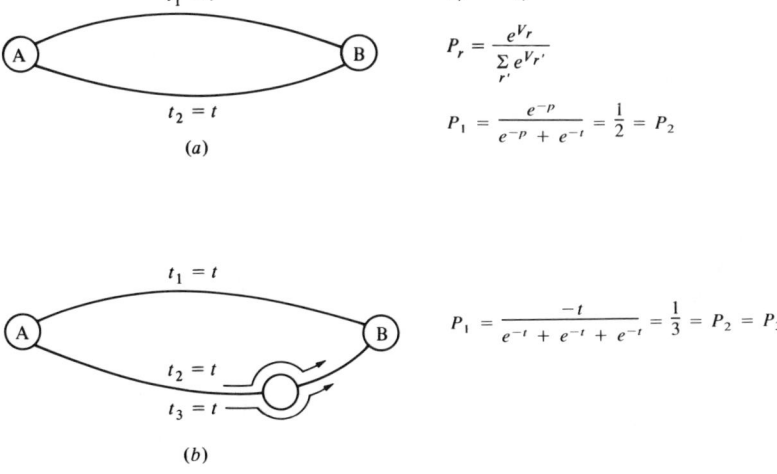

Figure 7-11 Example violation of the independence of irrelevant alternatives property: (a) sequential decision process; (b) joint decision process. (*Draganzo and Sheffi [1977]*.)

available) or rather a direct result of applying the logit model to a choice set that clearly violates the IIA assumption: alternatives 2 and 3 are *not* independent of each other; rather they are highly dependent, and the probability of choosing one is highly correlated with the probability of choosing the other.

Tests are available for identifying violations of the IIA assumption [Hensher and Johnson, 1981]. If the choice set does appear to violate the IIA assumption to the extent that the logit model is untenable, then modeling options include using a probit model, which is capable of handling correlation among alternatives [Daganzo, 1979; Hausman and Wise, 1978], or restructuring the decision structure assumed (discussed further below) so as to reduce or eliminate the dependence between alternatives.

Decision structure One approach for resolving the IIA violation in the route-choice problem discussed above is to consider the problem as a two-stage decision process in which choice is first made between the two "major" routes, and then a second choice is made, if required, between the two "subroutes." Figure 7-12 presents the *decision tree* representation of this two-stage or *sequential* decision process and contrasts it with the corresponding one-stage or *joint* decision process previously discussed.

In any complex choice situation, a number of decision structures are generally conceivable. In Sec. 7-4 it was observed that UTMS implicitly assumes a sequential

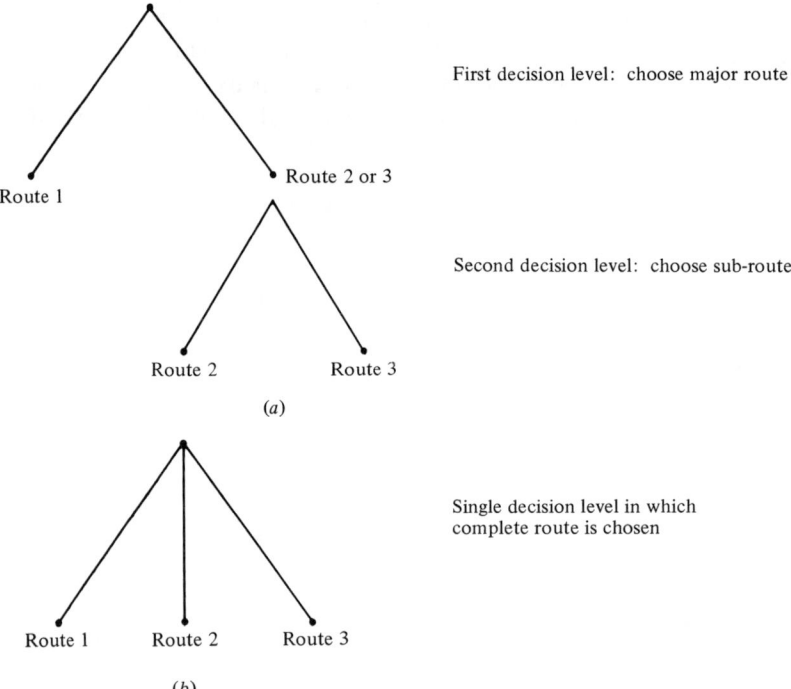

Figure 7-12 Alternative decision structures for a route choice problem. (*a*) Sequential decision process; (*b*) joint decision process.

process consisting of decisions concerning whether to make a trip, where to go given that a trip is made, what mode to use given the trip destination, and what route to use through the chosen mode's network to reach the chosen destination. An alternative decision structure is to assume that the decisions of whether to make a trip, where to go, and what mode to use to get there are all made simultaneously, that is, that a joint decision process exists.

Ben-Akiva [1974] has suggested the *choice hierarchy* shown in Fig. 7-13 for representing travel decisions. Higher-level decisions in the choice hierarchy are made prior to lower-level decisions, which in turn are *conditional* decisions based on the higher-level choices. Thus, nonwork travel decisions are assumed to depend on prior work-trip decisions which, among other things, determine the number of household autos that will be available for nonwork trips. Decisions within each level are generally assumed by Ben-Akiva to be made jointly, although "subhierarchies" are conceivable.

The determination of what choice structure to adopt is primarily based on theoretical grounds, although data availability, problem context, and calibration issues can also play a role. The key point, however, is that an assumption of a decision structure is exactly that: a behavioral assumption concerning the trip maker's decision-making process. As such, its validity should be tested to the extent that this is possible.

One approach to empirically testing decision structure hypotheses, as well as to providing an alternative decision structure "in between" the pure joint and pure sequential structures discussed to this point, is to adopt the so-called *nested* decision structure [McFadden, 1979]. In a nested structure, decisions are still made sequentially, but a higher-level decision (i.e., one made early in the decision process) may include in its calculations expectations concerning subsequent lower-level decisions (i.e., ones made later in the decision process). In particular, the *expected maximum utility* associated with the next stage in the decision process is included in the current stage's utility function. This "feedback" of expected lower-level decisions into the upper-level utility calculations is illustrated in Fig. 7-13 by the dashed arrow leading

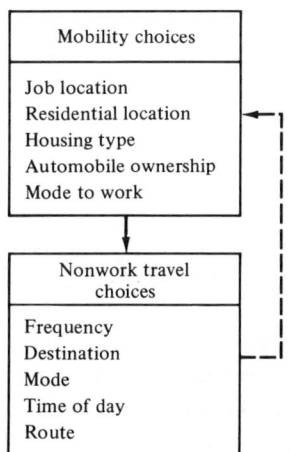

Figure 7-13 A transportation demand choice hierarchy. (*Ben-Akiva, [1974].*)

from the lower-level nonwork trip decisions to the upper-level mobility bundle decisions.

Other, more complicated functional forms for handling correlation among alternatives or "nestedlike" decision structures, such as the *generalized extreme value* model [McFadden, 1979] and the *dogit* model [Gaudry and Dagenais, 1979], are also available. The mathematical details of these models, however, are somewhat complex and are omitted here.

Utility function specification In the theoretical development of the choice model, it is simply assumed that a systematic utility function V_{it} exists for each individual t and alternative i. In practice, the specification of this utility function constitutes a major task in the model-building process. While it is possible to develop utility functions for each individual observed [Lerman and Louviere, 1978], conventional practice involves either categorizing individuals into relatively homogeneous groups and then developing utility functions for each group or developing generalized utility functions within which an individual's socioeconomic characteristics enter directly.

Variables within a utility function can be either *generic* or *alternative-specific* in nature. A generic variable is one which is included in every alternative's utility function with exactly the same weight (i.e., the same parameter value). An alternative-specific variable, on the other hand, has different weights for different alternatives, including an a priori specified weight of zero (i.e., it does not enter into a particular alternative's utility function). A special type of alternative-specific variable is the alternative-specific constant or bias term which is often employed to capture systematic, "all else being equal" preferences exhibited within a sample.

Some of these concepts can be illustrated with a simple modal choice problem consisting of two modes, auto *(a)* and transit *(t)*. Transportation variables chosen to characterize the system are in-vehicle travel time (IVTT), out-of-vehicle travel time (OVTT), and out-of-pocket travel costs (OPTC). Two socioeconomic variables are used to characterize each traveler: household income (INC) and household auto-ownership level (AO). A simple modal split model using these variables might be specified by the following utility functions:

$$V_a = b_1 + b_2 \text{IVTT}_a + b_4 \text{OVTT}_a + b_5 \frac{\text{OPTC}_a}{\text{INC}} + b_6 \text{AO} \qquad (7\text{-}21a)$$

$$V_t = b_3 \text{IVTT}_t + b_4 \text{OVTT}_t + b_5 \frac{\text{OPTC}_t}{\text{INC}} \qquad (7\text{-}21b)$$

Several points concerning Eqs. (7-21a) and (7-21b) should be noted:

1. OVTT and the composite variable OPTC/INC are generic variables since they enter both utility functions with the same parameter value (that is, b_4 and b_5, respectively).
2. IVTT is an alternative-specific variable since it enters the two equations with different weights (that is, b_2 and b_3). This reflects the hypothesis that a minute spent riding a bus is perceived (weighted) differently than a minute spent driving in a car.

3. While the utility functions are "linear in the parameters," nonlinear composite variables (such as the OPTC/INC term) can be included.
4. b_1 is an alternative-specific constant for the auto mode. No transit constant is specified (or, more correctly, the transit constant is arbitrarily set equal to zero) because in an n alternative choice set, at most $n - 1$ alternatives are statistically identifiable.
5. Because socioeconomic characteristics for a given individual do not vary across alternatives, socioeconomic variables must enter the utility functions as alternative-specific variables (such as AO) or generically in functional combination with a system variable (e.g., the OPTC/INC term). That is, a generic socioeconomic variable will add exactly the same value to every alternative's utility function and will thus have absolutely no impact on the choice probabilities.

Aggregation Individual choice models generate predictions of the probabilities associated with given individuals choosing a particular outcome from a set of alternatives. As such, these probabilities are of little direct use for planning purposes. That is, a planner is rarely interested in the probability that a specific individual will choose transit; rather he is interested in the total number of people in a zone or in an urban area likely to choose transit. Thus, some procedure must be employed to *aggregate* the individual choice predictions of the model to yield the total demand predictions required for planning purposes.

In principle, the simplest aggregation procedure is to enumerate all individuals within the study area and sum their probabilities of choosing a given alternative. The problem with *total enumeration,* as this procedure is called, is that one rarely, if ever, has complete information concerning each and every individual within a study area; and, even if one did, the calculations involved are likely to be extremely cumbersome, if not prohibitively expensive. Some other aggregation procedure is generally required. While a range of procedures exist [Koppleman, 1975], the three most commonly discussed are:

1. "Naive" aggregation
2. Classification with naive aggregation
3. Sample enumeration

Naive aggregation involves treating the individual choice model as if it were an aggregate model by using zonal average values for the utility function variables in order to compute an "average" zonal probability. Since logit model probabilities are nonlinear functions of the utility function variables, however, such use of average values will not generate the correct average probability. The errors which can occur through the use of naive aggregation can be substantial, and one should avoid the use of this technique whenever possible.

Aggregation errors can generally be reduced if the population is classified into relatively homogeneous groups with respect to one or more key variables prior to the use of naive aggregation. Koppleman identifies auto ownership and transit availability as two key variables to be used in classification for the modal split case [Koppleman,

1975], although other researchers have found that the key variables may differ from one urban area to another, as does the accuracy of the procedure [Reid, 1978].

While total enumeration is generally impractical if not infeasible, very often a representative sample of the population is available to the analyst. In such cases this sample can be enumerated, and the resulting sample prediction can be used as an estimate of the population prediction (with appropriate "grossing up," if required). For short-run analyses the calibration data set or some similar sample is generally available and can be used. For longer-run analyses, or in the absence of a current sample, a sample can often be synthesized from census data, zonal population forecasts, etc. if reasonable assumptions about the distributions of sample characteristics can be made. Provided that a representative sample is available or can be reliably generated, sample enumeration is generally the preferred aggregation procedure.

Table 7-3 provides a numerical example which illustrates the use of the enumeration, naive, and classification approaches to aggregation for the bimodal logit model specified by Eq. (7-21). The table presents the coefficient values assumed for the example (Table 7-3a) and the values of the explanatory variables in the utility functions for 10 observations (Table 7-3b). The final column of Table 7-3b presents the probabilities of choosing the auto mode for each observation. To aggregate by enumeration, one simply adds up these individual probabilities and divides by the total number of observations (10). This yields the true expected aggregate probability of 0.88635.

Table 7-3c illustrates the naive aggregation procedure. In this table, the average values for the utility function variables are shown. Using these average values in Eq. (7-21) results in the "average" probability of choosing auto (0.91505) shown in the last column of the table—a value about 3 percent higher than the true expected value computed in Table 7-3b. This result is typical of all naive aggregation predictions in that it represents an overprediction of the "dominant" alternative, in this case, the auto mode.

Finally, classification with naive aggregation is illustrated in Table 7-3d. This table shows the number of observations falling into each income–auto-ownership category, the average values for the utility function variables *within* each category, and the naive "average" probability of choosing auto for each category (computed by substituting the within-category average values into Eq. [7-21]). The aggregate "average" value is then computed by taking an average of these probabilities, weighted by group size. That is, the aggregate "average" probability computed by the classification procedure is equal to

$$\frac{3(0.81038) + 2(0.93913) + 1(0.978851) + 2(0.85516) + 2(0.96390)}{3 + 2 + 1 + 2 + 2}$$

or 0.89260. Thus, while the classification procedure still overpredicts auto usage, it performs much better than the pure naive approach in that it differs, for this test example, by less than 1 percent from the true average value.

The need to aggregate individual choice model predictions is sometimes viewed as a liability of the technique. In fact, it represents a major strength in that it means that the model can be applied at any level of spatial aggregation. Conventional aggregate

Table 7-3 Numerical example of aggregation procedures

(a) Utility function coefficients

$b_1 = 0.25 \quad b_3 = -0.11 \quad b_5 = -0.0007$
$b_2 = -0.10 \quad b_4 = -0.20 \quad b_6 = 0.25$

(b) Utility function variables and choice probabilities for individual observations

Obs. no.	IVTT$_a$	IVTT$_t$	OVTT$_a$	OVTT$_t$	OPTC$_a$	OPTC$_t$	INC	AO	P_{auto}
1	20	25	5	10	250	50	1	1	0.89187
2	25	35	5	15	300	50	3	2	0.98274
3	15	18	3	8	225	50	2	2	0.89741
4	30	40	5	15	400	50	3	1	0.97851
5	20	30	5	10	300	50	2	1	0.93776
6	10	12	3	5	150	50	1	1	0.75951
7	15	25	8	5	100	50	2	2	0.79939
8	35	40	5	10	600	75	3	2	0.92605
9	30	40	5	10	450	50	2	1	0.94048
10	10	15	5	5	125	50	1	1	0.74979
Average P_{auto}									0.88635

(c) Naive aggregation

	IVTT$_a$	IVTT$_t$	OVTT$_a$	OVTT$_t$	OPTC$_a$	OPTC$_t$	INC	AO	P_{auto}
Average values:	21.0	28.0	4.9	9.3	290.0	52.5	2.0	1.4	0.91505

(d) Classification with naive aggregation

No. of obs.	IVTT$_a$	IVTT$_t$	OVTT$_a$	OVTT$_t$	OPTC$_a$	OPTC$_t$	INC	AO	P_{auto}
3	13.3	17.3	4.3	6.7	175.0	50	1	1	0.81038
2	25.0	35.0	5.0	10.0	375.0	50	2	1	0.93913
1	30.0	40.0	5.0	15.0	400.0	50	3	1	0.97851
0							1	2	
2	15.0	21.5	5.5	6.5	162.5	50	2	2	0.85516
2	30.0	37.5	5.0	12.5	450.0	62.5	3	2	0.96390
Weighted average P_{auto}									0.89260

Note: All times are in minutes. All costs are in cents. Income is expressed as a code (1, 2, 3).

models can only be used in conjunction with the zonal system for which they were calibrated, since this calibration includes (in unknown ways) all the idiosyncrasies of the spatial aggregation implicit in the zonal system adopted. Thus, once calibrated, an aggregate model can only perform analysis at one level of spatial aggregation, regardless of whether this level is too coarse or too fine for the given problem application. Individual choice models, on the other hand, can be aggregated to any desired level, depending upon data availability and the problem context.

Data requirements Individual choice models are more efficient than corresponding aggregate models in their use of data. This is because aggregate models typically employ zonal averages which require a fair number of observations to construct, whereas individual choice models (and disaggregate models in general) employ every observation directly in their calibration. Thus, individual choice models require fewer observations to construct, for a given level of accuracy. Given the high cost of data collection and the very large samples typically gathered in the past to construct aggregate models, this is a very important strength of the individual choice model technique.

The nature and the detail of the data required by individual choice models, however, are often greater than that collected for aggregate models. A wider range of socioeconomic information and a more detailed representation of the level of service variables (including service characteristics for "unchosen" alternatives) experienced by the observed travelers are typically required. Further, this more detailed information must be available for the future situations for which predictions are required. As a rule, then, while individual choice models require less quantity of data (in terms of the number of observations in the sample), they often require higher quality data (in terms of the information obtained per observation).

Model transferability Since individual choice models are not tied to a specific zone structure within a specific city and since they possess the potential for a relatively rich representation of the factors affecting a traveler's decision making, it has been argued that such models should be capable of being transferred from one geographical location to another. The benefits of such transferability would be enormous in that it would significantly reduce in a number of cases the data requirements, calibration time and costs, and detailed analytical expertise required by planners to perform demand analyses. Atherton and Ben-Akiva [1976] performed the first major investigation into the transferability properties of individual choice models. In general, they found that logit mode split models could be transferred from one city to another, particularly if some "updating" of the model parameters was performed, using either available aggregate data (which is used to adjust the modal constants within the model) or a small local sample (in which case all or most of the model parameters can be adjusted).

McCoomb [1982] used data gathered by Statistics Canada as part of the 1976 labor force survey to calibrate identical work-trip mode split logit models for 10 Canadian cities, including the 9 largest census metropolitan areas (CMAs) in Canada, and then compared them using a range of qualitative and statistical tests. Based on the results of these tests, McCoomb found no universally transferable model but concluded that models were transferable on a specific city-pair basis, provided that the two cities were similar in size, structure, transportation system, and major market segments. Further, it appears possible to identify trends in the value of key model coefficients as functions of city size, structure, etc., which might obviate the need for the small sample updating procedures suggested by Atherton and Ben-Akiva.

7-5-2 Choice Model Applications

By far the most common application to date of individual choice models to transportation demand modeling has involved modeling the choice of mode (usually for the work trip) given a known trip origin, destination, and purpose. The modal choice problem is in many ways a "natural" for choice model applications in that it consists of a relatively small and reasonably well-defined discrete choice set from which one and only one alternative can be chosen for any given trip; the notion of utility is readily operationalized in terms of the times and costs associated with the available modes; and the logit model itself in many ways represents a mathematical formalization of the empirically derived diversion curves which were commonly used prior to the introduction of choice model concepts.

Tables 7-4 and 7-5 present the variable definitions and calibrated model coefficients for a "typical" logit work-trip mode split model for three modes (auto drive alone, auto shared ride, and transit) calibrated for the Washington, D.C. area, using 1968 home interview survey data. The characteristics of this model that are worth noting include:

1. Composite variables OPTC/INC and OVTT/DIST are used to modify the impact of the pure level-of-service variables OPTC and OVTT. That is, it is hypothesized that out-of-pocket travel costs are perceived as being less onerous by higher-income people than by lower-income people; similarly, out-of-vehicle travel time is hypothesized as becoming less important as the length of the trip increases.
2. Dummy variables BW_c, GW_s, etc. are used to capture observed systematic effects that are not captured by the conventional transportation, activity system, or socioeconomic variables. Each such variable represents a specific hypothesis concerning the system being modeled. For example, BW_c represents the hypothesis that the "breadwinner" or principal worker in the household receives priority in the allocation of a household's automobiles and hence is more likely to drive alone than is a nonbreadwinner. Similarly, GW_s represents the hypothesis that government workers possess a higher opportunity for car pooling than nongovernment workers because of federal government incentives to car-pool.
3. Socioeconomic variables (such as AALD, DINC, and NWORK) and activity system variables DCITY and DTECA all enter the utility functions as alternative-specific variables in ways which again represent hypotheses about system behavior. It is hypothesized, for example, that the higher the ratio of the number of automobiles owned to the number of licensed drivers within a household, the more likely it is that a worker will use automobile transportation rather than transit—either through the shared-ride mode or, even more likely, by driving alone. That

Table 7-4 Work mode choice model: Definition of variables

Variable code	Definition
1. D_c	1, for drive alone 0, otherwise
2. D_s	1, for shared ride 0, otherwise
3. OPTC/INC	Round trip out-of-pocket travel cost, in cents/household annual income, in dollars
4. IVTT	Round trip in-vehicle travel time, in minutes
5. OVTT/DIST	Round trip out-of-vehicle travel time, in minutes/one-way distance, in miles
6. $AALD_c$	Ratio of autos to licensed drivers, for drive alone 0, otherwise
7. $AALD_s$	Ratio of autos to licensed drivers, for shared ride 0, otherwise
8. BW_c	1, if worker is the breadwinner, for drive alone 0, otherwise
9. GW_s	1, if worker is a civilian employee of the federal government, for shared ride 0, otherwise
10. $DCITY_c$	1, if workplace is in the CBD, for drive alone 0, otherwise
11. $DCITY_s$	1, if workplace is in the CBD, for shared ride 0, otherwise
12. $DINC_{c,s}$	Household annual income $-$ [800 $\times$ number of persons in the household], in dollars, for drive alone and shared ride 0, otherwise
13. $NWORK_s$	Number of workers in the household, for shared ride 0, otherwise
14. $DTECA_s$	Employment density at the work zone (employees per commercial acre) $\times$ one-way distance, in miles, for shared ride 0, otherwise

Alternative: c = drive alone, s = shared ride (car pool), t = transit
Source: Atherton and Ben-Akiva [1976].

is, the a priori expectation is that the coefficients of $AALD_c$ and $AALD_s$ should be positive in value and that $AALD_c$ should be greater in magnitude than $AALD_s$ (which, as is shown in Table 7-5, proves to be the case).

Individual choice models have been used in a wide variety of planning applications, including [Spear, 1977; Ben-Akiva, 1977]:

1. To analyze the effects of various auto-restricted zone concepts in selected United States cities.

Table 7-5 Work mode choice model: the model coefficients

Variable		Coefficient	t-statistic
1. Drive alone constant	D_c	−3.24	−6.86
2. Shared-ride constant	D_s	−2.24	−5.60
3. Out-of-pocket travel cost divided by income	OPTC/INC	−28.8	−2.26
4. In-vehicle travel time	IVTT	−0.0154	−2.67
5. Out-of-vehicle travel time divided by distance	OVTT/DIST	−0.160	−4.08
6. Auto availability (drive alone only)	$AALD_c$	3.99	10.08
7. Auto availability (shared ride only)	$AALD_s$	1.62	5.31
8. Breadwinner (drive alone only)	BW_c	0.890	4.79
9. Government worker (shared ride only)	GW_s	0.287	1.78
10. CBD workplace (drive alone only)	$DCITY_c$	−0.854	−2.75
11. CBD workplace (shared ride only)	$DCITY_s$	−0.404	−1.36
12. Disposable income (drive alone and shared ride only)	$DINC_{c,s}$	0.0000706	3.46
13. Number of workers (shared ride only)	$NWORK_s$	0.0983	1.03
14. Employment density (shared ride only)	$DTECA_s$	0.000653	1.34

No. of observations = 1114
No. of alternatives = 2924
Log likelihood at zero = −1054.0
Log likelihood at convergence = −727.4

Source: Atherton and Ben-Akiva [1976].

2. To analyze TSM policies such as parking tax increases on automobile use in downtown Chicago, pricing policies for BART and the Alameda-Contra Costa Bus Company, strategies to reduce pollution emissions such as gasoline taxes and nonresidential parking surcharges in Los Angeles and Denver, and car pooling incentives in Washington, D.C.
3. To forecast demand for new services such as dual mode transit to provide areawide transit service, commuter rail access modes in Chicago, park-and-ride services in New York State, light rail and express bus systems in Portland, Oregon, a "people-mover" system for internal circulation within the Los Angeles central business district, alternative guideway transit strategies for Milwaukee, and an areawide public transit system in suburban Illinois.

Applications of individual choice models have ranged from the use of mode choice models to predict the impacts of relatively simple changes in the transportation system to the integrated application of a number of separately calibrated choice models to analyze a broad range of impacts. Figure 7-14 presents the modeling system structure for the most ambitious planning application of individual choice models yet attempted,

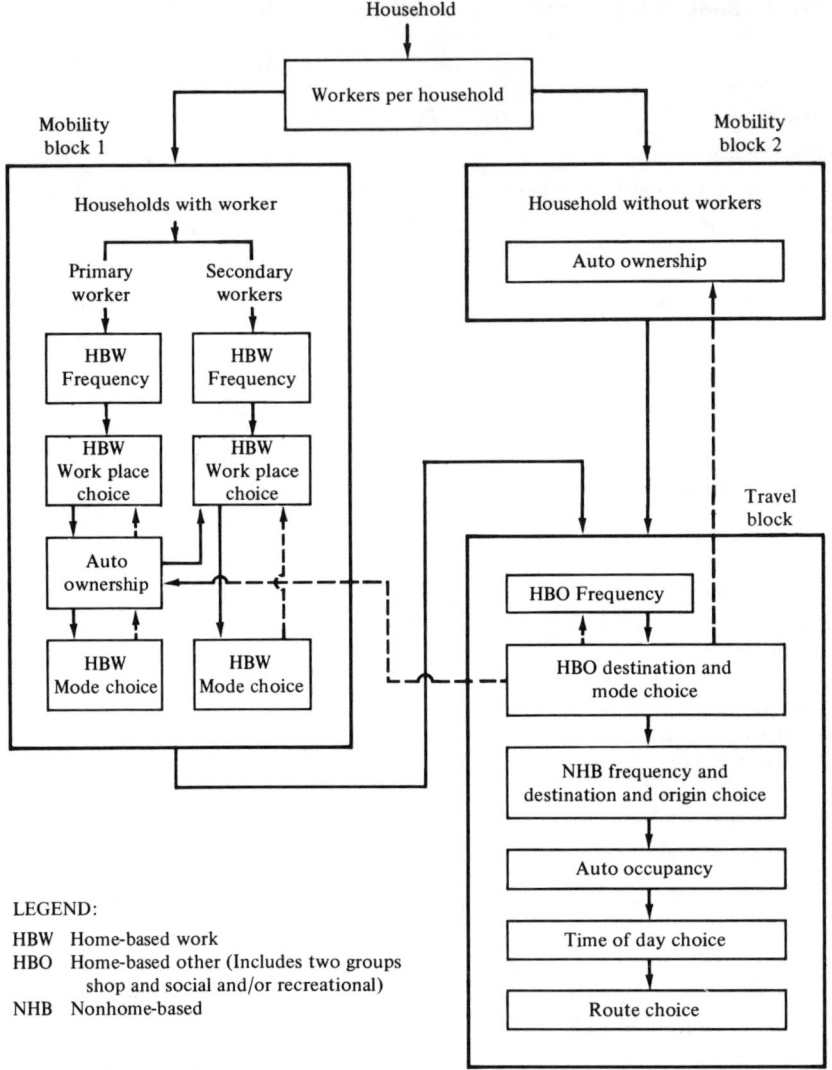

Figure 7-14 The MTC travel demand modeling system. (*Ben Akiva [1977]*.)

the San Francisco region's Metropolitan Transportation Commission (MTC) travel demand modeling system. This system was designed to replace a traditional aggregate UTMS system in the analysis of "conventional" regional urban transportation planning studies. It is fully compatible with the Urban Mass Transportation Administration's UTPS computer package in terms of its file structures and, in fact, employs UTPS subroutines and programs where they are applicable. Otherwise, all the transportation demand choices indicated in Fig. 7-14 are modeled by disaggregate logit models [Ruiter and Ben-Akiva, 1978].

Individual choice models have also been applied in a more experimental way to a number of planning issues including modeling the choice of the "mobility bundle" (i.e., the choice of residential location, auto ownership, and work-trip mode) [Lerman, 1976; Weisbrod, 1978; Pollakowski, 1982], auto-ownership choices [Lerman and Ben-Akiva, 1976; Lave and Train, 1979; Manski and Sherman, 1980; Train, 1980], nonwork travel choices [Adler and Ben-Akiva, 1976; Horowitz, 1980], route choice [Dial, 1971; Daganzo and Sheffi, 1977], retail location choice [Miller and Lerman, 1981; Wolfe, 1981], and sketch-planning applications [Watanatada and Ben-Akiva, 1978; Cambridge Systematics, 1979; McCoomb, 1982].

7-6 ANALYZING TRANSPORTATION DEMAND

The previous sections have outlined a number of techniques which can be used, given appropriate circumstances, in the analysis of transportation demand. This section focuses on the demand analysis process itself, which is largely independent of the actual techniques employed. As shown in Fig. 7-15, this process consists of six basic tasks:

1. Problem identification
2. Choice of analysis technique
3. Data collection
4. Model calibration
5. Model validation
6. Forecasting

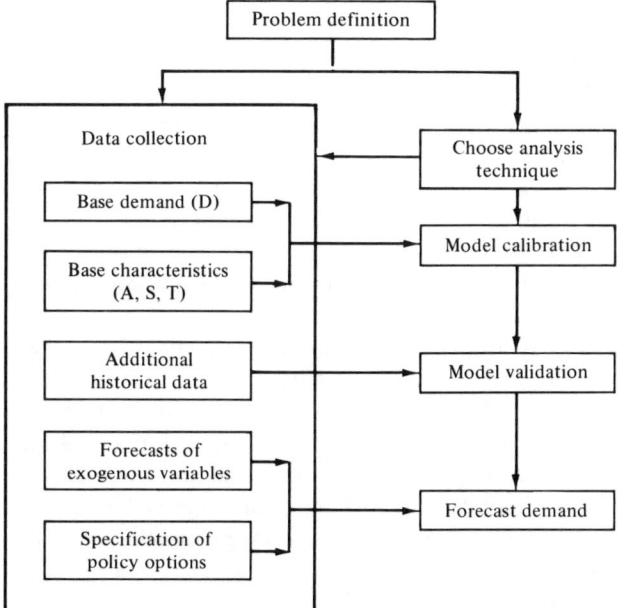

Figure 7-15 The demand analysis process.

Although Fig. 7-15 depicts demand analysis as a relatively linear process, the tasks involved are, in fact, highly interrelated. In particular, problem definition, choice of analysis technique, data collection, and model calibration are very much interconnected in a majority of cases. Data availability, for instance, often determines the analysis technique employed rather than the converse shown in Fig. 7-15. Similarly, model calibration issues often help determine model functional forms and specifications. Figure 7-15 is thus a simplification of the iterative, circular nature of most demand analyses, and is intended to illustrate some of the key aspects of the demand analysis process. Each of the major tasks shown in this figure is discussed in turn in the following subsections.

7-6-1 Problem Definition

Problem definition is largely determined outside of the demand analysis per se in that problems are usually identified in the diagnosis phase of the planning process. Such problem definitions, however, tend to be fairly general and abstract in nature (e.g., "examine short-term TSM strategies for relieving road congestion," or "assess long-term regional transit needs"). In order to perform a demand analysis the problem definition typically needs to be "sharpened" in terms of its detailed specifications. In particular, the analyst must define (or have defined for him):

1. *The specific planning period for the analysis.* The planning period is typically defined in terms of a *base year* and a *horizon year*. Many analyses provide only a horizon year forecast. If interim forecasts are also required (e.g., yearly ridership forecasts for the next 5 years), then it must be made explicit at the outset, since this will have implications for the data requirements and, possibly, for the analysis techniques used.
2. *The study region and zonal structure for the analysis.* The boundary of the study region, the zonal system within the study region, and whether or not trips across the study boundary to and from "external" zones are of interest and must all be defined. These decisions obviously depend highly on the particular problem context and, typically, on the existence of data for previously defined zone systems (census tracts, traffic analysis zones, planning district, etc.).
3. *The temporal unit of demand.* Is the desired temporal unit of demand the peak period, the day, the year? This decision again depends on the problem context and data availability.
4. *The policy variables.* What are the policy options available to the decision maker and how do these translate into measurable, observable variables? Clearly data must be available to characterize the alternatives of interest in terms of the relevant policy variables, and the demand technique used must be able to incorporate these variables, if the analysis is to be useful in judging the relative merits of the various alternatives. For example, a trip distribution model which does not include travel cost in its impedance function will not be of use in analyzing potential impacts of increasing energy costs on urban trip patterns.

5. *The measures of effectiveness required for evaluation.* Just as the policy variables characterizing the policy options or alternatives can be viewed as the "inputs" into the demand analysis, the "outputs" of the analysis are a set of measures of effectiveness which characterize the impacts which these alternatives are predicted to have on the urban system (e.g., average travel time within the system, volume-capacity ratios on major roadways, annual transit ridership by route). These effectiveness measures are then used within the evaluation phase to assist with the choice among the proposed alternatives (see Chap. 9). Clearly, the demand analysis must be able to generate the required measures if it is to contribute successfully to the evaluation (and, ultimately, to the overall planning) process. A particularly important consideration is whether or not these measures are required for different market segments. That is, are systemwide or general totals, averages, etc. sufficient, or should these be broken down by socioeconomic group (e.g., sex, income level, age group), geographic location (e.g., downtown, suburb), and so on, so that the *distribution* of impacts within the system can be assessed?

7-6-2 Choice of Analysis Technique

The choice of an analysis technique obviously depends upon the problem being addressed and will be heavily influenced by the problem definition issues discussed above: the analysis time frame, the spatial scale, the policy variables, and measures of effectiveness of interest, and so on. A typology of "appropriate techniques" for various spatial scales and time frames is difficult to construct because a given technique can typically be applied at various spatial scales (e.g., individual choice models can be employed at virtually any level of aggregation provided that a suitable aggregation procedure is available) and for various time frames (e.g., UTMS-type aggregate models are used in a wide range of planning activities, from assessing the immediate impacts of the opening of a new shopping center to estimating peak-period freeway flows over a 20- or 30-year horizon). As a generalization, however, two conflicting trends seem to exist. The first is that as the spatial scale and/or analysis time frame increases, so does the complexity and comprehensiveness of the analysis technique required to adequately address the planning problem. That is, as the "boundaries" of the problem expand, additional factors and relationships can no longer be considered to hold constant, and the analysis techniques and assumptions used must reflect this expansion of the problem context.

On the other hand, as spatial scale and time frame increase, so do the data, cost, and time requirements of the analysis. More fundamentally, the ability to observe detailed interactions, to hypothesize behavioral relationships, and to predict future system states decreases as spatial scale and time frame increase. Hence, a sort of "social Heisenberg principle" seems to exist in which as the need to be more comprehensive increases, the ability to do so decreases because of the volume, quality, and, ultimately, the availability of the data required.

Figure 7-16 qualitatively illustrates this proposition, suggesting that analysis complexity typically first increases in response to increasing problem scale but then

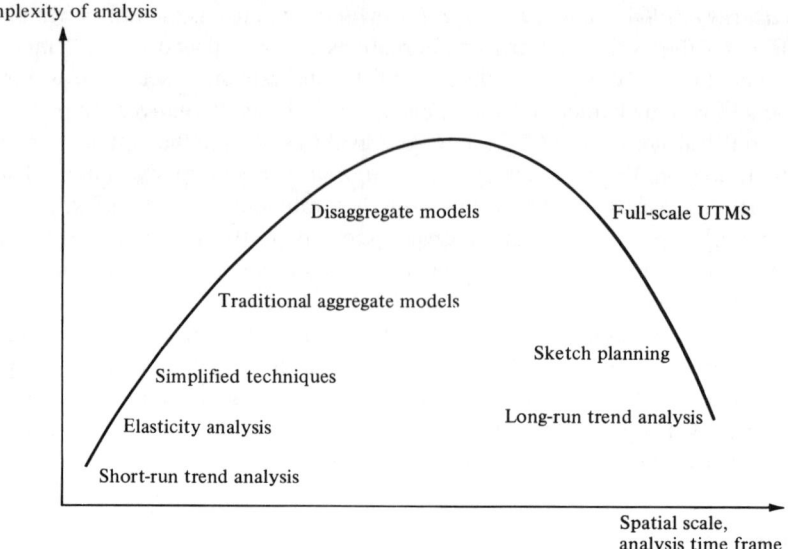

Figure 7-16 Relation between problem scale and analysis complexity.

ultimately decreases, reverting to simpler techniques, as limitations in available data and theory begin to dominate. The techniques discussed in this chapter have been distributed along the curve so as to approximate their typical "scale-complexity" placements, although, as discussed above, this can vary for a given technique from problem to problem.

7-6-3 Data Collection

Given the problem definition and the choice of an analysis technique, considerable data are typically required to perform the analysis. Two major types of data are needed for most analyses:

1. *Historical data* on travel behavior and the associated socioeconomic, activity system, and transportation system variables of interest
2. *Forecasts* or specifications of future values of socioeconomic, activity system, and transportation system variables required to predict future demand for each alternative under consideration

The historical data are required for the calibration and validation phases of the demand analysis discussed below. Chapter 4 dealt in some detail with data collection procedures and issues, and little more needs to be said at this point about the topic. Of greater immediate interest is the generation of data characterizing expected future system states required by the forecasting phase of the analysis. These data can be divided into two types: policy variables characterizing the alternatives under consideration and nonpolicy variables.

Policy variables (typically the transportation variables in the model and possibly some of the activity system variables) are not forecasted; they are simply specified as part of the process of defining the alternatives (e.g., links 400 to 425 inclusive will be a four-lane, controlled-access highway with a capacity of 2000 vehicles per lane per hour and a free-flow speed of 55 miles per hour). As such they pose no special difficulty to the demand analyst. Far more problematic are the nonpolicy variables (typically the socioeconomic and activity system variables) required by the demand model as exogenous inputs (e.g., population and employment by income level for each zone in the study region). Such variables typically must be themselves forecasted by some process. As with any forecasting exercise, the difficulty and complexity of this task depend very much on the forecast horizon year. In the very short run, the spatial distribution of people, buildings, and activities will change very little, and hence forecasting consists, at most, of minor updating of current conditions; while in the very long run all of these factors may well change dramatically in terms of their magnitude and spatial distribution, in which case forecasting may require an extensive and complex analysis of activity system trends and interactions.

Chapter 6 presented an overview of land use forecasting techniques. As discussed in Chap. 6, the large-scale land use models developed during the 1960s and early 1970s have largely fallen into disuse over the past decade. Little in the way of new techniques has emerged to take their place. This could ultimately impose a serious limitation on the application of new demand analysis techniques beyond relatively short-range contexts, particularly in the case of individual choice models with their relatively detailed data requirements.

7-6-4 Calibration

Virtually all transportation demand models effectively consist of a dependent variable—the demand for transportation—expressed as a function of one or more independent (or explanatory) variables. If D denotes demand and X denotes the vector of explanatory variables, then the demand model can generally be represented by the equation

$$D = f(X, \theta) \quad (7\text{-}22)$$

where θ is a vector of parameters or coefficients (the two terms are used interchangeably within this book) which determine the ''shape'' of the demand curve, the relative ''weights'' of the various terms within the demand function, etc. The elasticity value in a pivot-point analysis, the travel time exponent in a gravity model, and the utility function coefficients in a logit model are all examples of model parameters.

In the derivation of a demand model, the model parameters are assumed to be known. In actual fact, these parameters are not known, are likely to vary from city to city (as well as over time), and must be estimated for a given problem application from historical data. This estimation or calibration process involves a comparison of observed demand levels with the demand levels predicted by the model, given an assumed set of parameter values, followed by adjustment of these parameter values until the predicted demand levels match the observed demand as best as possible.

The archetypal calibration procedure is regression analysis. Figure 7-17 shows a plot of hypothetical zonal trip productions P_i vs. average zonal income Y_i. A simple trip production model suggested by these hypothetical data would be

$$P_i = \theta_1 + \theta_2 Y_i \qquad (7\text{-}23)$$

where P_i is the predicted number of daily trip productions in zone i.

Regression analysis can be used to find the values of θ_1 and θ_2 which cause Eq. (7-23) to "best fit" the observed data, where best fit is defined as minimizing the sum of squares of the differences between the observed and predicted trip productions. In-depth discussions of the procedures used to accomplish this task and issues in the use of regression analysis can be found in any standard econometrics text [Wonnacott and Wonnacott, 1970; Kmenta, 1971; Theil, 1971; Koutsoyiannis, 1977]. The point of interest here is that regression typifies the calibration process in that:

1. It involves an explicit definition of what is meant by a model best fitting observed data.
2. It employs a statistical estimation procedure which in both a computational and a statistical sense efficiently identifies the best-fit set of parameters.

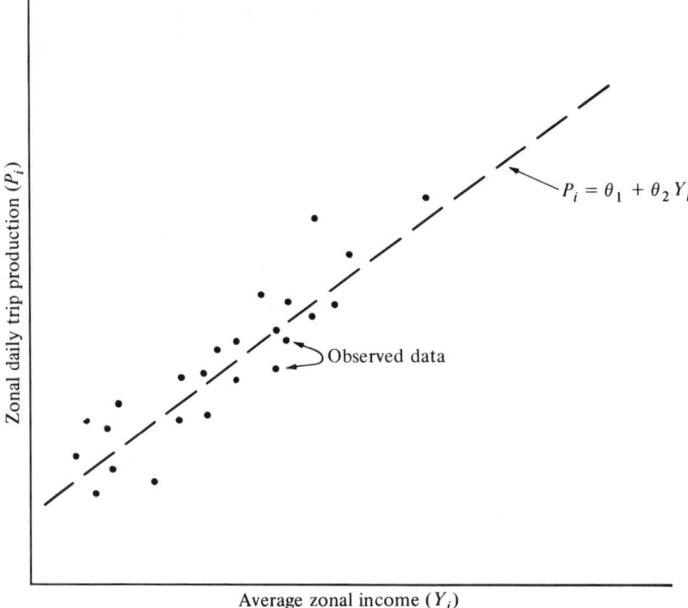

Figure 7-17 Hypothetical plot of zonal trip productions versus average income.

3. It facilitates the computation of a set of statistics which characterize the goodness of fit achieved by the model (such as the R^2 and F statistics) as well as the statistical significance of the individual parameters within the model (e.g., the t-statistic).

Regression analysis is an extremely powerful tool. A number of standardized, readily available computer packages exist for performing regression analysis, including SPSS [Nie et al., 1975] and TSP [Hall, 1975]. Unfortunately, many common transportation demand models cannot be expressed in a linear form that is suitable for regression. Instead, various nonlinear calibration techniques must be employed. A majority of these techniques take the principle of maximum likelihood as their starting point, in which the "most likely" set of parameters is determined, given the assumed model structure and the observed data. Maximum likelihood represents an econometric generalization of the notion of best fit introduced above. Indeed, it can be shown that, under certain assumptions, least-squares regression is a maximum likelihood procedure. Although it is used in a wide variety of applications, maximum likelihood estimation is primarily of interest to transportation planners because it represents the standard procedure for the calibration of individual choice models. A number of standardized computer packages exist for model estimation, including ULOGIT (available from the Urban Mass Transportation Administration), SLOGIT [Cambridge Systematics, 1976], BLOGIT [Hensher and Johnson, 1981], QUAIL [Berkman et al., 1977], and, for probit model estimation, CHOMP [Daganzo and Schoenfeld, 1978].

Statistical estimation procedures should be used whenever possible because of their rigor, efficiency, and the capability which they provide for making statistical statements about model goodness of fit, parameter significance, etc. Occasionally a model is developed which cannot be statistically estimated. One very common example of this is the standard gravity model when graphical friction factors are used in place of a mathematical function to represent travel impedance. In such a case an ad hoc, trial-and-error procedure must be employed. In the gravity model case, for instance, the graphical friction factors are often manually adjusted until the observed and predicted trip-length distributions for the system being modeled are "close" to one another, and the observed and predicted average trip lengths differ by no more than 3 percent [Bureau of Public Roads, 1965].

A final point to note concerning calibration is that since one is always dependent upon historical data to calibrate a model, one is inevitably making the major assumption that the past weights, preferences, attitudes, and all other social, psychological, and spatial factors which somehow combine to determine the calibrated values of the model's parameters will remain constant over time. One can hope that the more "behavioral" or "causal" the model is (including, possibly, dynamic submodels of how attitudes, etc. might change over time), the more fundamental or intrinsic these parameter values are likely to be and hence the less likely they are to change significantly over time. But this is ultimately only a hope which may or may not be realized.

7-6-5 Validation

Calibration produces a model which best reproduces the historical data used in the calibration process. Before using this model to predict future demand, the analyst should satisfy himself as best as possible that this model is, indeed, capable of predicting reasonably well. Testing the model's predictive capabilities is known as *validation*. At least three procedures exist for model validation, and each is discussed briefly below.

At a minimum, a demand model should be tested in terms of its "reasonableness." Much of this sort of testing is performed during the calibration phase, when coefficients are examined for statistical significance and a priori expected signs ($+$ or $-$). For example, travel time and cost always have negative impacts on travel demand; no demand model with a positive time or cost coefficient would be considered a reasonable or valid model. Other tests are possible as well. Model elasticities can be computed to see if they appear to lie within reasonable ranges; "sensitivity tests" can be performed on hypothetical data to explore the model's performance over expected ranges of input data; and so on. The objective within all such tests is simply to ensure that the model does not violate theoretical expectations (and, if it does, to try and determine which is "wrong"—the model or the expectations), that it does not exhibit any pathological tendencies, and that it is internally consistent (i.e., its predictions do not violate any assumptions used to generate them).

A far more rigorous test of the model's predictive capabilities involves using the model to predict demand for some time period other than that used for the calibration and then comparing this prediction with the demand actually observed during this second time period (using, for example, the same goodness-of-fit measures used during calibration). Whenever data for two or more time periods are available, this procedure provides the best test for the model. In practice, such a procedure is rarely performed in transportation demand analysis, presumably because suitable historical data for more than one time period are a luxury few planners enjoy.

Table 7-6 summarizes the results of one such validation exercise, in which the forecasts from 44 transportation planning studies in Great Britain for the time period 1962–1971 were compared with the actual observed system characteristics [Mackinder and Evans, 1981]. For each variable shown, the table indicates the number of observations (studies) used to compile the data, the average observed percentage increase in the variable 10 years after the study's base year, the average forecasted percentage increase for the same 10-year time horizon, and the average percentage error in these forecasts (all percentages are calculated relative to base year values). It is clear from this table that these studies significantly overpredicted future system values, although this result is largely due to the overprediction of the "land use" variables—population, employment, etc.—rather than of the "transportation" variables per se. This is perhaps not surprising given the relatively optimistic outlook among planners and others during the 1960s about future conditions—an outlook that did not include the staggering increases in the price of energy and the economic stagnation which were actually experienced in the 1970s.

Table 7-6 Comparison of predicted and observed changes for a sample of British transport studies

Forecast item	Number of observations	Average observed increase, %	Average forecast increase, %	Average forecast error, %	Root-mean-square forecast error, %
Population	39	5	15	10	14
Households	21	12	17	5	11
Employed residents	16	2	11	9	13
Employment	25	4	14	11	14
Cars per head	38	40	67	21	27
Household income	9	13	34	20	24
Highway trips	18	37	72	30	44
Public transport trips	11	−29	−4	35	41
Total person trips (private and public modes combined)	9	5	32	27	30
Screenline trips	34	41	55	13	28
External trips	14	49	76	24	38
Through trips	8	17	59	49	76

Source: Mackinder and Evans [1981].

A second quite different example of a validation exercise is provided by Florian and Nguyen [1976] in which they compared the predictions of their equilibrium assignment procedure with observed road network values for Winnipeg. Figure 7-18 presents graphical comparisons of predicted and observed link volumes and route travel times. In general, it appeared that the algorithm was rather sensitive to network aggregation effects (for a detailed investigation of such effects, see Bovy and Jansen, [1981]) and that the volume-delay curves used tended to overpredict intersection delays. Overall, however, it was judged that the assignment model replicated existing flow patterns well, particularly given that the observed flows are not "hard and fast" data points but rather random variables possessing considerable inherent variation.

A more restricted validation test that can be performed when multiple time period data are not available involves randomly splitting the one-period data set into two groups, using one group to calibrate the model and then using the calibrated model to predict the second group's demand. Thus, the model's predictive capability is validated against an independent set of observations, although the validation is clearly limited by the lack of temporal variation between the calibration and validation groups. This approach is particularly useful in the case of individual choice models in that one almost always has a large enough sample to split into two subsamples.

A major criticism of transportation demand modeling is the general lack of concern for, and effort put into, the validation phase of the analysis. To a certain extent this lack of concern is justifiable because of the time, budget, and data constraints which analysts typically experience in the course of any given demand analysis. Ultimately, however, the improvement in the predictive capabilities of transportation demand models, and in the credibility of these models with decision makers, rests to a

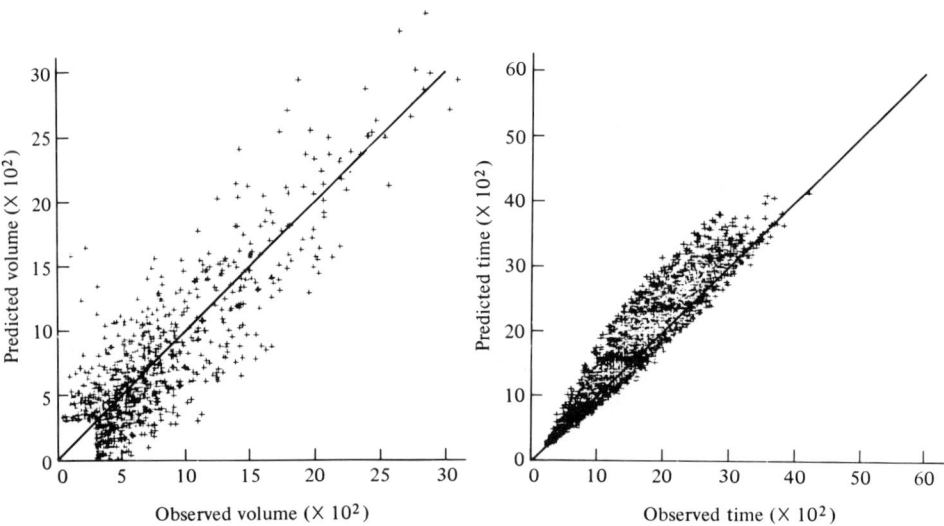

Figure 7-18 Validation of an equilibrium assignment procedure. (*Florian and Nguyen [1976].*)

large extent on the analyst's ability to validate the procedures used, and it can only be hoped that greater emphasis in the future will be placed on this phase of the analysis.

7-6-6 Forecasting

The final stage in the demand analysis process is the use of the calibrated and validated analysis technique to generate demand forecasts for each policy alternative and forecast year under consideration. This, of course, is the ultimate purpose of the whole demand analysis process. As such, the time and effort dedicated to this task should be commensurate with its importance within the overall analysis process. Unfortunately, this often does not prove to be the case: so much time and money are often spent in data collection and model development that very little is left for the forecasting phase. This problem is particularly typical of large-scale comprehensive modeling efforts, some of which have been known to never make it to the forecasting stage at all.

Ideally one would like to generate a wide range of forecasts corresponding to a full set of possible alternatives and future scenarios. The sensitivity of the forecasts to key modeling assumptions should also ideally be examined. The extent to which this is actually done depends heavily upon the problem under study, the budget and staff available to perform the work, and how successful the analysis team has been in saving budget and staff for the forecasting phase. Again, large-scale comprehensive studies are typically the worst in terms of their ability to investigate a very limited number of alternatives (often only two or three) under an even more limited number of future system states (often only one forecast is used), because of the cost and time involved in data assembly and model computations associated with each run of the model.

This need to investigate a wide range of alternatives and scenario assumptions represents a major force underlying the movement toward the development of sketch-planning techniques, "quick response" methods, and so on (see Sec. 7-3-3), which are intended to eliminate or at least significantly reduce the time and effort spent on model development and model execution so as to maximize the time and effort spent actually analyzing alternatives and investigating alternative scenarios.

7-7 CHAPTER SUMMARY

1. Predicting how many people of what type and for what purposes will use the transportation system (i.e., demand analysis) is an important task in transportation planning. Indeed, for many years, much of the effort in transportation planning focused almost exclusively on developing and using demand analysis methods.
2. There are several important concepts related to the analysis of travel demand. First, demand for transportation services is a *derived demand* in that people do not travel for the sake of the traveling experience itself. Rather, people travel so that they can participate in activities located at various locations within the urban area. Second, travel has associated with it a *disutility* or *generalized cost,* measured in

terms of time, monetary cost, inconvenience, etc. Third, the demand for travel manifests itself as *trips* which can be characterized along several dimensions such as trip purpose, origin, destination, etc. Fourth, demand analysis usually deals with *aggregate* levels of trip making, rather than at the individual trip-maker level. This aggregation can occur along spatial, temporal, and socioeconomic dimensions. Fifth, demand analysis methods can be classified into three broad categories: *simplified techniques,* the *urban transportation modeling system* (UTMS), and *individual choice models.*

3. Simple demand analysis techniques are often used in small-area, short-range planning issues, in preliminary "order-of-magnitude" analyses, in situations where more detailed analysis techniques are not available, or in the "screening" of a wide range of alternatives to select a smaller set of options for more detailed analysis (called *sketch planning*). Examples of simple demand analysis techniques include *trend analysis, elasticity-based models,* and *manual techniques.*
4. The urban transportation modeling system (UTMS) has been (and continues to be) the approach most commonly used in regional transportation studies. The UTMS consists of four major stages, each having its own modeling approach. These stages are *trip generation, trip distribution, modal split,* and *trip assignment.*
5. Individual choice models have been developed to model the decision process of individual trip makers. These models are based on the concept of *utility maximization,* that is, on the assumption that an individual traveler will choose an alternative that maximizes the benefits (e.g., provides minimum travel time and cost, maximum comfort and convenience, etc.). Individual choice models have been used to predict modal splits, to analyze the effects of traffic management schemes, and to forecast the demand for new services.
6. The demand analysis process consists of several steps, including problem identification, choice of analysis technique, data collection, model calibration, model validation, and forecasting.
7. Because the environment of planning changes over time, demand analysis must also be flexible in addressing new policy issues in a timely, responsive, and cost-effective manner. It is also important for the planner to understand the underlying assumptions and limitations of demand analysis, in order to place it in proper perspective with respect to the overall transportation planning process.

QUESTIONS

1. Much of travel demand modeling is predicated on the assumption of one-worker households. Comment on the implications of the growing numbers of multiworker households for:
    a. Characteristics of travel demand
    b. Modeling assumptions and techniques
    c. Analysis data requirements

2. Given that the demand for travel is a derived demand, what variables do you think might be of importance in explaining the demand for grocery shopping trips in an urban area? Explain your reasoning.
3. A trip production regression equation was developed using the data given in Fig. 7-7. The resulting equation is

$$O_i = 0.091 + 0.735(SIZE_i) + 0.945(AO_i)$$

where O_i = total daily trips per household produced in zone i
$SIZE_i$ = average household size in zone i
AO_i = average auto-ownership level in zone i

Using this equation and the data from Fig. 7-7c, compute the total daily trip productions for the given zone. Compare your results with those of Fig. 7-7d. Can you explain the differences?

4. Figure P7-4a presents a simple three-zone system, the link travel times for this

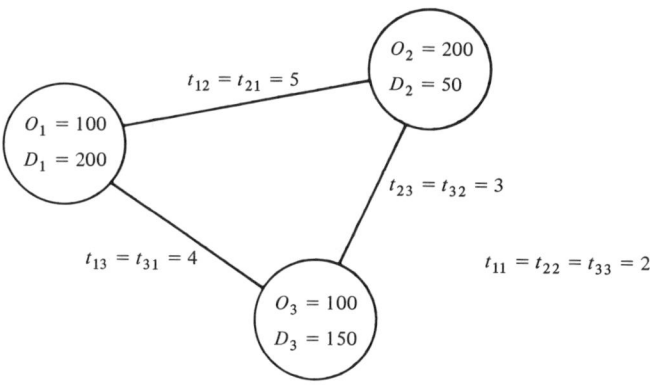

Figure P7-4a Three-zone system.

system, and the zonal productions and attractions. Assume a gravity model of the form

$$T_{ij} = \frac{O_i D_j^*(t_{ij})^{-b}}{\sum_{j'} D_{ij'}^*(t_{ij})^{-b}}$$

where D_j^* is a "modified attraction term" defined by the algorithm shown in Fig. P7-4b which ensures that the predicted trips to a given zone $\sum_i T_{ij}$ equal the true zonal attractions D_j. Compute O-D flows for this system for values of b of 1.0, 1.5, and 2.0. Table P7-4 presents the observed O-D flows for this system. Which values of b provide the "best fit"? Define explicitly how you are measuring goodness of fit.

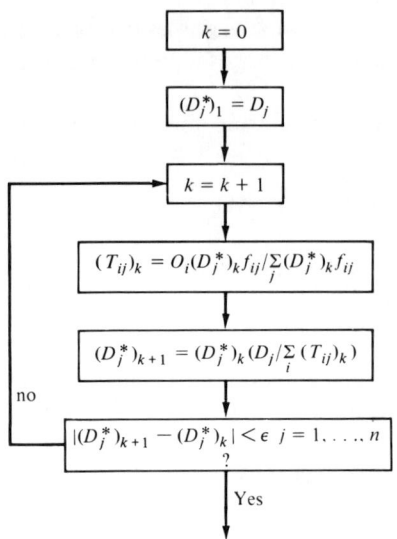

Figure P7-4b Gravity model balancing procedure.

Table P7-4 Observed O-D flows for the three-zone system

From	To		
	1	2	3
1	80	5	15
2	80	40	80
3	40	5	55

5. For the network shown in Fig. P7-5 and the O-D flow matrix shown in Table P7-5a, compute link flows using:
   a. All-or-nothing assignment.
   b. Incremental assignment, using the procedure shown in Fig. 7-10, modified so that instead of choosing an origin zone at random and assigning flow to all destinations, you choose individual O-D pairs at random and assign flows for each pair in turn. Assume a volume-delay curve of the form

$$t_\ell = \frac{t_{0\ell}}{1 - \dfrac{V_\ell}{C_\ell}}$$

Figure P7-5 Five-link network.

Table P7-5a O-D flow matrix

From	To			
	1	2	3	4
1	0	100	100	100
2	0	0	50	50
3	0	0	0	100
4	0	0	0	0

where t_ℓ = travel time on link l

$t_{o\ell}$ = travel time on link l under zero flow conditions

V_ℓ = volume flow on link l

C_ℓ = capacity of link l

Table P7-5b provides the values of $t_{o\ell}$ and C_ℓ for the links in the network. Assign 50 percent of an O-D pair's flow per iteration. Table P7-5c provides the "random" order in which you should choose O-D pairs for assignment.

Table P7-5b Link characteristics

Link	1	2	3	4	5
$t_{o\ell}$	10	15	3	5	4
c_ℓ	300	500	150	200	200

Table P7-5c "Random" order for O-D flow assignment

O-D pair	Assignment order for iteration no.	
	1	2
(1,2)	1	3
(1,3)	6	6
(1,4)	2	4
(2,3)	3	2
(2,4)	5	5
(3,4)	4	1

6. The buses in the numerical example of a logit mode split model presented in Sec. 7-5-1 (i.e., Eq. 7-19) are operated by the Red Bus Transit Co. Assume that a new operator, Blue Coach Lines, introduces a service that is identical to that of the Red Bus Transit Co. (i.e., 15-minute travel time, 50-cent fares), except that the service is provided by blue buses rather than red. We now have four "modes" in the choice set: auto, red bus, blue bus, and walk. Compute the probabilities of each of these four modes being chosen using Eq. (7-19) (and assuming that the blue bus utility function is the same as the red bus function). Compare these probabilities with those for the three-mode example in Sec. 7-5-1. Are these results reasonable, especially given that the model ignores frequency of service? Why or why not?
7. Ignoring data limitations (at least within "reasonable" limitations!), how (and why) would you modify the mode split model defined by Eq. (7-19) in Sec. 7-5-1 so as to improve its predictive capability and/or its policy sensitivity?
8. What options exist for structuring the decision process for an individual's choice of mode for work *and* access mode if transit is used (i.e., walk, park-and-ride, kiss-and-ride, etc.)? If you were modeling this process, what approach would you adopt?
9. The logit model was applied to the choice of mode for work trips in the San Diego area. Two models were formulated. The first model was estimated for CBD-

oriented trips where relatively good transit service is available, while the second model was estimated for non-CBD-oriented trips. For both models, the utility functions were defined as

For auto passenger: $U_P = -cX3_P - dL3_P - eCH_P$
For auto driver: $U_D = -cX3_D - dL3_D - eCH_D + a\,T135 + b$
For transit passenger: $U_T = -cX3_T - dL3_T - eCH_T + f$

where $X3_i$ = excess time for mode i
$L3_i$ = line-haul time for mode i
CH_i = cost for mode i
$T135$ = transformed household income
$100[1 - \exp(-0.035 \times INC)]$
a, b, c, d, e, f = model parameters

Table P7-9 presents the calibrated parameter values for both models.

Table P7-9 San Diego logit model parameters

Parameter	CBD model	Non-CBD model
a	0.0295	0.0268
b	−1.4809	−0.5441
c	0.0916	0.1314
d	0.0563	0.0192
e	0.0106	0.0184
f	1.1635	1.6600

a. Discuss the specification of this model. How would you modify it?
b. Evaluate the estimated models:
  i. Does each coefficient have the proper sign?
  ii. What statistical tests would you perform on the model? What do you expect to learn from these tests?
  iii. Outline the procedure you would follow in computing direct and cross elasticities in this model.
c. Compare the estimated coefficients of the two models and discuss the differences in terms of your a priori expectations. Can you suggest a more general model specification which can be applied to both CBD- and non-CBD-oriented trips? Explain.

REFERENCES

Adler, T. J., and M. E. Ben-Akiva: "Joint-Choice Model for Frequency, Destination, and Travel Mode for Shopping Trips," *Transportation Research Record*, No. 569, 1976, pp. 136–150.

———: "A Theoretical and Empirical Model of Trip-Chaining Behaviour," *Transportation Research*, vol. 13B, no. 3, 1979, pp. 243–258.

Amemiya, T.: "Qualitative Response Models: A Survey," *Journal of Economic Literature*, vol. 19, December 1981, pp. 1483–1536.

Atherton, T. H., and M. E. Ben-Akiva: "Transferability and Updating of Disaggregate Travel Demand Models," *Transportation Research Record*, No. 610, 1976, pp. 12–18.

Ben-Akiva, M. E.: "Structure of Passenger Travel Demand Models," *Transportation Research Record*, No. 526, 1974.

———: "Passenger Travel Demand Forecasting: Applications of Disaggregate Models and Directions for Research," in E. J. Visser, (ed.), *Transport Decisions in an Age of Uncertainty*, Martinus Nijhoff, The Hague, 1977, pp. 183–193.

Berkman, J., D. Brownstone, G. M. Duncan, and D. McFadden: *QUAIL 3.0 User's Manual*, University of California, Department of Economics, Berkeley, 1977.

Bovy, P. H. L., and G. R. M. Jansen: "Network Modelling Effects in Equilibrium Assignments: An Empirical Investigation," Presented at the "Frontiers in Transportation Equilibrium and Supply Models International Symposium," Montreal, November 1981.

Brokke, G. E.: *Evaluating Trip Forecasting Methods with an Electronic Computer*, Highway Research Board Bulletin No. 203, Washington, D.C., 1958.

Bruynooghe, M., A. Gibert, and M. Sakarovitch: "Une methode d'affectation du trafic," in Fourth Symposium of the Theory of Traffic Flow, Karlsruhe, Germany, 1968.

Bureau of Public Roads: *Calibrating and Testing a Gravity Model for Any Sized Urban Area*, U.S. Dept. of Commerce, Washington, D.C., 1965.

Burrell, J. E.: "Multipath Route Assignment and Its Application to Capacity Restraint," Presented at the Fourth International Symposium on the Theory of Traffic Flow," Karlsruhe, Germany, 1968.

Cambridge Systematics: *Multinomial Logit Estimation Package Program Documentation*, Version 2, Mod 4, Cambridge, Mass., November 1976.

———: *Transportation Air Quality Analysis—Sketching Planning Methods, Volume I, Analysis Methods*, Office of Transportation and Land Use Policy Report No. EPA 400/1-800-001a, Environmental Protection Agency, Washington, D.C., 1979.

Dafermos, S. C.: "An Extended Traffic Assignment Model with Applications to Two-Way Traffic," *Transportation Science*, vol. 5, 1971, pp. 366–389.

Daganzo, C. F., and Y. Sheffi: "On Stochastic Models of Traffic Assignment," *Transportation Science*, vol. 11, no. 3, 1977, pp. 253–274.

Daganzo, C. F., and L. Schoenfeld: *CHOMP User's Manual*, Institute for Transportation Studies, Research Report UCB-ITS-RR-78-7, University of California, Berkeley, 1978.

Daganzo, C. F.: *Multinomial Probit*, Academic Press, New York, 1979.

Damm, D.: "Toward a Model of Activity Scheduling Behavior," Unpublished Ph.D. thesis, MIT, Dept. of Civil Engineering, Cambridge, Mass., 1979.

de Neufville, R.: *Airport Systems Planning*, MIT Press, Cambridge, Mass., 1976.

Dial, R. B.: "A Probabilistic Multipath Traffic Assignment Model Which Obviates Path Enumeration," *Transportation Research*, vol. 5, 1971, pp. 83–111.

Dickey, J. W. (senior author): *Metropolitan Transportation Planning*, Scripta, McGraw-Hill, New York, 1975.

Domencich, T., and D. McFadden: *Urban Travel Demand: A Behavioral Analysis*, North Holland, Amsterdam, 1975.

Federal Highway Administration: *Traffic Assignment*, U.S. Dept. of Transportation, Washington, D.C., 1973.

———: *Trip Generation Analysis*, U.S. Dept. of Transportation, Washington, D.C., 1975.

Florian, M., and S. Nguyen: "An Application and Validation of Equilibrium Trip Assignment Methods," *Transportation Science*, vol. 10, no. 4, 1976, pp. 374–390.

Florian, M., R. Chapleau, S. Nguyen, C. Achim, L. James-Lefebvre, S. Galarneau, J. Lefebvre, and C. Fisk: *Validation and Application of EMME: An Equilibrium Based Two-Mode Urban Transportation Planning Method*, Centre for Transportation Research Publication No. 103, University of Montreal, 1979.

Fratar, T. J.: "Forecasting Distribution of Inter-Zonal Vehicular Trips by Successive Approximations," *Proceedings, Highway Research Board,* vol. 33, Washington, D.C., 1954.

Gaudry, M. J. I.: *An Aggregate Time-Series Analysis of Urban Transit Demand: The Montreal Case,* Center for Transportation Research Publication No. 6, University of Montreal, April 1975.

Gaudry, M. J. I., and M. G. Dagenais: "The Dogit Model," *Transportation Research B,* vol. 13, no. 2, 1979, pp. 105-112.

Golding, S., and K. B. Davidson: "A Residential Land Use Prediction Model for Transportation Planning," *Proceedings, Australian Road Research Board,* Melbourne, 1970, pp. 5-25.

Hall, B. H.: *TSP: Time Series Processor,* Version 2.7, Harvard Institute of Economic Research Technical Paper No. 12, Harvard University, Cambridge, Mass., 1975.

Hausman, J. A., and D. A. Wise: "A Conditional Probit Model for Qualitative Choice: Discrete Decisions Recognizing Interdependence and Heterogeneous Preferences," *Econometrica,* vol. 46, no. 2, 1978, pp. 403-426.

Hensher, D. A., and L. W. Johnson: *Applied Discrete-Choice Modelling,* Croom Helm, London, 1981.

Hinkle, J. J., R. H. Watkins, J. D. O'Doherty, M. Iwabuchi, and G. W. Schultz: *Transit Corridor Analysis—A Manual Sketch Planning Technique,* U.S. Dept. of Transportation Report No. URD.DCCO.74.2.3, UMTA, Washington, D.C., 1976.

Horowitz, J.: "A Utility Maximizing Model of the Demand for Multidestination Non-Work Travel," *Transportation Research B,* vol. 14, no. 4, 1980, pp. 369-386.

Hutchinson, B. G.: *Principles of Urban Transportation Systems Planning,* Scripta, McGraw-Hill, New York, 1974.

Kanafani, A.: *Transportation Demand Analysis,* McGraw-Hill, New York, 1983.

Kates, Peat, Marwick & Co.: *Calibration of a Regional Traffic Prediction Model for the A.M. Peak Period,* prepared for the Metropolitan Toronto and Region Transportation Study, Toronto, Ontario, 1967.

Kmenta, J.: *Elements of Econometrics,* Macmillan, New York, 1971.

Koppleman, F. S.: *Travel Prediction with Models of Individual Choice Behavior,* Center for Transportation Studies Report No. 75-7, MIT, Cambridge, Mass., June 1975.

Koutsoyiannis, A.: *Theory of Econometrics,* 2d ed., Macmillan, London, 1977.

Lave, C. A., and K. Train: "A Disaggregate Model of Auto-Type Choice," *Transportation Research A,* vol. 13A, 1979, pp. 1-9.

LeBlanc, L. J., E. K. Morlok, and W. P. Pierskalla: "An Efficient Approach to Solving the Road Network Equilibrium Traffic Assignment Problem," *Transportation Research,* vol. 9, 1975, pp. 309-318.

Lerman, S. R.: "Location, Housing, Car Ownership and Mode to Work: A Joint Choice Model," *Transportation Research Record,* no. 610, 1976, pp. 6-11.

Lerman, S. R., and M. E. Ben-Akiva: "Disaggregate Behavioral Model of Automobile Ownership," *Transportation Research Record 569,* Transportation Research Board, Washington, D.C., 1976, pp. 34-55.

Lerman, S. R., and J. J. Louviere: "On the Use of Functional Measurement to Identify the Functional Form of the Utility Expression in Travel Demand Models," *Transportation Research Record,* no. 673, 1978, pp. 78-86.

Luce, R. D., and P. Suppes: "Preference, Utility and Subjective Probability," Chapter 19 in R. D. Luce, R. R. Bush, and E. Galanter (eds.), *Handbook of Mathematical Psychology,* vol. 3, Wiley, New York, 1965, pp. 249-410.

Mackinder, I. H., and S. E. Evans: *Predictive Accuracy of British Transport Studies in Urban Areas,* Transport and Road Research Laboratory SR 699, Crowthorne, U.K., 1981.

Manski, C. F.: "The Stochastic Utility Model of Choice," Unpublished Ph.D. thesis, MIT, Department of Economics, Cambridge, Mass., 1973.

─────: "Structural Models for Discrete Data: The Analysis of Discrete Choice," *Sociological Methodology,* 1981.

Manski, C. F., and L. Sherman: "An Empirical Analysis of Household Choice among Motor Vehicles," *Transportation Research A,* vol. 14A, 1980, pp. 349-366.

Manski, C. F., and D. McFadden (eds.): *Structural Analysis of Discrete Data with Econometric Applications,* MIT Press, Cambridge, Mass., 1981.

Mayworm, P., A. Lago, and J. M. McEnroe: *Patronage Impacts of Changes in Transit Fares and Services,*

Report DOT-UT 90014, report prepared by Econsometrics, Inc., for the U.S. Dept. of Transportation, September 3, 1980.

McCoomb, L. A.: "Simplified Urban Transportation Planning Procedures Using Census Data," Unpublished Ph.D. thesis, University of Toronto, Dept. of Civil Engineering, Toronto, 1982.

McFadden, D.: "Modelling the Choice of Residential Location," Presented at the Conference on Spatial Interaction Theory and Planning Models," Bastad, Sweden, 1977.

———: "Qualitative Methods for Analyzing Travel Behavior of Individuals: Some Recent Developments," in D. A. Hensher and P. R. Stopher (eds.), *Behavioral Travel Modelling,* Croom Helm, London, 1979.

Miller, E. J., and S. R. Lerman: "Disaggregate Modelling and Decisions of Retail Firms: A Case Study of Clothing Retailers," *Environment and Planning A,* vol. 13, 1981, pp. 729-746.

Miller, E. J.: "Transit Planning and Land Use Trends: Issues and Research Needs," *RTAC Forum,* vol. 4, no. 2, 1982.

Morlok, E. K.: *Introduction to Transportation Engineering and Planning,* McGraw-Hill, New York, 1978.

Murchland, J. D.: "Road Network Traffic Distribution in Equilibrium," Paper presented at the Conference on Mathematical Methods in the Economics Sciences, Mathematisches Forschungsinstitut, Oberwolfach, 1969.

Nguyen, S.: "An Algorithm for the Traffic Assignment Problem," *Transportation Science,* vol. 8, 1974a, pp. 203-216.

———: "Une approache unifee des methods d'equilibre pour l'affectation du trafic," Department d'Informatique Publication No. 171, Universite de Montreal, 1974b.

Nie, N. H., C. H. Hull, J. G. Jenkins, K. Steinbrenner, and D. H. Bent: *SPSS: Statistical Package for the Social Sciences,* 2d ed., McGraw-Hill, New York, 1975.

Ontario Ministry of Transportation and Communications: *Systems Planning Branch, Modal Split: Toronto Area Regional Model Study,* Toronto, 1970.

Pollakowski, H. O.: *Urban Housing Markets and Residential Location,* D.C. Heath, Lexington, Mass., 1982.

Reid, F. A.: "Systematic and Efficient Methods for Minimizing Error in Aggregate Predictions from Disaggregate Models," *Transportation Research Record* 673, 1978, pp. 59-65.

Ruiter, E. R., and M. E. Ben-Akiva: "System of Disaggregate Travel Demand Models: Structure, Component Models, and Application Procedures," Presented at the 57th annual meeting of the Transportation Research Board, Washington, D.C., 1978.

Schneider, M.: *Panel Discussion on Inter-Area Travel Formulas,* Highway Research Board Bulletin No. 253, Washington, D.C., 1960.

Smith, D. P., and B. G.: Hutchinson, "Goodness of Fit Statistics for Trip Distribution Models," Dept. of Civil Engineering, University of Waterloo, Waterloo, Ont., 1979.

Sosslau, A. B., A. B. Hassam, M. M. Carter, and G. V. Wickstrom: *Quick-Response Urban Travel Estimation Techniques and Transferable Parameters, User's Guide,* National Cooperative Highway Research Program Report 187, Transportation Research Board, Washington, D.C., 1978.

Spear, B. D.: *Applications of New Travel Demand Forecasting Techniques to Transportation Planning—A Study of Individual Choice Models,* Federal Highway Administration, U.S. Dept. of Transportation, Washington, D.C., March 1977.

Steuart, G. N. (ed.): *Urban Transportation Planning Guide,* University of Toronto Press, Toronto, 1977.

Stopher, P. R., and A. H. Meyburg: *Urban Transportation Modeling and Planning,* Lexington Books, D.C. Heath, Lexington, Mass., 1975.

Stouffer, S. A.: "Intervening Opportunities: A Theory Relating Mobility and Distance," *American Sociological Review,* vol. 5, no. 6, 1940, pp. 845-867.

Theil, H.: *Principles of Econometrics,* Wiley, New York, 1971.

Thurstone, L.: "A Law of Comparative Judgement," *Psychological Review,* vol. 34, 1927, pp. 278-286.

Train, K.: "A Structural Logit Model of Auto Ownership and Mode Choice," *Review of Economic Studies,* vol. 47, 1980, pp. 357-370.

U.S. Department of Transportation: *Patronage Impacts of Changes in Transit Fares and Services,* UMTA RR 135-1, Washington, D.C., September 1980.

Voorhees, A. M., and Associates: *Handbook for Transportation System Management Planning, Volume 2, Handbook for the Evaluation of Individual Transit-Related TSM Actions,* North Central Texas Council of Governments, 1977.
Wachs, M.: "Social Trends and Their Implications for Transportation Planning Methods," *Special Report 196,* Transportation Research Board, Washington, D.C., 1982.
Wardrop, J. G.: "Some Theoretical Aspects of Road Traffic Research," *Proceedings of the Institute of Civil Engineers,* vol. 1, 1952, pp. 325–378.
Watanatada, T., and M. E. Ben-Akiva: "Spatial Aggregation of Disaggregate Choice Models: Areawide Urban Travel Demand Sketch-Planning Model," *Transportation Research Record* 673, 1978, pp. 93–99.
Webber, M.: "Pedagogy Again: What is Entropy?" *Annals of the Association of American Geographers,* vol. 67, no. 2, 1977, pp. 254–266.
Weisbrod, G. E.: "Determinants of Intra-urban Household Mobility," Unpublished master's thesis, MIT, Department of Civil Engineering, Cambridge, 1978.
Wilson, A. G.: "A Statistical Theory of Spatial Distribution Models," *Transportation Research,* vol. 1, 1967, pp. 253–269.
Wolfe, R. A.: "An Econometric Bid-Rent Model of Urban Retail Store Location and Entry," Unpublished Ph.D. thesis, MIT, Dept. of Civil Engineering, Cambridge, Mass., 1981.
Wonnacott, R. J. and T. H. Wonnacott: *Econometrics,* Wiley, New York, 1970.

CHAPTER
EIGHT
SUPPLY ANALYSIS

8-0 INTRODUCTION

As was discussed briefly in Chap. 5, the *supply* of transportation services can be characterized in terms of the *performance* of the transportation system (its travel times, headways, capacities, etc.), the *impacts* that this system has on the environment (which includes nonusers of the system), and the *costs* incurred in building, maintaining, and using the system. An understanding of the supply side of transportation is clearly fundamental to planning and operating transportation systems. It is difficult, for example, to decide how many buses to operate on a given route at a certain frequency level without being able to compute the round-trip travel time for a bus as a function of the route length, the number and location of stops along the route, typical traffic conditions along the route, and other factors affecting performance. Similarly, the demand for a transportation service generally cannot be estimated until the travel times and costs associated with this service are known; nor can the merit of the service relative to other available alternatives be evaluated until the performance, impacts, and costs of all reasonable alternatives are known.

As with the previous two chapters, this chapter begins with a discussion of the role of supply analysis within the planning process (Sec. 8-1). The three sections that follow then deal in some detail with each of the three major components of supply—performance, impacts, and costs. In general, the material presented in this chapter is relatively qualitative in nature. For more rigorous, mathematical discussions of these techniques and issues, the reader should refer to several texts which deal with transportation supply analysis in much greater detail [Wohl and Martin, 1967; Newell, 1971; Kennedy et al.,1973; Institute of Traffic Engineers, 1976; Morlok, 1978; Manheim, 1979; Newell, 1980; Larson and Odoni, 1981; Vuchic, 1981; Daganzo, 1982; Sheffi, 1984].

8-1 THE ROLE OF SUPPLY ANALYSIS IN TRANSPORTATION PLANNING

Transportation-oriented policies and programs can include a variety of actions designed to achieve specified goals. For example, some actions might be designed to alter urban activity patterns in order to enhance the performance of transportation systems (e.g., zoning regulations to encourage higher-density residential and commercial development for more effective service by public transit systems). Other actions might attempt to alter travel demand patterns directly, such as flexible work-hour programs to reduce peak-period demand. By far the most common type of transportation action, however, involves changes to the transportation system itself and, hence, to the supply of transportation services. In characterizing supply-related transportation policies, one can speak of the *component* of the transportation system affected by the policy, the *type* of policy or action adopted, and the *actor* or *decision maker* responsible for establishing or implementing the policy.

Six major components of the transportation system can generally be subjected to supply-related policies of various types:

1. The transportation system *infrastructure,* which includes the rights-of-way over which vehicles operate (i.e., roads, tracks, sidewalks[1]), the signal systems which control flows along the rights-of-way, terminals, and all other fixed, physical facilities required to operate and maintain the transportation system (in particular, vehicle storage, servicing, and maintenance facilities)
2. The *vehicles* that operate within this infrastructure system
3. The *routes* and *schedules* (where applicable) that govern the operation of vehicles over the infrastructure
4. The *drivers* of the vehicles (and other employees involved in the provision of transportation services)
5. The *procedures* for operating the system, which include everything from government regulations (e.g., speed limits, licensing requirements, and service standards) to the labor agreements concerning driver working conditions
6. The *costs* borne by operators and/or users of the system, which are not only an outcome of decisions made concerning infrastructure, vehicles, and operating procedures but which are also directly influenced by regulations and subsidies

Types of supply-related policies or actions thus include [Dosman et al., 1980]:

1. *Construction* of transportation infrastructure
2. *Design* and/or *manufacture* of transportation equipment (most notably, vehicles and signal systems)
3. *Provision* of transportation services
4. *Maintenance* of transportation infrastructure and vehicles
5. *Regulation* of transportation services, systems, market entry, and competition

---
[1]In which case, the "vehicle" is the pedestrian.

6. *Enforcement* of transportation regulations
7. *Financing* of transportation infrastructure and vehicles
8. *Subsidization* of transportation system operating costs and/or users of the system
9. *Taxation* of transportation services and equipment
10. *Pricing* of transportation services

In general, policy types 1 through 4 primarily address system performance (and ultimately system costs and impacts). Policy types 6 through 10 are financial in nature and primarily influence system costs (and hence the "affordability" or "profitability" of various system configurations and their associated performance and impact characteristics). Policy type 5—regulation—is, in a sense, the most flexible form of policy, since it can be used to directly address performance (all vehicles sold must be capable of withstanding a front-end collision of x miles per hour without incurring any damage), cost (this transportation system must operate on a cost recovery basis), and impact (carbon monoxide emissions due to the transportation system must be reduced by y percent a year over the next 5 years). How these regulations are met, of course, may involve other actions, usually directed more specifically toward affecting system performance.

Given the large variety of actions that can be taken to influence transportation supply, the number of actors involved in decision making can become quite large as well. Major decision makers or actors involved in supply-related policy-making include *elected representatives* who pass legislation concerning the financing of transportation infrastructure construction, subsidizing transportation system operations, taxing transportation services and equipment, and regulating the transportation system. *Regulators,* typically civil servants or government appointees, are responsible for enforcing government regulations (e.g., the Interstate Commerce Commission in the United States, the Canadian Transport Commission in Canada). *Operators* or providers of transportation services generally do the detailed design of the routes and schedules of the service being provided, operate the service, maintain the equipment, establish and attempt to maintain their own service standards or regulations, possibly in addition to any government-mandated standards or regulations, and determine (or contribute toward the determination of) user charges, investment policies, and other financial matters relating to the service being provided. *Implementers* are responsible for planning, designing, and constructing the projects for the transportation system. *Contractors* usually have great influence on elected representatives and wish to maintain or enhance government construction and maintenance programs. Finally, *law enforcement officials* enforce transportation-related laws and often significantly influence the effectiveness of transportation actions through this enforcement, especially those aimed directly at changing travel behavior.

The above discussion indicates that system performance must be viewed as the outcome of complex interactions between the system's components, that is, its infrastructure, vehicles, employees, routes, schedules, and operating procedures (see Fig. 8-1). These system components can be altered, primarily through operator, legislative, or regulatory intervention. The system operates within a short-run context of a given level of demand and a given operating environment (weather conditions,

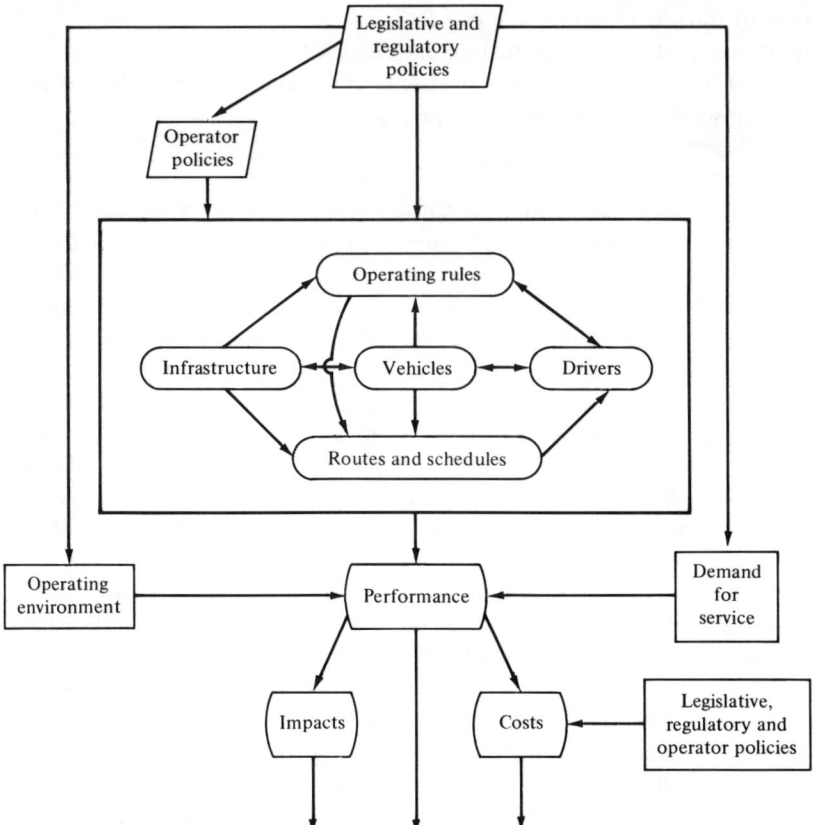

Figure 8-1 Supply-related interactions.

traffic-flow conditions on the street, etc.) which may or may not be amenable to short- or medium-term intervention by legislative or regulatory actions. Further, system costs are a function of both performance characteristics and direct operator, legislative, and regulatory actions.

Figure 8-2 further illustrates the role of supply analysis within the planning process by presenting a slightly expanded version of the analysis and evaluation component of the urban transportation planning process previously presented in Figs. 1-1 and 3-4. This figure indicates that supply analysis interacts with other components of the planning process in three major ways:

1. The performance and cost of transportation services, as perceived by potential users, are important determinants of the demand which actually results for these services. Transportation system performance, in turn, generally depends upon the levels of demand experienced, meaning demand and supply analyses are inherently linked. This linkage is typically most explicit in the trip assignment stage of

demand analysis (see Sec. 7-4-4) in which link flows (demand) and travel times (performance) are iteratively equilibrated. It is also implicit in other components of demand analysis (generally trip distribution and modal split, see Secs. 7-4-2 and 7-4-3) which employ system performance and cost as explanatory variables, as well as in most supply analyses which employ a ''given'' demand level as a key structural variable.
2. Over and above their influence on the demand for transportation, measures of system performance, impacts, and costs constitute important evaluation criteria in their own right (see Chap. 9).
3. The identification of current and proposed alternative system performance, impact, and cost characteristics can lead to the generation of improved alternatives for consideration, as well as contributing over time toward the monitoring and diagnosis planning functions. Further, the act of systematically exploring supply relationships and attempting to predict system supply measures should provide a mechanism for the planner to increase his understanding of the system and improve his perceptions of system problems and opportunities and the alternatives available for addressing them.

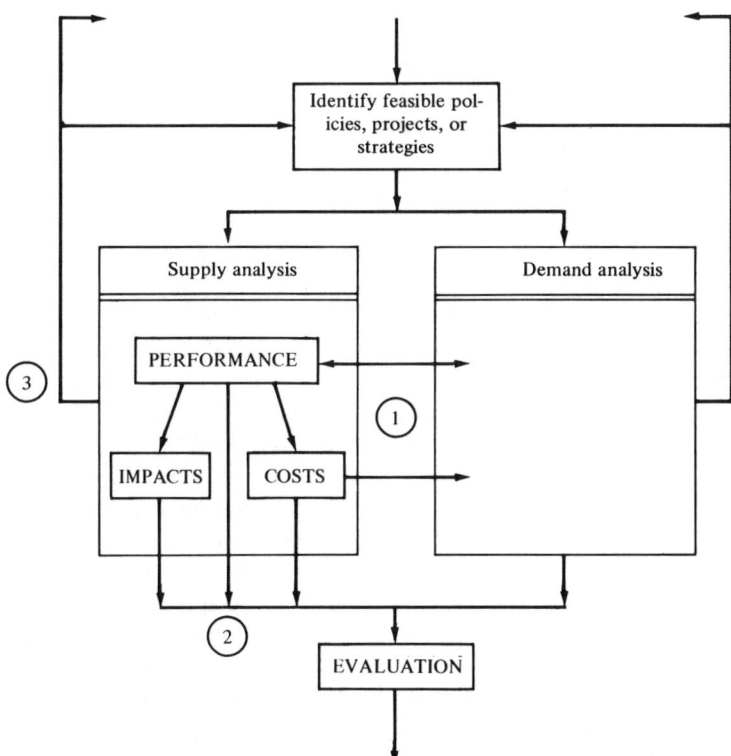

Figure 8-2 Supply analysis in transportation planning.

Figure 8-2 suggests that, in general, it is system performance that "drives" system impacts and costs. Or, in analytical terms, in order to analyze or predict system impacts and costs, one must first know or predict system performance. For example, the energy consumption or air pollution emissions on a section of highway depend on the speed of the vehicles using the highway, the number of speed-change cycles the vehicles undergo, and the number of vehicles using the highway per unit time. Similarly, the operating costs of providing transit service of a given frequency along a route with a certain demand level depend on the route cycle times, and in turn on the number of buses and drivers required to meet the schedule.

As with any planning analysis, supply analysis can be performed at many levels of the transportation planning process. Common planning contexts for supply analyses include:

1. *Regional or citywide planning exercises.* This level of planning generally involves the analysis of alternative modal networks, typically of a fairly aggregate, abstract nature. The planning time frame can range from the short run to the long term. Supply analysis in such cases usually involves determining equilibrium flow patterns on the modal networks using one of the assignment techniques discussed in Sec. 7-4-4, given the modal O-D flows determined by the demand analysis and a set of performance functions such as volume-delay curves for the links comprising the networks. These performance functions are generally simple, reflecting the abstract nature of the links being analyzed. The complexity of such analyses stems from the size of the networks being assessed, which can easily involve hundreds of zones and thousands of links, rather than from the level of detail of the analysis or the complexity of the technique being used per se.

2. *"Operational" or "tactical" planning.* The analysis or design of specific services or system components at the individual route or link level is a very common planning function, particularly within operating agencies. In these cases, only a small "network" consisting of the system component under study—such as a transit route or freeway section and, possibly, its linkages to the rest of the system—is considered, but this network is represented and analyzed in considerable detail. The planning time frame for such analyses is most often the short term (e.g., 1 year), given the nature of the decisions to be made (e.g., what changes to the bus routes should be made for next year's operations?) and the inability to generate detailed demand forecasts beyond the short term (e.g., one might know current passenger "ons" and "offs" by stop for a given transit route and assume that this pattern will be relatively stable over the next year; however, what will the ons and offs be for this route 10 years from now?). If longer term assessments are required (e.g., will this proposed freeway section have adequate capacity to handle peak-period flows 20 years from now?), then one must generally take a horizon-year demand forecast as the basis for the supply analysis (e.g., the estimated peak-period flows for 20 years from now) and/or explore the impact of different demand scenarios on the supply analysis results. The range of analytical techniques available for analysis at this level of planning is far broader than at the regional level and includes everything from simple "back of the envelope"

sketches to complex computer simulation programs. The choice of technique in any given problem application depends on the specific nature of the problem, the data available, the analytical capabilities of the planner, the time and budget available for the analysis, and the type of information (its accuracy, level of detail, etc.) required to address the issue at hand.

3. *Scheduling of transportation services.*[2] The assignment of transit vehicles to scheduled routes and the assignment of drivers to vehicles constitute a major planning issue for transit operators. The transit operator is clearly interested in scheduling vehicles and drivers in as efficient a manner as possible, that is, in scheduling them so as to minimize operating costs (and, in the longer run, minimize vehicle fleet size), subject to service standard constraints on the one hand and labor agreement constraints on the other (e.g., split shift regulations, rules on the use of part-time labor). The time frame for such scheduling processes is the very short run, generally less than 1 year. The scale of the analysis is the entire transit network (or at least large subnetworks—e.g., all routes serviced by a given garage), represented in considerable detail, although not generally as detailed as in route-level analyses. The technique used for scheduling (or "run cutting," as it is often called) typically involves a combination of manual and computerized procedures for heuristically finding "good" schedules. Ideally, one would like to find optimal (i.e., "best") schedules, but the problem is far too complex to be able to achieve this by using current analysis techniques.

The following sections of this chapter—which discuss performance, impact, and cost analysis techniques, respectively—focus on techniques and issues relating to regional and operational planning problems. Transportation scheduling techniques are discussed briefly in Sec. 8-2-3, which includes further references for the interested reader.

8-2 ANALYSIS OF TRANSPORTATION SYSTEM PERFORMANCE

The performance of the transportation system can be discussed from two perspectives: the *user* of the system and the *operator* of the system. Users of the system are interested in the travel cost and travel time which they experience when using the system. Travel time can be further broken down into *in-vehicle* time and *out-of-vehicle* time, which, in turn, consists of walking time to and from the transportation services, wait time, and transfer time. Other performance characteristics of importance to users include safety, comfort, and reliability of the service. In addition to these attributes, operators must be concerned with route frequencies, vehicle cycle times and capacities, and the operating cost associated with the provision of the service. Clearly, all of these concepts are related. Vehicle cycle times over a route translate into stop-to-stop travel times for passengers, average wait times at passenger stops are a function of

---

[2]Transportation scheduling problems other than the one discussed here exist. These include scheduling service vehicles (snowplows, garbage trucks, parcel delivery vehicles, etc.) and scheduling demand responsive transit services.

route frequency, passenger travel costs presumably bear some relationship to the cost of providing the services, and so on.

The estimation of operator and user costs is discussed in Sec. 8-4. In this section, techniques used to determine performance characteristics such as capacity, headway, and travel time are discussed. This discussion is divided into three parts. First, some basic concepts fundamental to the analysis of transportation system performance are introduced in Sec. 8-2-1. Section 8-2-2 then discusses a range of analysis techniques applicable to a wide variety of transportation supply analysis problems. Finally, Sec. 8-2-3 discusses some of the more common planning applications of these techniques in greater detail.

8-2-1 Basic Concepts

In developing or applying performance analysis techniques, the planner must consider several key aspects of the transportation system being analyzed. The first of these is the nature of the *components* comprising the system, which, as discussed in Sec. 8-1, include the system's *right-of-way* (infrastructure), *routes, schedules,* and *technology.* In general, system performance and the choice of techniques to analyze this performance depend on:

1. Whether the service operates on a shared right-of-way (e.g., a typical urban street, in which automobiles, buses, trucks, pedestrians, and bicycles all operate together on the same pavement) or on an exclusive or dedicated right-of-way (e.g., subway line, exclusive bus lane, or bicycle path)
2. Whether the service operates over fixed routes (e.g., conventional public transit) or is flexibly routed (e.g., the private auto, taxi, demand-responsive public transit)
3. Whether the service operates under a fixed schedule (conventional public transit) or not (private auto)
4. The type of technology employed in the system, particularly the guideway or suspension system (steel wheel on steel rail, rubber tire on pavement, etc.), the propulsion system (internal combustion diesel or gasoline engine, direct current electric motor with chopper control, etc.), and the system for controlling flow over the right-of-way (signalized intersections, "three-block" signalized control of rail lines, etc.)

Second, choice of analysis technique often depends on the *temporal* nature of the problem under study. The key distinction required here is whether one is interested in *steady-state* conditions (e.g., average travel times) or in *transient* phenomena (e.g., freeway conditions when one or more lanes are blocked by an accident or bus "bunching" due to operating conditions along a route).

Third, as previously discussed in Chap. 7 with respect to demand analysis, choice of analysis technique depends on the planning context of the analysis: the level of detail required, time and budget constraints, and the type of issues and policy variables that are of interest. Thus, for example, a quick "order of magnitude" estimate for sketch-planning purposes might be obtained through a simple hand calculation, whereas the analysis of the same system to provide performance measures for detailed evaluation purposes may well require a large computer simulation model.

Fourth, and most important, the analysis of transportation systems depends fundamentally on the *spatial* representation of the system. The real or physical transportation network must be represented with an "approximating network" [Newell, 1980] consisting of a connected set of *links* and *nodes*. As shown in Fig. 8-3, links represent roadways or other rights-of-way, while nodes represent intersections, terminals, or points of trip generation. This latter type of node is known as a *centroid*. Each zone in the system is represented by a centroid, and all trips into and out of the zone are assumed to be destined to or originate from the zone centroid. Centroids are connected to the network by *dummy links* which, unlike regular links in the approximating network, do not represent any real links in the physical network.

Network definition is perhaps the single most important step in the entire analysis process in that it determines the maximum level of accuracy and detail of analysis achievable, the quantity and quality of data required to represent and analyze the system, and the type(s) of analysis techniques which are suitable. It is also a particularly onerous task in terms of the time and cost involved in manually developing the network, coding and entering it into a computer, checking that the computerized version of the network is correctly coded and entered, and maintaining and updating the network over time. Standardized computer packages such as UTPS (provided by the Urban Mass Transportation Administration and Federal Highway Administration), PLANPAC (provided by the Federal Highway Administration) and System 33 (provided by the Ontario Ministry of Transportation and Communications)—which are used to develop, store, and manipulate transportation networks—are available for use by planning organizations. Nevertheless, the "overhead" associated with network approximations is high. The implication of this is that once a planning organization develops a network approximation, it tends to be "locked" into it for some time, given the time and expense involved in major network restructuring. This, of course, serves to emphasize the importance of making "correct" decisions at the design and development stages so as to ensure that the network will be a useful analysis tool for many years to come.

The links and nodes of the approximating network can be aggregated to form *routes* from point to point within the system. Analysis may well be performed on any of these system components, depending on the problem of interest. Examples include:

Links. Analysis of a section of an urban freeway
Nodes. Analysis of flow through an intersection or analysis of terminal operations
Routes. Analysis of the operation of a transit route
Networks. Analysis of network flows or analysis of route interactions with the network

An alternative approach to the use of networks to represent the transportation system is the use of *continuum models,* in which point-to-point network distances are approximated by the straight-line distances between such points. Advantages of such an approach include eliminating the dependence on a costly and cumbersome comput-

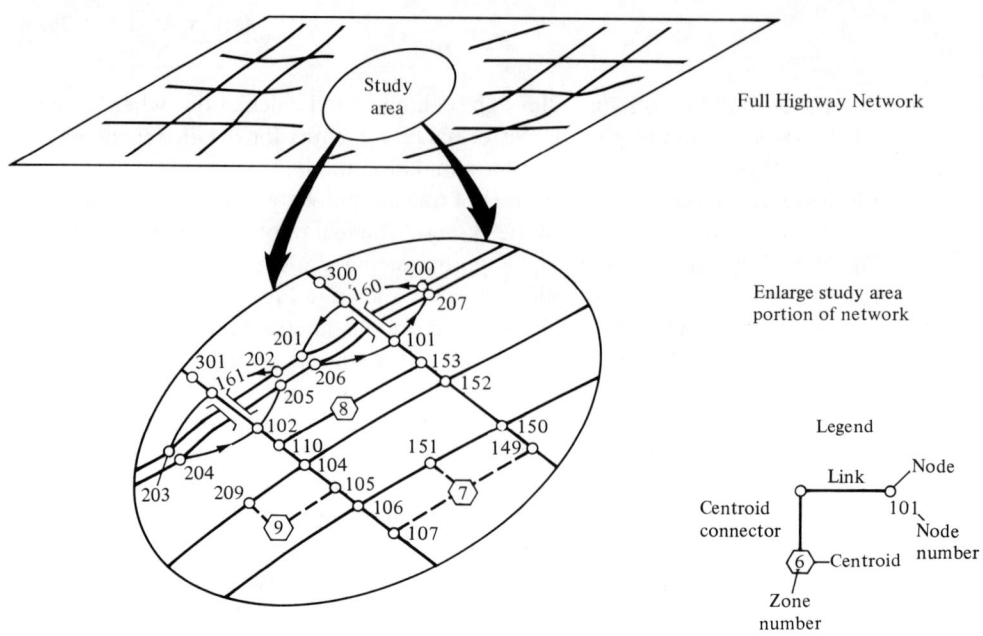

Full Highway Network

Enlarge study area portion of network

Legend

Study area network format

Typical format for display of network characteristics.[1/]

Link	Facility type	Lanes		Length, mi	Traffic control	Other
		Orientation	Number			
205–206	Freeway	One-way (NB)	3	0.6	Grade Separated	Industry
201–202	Freeway	One-way (SB)	3	0.6	Grade Separated	Industry
102–110	Arterial	Two-way	4	0.3	Signals	Commercial
106–107	Arterial	Two-way	6	0.6	Grade Separated	Industry
151–150	Arterial	Two-way	4	0.8	Signals	Residential

Continued

Node	Approach	Configuration[2/]	Traffic control	Other
160	N	Ramp – 2 lane	Stop	One-way link
	S	—No south approach – 1 way SB—		
	E	3T, 1L	No stop	No right turn
	W	3T	No stop	No left turn
150	N	2T	Signal (g/c = 0.4)	
	S	2T	Signal (g/c = 0.4)	
	E	2T, 1L	Signal (g/c = 0.6)	
	W	3T	Signal (g/c = 0.6)	No left turn

Continued

[1/] Refer to figure for diagram of network.
[2/] T = through lanes; L = left-turn lanes; R - right-turn lanes.

erized network and facilitating the analytical treatment of a number of transportation system performance measures (one simple example of which is the average zonal walk time calculations presented in Eqs. [8-32] to [8-34] in Sec. 8-2-3). The major disadvantage of such an approach is that it is not applicable to the analysis of explicit links or components of the transportation network, particularly with respect to situations in which link or system capacity is of importance.

A final concept which underlies all of transportation performance analysis is the *flow* of vehicles, people, and goods that occurs through the transportation network. As defined in Chap. 2, performance measures are related to the *volume* and *density* of this flow at a given point in the transportation network (typically along a given link or through a given node in the network), the *capacity* of given network components (i.e., the maximum volume which the given component can accommodate per unit time), and the *speed* at which individual elements of the flow are able to move through the network (or, equivalently, the *travel time* which individual elements experience in moving between two points within the network). All of these concepts are summarized in the *fundamental equation of traffic flow* introduced in Chap. 2 (see Fig. 2-10), which expresses the relationship between volume, flow, density, and speed for a given element of the network, namely,

$$q = \bar{V}k \tag{8-1}$$

where q = volume flow through network element, vehicles per hour
$\bar{V}$ = average speed of vehicles in network element, miles per hour
k = density of vehicles within network element, vehicles per mile

Equation (8-1) is derived in Sec. 8-2-2 through the use of time-distance diagrams. At this point, it is sufficient to observe that all of the techniques discussed in Secs. 8-2-2 and 8-2-3 represent various ways of conceptualizing flows within transportation networks and representing their relationships with characteristics of the network and the transportation system as a whole.

8-2-2 Performance Analysis Techniques

A number of performance analysis techniques are applicable to a range of transportation supply analysis problems. Before discussing specific applications, it is therefore useful to present some of these techniques in a generalized form. The techniques discussed in this subsection are:

1. Time-distance diagrams
2. Queuing theory
3. Fluid-flow approximations

Figure 8-3 Example transportation network (*Pedersen and Samdahl,* [*1982*]*.*)

4. Simulation
5. Mathematical programming

Each of these techniques is discussed briefly, in a relatively qualitative way. In each case, the interested reader is directed to references which deal with the technique in question in a more rigorous, mathematical manner. Although some examples are used for illustration, more detailed discussion of planning applications of these techniques is deferred until Sec. 8-2-3.

Time-distance diagrams[3] Undoubtedly the simplest (but often extremely effective) technique for analyzing transportation system performance is the time-distance or time-space diagram. The time-distance diagram is used to plot the trajectory of vehicles through time and distance, where "distance" means distance traveled along a route or link. Figure 8-4 illustrates the use of such a diagram. The diagram is constructed by choosing an arbitrary point in time and location along the route as the origin. The horizontal axis of the diagram is the time dimension; that is, the horizontal distance between the origin and any point in the diagram represents the time which has elapsed. The vertical axis of the diagram is the distance dimension; that is, the vertical distance between the origin and any point in the diagram represents the physical distance between that point on the route and the point on the route chosen as the origin. Most routes, of course, are not straight; they change direction in two-dimensional space (not to mention elevation in three-dimensional space) any number of times. For the purposes of the time-distance diagram, however, it is assumed that one can "straighten out" the route and characterize it solely in terms of the single dimension of length or distance traveled. This is, in fact, an easy and nonrestrictive assumption to make for the types of problems applicable to time-distance analysis.

Given these definitions, the location of a given vehicle within the system can be plotted for each point in time, as shown in Fig. 8-4. The locus of these location-time points (i.e., the connected line composed of these points) represents the time-distance trajectory of this vehicle through the system. As indicated in Fig. 8-4, the instantaneous velocity of the vehicle at any point is defined by the tangent to the vehicle's trajectory at that point (dx/dt), while the average speed of the vehicle between any two locations and points in time is defined by the slope of the arc connecting these two points. It follows from these observations that a straight-line trajectory implies that the vehicle is traveling at constant speed, that a trajectory with increasing slope implies that the vehicle is accelerating, conversely that a trajectory with decreasing slope implies deceleration, and that a horizontal trajectory indicates that the vehicle is stationary.

Figure 8-5 illustrates the derivation of the fundamental equation of traffic flow using a time-distance approach. This figure depicts the flow of vehicles along a route. A *time-distance domain* can be drawn, as shown in Fig. 8-5a, for a particular segment of the route and for a particular period of time (i.e., a particular observation period). If

---

[3]For further discussion of time-distance diagrams, see Morlok [1978]; Steuart [1979]; Daganzo [1982]; Sheffi [1984].

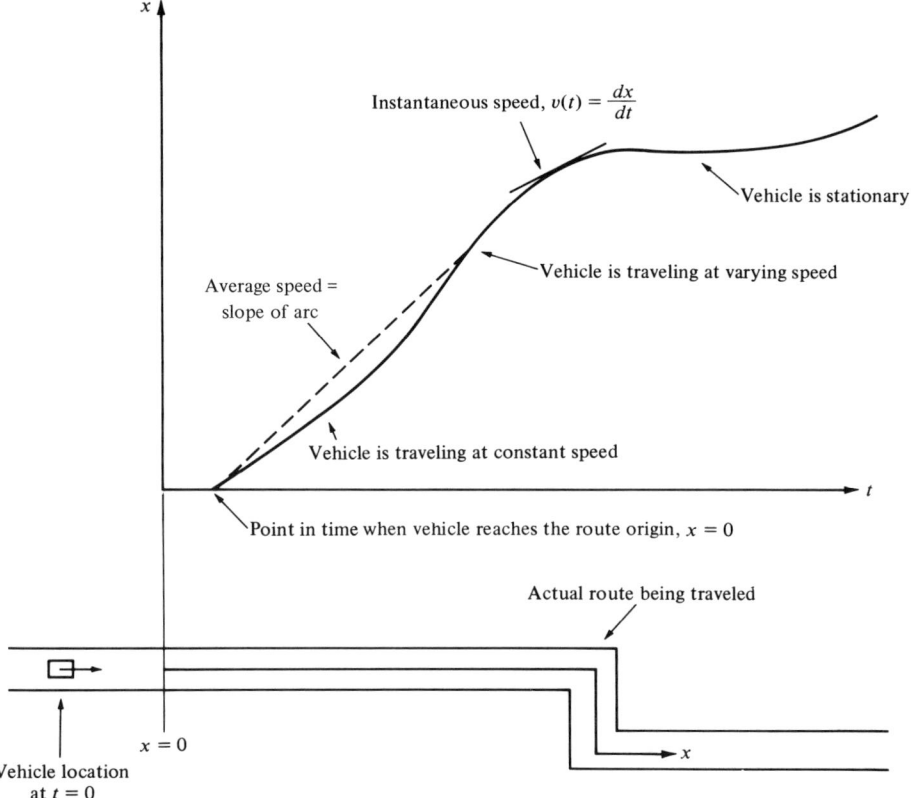

Figure 8-4 Example time-distance diagram.

the length of the route segment is X feet and the length of the observation period is T seconds, then the "area" of the domain is

$$A = XT \quad \text{foot seconds} \tag{8-2}$$

Using the subscript i to denote individual vehicles whose trajectories intersect the time-distance domain (i.e., vehicles which are within the route segment during the observation period), denote x_i as the distance traveled by vehicle i within the domain (i.e., the distance traveled by vehicle i along the segment during the observation period) and t_i as the time spent by vehicle i within the domain (i.e., the amount of time that the vehicle is within the route segment during the observation period).

The total number of "vehicle feet" of flow which occurs within the segment during the observation period is thus represented by $\sum_i x_i$. The area of the domain A expresses the total number of "feet seconds" used by this flow. The volume flow rate can thus be defined as the number of vehicle feet which pass through the system per foot second, or

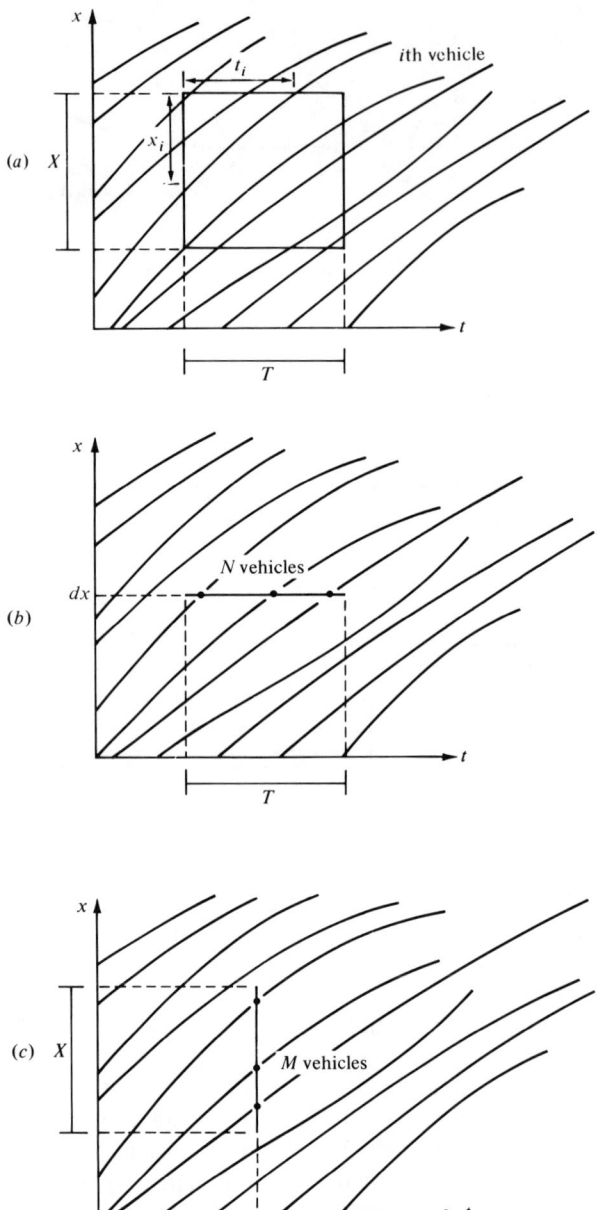

Figure 8-5 Derivation of the fundamental equation of traffic flow.

$$q = \frac{\sum_i x_i}{A} \quad \text{vehicles per second} \qquad (8\text{-}3)$$

Alternatively, if one "shrinks" the route segment down to a single point in space (with "width" dx), as shown in Fig. 8-5b, then the area of the time-distance domain is $T dx$, N vehicles pass through the domain, generating a total of $N\,dx$ vehicle feet and the flow rate is

$$q = \frac{N\,dx}{T\,dx} = \frac{N}{T} \quad \text{vehicles per second} \qquad (8\text{-}4)$$

which is perhaps a more intuitively obvious result.

Similarly, $\sum_i t_i$ represents the total number of "vehicle seconds" of flow within the route segment during the observation period. The density of vehicles within the domain shown in Fig. 8-5a can be defined as the number of vehicle seconds which occur within the system per foot second, or

$$k = \frac{\sum_i t_i}{A} \quad \text{vehicles per foot} \qquad (8\text{-}5)$$

Alternatively, shrinking the observation period to a single point in time (of "length" dt) yields a time-distance domain of area $X\,dt$ (see Fig. 8-5c). M vehicles pass through this domain (i.e., are within the route segment at the instant of time being considered), generating a total of $M\,dt$ vehicle seconds, and the density of flow is

$$k = \frac{M\,dt}{X\,dt} = \frac{M}{X} \quad \text{vehicles per foot} \qquad (8\text{-}6)$$

which, again, is the expected result.

Finally, the average speed of flow through the domain is equal to the total distance traveled by vehicles within the domain divided by the total time taken by these vehicles within the domain

$$\overline{V} = \frac{\sum_i x_i}{\sum_i t_i} \quad \text{feet per second} \qquad (8\text{-}7)$$

Equation (8-7), however, is equivalent to

$$\overline{V} = \frac{q}{k} \quad \text{feet per second} \qquad (8\text{-}8)$$

which is the fundamental equation of traffic flow.

Time-distance diagrams are an extremely simple but useful method for representing the actual flow of vehicles within a system. They can be applied to the analysis of either exclusive or shared rights-of-way, the analysis of intersection signals or other route control systems, the analysis of the interaction of conflicting flows, and so on. For simple problems, time-distance diagrams (plus associated side calculations) may well be all that the analyst requires for the analysis. The major limitation of the technique is that it quickly becomes cumbersome to use as the complexity of the analysis increases—particularly in terms of the number of vehicles being analyzed. In such cases, however, a time-distance diagram often aids in developing the more complicated analysis techniques required (many simulation models, for example, are ultimately nothing more than a complex operationalization of a time-distance analysis).

Queuing theory.[4] Queuing theory is used to analyze systems which can be characterized as consisting of one or more *servers* which perform a set of prescribed tasks for whatever *customers* present themselves to the server for service. As an example, an intersection might be considered to be a server performing the task of controlling the flow of vehicles from one street link to another, with the customers in this system being the vehicles wishing to pass through the intersection. The activities of the server are denoted in queuing theory as the *service process,* while the rate of arrival of customers is determined by the *arrival process.* Since the servicing of a given customer takes a finite amount of time, it is often the case that other customers will arrive during the time taken to serve this customer. In such cases, the customers must either wait until the server is free to serve them (and form a *queue),* or they must leave the system (i.e., forgo the service or perhaps return at another time).

Queuing systems are characterized in terms of:

1. The nature of the arrival process. The arrival process can be either *deterministic* (i.e., the time of each arrival is known with certainty) or *stochastic* (i.e., arrivals happen randomly, according to a known probability distribution).
2. The number of servers available.
3. The nature of the service process. Again, this process can be either deterministic or stochastic in nature.
4. The protocol for queue management. Are arrivals served on a first-come first-served basis, or does a priority system exist for servicing customers? If multiple servers exist, how is the queue allocated among the servers (e.g., a separate queue for each server; one queue, with the first member of the queue being served by the first available server)?

Many transportation system components can be thought of as queuing systems. Intersections have already been used as an example, in which the service process is determined by the signal cycle time, the arrival process is determined by the volume flow on the link preceding the intersection, and arrivals are processed on a first-come first-served basis—passing and turning movements aside. Other examples include freeway sections under "forced-flow" conditions, terminals, and passenger arrivals at transit stops.

Queuing theory is used to derive analytically key descriptors of system performance such as:

[4]The literature on queuing theory is immense. Examples include Prabhu [1965]; Clark and Disney [1970]; Newell [1971]; Bhat [1972]; Kleinrock [1975]; Larson and Odoni [1981].

1. The expected time a customer spends in the system
2. The expected wait time (delay) experienced by a customer in the system
3. The average queue length
4. The expected maximum queue size

For example, taking perhaps the simplest case of a single server queue, random arrival and service processes, both of which are described by a Poisson distribution[5] with an average arrival rate of λ customers per unit time and an average service rate of μ customers per unit time, it can be shown under steady-state conditions that the probability that the number of customers in the queue N at any given time equals a specific value (say n) is

$$P(N = n) = \rho^n(1 - \rho) \qquad \rho < 1 \qquad (8\text{-}9)$$

where ρ, often referred to as the *service ratio* or *traffic intensity*, is equal to λ/μ. The expected length of the queue N is

$$E(N) = \frac{\mu}{\mu - \lambda} \qquad (8\text{-}10)$$

and the expected time T spent by a customer in the system is

$$E(T) = \frac{1}{\mu - \lambda} \qquad (8\text{-}11)$$

Equation (8-11) is plotted in Fig. 8-6. As shown in the figure, expected time in the system increases as the service ratio ρ increases. In the limit, as ρ approaches 1 (i.e., the arrival rate equals the service rate), the queue length grows infinitely large, customers spend infinitely long in the system, and the system is said to be *saturated*, or at *capacity*.

[5]The Poisson distribution is used to describe the probability of n events occurring within a given period of time, given that the time between arrivals is a random number and that it is independent of the time of the previous arrivals. See, for example, Benjamin and Cornell [1970].

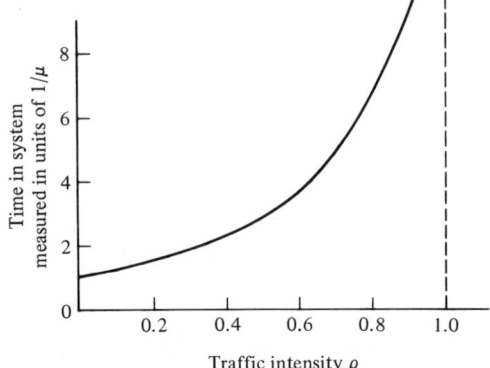

Figure 8-6 Wait time vs. traffic intensity for Poisson queuing process.

To illustrate the use of Eqs. (8-9) through (8-11), consider a loading dock which, on average, can unload a truck in 30 minutes or, in other words, has an average service rate μ of 2 trucks per hour. The average rate of arrival of trucks at the dock λ is 1 per hour. Thus, ρ equals 0.5 for this system. Assuming that both truck arrivals and the unloading of trucks can be represented as Poisson processes, from Eqs. (8-10) and (8-11) the expected queue length and time spent by a truck waiting and being unloaded are $1/(2-1) = 1$ truck and $1/(2-1) = 1$ hour, respectively. Similarly, the probability of 2 or more trucks being in the queue at any given time is

$$P(N \geq 2) = 1 - P(N = 0) - P(N = 1)$$

which, from Eq. (8-9), is

$$\begin{aligned} P(N \geq 2) &= 1 - \rho^0(1 - \rho) - \rho^1(1 - \rho) \\ &= 1 - 0.5^0(1 - 0.5) - 0.5^1(1 - 0.5) \\ &= 1 - 0.5 - 0.25 \\ &= 0.25 \end{aligned}$$

This simple example serves to illustrate the importance of randomness in influencing system performance, in that even though this system is far from saturated, the average queue length and service time vary considerably from the deterministic case (which would consist of a queue length of 0, a 0.5 hour service time, and the server being "idle" 50 percent of the time).

Queuing theory can be a very powerful analytical tool whenever it is applicable, examples of which include modeling toll booth performance and approximating freight terminal operations. Unfortunately, it cannot be used in transportation analysis as often as one might expect or hope. Reasons for this include:

1. Arrival and service processes can rarely be described by analytically convenient probability distributions. Thus, the number of problems which can be expressed in a tractable fashion is relatively small (although this number is increasing with time as useful approximations are developed for new problem applications [Larson and Odoni, 1981]).
2. Queuing theory deals with steady-state conditions. Transportation queuing phenomena of interest are often transient in nature and hence not well suited to this form of analysis.

Nevertheless, the concept of the queue is an important starting point for the conceptualization and analysis of transportation systems. It is the basis for simple fluid-flow approximations as well as many complex simulation models (both discussed below), which provide procedures for addressing queuing behavior in instances when formal queuing theory is analytically intractable or otherwise inapplicable.

Fluid-flow approximations.[6] Figure 8-7a depicts a typical arrival process for a transportation system component (e.g., vehicles at an intersection, passengers at a

---
[6]The seminal work in this field is Newell [1971].

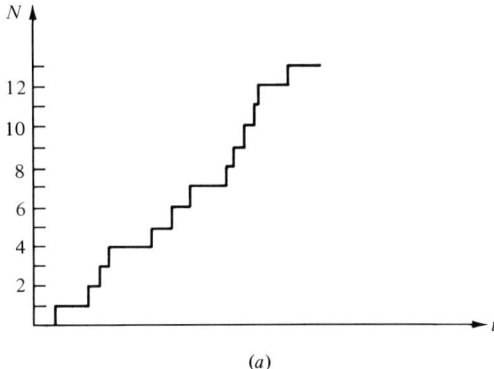

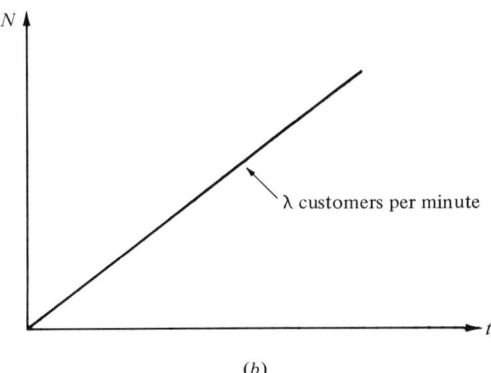

Figure 8-7 Discrete and continuous arrival processes. (*a*) Discrete customer arrivals. (*b*) Continuous customer arrivals.

transit stop). Each "step" in the curve indicates a new arrival, while the vertical height of the curve indicates the total number of arrivals which have occurred to the given point in time. In many transportation applications, the discrete event of the arrival and servicing of an individual customer is of little interest. What is of importance is the behavior of *flows* of customers through the system. Or, in other words, a single customer is a negligibly small quantity within the system, and the uncertainty due to random fluctuations in the number of arrivals is small compared to the observed number of arrivals [Steuart, 1979]. In such cases, the discrete step function of Fig. 8-7*a* can be replaced by the "fluid-flow" approximation of Fig. 8-7*b,* that is, by a continuous flow of (infinitesimally sized) arrivals.

The cumulative number of customers served by the system can be similarly plotted vs. time and overlaid on the cumulative arrival curve. Figure 8-8 illustrates this for the case of an intersection.[7] At the beginning of the process shown, the signal is green, no

---

[7] For simplicity of discussion, the representation of the intersection is idealized in that the amber portion of the signal cycle is ignored, as is the finite amount of time that it takes for a vehicle to pass through the intersection.

queue exists, and the arrival and departure curves coincide, since customers are served the instant they arrive. When the light turns red, the departure curve becomes horizontal (since no vehicles are departing), and a queue forms (indicated by the vertical gap between the arrival and departure curves). When the signal turns green again, the queue begins to dissipate, and if the arrival rate (i.e., the slope of the arrival curve) is sufficiently lower than the departure or service rate (i.e., the slope of the departure curve), then the queue ultimately vanishes. If, however, the arrival rate is large enough, then the queue does not vanish during one cycle of the signal and will tend to grow over time.

A number of important system descriptors can be obtained directly from diagrams such as Fig. 8-8. These include:

1. The queue length n at any point in time given by the vertical distance between the arrival and departure curves at that point
2. The waiting time w experienced by any arrival given by the horizontal distance between the arrival and departure curves
3. The total delay experienced by all customers in the system represented by the area between the two curves A
4. The average queue length $\bar{n}$ given by the area between the two curves, divided by the time interval over which this area is calculated, or

$$\bar{n} = \frac{A}{T} \tag{8-12}$$

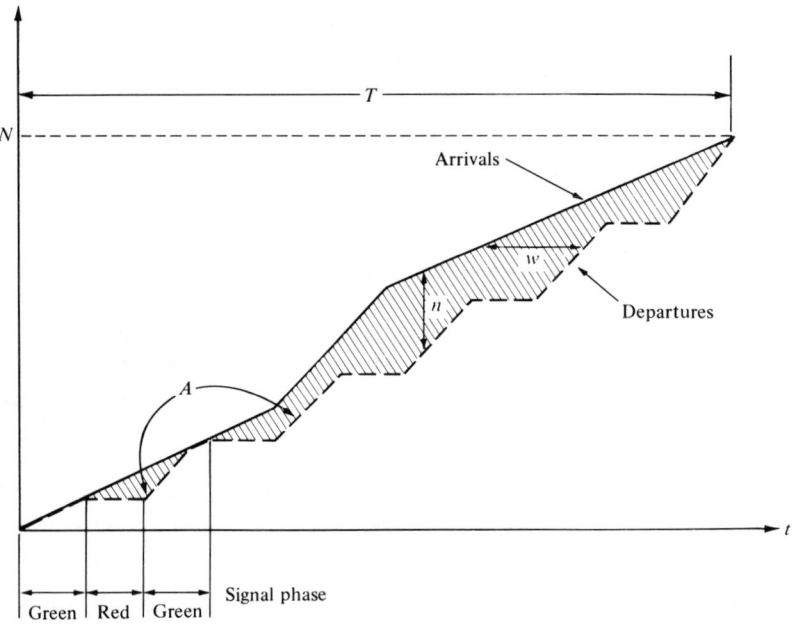

Figure 8-8 Fluid-flow approximation of a traffic signal's operation.

5. The average wait time or delay $\overline{w}$ given by the area between the two curves, divided by the number of arrivals, or

$$\overline{w} = \frac{A}{N} \tag{8-13}$$

Note that fluid-flow approximations indicate that zero delay occurs when the arrival rate is less than or equal to the service rate and no previously developed queue exists (e.g., during the first green phase of Fig. 8-8) and that finite delays occur when the arrival rate exceeds the service rate for finite periods of time. This can be contrasted with queuing theory results in which delay occurs when the service ratio is less than 1, and this delay grows infinitely large as the service ratio approaches unity. These seemingly contrary results highlight the differences between the fundamental assumptions underlying the two approaches. Queuing theory predicts steady-state results for a discrete system in which individual customers interact with individual servers. Since a server takes a finite amount of time to service a customer, customers arriving during this time period will experience delay, and this delay will tend to grow infinitely large as the arrival rate increases relative to the service rate. Fluid-flow approximations, on the other hand, adopt a more "macroscopic" view of the system. This view treats the server as a "channel" through which customers "flow." The service rate defines the channel capacity, while the arrival rate defines the volume flow through the channel. If this flow rate is less than the channel capacity, no delay occurs (since we are ignoring the "microscopic" interactions between the individual flow elements—i.e., customers—and channel-server). If it is greater than the capacity, however (or if the channel is temporarily "obstructed," for example, by a signal turning red), then the flow "backs up" and delay occurs. If this represents the "steady-state" condition, then this delay will be infinitely large. But, in general, the channel capacity is only exceeded for short periods of time (e.g., during the red phases of the signal cycle), and the queue can eventually dissipate (as shown by Fig. 8-8), resulting, in practice, in finite delays.

Which approach is the more "appropriate" representation depends, of course, on the system and problem being analyzed. In general, however, the two approaches are complementary rather than contradictory, in that queuing theory provides insight into how systems behave when operating in the region $\rho < 1$, while fluid-flow approximations describe their behavior in the region $\rho > 1$. Neither technique, however, appears to deal adequately with the case of $\rho \approx 1$, which may actually be the operating region of interest in many transportation planning problems (i.e., peak-period operations in which flows on critical links may be at or near capacity levels). In such cases, simulation models may be required to examine system performance in detail.

Strengths of fluid-flow approximations are that they do not require steady-state assumptions and that they are capable of handling virtually any level of complexity in the arrival and service processes, *provided* that arrivals and departures can be represented as continuous processes. For simple cases (yet ones too complex for queuing theory), the analysis can often be performed directly by graphical methods. For more complicated cases, the techniques can be computerized for analytical or numerical solution. In any event, the graphical representation can be extremely useful in assisting the analyst to "visualize" and understand the processes at work.[8] A major limitation of the approach, on the other hand, is that it generally involves the analysis of the system's performance over a single time interval. If conditions during this time interval are not "representative" of conditions during other time intervals, then the analysis must be repeated over an "ensemble" of intervals in order to derive "average" or "steady-state" values.

Simulation.[9] Simulation involves constructing a mathematical model of the system under study and then *operating* or exercising this model over time, as opposed to *solving* the model explicitly, as has been the case with the techniques discussed to this point. Simulation models have already been discussed with respect to their use in urban activity system modeling (Sec. 6-2-3). A generalization of the concepts presented in Chap. 6 is provided by the following equation:

$$y(t + \Delta t) = f[x(t + \Delta t), y(t)] \qquad (8\text{-}14)$$

where $y(t)$ = vector of variables which characterize system performance at time t

$x(t)$ = vector of exogenous variables which influence system performance at time t

$f(\cdot)$ = "procedure"[10] (i.e., system of mathematical equations, computer algorithms, probability distributions, etc.) which determines system performance at time $t + \Delta t$, given $x(t + \Delta t)$ and $y(t)$

For the case of the NBER urban simulation model presented in Sec. 6-2-3, $y(t)$ corresponds to the distribution of houses, population, and prices at time t; $x(t)$ corresponds to factors influencing these distributions over time (e.g., employment distributions, zone-to-zone travel times); and $f(\cdot)$ represents the system of equations and models programmed into the computer which express how these system variables interact over time.

Key characteristics of simulation models include:

1. They are explicitly dynamic; that is, they replicate system performance over time.
2. System performance at any point in time depends explicitly (and generally in complex ways) on system performance at previous points in time. Performance at time $t + \Delta t$ cannot be computed without knowing the performance at time t.
3. The "performance procedure" is sufficiently complex that it cannot be solved analytically. This complexity typically includes treating certain system processes probabilistically (e.g., random arrival and service rates).

If, as is typically the case, the simulation model is stochastic rather than deterministic (i.e., it includes probabilistic elements), then it must be exercised many times so that the frequency distribution or expected values of the outcomes associated with these

---

[8] A similar comment, of course, applies to time-distance diagrams, previously discussed.

[9] As with queuing theory, the simulation literature is vast. See, for example, Naylor et al. [1966]; Gordon [1969]; Larson and Odoni [1981].

[10] This terminology is used in the sense defined by Florian and Gaudry [1979].

stochastic processes can be determined. Simulation modeling is thus a form of experimentation, in which a series of trials of system performance is carried out under a range of operating conditions determined by the random processes embedded in the model.

Given the complexity and size of simulation models and the need to perform a large number of model runs or replications in order to generate usable information, simulation modeling is generally an expensive and time-consuming approach to analysis. This is particularly the case when no "off-the-shelf" model is available for use, in which case a new model must be developed, involving considerable time and cost to gather the data required, develop the computer programs, and make the programs operational. Simulation modeling is often characterized, therefore, as "the method of last resort."

Despite these constraints, simulation modeling remains an important and widely used analytical tool, for several reasons:

1. Often there is no other method which can analyze a given problem at the required level of detail and realism. In such cases, if the problem is to be analyzed at all, it must be analyzed using simulation techniques.
2. Often one is interested in analyzing very large and costly transportation systems. In such cases even very expensive simulation models represent a small portion of the total system development costs and may well be more than worth the expense in terms of their impact on system design and development.
3. Often standardized simulation packages exist (e.g., network simulation packages for traffic signal optimization) which eliminate the need for individual planners or planning organizations to develop their own model, greatly reducing the time and cost associated with the use of the model.

Mathematical programming.[11] A *mathematical program* consists of an *objective function* which is to be maximized or minimized (e.g., maximize the number of people carried by the available set of public transit vehicles; minimize the cost of operating a given service), subject to a set of *constraints* (e.g., all customers requesting service must be picked up and delivered; no driver will work more than an 8-hour shift). The objective function is a mathematical function of a set of *decision variables* (e.g., the number of buses to be assigned to each route in the system) which expresses how these decision variables are to be combined to yield the quantity to be maximized or minimized. The set of constraints is also a set of mathematical functions which define *feasible* ranges of values for these decision variables. A *linear program* is a special type of mathematical program in which the objective function and all the constraints are linear; while an *integer program* is one in which the decision variables are constrained to take on integer values (e.g., one cannot buy 0.637 buses or carry 142.94 passengers).

Figure 8-9 provides a simple but classical example of a transportation application of mathematical programming (in fact, it is often referred to as "the transportation problem" by mathematical programmers). In this system, goods are supplied at a set of

---

[11]Standard texts include Wagner [1975]; Hillier and Lieberman [1974]; Simmons [1972]; Avriel [1976]; de Neufville and Stafford [1971].

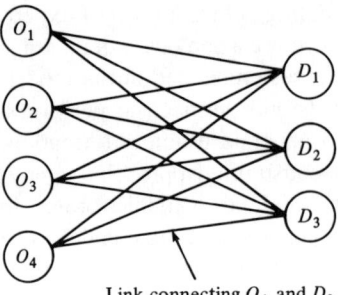

Link connecting O_4 and D_3

Figure 8-9 The "transportation" problem in mathematical programming.

origins, they are consumed at a set of destinations, and they must be shipped along transportation routes which involve certain unit costs. Thus, if

O_i = quantity of goods produced at origin i, $i = 1, \ldots, n$

D_j = quantity of goods required at destination j, $j = 1, \ldots, m$

x_{ij} = quantity of goods shipped from origin i to destination j

c_{ij} = cost per unit quantity of shipping goods from i to j

then the mathematical programming formulation of the problem which will determine a set of flows (i.e., a set of x_{ij}'s) that minimizes total shipping costs is

$$\min \sum_{i=1}^{n} \sum_{j=1}^{m} c_{ij} x_{ij} \qquad (8\text{-}15)$$

subject to

$$\sum_{j=1}^{m} x_{ij} \leq O_i \quad \text{for all } i, i = 1, \ldots, n \qquad (8\text{-}16)$$

$$\sum_{j=1}^{m} x_{ij} \geq D_j \quad \text{for all } j, j = 1, \ldots, m \qquad (8\text{-}17)$$

Equation (8-15) is the expression for the total shipping costs in the system for any given set of flows. The mathematical program must determine a set of flows which minimizes this function, subject to the constraints that the total flow out of each origin zone does not exceed the amount produced in the zone (Eq. [8-16]) and that the total flow into each destination zone is at least sufficient to meet the consumption requirements of the zone (Eq. [8-17]).[12]

Extremely powerful, efficient techniques exist for the solution of linear programs. These techniques can efficiently solve linear programs involving hundreds of constraints and essentially an unlimited number of decision variables, as well as provide extensive "postoptimality" sensitivity analyses of these solutions (e.g., if costs in-

---

[12]Note that this could have been written as an equality constraint (i.e., only flows sufficient to meet demands exactly would be assigned), but since the program is minimizing travel costs, no excess flow will be shipped in the optimal solution, and hence the equality constraint will be automatically satisfied.

crease by 10 percent, how will the solution change? If 15 more buses were available, how would the solution change?).

If the program to be solved is not linear but is integer or nonlinear, then the likelihood of being able to solve the program efficiently is much lower. The techniques used vary widely and depend greatly on the nature of the particular problem being addressed. Often specialized solution procedures must be specifically developed for a given problem in order to exploit the special "structure" or characteristics of the problem that facilitate its solution. Often *no* solution procedure can be found to solve the problem within reasonable limits of computer computation time and/or storage requirements. This is particularly true of the class of integer programming problems known as combinatorial optimization problems, in which the task is to choose an optimal set of items (e.g., schedules of pickups and deliveries for a fleet of demand-responsive transit vehicles) from among a very large set of feasible combinations of such items.

In cases where optimal solutions cannot be found using formal mathematical programming procedures, it is often possible to develop *heuristic* procedures which are designed to find "good" (but not necessarily optimal) solutions. Virtually all analytical procedures for addressing transportation scheduling problems, for example, involve the use of heuristics rather than optimizing procedures. This is because the complexity of practical-sized transportation scheduling problems typically renders formal optimizing extremely difficult, but it has proved possible to develop procedures which generate "good" schedules under most operating conditions.[13]

Transportation system analysis problems addressable within a mathematical programming framework include:

1. The scheduling of transportation services, vehicles, and drivers (typically through the use of heuristics)
2. The analysis of flows through networks
3. The calibration of models based on empirical data (typically through the maximization of a likelihood function)

8-2-3 Performance Analysis Applications

A detailed and comprehensive discussion of applications of transportation system performance analysis techniques is well beyond the scope of this book. In this section, only a selected number of "typical" or "key" applications are qualitatively discussed. For more detailed presentations, the reader should refer to, among others, Morlok [1978]; Vuchic [1981]; Newell [1980]; Larson and Odoni [1981]; and Daganzo [1982]. In structuring this discussion, it is useful to distinguish between the analysis of performance on exclusive right-of-way components, on shared right-of-way components, and on the network as a whole. Each of these categories relates to "in-vehicle" system characteristics. A fourth analysis category of interest is the calculation of "out-of-

---

[13]That is, it is almost always the case with any heuristic that one can find "pathological" cases which will result in the heuristic generating a relatively poor solution.

vehicle'' performance measures. Each of these four categories of analysis is discussed in turn below.

Exclusive right-of-way operations. The most common example of urban transportation operations on exclusive or dedicated rights-of-way is heavy-rail transit (subways and commuter rail). Other examples of exclusive right-of-way operations include light-rail transit on dedicated rights-of-way, ''advanced'' transit technologies (e.g., personalized rapid transit, intermediate capacity transit, and ''people movers''), and reserved lanes on roadways for buses and other ''high-occupancy vehicles'' (e.g., car pools). Performance on such systems is dictated by:

1. The technological capabilities of the vehicles using the right-of-way
2. The system used for controlling operations along the right-of-way
3. The spacing of stops along the right-of-way
4. Stop dwell times
5. Operating policies governing operations along the right-of-way (speed limits, etc.)

The techniques most often used to analyze performance on exclusive rights-of-way are simple analytical models (e.g., Lang and Soberman [1964]; Soberman and Hazard [1980]), time-distance diagrams (e.g., Steuart [1979]), and simulation models (e.g., Daskin [1978]; Sims and Miller [1982]). In this section, some simple analytical models dealing with route (or link) capacity, headway, fleet size, travel time, and average speed are discussed.

The most common models of transit-line performance assume that the system performs in a completely deterministic way or, equivalently, that random variations in system conditions and performance (resulting from, for example, interaction with other vehicles in the system or delays due to passenger boardings and unloadings) are negligible. As such, the simple relationships developed below are applicable to *any* service which can be assumed to be operating deterministically, although presumably such a condition is more likely to hold under exclusive right-of-way operations (with their greater degree of ''control'') than under shared right-of-way operations. Conversely, if random variations in system conditions cannot be ignored, then more complicated analytical approaches (such as simulation) must be employed in order to represent these effects adequately, regardless of the type of right-of-way.

Capacity, headway, and fleet size[14] The capacity q of a transportation facility is proportional to the frequency f of service on the facility, the number of vehicles n which are operated together per ''transit unit'' (e.g., a subway may operate 10-car trains, a light-rail system might operate two-vehicle trains, a busway involves the operation of single bus transit units), and the number of passengers p which can be accommodated per vehicle. That is

$$q = fnp \quad \text{passengers per hour} \tag{8-18}$$

---

[14]The discussion in this subsection draws heavily from Soberman and Hazard [1980], pp. 254–258 and 272–277.

or

$$q = \frac{60np}{h} \quad \text{passengers per hour} \qquad (8\text{-}19)$$

where the service frequency is expressed in transit units per hour and h is the service *headway* (i.e., the time between arrivals) in minutes. That is, by definition, $f = 60/h$.

The fleet size required to maintain the specified headway, and to provide the desired capacity, can be computed with the information that the cycle or round trip travel time for a single vehicle on the route c is given by

$$c = \frac{120L}{\overline{V}} \quad \text{minutes} \qquad (8\text{-}20)$$

where L is the one-way route distance in miles and $\overline{V}$ is the average speed over the route in miles per hour. Since, by definition, c/h transit units must pass by any point in the system during the c minutes it takes for one unit to complete a cycle, and since each transit unit consists of n vehicles, it follows that the total number of vehicles required to maintain the desired headway N is

$$N = \frac{cn}{h} = \frac{120Ln}{h\overline{V}} \quad \text{vehicles} \qquad (8\text{-}21)$$

Alternatively, planners may be faced with a fixed fleet size. In such cases, Eq. (8-21) can be rearranged to solve for the minimum headway achievable with this fleet size, and this result can be substituted into Eq. (8-19) to yield the system capacity which can be obtained with the given fleet size. Performing these manipulations yields

$$q' = \frac{p\overline{V}N'}{2L} \quad \text{passengers per hour} \qquad (8\text{-}22)$$

where the primes indicate that a fixed fleet size is being used as the basis for the calculation.

Minimum achievable headways are a function of vehicle performance characteristics (in particular, the time required to brake to a stop from a given operating speed), route operating speed, driver reaction time, and the control system used for regulating flows along the route. For the block signal systems used in most rail-transit operations in North America, for instance, it can be shown that the minimum safe headway achievable is

$$h_{\min} = t + \frac{x}{V} + \frac{KV}{2d} + \frac{V}{2a} + \tau \quad \text{seconds} \qquad (8\text{-}23)$$

where t = stop dwell time, seconds
x = train length, feet
V = operating (cruise) speed, feet/second
d = deceleration rate, feet/second^2
a = acceleration rate, feet/second^2
K = safety factor
τ = driver reaction time, seconds

Travel time and average speed Given a stop-to-stop (i.e., link) distance of S feet, the time T which elapses from the instant that the transit unit comes to a stop at the first stop to the time it comes to rest at the second stop is the sum of:

1. The time spent at rest at the first stop (i.e., the dwell time t)
2. The time spent accelerating (assumed to be at a constant rate) to the operating speed (V/a)
3. The time spent at the operating speed ($S/V - V/2a - V/2d$)
4. The time spent decelerating (also at a constant rate) to a stop (V/d)

Summing these terms and simplifying yields

$$T = t + \frac{S}{V} + \frac{V}{2}\left(\frac{1}{a} + \frac{1}{d}\right) \quad \text{seconds} \tag{8-24}$$

If the spacing is too short to permit the desired operating speed V to be achieved, then a new operating speed V' must be chosen such that

$$\frac{(V')^2}{2a} + \frac{(V')^2}{2d} \leq S \tag{8-25}$$

before Eq. (8-24) can be correctly applied. Note that if V' is chosen so that Eq. (8-25) holds as an equality (i.e., the transit unit accelerates to V' and then immediately decelerates to a stop, with no intervening "cruise phase"), then Eq. (8-24) reduces to

$$T = t + V\left(\frac{1}{a} + \frac{1}{d}\right) \quad \text{seconds} \tag{8-24a}$$

Given Eq. (8-24), the average link speed is simply

$$\bar{u} = \frac{S}{T}$$

$$= \frac{S}{t + \frac{S}{V} + \frac{V}{2}\left[\frac{1}{a} + \frac{1}{d}\right]} \quad \text{feet per second} \tag{8-26}$$

If there are m stops on the route, and if r is the turnaround time (in seconds) required at one end of the route, then the average speed over the entire route is

$$\bar{V} = \frac{3600L}{\frac{mV}{2}\left(\frac{1}{a} + \frac{1}{d}\right) + r + \sum_{i=1}^{m}(t_i + S_i/V)} \quad \text{miles per hour} \tag{8-27}$$

where t_i and S_i are the dwell time for stop i and the length of the link preceding stop i, respectively; the denominator of Eq. (8-27) is simply the summation of Eq. (8-24) over all the stops on the route; and the constant value of 3600 converts the expression from miles per second to miles per hour.

Example calculations In order to illustrate the use of the equations developed above, consider an 8-mile light-rail transit route with stations uniformly spaced at half-mile intervals. The maximum operating speed on the route is 30 miles per hour. Assume acceleration and deceleration rates of 3 miles per hour per second, station dwell times of 20 seconds, and 5-minute turnaround times at the route ends. Vehicles are run in two-car trains. The capacity of each vehicle is 120 passengers, and a design flow of 12,000 passengers per hour is required for the route. Given this information, we wish to determine the number of light-rail vehicles required to provide the specified service.

In the notation presented above, we have

m = number of stops = $8/0.5$ = 16

S_i = length of the ith link = 0.5 miles = 2640 feet for all i

V = cruise speed = 30 miles per hour = 44 feet per second

r = turnaround time = 5 minutes = 300 seconds

a = acceleration = 3 miles per hour per second = 4.4 feet per second^2

d = deceleration = a = 4.4 feet/second^2

t_i = dwell time at stop i = 20 seconds for all i

Substituting these values into Eq. (8-27) yields

$\overline{V}$ = average route speed

$$= 3600 \times \frac{8}{(16 \times 44/2)(1/4.4 + 1/4.4) + 300 + 16(20 + 2640/44)}$$

= 16.55 miles per hour

Given that q equals 12,000 passengers per hour, n equals 2 vehicles per train, and p equals 120 passengers per vehicle, the train frequency f required to provide this design capacity is, from Eq. (8-18)

$$f = \frac{12,000}{2 \times 120} = 50 \text{ trains per hour}$$

which implies a headway h between trains of $60/50$ = 1.2 minutes. Thus the number of vehicles N required is, from Eq. (8-21)

$$N = \frac{120 \times 8 \times 2}{1.2 \times 16.55}$$

$$= 96.7 \text{ or } 97 \text{ vehicles}$$

Shared right-of-way operations. Virtually all streets, highways, and sidewalks operate as shared rights-of-way. In dealing with the performance of shared right-of-way facilities, an important distinction needs to be made between *controlled access* facilities (e.g., freeways) and *uncontrolled access* facilities (e.g., urban streets and sidewalks). Each of these is discussed in turn.

Controlled access facilities A typical urban freeway or controlled access roadway consists of two or more lanes for travel in each direction, physical separation of the traffic moving in each direction, no signalized control of operations,[15] and access and egress to the facility limited to a small number of interchanges spaced relatively far apart. Under normal operating conditions, traffic on such facilities is generally free-flowing and corresponds well to the fundamental relationship of traffic flow (see Secs. 2-2-1, 8-2-1, and 8-2-2). As flow levels increase, interchanges typically begin to act as "bottlenecks" to traffic flow because of weaving maneuvers and other phenomena associated with vehicles exiting and entering the flow. Accidents and vehicle breakdowns in the flow lanes also act as temporary obstacles to the flow.

Given these characteristics, useful performance analysis techniques include fluid-flow and time-distance diagrams for analyzing both "steady-state" flows and transient phenomena associated with lane blockages and interchange maneuvers, analytical models developed to study various aspects of steady-state and transient behavior (e.g., Hurdle [1981]), and simulation models for detailed analysis of freeway operations.

An example of a simulation model designed to analyze freeway flows is the FREQ6PL simulation model developed by the Institute of Transportation Studies at the University of California to study the operation of exclusive lanes on freeways. Characteristics of this model include [Cilliers et al., 1978]:

1. It is a deterministic, macroscopic model of freeway flows (i.e., it deals with flows of vehicles, rather than with individual vehicles).
2. It generates a range of *measures of effectiveness* (see Chap. 9) for the evaluation of design alternatives. These are the travel time, fuel consumption, vehicle emissions, construction costs, facility operating costs, and facility maintenance costs associated with the use of freeway sections. These measures of effectiveness (MOEs) are combined into an overall *performance index PI* which is defined as the sum of the yearly monetary costs associated with each of the six MOEs.
3. It is capable of analyzing a range of exclusive lane geometries.
4. It incorporates the influence of parallel arterials on freeway operations.
5. It is sensitive to temporal variations in demand as well as to varying demand levels along the length of the freeway section.
6. It realistically represents the physical characteristics of the freeway.
7. It predicts the demand response to implementation of the exclusive lane in terms of spatial shifts (i.e., freeway users shifting to parallel routes) and modal shifts (from nonpriority to priority modes).

Figure 8-10 presents the major steps in the simulation model. Steps 1 through 5 represent the input data required by the program, which include [Cilliers et al., 1978]:

1. Subsection lengths, capacities, and volume-delay curves, the number of lanes, the position and capacities of on and off ramps, grades and curves, and the surface texture of the roadway
2. Definition of the exclusive lane strategy in terms of its position, time period in use, and priority cutoff limit (i.e., minimum number of passengers per vehicle required for use of the exclusive lane)

[15]"Ramp metering" types of control aside.

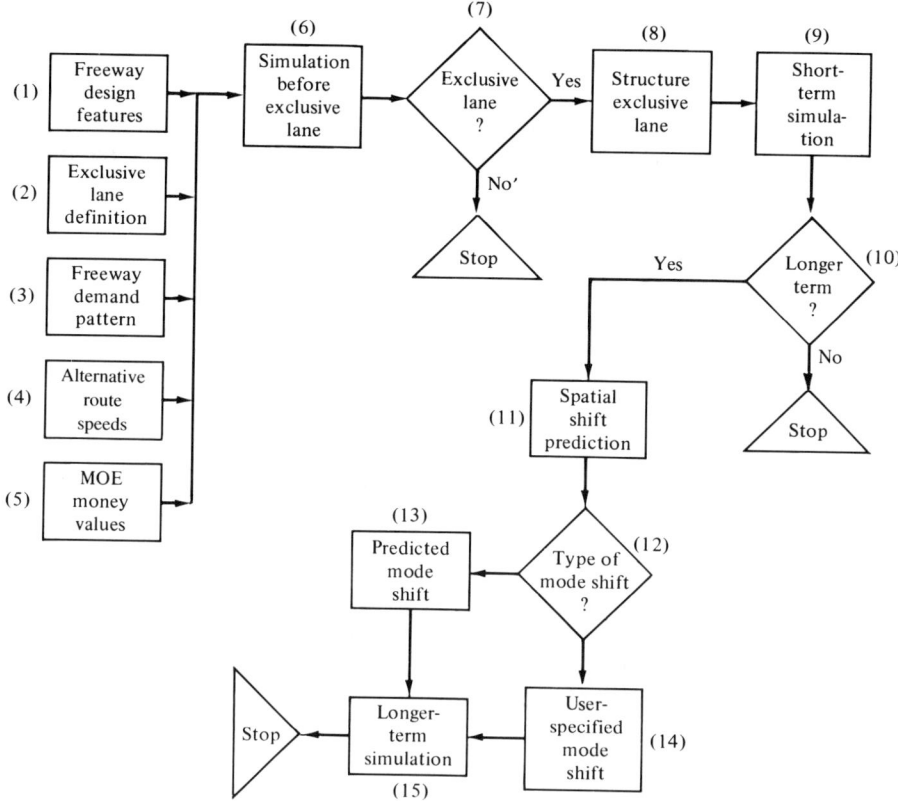

Figure 8-10 Structure of the FREQ6PL simulation model. (*Cilliers [1978]*.)

3. Origin-destination tables by time of day and vehicle occupancy distribution for each on ramp
4. Speeds for each section of the available parallel routes
5. User-specified monetary values for each of the measures of effectiveness considered

As indicated by Fig. 8-10, the model is capable of doing simulations for three different points in time: prior to implementation of the exclusive lane (which defines the base case for evaluation purposes), immediately after implementation of the exclusive lane, and 3 to 6 months after implementation (by which time it is assumed that demand will have adjusted to the change in supply). The third level of simulation thus represents a simple equilibration procedure in which demand adjusts over time to the service levels being supplied.[16]

[16]Note that demand responses other than those considered here are also possible, such as shifts in the time of day of the trip, choosing destinations not requiring use of the facility, and forgoing certain trips entirely.

"Mode shift" here refers to the shift from nonpriority modes (i.e., low-occupancy vehicles which cannot use the exclusive lane) to priority modes (i.e., bus and high-occupancy vehicles). Logit mode split models are used to estimate these shifts (or, alternatively, the user can directly input mode splits in order to explore "what if" questions concerning the impact of modal shifts on system performance). "Spatial shift" refers to the diversion of nonpriority freeway users to the parallel arterial roads. These diversions are calculated based on the following assumptions:

1. All trips using the freeway originating outside the study area will not be diverted to parallel routes by the implementation of the exclusive lane.
2. All trips using the freeway which have both their origins and destinations within the study area will be diverted to parallel routes if they save travel time by doing so.
3. Trips using the freeway originating within the study area but destined for points outside the study area will be incrementally diverted to parallel routes if travel-time savings exist, based on a "capacity-restraint" assignment procedure similar to the one shown in Fig. 7-10.

Table 8-1 presents example summary outputs from the model. This table presents and compares the measures of effectiveness for the Santa Monica Freeway in the Los Angeles metropolitan area, for the existing (or base) case, immediately after the implementation of an exclusive lane for buses and cars containing three or more people, and 3 to 6 months after implementation of the exclusive lane. As shown in the table, in the short run, total travel time increases by 74 percent, and all other MOEs increase with the exception of nitrous oxide emissions, resulting in an overall increase

Table 8-1 Sample outputs from the FREQ6PL simulation model*

Cost element	Before implementation of priority lane	After implementation of priority lane	After minus before	Percent difference
		Short term		
Time				
Freeway	6659	11605	4946	+ 74.3
Street	0	0		
Combined	6659	11605	4946	+ 74.3
Fuel				
Freeway	3488	3771	284	+ 8.1
Street	0	0		
Combined	3488	3771	284	+ 8.1
HC				
Freeway	616	844	229	+ 37.1
Street	0	0		
Combined	616	844	229	+ 37.1

Table 8-1 (*continued*)

Cost element	Before implementation of priority lane	After implementation of priority lane	After minus before	Percent difference
		Short term		
CO				
Freeway	47	69	22	+48.0
Street	0	0		
Combined	47	69	22	+48.0
NO_X				
Freeway	184	115	−69	−37.5
Street	0	0		
Combined	184	115	−69	−37.5
Construction	0	14	14	
Operating	0	60	60	
Maintenance	0	10	10	
Performance index	10993	16489	5496	+50.0
		Longer term		
Time				
Freeway	6659	5729	−930	−14.0
Street	0	1549		
Combined	6659	7298	640	+ 9.6
Fuel				
Freeway	3488	3022	−466	−13.3
Street	0	693		
Combined	3488	3715	228	+ 6.5
HC				
Freeway	616	530	−86	−13.9
Street	0	104		
Combined	616	634	18	+ 3.0
CO				
Freeway	47	41	−6	−13.4
Street	0	7		
Combined	47	48	1	+ 1.4
NO_X				
Freeway	184	160	−24	−13.2
Street	0	7		
Combined	184	166	−18	−9.6
Construction	0	14	14	
Operating	0	60	60	
Maintenance	0	10	10	
Performance index	10993	11946	953	+8.7

*All costs and the performance index expressed in thousands of dollars per year.
Source: Cilliers, Cooper, and May [1978].

in the performance index of 50 percent. In the longer run, however, freeway travel times, fuel consumption, and pollution emissions all decrease, although the associated increases in these measures on the parallel arterial streets—in combination with the construction, operating, and maintenance costs associated with the project—still result in an overall increase of 8.7 percent in the performance index.

Uncontrolled access facilities In contrast to controlled access facilities, typical urban streets have intersections which may or may not be signalized, signed, or otherwise regulated at regular, shortly spaced intervals. Urban streets also may or may not be physically segregated by direction of flow, they may or may not have parking permitted on their outside lanes, and they generally are used by a far greater variety of "vehicles" (automobiles, trucks, buses, streetcars, motorcycles, scooters, bicycles, pedestrians) for a far greater mix of purposes than controlled access facilities. As a result the urban street is in many ways a far more complicated system to analyze than is the urban freeway. Given this complexity, it is often difficult to develop analytically tractable models of urban street performance. In the absence of such models, simpler techniques, based on the use of empirically derived tables and nomographs codified in standard traffic engineering manuals, are often used [Institute of Traffic Engineers, 1976; Transportation Research Board, 1980; American Association of State Highway and Transportation Officials, 1984].

The starting point for progressing beyond these empirical performance tables and nomographs consists of the observation that the performance of urban streets tends to be dominated by the performance of intersections, rather than by the streets themselves. That is, the majority of the delay experienced by traffic on urban streets is caused by delays incurred while passing through intersections, not by delays caused by events originating in midstreet. The urban street system can therefore perhaps be best thought of as a giant queuing system. This, in turn, implies that appropriate performance analysis techniques for urban streets include queuing theory (typically for simple problems, such as the analysis of simple flows into a single intersection), time-distance diagrams (for tracing the interaction between flows of vehicles and signal cycles, conflicting flows, etc.), fluid-flow approximations (in which the departure process from one intersection will define the arrival process for the next intersection "downstream"), and simulation.

It is, for example, possible to develop a simple link travel time model which is based on the queuing formulas presented in Sec. 8-2-2. Given the following definitions:

q = volume of flow using link, vehicles per hour

c = capacity of link, vehicles per hour

t_0 = zero-flow link travel time, minutes (i.e., time required to traverse link by single vehicle in absence of any other flow on the link)

then the link travel time t associated with a given volume flow q is [Davidson, 1966]

$$t = \frac{t_0}{1 - q/c} \quad \text{minutes} \tag{8-28}$$

where the *volume-capacity ratio* q/c is equivalent to the queue service ratio ρ, and Eq. (8-28)—often referred to as a volume-delay curve—is analogous to Eq. (8-11). To account for the fact that links are interconnected and that what is actually being modeled is a series of interdependent queues rather than a single queue in isolation, Davidson [1966] suggests the use of a factor (denoted J) which modifies the expected delay as a function of road type and frequency of intersections (or other delay-causing locations). Introduction of this factor results in a new expression for total link travel time of [Davidson, 1966]

$$t = t_0\left(1 + \frac{J\rho}{(1-\rho)}\right)$$

$$= t_0 \frac{1 - \rho(1 - J)}{1 - \rho} \tag{8-29}$$

where $\rho = q/c$, and J is by definition less than 1.0 in value. Figure 8-11 presents plots of Eq. (8-29) for various values of J, while Fig. 8-12 presents typical volume-delay curves, used in capacity-restrained assignment procedures, which are based on equations similar to (8-29).

A second technique applicable to the analysis of urban streets is the *critical lane* method for analyzing intersection capacity [McInerney and Petersen, 1971; Sosslau et al., 1978]. This method involves determining a critical intersection volume and then comparing this volume with the volumes shown in Table 8-2 in order to determine a level of service rating for the intersection. The steps involved in the method are [Sosslau et al., 1978]:

1. Determine the net through volume for each approach to the intersection.
2. Determine the equivalent lane volume for each approach to the intersection by

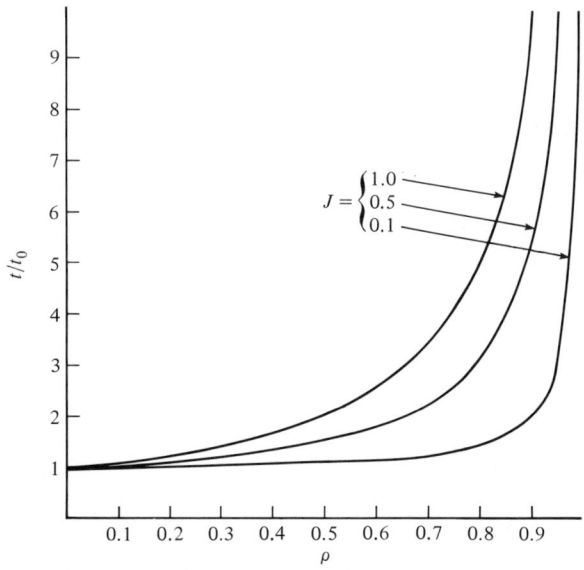

Figure 8-11 Total travel time on a street using Davidson's formula.

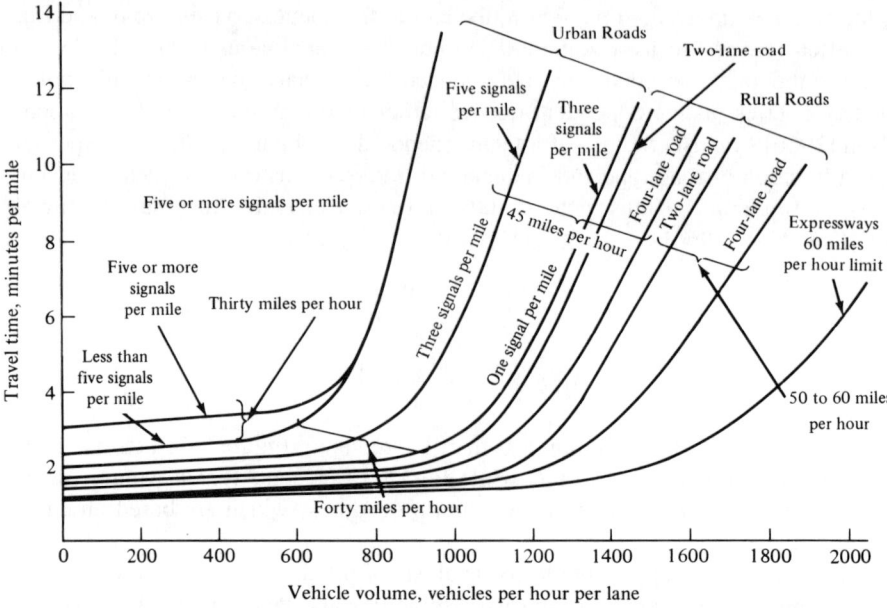

Figure 8-12 Example volume-delay curves, various road types. (*Hutchinson [1974].*)

applying the factors contained in Table 8-3 (alternatively, if lane volumes are known, choose the maximum lane volume for each approach).
3. Determine the left-turn volume for each approach to the intersection.
4. Determine the critical lane volume for each approach by adding the through volume and the opposing left-turn volume together.
5. Select maximum north-south and east-west volumes and sum them to obtain the critical movement summation (CMS).

Table 8-2 Intersection capacity by level of service

Level of service	Range of capacity, vph	
	Low	High
A	0	900
B	901	1050
C	1051	1200
D	1201	1350
E	1351	1500
F	(Special case)	1500

Source: Sosslau, Hassam, Carter, and Wickstrom [1978].

Table 8-3 Lane-use factors

Approach lanes	Lane-use factor
1	1.00
2	0.55
3	0.40
4	0.30

Source: Sosslau, Hassam, Carter, and Wickstrom [1978].

6. Compare the CMS to the volume ranges given in Table 8-2 in order to determine the intersection's service level.

Figure 8-13 illustrates an application of this procedure to a typical intersection.

A final example of performance analysis techniques applied to urban streets is the simulation model of street performance, similar in style to those models previously discussed for urban highways which have been developed to analyze policies such as traffic signal optimization (discussed briefly under network analysis below), turning movements at intersections, and the use of exclusive bus lanes in combination with shared-use lanes [Jovanis et al., 1977].

Network analysis. The preceding discussions have focused on "component-level" analyses. Many analysis problems, however, exist at the level of the network as a whole. Such problems include:

1. Determination of signal cycle times and offsets over road network segments
2. Determination of equilibrium flows for every link in a network, given an origin-destination demand pattern
3. A range of logistical or scheduling problems

Each of these is discussed briefly below.

Signal optimization There are several large-scale simulation and/or optimization packages designed to determine signal settings for a road network so as to minimize various performance measures such as total delay and total number of stops (and, more recently, systemwide fuel consumption). These packages include TRANSYT-7F [Wallace et al., 1983] and SSTOP [Schroeder and Allen, 1979; DelCan, 1981].

Major characteristics of TRANSYT-7F, which are typical of this class of model, are as follows:

1. It is a macroscopic deterministic simulation model.
2. It represents vehicles in terms of *platoon* shapes (i.e., closely bunched groups of vehicles), which change as vehicles proceed through the system being analyzed.
3. The arterial is represented as a set of nodes (intersections) connected by a series of bidirectional links.

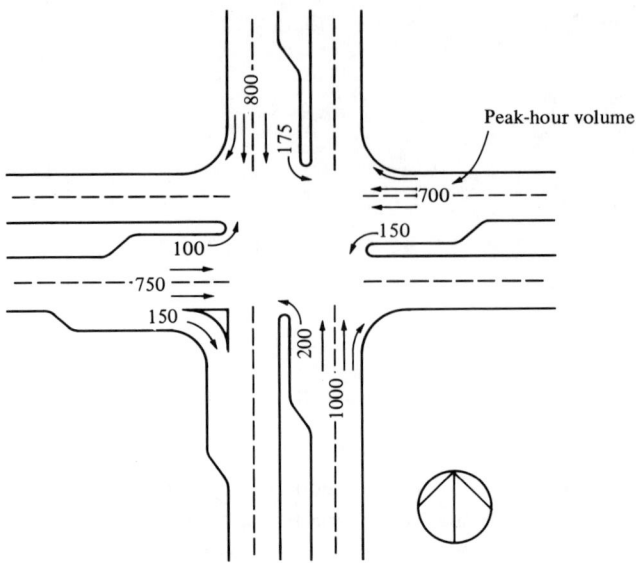

1. Determine the net approach volume (through volume) and multiply by the appropriate lane-use factor to obtain lane volume. (If lane volumes are available, this step is not necessary.) For the flows shown in the figure, this yields:

Direction	Net approach volume	Lane-use factor	Lane volume
Northbound	1000	0.55	550
Southbound	800	0.55	440
Eastbound	750	0.55	413
Westbound	700	0.55	385

2. Determine the critical lane volume for each approach:

	N-bound	S-bound	E-bound	W-bound
Through volume	550	440	413	385
Opposing left-turn volume	175	200	150	100
Total	725	640	563	485

3. Select maximum north-south and east-west volumes and sum to determine the critical movement summation (CMS):

$$\begin{aligned} CMS &= \text{northbound} + \text{eastbound} \\ &= 725 + 563 \\ &= 1288 \text{ vehicles} \end{aligned}$$

4. Compare CMS to volume ranges given in Table 8.3 to determine intersection operating service level. This yields a result for this example of a service level of D.

Figure 8-13 Critical lane method—example calculations. (Sosslau, Hassam, Carter, and Wickstrom [*1978*].)

4. Model inputs include flows, journey times, saturation flows, link lengths for every node in the system, and signal timing parameters.
5. Model outputs, by link, include total time spent, total distance traveled, uniform and random delay encountered, number of stops made, maximum uniform queue size, the degree of saturation, and fuel consumption.

The system is optimized by defining a *performance index* (PI) and employing a search procedure designed to find the set of *decision variables* which minimize the PI. For example, in version 7F of TRANSYT, the PI is

$$\text{PI} = \sum_{i=1}^{n} (d_i + ks_i) \tag{8-30}$$

where d_i = delay (in vehicle hours) experienced on link i,
s_i = number of stops per second experienced on link i
k = user-defined weighting factor.

The decision variables that can be adjusted in order to minimize PI are the traffic signal splits (i.e., the fraction of the signal cycle allocated to the green light) and the signal offsets (i.e., the staggering of signal cycles as one moves from signal to signal along the route).

Network flow analysis[17] Network flow analysis problems include:

1. Determination of the maximum flow through a network with links of finite capacity
2. Determination of the equilibrium flows through a network, given a known set of origin-destination flows
3. Determination of shortest paths between nodes within the network

Discussion of maximum flow problems is beyond the scope of this text; the interested reader will find further discussion of these techniques in the references listed in footnote 17. Equilibrium flow assignment techniques have already been briefly discussed in Sec. 7-4-4 (also, see references in footnote 17 for further details). Fundamental to virtually all network analyses, however, is the calculation of *shortest* or *minimum*, paths between selected points (i.e., nodes) in the network. Equilibrium assignment techniques, for example, typically require the calculation of minimum paths from all origin nodes (centroids) to all destination centroids at each iteration of the algorithm. The need thus clearly exists for efficient algorithms which can quickly compute shortest paths for large numbers of origins and destinations. One example of such an algorithm follows.

Given the following notation:

N = set of all nodes in the network

---

[17]For detailed treatments of network flow analysis, see, among others, Ford and Fulkerson [1962]; Potts and Oliver [1972]; Newell [1980]; Daganzo [1982]; Sheffi [1984].

M = set of "labeled" nodes (defined below)

$\overline{M}$ = set of unlabeled nodes ($M \cup \overline{M} = N$)

n_i = ith node

$c(n_i, n_j)$ = "cost" (travel time, distance, etc.) of traveling on the link from n_i to n_j [$c(n_i, n_j) \geq 0$ for all i, j]

$C(n_i)$ = total cost of travel between "home" node (defined below) and node n_i

a typical shortest path algorithm can be defined by the following steps:

1. Set $k = 1$. Choose a node as a home node (i.e., the origin from which minimum paths are to be computed). Label this node $[-, 0]$, where the minus sign indicates that there is no predecessor node, and the zero indicates that there is zero cost associated with reaching this node. Set M equal to $\{n_1\}$, where n_1 is equal to the node number for the chosen home node.
2. Set $k = 2$. Find an unlabeled node n_2 such that $c(n_1, n_2)$ is a minimum. Assign n_2 the label $[n_1, c(n_1, n_2)]$. That is, n_1 is its predecessor node (i.e., it is linked to n_1), and the cost of reaching n_2 from the home node is $c(n_1, n_2)$. Add n_2 to the set of labeled nodes (i.e., M now equals $\{n_1, n_2\}$).
3. Set $k = k + 1$
4. Find an unlabeled node n_k, such that

$$C(n_k) = \min_{n_x \in M} \left\{ C(n_x) + \min_{n_y \in \overline{M}} [c(n_x, n_y)] \right\}$$

$$= C(n_i) + c(n_i, n_k) \qquad \text{for some } n_i \in M, n_k \in \overline{M} \qquad (8\text{-}31)$$

Assign n_k the label $[n_i, C(n_k)]$ and add n_k to M. In words, Eq. (8-31) involves searching over all currently labeled nodes (i.e., all nodes already connected to the home node) that possess links with unlabeled nodes (i.e., nodes which are not yet connected to the home node) for a new node to connect to the home node (i.e., to add to the labeled set), such that the path to the new node has the lowest cost of travel from the home node.
5. If all nodes have been labeled (i.e., all nodes have been connected to the home node), stop. Otherwise go to step 3.

The final product of this algorithm is a *shortest path tree* rooted at node n_1; that is, it is a tree which identifies the minimum paths between the home node n_1 and all other nodes in the network. Figure 8-14 illustrates the use of this algorithm for the case of a simple six-node network.

Logistics and scheduling problems These include a wide range of transportation problems related to operations research, for example:

1. *Run cutting* assigns drivers to transit vehicles. Computerized run-cutting packages include RUCUS [Wilhelm, 1974] and HASTUS [Blais et al., 1976; Blais, 1978].

SUPPLY ANALYSIS **333**

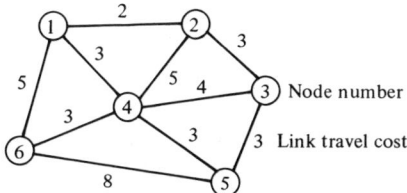

Objective: Build a shortest path tree from node 6.

Step 1: $n_1 = 6$ Label = $(-, 0)$
        $M = \{6\}$ $\overline{M} = \{1,2,3,4,5\}$

Step 2: $n_2 = 4$ Label = $(6,3)$
        $M = \{6,4\}$ $\overline{M} = \{1,2,3,5\}$

Step 3: $C(6) + c(6,1) = 5$ $C(4) + c(4,1) = 3 + 3 = 6$
        $C(6) + c(6,5) = 8$ $C(4) + c(4,2) = 3 + 5 = 8$
                                   $C(4) + c(4,3) = 3 + 4 = 7$
                                   $C(4) + c(4,5) = 3 + 3 = 6$
        $n_3 = 1$ Label = $(6, 5)$
        $M = \{6,4,1\}$ $\overline{M} = \{2,3,5\}$

Step 4: $C(6) + c(6,5) = 8$ $C(4) + c(4,2) = 8$ $C(1) + c(1,2) = 5 + 2 = 7$
                                   $C(4) + c(4,3) = 7$
                                   $C(4) + c(4,5) = 6$
        $n_4 = 5$ Label = $(4,6)$
        $M = \{6,4,1,5\}$ $\overline{M} = \{2,3\}$

Step 5: $C(4) + c(4,2) = 8$ $C(1) + c(1,2) = 7$ $C(5) + c(5,3) = 6 + 3 = 9$
        $C(4) + c(4,3) = 7$
        $n_5 = 3$ Label = $(4,7)$
        $M = \{6,4,1,5,3\}$ $\overline{M} = \{2\}$

Step 6: $C(4) + c(4,2) = 8$ $C(1) + c(1,2) = 7$
        $n_6 = 2$ Label = $(1,7)$
        $M = \{6,4,1,5,3,2\}$ $\overline{M} = \{\phi\}$

Result: The shortest path tree is

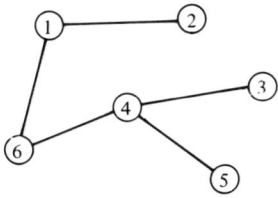

Figure 8-14 Example shortest path calculation.

2. *Demand-responsive vehicle scheduling* determines vehicle tours in demand-responsive service situations in which the origins, destinations, and desired pickup (and/or delivery) times of the passengers determine the vehicle routes and schedules [Bodin, 1975; Wilson and Miller, 1977; Haines et al., 1977; Miller et al., 1980].
3. The *transportation problem,* discussed in Sec. 8-2-2, assigns flows to a network so as to minimize total transportation costs for the system, subject to zonal production and attraction constraints. Transportation problem formulations are

often used to model intercity freight flows and as a planning tool for large organizations to determine "internal" flows (e.g., how best to supply a set of stores with goods from a set of warehouses) [Wagner, 1975; Hillier and Lieberman, 1974].
4. The *traveling salesman problem* involves finding the minimum cost route for a vehicle through a set of points, given that each point must be visited at least once. Routings of service vehicles, newspaper delivery trucks, and parcel pickup and delivery trucks are all examples of "traveling salesman" type problems [Larson and Odoni, 1981].
5. The *Chinese postman problem* (so called because it was first discussed in the journal *Chinese Mathematics*) involves finding the minimum cost route through a network, given that every link must be traveled at least once. Applications include determining postal routes and the routing of snowplows [Mei-Ko, 1962; Larson and Odoni, 1981].

Although all of these problems can be formulated as mathematical programming optimization problems, such programs cannot be feasibly solved for many practical-sized problems. For example, optimal solutions of the traveling salesman problem can only be derived within practical computer storage and computing limits for networks of 70 nodes or less [Held and Karp, 1971]. Similarly, no practical solution technique exists for the determination of optimal schedules for large-scale, multivehicle demand-responsive transit services. In such cases, *heuristics* must be employed to find "good," rather than optimal, solutions to the problem.

An example of a heuristic procedure developed for scheduling demand-responsive vehicles is the UMTA/MIT algorithm [Wilson and Miller, 1977]. This algorithm was designed to find the best insertion of a new customer (as represented by a pickup stop and a delivery stop) into an existing set of vehicle tours, where "best" was defined as the insertion which minimized an objective function consisting of the weighted sum of the marginal disutilities experienced by all passengers in the system due to the insertion and the expenditure of system resources implied by the insertion.

Although the algorithm finds the "best" insertion possible under the defined circumstances, the solution is suboptimal because previous decisions are not reevaluated by the algorithm. The optimal solution may involve rearranging previous assignments so as to better serve the passenger currently being assigned. Thus, the algorithm is "myopic" in that it does not incorporate all the information available in determining its solutions. It is also "greedy" in that it irrevocably commits system resources to customers; these resources might be better utilized serving "later" customers. Both of these problems are typical of heuristic procedures and serve to illustrate the nature of the trade-offs that must be made between the degree of optimality achieved (which is typically hard to conclusively determine) and having a workable, efficient solution procedure (which typically implies working with a limited amount of information and exploring a limited number of solution alternatives).

Out-of-vehicle performance measures. Out-of-vehicle performance measures typically of interest to planners include *walk* times to and from the transportation, *wait* times associated with waiting to board a vehicle, and *transfer* times, if one or more transfers between vehicles and/or routes are made during the course of the trip. In the case of the automobile, the only out-of-vehicle time component considered is the walk time which occurs at the destination end of the trip, since one generally has to park at a location which does not coincide with the actual destination of the journey. Wait and transfer times are meaningless concepts for the automobile mode, and access (or "home-based") walk times (e.g., from one's doorstep to one's garage) are generally assumed to be negligibly small.

Walk times The typical analysis problem faced by transportation planners with respect to walk times involves estimating average zonal walk times, either between two randomly located points within the zone (e.g., compute the average distance walked to work by people living and working within the same zone) or to a specified point in the zone (e.g., compute the average walking distance to the zone centroid, a transit stop, a shopping center). If trips can be assumed to be generated uniformly over the area of the zone (i.e., a uniform trip generation probability density function exists for the zone), then it is relatively easy to show from basic probability principles (see, for example, Larson and Odoni, [1981]) that:

1. The expected walk time between two randomly located points in a rectangular zone of dimensions x and y in which people must walk in directions parallel to the zone sides (i.e., "right-angled" or "Manhattan" distances corresponding to paths through a rectangular grid network are assumed) is

$$E(\text{WT}) = \frac{x + y}{3w} \qquad (8\text{-}32)$$

   where WT is walk time and w is walking speed (see Fig. 8-15a).

2. The expected right-angled walk time between a randomly located point within a rectangular zone and a corner of the zone (see Fig. 8-15b) is

$$E(\text{WT}) = \frac{x + y}{2w} \qquad (8\text{-}33)$$

3. The expected right-angled walk time between a randomly located point and a specified point within a rectangular zone (see Fig. 8-15c) is

$$E(\text{WT}) = \frac{1}{2Aw}\left[\sum_{i=1}^{m}(x_i + y_i)a_i\right] \qquad (8\text{-}34)$$

   where x_i, y_i = dimensions of ith zone section, $i = 1, \ldots, m$
   a_i = area of ith zone section = $x_i y_i$
   A = area of zone = $\sum_{i=1}^{m} a_i$

Similar results can be obtained for circular zones (or zones of more complex shapes) and for nonuniform probability distributions, although the computational complexity involved typically increases considerably. Ultimately, a point is reached where the analysis is no longer analytically tractable, and alternative techniques such as simulation must be employed.

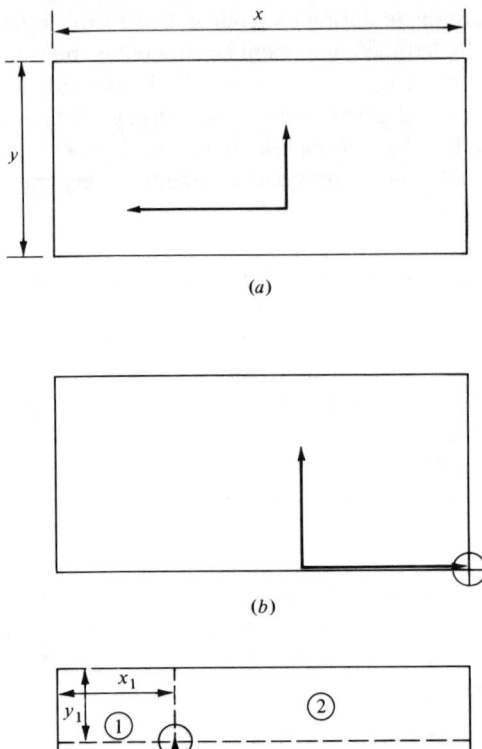

Figure 8-15 Average walk time calculations: (*a*) average distance between two random points; (*b*) average distance to a zone corner; (*c*) average distance to an interior point.

Wait times The wait times that passengers experience at transit stops are a function of the scheduled headway of the transit service, the schedule adherence of the service, and the extent of the passengers' knowledge of the service schedule. For simple analyses it is generally assumed that:

1. For services with relatively short headways (e.g., 15 minutes or less), passengers arrive randomly at the transit stop, with a uniform arrival rate.
2. Transit vehicle arrivals are exactly on schedule, as determined by their design headway.
3. For services with relatively long headways (e.g., greater than 15 minutes), passengers will have some information about the scheduled vehicle arrival times and plan their own arrivals accordingly.

Given these assumptions, an average wait time curve can be drawn as a function of scheduled headway. Figure 8-16 presents an example of one such function, in which two "headway regimes" exist: the "short headway regime," in which passengers arrive randomly relative to the bus arrival time and, on average, experience a wait time of half the headway; and the "long headway regime," in which passengers make use of some knowledge concerning expected vehicle arrival times to reduce their wait times to below the half-headway value. The actual values shown for the "break point" between the two regimes and the slope of the line in the "long headway regime" were empirically developed by Pecknold et al. [1972], and need not be universally representative.

Approaches to calculating transit wait times such as Fig. 8-16 break down in situations in which vehicles' capacities might be exceeded by the number of passengers wishing to board the vehicles. In such cases, some passengers will have to wait for one or more succeeding vehicles before they can board, hence increasing their expected delay. In such cases it becomes necessary to treat the phenomenon as a more complicated queuing system, in which passenger arrivals follow some theoretical or empirical probability distribution, bus arrivals are a function of scheduled headways and stochastic roadway conditions, and, in general, waiting times at any given stop along the route are dependent on the "upstream" stops on the route (e.g., heavy passenger "ons" or "offs" at an upstream stop will generally increase the delays experienced by passengers waiting at downstream stops). While queuing theory or fluid-flow approximations might be applied to fairly simple formulations of this problem, simulation is the only feasible approach to the problem in its general form.

Transfer times Transfers between routes can be treated in a manner similar to wait times if it can be assumed that the arrival times of the passengers on the first route and

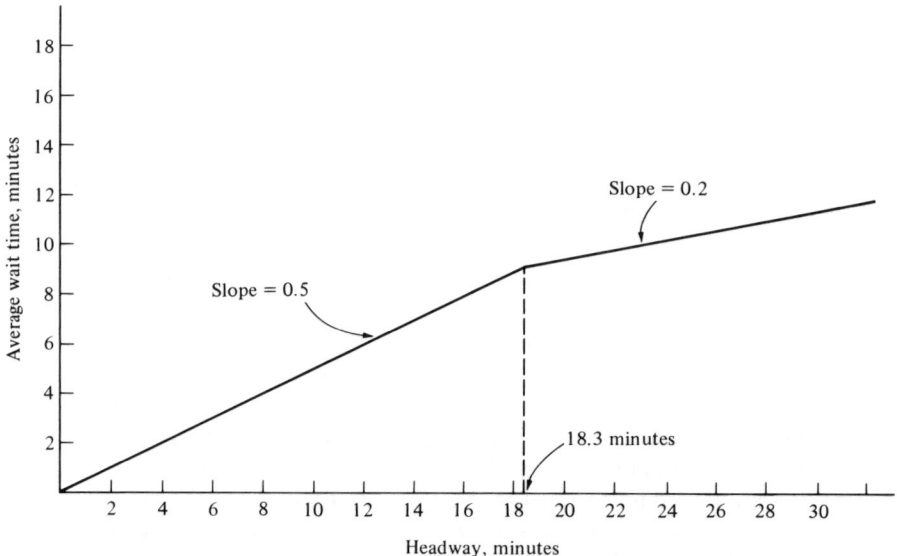

Figure 8-16 Average transit wait times vs. service headway. (*Pecknold, Wilson, and Kullman* [*1972*].)

the vehicle on the second route to which they are transferring are randomly related to each other. In such cases, the expected transfer time can be taken as half the headway of the second route. If timed transfer operations are in effect, then the scheduled transfer time can generally be used as the average transfer time. As with wait times, if more detailed analysis is needed, then more complicated techniques such as simulation are likely to be required.

8-3 IMPACT MODELS

A second area of concern in supply analysis involves an assessment of the environmental impacts associated with system performance. The three major impacts most commonly assessed by transportation planners are the impacts of transportation system performance on air quality, noise levels, and fuel consumption. Each of these impacts will be discussed in the following sections. Similar to performance models, impact models can vary in scale of application, degree of sophistication, and overall approach. The discussion below is designed to illustrate the different levels of complexity that can emerge in impact modeling.

8-3-1 Air Quality Impact

Ever since the relationship between automobile emissions and air quality was established, the impact on air quality of transportation system and facility performance has been a concern of transportation planners in many cities. As was discussed in Sec. 8-2-3, performance models have been developed to estimate the levels of pollutant emissions that result from different system performance characteristics. The importance of estimating air quality impact in transportation planning has also spurred the development of separate air quality impact models of varying sophistication. The simplest of these models consists of nomographs which relate pollutant emissions (in grams per unit distance) to the average vehicle speed, as determined from performance models. This rate of pollutant emissions (by mode) is then multiplied by the estimated total vehicle miles attributable to a specific level of facility performance to determine the total amount of pollutant emissions associated with that performance level. Nomograph techniques are primarily used to estimate levels of pollutants that tend to have a regional impact (such as nonmethane hydrocarbons). Figure 8-17 shows a graph of pollutant emissions related to average vehicle speed developed for planning use in Dallas [Voorhees and Associates, 1977].

Although useful for preliminary "sketch" estimates of air quality impact, the simple models represented by Fig. 8-17 do not realistically represent the complex set of interactions that underlie the formation and dispersion of pollutant concentrations (such as carbon monoxide) resulting from transportation sources. Accurate estimates of such concentrations must account for factors like vehicle mix in the traffic flow, emission factors based on vehicle type and average speed, meteorological conditions, highway design, and topographical characteristics. The influence of each of these factors on resultant pollutant concentrations at a given location can be significant and can be

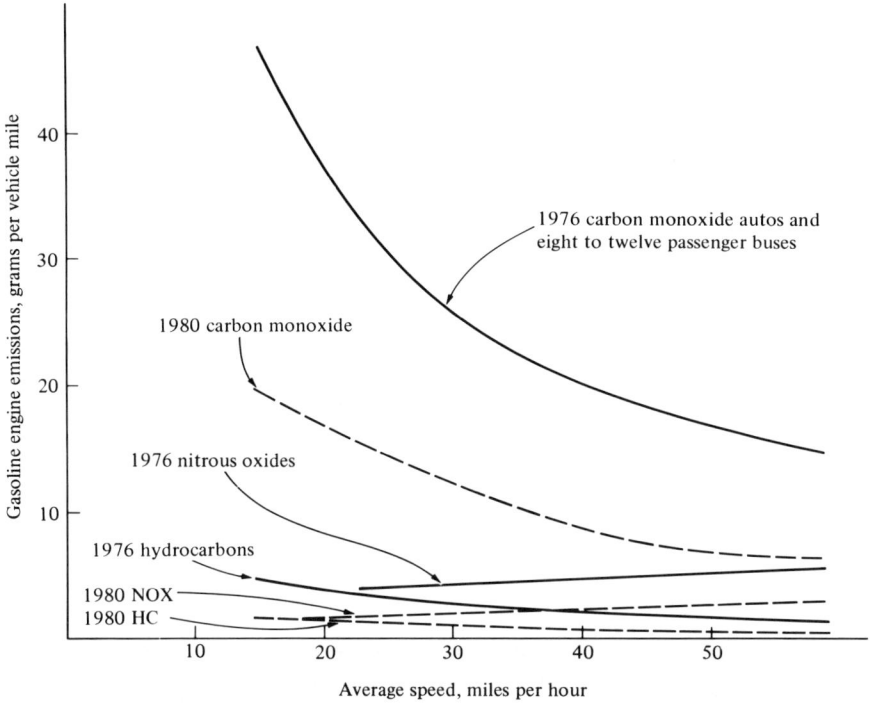

Figure 8-17 Pollutant emissions vs. average vehicle speed, Dallas. (*Voorhees and Associates* [*1977*].)

difficult to represent in simple models (for an excellent treatment of the scientific and theoretical foundation of air quality modeling, see Horowitz [1982]).

Because valid estimates of air quality impact must be based on approaches that take into account the factors mentioned above, two types of more complicated models, which use theoretical concepts relating to pollutant formation and transport, have been developed. The first category consists of models that convert information on driving conditions and other key variables into estimates of motor vehicle emissions. Known as emission models, these models can be used in concert with facility performance models to estimate the total level of pollutant emissions associated with facility performance. The second category consists of models that use data on emissions, meteorological conditions, and topographic characteristics to compute the dispersion of pollutants in the atmosphere, producing output data on the concentration of pollutants at sensitive receptor locations over specified time periods. These models are called dispersion models. Because both types of model are often used in transportation planning, each is discussed in more detail below.

Emission models are based on equations which relate vehicle emission factors to a set of key variables. One of the earliest models of this type, called the federal test procedure (FTP) method, illustrates the type of relationship usually contained in these models [U.S. Environmental Protection Agency, 1976]. The FTP method—capable of computing only CO, HC, and NO$_x$ composite exhaust factors—is based on the following equation:

$$e_{npstwx} = \sum_{i=n-12}^{n} c_{ipn} \cdot m_{in} \cdot v_{ips} \cdot z_{ipt} \cdot r_{iptwx} \quad (8\text{-}35)$$

where e_{npstwx} = composite emission factors in grams per mile for calendar year n, pollutant p, average speed s, ambient temperature t, percentage of cold-start operation w, and percentage of hot-start operation x.

c_{ipn} = FTP mean emission factor for the ith model year vehicles during calendar year n and for pollutant p

m_{in} = fraction of annual travel by ith model year vehicles during calendar year n

v_{ips} = speed correction factor for the ith model year vehicles for pollutant p and average speed s

z_{ipt} = temperature correction factor for ith model year vehicles for pollutant p and ambient temperature t

r_{iptwx} = hot and/or cold vehicle operation correction factor for ith model year vehicles for pollutant p, ambient temperature t, percentage cold-start operation w, and percentage hot-start operation x

Clearly, the calculation of these emission factors would require access to a great deal of technical information on vehicle technology as well as significant computation resources. To simplify the impact assessment process, several computerized programs have been developed to provide planners with a relatively easy-to-use tool for estimating vehicle emissions. The most recent computer model, called MOBILE-2, computes HC, CO, and NO$_x$ emissions for different vehicle types in three major geographic regions of the United States (low altitude, high altitude, and California) [U.S. Environmental Protection Agency, 1981]. A planner using this model is able to input data on vehicle mix in the traffic flow, annual mileage rates and vehicle registration distributions for each vehicle type, basic emission rates for vehicle types, the existence of a vehicle inspection and/or maintenance program, average trips and miles traveled per day for each vehicle type, and specific characteristics of the region in which the highway facility is located. Figure 8-18 shows an example of output produced by MOBILE-2 for different scenarios.

Dispersion models are more complex than emission models in that they must account for the transport of pollutant emissions over specified distances from the source. Several models based on alternative conceptualizations of how this transport phenomenon can best be represented have been developed. One of the earliest models assumes that pollutant concentrations are uniform throughout a specific area, with a rectangular "box" defining the air quality space over the facility and forming the boundary of analysis. The steady-state concentration of pollutants is then related to the emission rate and to other variables through a mathematical relationship (for an example of such a model, see U.S. Department of Transportation [1976]).

The most common dispersion modeling approach is called Gaussian plume modeling. This approach represents the concentration of pollutants as a function of the

```
CAL. YEAR: 1983     REGION: 49-STATE LOWALT,   ALT: 500. FT.
                    TAMB: 20.0(F)              50.0/ 10.0/ 50.0

VEH. TYPE:      LDGV    LDGT1   LDGT2   LDGT    HDGV    LDDV    LDDT    HDDV    MC      ALL VEH
VEH. SPD.:      5.0     5.0     5.0             5.0     5.0     5.0     5.0     5.0
VMT MIX:        0.763   0.085   0.046           0.042   0.019   0.003   0.033   0.009

COMPOSITE EMISSION FACTORS (GM/MILE)
NO-MTH HC:      26.64   25.65   24.90   25.39   39.22   1.14    2.15    8.15    33.62   25.90
EXHST CO:       389.61  366.18  318.13  349.33  715.38  4.36    6.61    35.01   246.01  376.51
EXHST NOX:      2.38    2.85    2.97    2.89    9.35    2.21    3.33    40.29   0.91    3.97


CAL. YEAR: 1987     REGION: 49-STATE LOWALT,   ALT: 500. FT.
                    TAMB: 20.0(F)              50.0/ 10.0/ 50.0

VEH. TYPE:      LDGV    LDGT1   LDGT2   LDGT    HDGV    LDDV    LDDT    HDDV    MC      ALL VEH
VEH. SPD.:      10.0    10.0    10.0            10.0    10.0    10.0    10.0    10.0
VMT MIX:        0.728   0.081   0.046           0.042   0.054   0.008   0.033   0.009

COMPOSITE EMISSION FACTORS (GM/MILE)
NO-MTH HC:      9.76    9.79    7.12    8.82    15.67   0.87    1.50    5.93    16.74   9.28
EXHST CO:       144.63  124.87  81.40   109.12  292.32  3.05    4.76    24.14   111.48  133.29
EXHST NOX:      1.89    2.18    1.56    1.96    8.05    1.47    2.14    24.59   0.89    2.87


CAL. YEAR: 1992     REGION: 49-STATE LOWALT,   ALT: 500. FT.
                    TAMB: 20.0(F)              50.0/ 10.0/ 50.0

VEH. TYPE:      LDGV    LDGT1   LDGT2   LDGT    HDGV    LDDV    LDDT    HDDV    MC      ALL VEH
VEH. SPD.:      5.0     5.0     5.0             5.0     5.0     5.0     5.0     5.0
VMT MIX:        0.669   0.074   0.046           0.042   0.112   0.016   0.033   0.009

COMPOSITE EMISSION FACTORS (GM/MILE)
NO-MTH HC:      10.35   9.83    7.81    9.06    13.76   1.14    1.88    6.87    28.59   9.22
EXHST CO:       202.75  133.06  96.81   119.22  224.67  4.54    7.13    35.01   231.63  163.07
EXHST NOX:      1.51    1.20    0.95    1.10    4.84    1.68    1.67    16.57   0.99    2.11
```

Figure 8-18 Example output from pollutant emissions model (Mobile-2).

emission rate, wind speed and direction, length of line source, and coefficients which reflect the assumed dispersion process (based on the Gaussian or normal distribution function). A discussion of the specific equations applicable in certain situations is beyond the scope of this textbook. Interested readers are referred to Rau and Wooten [1980] and Horowitz [1982].

As with emission modeling, several dispersion model computer packages have been developed to provide planners with easy-to-use tools for estimating pollutant concentrations. Two of the more recent packages include HIWAY-2 and CALINE-3 [Benson, 1979; Petersen, 1980]. An example of output from CALINE-3 is shown in Fig. 8-19. In this example, the planner inputs estimates of site characteristics like wind speed u, wind direction relative to the y axis BRG, a measure of atmospheric stability CLAS, the mixing height of pollutant concentrations MIXH, the averaging time for concentration formation ATIM, a measure of roughness of the surrounding land surface ZO, the velocity of deposition and settling VD and VS, and ambient air quality; link characteristics such as coordinates, use VPH, emission factor EF, height H, width W, and type; and the location of sensitive receptors where pollutant concentrations are to be estimated. CALINE-3 can also be used to estimate carbon monoxide concentrations from queued vehicles at a series of intersections. Given these inputs, the model produces an estimate of the pollutant concentrations in parts per million.

In using both the emission and dispersion models, planners often generate worst-case development scenarios and estimate air quality impacts for several years—the current year (or the latest year for which data are available), the year in which the project is targeted to open, and a future year in which maximum utilization is expected. Computer models like MOBILE-2 and CALINE-3 provide planners with tools that can quickly estimate the impact of transportation facility performance on air quality over a period of years. Although such models represent the current approach to air quality impact modeling, advancements in computer technology and increased understanding of the underlying phenomena of air pollution will likely result in the development of more accurate models in the future.

8-3-2 Noise Impact

As discussed in Sec. 2-2-3, traffic noise is predicted and evaluated in sound level units known as decibels, weighted with a standard "A" filter (dbA). The A filter reduces the intensity of the noise at low and very high frequencies for which the human ear has reduced sensitivity. It also gives additional weight to the more annoying high frequencies in the frequency spectrum. The dbA measure thus has frequency-response characteristics that correlate with a subjective human impression of loudness.

A widely used measure of noise is the percent of time certain noise levels are exceeded during a specified time interval. Common levels include

L_{90} = noise level exceeded 90 percent of the time

L_{50} = noise level exceeded 50 percent of the time

L_{10} = noise level exceeded 10 percent of the time

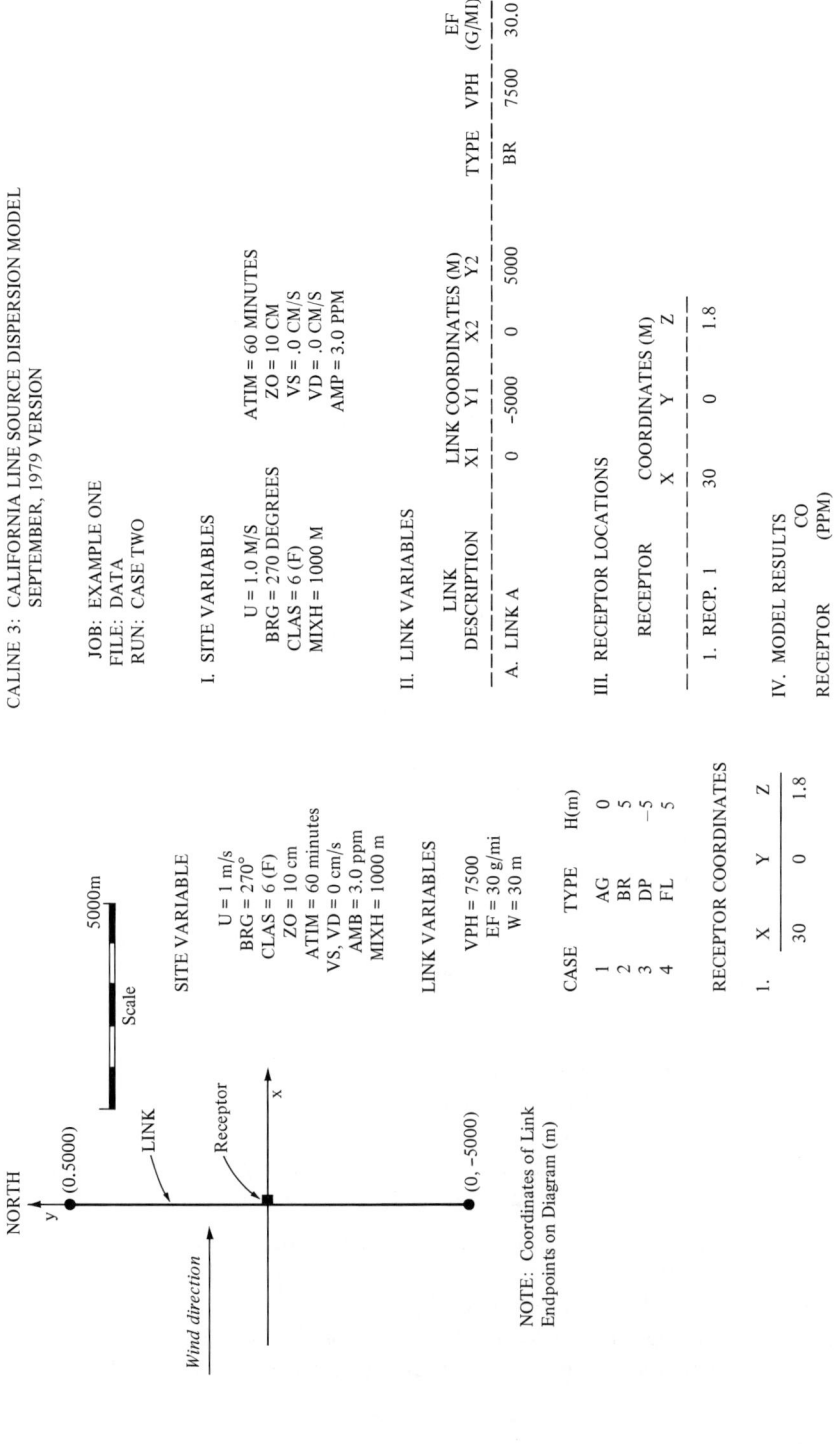

Figure 8-19 Example output air pollution dispersion model.

Perhaps the most common measure, however, is called the "equivalent sound level," L_{eq}, which represents the average energy level reaching an observer over a specified period of time. The advantage of L_{eq} over the other measures is that it is not as dependent on the characteristics of traffic flow (such as peaking factors and the assumption of uniform vehicle spacing) and it provides good estimates in low volume situations, whereas the L_{90}, L_{50}, L_{10} measures can be very sensitive to traffic-flow characteristics.

The methods used by planners to estimate noise impact range from handbook techniques to simulation. Most manual techniques are based on a series of equations that relate key input variables to noise output. For example, one of the most used manual methods is the FHWA Highway Traffic Noise Prediction Model. In this model, the predicted noise level is determined through a series of adjustments to a reference energy mean emission level for a specific vehicle type. The basic equation for this method when the distance from the centerline of traffic to the observer is greater than 15 meters is as follows: [Barry and Reagan, 1978; Bowlby, 1981]:

$$L_{eq}(h)_i = (\overline{L_0})_{Ei} \quad \text{reference energy mean emission level}$$

$$+ 10 \log \left(\frac{N_i \pi D_0}{S_i T} \right) \quad \text{traffic-flow adjustment}$$

$$+ 10 \log \left(\frac{D_0}{D} \right)^{1+\alpha} \quad \text{distance adjustment}$$

$$+ 10 \log \left(\frac{\psi_\alpha(\phi_1, \phi_2)}{\pi} \right) \quad \text{finite roadway adjustment}$$

$$+ \Delta_s - 13 \quad \text{shielding adjustment} \quad (8\text{-}36)$$

where $L_{eq}(h)_i$ = hourly equivalent sound level for the ith vehicle type
$\overline{L}_{0Ei}$ = reference energy mean emission level for vehicle type i
N_i = number of class i vehicles passing a specified point during time T
S_i = average speed for the ith vehicle class, kilometers per hour
T = period for which L_{eq} is desired
D = location where noise level is desired, meters from centerline of traffic lane
α = site condition parameter
ψ = function used for segment adjustments, i.e., an adjustment for finite length roadways
Δ_s = attenuation, in decibels, provided by some type of shielding such as barriers, rows of houses, densely wooded area, etc.

Because each component of Eq. (8-36) provides an important contribution to noise measurement, each will be discussed below. More detailed information on each measure can be found in the listed references.

There are three classes of vehicles in the FHWA model: auto (A), medium truck (MT), and heavy truck (HT). The reference energy mean emission level for each vehicle class i, $(\bar{L}_0)_{E_i}$, is based on research conducted by FHWA and is represented by the following equations:

$$(\bar{L}_0)_{EA} = 38.1 \log(S_A) - 2.4 \qquad (8\text{-}37)$$

$$(\bar{L}_0)_{EMT} = 33.9 \log(S_{MT}) + 16.4 \qquad (8\text{-}38)$$

$$(\bar{L}_0)_{EHT} = 24.6 \log(S_{HT}) + 38.5 \qquad (8\text{-}39)$$

where S_i is the average vehicle speed in kilometers per hour of vehicles of class i.

Because vehicle characteristics can vary from one region to another, Eqs. (8-37) to (8-39) might not be appropriate for all areas. Also, these equations are based on assumed cruise conditions on a flat roadway between 50 and 100 kilometers per hour. Local planners might therefore need to develop their own reference levels (see Federal Highway Administration [1978]).

The first adjustment to the reference energy mean emission level for a single vehicle relates to the fact that planners are interested in noise from traffic flows, rather than from a single vehicle. The second term in Eq. (8-36) represents this adjustment. Taking into consideration constants, this term can be simplified to $10 \log(N_i D_0/S_i) - 25$. From this simplification, one can see that if the total number of vehicles is held constant, the adjustment factor decreases at a rate of 3 dBA per doubling of the speed. Likewise, holding average speed constant and doubling the volume produces a 3-dBA increase.

The second adjustment term takes into account the impact of measuring noise at distances greater than 15 meters. This term also considers the acoustic nature of the surface between the roadway and the observer. When the surface is such that sound is reflected, the surface is called "hard" and α in the adjustment term is equal to zero. With such a surface, the doubling of distance results in a decrease of 3 dBA in the equivalent sound level. When the ground is absorptive (or "soft"), α is approximately equal to ½ and the drop off in dBA's is 4.5 dBA per doubling of distance.

The third adjustment to $(\bar{L}_0)_{E_i}$ recognizes that it is often necessary to divide a road into segments of finite length to account for changes in topography, traffic flows, and area exposed to the observer. This adjustment factor becomes complicated by the fact that length adjustments not only have to be made but the nature of the terrain must also be included. The easiest way of explaining how this adjustment term is calculated is through Figs. 8-20 and 8-21. Figure 8-20 shows three possible locations of a road segment and the resulting angle measurements with regard to an observer's location. Note that angles measured to the left of a perpendicular line connecting the observer and the road segment are negative, while those to the right are positive (ϕ is always the angle connecting the observer and the leftmost end of the segment). The value of this adjustment term can then be found for both hard and soft sites by using the graphs shown in Fig. 8-21, where $\Delta\phi = \phi_2 - \phi_1$.

The final adjustment is made for cases where an object located between the road and observer interferes with the propagation of sound waves. Research has shown that certain types of objects, such as dense woods or rows of houses, provide specific levels of dBA reductions. For example, dense woods 30 meters in depth, with trees extending at least 5 meters above the line of sight, can reduce the equivalent sound level by

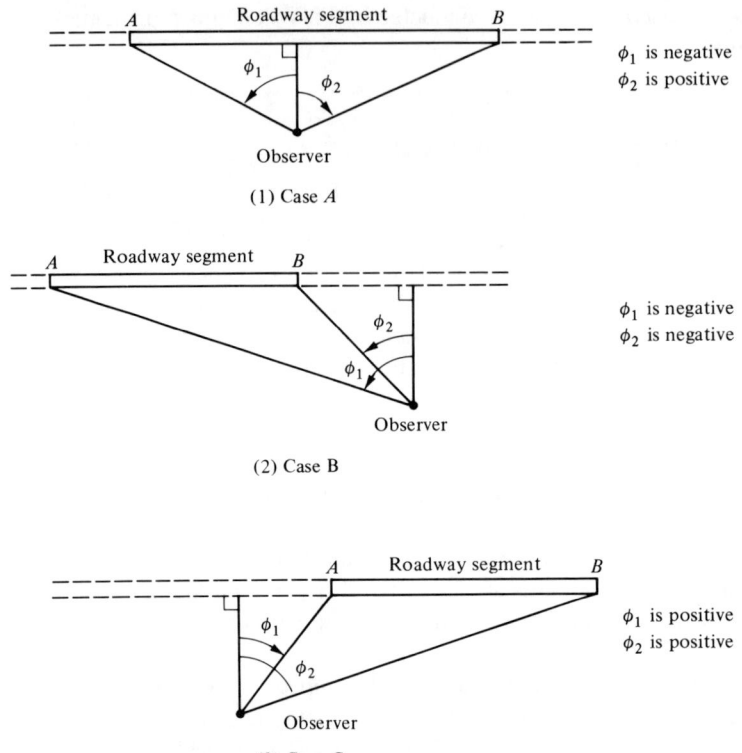

Figure 8-20 Angle identification of roadway segments for noise assessment. (*Barry and Reagan* [*1978*].)

5 dbA. In those instances where barriers are constructed to reduce noise, the level of reduction depends on the shape of the barrier, material of construction, and how much of the roadway is shielded from the observer. The calculation of the shielding adjustment term is often complex and will not be discussed in this text (see Barry and Reagan [1978]).

Equation (8-36) gives the hourly equivalent sound level for one class of vehicle. The total hourly equivalent sound level $L_{eq}(h)$ is given by

$$L_{eq}(h) = 10 \log(10 \frac{L_{eq}(h)_A}{10} + 10 \frac{L_{eq}(h)_{MT}}{10} + 10^{L_{eq}(h)_{HT}/10}) \quad (8\text{-}40)$$

The following example illustrates the application of Eq. (8-36). Assume that the eastbound lane of a two-lane highway carries an hourly volume of 400 automobiles, 30 medium trucks, and 40 heavy trucks, whereas the westbound lane carries 350 automobiles, 20 medium trucks, and 30 heavy trucks. Average speeds are 60 kilometers

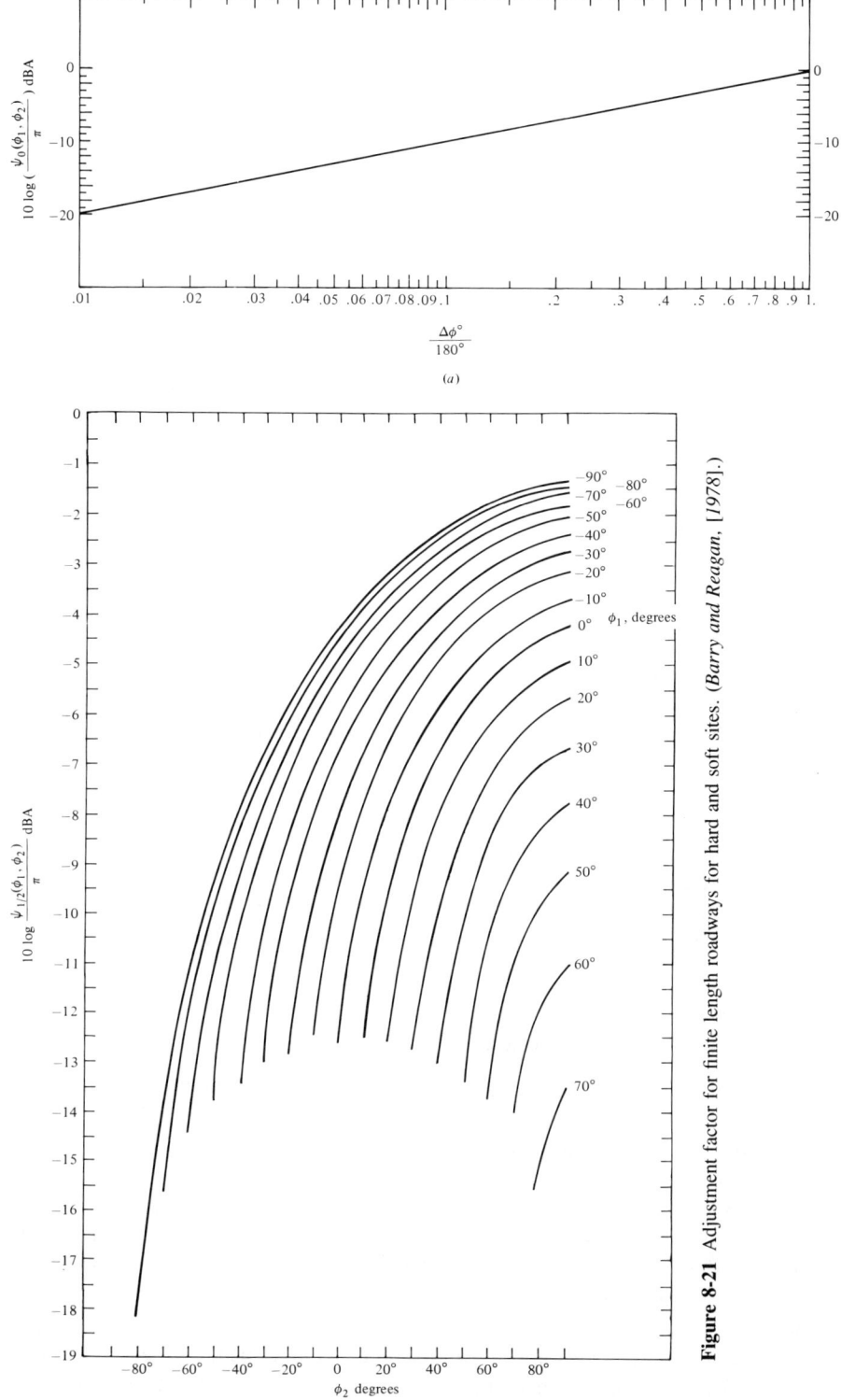

Figure 8-21 Adjustment factor for finite length roadways for hard and soft sites. (*Barry and Reagan*, [1978].)

per hour for trucks and 85 kilometers per hour for automobiles. The lane width is 3.66 meters. The observer is 50 meters south of the centerline of the eastbound lane, with ϕ_1 equal to $-45°$ and ϕ_2 equal to $+45°$. The ground surface between the road and the observer is reflective, with no obstructions. What is the total hourly equivalent sound level?

The reference energy mean emission levels for the three vehicle types are determined from Eqs. (8-37) to (8-39), which yield 71.1 dbA, 76.7 dbA, and 82.2 dbA for automobiles, medium trucks, and heavy trucks, respectively. Starting from 71.1 dbA, adjustments are made relating to the characteristics of the situation. For the eastbound lane, the traffic-flow adjustment is 10 log (400 × 15/85) − 25, which equals −6.5 dbA. Likewise, for the westbound automobile traffic the adjustment is −7.1 dbA. The distance adjustment for the eastbound lane is 10 log(15/50)$^{1+0}$, which equals −5.2 dbA. For the westbound lane the adjustment is 10 log [15/(50 + 3.66)]$^{1+0}$, which equals −5.5 dbA. From Fig. 8-21, one can see that the adjustment for finite road length, where $\Delta \phi = 90°$ is −3 dbA. There is no shielding adjustment in this case. The $L_{eq}(h)$ for automobiles for the eastbound lane is thus 71.1 − 6.5 − 5.2 − 3 = 56.4 dbA. Similar calculations can be made for trucks, which result in $L_{eq}(h)_{MT}$ = 52.3 dbA and $L_{eq}(h)_{HT}$ = 59 dbA. The total hourly equivalent sound from the eastbound lane is $L_{eq}(h)_{EB}$ = 10 log ($10^{5.64} + 10^{5.23} + 10^{5.9}$) = 61.5 dbA. Using the same method as above, the $L_{eq}(h)$ for the westbound lane is 60.1 dbA. The total noise heard by the observer is thus $L_{eq}(h)$ = 10 log($10^{6.15} + 10^{6.01}$) = 63.9 dbA.

The method discussed above has been put into nomograph form and is available for programmable calculators [Barry and Reagan, 1978]. Computer packages have also been developed to estimate noise impacts resulting from implementation of planned projects or programs. One of the most recent computer models developed by FHWA, called SNAP1.1, allows the user to predict traffic noise for multilane highways, four vehicle types, different roadway types, and varying vehicle speeds [Bowlby, 1980]. A sample printout from SNAP is shown in Fig. 8-22. Another set of computer packages, called STAMINA 2.0 and OPTIMA, also provides noise predictions, with the OPTIMA package calculating cost-effectiveness ratios for alternative designs of noise barriers [Bowlby et al., 1982].

8-3-3 Fuel Consumption Impact

The impact which transportation actions have on the consumption of gasoline has become a major concern only in recent years. Consequently, the methodology that has been developed to estimate fuel consumption impact is only now reaching a level of sophistication equivalent to that for air quality and noise impact analysis. In fact, the most common approach currently used is to estimate the change in number of vehicle miles associated with a particular project and multiply by a fuel consumption factor which reflects the average amount of fuel consumed per vehicle mile per vehicle type by year of make (see Fig. 8-23).

One of the first improvements to the approach described above was to develop relationships between fuel consumption and vehicle average speed. As was the case for both air quality and noise impact models, nomographs have been developed for

FHWA highway traffic noise prediction model (SNAP 1.1)

Receiver shielded by first row of buildings

			Receiver coordinates, meters				
			East, X 0.0	North, Y −60.00	Elevation, Z 1.50		
ROAD. no.	Alpha	Sound level descriptor	Cars	Medium trucks	Heavy trucks	Type 4	Road totals
1	0.0	LEQ	66.8	61.2	71.7	63.0	73.6
		L10	68.6	64.6	74.9	66.4	76.6
2	0.0	LEQ	62.3	58.6	65.3	56.9	68.0
		L10	64.2	62.0	68.6	60.3	71.0
Vehicle Totals		LEQ	68.2	63.1	72.6	64.0	74.7
		L10	69.9	66.5	75.8	67.3	77.6

Figure 8-22 Example output from a noise model. (SNAP1.1). (*Bowlby [1981]*.)

different vehicle types for use in identifying appropriate fuel consumption rates based on average vehicle speed (see, for example, Federal Highway Administration [1981]). Because fuel consumption depends significantly on engine technology, an analysis of fuel consumption impacts based on this approach must take into account the mix of vehicle types in the traffic flow and the changing characteristics of fuel efficiency that can occur in vehicle types from one year to the next.

Two other approaches for estimating fuel consumption impact have also been developed. The first is based on mathematical relationships developed with linear regression techniques which relate fuel consumption rates to vehicle speeds and road grades. Such an approach was originally used to estimate the fuel consumption impact of traffic engineering improvements [Hall, 1980]. Based on the results of several hundred vehicle test runs, an equation was formulated to predict vehicle fuel consumption rates, which were then used to estimate the total amount of fuel used under specific traffic control strategies. The estimated fuel savings for a variety of traffic engineering actions are shown in Table 8-4.

The second approach uses a simulation model of vehicle engine performance together with the factors affecting this performance to estimate the impact of alternative vehicle control strategies on fuel consumption. The major purpose of the simulation model is to calculate the propulsive and resistive forces that act on a vehicle as it proceeds along a given route. Sims and Miller [1982], for example, used a computer simulation model to assess the energy efficiency of alternative fixed-route transit modes. In this model, the resistive force consisted of the sum of rolling friction, aerodynamic drag, and forces due to the grade and curvature of the way. Propulsive forces were directly related to the engine technology employed, with the user being able to specify engine performance curves for different modes. This simulation model

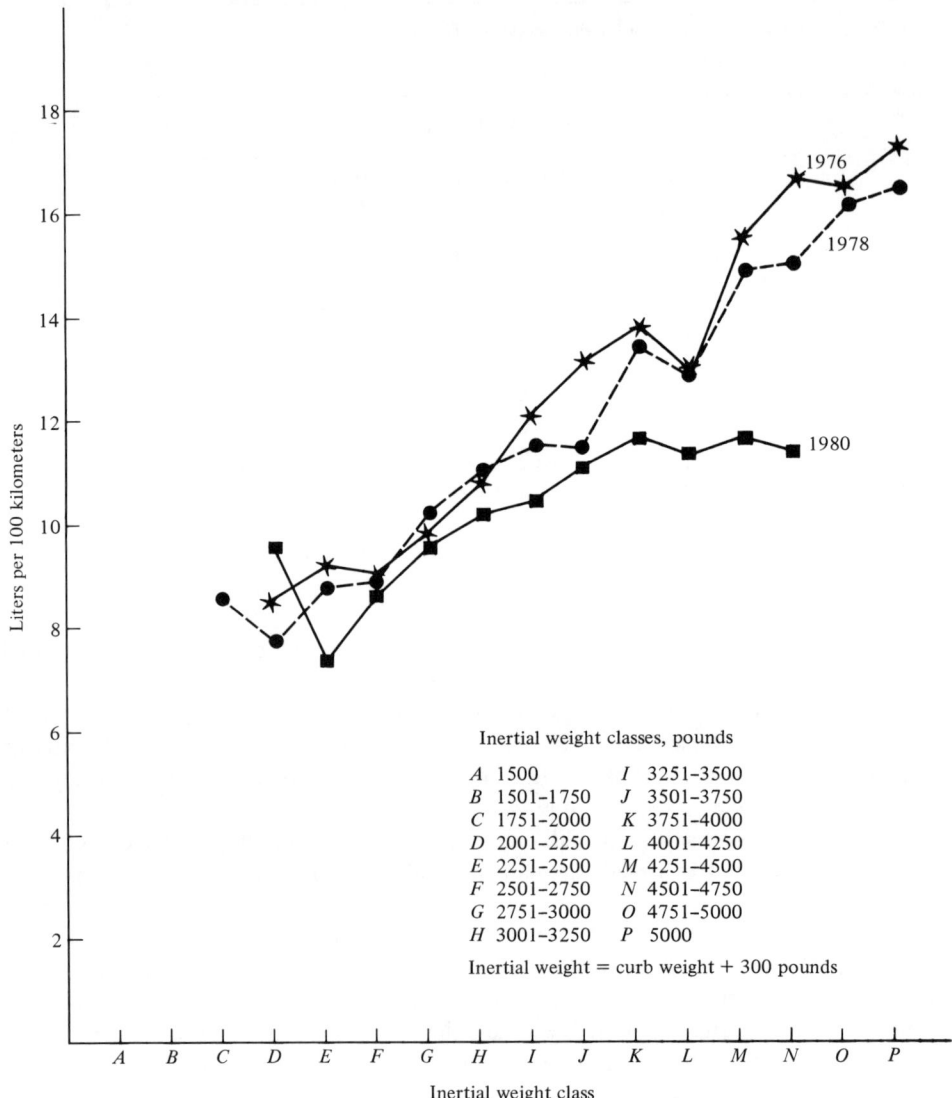

Figure 8-23 Automobile fuel consumption rates by vehicle weight and year, Canada. (*Department of Energy, Mines, and Resources* [*1982*].)

Table 8-4 Estimated annual fuel savings for traffic engineering actions

Improvement	AG/KV[a]	Realistic saving[b]
One-way street[c]	4600	4000
Coordinated signals[d]	4600	8000
STOP sign removal	3600	7000
School pedestrian crossing[e]	1090	2700
Right-turn lane	960	1000
Two-way, left-turn lane[f]	910	500
Curb radius (10'–30')	580	300
Flashing signal operation[g]	560	1000
Speed limit (25–30 mph)[h]	300	0–1000
Neighborhood diverter	−1800	−300

[a] Gallons of fuel saved/year/1000 affected vehicles per day.

[b] Annual gallons of fuel saved per improvement, under conditions of moderate volume, reasonable motorist compliance with regulations, and other conditions.

[c] Two miles long, good signal coordination.

[d] Half-mile section, one direction, with signing.

[e] Grade separation, crossings 3 hours per day.

[f] One block long, replacing previous median barrier.

[g] Operation for 8 hours per day vs. isolated pretimed signal.

[h] Optimistic assumption of motorist compliance with 25 mph limit for AG/KV calculation.

Source: Hall [1980].

was used to investigate the effect on vehicle fuel consumption of certain variables, including vehicle speed, stop spacing, grade, curvature, head wind, stop dwell times, and acceleration rates. Several results from this simulation model are shown in Fig. 8-24.

8-4 COST MODELS[18]

The two most common analysis problems related to the cost of urban transportation services involve estimating the costs associated with the construction and operation of transit services and estimating the user costs associated with the use of the private automobile. These problems are discussed in Secs. 8-4-2 and 8-4-3, respectively. In the estimation of transportation costs, a number of definitional issues are of importance, and these are discussed in Sec. 8-4-1.

---

[18]This section is based largely on Soberman and Hazard [1980]; Biemiller and Munro [1981]; Cherwony et al. [1981]; and Lang and Soberman [1964]. The reader should see these references for more detailed discussion of the topic.

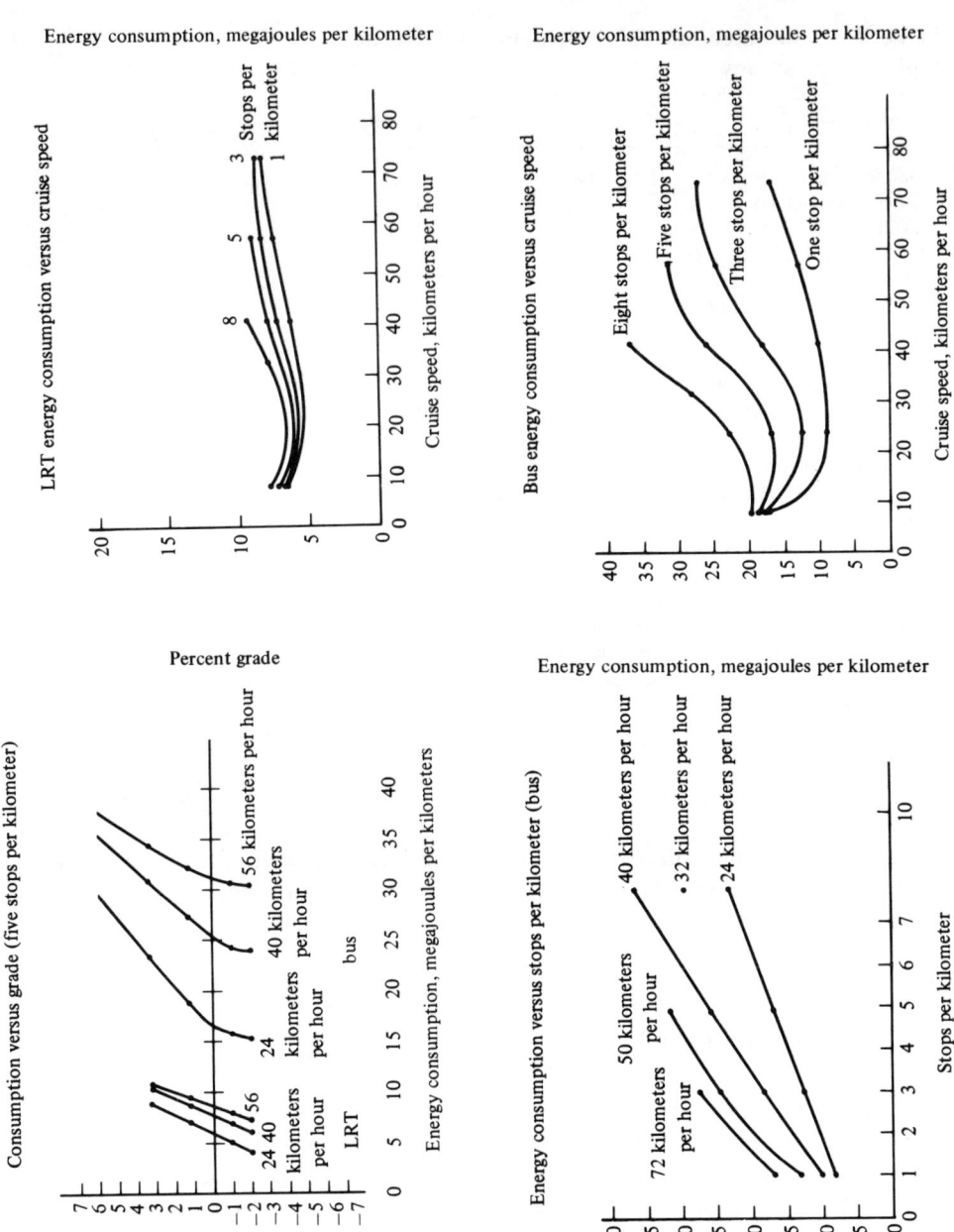

Figure 8-24 Simulation of transit energy consumption. (*Sims and Miller* [*1981*].)

8-4-1 Basic Concepts

Transportation system costs are either *fixed* or *variable* in nature. Fixed costs (which are generally equivalent to *capital* costs) are those associated with the construction of the system and purchase of equipment. That is, they are the costs associated with putting an operational system into place. Variable costs (which are generally equivalent to *operating* costs) are then the costs associated with the actual operation of the system. Fixed costs do not vary with the level of day-to-day operations, whereas variable costs do. *Average* or *unit* costs can be determined by dividing cost by the level of output achieved in order to obtain an average cost per unit of output. Figure 8-25 illustrates these concepts by showing "typical" fixed, variable, and total (i.e., fixed plus variable) cost curves, as well as by showing how these translate into average unit cost curves.

A second type of unit cost is the *marginal* cost. The marginal cost of production is the cost associated with the production of the last unit of output, or, mathematically, the marginal cost at any output level is given by the slope of the total cost curve at that output point. Figure 8-26 illustrates this point and provides a comparison between typical marginal cost and average cost curves. As indicated by this figure, it is typically the case that marginal costs are minimized at a lower level of output than average costs.

Fixed costs generally consist of costs associated with construction, plant (infrastructure), and vehicles, as well as engineering design and right-of-way acquisition. Table 8-5 summarizes typical fixed costs associated with the development of new public transit services.

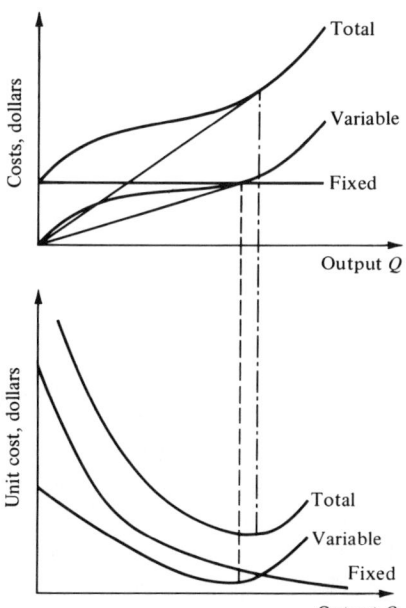

Figure 8-25 Fixed, variable and unit costs. (*Soberman and Hazard* [*1980*].)

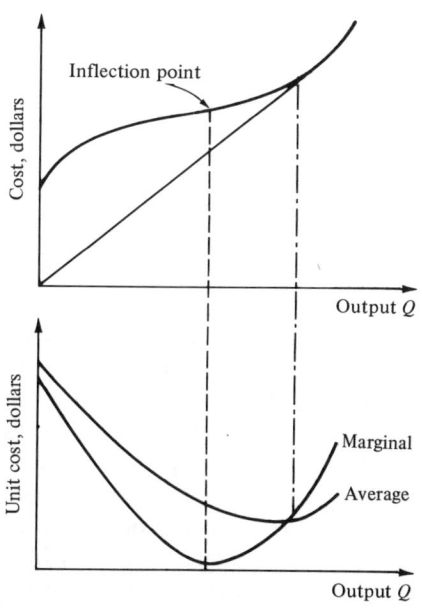

Figure 8-26 Average and marginal costs. (*Soberman and Hazard* [*1980*].)

Table 8-5 Elements of public transit fixed costs

Cost element	Diesel bus	Electric trolley	Streetcar	Commuter rail	LRT	Rapid transit
Engineering		✔	✔	✔	✔	✔
Right-of-way acquisition	*	*	*	✔	✔	✔
Construction						
Loading bays	✔	✔	✔			
Shelters	✔	✔	✔			
Preparation of road bed			✔	✔	✔	✔
Structures				✔	✔	✔
Stations				✔	✔	✔
Parking				✔	✔	✔
Access roadways				✔	✔	✔
Substations		✔	✔		✔	✔
Garages	✔	✔				
Shops	✔	✔	✔	✔	✔	✔
Storage yards			✔	✔	✔	✔
Utility relocation					✔	✔
Plant						
Track		✔	✔	✔	✔	✔
Electrification		✔	✔		✔	✔
Signal system				✔	✔	✔
Communications				✔	✔	✔
Ventilation						✔
Station equipment				✔	✔	✔
Maintenance equipment	✔	✔	✔	✔	✔	✔
Shop equipment	✔	✔	✔	✔	✔	✔
Vehicles						
Powered vehicles	✔	✔	✔		✔	✔
Unpowered vehicles				✔		
Locomotives				✔		
Maintenance vehicles	✔	✔	✔	✔	✔	✔

*Limited right-of-way acquisition for loading bays and storage facilities.
Source: Soberman and Hazard [1980].

 Variable costs can be further categorized as being *direct, indirect,* or *joint.* Direct costs are attributable to specific components such as labor, fuel, and maintenance associated with the operation of a given transit route, as opposed to indirect costs, which cannot be identified with specific components except in rather arbitrary ways or with difficult and costly experiments (e.g., heating and lighting costs of maintenance facilities). Finally, joint costs are those which are shared by two or more services (e.g., streetcar routes drawing power from the same substation or a commuter rail line sharing track maintenance costs with intercity passenger and freight lines).

 A more detailed definition of variable costs requires rather complex assumptions and accounting procedures, which, until recently, were not necessarily standardized from transit system to transit system. In the United States, Section 15 of the Urban

Mass Transportation Act (UMTA) mandated the development of a "uniform system of accounts and records." This system consists of categories of expense objects (e.g., labor, materials), functions (e.g., operating vehicles, vehicle maintenance), and operating data (e.g., vehicle hours of operation).

For the automobile user, fixed and variable costs approximately correspond to ownership costs (depreciation, insurance, residential parking charges) and operating costs (gasoline, oil, tires, maintenance, parking charges at trip destinations), respectively. It is generally assumed that automobile users rarely consider their true costs when making travel decisions (except, perhaps, when making vehicle purchase decisions, at which time they may roughly calculate the expected total costs associated with the purchase and use of the vehicle under consideration).[19] Rather, travel patterns are affected by perceived costs, which are generally considered to consist of the *out-of-pocket* costs (gasoline, oil, parking, with perhaps some allocation for "normal" maintenance costs) associated with the trip in question. Research indicates that, in general, not only do people not consider the full range of variable costs associated with a trip in their decision making, but their perceptions of these cost elements tend to vary considerably, in relatively unpredictable ways, from the "true" values [Adiv, 1982; Clark, 1982].

8-4-2 Transit Cost Models

Accurate determination of the fixed or capital costs associated with a new transit service (or a modification to an existing service) generally requires detailed engineering costing of the new system. Less detailed cost estimates, suitable for "ballpark" calculations or very preliminary evaluations, however, can be calculated on a per unit basis. For example, costs per mile of right-of-way acquisition and construction, costs per vehicle purchased, or costs per station constructed are estimated and then multiplied by the number of route miles to be constructed, the number of vehicles to be purchased, or the number of stations to be constructed. These unit costs are highly dependent on the technology used, details of the system design and local conditions, the rate of inflation, and so on.

With respect to estimating variable or operating costs, Biemiller and Munro [1981], observe:

> Two basic approaches can be used to construct a model relating route cost to route operating variables. One approach is the "cost allocation" or "unit cost" method which involves examination of individual cost components or "expense functions" (e.g., "equipment maintenance") and assignment of these on logical or empirical grounds to one or more operating variables (e.g., vehicle hours operated, or peak vehicles required per route). . . . The other approach is to use multivariate statistical techniques in which a number of observations relating total or operating costs to operating variables are used to determine a multiple regression equation specifying the relationship between operating costs and operating variables. Typically, data from a number of different transit systems is used to provide observations. Observations from one system over time can also be used. . . . Both methods ultimately

---

[19] By "true" costs we mean the true costs incurred by the user of the automobile. The total true *social* costs (i.e., the total costs borne by society as a whole associated with this usage, discussed in Sec. 2-1-5) are larger than the strict user costs and, it is safe to say, are *not* perceived by the user.

express the relationship between route cost (per day, week or year) in terms of an equation summing costs associated with each operating variable used.

Examples of how the multivariate regression approach can be used include Pozdena [1975] and Roess [1974]. Examples of the unit cost approach are provided by Ferreri [1979]. The multivariate approach is often difficult to apply in that:

1. Costs often vary dramatically from system to system because of differences in labor agreements, equipment, and scale of operations, rendering the pooling of data from several systems suspect.
2. Within a given system there may be insufficient variation in operating characteristics over the observation period to generate reliable regression estimators.

The unit cost approach is therefore the more commonly adopted of the two approaches.

The major difficulty in applying the unit cost approach involves determining which operating variables to use to explain costs and then allocating the various cost components to these variables. A number of different procedures for allocating costs over the years have been attempted. For reviews of these models, see Cherwony, et al. [1981] and Biemiller and Munro [1981]. One example of a unit cost model is [Biemiller and Munro, 1981]:

$$\begin{aligned} \text{Annual variable costs} = \\ a \text{ (vehicle or train hours)} + \\ b \text{ (vehicle miles)} + \\ c \text{ (peak vehicles)} + \\ d \text{ (route miles)} + \\ e \text{ (stations)} + \\ f \text{ (station man-hours)} + \\ g \text{ (modal fixed costs)} + \\ h \text{ (system fixed costs)} \end{aligned} \qquad (8\text{-}41)$$

The model coefficients a through h are the unit costs associated with each of the operating variables (e.g., each vehicle mile operated results in b dollars being spent). These unit costs are determined by allocating cost components to each operating variable and then computing average costs. Table 8-6 summarizes the cost allocations associated with Eq. (8-41). Note that the modal and system "fixed costs" correspond to indirect and joint variable costs, as defined in Sec. 8-4-1.

This particular model is a relatively general one in that it can be applied to all fixed-route transit modes (it was originally developed for the Toronto Transit Commission, which operates subways, streetcars, trolleybuses and diesel buses), and it is reasonably compatible with most systems' cost accounting procedures. The actual

Table 8-6 Allocations of transit costs by annual route cost variables

Cost variable	Cost components
Vehicle or train hours	Operators, inspectors*
Vehicle miles	Diesel fuel† Vehicle maintenance† Streetcar and trolley coach overhead maintenance
Peak vehicles	Electrical energy Vehicle servicing Licenses
Route miles	Track, signal, and communications maintenance Maintenance of stops, loops, safety zones, etc. Snow clearing
Station collector hours	Station collectors
Stations	Station maintenance
Modal fixed costs	Maintenance of nonrevenue equipment Machinery repair, etc. Maintenance and operation of buildings, grounds, etc. Taxes
System fixed costs	Administration

*Vehicle hours could be segregated into peak and off-peak.

†Available evidence suggests that vehicle mileage is the principal variable affecting fuel and vehicle maintenance costs. However, experimental data are needed to properly allocate these costs on slow, congested urban routes.

Source: Biemiller and Munro [1981].

values of the model coefficients (unit costs), however, would have to be determined specifically for the system being analyzed. Table 8-7, for example, provides typical transit unit costs for two Canadian cities, Toronto and Edmonton. Thus, if a transit system operates 800 peak-period buses, 4 million bus hours annually, and 50 million bus kilometers annually, then using the Toronto data from Table 8-7, the total annual operating costs for this system would be

$$\$13.38 \times 4 \times 10^6 + 0.239 \times 50 \times 10^6 + 9041 \times 800 = \$72.70 \text{ million}$$

Doing the same calculation using the Edmonton data from Table 8-7 yields a very similar total annual operating cost of $72.41 million.

A variation on the cost allocation model involves treating "direct driver costs" separately, in greater detail than the rest of the costs. In particular, the contributions of the peak and base periods of operations to direct driver costs are specifically taken into account. An example of such an approach is provided by the "Arthur Andersen model," which uses the following procedure to compute direct driver costs [Arthur Andersen, 1974; Cherwony et al., 1981]:

Table 8-7 Representative 1978 operating and maintenance costs for Toronto and Edmonton

Mode	Toronto	Edmonton
Diesel Bus		
Dollars per vehicle hour	13.38	11.14
Dollars per vehicle kilometer	0.239	0.268
Dollars per peak vehicle (annual)	9,041	18,062
Trolley Coach		
Dollars per vehicle hour	13.38	
Dollars per vehicle kilometer	0.229	
Dollars per peak vehicle (annual)	8,059	
Dollars per route kilometer (annual)	16,940	
Streetcar		
Dollars per vehicle hour	13.38	
Dollars per vehicle kilometer	0.327	
Dollars per peak vehicle (annual)	10,930	
Dollars per route kilometer (annual)	48,170	
LRT		
Dollars per vehicle hour		15.63
Dollars per vehicle kilometer		0.511
Dollars per peak vehicle (annual)		45,220
Dollars per route kilometer (annual)		125,000
Dollars per station (annual)		285,000

Source: Soberman and Hazard [1980].

1. Define the peak and base operating periods.
2. Obtain from a sample of shifts data on the number of driver pay hours, the number of peak-period vehicle hours, the number of base-period vehicle hours, and the total number of vehicle hours.
3. Plot driver pay hours per vehicle hour vs. peak-period vehicle hours per vehicle hour for these data, as shown in Fig. 8-27.
4. Fit a regression line through the plotted data.
5. Determine the coefficients a_1 and a_2 for the equation

$$D_a = a_1 P + a_2 B \tag{8-42}$$

where D_a = total driver pay hours
a_1 = pay hours per peak-period vehicle hour
a_2 = pay hours per base-period vehicle hour
P = peak-period vehicle hours
B = base period vehicle hours

As shown in Fig. 8-27, a_1 is the "Y" value of the regression line when "X" equals 1, while a_2 is the Y axis intercept.

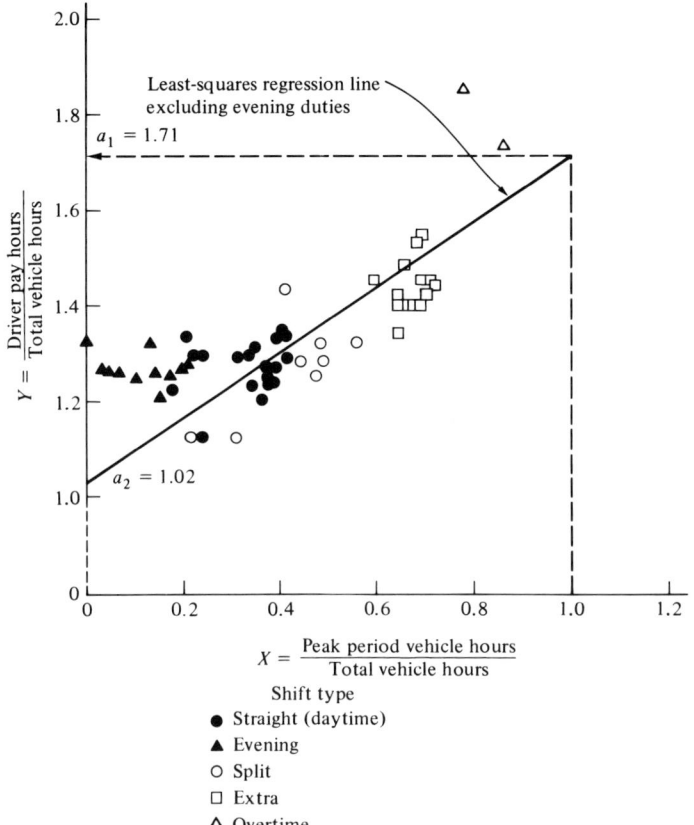

Figure 8-27 The Andersen cost allocation model. (*Andersen and Co.* [*1974*].)

6. Direct driver costs C_D are then simply

$$C_D = D_a \times W \qquad (8\text{-}43)$$

where W is the driver wage rate.

The Arthur Andersen model represents the point of departure for a bus cost estimation technique under development by UMTA, which is designed to assess the operating costs associated with incremental changes in bus operations. The characteristics of this technique can be summarized as follows [Cherwony and Porter, 1981]:

1. The Section 15 "function-object" classification scheme is used to define "marginal expense accounts," that is, expense items which will change because of incremental changes in bus service.
2. Most marginal expense accounts are treated in a conventional "cost allocation" way (i.e., in a manner similar to the Biemiller and Munro model).

3. Driver wages and benefits are given special treatment by:
    a. Determining the number of drivers required by the service change
    b. Relating driver unit costs to specific labor provisions (agreements concerning split shifts, etc.).

8-4-3 Automobile User Costs[20]

Automobile ownership costs depend on the type of vehicle operated, residential parking charges, licensing costs, and so on. Similar to transit fixed costs, automobile ownership costs can be computed on a unit cost basis as a function of the specific characteristics of the problem being analyzed.

While it is possible to develop detailed automobile operating cost functions that incorporate a range of operating variables such as vehicle weight, operating speed, route geometry, and traffic flow conditions (e.g., Claffey [1971]), the uncertainty associated with how these costs are actually perceived by auto users, as well as the level of detail generally required in planning studies (which is lower than that required by such detailed models) results in the adoption of a far simpler, cruder approach in most cases. In general, the out-of-pocket costs associated with a given two-way trip OPTC can be simply expressed as

$$\text{OPTC} = \text{CPM} \times \text{DIST} + \text{PARK} \tag{8-44}$$

where CPM = systemwide average cost per mile of operating an automobile
DIST = round-trip distance in miles for trip in question
PARK = parking cost at destination end of trip

Travel distances are computed from network minimum time paths. The unit travel cost CPM is generally set equal to the average cost of fuel (e.g., dollars per gallon) multiplied by the average automobile fuel consumption rate (i.e., gallons consumed per mile of travel), perhaps with an extra few cents per mile added in to account for oil, tire, and "normal" maintenance costs. Fuel consumption rates, in turn, are calculated by one of the methods discussed in Sec. 8-3-3.

Thus, for example, using the average fuel consumption rates by year of car shown below and making the following assumptions:
1. The model year distribution of the vehicle fleet is:
    5 percent 1974 and older   7.5 gallons per 100 miles
    8 percent 1975   7.6 gallons per 100 miles
    12 percent 1976   7.2 gallons per 100 miles
    25 percent 1977   7.0 gallons per 100 miles
    25 percent 1978   5.5 gallons per 100 miles
    25 percent 1979   5.9 gallons per 100 miles
2. The average price of gasoline is $1.13 per gallon.

[20]See also Sec. 2-1-5.

3. No additional operating costs (oil, etc.) are to be considered in out-of-pocket costs.

then Eq. (8-44) becomes

$$\text{OPTC} = \text{PARK} + (0.05 \times 7.5 + .08 \times 7.6 + 0.12 \times 7.2 + 0.25 \times 7.0 \\ + 0.25 \times 5.5 + 0.25 \times 5.9) \times \frac{\text{DIST}}{100} \times 113$$

$$= \text{PARK} + 7.29 \times \text{DIST}$$

where OPTC and PARK are expressed in cents and DIST is expressed in miles.

Unless individual trip records containing actual parking charges experienced (or at least perceived) by the individual auto users are being used in the analysis, determining the appropriate value of parking charges can be a difficult task, particularly for central city areas. Parking costs in such areas vary dramatically, from zero (for free off-street parking provided by employers and retailers, as well as for free—legal or otherwise—on-street parking) to several dollars a day (for parking garages and lots). In such cases, "average" parking costs are relatively meaningless because of the very high variance associated with them, implying that the analyst should try to categorize travelers to the zones in question into more homogeneous groups with respect to their parking opportunities and costs.

8-5 CHAPTER SUMMARY

1. The *supply* of transportation services can be characterized in terms of the *performance* of the transportation system (its travel times, headways, capacities, etc.), the *impacts* which this system has on the environment (which includes nonusers of the system), and the *costs* incurred in building, maintaining, and using the system.
2. Six major components of the transportation system which are generally addressable by supply-related policies are the transportation *infrastructure* (rights-of-way, signal systems, other fixed facilities), the *vehicles* which operate within this infrastructure, the *routes* and *schedules* for the system, the *drivers* of the vehicles, the *procedures* or rules for operating the system, and the *costs* borne by operators and users of the system.
3. Types of supply-related policies or actions include *construction* of transportation infrastructure, *design* and *manufacture* of transportation equipment (most notably, vehicles and signal systems), *provision* of transportation services, *maintenance* of transportation infrastructure and vehicles, *regulation* of transportation services and systems, *enforcement* of transportation regulations, the *financing* of transportation infrastructure and vehicles, *subsidization* of transportation system operating costs and/or users of the system, *taxation* of transportation services and equipment, and *pricing* of transportation services.
4. Major decision makers or actors involved in supply-related policy-making include

elected representatives, regulators, operators, implementers, contractors, and *law enforcement agencies.*
5. Supply analysis interacts with the planning process in three major ways. First, performance and cost characteristics are important determinants of the demand for transportation, while demand levels in turn affect system performance. Second, measures of system performance, impacts, and costs are important evaluation criteria. Third, supply analysis contributes toward the monitoring and diagnosis planning functions.
6. *Network* definition, consisting of the representation of the real or physical network by an "approximating network" composed of a connected set of *links* and *nodes,* is perhaps the single most important step in the entire analysis process in that it determines the maximum level of accuracy and detail of analysis obtainable, the quantity and quality of data required to represent and analyze the system, and the type(s) of analysis techniques that can be applied.
7. The *fundamental equation of traffic flow* $q = \overline{V}k$ summarizes the fundamental relationship between *volume q,* average *speed* $\overline{V}$, and *density k* for flows on transportation links.
8. *Time-distance diagrams* are used to plot vehicle trajectories through time and space (i.e., to identify vehicle locations along a route at any point in time). They can be applied to a range of simple performance analysis problems involving either shared or exclusive rights-of-way, the analysis of intersection signal systems, the analysis of conflicting flows, and so on.
9. *Queuing theory* is used to analyze systems in which *customers* must queue up in order to receive *service* (e.g., cars waiting at an intersection for the light to turn green). While transportation queuing theory applications are somewhat limited because of the nature of most transportation problems, the concept of the queue is a most important one and forms the basis for many analysis techniques (e.g., fluid-flow approximations and many simulation models).
10. *Fluid-flow approximations* are used to analyze transportation queuing problems in which customer arrivals and servicing can be treated in terms of continuous *flows* of customers (e.g., flows of vehicles on a street), rather than in terms of discrete, individual customers.
11. *Simulation* involves constructing a mathematical model of a system and then operating or exercising this model over time. Simulation models are *dynamic* in that they replicate system performance over time. That is, system performance at time $t + \Delta t$ cannot be computed without knowing the performance at time t. In addition, simulation models typically include *stochastic* or probabilistic elements which represent events or processes which cannot be modeled deterministically.
12. *Mathematical programming* techniques are used to find optimal values for a set of *decision variables,* where optimality is defined in terms of an *objective function* which is maximized (or minimized) subject to a set of *constraints* that define feasible ranges for the decision variables.
13. The choice of an appropriate technique to analyze transportation system performance depends on the level of detail required, data availability, the time and budget available for the study, and so on. It also depends on the nature of the

system being analyzed. In particular, techniques vary according to whether one is analyzing exclusive or shared rights-of-way, whether access to the shared right-of-way is controlled or uncontrolled, and whether one is analyzing a component of a network (e.g., a link or a route) or the network as a whole.

14. Transportation *impacts* include *air quality* impacts, *noise* impacts, and *fuel consumption* impacts. In general, transportation impacts can be analyzed by a variety of techniques, ranging from the use of simple nomographs or other "handbook" techniques to the use of complex computer simulation models of the system's performance as it relates to the generation of the impacts of interest.

15. Transportation costs are either *fixed* or *variable* in nature. "Ballpark" estimation of fixed or capital costs can be done on a *unit cost* basis. That is, the cost per unit (e.g., cost per vehicles or cost per mile of right-of-way) is determined and then multiplied by the number of units required. Variable or operating costs are modeled through the use of *cost allocation* techniques or the use of multivariate statistical techniques (usually regression analysis). Cost allocation involves assigning each cost component (e.g., driver wages) on logical or empirical grounds to a system performance characteristic (e.g., vehicle hours of operation). Average unit costs for each operating variable can then be determined (e.g., dollars per vehicle hour of operation), and total operating costs for any given service can be computed by multiplying these unit costs by the relevant operating variables and summing over all such terms.

QUESTIONS

1. Consider a section of one-way roadway which at time $t = 0$ is empty, with a vehicle about to enter (i.e., the location of the leading edge of the vehicle is $x = 0$ at $t = 0$) and with a stream of vehicles uniformly spaced behind the lead vehicle at a density of 100 vehicles per mile. All vehicles (including the lead vehicle) are moving at a uniform speed of 30 miles per hour. At $t = 1$ second a traffic signal turns red at location $x = 500$ feet. Assuming that the first vehicle stops instantaneously when it reaches the stop light location (i.e., $x = 500$) and that each succeeding vehicle stops instantaneously such that its leading edge is exactly 15 feet behind the leading edge of the vehicle in front of it, draw a time-distance diagram which shows the trajectories of the leading edges of the first five vehicles entering the section. Given this diagram:

   (a) Connect the points representing the time-distance locations at which each vehicle comes to rest. What shape is the curve which results?

   (b) This line is known as a *shock wave*. Physically, what does it represent?

   (c) Compute the slope of this line. Physically, what does it represent?

   At $t = 31$ seconds the light turns green. Assuming that the vehicles instantaneously accelerate to 30 miles per hour once they start moving and assuming that there is a ½-second response time between the time when the first vehicle and the second vehicle (the second and the third, etc.) start moving, do the following:

   (d) Draw the time-distance diagram showing the initialization of movement of the first five vehicles in the queue.

(e) Draw on this diagram the shock wave associated with the initialization of movement through the queue.
(f) Compute the slope of this line.
(g) Explain the physical interpretation of these results.
  Given the results of your analysis, draw a new time-distance diagram at a larger scale that will enable you to calculate graphically the total number of vehicles stopped by the red light.
2. For the system analyzed in Question 1, use a fluid-flow diagram to calculate:
  (a) The total number of vehicles stopped by the light.
  (b) The maximim queue length of vehicles stopped at the light
  (c) The average delay experienced by vehicles because of the red light
3. Consider a simple intersection of 2 one-way streets, one of which is a major "through" street and the other is a minor street controlled by a stop sign. Vehicles arrive along the minor approach according to a Poisson process at an average rate of 2 vehicles per hour. In order for a vehicle on the minor street to cross the major street, a *gap* in the flow of vehicles along the major street of sufficient size for the vehicle to cross safely must occur. Assume that such gaps in the major street flow arrive at the intersection according to a Poisson process at an average rate of μ gaps per hour (actually gap arrivals tend to be determined by more complicated processes than the Poisson; see, for example, May [1965]; or Athol [1965]). Using the queuing theory results presented in this chapter, plot average wait times and queue lengths for vehicles on the minor street vs. λ for the cases of μ equal to 200, 100, and 50. What criteria would you use to determine the flow levels at which it might be worthwhile to signalize the intersection? What additional information would you require to make this determination?
4. One approach to obtaining a more detailed analysis of the intersection examined in Question 3 is to use a simulation model. Develop a flowchart of the major tasks and information required to construct such a simulation model. In developing the flowchart, discuss:
  (a) How stochastic elements of the system are to be treated
  (b) Data requirements of the model
  (c) System performance measures required and how these will be computed
5. Consider a typical transit passenger stop which experiences average arrival rates of passengers over time as given in Table P8-5a. Buses with a design capacity of 80

Table P8-5a Average passenger arrival rates

Time period	Arrival rate, passengers per minute
9:00–9:15 a.m.	1
9:15–9:30 a.m.	2
9:30–10:00 a.m.	1

Table P8-5b Bus arrival times and loadings

Bus no.	Arrival time	No. of passengers on board
1	9:10	40
2	9:20	65
3	9:25	30
4	9:44	75
5	9:47	70
6	9:50	60
7	10:00	50

passengers (seated and standing) arrive at the stop at the times shown in Table P8-5b with the loadings shown in the same table. Assuming that the buses load passengers instantaneously at the stop (up to their maximum of 80), draw a fluid-flow diagram of operations at this stop for the time period 9 a.m. to 10 a.m., given that at 9 a.m. there are no passengers waiting at the stop. Calculate for this system the average wait time experienced, the maximum wait time, the average number of passengers waiting, the largest number of passengers ever waiting, and the average number of passengers on board the bus as it leaves the stop.

6. Consider the simple transit system shown in Fig. P8-6, consisting of three links, four nodes, and two bus routes. Table P8-6a provides the data characterizing this system, using the notation of Sec. 8-2-3. Table P8-6b provides the O-D flow matrix for the morning peak period for this system. Define N_1 and N_2 as the number of buses to be assigned to routes 1 and 2, respectively. If peak-period bus operations for this system cost C dollars a year per peak-period vehicle used, then:

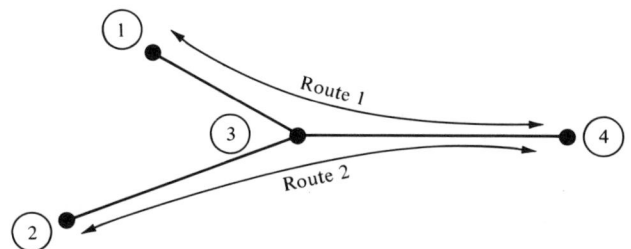

Figure P8-6 Two-route transit system.

Table P8-6a Transit system data

Characteristic	Route 1	Route 2
P	80 pass.	80 pass.
L	4 miles	5 miles
$\bar{V}$	20 mph	15 mph

Table P8-6b Morning peak-period O-D flow matrix

From node	To node			
	1	2	3	4
1	0	0	200	300
2	0	0	240	300
3	0	0	0	200
4	0	0	0	0

(a) Write the linear program (LP) which solves for the optimal (i.e., minimum annual operating cost) values of N_1 and N_2, subject to the constraints that demand on all links is carried.

(b) Plot the constraint equations for this LP on a graph in which N_1 and N_2 are the horizontal and vertical axes, respectively. Indicate the feasible region for the problem on this graph.

(c) For a given annual system operating cost (say, $5C$ dollars), plot the "iso-cost" line on this graph which defines the set of N_1, N_2 combinations which generate this operating cost.

(d) Noting that a family of parallel iso-cost curves can be drawn corresponding to a range of operating costs, graphically solve the LP for the minimum cost combination of N_1 and N_2.

(e) Can you draw any generalizations about the geometric properties of the solutions to linear programs from this example?

(f) What is the frequency of service on each of the two routes, given the optimal bus assignments? Are these frequencies reasonable? Is there any way to modify your LP so as to induce it to generate more reasonable frequencies?

7. Compute minimum path trees from nodes 2 and 5 for the network shown in Fig. P8-7.

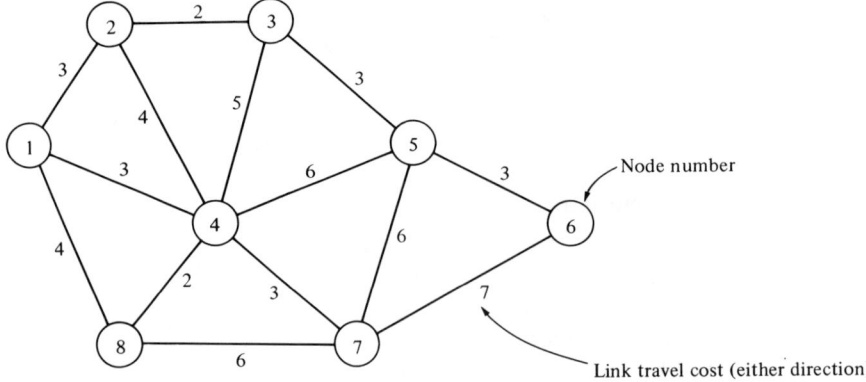

Figure P8-7 Network for minimum path calculations.

8. Compute the probability of a person using transit to go from zone 1 to zone 2 in Fig. P8-8 as a function of roadway congestion, given the two-mode network shown and given the following logit mode split model:

$$P_t = \frac{e^{V_t}}{e^{V_t} + e^{V_a}}$$

where
$V_a = 0.1 - 0.01 \text{ IVTT}_a - 0.025 \text{ OVTT}_a$
$V_t = - 0.01 \text{ IVTT}_t - 0.025 \text{ OVTT}_t$
IVTT_m = in-vehicle travel time in minutes for mode m
  ($m = a$ for auto; $m = t$ for transit)
OVTT_m = out-of-vehicle travel time in minutes for mode m
  = (average wait time) + (average access walk time)
  + (average egress walk time) for transit
  = (average egress walk time) for auto

Transit in-vehicle travel time and out-of-vehicle wait time can be computed using

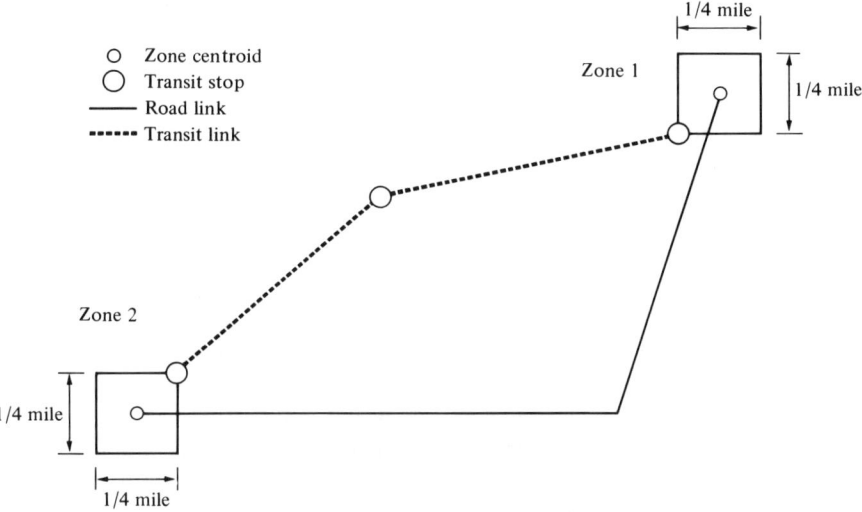

Figure P8-8 Two-mode network.

Table P8-8 Transit Link Characteristics

Characteristic	Link 1	Link 2
s	3 miles	3 miles
V	60 feet per second	60 feet per second
a	4 feet per second squared	4 feet per second squared
d	4 feet per second squared	4 feet per second squared
f	12 trains per hour	12 trains per hour

All stop dwell times are 20 seconds.

the data provided in Table P8-8 and equations developed in Sec. 8-2-3. Average zone-to-zone in-vehicle auto travel time is given by

$$\text{IVTT}_a = \frac{15}{1 - v/2000}$$

where v equals the volume of traffic using the roadway in vehicles per hour.
Walk times can be computed using equations from Sec. 8-2-3 and assuming:
(a) The probability of the trip originating at any point within zone 1 is uniformly distributed over the zone.
(b) The probability of the trip ending at any point within zone 2 is uniformly distributed over the zone.
(c) The probability of the parking location of the car (if auto is chosen) being at any point within zone 2 is uniformly distributed over the zone.
(d) People walk at an average rate of 3 miles per hour.

Plot P_t vs. v. If 1000 people wish to travel from zone 1 to zone 2 during the morning peak hour and the loading on the roadway due to other zones' traffic is 600 vehicles, what will be the equilibrium transit patronage for this system, assuming an auto occupancy rate of 1.0 passengers per vehicle? If the auto occupancy doubles to 2.0 passengers per vehicle, what does this do to the equilibrium transit patronage (assume that the "background" traffic of 600 vehicles per hour remains constant)? Does this result have any implications for the impact which car-pooling programs might have on transit ridership?

9. Given a total cost curve of the form

$$TC = a + bQ + cQ^2$$

where Q is the quantity produced, derive the corresponding average and marginal cost curves. Plot these curves given $a = 100$, $b = 1$, and $c = 0.001$. Indicate the points of minimum average and minimum marginal costs. Why are these points not the same?

10. Given the LRT system described in the example calculations in Sec. 8-2-3 and the Edmonton unit costs shown in Table 8-7, compute the annual operating costs for this system. The route capacity of 12,000 passengers per hour given in the example calculation should be assumed to be the peak-period capacity. Assume an off-peak design capacity of 4000 passengers per hour. Assume the system operates 18 hours per day, 6 hours of which are peak-period hours.

REFERENCES

Adiv, A.: "Perception of Travel Cost by Automobile to Work: Empirical Study in San Francisco Bay Area," Presented at the 61st annual meeting of the Transportation Research Board, Washington, D.C., January 1982.

American Association of State Highway and Transportation Officials: *Design of Urban Highways and Arterial Streets*, Washington, D.C., 1984.

Arthur Andersen and Co.: *Bus Route Costing for Planning Purposes*, Transport and Road Research Laboratory Supplementary Report 108UC, Crowthorne, U.K., 1974.

Athol, P.: "Headway Groupings," *Highway Research Record 72,* Highway Research Board, Washington, D.C., 1965, pp. 137–155.

Avriel, M.: *Nonlinear Programming: Analysis and Methods,* Prentice-Hall, Englewood Cliffs, N.J., 1976.

Barry, T. M., and J. A. Reagan: *FHWA Highway Traffic Noise Prediction Model,* Federal Highway Administration Report FHWA-RD-77-108, U.S. Department of Transportation, Washington, D.C., December 1978.

Benjamin, J. R., and C. A. Cornell: *Probability, Statistics and Decision for Civil Engineers,* McGraw-Hill, New York, 1970.

Benson, P. E.: *CALINE-3—A Versatile Dispersion Model for Predicting Air Pollutant Levels near Highways and Arterial Streets,* California Department of Transportation Report FWHA/CA/TL-79/23, Sacramento, Calif., November 1979.

Bhat, U. N.: *Elements of Applied Stochastic Processes,* Wiley, New York, 1972.

Biemiller, A., and S. Munro: *Estimating Annual Costs of Operating Urban Transit Routes by Mode,* University of Toronto–York University Joint Program in Transportation Research Report No. 71, Toronto, July 1981.

Blais, J. Y., G. Lapointe, R. Lessard, J. M. Rousseau, and F. Soumis: *The Problem of Assigning Drivers to Bus Routes in an Urban Transit System,* Centre for Transportation Research Publication No. 44, University of Montreal, Montreal, August 1976.

———: *Manual d'Utisation de HASTUS-MACRO,* Centre for Transportation Research Publication No. 93 University of Montreal, Montreal, February 1978.

Bodin, L. D.: "A Taxonomic Structure for Vehicle Routing and Scheduling Problems," *Computers and Urban Society,* vol. 1, 1975, pp. 11–29.

Bowlby, W.: *SNAP 1.1: A Revised Program and User's Manual for the FHWA Level 1 Highway Traffic Noise Prediction Computer Program,* Federal Highway Administration Report FHWA-DP-45-4, U.S. Department of Transportation, Washington, D.C., December 1980.

Bowlby, W. (ed.): *Found Procedures for Measuring Highway Noise: Final Report,* Federal Highway Administration Report FHWA-DP-45-1R, U.S. Department of Transportation, Washington, D.C., August 1981.

Bowlby, W., J. Higgins, and J. Reagan: *Noise Barrier Cost Reduction Procedure STAMINA 2.0/OPTIMA: User's Manual,* Federal Highway Administration Report FHWA-DP-58-1, U.S. Department of Transportation, Washington, D.C., April 1982.

Cherwony, W., C. Gleichman, and B. Porter: *Bus Route Costing Procedures Interim Report No. 1: A Review,* Urban Mass Transportation Administration, U.S. Department of Transportation, Washington, D.C., May 1981.

Cherwony, W., and B. Porter: *Bus Route Costing Procedures Interim Report No. 2, Proposed Method,* Urban Mass Transportation Administration, U.S. Department of Transportation, Washington, D.C., June 1981.

Cilliers, M. P., R. Cooper, and A. D. May: *FREQ6PL—A Freeway Priority Lane Simulation Model,* Institute of Transportation Studies Research Report UCB-ITS-RR-78-8, University of California, Berkeley, August 1978.

Claffey, P.: *Running Costs of Motor Vehicles as Affected by Road Design and Traffic,* Transportation Research Board NCHRP Report No. 111, Washington, D.C., 1971.

Clark, J. E.: "Modeling Travelers' Perception of Travel Time," Presented at the 61st annual meeting of the Transportation Research Board, Washington, D.C., January 1982.

Clarke, A. B., and R. L. Disney: *Probability and Random Processes for Engineers and Scientists,* Wiley, New York, 1970.

Daganzo, C. F.: *Transportation Supply,* Textbook in progress, 1984.

Daskin, M. S.: "Issues in the Design and Analysis of Airport Ground Transport Systems," SAE Technical Paper 780519, Presented at the Air Transportation Meeting of the SAE, Boston, May 1978.

Davidson, K. B.: "A Flow-Travel Time Relationship for Use in Transportation Planning," *Proceedings,* Australian Road Research Board, Melbourne, vol. 3, 1966, pp. 183–194.

DelCan: *SSTOP User's Manual,* Toronto, 1981.

de Neufville, R., and J. H. Stafford: *Systems Analysis for Engineers and Managers,* McGraw-Hill, New York, 1971.

Dosman, E., E. J. Miller, R. G. Rice, R. M. Soberman, G. N. Steuart: *Preliminary Analysis of Policy Options for Federal Involvement in Urban Transportation,* University of Toronto–York University Joint Program in Transportation, Toronto, November 1980.

Federal Highway Administration, *Determination of Reference Energy Mean Emission Levels,* Report FHWA-OEP/HEV-78-1, Washington, D.C., July, 1978.

―――――: *A Method for Estimating Fuel Consumption and Vehicle Emissions on Urban Arterials and Networks,* U.S. Department of Transportation Report No. FHWA-TS-81-210, Washington, D.C., April 1981.

Ferreri, M. G.: "Comparative Costs of Transit Modes," in G. G. Gray and L. A. Hoel (eds.), *Public Transportation: Operations and Management,* Prentice-Hall, Englewood Cliffs, N.J., 1979, pp. 226–252.

Florian, M., and M. Gaudry: *A Conceptual Framework for the Supply Side in Transportation Systems,* Centre for Transportation Research Publication No. 35, University of Montreal, Montreal, 1979.

Ford, L. R., and D. R. Fulkerson: *Flows in Networks,* Princeton University Press, Princeton New Jersey, 1962.

Gordon, G.: *System Simulation,* Prentice-Hall, Englewood Cliffs, N.J., 1969.

Haines, G., R. N. Wolff, P. D. Bunt, and G. N. Steuart: *Demand Responsive Systems—A Study of Task Complexity,* University of Toronto–York University Joint Program in Transportation, Toronto, 1977.

Hajek, J.: *Ontario Highway Noise Prediction Method,* Ontario Ministry of Transportation and Communications Research Report 197, Toronto, 1975.

Hall, J.: *Traffic Engineering Improvement Priorities for Energy Conservation,* New Mexico Energy Institute NMEI Report No. 78-1128, Albuquerque, N.M., May 1980.

Held, M., and R. M. Karp: "The Traveling Salesman Problem and Minimum Spanning Trees, Part II," *Mathematical Programming,* vol. 1, no. 1, 1971, pp. 6–25.

Hillier, F. S., and G. J. Lieberman: *Operations Research,* 2nd ed., Holden-Day, San Francisco, 1974.

Horowitz, J. L.: *Air Quality Analysis for Urban Transportation Planning,* MIT Press, Cambridge, Mass., 1982.

Hurdle, V. F.: "Equilibrium Flows on Urban Freeways," *Transportation Science,* vol. 15, no. 3, 1981, pp. 255–293.

Hutchinson, B.: *Principles of Urban Transportation Systems Planning,* Scripta Books, New York, 1974.

Institute of Traffic Engineers: *Transportation and Traffic Engineering Handbook,* Prentice-Hall, Englewood Cliffs, N.J., 1976.

Jovanis, P. P., A. D. May, and A. Deikman: *Further Analysis and Evaluation of Selected Impacts of Traffic Management Strategies on Surface Streets,* Institute of Transportation Studies Research Report UCB-ITS-RR-77-9, University of California, Berkeley, October 1977.

Kennedy, N., J. H. Kell, and W. S. Hamburger: *Fundamentals of Traffic Engineering,* 8th ed., Institute of Transportation and Traffic Engineering, University of California, Berkeley, 1973.

Kleinrock, L.: *Queuing Systems Vol. I: Theory,* Wiley, New York, 1975.

Lang, A. S., and R. M. Soberman: *Urban Rail Transit: Its Economics and Technology,* MIT Press, Cambridge, 1964.

Larson, R. C., and A. R. Odoni: *Urban Operations Research,* Prentice-Hall, Englewood Cliffs, N.J., 1981.

Manheim, M.: *Fundamentals of Transportation System Analysis,* MIT Press, Cambridge, Mass., 1979.

May, A. D.: "Gap Availability Studies," *Highway Research Record 72,* Highway Research Board, Washington, D.C., 1965, pp. 101–136.

Mei-Ko, K. "Graphic Programming Using Odd and Even Points," *Chinese Mathematics,* vol. 1, no. 3, 1962, pp. 237–277.

McInerney and Peterson: "Intersection Capacity Measurement through Critical Movement Summations: A Planning Tool," *Traffic Engineering,* January 1971.

Miller, E. J., F. J. Ahlin, P. D. Bunt, J. H. Bookbinder, and R. N. Wolff: *Wheel-Trans: Feasibility of Computer-Aided Reservations, Scheduling and Dispatching,* University of Toronto–York University Joint Program in Transportation Research Report No. 73, Toronto, November 1980.

Morlok, E. K.: *Introduction to Transportation Engineering and Planning,* McGraw-Hill, New York, 1978.

Naylor, T. H., J. L. Balintfy, D. S. Burdick, and K. Chu: *Computer Simulation Techniques,* Wiley, New York, 1966.

Newell, G. F.: *Applications of Queuing Theory,* Chapman and Hall, London, 1971.

———: *Traffic Flow on Transportation Networks,* MIT Press, Cambridge, Mass., 1980.
Pecknold, W. M., N. H. M. Wilson, and B. Kullman: *An Empirical Demand Model for Evaluating Local Bus Service Modifications,* Department of Civil Engineering, MIT, Cambridge, Mass., 1972.
Pedersen, N., and D. Samdahl: "Highway Traffic Data for Urbanized Area Project Planning and Design," *National Cooperative Highway Research Program Report 255,* Transportation Research Board, Washington, D.C., 1982.
Peterson, W. B.: *User's Guide for HIWAY-2: A Highway Air Pollution Model,* U.S. Environmental Protection Agency Report No. EPA-600/8-80-018, Washington, D.C., May 1980.
Potts, R. B., and R. M. Oliver: *Flows in Transportation Networks,* Academic Press, New York, 1972.
Pozdena, R. J.: *A Methodology for Selecting Urban Transit Projects,* Institute of Urban and Regional Development Monograph No. 23, University of California, Berkeley, 1975.
Prabhu, N. U.: *Queues and Inventories,* Wiley, New York, 1965.
Rau, J. G., and D. C. Wooten (eds.): *Environmental Impact Analysis Handbook,* McGraw-Hill, New York, 1980.
Roess, R. P.: "Operating Cost Models for Urban Public Transportation Systems and Their Use in Analysis," *Transportation Research Record 490,* 1974, pp. 40–54.
Schroeder, E. C., and B. Allen: *SSTOP—Off Line Signal System Optimization Package—Volume 1, Project Summary,* Traffic Research Group, Department of Civil Engineering, McMaster University, Hamilton, 1979.
Sheffi, Y.: Urban Transportation Networks, Prentice-Hall, Englewood Cliffs, N.J., forthcoming.
Simmons, D. M.: *Linear Programming for Operations Research,* Holden-Day, San Francisco, 1972.
Sims, D., and E. J. Miller: "Energy Consumption of Alternative Fixed-Route Transit Modes," *RTAC Forum,* vol. 5, no. 1, 1982.
Soberman, R. M., and H. A. Hazard (eds.): *Canadian Transit Handbook,* University of Toronto–York University Joint Program in Transportation, Toronto, January 1980.
Sosslau, A. B., A. B. Hassam, M. M. Carter, and G. V. Wickstrom: *Quick-Response Urban Travel Estimation Techniques and Transferable Parameters, User's Guide,* Transportation Research Board National Cooperative Highway Research Program Report 187, Washington, D.C., 1978.
Steuart, G. N.: "Urban Transport Supply," Unpublished lecture notes, University of Toronto/MIT, summer course, *Transport Planning in Developing Countries,* August 1979.
Transportation Energy Division, Department of Energy, Mines, and Resources: *Fuel Consumption and Associated Trends in New Automobiles, 1975–1980,* Report TE-82-2, Ottawa, 1982.
Transportation Research Board: *Interim Materials on Highway Capacity,* Transportation Research Circular 212, January 1980.
U.S. Department of Transportation: *Fundamentals of Air Quality,* Federal Highway Aministration Implementation Package 76-5, Washington, D.C., 1976.
U.S. Environmental Protection Agency: *Compilation of Air Pollutant Emission Factors,* Office of Air Quality Planning and Standards, EPA Report No. AP-42, February 1976.
———: *User's Guide to Mobile 2,* Report EPA-460/3-81-006, February 1981.
Voorhees, A. M., and Associates, Inc.: *Handbook for Transportation System Management Planning,* vol. 2, Prepared for the North Central Texas Council of Governments, August 1977.
Vuchic, V. R.: *Urban Public Transportation Systems and Technology,* Prentice-Hall, Englewood Cliffs, N.J., 1981.
Wagner, H. M.: *Principles of Operations Research,* 2d ed., Prentice-Hall, Englewood Cliffs, N.J., 1975.
Wallace, C. E., K. G. Courage, D. T. Reaves, G. W. Schoene, and G. W. Euler: *TRANSYT-7F User's Manual,* Federal Highway Administration, U.S. Department of Transportation, Washington, D.C., February 1983.
Wilhelm, E. G.: *Overview of the RUCUS Package Driver Run Cutting Program,* Urban Mass Transportation Administration, U.S. Department of Transportation, Washington, D.C., December 1974.
Wilson, N. H. M., and E. J. Miller: *Advanced Dial-a-Ride Algorithms Research Project Phase II: Interim Report,* Department of Civil Engineering Research Report No. R77-31, MIT, Cambridge, Mass., July 1977.
Wohl, M., and B. V. Martin: *Traffic Systems Analysis for Engineers and Planners,* New York, McGraw-Hill, 1967.

CHAPTER
NINE

TRANSPORTATION SYSTEM AND PROJECT EVALUATION

9-0 INTRODUCTION

The preceding chapters have identified numerous analytic tools that can be used to predict travel demand and impacts of transportation alternatives. Decision makers, however, often require more information on the consequences of alternative projects and plans than quantitative estimates of use and impact. For example, information on the process of implementing alternative projects, the distribution of costs and benefits among affected groups, and the net social value of the alternatives under consideration can be important to the decision-making process. In this chapter, we will discuss *evaluation*, the process of assessing the advantages and disadvantages of different courses of action and presenting this information to decision makers in a comprehensible and useful form.

There are two important distinctions made in this chapter that are not made in most transportation planning texts. First, distinction is made between evaluation *techniques* (e.g., cost and benefit analysis) and the evaluation *process* (e.g., the interaction among key participants in planning). The latter concept receives a great deal of attention in this chapter because of our belief that transportation planning is as much a political process as it is a technical one.

A second distinction is made between a priori evaluation (i.e., the evaluation of plan or project alternatives yet to be implemented) and ex post evaluation (i.e., the evaluation of projects or programs after implementation). With a growing interest within the transportation planning profession in service-oriented transportation actions, the latter approach to evaluation is becoming more important. A careful consideration of the impacts of previously implemented projects can provide transportation officials with potentially useful information on the desirability of implementing similar projects elsewhere. From a political perspective, the potential for an ex post evaluation can create pressure on public agencies to implement the selected alternative very carefully, so that an ineffective project or program cannot be blamed on poor implementation procedures.

In the next section, the general principles that guide successful evaluation efforts are discussed. The key questions that form the basis of any type of evaluation are outlined, and a framework is suggested for conducting evaluations. In Sec. 9-2 a major component of evaluation, the measures of effectiveness used to determine project or plan desirability, is discussed. In Secs. 9-3 and 9-4, the technical concepts underlying the use of evaluation techniques are presented, and the evaluation techniques themselves are outlined. A case study of the evaluation process in a regional transit planning process for Milwaukee, Wisconsin, is found in Sec. 9-5. An example of an evaluation process for the analysis of transportation corridors is presented in Sec. 9-6. Ex post evaluation, including both the underlying concepts and alternative experimental designs, is discussed in Sec. 9-7. A more detailed discussion of environmental impact assessment is found in Appendix B.

9-1 A FRAMEWORK FOR EVALUATION

Evaluation serves three major purposes in the transportation planning process. First, evaluation is the process of determining the value of individual alternatives and the desirability of one alternative over another. The key methodological issues in this determination are (1) defining how value is to be measured and (2) estimating the source and timing of the benefits and costs of the proposed actions. Second, evaluation provides information to decision makers on the impact of policy proposals, trade-offs, and major areas of uncertainty. Not only does the magnitude of the impact have to be identified, but the parties that are positively or negatively affected by each action have to be specified as well. Finally, evaluation provides planners with an opportunity to identify areas of further study. Thus, evaluation not only provides a linkage between planning and decision making, it can also link together the many studies conducted in transportation planning.

As noted in Chap. 3, transportation planners for many years focused their efforts on the first of these purposes. More specifically, most evaluation efforts emphasized quantifying the many impacts of proposed alternatives and assigning monetary values to project benefits and costs. The value of an individual project was thus determined by the relationship between monetary benefits and costs. Beginning in the late 1960s and early 1970s, transportation planners became increasingly interested in the consequences of transportation projects that could not be easily measured in monetary terms. In part because of laws and regulations, issues such as project impact on air quality, community cohesion, energy consumption, equitable distribution of resources, and economic development were incorporated into the evaluation process.

With this change in the focus of evaluation, questions other than: "Which alternative maximizes the monetary benefits returned for the costs incurred?" became important in the evaluation process. Evaluation began to involve questions related to the effectiveness of alternative projects, the efficiency of resource allocation, the impact on an equitable distribution of resources, and the administrative and legal feasibility of alternative project implementation. Because these questions (shown in Table 9-1) address many issues that are often a part of transportation decision making, they are proposed as the basis of effective evaluation efforts.

In developing an overall framework for evaluation that addresses the questions listed in Table 9-1, several fundamental characteristics of the evaluation process should be considered. As first discussed in Chap. 5, evaluation should:

1. Focus on the decision to be made and the key issues to be faced by decision makers
2. Incorporate as much information in the analysis as the planner feels is relevant
3. Relate the consequences of alternatives to goals and objectives

Table 9-1 Questions that form the basis of evaluation

Appropriateness	*Efficiency*
What information on impacts and trade-offs is required for the decisions that need to be made?	Does the alternative provide sufficient benefits to justify the costs?
Do the objectives attained by the alternative reflect previously specified community goals and objectives?	In comparison with other alternatives, are the additional benefits provided (or forgone) worth the extra cost (or cost savings)?
What is the distribution of benefits and costs among members of the community (equity consideration)?	*Implementation feasibility*
	Will the funds be available to implement the alternative on schedule?
Do any groups pay shares of the costs which are disproportionate to the benefits they receive (equity consideration)?	Are there any administrative or legal barriers to alternative implementation?
Effectiveness	Does the organizational capability (e.g., staff and expertise) exist to implement the alternative?
Is the alternative likely to produce the desired results?	Are there groups who are likely to oppose the alternative?
To what extent are planning and community goals attained through the implementation of the alternative?	*Sensitivity analysis*
Adequacy	How are the predicted impacts modified when analysis assumptions are changed?
Does the alternative correspond to the scale of the problem and to the level of expectation of problem solution?	What is the likelihood of these changes occurring?
Are there other alternatives which might be considered?	

4. Determine how particular interests are affected by transportation proposals
5. Be sensitive to the timeframe in which project impacts are likely to occur
6. In the case of regional transportation planning, produce information on the likely impacts of alternatives at a level of aggregation that permits both system and subarea impact assessment
7. Analyze the implementation requirements of each alternative
8. Provide information to decision makers on the value of alternatives in a readily understandable and useful form and in a timely fashion

These eight characteristics imply an evaluation framework which provides involvement for interested parties, which summarizes in understandable terms the key issues to be considered by decision makers, and which guides much of the technical analysis activity during the planning process. As reflected in the first characteristic above, the evaluation process should be tailored to the types of decisions faced by decision makers. Tailoring the evaluation process requires the planner to determine what information is *needed* in the decision-making process over and above what is *wanted* by decision makers. Clearly, the type of evaluation conducted for a series of intersection improvements would be different from that for an examination of future transportation network configurations. In the case of intersection improvements, the benefits of the improvements could be easily estimated because of the short time frame involved. The evaluation of alternative system plans, however, would be a much more comprehensive and complex effort. Planners would have to consider a large set of "benefits" and "costs," the measurement of which could create significant problems. To be useful to planners, therefore, a framework for evaluation must, above all, be adaptable to different problem contexts. A framework having such flexibility can be found in a modified version of the *cost-effectiveness* approach to evaluation.

The cost-effectiveness approach is concerned with how each alternative contributes to the attainment of community goals and objectives [Thomas and Schofer, 1970]. The basis of this assessment is the identification of criteria that serve as the dimensions against which each alternative will be evaluated. These criteria, referred to as *measures of effectiveness,* reflect community or decision-maker goals and objectives or any other consequences of plan and/or project implementation that might be of interest to decision-makers. The "effectiveness" of an alternative is usually represented as a scaled quantity relating to a specific objective (e.g., number of car pools formed, the reduction in air pollution in tons of pollutant, or number of people having access to special transportation services). Cost-effectiveness ratios can thus be calculated to show the degree of goal attainment achieved per dollar of net expenditure [Hudson, Wachs, and Schofer, 1974]. Examples of such cost-effectiveness ratios are found in Secs. 9-5 and 9-6.

The significance of the cost-effectiveness approach is its recognition that the final authority and responsibility for choice lie with decision makers. The "correct" decision does not result from the evaluation process; rather, the cost-effectiveness approach produces a structured set of information which can be used for input into the decision-making process. Most important, the cost-effectiveness approach illustrates the possible trade-off between level of effectiveness and costs.

A simple example of how the cost-effectiveness approach can provide the opportunity for trade-off assessment is shown in Fig. 9-1. In this instance, ten alternatives are considered at different budget levels, with each exhibiting different levels of effectiveness in terms of two measures. Those alternatives at a given budget level which are not dominated by another alternative (i.e., where more effectiveness can be gained for the same cost) lie on an "efficiency frontier." In Fig. 9-1, alternatives 1, 2, and 4 lie on such a frontier. The decision of which alternative to choose at this budget level, or of increasing or decreasing the budget level, is inherently a value-laden one and depends on the willingness of the decision makers to trade one measure of effectiveness for another.

One difficulty with the cost-effectiveness approach is that it does not provide information on the relative value of alternatives. Because this information can often be extremely important to decision makers, some effort should be made to incorporate such information into the results of evaluation. Two approaches for producing this type of information have been used by transportation planners. Perhaps the best known approach is one which uses economic evaluation techniques (e.g., benefit and cost, annual cost, present value, and rate of return) to estimate quantitatively the individual and comparative worth of alternatives. In this approach the costs and benefits for each year of the useful life of a project are estimated, discounted to a base year for comparison, and then compared on the basis of some decision rule (e.g., the ratio of benefits to costs must be greater than 1).

Although extensively used in the evaluation process, the economic evaluation approach does not provide, by itself, answers to the questions shown in Table 9-1. By reducing the benefits and costs of a project to a single scalar dimension of dollars, this

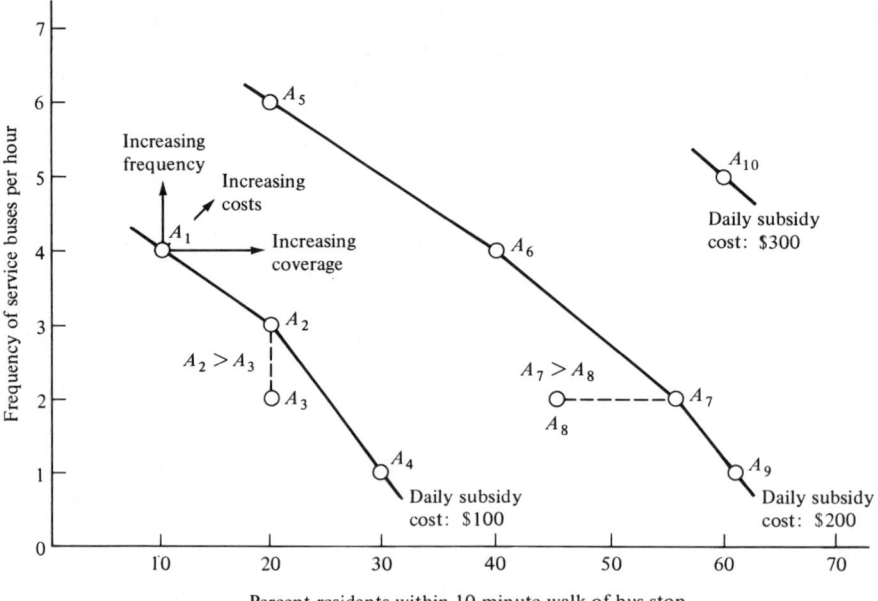

Figure 9-1 Example of cost effectiveness analysis. (*Schofer* [*1978*].)

approach can in fact ignore some of the more important nonmonetary consequences of project implementation.

Another common evaluation approach, developed partly in response to the deficiencies of the economic evaluation approach, uses scoring techniques or weighting schemes to produce a scalar measure of project attractiveness. The advantages of this approach are that community objectives can be weighted to reflect the preference of decision makers, and impacts need not be expressed in monetary terms [Hill, 1973; Jessiman et al., 1967; Cohen et al., 1978]. The weights assigned to the objectives or evaluation criteria have in the past been determined by panels of experts or representatives of community groups. Often, estimates of impacts have also been determined in the same manner. A quantitative score for each alternative could then be obtained by summing the separate scores for each objective-impact category.

Although offered as an improvement over the economic evaluation approach, the rating approach exhibits as many, if not more, problems. For example, subjective weighting procedures always raise questions as to whose values are being applied in the assessment. Also, the rating approach does not provide useful information on the relative effectiveness of alternatives and does not indicate whether the costs of alternatives are justified by the benefits expected.

These two approaches to comparative assessment—economic evaluation and rating schemes—have been used in many transportation studies. In both cases, there exist serious deficiencies which limit their use as a *sole* means of evaluation. In the context of transportation planning, as defined in this book, the most serious problem with each is that both have been used to choose the "best" alternative, rather than to provide full information to decision makers. Consequently, such techniques are best used within the context of an overall cost-effectiveness framework for evaluation, which is the approach adopted in this book.

As shown in Fig. 9-2, the results of both the measure of effectiveness analysis and the comparative assessment can be presented in an information tableau or effectiveness matrix. The information provided in this matrix can in itself be the final product of the evaluation process (except in cases where other studies are identified by planners), or a scoring function could be used to rank the alternatives according to a predetermined set of weights, similar to the rating schemes discussed above.

In summary, the cost-effectiveness approach provides a basis for an overall framework for structuring an evaluation process. At its foundation, the cost-effectiveness approach is based on the belief that the most important consequences of changes to the transportation system are not necessarily those measured strictly in monetary terms and that affected interests can play an important role in the evaluation and planning processes. Nonmonetary effectiveness and equity implications can be much more important than an efficient expenditure of funds. Because the cost-effectiveness approach is tied so closely to community goals and objectives, planners using this approach should be concerned with providing opportunities for public involvement in the evaluation process. The *process* becomes as important as the *techniques* used in evaluation.

For all its advantages, however, the cost-effectiveness approach does not provide information on the relative worth of alternatives, an important piece of information for decision makers. Therefore, the framework for evaluation suggested in this book, and

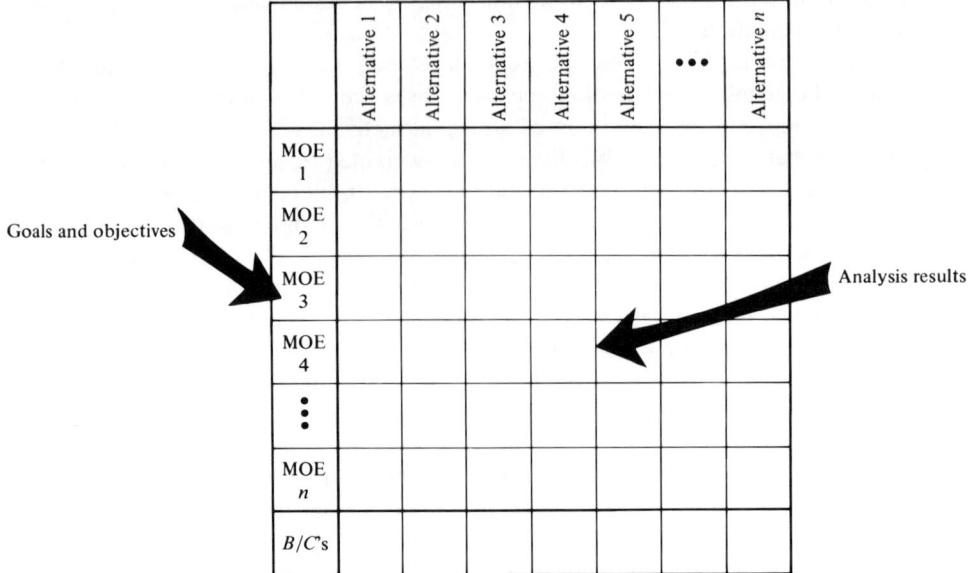

Figure 9-2 The evaluation matrix.

illustrated in Fig 9-2, adopts a modified cost-effectiveness approach in which measures of effectiveness and methods of comparative evaluation are combined into one process. For projects where large-scale impacts are not anticipated, this framework can be simplified to include the measures or the comparative evaluation information which is considered most appropriate given the available resources and scope of the problem. These two major components of the evaluation framework—measures of effectiveness and comparison assessment methods—will be discussed in greater detail below.

9-2 MEASURES OF EFFECTIVENESS IN EVALUATION

Measures of effectiveness (MOEs) are the criteria against which all alternatives are measured and serve as a major link between technical analysis and the goals and/or objectives of decision makers. Such measures have been developed for different planning contexts (e.g., long-range and short-range planning), alternative project types, and different decision purposes. To be of use in the evaluation process, MOEs should exhibit six major characteristics. They must be [Schofer, 1978; Abrams and DiRenzo, 1979]:

1. *Relevant to objectives.* Each MOE should be clearly related to an objective defined for the decision-making process (see Sec. 4-4-1).
2. *Measurable.* The data and analysis techniques required to produce the necessary information for the MOE should be readily available, and the costs for data collection and analysis should be commensurate with the value of information produced.

3. *Sensitive.* Each MOE should be specified at the level of detail and sensitivity to change appropriate for the decision being made. Measures might also pertain to various community groups likely to be impacted by the alternatives. This implies that different MOEs would likely be used at different scales of analysis or in different operating environments.
4. *Unbiased.* The measures should be applicable to a wide range of alternatives and not favor one mode over another (e.g., *vehicle* miles of travel vs. *person* miles of travel).
5. *Manageable.* The number of measures used in the evaluation should be as small as possible, subject to the needs of decision makers. Providing too much information is often as ineffective as not providing enough.
6. *Understandable.* Because the major purpose of an MOE is to provide information to decision makers, the measure must be understandable to those who will make the decisions.

A list of candidate MOEs for the evaluation of alternative *projects* is shown in Table 9-2. Clearly, not all of these measures would be used in an evaluation process, not only because most planning efforts have a smaller set of specific objectives, but also because of the high cost of collecting and analyzing the required data. These MOEs are often used with more specific characterizations of time period, modal use, geographic area, and special data groupings (e.g., person hours of travel in peak hours, number of car pools in a corridor of travel, and average trip time for work travel).

Table 9-2 Example measures of effectiveness for project evaluation

Objective: *minimize travel time*
  *Person hours of travel
  *Point-to-point travel time
  Response time for dial-a-ride transit
  *Vehicle delay
  *Vehicle hours of travel
  Vehicle stops

Objective: *minimize travel costs*
  Parking cost
  Point-to-point out-of-pocket travel costs
  Point-to-point transit fares

Objective: *maximize safety*
  Accidents
  Accident rate
  Freeway incident rate
  Traffic violations

Objective: *maximize security*
  Crimes

Objective: *maximize pedestrian and bicycle travel*
  Bicycle counts
  Pedestrian counts

Objective: *maximize capacity*
  Critical lane volume
  Level of service
  Parking supply
  *Volume/capacity ratio

Objective: *maximize productivity*
  Active revenue vehicles
  Inspection and maintenance cost per labor hour
  Length of queue
  *Operating cost per passenger trip
  Operating cost per revenue vehicle mile
  Operating revenue/operating costs
  *Passengers per revenue vehicle hour
  Passengers per revenue vehicle mile
  *Revenue vehicle miles per active revenue vehicle

Table 9-2 *(continued)*

Objective: *maximize comfort and convenience*
    Active revenue vehicles with working air conditioning and heating
    Frequency of transit service
    Hours of transit operation
    Parking accumulation
    Comfort and convenience
    Transfers per transit passenger
    Transit load factor
    Transit transfer time
    Trip distance
    Walking distance from parking location to destination

Objective: *maximize reliability*
    Freeway incident delay
    Perceived reliability of service
    Schedule adherence
    Transit vehicle breakdowns
    Variance of average point-to-point travel time

Objective: *minimize auto usage*
    Intersection vehicle turning movements
    Number of car pools
    *Number of vehicles by occupancy
    *Person miles of travel
    Person trips
    *Traffic volume
    *Vehicle miles of travel

Objective: *maximize transit usage*
    Information requests
    *Passenger miles of travel
    *Transit passengers

Objective: *minimize operating costs*
    *Operating and maintenance costs
    Operating deficits
    Operating revenue

Objective: *minimize capital costs*
    *Capital cost

Objective: *minimize noise impacts*
    Noise levels

Objective: *minimize air pollution*
    Concentration of pollutants
    *Tons of emissions

Objective: *minimize energy consumption*
    Energy consumption

Objective: *maximize transportation disadvantaged ridership*
    Transportation disadvantaged ridership

Objective: *minimize economic impacts*
    Dollar sales
    Employment

Objective: *maximize equity*
    Point-to-point travel costs to major activity centers
    Point-to-point travel time to major activity centers
    Population within .25 mile of bus route

Objective: *minimize displacement*
    Acres of land acquired
    Structures displaced

*Indicates an MOE that is commonly used in project evaluation.
Source: Abrams and DiRenzo [1979].

Measures of effectiveness for the evaluation of transportation *plans* can be similar to those shown in Table 9-2, although the types of analysis tools necessary to determine impacts might be much different. For example, a determination of average trip time in alternative transportation network configurations would require simulation of person and vehicle flows on each network. The average trip time could be computed by dividing the total passenger hours of travel by total number of passenger trips made. Because of the added complexity of determining the values of MOEs in the evaluation of alternative plans, a set of MOEs for plan evaluation must be chosen with special consideration to the costs associated with producing the required information.

An example of the MOEs that could be used in plan evaluation is a set of measures proposed by planners in Chicago [Schulz, 1975]. The measures were divided into eight major categories relating to (1) transportation system performance, (2) equity, (3) environmental impact, (4) energy, (5) social and neighborhood impact, (6) economic impact, (7) regional development, and (8) capital and operating costs. The specific measures proposed in each category are shown in Table 9-3. Note the wide range of data that has to be collected to produce these MOEs. Some data have to come from the results of complex modeling efforts, while other data can be determined simply by looking at a map of the area surrounding proposed transportation facilities.

An important characteristic of MOEs and their use in evaluation is that estimates of the impact they represent are usually made in the beginning of the process. If these initial estimates indicate that the impact will not have significant consequences, they can be used without further detailed analysis. In many cases, however, initial estimates will indicate that the impact is close to, or exceeds, a certain threshold level (or standard as described in Chap. 4). Further analysis is then required to determine in more detail the magnitude and distributional consequences of the impact.

Another important characteristic of MOEs is that they can be specified for affected interests or geographic areas. These two categories—socioeconomic classes and geographic areas—form the basis of assessments of the distributional consequences of transportation projects. There are three aspects of such an assessment that planners should recognize. First, every program or project will have *some* distributional consequence, either in the benefits that accrue or in the costs that will be borne by groups in the community [Starling, 1979]. These consequences can include the equity impacts of transportation services provided or the distribution impacts of the externalities associated with the project (e.g., increased noise, reduced air quality). Second, the determination of which distributional impacts are desirable, or at least tolerable, as opposed to those that are clearly unacceptable is a value judgment that is generally made as part of the political decision-making process. Third, in cases where distributional consequences are an articulated policy objective, the changes selected should be those that attain the objectives in the least costly fashion, other factors being equal.

Table 9-3 Chicago example of MOEs for plan evaluation

Transportation system performance
  Average trip time (by mode, trip type, and income)
  Average trip speed (by mode and trip type)
  Peak-period corridor and link volume/capacity ratios
  Percent of population within 10 minutes walking time of an entry point of a transit system with headways of 15 minutes or better (also computed for 30- and 60-minute headways)
  Vehicle miles of travel within various volume/capacity ratio ranges
  Mode split for entire region and subareas

Social and neighborhood impact
  Estimated monetary residential relocation costs
  Number of relocated households
  Number of relocated community facilities
  Number of historic sites taken

Economic impact
  Number of jobs relocated or eliminated (by income and area)
  Number of commercial establishments relocated
  Tax base removed
  Man-years of construction employment

Table 9-3 *(continued)*

Environmental impact
  Noise levels (by geographic area)
  Air pollution emissions
  Area exceeding air quality standards
  Cumulative percent of population working or residing in areas above air quality standards
  Maximum concentrations of pollutants
  Number of acres of open space consumed by plan implementation

Energy
  Total annual fuel consumption
  Fuel consumption per passenger mile

Regional development
  Accessibility maps to the central business district and to regional centers
  Percent of designated regional centers within 1 mile of a major transportation service
  Average frequency of transit service
  Average number of transfers
  Percent standing passengers
  Average annual total transportation cost per user
  Average out-of-pocket cost per trip (by trip purpose)
  Total number of accidents
  Total number of accidents per passenger mile

Equity
  Average travel times for the elderly, handicapped, and poor
  Relative average time between majority and minority
  Accessibility maps for minorities and poor
  Number of low-income jobs within 60 minutes by transit

Capital and operating costs
  Total annual cost of transportation for all modes
  Total public capital cost
  Total operating and maintenance costs
  Route miles of construction

Source: Memorandum from D. Schulz to CATS Technical Staff, "Evaluative Measures," Chicago Area Transportation Study, July 17, 1975.

The most common way in transportation planning of portraying distributional consequences is through the use of an impact-incidence matrix. As shown in Fig. 9-3 such a matrix contains information concerning the impacts on groups directly or indirectly affected. By seeing the impact information displayed in this way, decision makers can identify which groups are adversely affected and the level of compensation that might be necessary for the costs they incur. The level of aggregation of the information provided in such a matrix depends on the stage of the planning process in which it is to be used; less detail is required in the early alternatives screening phase, while more disaggregate information is needed as the process nears design evaluation.

In summary, measures of effectiveness are the critical variables in the evaluation of transportation projects and plans. As such, planners must be careful that the set of MOEs used in evaluation reflects community goals and objectives and produces the information needed by decision makers. At the same time, the greater the number of MOEs used in evaluation, the greater the cost of data collection and analysis. It is thus

			Impacts						
			MOE 1	MOE 2	MOE 3	MOE 4	MOE 5	••••	MOE *n*
Groups impacted	Indirect	1							
		2							
		3							
		4							
	Direct	1							
		2							
		3							

Figure 9-3 The impact-incidence matrix.

important that planners interact with decision makers early in the planning process to determine the MOEs most important to the evaluation. Again, this does not imply that only those MOEs wanted by decision makers should be included in the evaluation. Given the typically long lead time between planning and project implementation, planners must use their professional judgment in predicting the important concerns that could surface by the time the evaluation steps in planning are reached. The process of selecting an appropriate set of MOEs thus includes an identification of information *desires* of decision makers as well as their likely information *needs*.

9-3 TECHNICAL CONCEPTS UNDERLYING ECONOMIC EVALUATION METHODS

Several characteristics of project consequences can have significant impact on the approaches used in evaluation. One such characteristic, that an alternative can impact many different groups in a community, was discussed in the previous section. From the perspective of the economic evaluation approach, three other characteristics merit special attention. First, the definition of "benefits" and "costs" depends on which group is defining the terms. For example, economic evaluation techniques discussed in this section reduce all benefits and costs to dollar terms. Second, the benefits and costs of alternatives will occur in the future, meaning some mechanism for comparison over time is required. Third, impacts can rarely be assessed with a great deal of certainty. Planners should thus adopt certain strategies in evaluation to determine the sensitivity of the results to the uncertainties of key variables. Each of these features—the economic definition of benefits and costs, dealing with the time dimension of impacts, and handling uncertainty—is discussed in the following sections.

9-3-1 Impacts of System and Project Alternatives: Characteristics of Benefit and Cost Measurement

Almost all evaluation in transportation planning requires some determination of the benefits and costs associated with the alternatives under consideration. The definition of benefits and cost, and the relative weighting of each, however, is very much dependent upon the groups likely to experience the impacts of different alternatives. For example, a new transportation facility might be considered beneficial to users of the facility because it will reduce the amount of time needed by commuters to travel to work. On the other hand, this same facility might inflict on nearby residents the costs of increased noise, worsened local air quality, and disruptions to normal social interaction.

Historically, evaluation has focused almost exclusively on the benefits realized and the costs incurred by the users, with only the benefits and costs readily expressable in dollar terms being included in the evaluation process. As has been noted throughout this book, however, the transportation system is complex, as is its interrelationship with the socioeconomic activity systems. Any changes to this system can have significant impacts, both direct and indirect, on the performance of the transportation system and on socioeconomic activities in an urban area. The challenge to planners in evaluation is to understand this complex relationship and to identify a set of benefits and costs of alternatives that accounts for the diverse interests associated with any particular action.

Before the types of benefits and costs usually considered in evaluating transportation system changes are discussed in detail, several basic characteristics of benefit and cost measurement should be explored. First, a distinction has to be made between *real* and *pecuniary* impacts. Real benefits are those realized by the final consumers of a project or those which add to a community's overall welfare, while pecuniary benefits are those that are gained at the expense of other individuals or groups (i.e., a redistribution of income). Rising land values resulting from improved transportation accessibility is a good example of a pecuniary benefit. Although the owners of the land will benefit monetarily from changes to the transportation system, consumers of the land will ultimately have to pay these costs in terms of increased land values. From a societal viewpoint, there will be no net welfare gain for the economy. In general, strictly pecuniary effects should not be included in an evaluation, unless a redistributional impact among income groups is a major objective of the investment [Musgrave and Musgrave, 1976]. From a political perspective, however, the identification of such pecuniary impacts might be important to the identification of groups that would support or oppose specific alternatives.

Another point worth noting at the outset is that real benefits and costs can be *direct* or *indirect*. Direct benefits and costs are those specifically related to the major program or planning objectives, while indirect benefits and costs are, in some sense, by-products of system investment. For example, a transit improvement project can provide direct benefits to users in terms of reduced travel times and indirect benefits to the community of improved safety and air quality. Another indirect impact of such an improvement might be the short-term benefits realized by users of other facilities in terms of improved personal travel times (resulting from the absence of travelers who have abandoned their previous mode to use the new service).

In many cases, the distinction between direct and indirect *benefits* is difficult to specify. For this reason, a clear statement of planning goals and objectives, along with a statement of how the alternatives under consideration relate to these goals, is important to the planner undertaking an evaluation.

The real *costs* associated with an investment can also be both direct and indirect. The direct costs of an alternative include its initial capital costs, as well as the costs associated with facility or service operation and maintenance. Indirect costs include expenditures required of other government agencies (e.g., additional costs for police agencies to enforce speed limits and parking restrictions or to provide protection at transit terminals) and the social costs of additional air and noise pollution, increased congestion, and any adverse impacts on the viability of alternative transportation services (such as public transit in the case of highway investment).

Differences in the degree to which benefits and costs can be "measured" result in *tangible* or *intangible* effects. In economic terms, tangible benefits and costs are those which can be assigned monetary values for market purposes, with benefits being measured by the price a service would command in the marketplace and costs being measured by the price of the inputs needed to deliver the service. Intangible benefits and costs, conversely, are those which cannot be easily measured or associated with prices in the marketplace (e.g., the aesthetic value of transit station design). These intangible benefits and costs can nevertheless play an important role in the decision-making process and are thus important to include, in some form, in alternatives assessment. They should be described as explicitly as possible and, where feasible, described in nonmonetary, though quantitative, terms [Haveman and Weisbrod, 1977].

Another distinction needs to be made between the benefits and costs that are *internal* and *external* to geographic boundaries of the planning study. Major improvements to urban transportation facilities are often paid for by local municipalities (e.g., those belonging to a regional transit district), while the benefits of such improvements, both indirect and direct, can accrue to groups beyond the jurisdictional boundaries of these municipalities. For example, improvements to line-haul facilities can benefit both short-distance and long-distance travelers, making a determination of exactly who will benefit somewhat difficult. Similarly, an improvement in air quality due to transportation improvements in one region could benefit another region downwind. Planners must therefore be careful in defining benefits and costs to consider the extent of such effects.

Especially relevant to transportation is the distinction between *user* and *nonuser* costs. For many years, the most commonly used evaluation criteria related to the impacts on the users of a system or facility. For example, the monetary value of the user travel time saved was an important benefit incorporated into evaluation. User benefits and costs were usually measured in monetary terms. In recent years, the benefits and costs of transportation changes to the general community, or nonusers, have become increasingly important in evaluation. These nonuser impacts include dislocation of businesses and homes, environmental degradation, and impacts on land-use patterns. It is partly because of the importance of these nonuser impacts that the modified cost-effectiveness framework for evaluation shown in Fig. 9-2 has been suggested in this text.

A final distinction should be made between *total* and *incremental* costs and benefits. An estimate of total costs, for instance, includes the total outlay of dollars used to construct and operate the system under consideration. Incremental costs are those that are directly related to proposed changes to existing systems. The incremental cost approach should be undertaken with regard to the major groups to be affected by

Table 9-4 Incremental costing of an express bus example

A. Incremental costs to transit operator
  1. Cost of additional buses required, if any
  2. Reduced cost of new vehicles purchased if existing and new services can be provided with fewer units due to higher round-trip speeds
  3. Cost of modifying existing buses (high-speed tires, etc.)
  4. Changes in maintenance costs for vehicles operating on freeways rather than local streets
  5. Changes in the cost of driver wages
  6. Changes in general transit vehicle operating costs
  7. Cost of lost patronage on parallel nonexpress transit routes due to passenger diversion
  8. Others

B. Incremental costs to freeway operator
  1. Changes in maintenance costs for traveled way (pavements, structures, etc.)
  2. Costs of specialized facilities, such as freeway stops, modified acceleration and deceleration lanes
  3. Others

C. Incremental costs to freeway users (presence of buses may modify operating characteristics of the freeway in that their size and performance characteristics are different; their effect on the traffic stream may be favorable or unfavorable; the new service may also divert some people from their cars, resulting in a favorable effect on congestion)
  1. Changes in operating costs (fuel, tires, etc.)
  2. Changes in time costs (particularly important if a freeway lane is reserved for buses in the peak hour)
  3. Changes in accident costs due to changes in the risk of an accident as well as the consequences of accidents
  4. Others

D. Incremental costs to users of bus transit
  1. Fare costs to new express riders
     a. Costs to persons making new trips
     b. Costs to persons diverted from automobiles (transit fare less previous auto costs)
     c. Costs to persons diverted from local transit service (express fare less previous fare)
     d. Changes in costs to persons remaining on arterial bus routes with reduced service
  2. Changes in terminal costs
     a. Getting to the bus stop from origin
     b. Getting to destinations from bus stop
  3. Changes in time costs
  4. Others

Source: Thomas and Schofer [1970].

system changes. An example of such an approach is provided by Thomas and Schofer in the case of a proposal to offer express bus service on freeways, instead of continuing the existing service on local streets [Thomas and Schofer, 1970]. As shown in Table 9-4, the incremental costs of such a proposal can accrue both to the operators of the freeway and transit system and to the users of both facilities.

A systematic examination of the various effects of a proposal on system cost elements, as was done in Table 9-4, can provide additional information to planners and decision makers. By using the incremental cost method, planners can (1) gain a better understanding of the interrelationship between transportation system components, (2) clearly identify the separable costs associated with project implementation so that decision makers are aware of the highest cost components and the subsequent demands on different revenue sources needed to cover additional costs, and (3) obtain information on the sensitivity of certain components of the proposed change (e.g., those components which have high costs associated with them, and yet whose impacts are uncertain, are possible targets for more detailed analysis). In order to use the incremental cost model in evaluation, the planner must also have the capability to perform marginal or incremental assessments on the other consequences of project implementation. This capability exists in some cases, especially for determining short-term and intangible impacts. The difficulty lies in assessing the likely consequences over the long term, especially for intangible impacts.

The above six distinctions in the measurement of benefits and costs—real vs. pecuniary, direct vs. indirect, tangible vs. intangible, internal vs. external, users vs. nonusers, and total vs. incremental—are important in assessing the value of transportation actions. The definition of what constitutes a benefit or a cost, however, is central to the entire notion of evaluation. Of the two, the definition of a benefit has been the more difficult for planners to specify and hence will be addressed first.

9-3-2 Impacts of System and Project Alternatives: Measurement of Benefit and Cost

Benefits. In simple terms, benefits are the desirable effects of investment, where "desirable" suggests some positive impact on community, agency, or individual goals and objectives. Much of the academic discussion of benefits has related to economic interpretations of how a change in price will affect consumer welfare or, in other words, the value to a consumer (i.e., his "willingness to pay") of a change in the price of a good. As discussed in Sec. 5-2, the quantity to be measured in this case is the amount the consumer would pay or would need to be paid in order to be as well off after a price change as he was before the change. The two economic measures that represent this benefit accurately were identified as compensating variation and equivalent variation measures. As was also discussed in Sec. 5-2, one approach to estimating these measures is through the use of disaggregate travel demand models.

In practice, however, most measurements of economic benefit are based on the concept of consumer surplus. As shown in Fig. 9-4, consumer surplus is the area under the market demand curve which represents the total user benefit minus the cost to

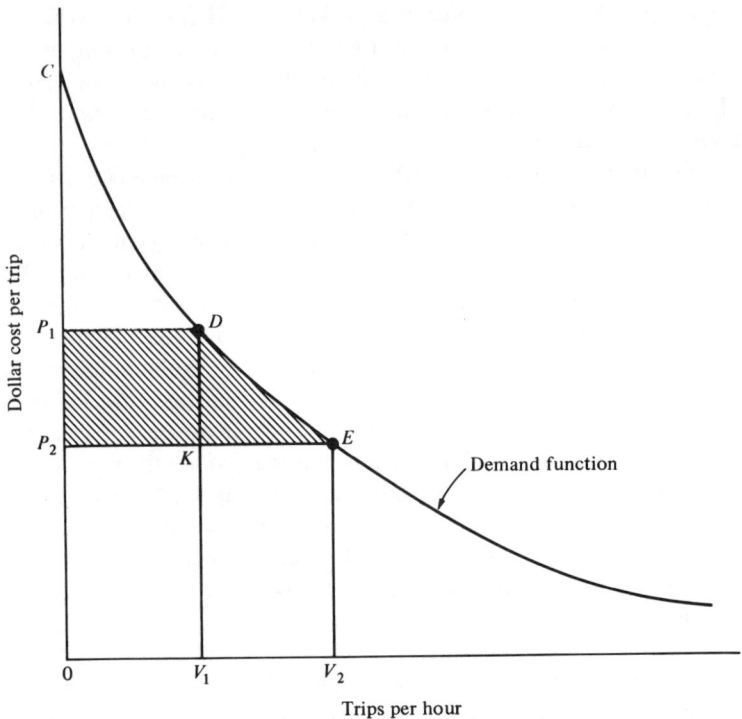

Figure 9-4 The measurement of consumer surplus.

users. At the original price of travel P_1 (which includes out-of-pocket costs, travel time, and other factors that influence travel behavior) travelers would be willing to pay amounts to the left of point D for use of that facility, or the total benefit to the V_1 travelers would be equal to the area under the demand curve to the left of point D (area $OCDV_1$). The net benefit or "consumer surplus" to users of the facility at price P_1 is this area $OCDV_1$ minus area OP_1DV_1, or area P_1CD. A change in total net user benefit stemming from a price change would thus be the change in consumer surplus, which in Fig. 9-4 would be area P_2CE minus P_1CD, or the shaded area P_2P_1DE. This total net user benefit consists of two types of benefit: that gained by the original V_1 travelers (represented by area P_2P_1DK) and that realized by the users of the facility induced to travel because of a "lower" travel price (represented by area KDE). It is important to note that the "change in price" which produces a benefit to users can consist of many components, and great care must be used in defining this change. Most important, from a theoretical perspective, the dynamics of this change over time (i.e., how and when a new equilibrium is established) are significant considerations.

Based on this concept of total net user benefits, numerous equations and theoretical formulations have been developed to define benefits according to different underlying assumptions. Through simple geometry, the change in consumers' surplus can be approximated as

$$N = \tfrac{1}{2}(P_1 - P_2)(V_1 + V_2) \tag{9-1}$$

where NB = net benefits to users

P_1 = original price of travel

P_2 = reduced price of travel

V_1 = volume of travel at P_1

V_2 = volume of travel at P_2

The best known procedure for engineering economic studies based on Eq. (9-1) is found in the American Association of State Highway and Transportation Officials (AASHTO) *Manual of User Benefit Analysis of Highway and Bus-Transit Improvements* [AASHTO, 1977].

As can be seen from the above discussion, the evaluation of user benefits is primarily a process of determining how great a reduction in negative effects will occur if an improvement is made (e.g., the reduction in the price of travel due to an improvement). There can thus be a definition problem of what constitutes a benefit and a cost. Reductions in costs are usually considered benefits (note, for example, that categories C and D of incremental costs shown in Table 9-4 could also be considered benefits if the effects on users and nonusers were favorable). From the perspective of the user, reductions in the number of accidents, travel costs, and travel time comprise the most direct benefits of transportation projects, the most significant of which (relative to most of the costs of major projects) is the reduction in user travel times (e.g., between 72 percent and 81 percent of the benefits of the U.S. interstate highway system have been attributed to travel time savings) [Fallon et al., 1970].

These types of benefits are usually incorporated into the evaluation process by applying a unit value to each measure and then multiplying this value by the total amount of savings (i.e., the highway engineer's benefit approach). In each case, however, the determination of appropriate unit values has created considerable controversy among researchers and practitioners, a good illustration being the appropriate measure for "value of time."

Benefits from travel time savings As mentioned in Chap. 2, the underlying basis for assigning a monetary value to travel time is that time not spent in travel can be used for other activities. In the case of work travel, a reasonable estimate of the value of time for work trips can be related to the traveler's wage. For other trip purposes, the value of travel time becomes less obvious. Still, different dollar values have been used to represent the value of time, which has been found to be sensitive to trip purpose, a traveler's income level, and the amount of time savings per trip [Thomas and Thompson, 1971]. These values of time measures can be found in tabular or graphical form in many evaluation handbooks (see Fig. 9-5). A 1977 study of value of time measures recommended the values shown in Fig. 9-5, where the values in dollars per traveler

		Trip purpose, dollars	
Annual family income, dollars	Time saving, minutes	Average trips	Work trips
5,000	0–5	0.07	0.15
	5–15	0.58	0.77
	Over 15	1.26	1.26
10,000	0–5	0.13	0.31
	5–15	1.16	1.55
	Over 15	2.52	2.52
15,000	0–5	0.21	0.48
(average)	5–15	1.80	2.40
	Over 15	3.90	3.90
20,000	0–5	0.27	0.62
	5–15	2.32	3.10
	Over 15	5.03	5.03
30,000	0–5	0.41	0.92
	5–15	3.48	4.65
	Over 15	7.55	7.55

(a)

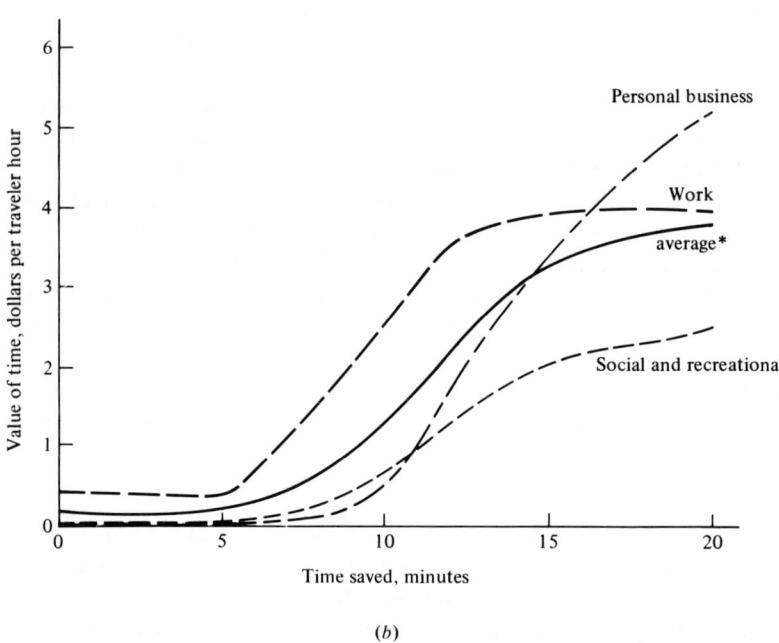

(b)

Figure 9-5 Value of time estimates (1975 dollars). (a) *American Association of State Highway Transportation Officials* [*1973*]; (b) American Association of State Highway and Transportation Officials [*1977*].

hour can be converted to dollars per vehicle hour by applying vehicle occupancy rates (e.g., 1.22 adults per vehicle for work trips, 1.98 for social-recreational trips, and 1.64 for personal business trips, for a total average of 1.56 adults per vehicle) [AASHTO, 1977].

In the case of transit, a distinction has to be made between value of time spent in and out of the vehicle. The same 1977 study recommended that out-of-vehicle travel time be weighted at 1.5 times the in-vehicle travel time.

Two important observations should be made about value of time measures. First, because the value of time depends on the traveler's income level, more benefit will be assessed for projects that improve travel time for higher-income individuals, a result that has significant equity implications. Second, the dependence of travel time value on income and trip length requires computation of different user travel times for each alternative under consideration, an analysis problem that exceeds the computational resources of most planning agencies. Because of this computational problem, planners sometimes use an average value of travel time by trip purpose for all users of the system (e.g., $3.00 per vehicle hour is used by the American Association of State Highway and Transportation Officials).

Benefit from reduction in accidents Another benefit attributable to facility improvement is the value associated with a potential reduction in accidents. As was the case with determining the value of travel time, an estimation of the cost of traffic accidents is a difficult task, as the costs vary from one urban area to another and differ by type of accident. In the case of a fatal accident, the difficult problem of estimating the value of a human life arises. One of the crucial steps in estimating accident costs is determining what elements should be included. Some choices that have to be made include using *net* future earnings vs. *total* future earnings of victims, including or excluding nonmonetary items such as loss to family or community service, and assigning value to pain and suffering as opposed to excluding them.

A representative set of accident costs is shown in Table 9-5. These values should be viewed with caution because of the variation in accident costs among urban areas, by accident type, and according to the socioeconomic status of those injured.

Benefit from reduced cost of vehicle operation The final user benefit usually considered in transportation project evaluation is the change in costs of vehicle operation. Included in this category of costs are fuel, oil, maintenance and repairs, and depreciation associated with vehicle wear. Typical unit values of operating costs for vehicles on freeways and arterial streets can be found in many handbooks [U.S. Department of Transportation, 1979]. These costs depend on the characteristics of the vehicles involved and of the vehicle mix, roadway design and traffic characteristics, driver and trip characteristic, and the costs in an urban area for each component of the operating costs. Several books provide extensive discussions of how average operating costs can be adjusted to account for these characteristics [AASHTO, 1973; Morlok, 1978; Oglesby and Hicks, 1982]. Adjusting vehicle operating costs to a specific urban context, however, can require considerable data collection and analysis. Such effort

Table 9-5 Representative values of accident costs

Source	Property damage only	Nonfatal injury	Death		
National Highway Traffic Safety Administration*	$471	Minor—$2276 Moderate—$4592 Serious—$10,260 Severe—$43,729 Critical—$190,010	$268,727		
National Safety Council (for cities with more than 10 deaths per year)†	$1090	$8000	$200,000		
National Safety Council (for cities with less than 10 deaths per year)	—	—	Age Under 5 5–14 15–24 25–44 45–64 65–over	Male $120,000 $180,000 $270,000 $310,000 $120,000 $18,000	Female $60,000 $80,000 $130,000 $160,000 $60,000 $17,000

*From National Highway Traffic Safety Administration, *The Economic Cost To Society of Motor Vehicle Accidents*, Report DOT HS 806 342, Jan. 1983; all costs in 1980 dollars.

†From National Safety Council, *Estimating the Cost of Accidents, 1982*, Bulletin, 1983; all costs in 1982 dollars.

might be appropriate in some cases (e.g., highway project planning) but is probably not warranted in most circumstances.

These three measures of user benefit—value of time, accident costs, and vehicle operating costs—are the most commonly used in the comparative assessment of project and system alternatives. As was shown above, these measures are based on assumptions that can be quite sensitive to environmental influences. Furthermore, because of difficulties of measurement, these measures are often considered with average unit values. Given that these measures are so important in evaluation, planners should (1) review with and gather input from decision makers on the unit values to be used in the assessment and (2) conduct tests on how sensitive the results of evaluation are to the values used.

Costs. The determination of costs is generally considered to be a much easier task than the assessment of project benefits. This is most likely the case for several reasons: (1) little distinction is typically made between dollar expenditures and total costs, the latter including some representation of the social costs and opportunity costs of investment; (2) nonquantifiable cost measures are customarily dismissed as noncost considerations or as negative benefits; and (3) benefits are considered to occur over longer periods of time while most costs are incurred early in project implementation [Quade, 1975].

Just as different definitions and classification schemes apply to the explanation of benefits, there are also different ways of defining and aggregating costs. The cost classification scheme chosen for an evaluation depends on the objectives of the planning effort, the amount of detailed data needed to determine costs, and the format requirements of government regulations. For example, costs could be determined on the basis of who must bear them (e.g., agencies, system users, or system nonusers), the components or commodities purchased (e.g., in the case of user costs, vehicle depreciation, fuel and oil costs, maintenance costs, insurance fees, time costs, and fares) or the activities with which they are associated (e.g., research and development, planning and design, right-of-way acquisition and construction, finance, operating, maintenance, and management).

In most cases, no single cost scheme will be appropriate for all purposes. As shown in Table 9-6, however, one possible approach to developing a generalized cost scheme for plan evaluation is to combine (or "nest") different approaches into an integrated cost framework. In this scheme, a distinction is made between centralized and decentralized costs (i.e., the incidence of resource outlays), activities supported by these costs, and the components of the activity actually purchased. As will be dis-

Table 9-6 Example of nested costing structure

Centralized costs	Safety services (policing, etc.)	*Decentralized costs*
Research and development	Materials and equipment	User costs
Planning and design	Durables	Operations
Construction and purchases	Nondurables	Usage-based
Right-of-way	Wages and benefits	Depreciation
Purchases	Overhead	Fuel and oil
Relocation	Accident costs	Parking
Legal fees	Maintenance	Tires
Construction	Materials and equipment	Insurance
Traveled way	Durables	Accidents
Special structures	Nondurables	Time costs
Terminals and yards	Wages and benefits	General usage-based
Purchases	Overhead	maintenance
Rolling stock	Management and	Nonuser costs
Special equipment	administration	
Financing charges	Monitoring system performance	
Operations		
Transport operations		
Energy costs (fuel, power)		
Materials and equipment		
Durable		
Nondurable		
Wages and benefits		
Overhead		

Source: Adapted from Thomas and Schofer [1970].

Table 9-7 Items in evaluation to avoid double counting

Cost item	Omit	Include
Fares	Always	
Tolls	If used for highway construction, finance, or operations and maintenance for that alternative	If used for covering costs of that alternative that are not covered elsewhere in cost estimate
Parking charges	If used to cover capital or operations and maintenance costs that are part of that alternative and are covered elsewhere in cost estimates	If used for covering costs of that alternative that are not covered elsewhere in cost estimates
Fuel taxes or other highway user fees	Always (it is a transfer payment; not a measure of resources consumed)	
Insurance costs	Portion attributable to accident costs (usually assume all of it is attributable)	
Land value increase	Always	

Source: Cohen, Stowers, and Petersilia [1978].

cussed in Sec. 9-3-3 the cost measures actually used in this analysis are annual costs, which require a discounting procedure to account for the changing value of money over time.

The above discussion of benefits and costs has explored the key concepts that provide a foundation for incorporating relevant costs and benefits into comparative assessment methods. One final observation needs to be made with respect to the concept of benefit and cost accounting. There is a danger, when determining impacts, that some impacts will be overlooked while others may be double-counted (see Table 9-7). The measurement of benefits and costs should thus be based on theoretically sound and empirically tested procedures. Perhaps most important, the evaluation framework *must* be applied consistently across all alternatives to provide a valid basis for comparative evaluation. This consistency is especially important in the application of the same definitions of costs and benefits to all alternatives under consideration.

9-3-3 Economic Concepts of Discounting and Capital Recovery

As discussed above, the dominant measure used in comparative assessment methods for defining benefits and costs is dollars. By determining monetary return or initial capital investment, decision makers are able to judge the worth of undertaking any individual alternative. Calculating the return on an initial investment in buses, for example, requires consideration of operating and maintenance costs over time, as well as the revenues produced by the subsequent service and the salvage value of the buses at the end of their useful life. A concept critical to the determination of these costs and benefits is the changing value of money over time, commonly known as the *real value of money*.

Quite simply, if one invests $10,000 today with an interest rate of 10 percent for a 1-year period, at the end of 1 year the investment will nominally be worth $10,000 + ($10,000) (0.10) = $11,000. Thus, $10,000 now is equivalent to $11,000 in 1 year at 10 percent interest, and the $10,000 is the *present* or *discounted* value of the future $11,000. In this case, the interest rate is the rate of return paid to the investor. For purposes of comparison between projects, a discount rate is usually used to represent the opportunity costs of capital (i.e., the rate of return that could be gained from alternative use of the capital).

In general, the equation used to compare sums of money which exist at distinct times is

$$F = P \times (1 + r)^n \tag{9-2}$$

where F = future amount of money
P = present amount of money
r = discount rate
n = periods of repayment or project life

Using the previous example, the future value of $10,000 after 2 years would be

$$F = \$10{,}000 \times (1 + 0.10)^2 = \$12{,}100$$

Alternatively, the present value of future cost or revenues can be determined by rearranging Eq. (9-2).

$$P = \frac{F}{(1 + r)^n} \tag{9-3}$$

Again using the previous example, the present value of a future sum of $12,100 with a 10 percent discount rate is

$$P = \frac{\$12{,}100}{(1 + 0.10)^2} = \$10{,}000$$

In Eq. (9-3), the factor $1/(1 + r)^n$ is called the *present worth factor* and can be found in tabular form with different discount rates in numerous project evaluation texts. Table 9-8 gives the present worth factors for discount rates of 5 percent, 8 percent, 10 percent, 12 percent, and 15 percent for different time periods. As shown in Fig. 9-6, the discounting that results from applying the present worth factor does not occur linearly over time. When determining present values for an entire time stream of costs, therefore, one should not use measures of costs and benefits for a single forecast year, a mistake commonly made in practice today.

In finance, an important consideration in investment is the present value of a constant stream of equal payments over several periods. This form of payment is common to most home and auto mortgages. Based on Eq. (9-2), it can be shown that

Table 9-8 Present worth and capital recovery factors

	Present worth factors				
Year	5%	8%	10%	12%	15%
1	0.9524	0.9259	0.9091	0.8929	0.8696
2	0.9070	0.8573	0.8264	0.7972	0.7561
3	0.8638	0.7938	0.7513	0.7118	0.6575
4	0.8227	0.7350	0.6830	0.6355	0.5718
5	0.7835	0.6806	0.6209	0.5674	0.4972
10	0.6139	0.4632	0.3855	0.3220	0.2472
15	0.4810	0.3152	0.2394	0.1827	0.1229
20	0.3769	0.2145	0.1486	0.1037	0.0611
50	0.0872	0.0213	0.0085	0.0035	0.0009
	Capital recovery factors				
Year	5%	8%	10%	12%	15%
1	1.0500	1.0800	1.1000	1.1200	1.1500
2	0.5378	0.5607	0.5762	0.5917	0.6151
3	0.3672	0.3880	0.4021	0.4163	0.4380
4	0.2820	0.3019	0.3155	0.3292	0.3503
5	0.2310	0.2505	0.2638	0.2774	0.2983
10	0.1295	0.1490	0.1627	0.1770	0.1993
15	0.0963	0.1168	0.1315	0.1468	0.1710
20	0.0802	0.1019	0.1175	0.1339	0.1598
50	0.0548	0.0817	0.1009	0.1204	0.1501

the relationship between an initial investment and the annual payment over n years needed to repay the value of the initial investment as it changes over time is [Shupe, 1980]

$$A = P\left[\frac{r(1 + r)^n}{(1 + r)^n - 1}\right] \tag{9-4}$$

where A is the uniform payments required over n periods.

The term $r(1 + r)^n/[(1 + r)^n - 1]$ is commonly called the *capital recovery factor* and represents the proportion of an initial investment that has to be recouped as benefits in each of n periods in order to return the same value as was invested (see Table 9-8). Using the previous example, the annual payment required over 10 years to return the value of a present amount of $10,000 is

$$A = (\$10{,}000)\left[\frac{(0.10)(1.10)^{10}}{(1.10)^{10} - 1}\right] = \$1{,}627$$

The value of money concept and associated equations are an extremely important component of plan and project evaluation in that, for comparative purposes, the benefits and costs of alternatives can be represented as occurring at a single point in

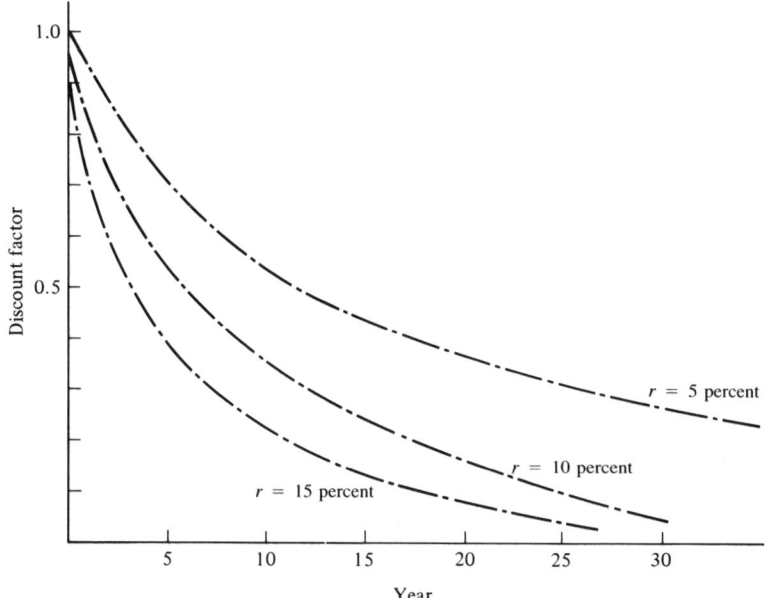

Figure 9-6 Impact of discount rate over time.

time. In most cases, for example, the time streams of benefits and costs are expressed in terms of present values or as equivalent annual costs. The present value method examines all benefits and costs over the project life as if they occur at the present time, while the equivalent annual cost method determines the series of payments over the project life that would have the same present values as the time stream of costs and benefits expected to occur if the project were implemented [de Neufville and Stafford, 1971]. An example of how these methods can be used is included later in this chapter.

The debate on how to select a discount rate for public investment evaluation has been extensive (see, for example, de Neufville and Stafford [1971]; Dasgupta, Sen, and Marglin [1972]; Layard [1972]; and Musgrave and Musgrave [1976]). The major options available for selecting a discount rate, which is expressed as net of inflation, include:

1. The percentage rate of return that the investment would otherwise provide in the private sector
2. The government borrowing rate for capital
3. The "social discount rate" which recognizes the additional societal value of investment in public services and infrastructure
4. A discount rate explicitly chosen to reflect the risk associated with an alternative

It is beyond the scope of this book to outline the advantages and disadvantages of each type of discount rate. It is important, however, that planners realize that the selection of a discount rate for evaluation, in essence a relative weighting of present vs.

future impacts, is a value judgment that should be related specifically to the context of the alternatives being considered. The discount rate can significantly influence whether one project is more desirable than another. The evaluation should be undertaken with different discount rates to determine how the relative assessment of the alternatives is affected by changes in the discount rate (i.e., a sensitivity analysis should be undertaken with respect to different discount rates). One transportation evaluation guide has suggested that the discount rates included in this sensitivity analysis should range from a low rate which reflects the current government borrowing rate for capital (a rate which many economists feel is artificially low because of tax exemptions and the reduction of risk attributable to government backing of such borrowing) to a high rate which represents an expected private-sector return on capital [Cohen et al., 1978].

By carefully considering the choice of discount rate and by recognizing the judgmental nature of the rate through sensitivity analysis, the analysts responsible for assessing project benefits and costs over time can generate information useful to decision makers. The underlying assumptions and consequences of discount rate selection should also be presented to decision makers so that they too can fully understand the explicit and implicit values incorporated into this selection.

9-3-4 Treatment of Uncertainty in Evaluation

No aspect of evaluation is as pervasive to the process, and yet as often ignored, as uncertainty. Uncertainty is present in all facets of transportation planning, from predicting the amount of travel demand for a facility in the future to incorporating the exogenous political, economic, and technological factors that can influence the travel behavior of urban residents. For example, many of the transportation plans developed prior to the 1973–1974 oil embargo implicitly assumed unlimited supplies of cheap gasoline. The result of the embargo and subsequent fuel shortages has been a greater public sensitivity to the cost and availability of gasoline, manifested in the marketplace through a decrease in vehicle miles traveled and the use of more fuel-efficient automobiles. It is unexpected events such as this that make transportation forecasting and prediction so difficult.

Uncertainty can be associated with more than just the technical process of prediction. Uncertainty can be categorized according to the aspect of analysis that it will influence. Quade [1975] notes that this means:

> Uncertainty might be (a) *conceptual:* What precisely is the problem? (b) *factual:* What are the relevant facts associated with the alternatives and the current situation? (c) *predictive:* What changes in the situation are likely to occur before any decision can take effect? And what are the likely consequences and reactions to the alternatives between which a choice must be made? (d) *strategic:* What counteractions may be expected to be taken by opposing interests? (e) *ethical:* What should the goals be and which of the potential outcomes would be preferable in the light of those goals?

To answer these questions, and thereby deal with the uncertainties they represent, planners have adopted several different approaches, including:

1. Assume the useful life of the project or system under design to be less than its economic life. By doing this, the initial capital outlay will be expected to be recouped over a reduced period of time, or the project will not be undertaken.
2. Add a "risk premium" to the discount rate used in evaluation. Although quite arbitrary in nature, increasing the discount rate reduces the expected value of net benefits and requires larger expected future benefits for the project to be chosen.
3. Build flexibility into the design of the system or facility. Projects can be staged over time so that the completion of one phase of construction initiates a reexamination of the future and consideration of alternative strategies for completing the planned facility [Manheim, 1979].
4. Use scenario planning approaches to identify alternative futures and transportation needs, given different future circumstances. This approach usually requires the input of experts in different areas (e.g., energy, economic development, social and community values) to identify alternative scenarios of the future, defined along dimensions determined to be critical for influencing future transportation needs.
5. Undertake sensitivity analyses of the important variables in the evaluation (e.g., discount rate, value of time, and other uncertain costs or benefits) to judge how the results of evaluation vary with changes in important input parameters.
6. Use decision theory techniques (e.g., decision flow diagrams, expected monetary value approaches, and game simulation) which employ probability distributions of events occurring to incorporate uncertainty into analysis [Raiffa, 1968; Schlaifer, 1968].

Most of these approaches focus on sensitizing technical analysis procedures to the concept of uncertainty. Two of the approaches—scenario building and plan and/or program flexibility—incorporate concerns over uncertainty into the planning process itself and into the product of that process. Because these approaches are generally absent from most other references, an example of each is provided here.

The use of scenarios in transportation planning was shown in the Milwaukee transit analysis case in Sec. 6-2. Another example of scenario building is provided by a "futures" conference held in Chicago in 1976 to identify alternative scenarios of the future socioeconomic environment of the region. The final report of this conference stated [Chicago Area Transportation Study, 1976]:

> Traditionally, planning has approached the uncertainty of the future by attempting to develop and apply increasingly more precise forecasting procedures. Beginning with extensive data collection efforts to describe existing relationships salient to transportation, predictive tools have been calibrated and applied to forecasting both point estimates of future characteristics of the region and precise values of the performance and impacts of proposed transportation alternatives. While there has always been an implicit recognition of the possibility of errors in these point estimates of the future, we face today an increasing need to accommodate this uncertainty explicitly. This is principally because of the wide— and relatively unanticipated—shifts in several key factors directly affecting transportation and other important elements of our society. These variables include energy price and availability, the state of the economy, the availability of public funds and social and institutional constraints on the development and application of technology.

The Year 2000 Alternative Transportation Futures Conference . . . abandons the attempt to develop the transportation plan best suited to meet the demands of the most likely or most desirable future. Instead, attempts are made to develop the most robust (i.e., adaptable) transportation plan capable of accommodating the range of possible futures. The objective of the conference was to define the range of possible futures in order to provide a basis for generating and evaluating transportation alternatives.

More than 100 individuals, each an expert in a relevant field, participated in this 1-day conference. Workshops were formed to identify important variables and to define ranges of values for these variables. The results of these workshops were then used in workshops focused exclusively on the definition of three future scenarios—an energy-abundant future, one of energy scarcity, and a no-change energy future. The first workshops were divided into six major topics: energy, regional economy, technology, financial resources, regulatory directions, and societal attitudes and behavior.

As shown in Table 9-9, the three scenarios were defined along several dimensions and included estimates of the likely change of several key variables. The results were designed to play an important role in defining alternative plans, in providing input into demand estimation and performance testing, and in evaluating alternative plans. Most important, the effort of defining alternative futures and the subsequent impacts on the transportation system sensitized local planners and officials to the importance of explicitly recognizing uncertainty in the planning process.

Table 9-9 Alternative futures used in Chicago transportation planning

Dimension Variable	Energy availability themes†		
	Abundant	Intermediate	Scarce
Energy			
A. Availability (petroleum)	130%	100%	75%
B. Price (petroleum)	100%	200%	400%
C. % use of nonpetroleum fuels (share of total fuel usage)	3%*	10%*	20%*
Regional economy			
A. Regional employment	120%	120%	106+%
B. Regional population	130%	115%	115%
C. Annual growth rate— gross regional product	110%	105%	100%
D. Service sector % total employment	120%	120%	Increase
E. Travel to fixed place of work	100%	90%	100%
F. Price of goods and services relative to income	105%	. . .	125%
G. (*a*) Level of per capita personal income	Decrease	150%	
(*b*) Level of per capita disposable income	Decrease	120%	

Table 9-9 (continued)

Dimension Variable	Energy availability themes†		
	Abundant	Intermediate	Scarce
Technology			
A. Communications as a substitute for travel	100%	104%	115%
B. Movement of goods by nonhighway or rail modes	. . .	150%	
C. Technological improvements to reduce environmental effects of highway vehicles	Increase	. . .	120%
D. Energy efficiency of highway vehicles	120%	150%(120%)‡	150%
E. Transit ridership changes due to technological improvement	100%(110–115%)	105%	115%
Financial resources			
A. Public funds for transportation 1976 $ (all modes)	80%(200%)	150%	200%(80%)
B. Public funds for highways 1976 $ (share of total public transport funds)	40%*	25%(30%)*	20%*
C. Public funds for mass transit 1976 $ (share of total public transport funds)	25%(50%)*	55%(60%)*	60%*
D. Public funds for air transport 1976 $ (share of total public transport funds)	15%(1%)*	5%(10%)*	8%*
E. Public funds for freight transport 1976 $ (share of total public transport funds)	20%(9)*	15%(10%)*	12%*
F. Funds derived from user charges	Increase		
Regulatory directions			
A. Regulation of project processing	150%	125%	200%
B. Regulation of interregional transport	100%	Some nationalization	75%
C. Regulation of urban area transport	Increase	Increase TSM	Transit—75%§ Auto—200%§
D. Local involvement in regulation	Limited metro government	100%	100%

Table 9-9 (continued)

Dimension Variable	Energy availability themes†		
	Abundant	Intermediate	Scarce
Societal attitudes and behavior			
A. Acceptance of high density			
(a) City	100%	125% (100, 150%)	100%
(b) Near suburbs	110% (80%)	100%(120%)	125%
(c) Far suburbs	150%	100%(150%)	150%
B. Acceptance of public transportation			
(a) Work trips	80%	140%	200%
(b) Nonwork trips	100%	150%(110,125,200%)	150%
C. Perception of crime on public transportation			
(a) Peak hours	100%	75%	80%
(b) Off-peak hours	200%	100%	70%
D. Societal polarization	120%	100%	120%
E. Ability of government to control land use—acceptance of constraints to preserve the environment and conserve resources	(100%) (increased)	200% (225%)	150%
F. Average trip length			
(a) Work trips—time	100%	90%	
(b) Work trips—distance	150% (120)%¶	80%	85%
(c) Nonwork trips—time	100%	80%	Largely reflects distance¶
(d) Nonwork trips—distance	150%	80%	

†Percentages are relative to the present value of each variable (i.e., 75% means a 25% decrease; 100% means no change; 125% means a 25% increase). Exceptions are indicated by asterisks (*).
‡Numbers in parentheses indicate minority opinions.
§Workshop divided regulation of urban area transport into two variables.
¶Several multicategory variables were collapsed into a single minority or majority forecast.
Source: Chicago Area Transportation Study [1976].

The second approach for recognizing uncertainty, program and/or plan flexibility, requires a systematic investigation of alternative strategies for system development over the long term and consideration of short-term actions that do not foreclose future options. A good example of this approach is a policy developed by the U.S. Department of Transportation in 1976 to guide investment in major urban mass transportation projects [Urban Mass Transportation Administration, 1976]. In this policy statement, federal officials encouraged the concept of "incremental development" whereby initial segments of system improvement would occur only in those corridors in which the need was justified in the short term. Other corridors were to receive improvements appropriate to their needs, with the level of service being progressively upgraded as demand developed. The purpose of this approach was "to ensure that high priority corridors receive initial attention; that appropriate balance is maintained between the transportation requirements of the entire region and those of local communities within the region, and between long range and short range needs for transportation improvements; that flexibility is preserved to respond to changing technology, land use patterns and growth objectives; and that the fiscal burden is spread over a long period of time." An example of this incremental development approach might be the construction of a fixed guideway rail in corridor 1, a detailed study of rail transit and implementation of temporary exclusive bus lanes in corridor 2, express bus on freeway in corridor 3, and minor bus service changes in corridor 4.

9-4 COMPARATIVE ASSESSMENT METHODS

The previous discussion has explored some of the important characteristics of evaluation and identified one of the important trade-offs that must be taken into account in the evaluation process—present expenditures in exchange for future benefits. In this section, two types of comparative assessment methods are discussed, one relating to a single objective of maximizing net monetary benefit and the other incorporating multiple objectives into the assessment method.

9-4-1 Single Objective Assessment Methods

Much of the comparative assessment that has occurred in transportation planning has reduced the benefits and costs of alternatives to monetary terms and then determined which alternative provided the most net benefit. Planners have used four major methods to compare alternatives on such a commensurate basis [Shupe, 1980].

1. *Present worth method.* Using the discount rate, convert the costs and benefits for each alternative to its equivalent present value and then compare these present values.
2. *Annual cost method.* Using the discount rate, determine the average annual cost for each alternative and then compare these annual costs.
3. *Benefit/cost method.* Using the discount rate, and separating costs from benefits, convert the case flows to their equivalent annual (or present) values and compare the equivalent benefits to the equivalent cost for each alternative. A benefit to cost ratio is determined for each alternative.
4. *Return-on-investment method.* Find the interest rate that balances present and future cash flows and compare it to a minimum attractive return rate determined before the evaluation.

The use of these methods can be illustrated with the example time stream of benefits and costs shown in Fig. 9-7. The costs represent the capital costs for construc-

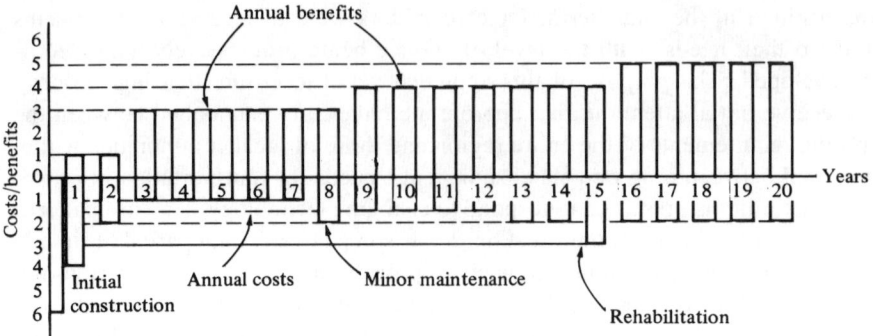

Figure 9-7 Time stream of benefits and costs for a hypothetical project.

tion, continuing costs of operation and maintenance, capital costs for vehicles and terminals, and user costs; while the benefits represent user and nonuser benefits. (A good discussion of how benefits and costs can be calculated for different types of alternative investment strategies can be found in Stopher and Meyburg [1976].)

For the present worth method, the present value of benefits and costs is equal to the summation of the value of these impacts multiplied by the present worth factor appropriate to the period over which the effects occur. The net present value of an alternative equals the difference between the present value benefits and present value costs. In mathematical terms,

$$\text{NPV}_r = \sum_{t=0}^{n} (\text{pwf}_{r,t})(\text{benefits}_{y,t}) - \sum_{t=0}^{n} (\text{pwf}_{r,t})(\text{costs}_{y,t}) \qquad (9\text{-}5)$$

where
NPV_r = net present value with discount rate r

$\text{pwf}_{r,t}$ = present worth factor with discount rate r and time t

$\text{benefits}_{y,t}$ = benefits of project y in time period t

$\text{costs}_{y,t}$ = costs of project y in time period t

n = economic life of project y

By applying Eq. (9-5) to the time stream of benefits and costs shown in Fig. 9-7, it can be shown that the net present value of the project with a discount rate of 10 percent is $26.149 − $21.208 = +$4.941 million.

In the annual cost method, the discounted costs are summed and multiplied by the appropriate capital recovery factor. In the case above, the summation of the discounted costs is equal to $21.208 million, and the capital recovery factor for a 20-year time period at a discount rate of 10 percent is 0.1175. The equivalent annual cost for the project is thus ($21.208) (0.1175) = $2.492 million.

The benefit/cost (B/C) method simply uses the total discounted benefits and costs to develop a ratio of benefits over costs. If the alternative has a B/C ratio of less than 1.0, it is a likely candidate for rejection. (Once again, the ultimate decision for rejection rests with the decision makers; the B/C measure is simply an indication of efficient use of resources.) In the above case, the total discounted benefits were equal to $26.149 million, and the total discounted costs equaled $21.208 million. The ratio of benefits to costs for this alternative is thus $26.149/$21.208 = 1.23.

Finally, the rate of return method determines the discount rate at which the present value of both the present and future cost will equal the present value of both the present and future benefits. In mathematical terms, we are trying to determine the discount rate r in which

$$\sum_{t=0}^{n} (\text{pwf}_{r,t})(\text{costs}_{y,t}) = \sum_{t=0}^{n} (\text{pwf}_{r,t})(\text{benefits}_{y,t}) \qquad (9\text{-}6)$$

where the terms are the same as in Eq. 9-6. Unfortunately, the process of determining the discount rate involves an iterative procedure which, unless performed on computer, is quite tedious. When the discount rate is identified from this process, it can be compared to a predefined acceptable rate of return. If the rate of return from the alternative is greater than this acceptable rate, the project can be considered desirable. In the above example, the rate of return for the project is just over 15 percent, which says that if the required rate of return has been set less than or equal to 15 percent by decision makers, this project would be desirable.

In the above examples, the four major methods used in comparative assessment have been used to evaluate the utilization of resources and benefits gained for one project. In practice, of course, planners must use these methods to determine the worth of alternatives relative to one another. In such instances, each method has its strengths and weaknesses. The annual cost method provides the smallest amount of information to decision makers in that the benefits associated with each alternative are not explicitly considered in the assessment. The net present value and rate of return methods will often produce the same recommended alternative, if the same project life cycle is assumed for each. However, the rate of return method has associated with it serious computational problems and the chance of producing ambiguous results.[1]

The benefit/cost method must be used with each successive pair of projects and the "do-nothing" alternative such that the B/C assessment between alternatives 1 and 2 is

$$\text{B/C}_{1,2} = \frac{B_1 - B_2}{C_1 - C_2} \qquad (9\text{-}7)$$

which must be greater than 1.0 if alternative 1 is preferred over alternative 2. To avoid inconsistencies in this assessment, the higher-cost alternative should always be compared to the lower-cost alternative [i.e., the higher-cost alternative in Eq. (9-7) is alternative 1]. The best alternative is the one with the highest cost, which has a B/C ratio greater than 1.0, and whose B/C ratios with all lower-cost alternatives are also greater than 1.0. As stated previously, benefits are usually considered as the reduction

---

[1] This is because Eq. (9-6) assumes that the interest rate of reinvestment of funds is the internal rate of return r. In general, this will not be the case, meaning a straightforward application of Eq. (9-6) can lead to results which are not consistent with those which would be obtained by one of the other methods. Equation (9-6) can be modified to correct this inconsistency, but this further complicates the calculations required.

in user costs; thus Eq. (9-7) should not be construed as meaning that the benefits of the two alternatives can be assessed separately. In practice, Eq. (9-7) is applied as the ratio of the change in user costs to the change in system costs for the two alternatives.

The use of Eq. (9-7) is shown in Fig. 9-8. The first part of this figure shows the present value of all costs (in millions) associated with five alternatives. In this simple case, the user costs of the do-nothing alternative are quite high because of increased travel time delays which would result if no improvements are made. The second part of Fig. 9-8 presents the first benefit/cost assessment, which indicates that all of the alternatives, when compared to the do-nothing alternative, would be justified on economic grounds. It now becomes necessary to compare each alternative with the other to determine which one provides the greatest return for the dollars expended. Such an assessment is shown in the third part of Fig. 9-8, in which each alternative is compared with all other lower capital cost alternatives, leading to the identification of alternative number 3 as the "best" alternative in benefit/cost terms.

Although the benefit/cost method has seen extensive use in transportation planning, there are serious problems with it. In many cases, the benefit/cost ratio is ambiguous and can generate information that is based on arbitrary definitions of cost and benefits. Also, it is difficult to judge the significance of two benefit/cost comparisons that produce ratios marginally different from one another.

Each of the above comparative assessment methods is in use today. Even though one might be more appropriate than another in a given situation, in general, the net present value method provides the most useful information to decision makers and is thus recommended for use in efficiency evaluation [AASHTO, 1977; Wohl, 1979]. Of course, each of these methods suffers from the problem of assigning a monetary value to the benefits and cost of the alternatives under consideration. For this reason, we once again emphasize a point made earlier—*comparative assessment must take place within the overall context of a cost effectiveness evaluation framework.*[2]

9-4-2 Multiobjective Assessment Methods

The methods discussed above have one major characteristic in common; that is, the many dimensions of a transportation problem are reduced to dollar terms so that a single objective—maximization of net benefits—can be attained. As has been stated throughout this book, however, the transportation planning process includes many different objectives, reflecting the role of wide-ranging interests in the decision-making process. Thus, while the methods that seek to maximize net benefits can provide useful information to the planning process, they do not systematically incorporate multiple, often conflicting, objectives into the assessment process.

Several assessment methods have been developed which attempt to assess the relative importance of projects or plans based on multiobjective analysis. One of these

---

[2] A detailed discussion on the use and advantages and disadvantages of economic evaluation methods is beyond the scope of this book. Such discussion is found elsewhere [Wohl and Martin, 1967; de Neufville and Stafford, 1971; Stopher and Meyburg, 1976; Shupe, 1980].

	Present value of costs, $ millions		
Alternative	User cost	Operating and maintenance	Capital
0 do nothing	250	150	3
1	150	170	10
2	200	175	12
3	125	125	20
4	110	130	35

(a)

	B/C comparison with "do nothing"		
Alternative	Change in user, O&M costs	Change in capital costs	B/C ratio
0			
1	80	7	11.4
2	25	9	2.8
3	150	17	8.8
4	160	32	5.0

(b)

			B/C ratios in comparing alternatives		
Alternative	User + O&M costs	Cap. costs	Alt. 2	Alt. 3	Alt. 4
1	320	10	$-\$55/2 = -27.5$ (no benefit)	$70/10 = 7.0$	$80/25 = 3.2$
2	375	12	. . .	$125/8 = 15.6$	$135/23 = 5.9$
3	250	20	. . .		$10/15 = 0.7$
4	240	35			

(c)

Alternative 2 is not justified because it shows no benefit over alternative 1. Alternative 3 is possibly justified because it dominates alternatives 1 and 2. Alternative 4 also dominates alternatives 1 and 2 but has a B/C ratio with alternative 3 of less than 1. Therefore, alternative 3 is the best alternative based on economic efficiency. Note that the alternative with the highest B/C ratio when compared with the do-nothing alternative did not result in the best alternative.

Figure 9-8 Example benefit/cost assessment.

methods, similar to the evaluation framework shown in Fig. 9-2, is called the goals-achievement matrix [Hill, 1973]. The goals-achievement matrix assigns relative weights to each objective and evaluation group, the weighted indices of goals achievement are then summed, and the preferred plan is the one with the largest benefits to costs comparison. The benefits and costs are always defined in terms of goal achievement. If measured in quantitative units, the benefits and costs for each objective should be defined in the same units.

A modification to this goals-achievement matrix involves the use of a simple assessment scale to determine whether goal attainment is enhanced ($+1$), decreased (-1), or if there is no effect (0). The weights of individual objectives and their incidence can be introduced, and an overall index for each plan can be determined.

One of the appealing aspects of the goals-achievement approach is that the planner is able to determine how particular community groups will be impacted by proposed alternatives. The weights associated with these groups also indicate how each community perceives different objectives. Another major advantage of the goals-achievement approach is that it permits the determination of the extent to which threshold values or standards are being met [Hill, 1973]:

> By determining how various objectives will be affected by proposed plans the goals-achievement matrix can determine the extent to which certain specified standards are being met. Is the transportation plan likely to meet minimum accessibility requirements and minimum standards of comfort and convenience? Are the levels of air pollution and noise likely to exceed specified standards? . . . These are the types of questions that the goals achievement matrix is designed to answer.

The major drawback of this assessment approach is that even though the weights associated with the objectives of the community group are supposed to be objectively determined, there is no unambiguous way to do this. If the weights do not reflect the true preference of these groups, this approach is not very helpful. One of the other problems with the goals-achievement approach is the aggregation of the costs and benefits across objectives to derive a weighted index.

Another type of multiobjective assessment method is based on expected utility theory and is arguably the most widely accepted formal methodology used in the analysis of decisions in an uncertain environment [Raiffa, 1968; Keeney and Raiffa, 1976]. The basis of this method is the multiattribute utility function which assigns a unique value to any combination of levels for the various dimensions of the impacts. The concept of a multiattribute utility function is similar to the utility function discussed in Chap. 7 with regard to demand analysis. The utility for a specific alternative is thus a function of the utilities of the various attribute levels associated with the alternative. For example, in some cases, the utility of an impact can be expressed in the following forms:

$$U(X) = \sum_i K_i U_i(X_i) \qquad (9\text{-}8)$$

where $U(X)$ = overall utility for impact X

K_i = scaling factors

$U_i(Xi)$ = single dimensional utility over attribute X_i

The problem for the planner is to establish the functional form of the utility functions over each dimension and the scaling factors of the overall function.

One example of the use of such functions is the evaluation of a new airport for Mexico City [Keeney and Raiffa, 1976]. In this case, six objectives were identified as being important to the analysis: (1) minimize total construction and maintenance costs, (2) provide adequate capacity to meet air traffic demands, (3) minimize access time to the airport, (4) maximize safety of the system, (5) minimize social disruption of a new airport, and (6) minimize effects of noise pollution due to air traffic. Measures of effectiveness were developed for each objective, and interviews with key decision makers were used to identify characteristics of the utility function associated with each measure (e.g., at what point were decision makers indifferent as to the direction and magnitude of the measure of effectiveness). After determining the parameters of the overall utility function (which was found to be the product of the individual utility functions) the expected utility for specified alternatives was determined, and a listing was developed showing the best solutions based on the decision makers' own judgment of how important the evaluation criteria were.[3]

Although potentially more valid from the perspective of representing true preferences, the multiattribute utility method presents significant computational and conceptual problems. For example, the specification of the utility functions will greatly influence the results of the assessment. However, it is possible that further research in this area could result in important and easy-to-use assessment methods.

A final example of multiobjective assessment methodology is the result of recent advances in computer technology. Microcomputers and interactive graphics have provided planners with a powerful tool for assessing the consequences of alternatives. By changing the weights associated with certain objectives, or specifying alternative threshold values, the planner can quickly identify the most desirable set of consequences. For example, one interactive computer planning approach focuses on the design of transit route networks in an urban area. The planner in this instance can input data on hourly driver cost, operating costs, and the values of transfer and wait time. The computer then produces the network design that achieves a specified objective (e.g., minimize costs) [Andreasson, 1977].

With further advances in computer technology, the ability of the planner to illustrate to decision makers the desirability of alternatives under different conditions will be greatly enhanced. The microcomputer will most likely have an important role to play in such assessments. These tools, however, must be used very carefully, since the validity of the assessment results is dependent upon the explicit and implicit assumptions incorporated into the algorithms which produce the results.

---

[3] Where either the determination of a well-behaved utility function requires too much effort or the assumptions underlying such a determination are too restrictive, another class of method, based on outranking relations, may be appropriate. These methods, known as ELECTRE, have recently been applied to the assessment of possible subway line extensions in Paris [Roy and Hugonnard, 1982]. The attributes considered most important in the evaluation were (1) population and jobs served per kilometer of line, (2) passenger volumes entering new stations per kilometer of line, (3) capital cost per kilometer of line, (4) internal rate of return, (5) impact on the organization of public transit, and (6) impact on the urban area.

9-5 EVALUATION OF ALTERNATIVE TRANSIT SYSTEM CONFIGURATIONS: THE SOUTHEASTERN WISCONSIN EXAMPLE

In 1979, the Southeastern Wisconsin Regional Planning Commission (SEWRPC) undertook a study to (1) identify the travel corridors within the greater Milwaukee area that could support fixed guideway transit facility development and (2) identify the transit modes that could best provide service within those corridors. Because this effort illustrates many of the concepts of evaluation discussed earlier, the planning process used by SEWRPC officials will be described here in detail.

The overall planning process for the SEWRPC study, shown in Fig. 9-9, was based on the alternative futures approach discussed in Sec. 9-3-4. The reason for choosing this approach was stated as follows [SEWRPC, 1980]:

> The purpose of this approach is to permit the evaluation of the performance of alternative systems plans over a variety of possible future conditions in order to identify those alternatives that perform well under a wide range of conditions. . . . In this way, "robust" system plans that can be expected to remain viable under greatly varying future conditions can be identified.

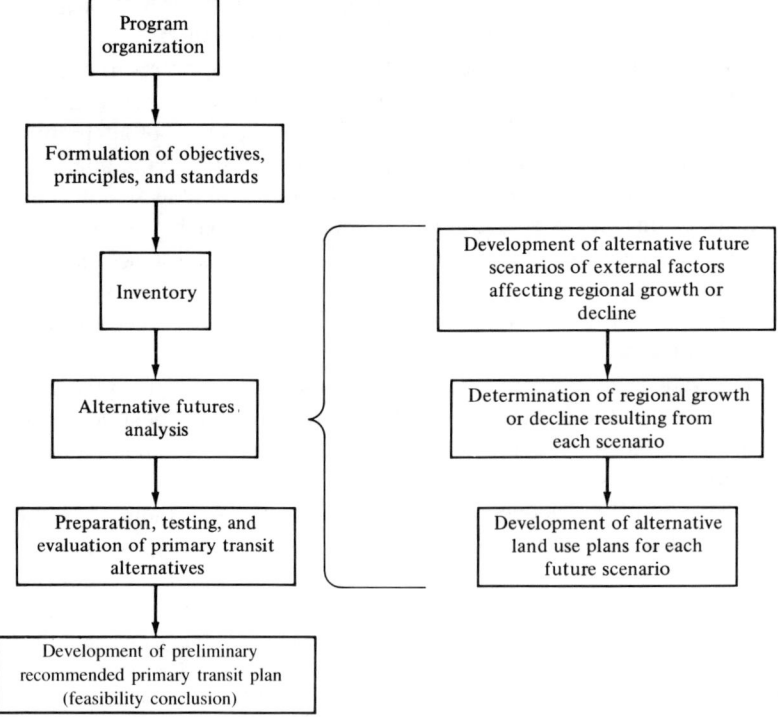

Figure 9-9 The Milwaukee area transit system alternatives analysis planning process. (*Southeastern Wisconsin Regional Planning Commission [1982].*)

The use of alternative futures represented a recognition that future conditions—such as price and availability of fuel, automobile technology, economic growth, lifestyles, and population distribution—will strongly influence the performance of the transit system. Four alternative futures were postulated in the study, and the "best" transit plan for each scenario was then developed. The final recommended system plan consisted of those elements of the alternative future plans that the analysis and evaluation indicated would perform well under varying alternative future scenarios. Those elements of alternative future plans that were unique to specific plans and not deemed critical to system effectiveness were left for future consideration, when economic and technological conditions would become more certain (see Fig. 9-10a).

The process of developing and testing the best primary transit system plan for each alternative future consisted of five major steps (see Fig. 9-10b). The first step was to design the most extensive transit network possible for each transit alternative considered. Seven major transit technologies were initially considered, including bus operation in mixed freeway traffic (the do-nothing alternative), bus operation in mixed traffic on operationally controlled freeways, bus operation on reserved freeway lanes, bus operation on busways, commuter-rail transit, rail transit, and heavy-rail transit. Three networks were examined in the analysis, serving all identified major corridors of transit demand: one for bus-on-freeway, one for commuter rail, and one for fixed guideway alternatives (i.e., light rail, heavy rail, and busway). The initial identification of maximum extent networks was heavily influenced by estimates of corridor travel demand and the availability of rights-of-way.

The second step in this planning process involved refining the initial networks to the level of specific alignments for each type of guideway technology under consideration. Four factors were considered in selecting preferred alignments: construction cost, community disruption, travel time advantage, and number of residences and jobs served.

The third and fourth steps in the process concerned the preparation and testing of system plans for each primary technology under each alternative future. The best plan for each alternative future was selected, and the overall plan for the system was chosen from the elements of these alternative future plans in step 5 of the planning process. Because these last three steps are directly concerned with evaluation, they will be discussed in greater detail below.

The evaluation of the system plans for each alternative future was limited to measures of transit ridership, cost, and cost-effectiveness. Estimates of transit ridership were obtained through the use of travel forecasting models based on the trip generation, trip distribution, mode split, and trip assignment approach discussed in Chap. 7. Estimates of capital and operating costs were developed by applying average unit prices to each alternative. The system designs were considered cost-effective if the total cost per passenger approximated that of the base plan (i.e., the do-nothing alternative) and if the individual transit routes, and the system as a whole, recovered at least 50 percent of estimated design-year operating and maintenance costs from farebox revenues.

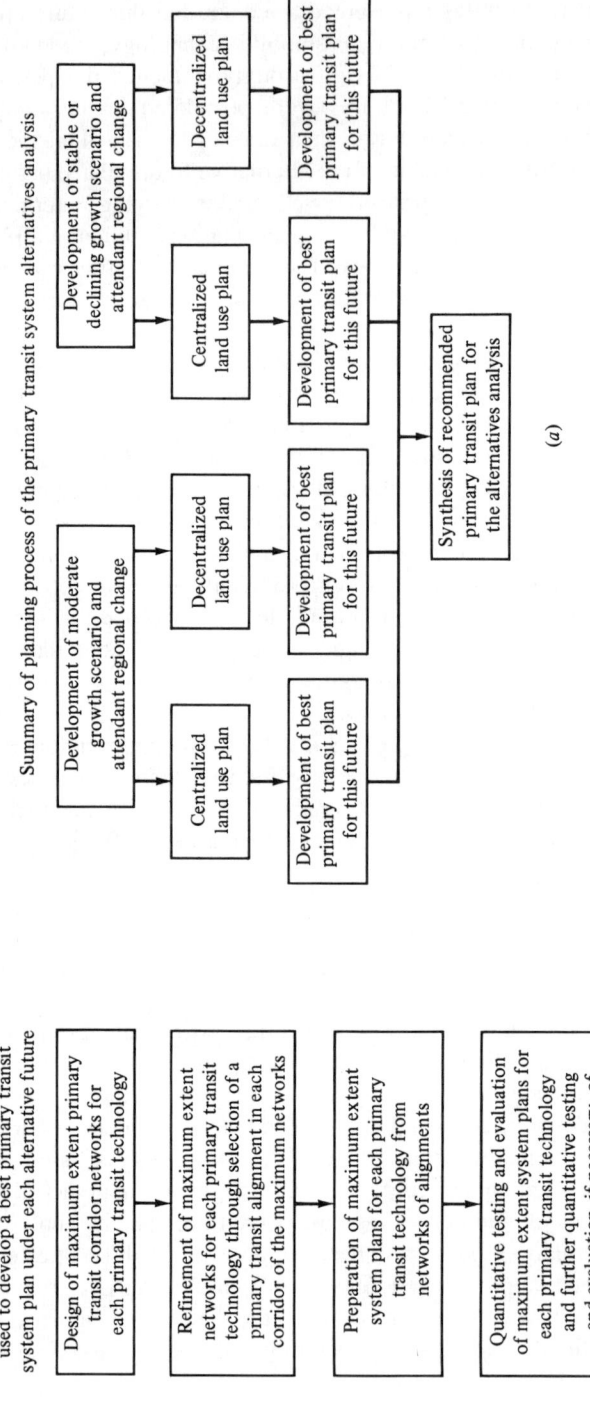

Figure 9-10 Subcomponents of the Milwaukee alternatives analysis process. (*Southeastern Wisconsin Regional Planning Commission [1982]*.)

A total of 21 plans were tested and evaluated under the conditions of each alternative future scenario. The elements of the plans not meeting the above tests for cost-effectiveness were eliminated from further consideration (e.g., bus routes not recovering 50 percent of the cost), and the resulting "truncated" plans were then reevaluated under each alternative future. This second evaluation was more comprehensive in that the measures of effectiveness included transit system cost and ridership, accessibility, level of service, energy consumption, air pollution, and community disruption. Other intangible impacts included the potential for public transit to influence land development and redevelopment, the potential for continued and expanded public transit operation during a severe petroleum energy shortage, the potential for public transit to reduce localized environmental impacts of public transit, the potential for public transit to increase the reliability and safety of public transit operations, and rider preference for rail/transit service over bus/transit service (see Table 9-10).

The results of the evaluation process showed that three system plans—bus-on-metered-freeway, bus-on-busway, and light-rail transit—would perform equally well under a wide range of conditions. The only significant measurable difference between

Table 9-10 Summary of intangible benefits in Milwaukee transit plans

	Rapid-transit mode		
Benefit or consideration	Light-rail transit	Bus way	Commuter rail
Intangible benefits			
Ability to influence land development and redevelopment	●	○	○
Continued operation during severe petroleum shortage	●		
Reduce localized adverse environmental impacts	●		
Increased public transit reliability	●	●	●
Increased public transit safety	●	○	●
Rider preference	○		○
Other subjective considerations			
Operation during labor disruptions	○		○
Importance in light of possible deferred highway maintenance	●	●	●
Operation during widespread emergency situations	○	●	○
Local climatic conditions	●	○	○
Usefulness with respect to long-range advances in transit technology	○	○	
Impact of current land use decentralization trends	○	○	
Probability of implementation	○	○	○

Legend
● Benefit or consideration appears to definitely support this transit mode.
○ Benefit or consideration may support this transit mode.
Source: Southeastern Wisconsin Regional Planning Commission [1982].

these three alternatives was the capital cost incurred in their implementation. The bus-on-metered-freeway was found to be the least expensive alternative under each of the four alternative futures. The bus-on-busway was estimated to cost between 14 and 19 percent more, and the light-rail plan, between 25 and 30 percent more. However, it was also determined that the two fixed guideway alternatives would probably have a greater, although uncertain and unmeasurable, potential to influence land development and would provide a more reliable and safer public transit system. Because of its high passenger-carrying capacity, light rail was also considered to have greater usefulness in labor disruptions and fuel shortages, an advantage with respect to operation in a cold climate, and flexibility in responding to new transportation technologies. The bus-on-metered-freeway alternative was found to have one major intangible advantage—greater flexibility for responding to geographically widespread system disruptions (e.g., due to natural disaster).

Based on this assessment, SEWRPC planners recommended two options to decision makers (see Table 9-11). The first option was the implementation of the bus-on-metered-freeway alternative. The second option included implementation of a basic bus-on-metered-freeway system plan along with a light-rail facility in one corridor (the tier 1 program). The bus-on-metered-freeway facilities recommended for implementation in other corridors where light rail or commuter rail were considered feasible under certain future conditions could be modified to allow eventual upgrading to light-rail operation. Light-rail and commuter-rail facilities (tier 2) would not be implemented unless future conditions warranted such an action or unless the initial light-rail facility demonstrated significant impact in terms of the previously discussed intangible benefits.

To supplement the information shown in Table 9-11, SEWRPC planners conducted a benefit and cost analysis to demonstrate the economic value of the alternative system plans. The direct benefits assumed included reductions in the cost of automobile ownership and operation, in the cost of travel time, and in accidents. The direct costs included were capital, operating, and maintenance costs to public agencies. As shown in Table 9-12, this benefit/cost analysis indicated that the bus-on-metered-freeway alternative would provide the best investment based on this criterion.

There are several characteristics of the SEWRPC planning process that closely reflect the proposed model of planning and evaluation outlined in this text. First, SEWRPC planners explicitly addressed the issue of uncertainty by using the alternative futures concept. By examining the performance of alternative system configurations under different assumed future conditions, the planners were able to identify specific projects that could provide cost-effective service under future circumstances.

Second, a screening process was used to determine which alternatives were not feasible given certain constraints. This process, which produced the set of maximum extent network plans for each alternative future, was based on a small set of evaluation criteria, the most important being a determination of cost-effectiveness and a 50 percent recovery of costs. Because planners conducted this screening process, important financial and personnel resources were not wasted on detailed evaluations of alternatives that had a small likelihood of implementation.

Table 9-11 Overall evaluation matrix for Milwaukee transit plans

	Alternative							
	Base plan		Bus-on-metered-freeway plan				Lower tier of the two-tier system plan	
Evaluative measure	Optimistic scenario Moderate growth—centralized land use plan	Pessimistic scenario Stable or declining growth—decentralized land use plan	Optimistic scenario Moderate growth—centralized land use plan	Pessimistic scenario Stable or declining growth—decentralized land use plan			Optimistic scenario Moderate growth—centralized land use plan	Pessimistic scenario Stable or declining growth—decentralized land use plan
Objective no. 1—*serve land use*								
Accessibility								
Average overall travel time of transit trips to the Milwaukee central business district, minutes	35	35	34	34			34	34
Objective no. 2—*minimize cost and energy use*								
Cost								
Total public cost to design year (capital cost and operating and maintenance deficit)	$579,742,000	$483,703,200	$722,873,900	$567,488,900			$812,880,000	$819,931,500
Average annual total public cost	27,606,600	23,033,500	34,422,600	27,023,100			38,706,600	29,520,500
Capital cost								
Capital cost to design year	148,840,000	107,761,000	214,323,900	160,906,900			306,300,000	217,931,500
Average annual capital cost	7,087,600	5,131,500	10,205,900	7,662,200			14,585,700	10,377,700
Capital investment to design year	233,328,700	161,597,700	329,729,600	229,867,300			470,700,000	364,526,300
Average annual capital investment	11,110,900	7,695,100	15,701,400	10,946,000			22,414,300	17,358,400
Operating and maintenance deficit (net cost)								
Deficit in design year	23,198,300	16,328,700	32,904,700	20,158,500			32,658,400	19,481,200
Deficit to design year	430,900,000	375,942,200	508,550,000	406,580,000			506,580,000	402,000,000
Average annual deficit	20,519,000	17,902,000	24,216,700	19,360,900			24,122,900	19,142,900
Cost-effectiveness								
Total public cost to design year per passenger	0.39	0.43	0.46	0.50			0.52	0.54
Capital cost to design year per passenger	0.10	0.10	0.14	0.14			0.20	0.19
Operating deficit to design year per passenger	0.29	0.33	0.32	0.36			0.32	0.35
Total public cost to design year per passenger mile	0.10	0.11	0.09	0.12			0.10	0.13
Capital cost to design year per passenger mile	0.03	0.03	0.03	0.03			0.04	0.05
Operating deficit to design year per passenger mile	0.07	0.08	0.06	0.09			0.06	0.08

Table 9-11 (*continued*)

	Alternative							
	Base plan		Bus-on-metered-freeway plan		Lower tier of the two-tier system plan			
Evaluative measure	Optimistic scenario Moderate growth—centralized land use plan	Pessimistic scenario Stable or declining growth—decentralized land use plan	Optimistic scenario Moderate growth—centralized land use plan	Pessimistic scenario Stable or declining growth—decentralized land use plan	Optimistic scenario Moderate growth—centralized land use plan	Pessimistic scenario Stable or declining growth—decentralized land use plan
Percent of operating and maintenance cost met by fare-box revenue in the design year						
Total transit system	62	53	61	52	61	52
Primary element	56	49	50	45	63	47
Energy						
Total transit system energy use to design year (million BTU)	20,278,020	15,037,280	22,305,100	16,120,900	23,213,700	16,551,300
Total transit construction energy use to design year (million BTU)	1,498,400	1,044,480	1,840,100	1,335,200	2,414,700	1,875,800
Total transit operating and maintenance energy use to design year (million BTU)	18,779,620	13,992,800	20,465,000	14,785,700	20,799,000	14,675,500
Total transit system energy use per passenger mile traveled to design year (BTU)	3,330	3,530	2,730	3,380	2,830	3,640
Total transit passenger miles per gallon of diesel fuel to design year (BTU)	40.9	38.5	49.8	40.1	48.1	39.4
Dependence on petroleum-based fuel	All trips dependent	All trips dependent	All trips dependent	All trips dependent	8 percent of transit trips not dependent	8 percent of transit trips not dependent
Petroleum-based fuel use by transit to design year (gallons of diesel fuel)	134,355,000	100,744,850	144,697,000	114,936,000	124,502,200	112,450,000
Automobile propulsion energy use in design year (gallons of gasoline)	404,800,000	338,400,000	395,200,000	332,800,000	395,200,000	332,800,000

Objective nos. 3 and 5—Provide appropriate service and quick travel						
Average weekday transit trips in design year						
Total transit system	326,800	169,400	371,300	176,000	372,900	176,300
Primary element	15,000	9,500	75,000	22,500	96,300	34,200
Percent of transit trips using primary element	4	6	20	12	26	19
Service coverage						
Population served within a one-half-mile walking distance of primary transit service	257,100	181,500	373,500	250,100	392,200	260,100
Population served within a three-mile driving distance of primary transit service	1,012,400	698,800	1,620,700	933,167	1,300,000	930,600
Jobs served within one-half-mile walking distance of primary transit service	237,000	194,600	293,600	253,100	309,300	250,200
Average speed of transit vehicle (mph)						
Primary element	19	24	29	27	29	27
Total system	14	15	18	17	18	17
Average speed of passenger travel on vehicle (mph)						
Primary element	25	25	34	32	32	30
Total system	15	15	20	18	21	19
Objective no. 4—minimize environmental impacts						
Community disruption						
Homes, businesses, or industries taken	None	None	None	None	None	None
Land required (acres)	12	10	70	20	120	80
Air pollutant emissions—total transportation system (highway and transit) in design year (tons per year)						
Carbon monoxide	171,200	165,800	167,400	163,100	167,300	163,100
Hydrocarbons	17,400	16,700	16,900	16,400	16,900	16,400
Nitrogen oxides	30,700	30,100	30,000	29,200	30,000	29,200
Sulfur oxides	2,500	2,400	2,500	2,400	2,600	2,400
Particulates	4,100	4,000	4,000	3,900	4,000	3,900
Objective no. 6—maximize safety						
Proportion of total person trips made on transit	0.074	0.047	0.064	0.060	0.084	0.050

Source: Southeastern Wisconsin Regional Planning Commission [1982].

Table 9-12 Benefit/cost estimation for Milwaukee transit plans

Alternative plan		Costs: 1980-2000				Benefit-cost ratio
Land use plan	Transit plan	Discount rate, percent	Transit system user	Capital, operating, and maintenance	Benefits*	Cost†	
Moderate growth centralized land use plan	Base plan	6 10	$1,317,414,000 932,992,000	$333,200,000 208,700,000			
	Bus-on-metered-freeway plan	6 10	1,202,062,000 866,230,000	400,200,000 289,600,000	115,352,000 66,762,000	67,000,000 80,900,000	1.72 0.83
	Two-tier plan	6 10	1,197,637,000 863,669,000	427,600,000 308,600,000	119,777,000 69,323,000	94,400,000 99,900,000	1.27 0.69
Stable or declining growth—decentralized land use plan	Base plan	6 10	1,032,113,000 767,869,000	268,500,000 199,500,000			
	Bus-on-metered-freeway plan	6 10	987,317,000 741,942,000	313,000,000 235,200,000	44,796,000 25,927,000	44,500,000 35,700,000	1.01 0.73
	Two-tier plan	6 10	983,259,000 739,594,000	345,200,000 266,800,000	48,854,000 28,275,000	76,700,000 67,300,000	0.64 0.42

*Benefits are defined as the difference—or "savings"—in transit system user costs resulting from the implementation of either the bus-on-metered-freeway-plan option or the two-tier-plan option instead of the base plan under the appropriate alternative future.
†Costs are defined as the difference—or "additional capital and operating expense"—incurred because of the implementation of either the bus-on-metered-freeway-plan option or the two-tier-plan option instead of the base plan under the appropriate alternative future.

Source: Southeastern Wisconsin Regional Planning Commission [1982].

Third, the options presented to decision makers incorporated within them flexibility for implementing future projects or modifying existing ones. The two-tiered approach of the second option is a good example of this flexibility.

Fourth, the sensitivity of important variables to uncertainty is addressed not only in the use of alternative futures, but also in the different interest rates used in the benefit and cost analysis. By performing sensitivity analyses, planners could determine the impact on the recommended options of changes in key variables.

Fifth, the evaluation process was linked directly to community goals and objectives. Both the tangible and intangible measures of effectiveness were related to the major decision-maker concerns, as shown in the evaluation matrix in Table 9-11. To ensure that community and decision-maker concerns were reflected in the evaluation process, numerous public information meetings, a public hearing, and an advisory committee were used for public involvement opportunities.

Sixth, the benefit and cost assessment was used within an overall cost-effectiveness framework. The assessment was simply one more piece of information for decision makers. In fact, a technical report generated in the process noted that "such an assessment alone is not a conclusive measure of the relative value of primary transit alternatives, but should be viewed together with the results of the cost-effectiveness analysis" [SEWRPC, 1982].

Finally, and most important, the overall approach to the planning process was one of providing information to decision makers. Decision-maker concerns were explicitly incorporated into the evaluation criteria, and special analyses were undertaken in response to questions which decision makers had during the process. The result of planning was a set of information that could be used by decision makers to determine the best alternative from their perspective of maximizing community welfare.

Such a decision-oriented planning process at the regional level is not undertaken effectively without some cost. The process is dependent upon an analysis capability that can permit a broad examination of numerous issues. In the SEWRPC case, for example, many different alternative system configurations had to be simulated and the performance results interpreted. The process is also dependent on a close interaction between planners and decision makers which requires substantial staff time for meetings and presentations. Even with these costs, the results of the planning process, because of this close relationship to the decision-making process, become an important source of information to decision makers. Given the important trade-offs that are often necessary in such decisions and the need for cost-effective public investment, these planning costs are justified in most cases.

9-6 EVALUATION OF TRANSPORTATION CORRIDORS: THE BALTIMORE EXAMPLE[4]

As part of an extensive air quality–transportation planning effort, the Baltimore region was divided into a series of corridors which became the focus of site-specific analysis

---

[4] Another good example of corridor-level analysis can be found in Golenberg and Havard [1983].

of problems and opportunities that could be addressed with short-term TSM strategies [Samdahl, Reightler, and Lippman, 1983]. Six corridors, ranging from 7 miles to 20 miles in length, were selected for analysis. Each corridor study received technical guidance from a project management committee, consisting of technical staff from affected jurisdictions and state agencies. Numerous public meetings and public outreach activities provided affected communities with a chance to identify problems, opportunities, and potential actions and to provide feedback to planners on the actions being considered.

The first step in the corridor planning process was to identify a set of study goals and objectives. Given the nature of the studies, the goals, not surprisingly, were defined as reducing air pollution, reducing energy consumption, and improving the efficiency and productivity of the transportation system. Ten specific objectives were elected to operationalize these goals: reducing air pollutant emissions, reducing vehicle miles of travel, increasing transportation system productivity, reducing delay and travel time, reducing energy consumption, improving system safety, promoting desirable (and minimizing undesirable) social and economic impacts due to transportation improvements, spending funds in the most cost-effective manner, constructing projects which were compatible with one another, and implementing projects that would be positively received by local constituencies. From these 10 objectives, 27 measures of effectiveness (MOEs) were identified which formed the basis of the corridor evaluation process. For each action or combination (package) of actions, these 27 MOEs became the criteria for comparison (see Fig. 9-11).

Each action was then given a relative rating in each objective category and a priority level. Priority level 1 was assigned to those actions which favorably met the mobility, energy, and air quality objectives, had a good cost-effectiveness result, and were implementable. Priority level 2 included actions having negligible impacts on mobility, energy, and air quality but which met other objectives like improved safety. Priority level 3 was given to those actions not recommended for implementation. Table 9-13 illustrates the results of this assessment.

Once this assessment was undertaken for all of the actions and action packages, a recommended TSM strategy for each corridor was developed which identified specific actions, priorities, agency responsibilities, key costs, and environmental impact data (see Table 9-14). In the six corridors studied, 134 actions were recommended—representing an estimated total daily reduction of 25,800 gallons of gasoline, 735 kilograms of HC, 1460 kilograms of NO_x, 9390 kilograms of CO, 513,200 vehicle miles traveled, and costing $9.6 million to build with annual operating costs of $440,000.

As in the Milwaukee transit planning case, the Baltimore Corridor study illustrates quite well several of the characteristics of the planning and evaluation process proposed in this book. Interestingly, the Baltimore case shows an evaluation process oriented toward small-scale, operations types of improvements, and one not focusing on large-scale, capital intensive alternatives.

The first noteworthy characteristic of this Baltimore example is the scale of analysis. One of the key characteristics of analysis and evaluation noted in Chap. 5 was that the scale of analysis and evaluation must correspond to the types of problems and

Corridor: MD 2

TSM-TCP action: Provide intersection and traffic-flow improvements at MD 2 and College Parkway

Description of action:
Implement intersection improvements to include:
 Extending right turn lane merge (at MD 2 and College Parkway) from westbound College Parkway to northbound MD 2
 Extending double left turn lane from southbound MD 2 to eastbound College Parkway

In addition to the above:
 a) Coordinate signals at MD 2/College Parkway and College Parkway/Peninsula Farm Rd. to accommodate eastbound traffic*
 b) Coordinate signals at MD 2/College Parkway and College Parkway/Peninsula Farm Rd. to accommodate westbound traffic†

Air quality
1. Changes in HC (kg/day)   (a) − 2.9   (b) − 1.2†
2. Changes in NO$_x$ (kg/day)   (a) − 3.9   (b) − 1.0†
3. Changes in CO (kg/day)   (a) − 31.9   (b) − 13.4†

Energy
4. Changes in fuel consumption (gal/day)   (a) − 43.2   (b) − 15.8†

Transportation system productivity
5. Changes in VMT (veh. mi/day)   (a) Negligible   (b) Negligible
6. Changes in mode split   (a) No effect   (b) No effect
7. Changes in vehicle occupancy   (a) No effect   (b) No effect

Transportation system efficiency
8. Changes in travel time/speed   (a) Negligible   (b) Negligible
9. Changes in delay/level of service   (a) − 34.4 veh. h/day   (b) − 23.5 veh. h/day†
10. Changes in VHT (veh. h/day)   (a) − 34.4   (b) − 23.5†

Safety
11. Changes in system safety (a) and (b) Both options will reduce conflicts between through and turning traffic on MD 2. Negligible change on College Parkway.

Cost
12. Capital cost ($)   (a) $72,000   (b) $60,000†
13. Operating cost ($/yr)   (a) $1,600 (maintain interconnect)   (b) Negligible†
14. Total annualized cost ($/yr)   (a) $14,350   (b) $10,620†

Cost-effectiveness
15. Cost‡/emission change ($/kg)   HC $190.60
16.   NO$_x$ $190.60
17.   CO $ 17.30
18. Cost‡/fuel consumption changes ($/gal) $ 13.60
19. Cost‡/VMT change ($/veh. mi)   High
20. Cost‡/VHT change ($/veh. h) $10.60

Social and economic
21. Social impacts: Negligible
22. Economic impacts: Will improve accessibility to industrial parks on Patuxent Range Road.

Compatibility
23. Compatibility with other actions: Compatible with all actions, particularly Action #1.

Implementability
24. Likely public/political reaction: Expected to receive positive reaction from truckers. Other reaction should be minimal.
25. Implementation process: Include in state (SHA) capital program. Probably not a separate CIP project
26. Funding source(s): State (SHA); possible contribution from industrial park
27. Time required for implementation 1 to 2 years

Comments

*The analysis of the phasing at this intersection indicated that a separate southbound left turn phase is not necessary to accommodate this movement. At the same time, total intersection delay would increase if a separate phase were implemented.

†Coordination of this signal with Baltimore Street could feasibly be implemented along with Action #1, although this impact was not evaluated.

‡ = Total annualized cost.

Figure 9-11 Example display of impacts in Baltimore Corridor study. (*Samdahl, Reightler, and Lippman* [1983].)

Table 9-13 Comparative assessment of corridor actions

Action number	Location	TSM-TCP action	Measure of effectiveness										Priority level	Reason for priority level
			Air quality	Energy	Cost	Cost-effectiveness	Productivity	Efficiency	Safety	Social-Economic	Compatibility	Implementability		
1	MD 2/US 50/301	Improve signs and lane markings	O	O	+	+	O	+	++	O	+	+	1	Low cost; very good safety benefits; good compatibility with other actions
2a	MD 2/College Parkway	Provide intersection and traffic-flow improvements	+	+	−	O	O	+	+	O	+	+	1	Moderate air quality, energy savings, and cost-effectiveness; slight safety improvement; high capital cost
2b	MD 2/College Parkway	Provide intersection and traffic-flow improvements	+	+	−	−	O	+	+	O	+	+	3	Only slight air quality and energy savings; high cost and poor cost-effectiveness

3	Robinson/Benfield	Install traffic signal	−	−	○	−	○	++	+	+	+	2	In spite of negative air quality impacts, action offers very good safety benefits at a moderate cost.
4	MD 2/Robinson/ MD 648	Provide intersection improvements	+	○	○	−	○	+	++	○	+	+	2	Moderate air quality and energy improvements; good safety benefits; moderate cost
5	MD 2/Pasadena	Provide intersection improvements	+	○	○	○	○	+	+	○	+	+	2	Slight air quality and energy improvements; good system efficiency and safety benefits; moderate cost
6	MD 2/Jumpers Hole	Provide intersection improvements	+	○	−	−	○	+	○	+	+	+	2	Slight air quality, energy, and efficiency improvements; good compatibility with other actions; relatively high cost

Source: Samdahl, Reightler, and Lippman [1983].

Table 9-14 Example of recommended corridor study actions

TSM-TCP package	TSM-TCP action	Priority level	Primary implementing agencies				Cost		Package impacts			
			Balt City	AA CO	State SHA	State MTA	Capital $	Operating $/yr	Δ HC, kg/day	Δ NO$_x$, kg/day	Δ CO, kg/day	Δ Fuel, kg/day
Traffic operations	Improve signs and lane markings at MD 2/US 50/301 (1)	1			x		4,000	Negl.	−0.4	−0.5	−5.5	−3.0
	Provide intersection and traffic flow improvements at MD 2/College Parkway (2a)	1		x	x		72,000	1,600	−2.9	−3.9	−31.9	−43.2
	Install traffic signal at Robinson Road/Benfield Road (3)	2		x			30,000	3,000	+3.9	+6.2	+40.4	+46.9
	Provide intersection improvements at MD 2/Robinson Road/MD 648 (4)	2			x		50,000	Negl.	−1.0	−0.8	−10.5	−11.7
	Provide intersection improvements at MD 2/Pasadena Road (5)	2		x			25,000	Negl.	−0.6	−0.9	−6.2	−8.9
	Provide intersection improvements at MD 2/Jumpers Hole Road (6)	2		x	x		80,000	Negl.	−0.6	−0.5	−6.0	−7.4
	Improve signs and lane markings at MD 2/ MD 100 (7)	1			x		40,000	Negl.	−0.7	−0.8	−9.8	−4.1
	Provide intersection improvements at MD 2/Aquahart Road (8)	1			x		100	Negl.	Negl.	Negl.	Negl.	Negl.
	Provide intersection improvements at MD 2/Burwood Avenue/New Ordinance Road (10a)	1		x	x		37,000	Negl.	−3.5	−2.5	−40.2	−45.3

Traffic operations	Provide traffic safety improvements at MD 2/MD 648 connector north of College Parkway (12b)	2		x		75,000	Negl.	−2.0	−2.8	−28.9	−21.9
	Provide intersection improvements along Hanover Street north of Patapco River Bridge (24)	1	x			8,000	5,000	−1.6	−1.3	−16.6	−18.9
	Improve directional sign messages along MD 2 within Baltimore City (26)	1	x			1,000	Negl.	Negl.	Negl.	Negl.	Negl.
	Priority 1: subtotal					428,000	12,700	−123.6	+36.4	−1517.9	−1720.3
	Priority 2: subtotal					440,000	3,000	−.7	+.5	−26.5	−17.8
	Total package					868,100	15,700	−124.3	+36.9	−1544.4	−1738.1
HOV priority treatments	Improve signage for Glen Burnie park and ride lot (9)	1			x	1,000	500	−0.2	−0.5	−2.3	−8.1
	Provide parking lot improvements to Hanover Street park and ride lot (21)	1	x		x	6,700	+7,030 savings	−0.4	−1.1	−5.3	−18.6
	Establish and promote park-and-ride lots utilizing off-street locations (31)	1		x	x	206,450	+9,400 savings	−4.3	−12.1	−56.9	−198.1
HOV priority treatments	Priority 1: subtotal					214,150	+15,930	−4.9 savings	−13.7	−64.5	−224.8
	Priority 2: subtotal					—	—	—	—	—	—
	Total package					214,150	+15,930 savings	−4.9	−13.7	−64.5	−224.8

Source: Samdahl, Reightler, and Lippman [1983].

opportunities being examined. Thus, while many cities have undertaken air quality–transportation planning efforts at a regional level, Baltimore chose to focus on subareas or corridors, exactly the scale of detail needed to address effectively the issue of air quality improvement through TSM actions.

Second, the Baltimore Corridor studies provided numerous opportunities for public input throughout the process. These were considered essential to the successful completion of the study and adoption of its recommendations. Not only was public input sought for reaction to proposed alternatives, but serious effort was made to seek public ideas on problem identification and ways to solve these problems.

Third, measures of effectiveness were the basis of the evaluation effort. These MOEs were directly linked to the study objectives and provided a common basis for comparison among alternatives.

Finally, the evaluation results were presented in an easily understood format with justification given for each recommendation. The communication linkage between planner and decision maker was thus quite strong.

9-7 EVALUATION OF IMPLEMENTED PROGRAMS AND PROJECTS (EX POST EVALUATION)

The discussion up to this point has focused on the evaluation of projects that have yet to be implemented. Another type of evaluation, which has become increasingly important in recent years, is the assessment of programs and projects after they have been implemented. The purpose of such ex post evaluation is to answer three basic questions: "What changes were made to the transportation system?" "What were the impacts of these changes?" and "Why did these impacts occur?" Not only does ex post evaluation show the level to which programs and projects achieve their objectives, the evaluation results should also provide guidance to decision makers on the effectiveness of the implementation strategy used.

The most important concern to the planner in ex post evaluation is to correctly establish the causal factors for the changes that occurred. In order to establish causality, evaluators often develop an experimental design or evaluation strategy to collect the information needed to determine causality. The experimental design can take many forms, ranging from simple case studies to before-and-after studies of both impacted population groups and a control group.

The impacts of system changes can be measured by many different strategies for comparing the state of the system before and after a change. There are three strategies, however, that are most commonly used: comparison at different points in time, comparison of different geographic regions or population groups, and comparison between real and hypothetical systems [Billheimer and Lave, 1975]. These three comparison strategies are illustrated in Fig. 9-12. Since each of the strategies has particular strengths and weaknesses, a combination of the three approaches might be necessary. The experimental design must take into account the strengths and weaknesses of comparison strategies, so that the selected strategy can address the problems likely to arise in establishing causality.

TRANSPORTATION SYSTEM AND PROJECT EVALUATION **427**

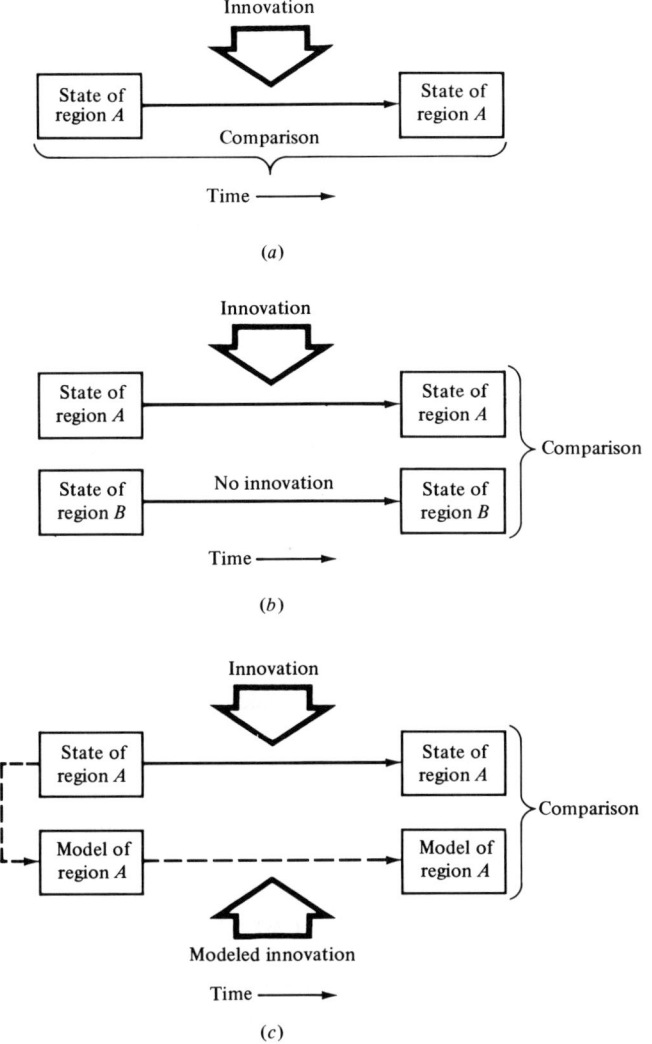

Figure 9-12 Alternative ex post evaluation comparison strategies. (a) Before and after approach. (b) Control region approach. (c) Modeling approach. (*Billheimer and Lave* [*1975*].)

Perhaps the best discussion of experimental designs can be found in Campbell and Stanley [1966], where a number of such designs are related to experimental conditions that "threaten" the validity of experiments and to those that affect external validity. Internal and external validity are defined as [Campbell and Stanley, 1966]:

> *Internal validity* is the basic minimum without which any experiment is uninterpretable: Did in fact the experiment treatments make a difference in this specific experimental instance? *External validity* asks the question of generalizability: To what populations, settings, treatment variables, and measurement variables can this effect be generalized?

Seven major threats to internal validity can be identified. The threats, along with transportation examples, were as follows:

1. *Exogenous influences.* Changes in the economy or social and political structure could occur at the same time as changes made to the transportation system. Thus, an explanation for the resulting impacts might be better related to these economic and sociopolitical forces than to the transportation change. For example, if transit service is being significantly improved at a time when the price of gasoline is rising rapidly, it might be difficult to distinguish between the two when trying to explain the response of ridership to new service. Other examples of exogenous influences include labor strikes, gasoline shortages, economic recession, and weather.
2. *Maturation.* The natural evolution of the physical and economic characteristics of an urban area might account for observed changes. For example, a deteriorating building stock might be the cause of new building construction or renovation, as much as the existence of a new transit station. Long-term trends in transit ridership, accident rates, and gasoline consumption could explain events after a change as much as the change itself.
3. *Testing.* The process of being interviewed or of answering a questionnaire might change an individual's behavior simply because of a new awareness due to being the subject of evaluation. A subsequent interview or questionnaire would identify a change in behavior but not the reason for it.
4. *Instrumentation.* A change in the survey instrument, interviewer, and coders between data collection efforts could result in different types of data being collected. For example, some interview questions may be considered ambiguous by respondents, who ask for clarification from the interviewer. This clarification, if not consistent across all interviewers, could result in different interpretations of the question from one group to the next.
5. *Statistical regression.* Sampling on the basis of one or two behavioral characteristics determined from previous surveys can result in wrong information. For example, on the day of a survey, one respondent could have reported taking a bus trip, an unusual event only made necessary by a malfunctioning car. If a subsequent survey is made, selected on the basis of bus riders, this respondent is likely to be reported as switching to an automobile, when in fact he always was an automobile driver.
6. *Selection.* The criteria used for selecting a sample population could introduce bias into the results. For example, a survey sample based on telephone numbers biases the results in that those not having telephones (e.g., those with low income) or those having unlisted numbers would not be represented.
7. *Sample mortality.* In those cases where different population groups are used in the evaluation, the differential loss of respondents from these groups could invalidate the results. For example, in those neighborhoods having a high percentage of renters, any survey that is to be made over a period of years is likely to face a significant problem of previous respondents having moved away.

The major threats to external validity are similar to those listed above but are related to the transferability of results to other situations. For example, one such threat was called "reactive testing" and was defined as a population group reacting differently once it had been surveyed.

Table 9-15 shows the type of experimental designs available and their impact on the threats to internal validity. The 0's in this table represent an observation or data-gathering effort for a population group A or B, while the X's represent a change introduced into the system. The R's mean a random sample is taken of that particular observation effort. A " + " indicates that the design addresses, to some extent, the threat to internal validity found in the column heading, a " − " indicates vulnerability, a "?" means that the effect depends on the application of the design, and a blank means the factor is not relevant.

It is beyond the scope of this text to discuss in detail the advantages and disadvantages of each experimental design. Such discussion can be found elsewhere [Charles River Associates, 1972]. Indeed, the most effective experimental design depends on the specifics of the program or project being evaluated, the time available, and the level of financial resources that can be allocated to the evaluation task. In most transportation cases, the before-and-after study approach seems to be the most utilized (designs g, h, and i in Table 9-15.)

Because the evaluation of implemented programs and projects is so susceptible to factors not under the control of evaluators, one should carefully plan the approach to be followed in such evaluations. This might require the development of an evaluation or impact assessment plan in which the objectives, experimental approach, data required, data analysis strategy, and limitations are clearly specified. Several books which outline appropriate experimental design strategies and the most effective design of evaluation tools such as surveys and interviews are available [Charles River Associates, 1972; Dillman, 1978; Billheimer and Trexler, 1980; Murphy, 1980].

As mentioned earlier, another purpose of ex post evaluation is to provide information on the implementation strategy used. Clearly, the institutional arrangements in an urban area, the coordination (or lack thereof) among agencies, and the timing of implementation can influence the results of any change to the transportation system. As noted by Williams, "the lack of concern for implementation is currently *the* crucial impediment to improving complex operating programs, policy analysis, and experimentation" [Williams, 1976]. An examination of the implementation of an auto-restricted zone in downtown Boston illustrated the importance of an implementation strategy in successfully developing a transportation project [Lloyd and Meyer, 1984]. This examination concluded that the context for policy, program, and project implementation is usually in constant flux, with political variables changing, major actors leaving and then later reappearing in the process with new demands, and key decision makers not making decisions until the consequences of such actions are clearly spelled out. Several important characteristics of an "implementation" perspective in evaluation were identified as:

1. Successful implementation of a program or policy requires an individual or group

Table 9-15 Experimental designs and impact on threats to internal validity

	Exogenous influences	Maturation	Testing	Instrumentation	Statistical regression	Selection	Sample mortality	Interactions of sources
a. One-shot case study $\times\ 0$	–	–				–	–	–
b. One-group pretest-posttest design $0_1 \times 0_2$	–	?	+	+	–	–	–	–

c. Static-group comparison
    $\times\ 0_A$
    0_B
	–	–	–	–	–	–	–	–

d. Pretest-posttest control group
    $R\ 0_{A1} \times 0_{A2}$
    $R\ 0_{B1}\ \ \ 0_{B2}$
	+	+	+	+	+	+	+	+

e. Posttest-only control group
    $R \times 0_A$
    $R\ \ \ 0_B$
	+	+	+	+	+	+	+	+

f. Time series $0_1\ 0_2\ 0_3\ 0_4 \times 0_5\ 0_6\ 0_7\ 0_8$	–	–	–	–	–	–	–	–

g. Before-and-after with control group
    $0_{A1} \times 0_{A2}$
    $0_{B1}\ \ \ 0_{B2}$
	–	–	+	+	–	–	–	–

h. Before-and-after user study
    $R\ 0 \times$
    $R\ \ \ \times 0$
	–	–	+	?	+	+	+	+

i. Randomized before-and-after study with control
  (A) $R\ 0 \times$
       $R\ \ \ \times 0$
  (B) $R\ 0$
       $R\ \ \ 0$
	+	+	+	?	+	+	+	+

-    Design is vulnerable to threat.
+   Design accounts for threat.
?   Design affects threat depending on application.
blank   Threat not relevant.

Source: Charles River Associates [1972].

of individuals who are committed to the project and who are able to orchestrate the often innumerable interactions necessary to overcome implementation obstacles. In this regard, there is a need for professionals who are comfortable serving multiple objectives, who are able to operate in complex political environments, who can provide expertise in a politically acceptable way, and who can operate at different levels or problem scales in response to different constituencies.
2. Because it is often difficult to predict with any certainty what the implementation characteristics of innovative or potentially controversial projects will be, project advocates must maintain a flexible approach with respect to how implementation will occur. Any implementation analysis that occurs prior to project adoption must remain flexible in the face of uncertainty and provide opportunities for compromise, if necessary.
3. The most important characteristic of successful implementation (where implementation here is considered as obtaining the desired project outcome) is the development of a constituency that can support the project in the adoption stages and then have enough at stake in the project to continue this support when project advocates begin new assignments. The more influential these constituencies, the easier it will be to implement and maintain the project.
4. Consistent communication and feedback are critical elements of successful implementation, required to gauge the response of constituent groups and modify strategy as appropriate. The media, which often report their own interpretations of project implementation, have an important role to play in shaping public perceptions and in determining the positions of key decision makers. In extremely controversial situations, the media might act as the only communication link between the major antagonists. Project proponents must develop and maintain credibility with the media and work to keep them informed about the project.
5. The success of the auto-restricted zone was attributed to, among other factors, the fact that the project proponents had strong professional values and goals that meshed closely with the political objectives of the chief decision maker—in this case, the mayor. The planners' desires to enhance the amenities of the downtown area and to limit the use of the automobile corresponded quite closely with the mayor's objectives of improving the business climate of the downtown area and maintaining the city for its citizens, not for those from the suburbs who commuted in every morning and left the city behind every night. The "marriage" between professional goals and political power proved to be a significant factor in the success of the auto-restricted zone.

The implementation process of system change is thus a critical part of the success or failure of that change. As such, ex post evaluation should explicitly consider this process and identify where pitfalls occurred.

In summary, ex post evaluation can be an important part of transportation planning. Not only does it provide useful information to decision makers on the achievement of previously implemented programs or projects, but it can also give them some idea of the feasibility of such programs or projects in other situations. The major challenge to evaluators is establishing the causality between project implementation and the resulting effect. To do this, careful consideration must be given to an experimental design or evaluation approach which takes into account possible threats to validity. The development of an evaluation plan before the program or project is implemented is necessary to ensure a successful evaluation effort.

9-8 CHAPTER SUMMARY

1. *Evaluation* is the process of determining the relative value of individual alternatives and the desirability of one alternative over another. Most important, evaluation provides information to decision makers on impacts, likely trade-offs, and major areas of uncertainty.
2. A modified version of the *cost-effectiveness approach* to evaluation is, in most cases, the best approach to use in the evaluation process. This approach includes an assessment of alternatives based on *measures of effectiveness,* along with results from comparative assessment methods.
3. An important characteristic of measures of effectiveness is that they can be specified for affected interests or geographic areas. The most common way of portraying these distributional consequences is through the use of an *impact-incidence matrix.*
4. There are several characteristics of benefits and costs that must be considered in evaluation. These include the distinctions between *real* and *pecuniary, direct* and *indirect, tangible* and *intangible, internal* and *external, user* and *nonuser,* and *total* and *incremental.*
5. The correct measures of net benefit are compensating variation and equivalent variation measures, both of which can be estimated from disaggregate travel demand models. In practice, however, most measures of benefit are based on the concept of *consumer surplus.* The evaluation of user *benefits* is primarily a process of determining how great a reduction in negative effects will occur if an improvement is made. User benefits can include the value to users of a reduction in travel time, a reduction in accidents, and decreased vehicle operating costs.
6. The *costs* used in comparative assessment methods include (1) the dollar outlays necessary to construct, operate, and maintain a facility; (2) the costs to users; and (3) the "costs" of environmental degradation.
7. Because costs and benefits of projects occur over time, a discounting procedure is needed to represent these impacts at a single point in time. The choice of a *discount rate* is extremely important because such a rate can significantly influence whether one project is more desirable than another.
8. There are two major types of comparative assessment methods. The first type focuses on minimizing net monetary benefits and includes such methods as *present worth, annual cost, benefit/cost,* and *return on investment.* The second type incorporates multiple objectives into the assessment method.
9. *Ex post evaluation* serves to answer three basic questions: "What changes were made to the transportation system?" "What were the impacts of these changes?" and "Why did these impacts occur?" Such evaluation also provides information to decision makers on the effectiveness of the implementation strategy used. To

answer the above questions, the evaluation process must be based on a valid *experimental design*.

QUESTIONS

1. Using the questions for evaluation found in Table 9-1, outline the type of information, and the likely sources of such information, needed to answer these questions.
2. For a transportation project with which you are familiar, develop a cost-effectiveness framework that you think (1) meets the needs of the decision-making process and (2) falls within the budget established for evaluation. Be specific concerning the MOEs to be defined and the comparative assessment techniques to be used.
3. Identify those MOEs in Table 9-2 that would be most useful in determining impacts on selected impact groups (i.e., which MOEs would most likely be found in an impact-incidence matrix?).
4. A four-lane highway which runs through a densely populated urban area provides the major east-west connection across the southern part of a metropolitan area. Because of increased commercial and residential construction in the surrounding community, this highway has experienced increased levels of congestion in recent years. Several options for improving the situation have already been suggested by local officials, including expansion to six lanes, addition of a fifth lane, traffic engineering improvements, and preferential treatment for high-occupancy vehicles. Outline an evaluation plan for a corridor planning study designed to address this problem. Be sure to specify the type of information needed and the techniques to be used in assessment. You are especially interested in the impact of prospective projects on existing travel flows and on the surrounding community. How would your evaluation plan change if the candidate highway were located in the city center and paralleled a rapid-transit line?
5. Given the benefits and costs schedule shown below for projects A, B, and C, determine which project is best from an economic efficiency point of view. Conduct the assessment for discount rates of 8 percent, 10 percent, and 12 percent. How does the discount rate affect the choice of the "best" project?

Year	Expected yearly cost			Expected yearly benefit		
	A	B	C	A	B	C
1	$10	$30	$10	$ 0	$ 0	$ 0
2	15	10	10	5	20	15
3	30	10	10	10	20	15
4	15	5	10	15	10	10
5	10	5	10	15	10	5
6	5	5	5	10	10	5
7	5	5	5	10	10	5
8	5	5	5	10	5	5
9	5	5	5	5	5	5
10	5	5	5	5	5	5

6. Select one of the approaches for dealing with uncertainty presented on pages 398 to 403. Discuss in detail the use of this approach and its advantages and disadvantages.
7. For the costs shown below, and assuming that benefits can be defined in terms of savings in costs relative to the do-nothing alternative, do a benefit/cost assessment to determine which alternative is preferred.

	Present value costs	
Alternative	User and operating costs	Capital
0 (do nothing)	$400	$ 5
1	$200	$40
2	$300	$20
3	$350	$25
4	$250	$30
5	$320	$15

8. The intangible benefits associated with the Milwaukee alternatives analysis study are shown in Table 9-13. Which of these intangible benefits could indeed be measured and incorporated into an impact matrix? Why was this most likely not done?
9. A new express bus service is about to be introduced in one corridor of a metropolitan area. Because of financial constraints, agency officials are interested to know what impact this service is likely to have on travel behavior in the corridor. Outline an experimental design structured to determine this impact.
10. To evaluate many innovative projects, planners are often asked to produce an evaluation plan that must be approved by sponsoring agency decision makers. Describe, in outline form, the contents of such a plan.

REFERENCES

Abrams, C., and J. Di Renzo: *Measures of Effectiveness for Multimodal Urban Traffic Management*, U.S. Department of Transportation Report FHWA-RD-79-113, Washington, D.C., December 1979.

American Association of State Highway and Transportation Officials: *A Policy on Design of Urban Highways and Arterial Streets*, Washington, D.C., 1973.

———: *Manual of User Benefit Analysis of Highway and Bus-Transit Improvements*, Washington, D.C., 1977.

Andreasson, I.: "Volvo Approach to Computer-Aided Transportation Planning," *Transportation Research Record 657*, Transportation Research Board, Washington, D.C., 1977.

Billheimer, J., and R. Lave: *Evaluation Plan for the Santa Monica Freeway Preferential Lane Project*, Contract No. DOT-TSC-1084, Submitted to the Transportation Systems Center, Cambridge, Mass., November 1975.

Billheimer, J., and R. Trexler: *Evaluation Handbook for Transportation Impact Assessment*, U.S. Department of Transportation Report UMTA-IT-06-0203-81-1, Washington, D.C., December 1980.

Campbell, D., and J. Stanley: *Experimental and Quasi-Experimental Designs for Research,* Rand McNally, Chicago, 1963.
Charles River Associates: *Measurement of the Effects of Transportation Changes,* Report CRA-166-2, Cambridge, Mass., August 1972.
Chicago Area Transportation Study: *Proceedings Year 2000 Alternative Transportation Plan Scenarios,* Chicago, 1976.
Cohen, H., J. Stowers, and M. Petersilia: *Evaluating Urban Transportation System Alternatives,* U.S. Department of Transportation Report DOT-P-30-78-44, Washington, D.C., November 1978.
Dasgupta, P., A. Sen, and S. Marglin: *Guidelines for Project Evaluation,* United Nations Industrial Development Organization, New York, 1972.
de Neufville, R., and J. Stafford: *Systems Analysis for Engineers and Managers,* McGraw-Hill, New York, 1971.
Dillman, D.: *Mail and Telephone Surveys,* Wiley, New York, 1978.
Fallon, G., et al.: "Benefits of Interstate Highways," U.S. Government Printing Office Committee Print (91-41), Washington, D.C., 1970.
Golenberg, M. and J. Howard, "A Short-range TSM Corridor Planning Case Study" and "A Major Capitol Improvement Subarea Planning Case Study," in Simplified Aids for Transportation Analysis series, Reports FHWA/PL/83/004 and FHWA/PL/83/005, U.S. Department of Transportation, Washington D.C., May 1983.
Haveman, R., and B. Weisbrod: "Defining Benefits of Public Programs: Some Guidance for Policy Analysts," in R. Haveman and J. Margolis (eds.), *Public Expenditure and Policy Analysis,* Rand McNally, Chicago, 1977.
Hill, M.: *Planning for Multiple Objectives,* Regional Science Research Institute Monograph Series No. 5, Amherst, Mass., 1973.
Hudson, B., M. Wachs, and J. Schofer: "Local Impact Evaluation in the Design of Large-Scale Urban Systems," *Journal of the American Institute of Planners,* vol. 40, no. 4, July 1974.
Jessiman, W., D. Brand, A. Tumminia, and C. R. Brussee: "A Rational Decision-Making Technique for Transportation Planning," *Highway Research Record 180,* Highway Research Board, Washington, D.C., 1967.
Keeney, R., and H. Raiffa: *Decisions with Multiple Objectives,* Wiley, New York, 1976.
Layard, A.: *Cost-Benefit Analysis,* Penguin, London, 1972.
Lloyd, E., and M. Meyer: "Strategies for Overcoming Opposition to Project Implementation," *Transport Policy and Decision Making,* vol. 2, no. 3, 1984.
Manheim, M.: *Fundamentals of Transportation Systems Analysis,* MIT Press, Cambridge, Mass., 1979.
Morlok, E.: *Introduction to Transportation Engineering and Planning,* McGraw-Hill, New York, 1978.
Murphy, J.: *Getting the Facts,* Goodyear, Santa Monica, Calif., 1980.
Musgrave, R., and P. Musgrave: *Public Finance in Theory and Practice,* McGraw-Hill, New York, 1976.
Oglesby, C., and T. Hicks: *Highway Engineering,* Wiley, New York, 1982.
Quade, E.: *Analysis for Public Decisions,* Elsevier, New York, 1975.
Raiffa, H.: *Decision Analysis, Introductory Lectures on Choices under Uncertainty,* Addison-Wesley, Reading, Mass., 1968.
Roy, B., and J. C. Hugonnard: "Ranking of Suburban Line Extension Projects on the Paris Metro System by a New Multicriteria Method," *Transportation Research,* forthcoming.
Samdahl, D. R., J. Reightler, and S. Lippman: "Getting Results from TSM Planning: Baltimore's Corridor Study Approach," Paper presented at the annual meeting of the Transportation Research Board, January 1983.
Schlaifer, R.: *Analysis of Decisions under Uncertainty,* McGraw-Hill, New York, 1968.
Schofer, J.: "Emerging Methods in Transportation Evaluation," in W. Brown (ed.), *Emerging Transportation Planning Methods,* U.S. Department of Transportation Report DOT-RSPD-DPB-50-78-2, Washington, D.C., March 15, 1978.
Schulz, D.: "Evaluative Measures," Memorandum to CATS Technical Staff, Chicago Area Transportation Study, July 17, 1975.
Shupe, D.: *What Every Engineer Should Know about Economic Decision Analysis,* Marcel Dekker, New York, 1980.

Southeastern Wisconsin Regional Planning Commission: *Alternative Futures for Southeastern Wisconsin,* Technical Report No. 25, 1980.

————: *Milwaukee Area Alternative Primary Transit System Plan Preparation, Test, and Evaluation,* Technical Report 26, March 1982.

Starling, G.: *The Politics and Economics of Public Policy,* Dorsey, Homewood, Ill., 1979.

Stopher, P., and A. Meyburg: *Transportation Systems Evaluation,* D. C. Heath, Lexington, Mass., 1976.

Thomas, E., and J. Schofer: "Strategies for the Evaluation of Alternative Transportation Plans," *NCHRP Report 96,* Washington, D.C., 1970.

Thomas, T., and G. Thompson: "The Value of Time for Commuting Motorists as a Function of Their Income Level and Amount of Time Saved," *Highway Research Record 314,* Highway Research Board, Washington, D.C., 1970.

U.S. Department of Transportation: *Characteristics of Urban Transportation Systems,* Report UMTA-IT-06-0049-79-1, June 1979.

Urban Mass Transportation Administration: "Major Urban Mass Transportation Investments," *Federal Register,* September 22, 1976.

Williams, W.: *The Implementation Perspective,* University of California Press, Berkeley, 1980.

Wohl, M., and B. Martin: *Traffic System Analysis,* McGraw-Hill, New York, 1967.

Wohl, M.: "Common Misunderstandings about the Internal-Rate-of-Return and Net Present Value Economic Analysis Methods," *Transportation Research Record 731,* Transportation Research Board, Washington, D.C., 1979.

CHAPTER
TEN

PROGRAM AND PROJECT IMPLEMENTATION

10-0 INTRODUCTION

An important product of the transportation planning process is the development of a program which outlines the projects to be implemented, the timetable for their implementation, and the financial resources necessary for each. *Project programming* is thus an important task in the transportation planning process and a focal point for decision-maker interest. Not only is the programming process an important step in planning, but both the process and the resultant document can be critical parts of an agency's program management efforts.

The purpose of this chapter is to examine the project programming process and alternative schemes for establishing project priorities. The central argument presented here is that, even though the ultimate decision as to which projects should be implemented is often a political one, there are several useful roles for technical methods in generating information for this decision process. Unfortunately, there is little information in the literature on metropolitan-level project programming. Much of the material in this chapter is drawn from experience with state or provincial programming procedures. Although different in geographic scale from the metropolitan level, the state- or provincial-level processes examined provide many useful concepts that can be applied to programming at any level.

10-1 CHARACTERISTICS OF A PROGRAMMING PROCESS

Programming has been defined as "the matching of available projects with available funds to accomplish the goals of a given period" [Transportation Research Board,

1978]. In the urban transportation sector, several types of programming often occur, including the programming of transportation projects for an entire metropolitan region and the programming of projects for specific agencies. In both cases, the programming process must necessarily take into account *resource availability,* both the absolute level and distribution of funds among modes, functional systems, political jurisdictions, and specific project types, as well as the commitment of organizational resources that will be needed to implement and monitor the projects as they progress through the project development process. The programming process must also be concerned with the *staging of projects over time* in such a way that any interdependence among projects is clearly recognized, the future implications of near-term decisions are understood, and the availability of funding in specific time periods is accounted for.

As has been the case with regard to other types of decisions in transportation planning, the decision-making approach adopted for project programming will differ from one urban area to the next (although in the United States, federal regulations have been developed in an attempt to provide a uniform programming process and document in each urban area). In some cases, decision makers may be concerned with specific projects and their chances of being programmed, whereas in other cases decision makers may be more concerned with overall funding levels and the need to either maximize expenditure of transportation funds (i.e., show a constituency that progress is being made) or minimize such use (i.e., show a constituency that government is responding to fiscal austerity). The programming problem in both cases is to determine which projects will be constructed when, thus meeting the objectives of the agency or regional transportation policy, while still satisfying as many individuals as possible [Humphrey, Meyer, and Salvucci, 1983].

A transportation program represents a commitment to the allocation of transportation resources in a metropolitan area and is thus subject to the politics inherent in any decision to expend public funds. It is rare that decision makers yield their own negotiating positions on the basis of the results of a technical analysis alone. For some decision makers, choosing one alternative over another is an opportunity to reward those who have given support in the past or whose support might be needed in the future [Lloyd and Meyer, 1984]. Technical information on the benefits and impacts of the alternatives will consequently have little influence in such cases. For other decision makers, the technical information may be perceived to be both useful and desirable, but when forced to make a commitment, they may trust their intuition over the analysis results. In yet other cases, decision makers may have to choose from a set of alternatives that have been prioritized. To them, a subset of these alternatives might be acceptable, whereas to the planner, one alternative clearly dominates the others (see Chap. 3 for a discussion of this type of decision making). In all of these situations, the relationship between technical information and its influence on decision making can prove to be a most frustrating one from the perspective of the planner.

The programming process can thus be heavily influenced by the politics of negotiation, legislative requirements, the quid pro quo of organizational commitments, and the level and origin of support for specific projects. Developing a transportation program, therefore, requires both an awareness of the impacts of alternative projects or project sets on the community *and* an understanding of the many local political agendas. A recent synthesis of programming practice included the following observations [Transportation Research Board, 1978]:

> These two elements (technical and institutional factors) are constantly interacting, and many final decisions are intuitive. It is rare that a decision regarding a major project is based on technical data only, although technical data can have a strong influence on a go-, no-go decision. Also, technical factors are often the major determinants of the priority of hundreds of smaller projects. However, a nontechnical factor—for example, the inappropriateness of a project for the time or conditions—can terminate the technical analysis of that project.

In spite of this need for a broad perspective on programming, much of the early work in developing a programming process focused on the technical methods that state or provincial transportation departments could use to determine priorities quantitatively for highway projects located within their jurisdiction. As funding for transportation investment became increasingly limited, the need grew for some mechanism to determine the most cost-effective investment strategy. In response, several computerized analysis packages were developed whose output provided a time-staged sequencing of projects with levels of funding for each time period [North Carolina Department of Transportation, 1972; U.S. Department of Transportation, 1973; Ontario Ministry of Transportation and Communications, 1974; U.S. Department of Transportation, 1976; Bellomo et al., 1979].

The basic analysis tool used in most of these packages was a linear programming model designed to maximize discounted net benefits subject to a series of constraints. An example of the inputs needed for such an analysis package and the expected outputs is shown in Fig. 10-1. Also shown is a priority implementation schedule for highway projects in Maryland that resulted from the analysis. As can be seen from the chart of inputs and outputs, a large amount of data is necessary for conducting the analysis, a requirement that reduces the attractiveness of such an approach. Nevertheless, the resulting project implementation schedule is a most useful source of information for decision makers and can serve as a good management tool.

Similar types of analysis techniques have not, in general, been used in the development of transportation investment programs for urban areas. There are several reasons for this. First, the goals and objectives of transportation policy in urban areas tend to be much more diverse than at higher levels of government. As disagreements over goals multiply, it becomes more difficult to develop an acceptable program for the urban area. For example, in many metropolitan areas, a major conflict often arises between center city and suburban interests over policies designed to enhance the economic health of the CBD. Transportation programs aimed in this direction are usually fought by suburban interests.

Second, major urban areas have several different types of transportation investment that need to be considered: highway projects, transit services, ride sharing, etc. It is often very difficult to determine trade-offs in a quantitative manner between these investment categories, with the result that such trade-offs are usually left to the political process.

Third, state and provincial officials often have a good estimate of the funds they will have available for the construction of projects, mainly because these funds

	Inputs		Outputs
General information needs	Specific variables and project information		
Vehicle operating costs	Highway adequacy rating		From user-benefit package
Fuel	Control of access		Vehicle operating costs
Oil	Lane width, number and types of lanes		Time
Tires	Shoulder width		Accidents: fatal
Mechanical labor	Passing sight distance (percent)		Accidents: injury
Vehicle depreciation	Length (miles)		Accidents: property damage
Time	Accidents/million vehicle miles		From edit and update, inflate and discount packages
Accidents	Grade		
Traffic inventory	Curvature		Master improvement list
Permanent traffic-count station data	Type of pavement		Salvage value
Average one-way flows	Capacity (volume per hour)		Annual added-maintenance calculation
Ratio of traffic-link flow to saturatic flow	Needs study		Surface maintenance-savings calculation
Percentage of trucks (base year and projected [assumed constant])	Average daily traffic (base and projected years)		Working improvement list
	Planning costs		From linear programming package
Terrain	Engineering costs		Inflated cost streams
Mountainous (western Maryland)	Right-of-way costs		Discounted benefit streams
Rolling (central and southern Maryland)	Construction costs		Cost-benefit ratios
Level (eastern shore)	Other		Project starting dates
Occupancy rates (persons/vehicle)	Median width (field survey)		
Urban = 1.5	Average highway speed (posted speed)		
Suburban = 1.6	Number of intersections (field survey)*		
Rural = 2.0	Cycle length (seconds) (estimated)*		
	Number of hours parking allowed (field survey)*		
	Environmental factor (not used)*		
	Maintenance costs (estimated)		

* Needed only for urban projects.

Project no.	Costs, $000											Total
	1977	1978	1979	1980	1981	1982	1983	1984	1992	1993	1994	1995–1996	
1	1,732	13,731	15,622	15,622	15,622	13,890	1,890						78,109
2	4,839	4,840	4,840	4,840	4,840								24,199
3						12,393	18,380	18					91,899
4								61	19,262				142,298
5	4,619	4,620	4,620	4,620	4,620								23,099
6													10,600
7							1,979						5,939
8													9,459
9					2	6,441	8,358	8,361					41,799
10													16,619
11													25,679
12							5,177						25,850
13							4,87						24,369
14				4,949	4,950	4,950	6,3						24,101
15								35	10,135				52,971
16								260	4,260				21,299
17	8,057	8,058	8,058	8,058	8,058				4,260	4,391	4,392		53,463
18	12,217	12,218	12,218	12,218	12,218				4,391	4,391	4,392		61,089
19	8,639	8,640	8,640	8,640	8,640								43,199
20													100,339
21					12,400	12,400							82,000
22				3,940	3,940	3,940		3,940	3,940				31,520
23	Not programmed												0
24			1,366	1,366	1,366	1,167							12,899
25			2,466	2,466	2,467								20,799
26						359	804						7,399
Total	40,103	52,107	57,830	66,721	85,562	57,2	0,881	51,883	47,596	4,391	4,392		1,010,996
Cumulative total	92,210	150,040	216,761	302,323				922,764	970,360	1,002,213	1,006,604	1,010,996	

Figure 10-1 Example inputs and outputs for a state highway programming model. *(Bellomo et al. [1978].)*

generally come from only one or two sources. At the metropolitan level, there are often many more funding sources, each having greater uncertainty associated with it, meaning estimates of funding levels beyond 3 or 4 years are difficult to make.

Fourth, from a technical perspective, on a state or provincial level network, the interdependence between alternative projects is probably not significant, meaning the linear programming formulation (more specifically, the additivity assumption in the objective function) can be used. In an urban context, however, the interdependence between several projects creates significant analysis problems.

Finally, the number of transportation projects considered in a large metropolitan area is typically greater than at state or provincial levels. In large cities, the number of projects considered on a yearly basis can range from 300 to 700. The effort needed to collect sufficient information on each project to satisfy the requirements of an analysis package would be beyond the resources of most government agencies.

Although the development of analytical tools for programming urban projects has not reached the level of state or provincial efforts, some progress has been made in recent years in the United States to establish a programming process for urban transportation improvements. In 1975, the U.S. Department of Transportation issued planning regulations which required that each urbanized area receiving federal funds develop a transportation improvement program (TIP). The TIP was defined as a staged, multiyear program of transportation improvements initially recommended in the regional transportation plan. The most important component of the TIP was its annual element, the first year's listing of projects. The development and update of the TIP were the responsibility of the Metropolitan Planning Organization (MPO) [U.S. Department of Transportation, 1975].

The TIP was to accomplish several tasks:

1. Identify transportation improvements recommended for advancement during the program period (3–5 years).
2. Indicate an urban area's priorities with respect to transportation.
3. Group improvements of similar urgency and anticipated staging into appropriate staging periods.
4. Include realistic estimates of total costs and revenues for the program period.
5. Include a discussion of how projects recommended in the transportation plan were merged into the TIP.

In response to this regulation, each urbanized area in the United States prepared a TIP document. The typical contents of such a document included information on the projects being considered, the level of funding required, the agency responsible for each project, and the staging over time of project construction. (As will be argued below, an effective programming document should also provide information on the policy objectives of the region and on the transportation priorities set by local governments.)

Although a programming document can be a source of useful information to decision makers, there are several factors which should be kept in mind when creating or updating a transportation program [Transportation Research Board, 1978]. First, the program is rarely new; it usually contains commitments made in previous years and to other agencies or groups. Second, the projects are in all stages of development from initial planning studies to final design; at any point and for any number of reasons, a project may be stopped temporarily and thrown off schedule. Third, the funds available may be restricted to certain categories of use, although there may be some flexibility with regard to the transfer of funds between categories or the reassignment of projects to different categories. Finally, priorities may be constantly changing because of changing philosophies, transportation needs, economic conditions, energy availability, political conditions, and other factors affecting individual or collective priorities.

By taking recent experience with project programming into account, and by relating such a process to the characteristics of decision making discussed in Chap. 3, several characteristics of an effective programming process and document become apparent.

1. The programming process must be closely linked to the planning steps that precede it. That is, the projects programmed for implementation should have already been subjected to analysis and evaluation procedures. This is important to ensure consistency between transportation policy and planning goals *as articulated in the plan* and the actual policy *as implemented in the program*. The transportation program should thus be considered as one step toward the realization of an adopted transportation system plan and as one component of managing an agency's investment program.
2. The transportation program should have a multiyear framework that integrates projects over time and location. This multiyear framework should provide a general direction for transportation investment and identify the interdependence between short-run investments and long-term outcomes. The different stages of project development—preliminary engineering, right-of-way acquisition, and construction—must also be considered in this program. As shown in Fig. 10-2, one possible format for the regional program could be to divide it into improvement programs for specific corridors. This figure also illustrates some important characteristics of such improvement programs—identification of potential project substitutions, operating and policy changes, and decision points where choices between alternatives could be made.
3. In every programming process, priorities are set for project implementation. Even in cases where a formal process of priority setting does not exist, the allocation of organizational and financial resources for the development of some projects over others is an implicit setting of priorities. What must be avoided is the "scattergun" approach to programming (i.e., satisfying everyone by allocating small amounts of resources to large numbers of projects but not providing a critical mass of resources to complete the implementation of any). Trade-offs, and the necessity of establishing priorities among policy and agency objectives, are critical components of the programming process.

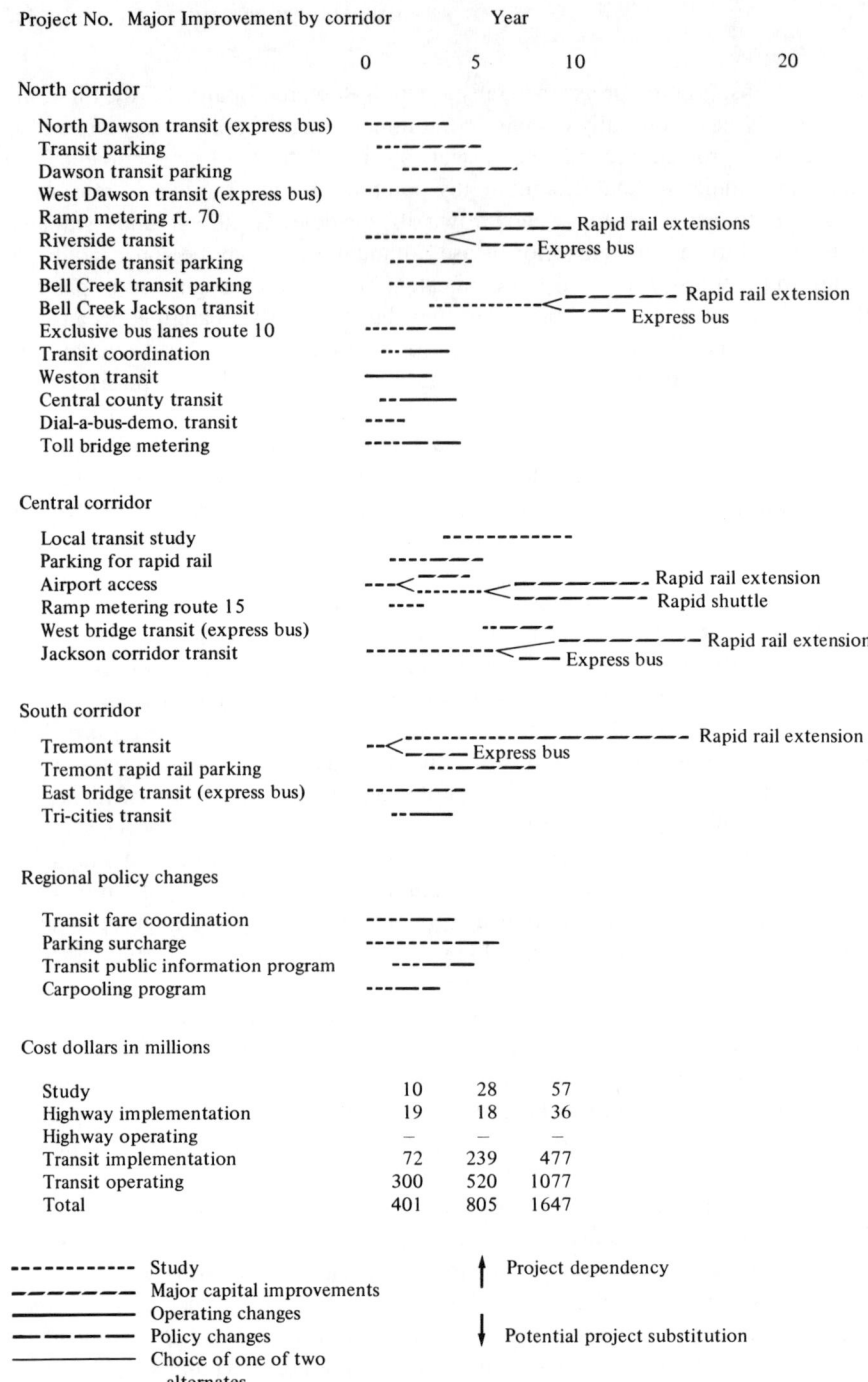

Figure 10-2 Corridor-based transportation improvement program. (*L. Neumann [1976].*)

4. Perhaps the most important consideration in the programming process, and certainly in the political bargaining process that accompanies it, is the amount of funding available for transportation investment. For the programming process to be effective and credible, the level of funds identified in the program must be a realistic estimate of what can be expected. This requires a good understanding of the many sources of funds that are used to finance urban transportation projects (see Fig. 10-3).
5. The transportation program should be useful to decision makers not only in identifying which projects are to be implemented, but also as a means of monitoring the progress of previously programmed projects, the degree to which the

---

United States

Typical local transit revenue sources

    Federal government (50 percent of operating costs and 80 percent of capital costs)
    State government (varies)
    Fares (usually between 20 percent to 60 percent of total revenues)
    Dedicated metropolitan sales tax
    Gasoline and auto-use taxes
    Employer payroll tax
    Advertisement
    Charter bus service

Highway projects

    Funding comes from general revenues of locality and other governments participating in project. Federal funding depends upon type of project but usually ranges from 50 percent to 90 percent of project cost.

Canada—Province of Ontario—Toronto

Transit operations 1979

Revenues	72%
Provincial subsidies	14%
Metropolitan Toronto	14%
	100%

Theoretical revenue/cost ratio set by province is 72.5 percent. In general, province pays 50 percent of deficit above constraint.

Capital 1979

Province	74%
Metropolitan	20%
Toronto Transit Commission	6%
	100%

In general, province pays for 75 percent of capital costs.

Highway projects

    Financing depends on whether project is a local street, regional and/or metropolitan road, or provincial highway. In general, three levels of government—province, metropolitan, and local (not federal)—will be involved in infrastructure projects.

Figure 10-3 Typical sources of transportation funding.

projects being implemented conform to regional policies, and the specific obstacles that must be overcome to implement programmed projects. An updated program document can thus become a major source of information to decision makers on the effectiveness of transportation policy and planning in the region.
6. Because the programming process represents an important stage in the effort to implement projects, opportunities should be provided for the involvement of interested parties, such as elected officials, representatives of implementing and planning agencies, and the general public. An "open" programming process will help assure consistency between the transportation program and the community goals and objectives outlined in the transportation plan or regional transportation policy.

10-2 THE TWO BASIC COMPONENTS OF PROGRAMMING

There are two tasks which play an important role in the programming process and which are critical to its success—setting priorities for project selection and determining the availability of funds. Each of these is discussed below.

10-2-1 Setting Priorities for Project Selection

If there were unlimited transportation resources in a metropolitan area, there would be no need to program project implementation because every project could be constructed immediately. However, the financial and organizational resources available for transportation investment are limited and may in some instances even be shrinking. In addition to the constraint of declining funding levels, the small number of construction firms in an urban area and the limited ability of government agencies to supervise project construction also limit the number of projects that can be implemented in any one year. Further, the limited capacity of government agencies to design facilities or to monitor the design process constrains the number of projects that can reach the programming stage. (An example of this last problem is provided by a recent U.S. Department of Transportation bridge replacement program, where the limited design capability for such work at the local level has left a large amount of unspent funds and local agencies struggling to complete the needed design work before construction can take place.) Given these circumstances, it becomes necessary to establish priorities for project implementation, that is, to determine which projects should receive immediate funding and which ones should be postponed or removed from consideration completely.

Several efforts have been made to develop comparative analysis techniques to rank projects along various dimensions. The most popular approach is the use of *priority indices* based on measures of user benefit, environmental impacts, safety, and current condition of the facility. For example, one rating system uses the assignment of points between 0 and 10 to indicate the level of highway condition with regard to several criteria, including pavement condition, drainage, roadway width, fatal and total accidents, peak-hour speed, and off-peak speed [Federal Highway Administration, 1980]. These ratings are then combined to identify critically deficient sections of the transportation system, with a project ranking resulting from the analysis based on the "total score" received by each project.

Another example of this type of priority setting is the priority programming process developed for Wayne County in southeastern Michigan [Politano, 1983]. Eight criteria are used in this process with the maximum allowable points assigned to each as follows:

Congestion and/or traffic operations improvement	maximum: 30 points
Safety	maximum: 30 points
Minimize cost	maximum: 20 points
Air quality	maximum: 5 points
Energy conservation	maximum: 5 points
Social, economic, and environment	maximum: 5 points
Maintenance and/or service	maximum: 10 points
Intermodal coordination	maximum: 5 points

The total points assigned between the first two criteria (i.e., congestion and safety) cannot be greater than 50 (so that the total score for a project will not exceed 100 points), although each could receive a maximum of 30 points individually. The number of points is summed for each project to yield a total point score for each project, which can then be used to rank projects. Alternatively, the total point score for each project, minus the cost minimization score, can be divided into the project cost to yield a cost-effectiveness measure (the cost minimization score is deleted from this calculation in order to avoid double-counting costs in the cost-effectiveness measure). Figure 10-4 illustrates the use of both the cost-effectiveness measure and the total point score in the identification of an implementation ranking for a set of projects.

More sophisticated analysis techniques based on computer packages are now beginning to be used by state and provincial governments. An example of such an analysis was shown in Fig. 10-1. Although the analysis style is more sophisticated in these computer packages, the basic objective is the same—to maximize the net benefits of the investment program.

Very little effort has been made to use similar approaches at the metropolitan level. The efforts that have been made most often use the results of the conventional demand models discussed in Chap. 7 to determine specific measures of project impact and the cost-effectiveness of alternative project sets. The projects that are the most cost-effective (e.g., largest ridership increase per dollar invested) receive priority in the programming process.

By far the most common approach to setting priorities is to establish priority project categories or priority problem areas and to require the project selection process to take these categories or areas into account as the program is developed. In Chicago, for example, the MPO reviewed various approved and publicly adopted plans that contained statements reflecting regional goals and objectives. A list of priorities was developed, and after negotiations with participating agencies, this list was adopted as

No.	Project description	Congestion operations (30-0)	Safety improvements (30-0)	Implementation cost (20-0)	Air quality (5-0)	Energy conservation (5-0)
		50 points maximum				
X1	Widen road from four to five lanes to provide center left turn lane; resurface pavement; remove angle parking in road R/W	Moderate congestion; primary impact (24)*	Potentially hazardous; secondary impact (8)	$500,000 (15)	Est. emission reduction 110 tons (2)	Est. fuel consumption reduction 9,000 gal (1)
X2	Change traffic signal operation to provide separate left turn phase for NB and SB approaches; modernize signal equipment, install pedestrian signals	Moderate congestion; no significant impact (0)	Very high accidents; primary impact (30)	$20,000 (20)	Est. emission reduction 10 tons (0)	Est. fuel consumption reduction 6,000 gal (1)
X3	Reconstruct and widen from two to five lanes; improve horizontal alignment at major intersection; upgrade signals and signing	Severe congestion; primary impact (30)	High accident experience; secondary impact (15)	$1,400,000 (6)	Est. emission reduction 225 tons (4)	Est. fuel consumption reduction 18,000 gal (3)
X4	Interconnect and modernize traffic signals along 3-mile section of arterial road; remove on-street parking; relocate and upgrade bus stops and shelters	Moderate congestion; primary impact (24)	Potentially hazardous; indirect impact (2)	$80,000 (19)	Est. emission reduction 205 tons (4)	Est. fuel consumption reduction 21,000 gal (4)
X5	Construct passing lane on arterial road at intersection with main hospital drives; rebuild shoulders	Occasional congestion; primary impact (12)	Potentially hazardous; secondary impact (8)	$75,000 (19)	Est. emission reduction 22 tons (0)	Est. fuel consumption reduction 3,200 gal (0)

*Numbers in parentheses indicate the operation used to derive a cost-effectiveness score for each project's criterion.

Figure 10-4 Priority setting by point allocation and cost-effectiveness. (*Politano* [1983].)

the set of project priority guidelines to be used by these agencies (see Fig. 10-5). These policies were not meant to prevent an implementing agency from designing a project that does not meet all the guidelines. They were meant to provide an overall direction for the programming process.

One of the more innovative attempts at structuring a framework to help decision makers in project selection occurred in a suburban county in the Chicago metropolitan region [Wilson and Schofer, 1978]. Before this framework was adopted for use, highway programming decisions were often made on the basis of which one was

TSM evaluation procedures—example projects

Social, economic, environmental (5-0)	Maintenance and/or service (10-0)	Intermodal coordination (5-0)	Total points (100-0)	Project cost	Cost-effectiveness
School, business, recreation access (lost parking) (2)	Resurface pavement; upgrade signals (6)	Bus route (1)	59	$500,000	$\frac{500{,}000}{59-15} = \$11{,}360$
Business, church access (2)	Modernize signals (4)	Improve pedestrian crossing (2)	59	$20,000	$\frac{20{,}000}{59-20} = \$510$
Residential access; curb and landscaping (noise increase) (1)	Roadway reconstructed; upgrade signals and signs (10)	Bus route (1)	70	$1,400,000	$\frac{1{,}400{,}000}{70-6} = 21{,}880$
Business, school, public services access, aesthetics (3)	Modernize signals and improve performance (6)	Bus route, bus stops and shelters improved (4)	66	$80,000	$\frac{800{,}000}{66-19} = \$1{,}700$
Emergency medical access (4)	Shoulder repair (1)	None (0)	44	$75,000	$\frac{75{,}000}{44-19} = \$3{,}000$

proposed first or according to the readiness of the project for immediate implementation. Twelve members of the county decision-making committee, with help from the technical staff, identified seven measures that they would consider in their decision:[1]

1. Change in peak-hour travel time
2. Change in equivalent property damage (EDP) rate of accidents
3. Change in average daily congestion (volume/capacity ratio)
4. Change in off-peak daily travel time
5. Change in noise pollution
6. Change in air pollution
7. Number of dwelling units taken

[1] Although there is a high level of correlation between some of these measures (e.g., the first and third), these measures were left as defined because of the direct concern expressed by the decision makers.

First level

1. Projects which aid in the interface between highways and transit should receive a high priority.
2. Projects which improve air quality should be increased in priority.
3. Projects which conserve energy should be increased in priority.

Second level

1. Projects which serve elderly and handicapped should be increased in priority.
2. Projects which improve the relative accessibility of the CBD should be increased in priority.
3. Projects which maximize the use of the transit system should be increased in priority.
4. Projects which improve user safety should be increased in priority.

Figure 10-5 Project priority guidelines in Chicago transportation programming process. (*Chicago Area Transportation Study* [1976].)

These measures were to be applied in two time periods: the (then) current year and 1985. A simple linear weighting scheme was used to determine the most desirable projects, and a Delphi process was used to identify the weights to be associated with each (see Appendix C). The values for these measures were then obtained from existing data sources and through the use of standard forecasting techniques. A measure of effectiveness score was obtained for each project by applying the weights assigned to each measure and adding across all measures; cost-effectiveness indices were then derived by dividing the effectiveness scores by capital costs. These cost-effectiveness indices were used to rank the projects, meaning that the most cost-effective program included the projects ranked by decreasing cost-effectiveness until the budget was consumed.

As shown in Table 10-1, the program identified from the cost-effectiveness framework was similar to the one finally selected by the decision makers, although there were some differences. Those who evaluated the process observed that "the differences between the rankings of the decision makers and those produced by the evaluation process is that the political process is still in control of investment decisions in the public sector and thus is still in a position to respond to the unique characteristics of the needs of individuals and groups" [Wilson and Schofer, 1978]. In other words, attempts to analytically structure the priority-setting process are a useful exercise for both planners and decision makers, but the final decision will be based on political judgment.

10-2-2 Determining Availability of Funding

The forecasting of future funding is perhaps the most complex area of transportation programming. The major reason for this is the large numbers of factors outside the control of planners which can influence the level of funding available in future years. These include unstable funding commitments from higher levels of government, reduced revenues from gas taxes because of more efficient automobile use, changes in

Table 10-1 Comparison of project selection by political and technical process

	Projects selected by ranking methodology			Projects selected by decision makers	
Project	Cost-effectiveness	Cost, $000,000	Project	Cost-effectiveness	Cost, $000,000
A	62.6	0.385	A	62.6	0.385
B	28.6	0.300	B	Not chosen	
C	16.1	0.912	C	16.1	0.912
D	14.2	0.610	D	Not chosen	
E	7.9	0.600	E	Not chosen	
F	7.4	3.300	F	7.4	3.300
G	Not chosen		G	6.0	1.065
H	5.7	0.172	H	Not chosen	
I	3.7	0.601	I	3.7	0.601
J	Not chosen		J	2.9	0.570
Total		6.88			6.833

Source: Wilson and Schofer [1978].

local priorities in public funding due to changes in administration, and the uncertainty of an inflationary economy. All of these factors can significantly influence the amount of funds that will be available for transportation investment, and yet each is very difficult to predict. To some extent, then, the determination of future funding is often a loosely structured process, based on the expectations and intuition of the programmer [Transportation Research Board, 1978].

> It [fund forecasting] requires a knowledge of transportation: trends in priorities and funding on the part of Congress, state legislatures, county boards, and city councils; departmental and executive-branch priorities and trends; and project development in various modes for different types of projects and the way projects might be affected by everything from environmental laws and citizen opposition to design delays.

In some instances, especially in the United States, certain funds are earmarked for specific projects or project categories, with the allocation being determined by a variety of measures such as metropolitan population, road mileage, or population density. If the overall amount of funding for the categories is known, the funding level for a metropolitan area in this project category can be determined by using an allocation formula. For other sources of funds, such as revenues from transit operations, simple trend estimates can be used to determine the following year's total revenue, while more sophisticated analysis techniques can be used to estimate ridership (and hence revenues beyond the 1-year time frame).

As an overall approach, a four-step process can be used to determine the availability of funding:

1. *Forecast future funds available from higher levels of government.* This step is probably the most difficult one in the entire process because it occurs at a level far

removed from the immediate concern of the programmer. In the United States, for example, this task would involve forecasting the amount of transportation money that will be coming from state government. At the state level, since a large percentage of transportation funds comes from taxes on gasoline consumption, forecasting the flow of funds requires an understanding of the impact on transportation funds of more fuel-efficient automobiles or decreased vehicle registrations. Often, officials in agencies of higher levels of government are able to estimate what funds they will have available, at least in the near term (see Fig. 10-6). At other times, these officials will be unable to provide this information because the appropriate legislative body has not yet decided on the level of funds to be allocated. Local programmers might thus find themselves developing estimates of the levels of funding from higher levels of government which in one year might be, at best, a rough approximation of what action the legislative body will take.

2. *Forecast future funds available from local government.* The programmer should be able to determine with some certainty the level of funding that will be provided for transportation purposes by local government. This can be done by closely monitoring the political and budgetary process of local governments or, in the case

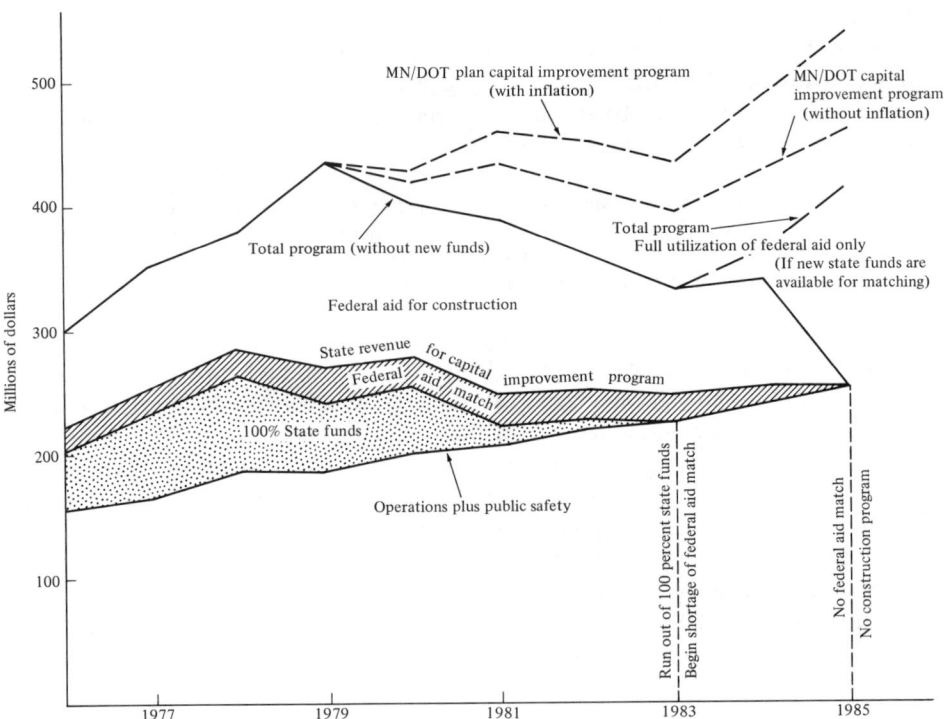

Figure 10-6 Historic and projected highway revenues and expenditures for Minnesota. (*Transportation Research Board [1980].*)

of dedicated funding sources (e.g., 1 percent sales tax for regional transportation purposes), estimating the likely trends associated with the source activity and the resultant level of funds to be made available for transportation purposes. In the case of revenue projections (e.g., from transit fares or highway tolls) the level of analysis can be relatively simple (for example, trend projections) or sophisticated (for example, transit ridership demand models). The specific analysis technique used in estimating the revenues would depend on the characteristics of the transportation system and on the operating environment. Clearly, adding a new line to a subway network or having the price of gasoline increase dramatically would affect the ridership and revenues on a transit system and would require a more sophisticated revenues analysis than a simple trend projection. Estimating the impacts of selected projects on budget availability is thus an important task for transportation planners concerned with programming.

3. *Determine cash flow requirements.* Although estimating the total level of funding available for transportation purposes is an important element of programming, an equally important task is determining the flow of those funds among project categories and over time. Many funding programs have provisions for separate agencies funding a different share of the project cost. For example, the interstate highway program in the United States was constructed with the federal government covering 90 percent of the project cost and state governments providing the rest. In situations where matching shares of project cost are feasible, the programmer is faced with the task of determining if sufficient local funds are available at the required time to match funds from other agencies.

Another cash flow problem can be related to the reimbursement policies of government agencies. For example, the costs of project design and right-of-way acquisition typically need to be paid when the work is being done, whereas for construction projects, the costs might not have to be paid until the contractor reaches certain stages of the construction work. The determination of costs for a specific project which involves preliminary engineering, right-of-way acquisition, and construction can thus extend beyond a short-term programming horizon and can cause problems for the programmer in terms of determining cash flow.

4. *Bring funding categories together to determine overall budget and deficit.* Once the funding levels have been estimated for specific program areas, they should be combined with estimates of operating and capital expenditures to provide a clear picture of the financial situation over the programming time horizon (see Fig. 10-7). Such a synthesis not only gives decision makers an indication of the absolute levels of funding available, but also provides an "early warning" system for identifying future areas with uncertain funding.

Because there are so many uncertainties associated with overall funding levels, some urban areas develop several funding scenarios and then choose the one most likely to occur. Transportation planners in Chicago, for example, developed the following funding scenarios based on alternative assumptions of state and local revenues, transfer of funds from a crosstown expressway project, and the cost escalation of providing existing services.

	1981 regional transportation improvement program					
	FY82	FY83	FY84	FY85	FY86	FY82–86 total
Expenditures						
State highway program	61,847	120,205	107,411	89,018	127,192	505,673
Local assistance						
highway	32,384	28,798	14,101	15,950	11,228	102,461
Transit—operating	60,273	73,388	82,689	92,847	109,823	419,020
Transit—capital	80,185	37,929	15,552	18,177	15,995	167,838
Bikeway	1,488	1,102	1,677	930	1,095	6,292
Aviation	3,767	9,115	10,164	5,036	64	28,146
Total	239,944	270,537	231,594	221,958	265,397	1,229,430
Revenues—federal						
Highway (FHWA)	47,436	108,257	86,385	79,253	106,260	427,591
Transit (UMTA)	29,086	24,316	26,396	27,588	26,385	133,771
Aviation (ADAP)	1,716	7,717	8,166	4,157		21,756
Federal—other					392	392
Revenues—nonfederal						
State highway	8,272	20,498	14,778	13,870	19,007	76,425
Prop 5 transit*	16,700	14,300	10,200	8,600	7,500	57,300
Toll bridge	826		930			1,756
SB620 state†	56,920	24,430				81,350
Bike lane acct.	153	102	154	228		637
Aviation (CAAP)	729	242	50	54	58	1,133
State—other	1,526	468	515	567	622	3,698
TDA/LTF‡	33,939	32,465	39,650	43,696	51,186	200,936
STAF (SB620)§	3,172	3,083	700	800	800	8,555
Local—other	39,479	33,156	40,784	38,408	47,499	199,326
Revenues—total	239,954	269,034	228,708	217,221	259,709	1,214,626
Deficit	+10	(1,503)	(2,886)	(4,737)	(5,688)	(14,804)

* Locally generated gas tax revenue returned to county.
† State transit discretionary funds generated by state sales tax.
‡ Local transportation fund generated by state sales tax.
* State transit assistance fund generated by state sales tax.

Figure 10-7 Revenue and expenditure summary for San Diego, in thousands of dollars.

Level A (start). Federal funds remain at existing levels with an impasse on the crosstown; state and local revenues remain at existing levels, but the cost of existing services escalates. Result: not enough local funds to match federal funds. $1,435,763,000

Level B (low-one). Federal funds remain at existing levels with an impasse on the crosstown; new state and local revenues are tapped. Result: all federal funds are matched. $1,648,524,000

Level C (low-two). Federal funds remain at existing levels, *and* the crosstown money is used; new state and local revenues are tapped. Result: all federal funds are matched. $2,627,424,000

Level D (high-one). Federal funds depict higher levels of spending and proportional increases in the regional federal funds. Impasse on the crosstown. Result: all potential state and local revenues are tapped. $3,093,795,000

Level E (high-two). Federal funds depict higher levels of spending and proportional increases in the regional federal funds, *and* the crosstown money is used. Result: all potential state and local revenues are tapped. $4,072,795,000

After analyzing the alternative sources of funding and the problem of increasing maintenance and operating costs, Chicago planners chose level B as the basis for developing the transportation investment program.

It should be noted that there are approaches other than this example from Chicago for establishing the overall programming budget for a metropolitan area. For example, one could develop different budget scenarios such as that shown above, but instead of choosing one to guide the programming process, alternative programs could be designed for each scenario. Each alternative could then be compared for similar projects. Desirable projects would receive priority for programming because, no matter which scenario actually occurred, these projects would be found in each program.

Another approach, which seems to occur often in practice, is to establish an estimate of the budget and then overprogram (i.e., list more projects in the programming document than there is money to build). The purpose of this approach is to have a large number of projects which could be implemented if extra funds unexpectedly became available or if one project is stopped and the funds could be used for other purposes. Transportation agencies often have completed preliminary engineering on such projects and are therefore able to commit construction money immediately if funding becomes available. This approach is especially helpful in capturing federal money unclaimed by other agencies, since such money must be committed within a short time frame.

10-3 DESIGN OF THE TRANSPORTATION IMPROVEMENT PROGRAM DOCUMENT

The transportation investment program is such an important component of the transportation planning process that the program document itself should be carefully designed to provide as much information as possible to decision makers on the status of the transportation program and on the progress being made toward the attainment of community goals. One possible format for a programming document is shown in Fig. 10-8. This format has been synthesized from the programming documents of several United States cities.

Some characteristics of this format merit special attention. First, the projects being considered are associated with the objectives of the transportation plan. The programming document thus indicates how successful the implementation of a regional transportation plan is and how specific objectives are being achieved. Second, a lead agency is designated for each project; the document identifies the agency to be contacted with questions on the status of the project and also establishes responsibility for moving the project through the development process. Third, the costs of the project are given in current dollars and inflated dollars to indicate the level of funding necessary to complete the project (and to indicate the cost of delay). The funding sources are also identified by major governmental unit. Finally, the type and status of environmental

Priority	Program area		Short-range plan objective				Long-range plan objective				Current costs, ($000)				Escalation rate %
	Project description	Lead agency	1	2	3	4	1	2	3	4	Fed.	State	Local	Total	

Escalated cost	Program year					Environmental documents	Comments
	1982–1983	1983–1984	1984–1985	1985–1986	1986–1987		

Figure 10-8 Example format for a transportation improvement program.

documents necessary to proceed with construction are indicated in one of the last columns. An "R" in this column means that the necessary documentation has been received by the MPO, and an "NR" means that it has not been received.

As shown by this example, the TIP can provide useful information apart from the sequence of project implementation over time. The TIP can also indicate the degree to which the transportation plan is being implemented, the agencies responsible for project implementation, the costs of project development (and delay), and the status of specific requirements that might delay the project. Along with this tabular summary of the projects scheduled for implementation, the programming document should provide a summary of the transportation issues facing the region, identify projects that can be substituted for those under consideration, and indicate other decisions on project implementation that need to be made. In this way, the TIP could serve as an extremely valuable management and decision-making document for the transportation planning process.

10-4 EXAMPLES OF SCHEDULING, BUDGETING, AND ESTABLISHING PRIORITIES

The following three examples are presented to give the reader an indication of how transportation planners have addressed the issues related to the programming process. It should be noted that these examples—a proposed regional transportation programming scheme for southeastern Wisconsin, a network scheduling procedure for the Atlanta subway system, and a budgeting process for the Portland transit agency—are simplified descriptions of very complex political and technical processes. They have been included here to illustrate many of the concepts discussed earlier.

10-4-1 A Proposed Method for Preparing a Regional Transportation Improvement Program: The Case of Southeastern Wisconsin

An effective programming process must reflect the transportation institutional structure of a metropolitan area and should be sensitive to the formal decision-making process which reconciles conflicting and often competing needs and interests. In most cases in the United States, this requirement has meant that the regional programming process has really been one of individual implementing agencies developing investment programs based on their own estimation of the funds available to them and then submitting these programs to the metropolitan planning organization for review to ensure consistency with other regional plans. The adopted regional transportation improvement program (TIP) is thus, in many cases, nothing more than a compilation of individual agency program lists [Meyer, 1978]. Under this process, little effort is made to compare investments between modes, resulting in an investment strategy which is not necessarily the best for the region. On the positive side, however, this type of programming process is relatively easy to update because areawide priorities do not have to be determined, it reflects the structure of institutional responsibility in the region, and it complements the structure of funding which, in the United States, is based along modal lines.

Step 1: Criteria development	Step 2: Needs identification	Step 3: Funds estimation	Step 4: Grouping and prioritization	Step 5: Project group and individual project selection
Task 1A—Development of project grouping criteria Task 1B—Development of group prioritization criteria Task 1C—Development of project selection criteria	Task 2A—Project submittal or proposal by implementing agencies Task 2B—Analysis of conformance or conflict of projects with regional transportation system plan Task 2C—(If needed) review of nonconforming or conflicting projects with implementing agency and resolution of differences	Task 3A—Estimation of availability of nondiscretionary funds by mode and funding category Task 3B—Estimation of availability of discretionary funds by mode and funding category	Task 4A—Categorization of all projects into high-, medium-, and low-priority preservation, improvement, and expansion for on-system highway and transit and for off-system highway, safety, and environmental enhancement for highway (utilizing project grouping criteria developed under task 1A) Task 4B—Prioritization of groups eligible under	Task 5A—Application of available discretionary funds in each funding category to project groups under that category arrayed in priority order; projects in groups wholly funded in each category are included directly in TIP Task 5B—Analysis of intermediate system resulting from adding nondiscretionary funded projects and projects from wholly funded groups to

each funding category (utilizing group prioritization criteria developed under task 1B)

Task 4C—Removal from prioritized groups of those projects programmed by implementing agencies for implementation with nondiscretionary funds and inclusion of them directly in TIP

existing transportation system; identification of system connectivity problems (gaps, bottlenecks, dead ends, etc.)

Task 5C—Selection of projects from unfunded groups sufficient to use remaining money (utilizing project selection criteria developed under task 1C, with emphasis on addressing system connectivity problems identified under task 5B)

Figure 10-9 Proposed methodology for preparing a transportation improvement program in southeastern Wisconsin. (*Schulz and Evenson [1978].*)

In 1977, the Southeastern Wisconsin Regional Planning Commission (SEWRPC) undertook a study of an alternative method for programming, one based on a decision-making structure in which the programming decisions were made by an advisory committee of the commission. This structure focused the debate and negotiation related to regional investment strategies on the trade-offs related to each, resulting in a transportation program that truly reflected the needs of the region [Schulz and Evensen, 1978].

As shown in Fig. 10-9, the programming method designed to support this decision structure consisted of five major steps. The first step, development of criteria for project grouping and prioritization, was extremely important in that these criteria dictated which projects would be considered and what level of competition each would receive from other projects. The first task in this step was to develop groupings which would serve to classify the projects being considered. Nine categories were proposed with each category having three levels of priority—high, medium, and low. The nine categories were:

1. *On-system highway preservation.* Projects which result in little or no increase in the traffic-carrying capacity of the existing highway system but which are necessary to maintain existing capacity and structural adequacy of the facility for which the project is proposed
2. *On-system highway improvement.* Projects which significantly increase the capacity of existing streets or highways (by definition, the conversion of roads from rural to urban sections is an improvement, even though it might result in marginal capacity improvement)
3. *On-system highway expansion.* Projects which significantly increase the capacity of the transportation system through development of new or extended streets or highways
4. *Transit preservation.* Projects which are necessary to maintain the current quality and level of service on the existing transit system
5. *Transit improvement.* Projects which improve the quality and level of service on the existing transit system
6. *Transit expansion.* Projects which either expand the existing transit system or create new transit systems or subsystems
7. *Highway off-system.* Projects on streets or highways which are not on a currently designated federal aid system
8. *Highway safety.* Projects designed to improve or eliminate existing unsafe conditions on the federal aid highway system as it currently exists
9. *Environmental enhancement.* Projects which, while materially reducing air, noise, or visual pollution, do not significantly affect system operations

Within each category, objective values were assigned to each project using weights related to specific criteria. An example of possible weights for projects in the transit expansion category is shown in Table 10-2. Threshold scores were set in order to classify projects as high, medium, or low priority.

Once these priority groups were identified, they were further grouped by funding category. For example, many types of highway projects can often be funded from the

Table 10-2 Example criteria for determination of project priorities

Criterion	Weight, points
Where a project sponsor is not local unit of government, an assurance that project implements local plans and has local support, as indicated by a letter from local government(s)	100
That a project directly provides or improves coordination between two or more transit systems as indicated by evaluation of the project submittal	50
Design provision for other modes	
Highway	25
Bicycle	25
Pedestrian	25
Service to special groups as indicated by evaluation of project submittal	
Elderly persons	75
Handicapped persons	100
Racial minorities	50
Functional criterion: type of service (total of 200 points available) as indicated by evaluation of the project submittal	
Primary	200
Secondary	150
Tertiary	100
Other	varies
Number of people served: proposed daily ridership	200
Surrogate for cost-effectiveness: passenger travel provided per cost of project	200

Source: Mason et al. [1979].

same source. It was also necessary to determine within each funding category which groups were more important than others (e.g., were medium-priority highway improvement projects more important than high-priority highway expansion projects?).

The final task in this first step of the programming process was to determine the criteria to be used for selecting projects that did not fall into any funding category. These criteria could include impact on specific community groups, geographical dispersion of projects due to political pressures, or any other criterion that related to the objectives of the metropolitan area or the requirements of the political process.

The second step in the method consisted of identifying transportation needs by type of project. Projects would be submitted by the transportation implementing agencies, and by any other interested group in the metropolitan area, to the MPO. These projects would then be reviewed by the MPO staff to determine their consistency with regional plans.

The third step, perhaps the most important and yet most susceptible to political and economic changes, was the estimation of available transportation funds. In this case, there were two distinct types of funding that had to be considered—nondiscretionary funds which were obtained from higher levels of government and which had to be applied to specific project types, and discretionary funds which the advisory committee could distribute as it saw fit.

The final two steps in the process were geared toward operationalizing the method. Step 4 involved taking the projects identified in step 2 and, using the criteria developed in step 1, placing them in categorical-priority groups. In cases where there was full funding available in a specific category, all candidate projects in this category were put directly into the programming document. Step 5 in the process consisted of allocating the discretionary funds to the projects in each category that were not yet funded. Although information on priorities of groups and projects was provided in this analysis, the allocation of discretionary funding very much depended on political bargaining and negotiation. The output of this programming process was a document which outlined the future transportation investments in the region and reflected the priorities set by the political process.

10-4-2 Network Phasing: The MARTA Subway System

In 1971, the voters of metropolitan Atlanta approved a referendum that provided local financial support for the construction of a 53-mile subway system, 8 miles of bus way, and an extensive feeder bus system. Although originally scheduled for completion by 1980, the lack of sufficient federal funds meant that only phase A was completed—13.7 miles of rail line with supporting local and feeder bus service. Because future funding for subway construction was uncertain, the Metropolitan Atlanta Rapid Transit Authority (MARTA) undertook a study to determine the best incremental implementation strategy given that future funding would be sufficient to cover the construction of only one or two parts of the network at any given time [Mason et al., 1979].

In the opening paragraphs of the final report, the difficulties in planning the development of a system such as MARTA's under uncertain environmental conditions were clearly identified [Metropolitan Atlanta Rapid Transit Authority, 1977]:

> No preconditions were considered in analyzing the most desirable sequence of extensions. In particular, the schedule of system completion which was included in the 1971 Engineering Report was not considered. That schedule was based on the assumption that the entire rail system would be opened over a period of only two years, and the sequence was determined primarily by technical considerations concerning construction and operations. The Phasing Study is based on longer intervals between extensions. It also reflects other conditions which have changed since 1971, such as development patterns, the energy crisis, and the changes which have been made in the system itself.

Over a period of only 6 years, several factors—rapid urban development, increasing cost and scarcity of gasoline, and improvements made to the transportation system—had changed the validity of previous analyses and thus had to be incorporated into the updated planning study.

The MARTA network, beyond the initial phase A system, was divided into 13 operational segments. These segments were then grouped into four test networks that served as the basis for a comparative analysis (see Fig. 10-10). Using the conventional modeling techniques discussed in Chap. 7 (in this case, UTMS) and other simpler analysis methods, MARTA planners were able to predict the following for each segment:

Total increase in transit system patronage
Total patronage on each segment

PROGRAM AND PROJECT IMPLEMENTATION **463**

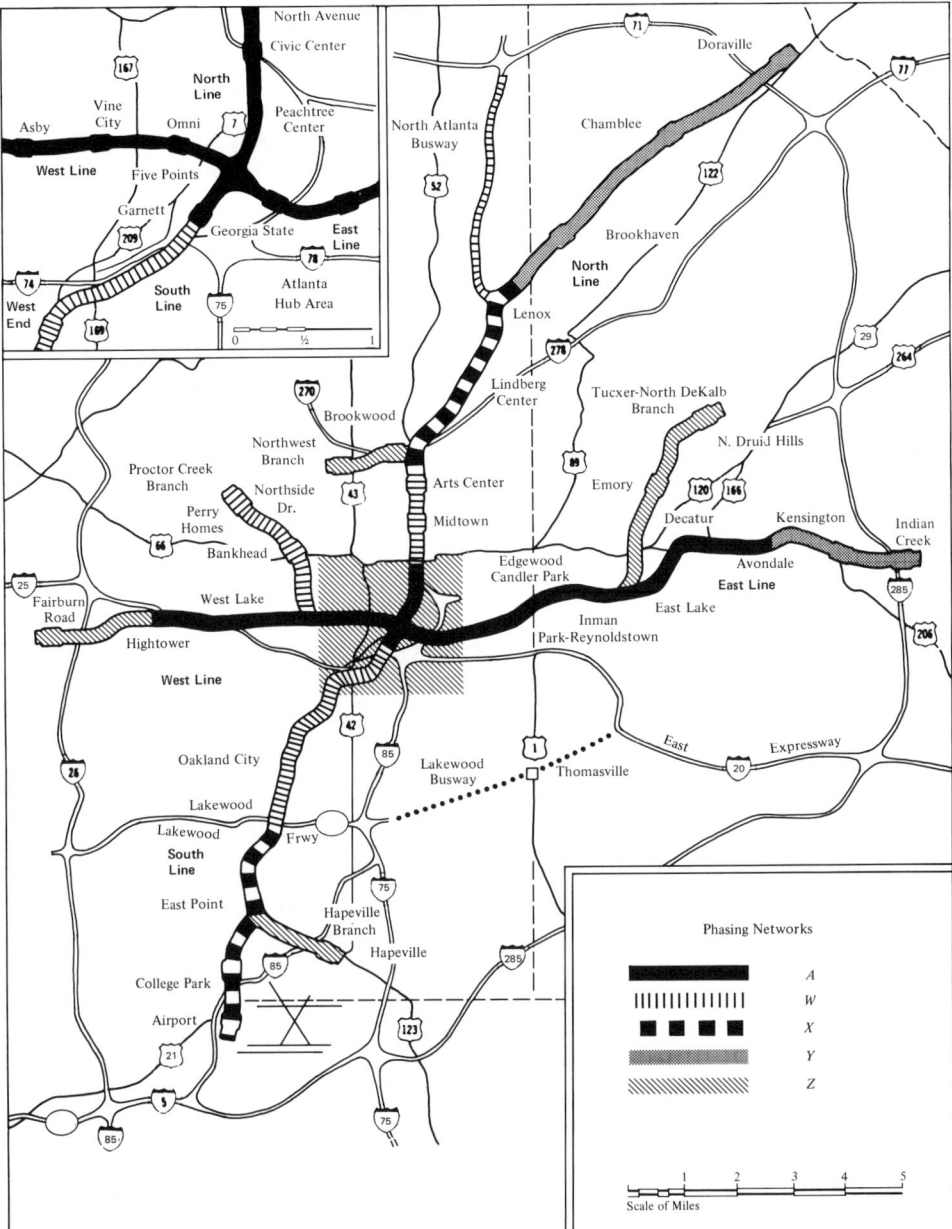

Figure 10-10 Network phasing alternatives for the Atlanta subway system. (*Metropolitan Atlanta Rapid Transit Authority [1977].*)

Total capital cost
Total increase in operating cost
Relative cost-effectiveness
Travel time improvements to major activity centers
Improvement of transit service to special groups (i.e., elderly, handicapped, and captive riders)
Impacts on land use and development patterns
Environmental impacts and energy consumption

This information was then used for ranking the segments in order of implementation priority.

Several characteristics of the method used in this analysis merit special attention. First, the analysis was conducted in an iterative manner. In the first iteration, only those segments that could potentially be added to the phase A system were considered, with those segments having the best rankings chosen for priority implementation. The phase A network plus the segments chosen from the first iteration then became the base case for the second iteration, and so forth. In each case, the addition of a new segment to the network changed the characteristics of travel (e.g., mode split) because new transit origins and destinations were added to the base system.

Second, both capital and operating costs were associated with each segment. Although the capital costs of construction were relatively straightforward to estimate, several problems were encountered in estimating the operating costs. One of the most difficult problems, for example, was determining the allocation to specific segments of costs common to the entire system, such as costs of administration and fare collection. The general approach followed by MARTA planners for determining operating costs was to calculate the increase of vehicle miles associated with a particular segment, multiply it by an operating cost per vehicle mile, and then add any costs associated with the operation of new stations along the segment. The common costs were assumed to be constant over each network tested ($1.20 per vehicle mile), but the operating cost changed in each iteration because of network scale factors. The costs estimated in this analysis were then related to the number of new riders attracted to the system by segment, and a cost per daily rider or a cost-efficiency figure was obtained (see Table 10-3).

Third, MARTA planners wanted to incorporate into the analysis some measures of service value per dollar invested. This was accomplished by determining the difference in travel time by transit, before and after adding a new segment, to major destination points in the Atlanta region. The time saved for each trip was multiplied by the estimated number of riders making the trip and then summed over all the trips made. This figure, the total number of person minutes saved for arrivals at these destinations, was then divided into the daily cost of providing the service, producing a *travel utility measure* of cost per person minute saved. To facilitate comparative analysis, these measures were divided by the lowest segment measure to generate a *travel utility index*. For example, if the measures for five segments were $0.10, $0.20, $0.35, $0.40, and $0.50 per person minute saved, the respective utility indices would be 1.0, 2.0, 3.5, 4.0, and 5.0. This implies that the second segment is only one-half as cost-effective in terms of travel time savings as the first segment, and so forth.

Table 10-3 Derivation of cost per daily rider for MARTA network phasing (1977 dollars)

		Total daily new systemwide riders	Total capital cost, $ millions	Daily capital cost, 50-year life for structures and 25-year life for equipment	Daily capital cost per new daily rider (1)	Operating increase, $ millions	Daily operating cost increase	Operating cost increase per new daily rider (2)	Total daily cost per new daily rider (1 + 2)
Iteration one	Garnett–Lakewood	18,300	$109	$ 9544	$ .52	$4.18	$14667	$ .80	$1.32
	Proctor Creek branch	4,390	$ 73	$ 6386	$1.45	$ .86	$ 3018	$ .69	$2.14
	Hightower–Fairburn Road	1,510	$ 48	$ 4211	$2.79	$1.32	$ 4632	$3.07	$5.86
	North Avenue–Arts Center	7,900	$ 63	$ 5474	$ .69	$1.23	$ 4316	$ .55	$1.24
	Tucker–North DeKalb branch	4,300	$ 90	$ 7860	$1.83	$1.73	$ 6070	$1.41	$3.24
	Avondale–Indian Creek	9,470	$113	$ 9895	$1.04	$3.50	$12281	$1.30	$2.34
Iteration two	Lakewood–Airport	21,260	$134	$11719	$ .55	$3.70	$12982	$ .61	$1.16
	Lakewood–bus way	2,300	$ 18	$ 1544	$ .67				$ .67
	Proctor Creek branch	4,590	$ 73	$ 6386	$1.39	$2.27	$ 7965	$1.74	$3.13
	Hightower–Fairburn Road	1,640	$ 48	$ 4211	$2.57	$1.09	$ 3825	$2.33	$4.90
	Arts Center–Lenox	10,000	$136	$11860	$ .59	$4.78	$16772	$ .84	$1.43
	Northwest branch	4,450	$ 88*	$ 7508	$1.69	$2.96	$10386	$2.33	$4.02
	Tucker–North DeKalb branch	9,710	$ 90	$ 7860	$1.67	$2.46	$ 8632	$1.83	$3.50
	Avondale–Indian Creek	11,700	$113	$ 9895	$ .85	$3.66	$12842	$1.10	$1.95
Iteration three	Hapeville branch	4,250	$ 60	$ 5053	$1.19	$1.75	$ 6140	$1.44	$2.63
	Proctor Creek branch	4,640	$ 73	$ 6386	$1.38	$2.03	$ 7123	$1.54	$2.90
	Hightower–Fairburn Road	1,720	$ 48	$ 4211	$2.45	$ .68	$ 2386	$1.39	$3.84
	Northwest branch	4,500	$ 78	$ 6807	$1.51	$1.20	$ 4211	$ .94	$2.45
	Lenox–Doraville	12,700	$166	$14456	$1.14	$5.04	$17684	$1.39	$2.53
	North Atlanta bus way	1,880	$ 20	$ 1754	$ .93				$ .93
	Tucker–North DeKalb branch	5,020	$ 90	$ 7860	$1.57	$1.95	$ 6842	$1.36	$2.93
	Avondale–Indian Creek	12,380	$113	$ 9895	$ .80	$4.01	$14070	$1.14	$1.94

* If Northwest branch is built before Lenox, cost of some prebranch track must be added.

Source: Metropolitan Atlanta Rapid Transit Authority [1977].

Finally, a set of "nonquantifiable" factors was considered for each segment. These factors included community and environmental impact, effect on land use and development, and service to special groups and transit-dependent persons. (Note that while MARTA planners considered these factors in a subjective way, such factors have been "quantified" in other studies.) The factors were then summarized in one rating for each segment with "A" being the most desirable and "E" being the least desirable. The following statement is an example of a segment given a "B" rating:

> The rail line follows a railroad corridor, and will have relatively little adverse impact. Areas where adverse impacts were anticipated are the McDaniel-Glenn apartments (relocation and noise) and Fort McPherson (historic and possible ecologic).
> Positive effects will include the stimulation of development in the West End area, and for the South side in general; improved service to lower-middle income areas with many elderly persons; and improved service to large concentrations of blue-collar employment.

Each of these evaluation criteria—ridership estimates, cost efficiency, travel utility, and nonquantifiable measures—was used in comparing the overall desirability of the segments. Such a comparison is shown in Table 10-4 for the first iteration of the phasing study. From this analysis, it was concluded that first priority should be given to the construction of the Garnett–Lakewood and North Avenue–Arts Center segments because of their dominance over other segments.

10-4-3 The Portland Transit Agency Financial Programming Process

Financial forecasting is a planning tool which extends beyond the accounting functions of the budgetary process to a consideration of the longer-run economic implications of a particular course of action. By taking into account the causes of cost and revenue trends, as well as the consequences of alternative investment strategies, financial forecasting enables Tri-Met, the transit agency in Portland, Oregon, to ensure that the annual budget is consistent with the first year of a longer-term financial strategy [Jones and Wentworth, 1981].

Table 10-4 Atlanta phasing study, iteration one

Segment	Net systemwide patronage increase	Cost-efficiency analysis	Total daily rail ridership	Travel utility index	Non quantifiable factors
Garnett–Lakewood	18,300	$1.32	57,100	1.00	B
Proctor Creek branch	4,390	$2.14	17,700	4.51	B
Hightower–Fairburn Road	1,510	$5.86	7,700	4.90	E
North Avenue–Arts Center	7,900	$1.24	54,100	1.29	A
Tucker–N. DeKalb branch	4,300	$3.24	12,200	4.18	D
Avondale–Indian Creek	9,470	$2.34	26,700	4.23	C

Source: Metropolitan Atlanta Rapid Transit Authority [1977].

The financial forecasting process involves a series of models, each used to estimate some aspect of costs or revenues. When applied together, these models are used to develop future cash flow estimates for the agency. Each forecasting model is a mathematical simulation of a particular cause-and-effect relationship involving operating costs or revenues. The input data for the equations are the causal factors which become the independent variables in the simulation. Changes in these causal factors are projected in order to forecast the consequent changes to the dependent variables, the actual costs or revenue items. Such forecasts are projections made under a set of *assumed* conditions, rather than predictions.

Tri-Met utilizes the financial forecasting system for both revenue and cost management. The system enables management to better understand the dynamics of transit revenues by examining (1) local tax bases, (2) returns on investments, (3) trends in fares, and (4) federal grant programs. The system also aids in cost management by assessing the impacts of service changes, service standards, work rules and employee benefits, maintenance activities, capital programming, and construction management. The main purpose of applying the financial forecasting system to each of these aspects of transit operations is to allow Tri-Met to anticipate the financial consequences of alternative policy options.

The two principal components of the financial forecasting system are the financial planning structure and the forecasting models (see Table 10-5). The financial planning structure is the analytical framework that provides a convenient and organized method

Table 10-5 Financial forecasting system

	Revenue models	Cost models	
Input	Revenue line items	Cost line items	Input
Noncapital revenues	Fare revenues Tax-base revenues Federal operating assistance (Section 5) Federal technical and demonstration grants Miscellaneous (interest on investments, etc.) State operating assistance Other	Bus operator costs Other transportation and operations costs Fuel Maintenance General and administrative including pension cost	Operating costs
Capital revenues	Federal capital State capital Local capital Other local assistance	Capital costs: Vehicles, facilities, and equipment Vehicle replacement Debt service Project scheduling Life-cycle costing	Capital costs
Output	Summary financial forecast		Output

Source: Jones and Wentworth [1981].

Table 10-6 Financial forecast for Tri-Met, optimistic scenario

	FY81	FY82	FY83	FY84	FY85
Revenues					
Noncapital revenue					
Fare-box revenue	18,700	21,114	25,415	28,781	32,371
Other operating revenue	678	753	835	926	1,029
Payroll tax	34,965	39,615	45,805	54,502	62,638
State operating assistance		900	1,000	1,400	1,600
Federal tech and demo assistance	1,654	3,185	2,873	3,065	2,783
Miscellaneous	2,647	2,938	3,261	3,587	3,946
New revenue source					
Federal operating assistance	5,890	5,890	3,887	1,944	
Total operating revenue	64,534	74,395	83,076	94,205	104,367
Capital revenue					
Federal (bus)	1,330	29,728	28,391	17,014	22,417
State (bus)	0	2,581	983	2,075	675
Subtotal (bus)	1,330	32,309	29,374	19,090	23,092
Federal (LRT)	414	39,819	31,005	42,115	66,056
State (LRT)	83	6,807	14,110	0	0
Subtotal (LRT)	497	46,626	45,115	42,115	66,056
Long-term financing	1,434	8,380	6,525	7,745	12,149
Total capital revenue	3,261	87,315	81,014	68,950	101,297
Costs					
Operating cost					
Operators	27,869	34,565	39,619	43,532	47,349
Fuel	4,944	6,615	8,402	9,410	10,539
Maintenance	11,400	12,944	14,738	16,212	17,833
Operators' administration and support	4,027	4,960	6,029	6,732	7,505
General and administration	11,452	13,017	14,539	15,993	17,592
Banfield LRT project	451				4,400
Total operating cost	60,143	72,101	83,327	91,879	105,218
Capital cost					
Vehicles (bus)	2,418	22,294	11,660	13,367	13,046
Facilities and equipment (bus)	3,570	18,397	24,239	8,100	14,975
Vehicles (LRT)		46,629	45,115	47,484	73,876
Facilities and equipment (LRT)					
Debt service	337	2,553	2,980	5,577	6,324
Total capital cost	6,325	89,870	83,994	74,523	107,621
Operating contingency					
Net change in working capital	1,327	(261)	(3,231)	(3,252)	(7,175)
Beginning working capital	14,684	16,011	15,750	12,519	9,267
Ending working capital	16,011	15,750	12,519	9,267	2,092

Source: Jones and Wentworth [1981].

for inputting the data and control parameters and for producing output reports. The validity of each model's output is dependent on the assumptions made about the causal relationships. Once formulated, each model is calibrated to match observed data and historical trends. Sensitivity analyses are then used to determine the range of variability of the forecasting process. An example of the output of this financial planning system is shown in Table 10-6.

10-5 CHAPTER SUMMARY

1. Project programming is a technical and political process that establishes priorities for transportation projects by assessing current and future resource availability in order to stage projects over time. Technical analysis and political considerations are elements of programming that are closely interrelated, with the relative impact of each on any one project decision varying greatly as decision makers seek to satisfy both the relevant transportation policies and the many interest groups involved.
2. Computer-based analytical tools for establishing project priorities on the basis of the cost-effectiveness of investments in highway construction are widely used by state and provincial transportation agencies. Urban agencies, however, generally have not made similar use of these techniques because of the greater complexity of transportation investment decisions at the metropolitan level. The 1975 U.S. Department of Transportation planning regulations requiring urban agencies to develop staged, multiyear transportation improvement programs were a first step toward structuring the project programming process in urban areas.
3. An effective programming process should:
    - Ensure that investment decisions made are related to established transportation policy and planning goals
    - Provide a general direction for transportation investment by integrating projects over time and location
    - Set priorities among policy and agency objectives
    - Include credible estimates of funding sources
    - Provide decision makers with a timely review of the effectiveness of transportation policy and planning in the region
    - Be open to those interested to assure consistency between the program and community goals
4. Setting priorities for project selection is a basic component of the programming process. Once again, most of the efforts to develop and use computer packages to rank project proposals according to various priority indices have occurred at higher levels of government rather than in urban areas. Project priority guidelines for decision makers and linear weighting schemes involving predetermined impact measures are more common approaches for determining the relative effectiveness of different transportation investments in urban areas. Even when such structured

techniques for ranking projects are used, however, political considerations tend to control the final investment decision.
5. Another basic component of the programming process is the forecasting of future funding availability. The diversity and uncertainty of transportation funding sources mean that experience and intuition on the part of the programmer can be just as important as the analytical techniques used. Several aspects of the forecasting component merit special note:

- Funds to be made available by higher levels of government are the most difficult to forecast, as funds allocations can be determined both by changing economic trends and by legislative decisions.
- Monitoring the budgetary processes of local governments and estimating the impacts of selected projects on future local budgets are crucial to developing accurate estimates of funding from local sources.
- The cash flow requirements of different project categories over time and the shares to be paid by different levels of government have to be determined, beyond the short-term programming horizon.
- Estimates of funding sources and availability have to be related to projected operating and capital expenditures in order to provide a complete picture of the financial situation over the programming horizon.

6. The transportation program document itself should be designed to inform decision makers of the program and the progress being made toward the attainment of transportation policy goals. A possible format could include outlines of the transportation projects programmed and indications of the relationships between the projects and specific policy objectives. In the document, a lead agency should be designated for each project, the costs and funding sources for each project should be identified, and any environmental or other requirements for its construction should be outlined. Along with the projects scheduled for implementation, other transportation issues and alternative projects could be described to maximize the amount of information the document provides to decision makers.

QUESTIONS

1. For your urban area, obtain a copy of a transportation programming document and discuss the following:
    (a) What are the major sources of funding for transportation projects in your urban area?
    (b) Which agencies seem to be actively involved in the programming process, based on the documentation?
    (c) What type of project seems to be receiving priority in the document?
    (d) For the major sources of funding, what factors are likely to hinder or help forecasting future contributions?

2. A multiyear framework for programming allows the planner to integrate projects over time and location. What problems are likely to arise in developing such a multiyear program?
3. Establishing priorities for resource allocation is an important element of the programming process. Most efforts to establish such priorities have focused on projects found in one funding category or in one modal group. Thus, for example, highway projects are often compared and ranked with other highway projects but rarely with transit projects. Outline a procedure for establishing priorities between highway and transit projects. What are the advantages of such a procedure?
4. Divide the class into groups and use the Delphi process, as described in Appendix C, to establish the importance of transportation problems facing university students. Use the process for two iterations. What happened to the relative importance of the identified problems?
5. Select a funding source for transportation programs sponsored by a local agency. Forecast the level of funds that will be available from this source next year, in 3 years, in 5 years, in 10 years. What are some of the problems associated with such forecasting?
6. Outline a public participation program that can be used to provide input into a regional transportation programming process.

REFERENCES

Bellomo, S. J., et al.: "Evaluating Options in Statewide Transportation Planning/Programming," *National Cooperative Research Program Report 199*, Transportation Research Board, Washington D.C., 1979.

Chicago Area Transportation Study: *Transportation Improvement Program FY 76-FY80, A Documentation of the Programming Process*, June 1976.

Federal Highway Administration: *Programming Projects*, U.S. Department of Transportation, Washington, D.C., 1980.

Humphrey, T., M. Meyer, and F. Salvucci: "An Organizational Analysis of a State DOT Program Development Process," *Transportation Research Record 949*, Transportation Research Board, Washington, D.C., 1983.

Jones, J., and D. Wentworth: "Use of Financial Forecasting in Dealing with Transit Funding Uncertainties," Paper prepared for presentation at the Conference on Urban Transportation Planning in the 1980s, Airlie House, Warrenton, Va., Nov. 9, 1981.

Lloyd, E., and M. D. Meyer: "Strategies for Overcoming Opposition to Project Implementation," *Transport Policy and Decisionmaking*, forthcoming.

Mason, J., et al.: "Determination of Priorities for Incremental Development of the MARTA System," *Transportation Research Record 698*, Transportation Research Board, 1979.

Metropolitan Atlanta Rapid Transit Authority: "Analysis of Priorities for the Completion of the Rapid Transit System," Atlanta, Ga., October 1977.

Meyer, M. D.: "A Review of Second-Year TSM Plans: Evolution of the Short-Range Transportation Planning Process," Center for Transportation Studies Working Paper 78-1, MIT, Cambridge, Mass., March 1978.

Neumann, L.: "Integrating Transportation System Planning and Programming: An Implementation Approach," unpublished Ph. D. dissertation, Department of Civil Engineering, MIT, Cambridge, Mass., 1976.

North Carolina Department of Transportation: *A Transportation Resource Allocation System for North Carolina,* June 1972.

Politano, A.: *Financing Urban Transportation Improvements, Report 1: Cost-Effectiveness Considerations in Corridor Planning and Project Programming,* Federal Highway Administration, U.S. Department of Transportation Report FHWA/PL/83/001, Washington, D.C., April 1983.

Ontario Ministry of Transportation and Communications: *Priority Analysis, Systems Manual,* Toronto, Ontario, September 1974.

Schulz, D. F., and P. C. Evenson: "Alternative Methods for Developing Transportation Improvement Programs for Urban Areas," *Transportation Research Record 680,* Transportation Research Board, 1978.

Transportation Research Board: *National Cooperative Highway Research Program Synthesis of Highway Practice 72,* Washington, D.C., 1980.

―――: "Priority Programming and Project Selection," *National Cooperative Highway Research Program Synthesis of Highway Practice 48,* Washington, D.C., 1978.

U.S. Department of Transportation: *Objective Priority Programming Procedures: Narrative and User's Documentation,* Washington, D.C., 1973.

―――: "Transportation Improvement Program," *Federal Register,* Sept. 17, 1975.

―――: *Highway Investment Analysis Package,* Washington, D.C., March 1976.

Wilson, D. I., and J. L. Schofer: "Decision-Maker-Defined Cost-Effectiveness Framework for Highway Programming," *Transportation Research Record 677,* Transportation Research Board, 1978.

APPENDIX
A

CHRONOLOGY OF SELECTED FEDERAL ACTIONS RELATED TO URBAN TRANSPORTATION PLANNING

Year	Action	Impact
1962	Federal-Aid Highway Act	Encouraged development of comprehensive transportation systems
		Directed states to develop long-range highway plans coordinated with other modes
		Required that all federally funded highway projects be based on a continuing, comprehensive, and cooperative planning process (3C) involving states and local communities
		Defined planning focus as the urban area
1963	Guidelines for Implementing the 3C Process	Resulted in quick development of relatively standardized planning process in all urbanized areas
1964	Urban Mass Transportation Act	Encouraged planning of areawide urban mass transportation systems
		Established federal support match for acquisition and construction of transit facilities at two-thirds of cost; federal share was limited to 50 percent when no comprehensive plan existed
		Required that all funds be channeled through public agencies to projects initiated locally
		Established program of mass transportation research, development, and demonstrations
1965	Housing and Urban Development Act	Authorized grants for comprehensive planning to regional organizations

473

Year	Action	Impact
1966	Amendments to UMT Act of 1964	Established program of two-thirds support for planning, engineering, and design of local transit projects which would lead to a federal grant application
		Established grants for transit management training
		Established program to develop new system technology
1966	Department of Transportation Act	Created U.S. DOT and provided focal point for coordinated federal transportation policy
		Provided for protection of publicly owned wildlife refuges, recreation areas, parks, and public or private historic sites from highway impacts (Section 4[f])
1966	Demonstration Cities and Metropolitan Development Act	Required review of federal aid applications (section 204) by an areawide agency for coordination with long-range comprehensive development plans
1967	U.S. DOT Policy and Procedure Memorandum 50-9	Specified the 3C process for urban transportation planning, including jurisdictions covered, plan elements, scope of studies, and citizen participation
1968	Federal-Aid Highway Act	Required that secretary of U.S. DOT not approve a program or project requiring use of publicly owned park recreation area or wildlife or waterfowl refuge unless (1) there is no prudent and feasible alternative and (2) all possible planning has been done to minimize harm
		Required public hearings
1968	Intergovernmental Cooperation Act	Required that national, state, regional, and local viewpoints be taken into account (to the extent possible) in planning of federally assisted development programs and projects
1968	Reorganization Plan No. 2 from the President to Congress	Established the Urban Mass Transportation Administration within DOT and transferred existing urban mass transportation programs from the Department of Housing and Urban Development to DOT
1968	U.S. DOT Instructional Memorandum 50-4-68	Required operations plans defining organizational structures and provided further specification of procedures for urban transportation planning
		Provided additional guidance for technical approaches and scheduling of plan reviews and reevaluation
1969	U.S. Office of Management and Budget Circular A-95	Encouraged establishment of project notification and review systems
		Required areawide comprehensive planning agencies to comment on the relationship of proposed projects to the planned development of the area
		Required that federal agencies notify governors of awards within their state
1969	Federal Highway Administration Policy and Procedure Memorandum 20-8	Required a two-public-hearing process for highway projects
		Required consideration of a full range of social, economic, and environmental impacts
1969	Environmental Quality Improvement Act	Established Office of Environmental Quality

Year	Action	Impact
1969	National Environmental Policy Act	Required the preparation of environmental statements (EIS) for major federal actions including a discussion of alternatives and unavoidable adverse effects
		Required a systematic interdisciplinary approach of planning and decision making
		Created Council of Environmental Quality to implement policy
1970	Amendments to Clean Air Act	Created the Environmental Protection Agency, authorized to set ambient air quality standards
		Required development of state implementation plans (SIP) to meet the standards
		Set deadlines for meeting EPA's ambient air quality standards
		Required focus on low-capital and traffic management actions
1970	Urban Mass Transportation Assistance Act	Required that transit systems consider special needs of the elderly and handicapped
		Required environmental impact hearings
1970	Federal-Aid Highway Act	Established the federal-aid urban systems (FAUS)
		Authorized expenditure of highway funds on bus transit projects
		Required promulgation of guidelines to assure that adverse economic, social, and environmental effects are fully considered in highway projects
		Increased federal share for noninterstate projects to 70 percent
		Amended Section 134 to require consultation with local officials before any highway project is built in urban areas with populations of 50,000 or more
1970	Historic Preservation Act	Required secretary of the interior to publish a national register of historic places; once selected, a site is subject to the Section 4 (f) requirements discussed above
1970	Fish and Wildlife Coordination Act	Required consultation and coordination between relevant agencies for any project that modifies any water body of the U.S. in which federal aid is used
1971	Federal Highway Administration Instructional Memorandum 50-3-71	Established annual certification of 3C processes
1972	Policy and Procedure Memorandum 90-4 "Process Guidelines"	Required states to develop their own action plans to describe organization and procedures for highway planning and allowed different procedures for different categories of projects
		Topics to be covered included social, economic, and environmental effects; alternative courses of action; involvement of other agencies and the public; responsibility for implementation; and fiscal and other resources
1972	UMTA Order 1000.2, the UMTA External Operating Manual, Appendix 2	Provided description of planning requirements related to urban mass transportation

Year	Action	Impact
1973	Federal-Aid Highway Act	Allowed expenditures of FAUS funds on mass transportation projects
		Allowed withdrawal of interstate segments and substitution of mass transit projects
		Made funds available to agency designated by state as responsible for 3C process in urban areas
		Required that programs for projects on the urban system be in accordance with Section 134 planning procedures
1973	CEQ, Preparation of Environmental Impact Statements	Provided guidelines to federal departments and agencies for preparing detailed environmental statements
		Directed individual agencies to establish formal procedures
1974	DOT Order 5610.1B	Formalized DOT procedures for environmental impact statements
1974	Interstate System Revisions	Implemented interstate withdrawal and substitution provisions of the 1973 Federal-Aid Highway Act
1974	National Mass Transportation Assistance Act	Authorized federal operating assistance for urban mass transit systems
1975	Endangered Species Act	Prohibited federal activity (including highway building) which may further jeopardize the existence of a plant or animal on the federal endangered species list
1975	FHWA-UMTA Joint Regulations on Urban Transportation Planning	Required, as condition for continuing federal assistance: Designation of a metropolitan planning organization (MPO) in each urban area by the governor
		A unified planning work program and a prospectus
		A short-range transportation systems management (TSM) plan
		A transportation improvement program (TIP) and an annual element detailing the next year's projects
		Special efforts to plan for needs of the elderly and handicapped
1976	UMTA, Major Mass Transportation Investments	Required an analysis of transportation alternatives and final environmental impact statement in order to be eligible for federal assistance for major investments
		Established principles and procedures for UMTA review of alternatives analysis
1977	Mass Transit and Special Use Highway Projects	Authorized the use of highway funds for projects related to transit and high-occupancy vehicles
1977	Federal Water Pollution Control Act	Prohibited dumping of dredged or fill material into wetlands unless a permit is obtained from the Army Corps of Engineers (section 404)
1978	UMTA Policy Toward Rail Transit	Clarified and supplemented earlier principles and procedures for UMTA review of alternatives analysis

Year	Action	Impact
1978	Surface Transportation Assistance Act	Set September 30, 1986, as date by which all remaining portions of interstate system must be under contract or be de-designated
		Made funds available for interstate system resurfacing as of FY 1980
		Required the secretary of DOT to create guidelines for interstate system maintenance
		Created highway bridge replacement and rehabilitation programs
		Created formula grant program for areas other than urbanized (Section 18 of UMT Act)
1980	Environmental Impact and Related Procedures: Final Rule	Established specific NEPA requirements to be followed by FHWA and UMTA
		Specified three classes of actions which prescribe the necessary level of documentation
		Outlined "scoping process" of agency review
1981	FHWA-UMTA, Urban Transportation Planning: Interim Final Rule	Simplified planning process for areas under 200,000
		Gave states and local governments more discretion in determining what is an acceptable MPO structure
		Encouraged metropolitan areas to follow suggested activities to a degree appropriate for the area
1981	FHWA-UMTA Policy on the Applicability of Urban Planning Requirements in Newly Designated Areas	Minimized burden of planning and programming requirements on 95 new urbanized areas (from 1980 census)
		Intended to provide 2-year transition period for new areas for complying with standards
		Allowed interim designations of MPOs in new areas, preferably existing agencies
1982	Surface Transportation Assistance Act	Provided additional funds for highway and transit projects
		Established separate mass transit account in highway trust fund
		Terminated transit operating assistance in FY 84
1983	FHWA-UMTA, Urban Transportation Planning, Final Rules	Increased role of state in directing urban transportation planning
		Reduced number of required products of planning process (e.g., a TSM plan no longer required)

APPENDIX B

ENVIRONMENTAL IMPACT STATEMENTS

	U.S. DEPARTMENT OF TRANSPORTATION **FEDERAL HIGHWAY ADMINISTRATION**	
SUBJECT GUIDANCE MATERIAL FOR THE PREPARATION OF ENVIRONMENTAL DOCUMENTS		**FHWA TECHNICAL ADVISORY** T 6640.8 February 24, 1982

1. PURPOSE. To provide guidance to Federal Highway Administration field offices and to project applicants on the various types of environmental studies and reports.

2. APPLICABILITY

   a. This material, which is not regulatory, has been developed to provide uniform guidance on the content and format of the various environmental studies and reports required by the National Environmental Policy Act (NEPA), 23 U.S.C. 109(h), and 23 U.S.C. 138 (Section 4(f) of the DOT Act).

   b. While this material was developed primarily to provide guidance for the development of environmental impact and Section 4(f) statements, it is also applicable (to the extent appropriate) to any environmental studies that may be needed prior to the advancement of a project with a finding of no significant impact or with a categorical exclusion determination.

Leon N. Larson
Leon N. Larson
Director, Office of
Environmental Policy

Attachment

DISTRIBUTION: H-WCCC/CR/PL)-1   H-W(EO)-2
H-W(EV/RW)-3   HD(ED/FH/RC/RW)-2
H-M-2
H-M(SH/HP)-4

OPI: HEV-11

Guidance Material for the Preparation of Environmental Documents

Background

The purpose of this material is to provide guidance to FHWA field offices and project applicants on National Environmental Policy Act (NEPA) actions and to provide the public with a further explanation of FHWA internal operating procedures in the development of the reports and documentation required by NEPA. This material also provides the guidance required by 23 U.S.C. 109(h) to assure the full consideration of possible adverse economic, social, and environmental effects of proposed FHWA projects. While the material was developed primarily to provide guidance in the development of environmental impact statements (EIS's), it is also applicable, to the extent appropriate, for environmental assessments and other environmental studies deemed necessary prior to the advancement of a project with a categorical exclusion determination or a finding of no significant impact. This material is not regulatory, but has been developed to provide uniform and consistent guidance for the development of environmental documents. Each project will need to be carefully evaluated and the appropriate environmental document developed based on each individual situation.

The FHWA fully subscribes to the Council on Environmental Quality (CEQ) philosophy that the goal of the NEPA process is better decisions and not more documentation. As noted in the CEQ regulations, EIS's should normally be less than 150 pages for most projects and not more than 300 pages for the most complex projects.

The FHWA considers the early coordination process to be a valuable tool to assist in identifying and focusing on the significant environmental issues. On April 30, 1981, the CEQ issued a memorandum entitled "Scoping Guidance" which discusses various techniques that will ensure participation in the scoping process. The CEQ also issued, on March 6, 1981, a memorandum entitled "Questions and Answers about the NEPA Regulations." Both of the documents are nonregulatory; however, they do provide CEQ views on various issues and are available from the FHWA Office of Environmental Policy (HEV-10).

SECTION	SUBJECT	PAGE
1	Environmental Assessment (EA)	3
2	Finding of No Significant Impact	4
3	EIS--Format and Content	5
4	Distribution of EIS's and Section 4(f) Evaluations	26
5	Record of Decision--Format and Content	27
6	Section 4(f) Evaluations--Format and Content	29
7	Predecision Referrals to CEQ	32
8	Other Agency Statements	32
9	Proposals for Legislation or Regulations	33

1. ENVIRONMENTAL ASSESSMENT (EA)

   Title 23, Code of Federal Regulations, Part 771, Environmental Impact and Related Procedures, describes those circumstances where the preparation of an EA is appropriate. The CEQ regulations require that an EA is to include the information listed in 40 CFR Part 1508.9. The following format, which assures this coverage, is suggested:

   a. Cover Sheet. There is no required format for the EA. However, it is recommended the EIS cover sheet format, as shown on page 5, be followed where appropriate. Since the EA is not formally circulated, there is no need to include the "comments due" paragraph listed on page 5.

   b. Description of the Proposed Action. Describe the locations, length, termini, proposed improvements, etc.

   c. Need. Identify and describe the problem which the proposed action is designed to correct. Any of the items discussed under the "Need" section in Section 3 (EIS - Format and Content) may be appropriate.

   d. Alternatives Considered. Discuss all reasonable alternatives to the proposed action which were considered. The EA may either discuss (1) the preferred alternative and the alternatives considered or (2) if the applicant has not identified a preferred alternative, the alternatives under consideration.

   e. Impacts. Discuss the social, economic and environmental impacts of the alternatives considered and describe why these impacts are considered not significant.

   f. Comments and Coordination. Describe coordination efforts and comments received from government agencies and the public. If the EA includes a Section 4(f) evaluation, the EA and the Section 4(f) evaluation may be circulated to the appropriate agencies for Section 4(f) coordination, or the Section 4(f) evaluation may be supplemented by any additional information necessary to properly explain the project and circulated as a separate document.

   g. Appendices (if any). Include only analytical information that substantiates an analysis which is important to the document. Other information should be incorporated by reference only.

2. **FINDING OF NO SIGNIFICANT IMPACT (FONSI)**

771.121 of 23 CFR 771, entitled Environmental Impact and Related Procedures, describes the approval process for a FONSI. Section 1508.13 of the CEQ regulations describes the content of a FONSI. The EA should be modified to reflect all applicable significant environmental comments received as a result of the public hearings or other significant environmental comments received as a result of the public and clearinghouse notification process. The EA, revised as appropriate, including appropriate responses to any comments received, is then submitted to the FHWA Division Administrator along with the applicant's recommendation. The basis for the applicant's recommendation should be documented in the EA. After review of the EA and any other appropriate information, the FHWA Division Administrator may determine that the proposed action has no significant impacts. This is documented by attaching to the EA a separate statement (example follows) which clearly sets forth the FHWA analysis of the EA along with any other supporting documentation that has resulted in a FONSI. As appropriate, the FHWA Division Administrator may choose to expand on the discussion in the sample FONSI to identify the basis for the decision. The EA/FONSI should document compliance with the requirements of all applicable environmental laws, Executive Orders, and other related requirements. If full compliance is not possible by the time the FONSI is prepared, it should reflect consultation with the appropriate agencies and provide reasonable assurance that the requirements will be met.

FEDERAL HIGHWAY ADMINISTRATION
FINDING OF NO SIGNIFICANT IMPACT
FOR
(Title of Proposed Action)

The FHWA has determined that this project will not have any significant impact on the human environment. This finding of no significant impact is based on the attached environmental assessment (reference other environmental documents as appropriate) which has been independently evaluated by the FHWA and determined to adequately and accurately discuss the environmental issues and impacts of the proposed project. It provides sufficient evidence and analysis for determining that an environmental impact statement is not required. The FHWA takes full responsibility for the accuracy, scope, and content of the attached environmental assessment.

_____   _____   _____
Date   Responsible Official   Title

3. EIS -- FORMAT AND CONTENT

Each EIS should have a cover sheet containing:

(EIS NUMBER)

<u>(Route, Termini, City or County, and State)</u>
Draft (Final)
Environmental Impact Statement
Submitted Pursuant to 42 U.S.C. 4332 (2) (c) (and
where applicable, 49 U.S.C. 1653(f)) by the
U.S. Department of Transportation
Federal Highway Administration
and
State highway agency (HA)
and
(As applicable, local highway agency (HA)

<u>Cooperating Agencies</u>
List Here

Date of Approval   For FHWA   Title

The following persons may be contacted for additional information concerning this document:

(Name, address, and telephone number of FHWA division office contact)

(Name, address, and telephone number of HA contact)

A one-paragraph abstract of the statement.

Comments on this draft EIS are due by <u>(date)</u> and should be sent to <u>(name and address)</u>.

The top left-hand corner of the cover sheet of all draft and final EIS's contains a number parallel to that in the following example:

FHWA-AZ-EIS-81-01-D(F)(S)

FHWA - name of Federal agency

AZ - name of State (cannot exceed four characters)

EIS - environmental impact statement

81 - year draft statement was prepared

01 - sequential number of draft statement for each calendar year

D - designates the statement as the draft statement

F - designates the statement as the final statement

S - designates supplemental statement

The EIS's should be printed on 8 1/2 x 11-inch paper with all graphics folded for insertion to that size. The wider sheets should open to the right with the title or identification on the right. The use of a standard size will facilitate administrative recordkeeping.

Summary

The summary should include:

a. A brief description of the proposed FHWA action indicating route, termini, type of improvement, number of lanes, length, county, city, State, etc., as appropriate.

b. A description of any significant actions proposed by other government agencies in the same geographic area as the proposed FHWA action.

c. A summary of major alternatives considered. (The final EIS should identify the preferred alternative.)

d. A summary of significant environmental impacts, both beneficial and adverse.

e. Any areas of controversy (including issues raised by both agencies and the public).

f. Any significant unresolved issues.

g. A list of other Federal actions required because of this proposed action (i.e., permit approvals etc.).

Table of Contents

a. Cover sheet.

b. Summary.

c. Table of Contents.

d. Purpose of and Need for Action.

e. Alternatives Including Proposed Action.

f. Affected Environment.

g. Environmental Consequences.

h. List of Preparers.

i. List of Agencies, Organizations, and Persons to Whom Copies of the Statement are Sent.

j. Comments and Coordination.

k. Index.

l. Appendices (if any).

Purpose of and Need for Action

Identify and describe the transportation problem(s) which the proposed action is designed to address. This section should clearly demonstrate that a "need" exists and must define the "need" in terms understandable to the general public. This discussion will form the basis for the "no action" discussion in the "Alternatives" section. The following is a list of items which may assist in the explanation of the need for the proposed action. It is by no means all-inclusive or applicable in every situation and is intended only as a guide.

a. System Linkage - Is the proposed project a "connecting link"? How does it fit in the system? Is it an "essential gap" in the Interstate System?

b. Capacity - Is the capacity of the present facility inadequate for the present traffic? Projected traffic? What capacity is needed? What is the level of service?

c. Transportation Demand - Including relationship to any statewide plan or adopted urban transportation plan.

d. Federal, State, or local governmental authority (legislation) directing the action.

e. Social Demands or Economic Development - New employment, schools, land use plans, recreation, etc. What projected economic development/land use changes indicate the need to improve or add to the highway capacity?

f. Modal Interrelationships - How will the proposed facility interface with and serve to complement airports, rail and port facilities, mass transit services, etc.

g. Is the proposed project necessary to correct an existing or potential safety hazard? Is the existing accident rate excessively high? Why? How will the proposed facility improve it?

Alternatives Including Proposed Action

The "Alternatives" section of the draft EIS should begin with a concise discussion of how the "reasonable alternatives" were selected for detailed study. It should also describe those "other alternatives" that were eliminated early in project development and the basis for their elimination. The alternatives to be considered in this section will normally include the following:

a. The "no-action" alternative, which would include those usual short-term minor reconstruction types of activities (safety improvements, etc.) that are a part of an ongoing plan for continuing operation of the existing roadway system in the project area.

b. A Transportation System Management (TSM) alternative which would include those types of activities designed to maximize the utilization and energy efficiency of the present system. Possible subject areas to include in this alternative are options such as fringe parking, ridesharing, high-occupancy vehicle (HOV) lanes on existing roadways, and traffic signal timing optimization. This limited construction alternative should be given appropriate consideration when major urbanized area construction activities are proposed. On major new urbanized area highway projects, the option of including and/or designating HOV lanes should be a consideration. Consideration of this alternative may be accomplished by reference to the regional transportation plan, when that plan considers this option. In the case of regional transportation plans which do not reflect consideration of this option, it may be necessary to evaluate the feasibility of this alternative. The effects that reducing the scale of a link in the regional transportation plan will have on the remainder of the system will need to be discussed during the evaluation of this alternative. While this discussion relates primarily to major projects in urbanized areas, the concept of achieving maximum utilization of existing facilities is equally important in rural areas. Before major projects on new location are proposed, it is important to demonstrate that reconstruction and rehabilitation of the existing system will not adequately correct the identified deficiencies. Appendix A of 23 CFR 450 provides additional discussion on the goals and scope of the TSM concept.

c. All other proposed "construction" alternatives discussions should include, where relevant, those reasonable and feasible alternatives (i.e., transit options) which may not be within the existing funding authority of FHWA. Some urban projects may be multimodal, thus requiring close coordination with the Urban Mass Transportation Administration (UMTA). In these situations, UMTA should be consulted early in the project development process. Depending on the extent of UMTA involvement and the possible use of UMTA funds for portions of the proposal, the need to request UMTA to be either a "lead agency" or a "cooperating agency" should be considered at the earliest stages of project development. Where applicable, cost-effectiveness studies that have been performed should be summarized in the EIS.

The discussion of alternatives in this section can be best accomplished by a brief written description of each alternative, supplemented with maps and other appropriate visual aids such as photographs, drawings, or sketches which would assist the reader in better understanding the various alternatives, impacts, and mitigation measures. In some situations, design level details may be appropriate to evaluate impacts. However, final design details are not normally available at this stage in project development. The material should provide a clear understanding of each alternative's termini, location, costs, and major design features (number of lanes, right-of-way requirements, median width, etc.) which will contribute to a reader's better understanding of each alternative's effects on its surroundings or the community.

Generally, each alternative should be developed to a comparable level of detail in the draft EIS. Normally, the draft EIS should state that all alternatives are under consideration and that a decision will be made only after the public hearing transcript and comments on the draft EIS have been evaluated. However, in those situations where the HA has identified a "preferred" alternative based on its early coordination and environmental studies, the HA may so indicate in the draft EIS. However, the EIS should include a comment to the effect that the final selection will not be made until the results of the EIS circulation and the public involvement process have been fully evaluated. The final EIS must identify the preferred alternative and discuss the basis for the selection.

Affected Environment

This section should provide a concise description of the existing social, economic, and environmental setting for the area affected by all of the alternative proposals. The description should be a single general description for the area rather than a separate one for each alternative. All environmentally sensitive locations or features should be identified. However, it may be desirable to exclude from environmental documents certain specific location data on archeological sites to prevent vandalism.

To reduce paperwork and eliminate the presentation of extraneous background material, the discussion should focus on significant issues and values. Prudent use of photographs, illustrations, and other graphics within the text can be effective in giving the reviewer an understanding of the area. The statement should describe other related Federal activities in the area, their interrelationships, and any significant cumulative environmental impacts.

Data and analyses in the statement should be in proportion to the significance of the impacts which will be discussed later in the document. Less important material should be summarized or referenced. This section should also describe the scope and status of the planning process for the area. The inclusion of a map of any adopted land use and transportation plan for the area would be helpful in relating the proposed project to the areawide planning process.

Environmental Consequences

This section will discuss the probable social, economic, and environmental effects of the alternatives and the measures to mitigate adverse impacts.

There are several ways of preparing this section. Normally, it is preferable to discuss the impacts and mitigation measures separately for each of the alternatives. However, in some cases (such as where there are few alternatives), it may be advantageous to present this section with the impacts as the headings. Where possible, a subsection should be included which would discuss the general impacts and mitigation measures that are the same regardless of the alternative selected. This would reduce or eliminate repetition under each of the alternative discussions.

When the final EIS is prepared, the impacts and mitigation measures associated with the selected alternative may need to be discussed in more detail than in the draft EIS. In discussing the impacts, both beneficial and adverse, the following should be included in both the draft and final EIS.

a. A summary of studies undertaken and major assumptions made, with enough data or cross referencing to determine the validity of the methodology.

b. Sufficient information to establish the reasonableness of the conclusions concerning impacts.

c. A discussion of mitigation measures. Prior to completion of the final EIS, these measures normally should be investigated in appropriate detail so that a commitment can be included in the final EIS.

Charts, tables, maps, and other graphics illustrating comparisons between the alternatives (i.e., costs, residential displacements, noise impacts, etc.) are useful as a presentation technique.

In addition to normal FHWA program monitoring of design and construction activities, special instances may arise when a formal program for monitoring impacts or mitigation measures will be appropriate. In these instances, the final EIS should describe the monitoring program.

Listed below are examples of the potentially significant impacts of highway projects. These factors should be discussed <u>to the extent applicable</u> for each alternative. This list is by no means all-inclusive and on specific projects there may be other significant impacts that require study.

<u>Social and Economic Impacts</u>

The statement should discuss:

a. Changes in the neighborhoods or community cohesion for various groups as a result of the proposed action. These changes may be beneficial or adverse, and may include splitting neighborhoods, isolating a portion of an ethnic group, new development, changed property values, or separation of residences from community facilities, etc.

b. Changes in travel patterns and accessibility (e.g., vehicular, commuter, bicycle, or pedestrian). If any cross streets are terminated, the EIS should reflect the views of the involved city or county on such street closings.

c. Impacts on school districts, recreation areas, churches, businesses, police and fire protection, etc.

d. The impacts of alternatives on highway and traffic safety as well as on overall public safety.

e. Regional economic impacts, such as the effects of the project on development, tax revenues and public expenditures, employment opportunities, accessibility and retail sales. Any significant impacts on the economic viability of affected municipalities should also be discussed together with a summary of any efforts taken and agreements reached for using the transportation investment to support both public and private development plans. To the extent possible, this discussion should rely upon reviews by affected State, county, and city officials and upon studies performed under 23 U.S.C. 134.

f. For projects that might lead to or support large commercial development, the EIS should provide information on any significant effects the pending action would have on established business districts, and any opportunities for mitigation by the public and/or private sectors.

g. The general social groups specially benefitted or harmed by the proposed action should be identified. Particular effects of a proposal on the elderly, handicapped, nondrivers, transit-dependent, or minorities should be described to the extent these can be reasonably predicted. For example, where minority impacts may be a significant concern, EIS's should contain, when applicable, the following information, broken down by race, color, and national origin: the population in the study area, the number of displaced residents, the type and number of displaced businesses, and the type and number of displaced employees. Secondary sources of information such as census data reports can be utilized for obtaining this type of background information. Changes in minority employment opportunities, the relationship of the proposed action to other Federal actions which may serve or affect the minority population, and proposed mitigation measures to reduce or avoid impacts on minority populations should also be discussed.

Relocation Impacts

The relocation information necessary for the draft EIS may be included in the draft statement, either in the form of a complete conceptual stage relocation plan, or summarized in sufficient detail to adequately explain the relocation situation along with a resolution of anticipated or known problems. When the relocation information is summarized, the conceptual stage relocation plan should be referenced in the draft EIS.

A discussion of the information listed below is to be included in the draft EIS to the extent appropriate for the project.

a. An estimate of households to be displaced, including the family characteristics (e.g., minorities, handicapped, income levels, the elderly, large families, length of occupancy, and owner/tenant status). Where the project is not complex from a relocation viewpoint and the impact on the community is slight, this information may be obtained by visual inspection and from available secondary sources. On complex relocation projects where the relocation will have a major impact on the community, a survey of affected occupants may be needed. This survey may be accomplished by a sampling process.

b. A discussion of available housing in the area and the ability to provide suitable relocation housing for each type of family to be displaced within the financial capabilities of the relocatees.

c. A description of any special advisory services that will be necessary for unique relocation problems.

d. A discussion of the actions proposed to remedy insufficient relocation housing, including a commitment to housing of last resort, if necessary.

e. An estimate of the number, type, and size of businesses to be displaced. The approximate number of employees for each business should be included along with the general impact on the business dislocation(s) on the economy of the community.

f. A discussion of the results of early consultation with the local government(s) and any early consultation with businesses potentially subject to displacement, including any discussions of potential sources of funding, financing, planning for incentive packaging (e.g., tax abatement, flexible zoning, and building requirements), and advisory assistance which has been or will be furnished along with other appropriate information.

g. Impact on the neighborhood and housing community services where relocation is likely to take place. If there will be extensive residential and/or business displacement, the affected community may want to investigate other sources of funding from local and State entities as well as HUD, the Economic Development Administration, and other Federal agencies, to assist in revitalization of the community.

h. The results of discussions with local officials, social agencies, and such groups as the elderly, handicapped, nondriver, transit-dependent, and minorities regarding the relocation impacts.

i. A statement that the housing resources are available to all relocatees without discrimination.

The effects on each group should be described to the extent reasonably predictable. The analysis should discuss how the relocation caused by the proposed project will facilitate or inhibit access to jobs, educational facilities, religious institutions, health and welfare services, recreational facilities, social and cultural facilities, pedestrian facilities, shopping facilities, and public transit services.

Air Quality Impacts

The EIS should contain a brief discussion of air quality effects or a summary of the carbon monoxide (CO) analysis if such an analysis is performed. The following provides additional guidance:

a. A microscale CO analysis to determine air quality impacts is probably unnecessary where such impacts are judged to be minimal or insignificant.

    The judgment on the degree of CO impacts may be based on: (1) previous analyses for similar projects, (2) previous general analyses for various classes of projects, or (3) simplified graphical or "table look-up" analyses.

b. If the impacts of CO are judged to be minimal or insignificant, a brief statement to this effect is sufficient. The basis for the statement should be given in the EIS.

c. If the project CO contribution plus the background level are known to be well below the 1- and 8-hour National Ambient Air Quality Standard or other applicable standard, then the air quality CO impact is judged to be insignificant.

d. For those projects where a CO microscale analysis is performed, then the total CO concentration (project contribution, plus estimated background) at identified reasonable receptor sites for all alternatives should be reported and compared with applicable State and national standards.

e. If a CO analysis is performed, a brief summary of the methodologies and assumptions used should be given in the EIS.

f. In addition to the CO impact assessment, one of the two following statements should be included in the EIS:

    (1) This project is in an area where the State implementation plan does not contain any transportation control measures. Therefore, the conformity procedures of 23 CFR 770 do not apply to this project.

    (2) This project is in an air quality nonattainment (or attainment) area which has transportation control measures in the State implementation plan (SIP) which was (conditionally) approved by the Environmental Protection Agency on (date). The FHWA has determined that both the transportation plan and the transportation improvement program conform to the SIP. The Federal Highway Administration has determined that this project is included in the transportation improvement program for the (indicate 3C planning area). Therefore, pursuant to 23 CFR 770, this project conforms to the SIP.

Noise Impacts

The EIS should contain a summary of the noise analysis including the following:

a. A brief description of noise sensitive areas, including information on the numbers and types of activities which may be affected. If the project has significant noise impacts, noise contours of the proposed action and alternatives may be appropriate to assist in understanding those impacts.

b. The extent of the impact (in decibels). This should include a comparison of the predicted noise levels with both the FHWA design noise levels and the existing noise levels.

c. Noise abatement measures which have been considered and those measures that would likely be incorporated into the proposed project.

d. Noise problems for which no prudent solution is reasonably available and the reasons why.

Energy

Draft and final EIS's should discuss in <u>general terms</u> the energy requirements and conservation potential of various alternatives under consideration. This general discussion might recognize that the energy requirements of various construction alternatives are similar and are generally greater than the energy requirements of the no-build alternative. Additionally, the discussion could point out that the post-construction, operational energy requirements of the facility should be less with the build alternative as opposed to the no-build alternative. In such a situation, one might then conclude that the savings in operational energy requirements would more than offset construction energy requirements and thus, in the long term, result in a net saving in energy usage. For most projects, a detailed energy analysis including computations of BTU requirements, etc., is not needed, but the discussion should be reasonable and supportable.

For major projects with potentially significant energy impacts (an example would be the Westway project in New York City), both the draft and final EIS should discuss any <u>significant</u> direct and/or indirect energy impacts of the proposed action. Direct energy impacts refer to the energy consumed by vehicles using the facility. Indirect impacts include construction energy and such items as the effects of any changes in automobile usage. The action's relationship and consistency with any State and/or regional energy plan should also be indicated.

The final EIS should identify any energy conservation measures that will be implemented as a part of the recommended alternative. Measures to conserve energy include the use of high-occupancy vehicle incentives, measures to improve traffic flow, and also pedestrian and bicycle facilities.

Wild and Scenic Rivers

If the proposed action could have an adverse effect on a river on the National Wild and Scenic Rivers System or a river listed in the Nationwide Inventory of Rivers with potential for inclusion in the National Wild and Scenic Rivers System, there should be early coordination with the National Park Service (NPS) or the Department of Agriculture (USDA). The EIS should identify any potential significant adverse effects on the natural, cultural, and recreational values of the inventory river. Adverse effects include alteration of the free-flowing nature of the river, alteration of the setting, or deterioration of water quality. If it is determined that the proposed action could foreclose options to designate the river under the act, the EIS should reflect consultation with the NPS or USDA on avoiding or mitigating the impacts. The final EIS should indicate measures which will be included in the action to avoid or mitigate impacts. The October 3, 1980, memorandum from the Office of Environmental Policy provides additional information on this subject area.

Floodplain Impacts

The draft EIS should contain a summary of the "Location Hydraulic Studies" required by FHPM 6-7-3-2, Location and Hydraulic Design of Encroachments on Floodplains. Exhibits defining the floodplains or regulatory floodway, as appropriate, should be provided whenever possible. When there is no practicable alternative to an action which includes a significant encroachment, the final EIS should contain the finding required by FHPM 6-7-3-2, paragraph 8, in a separate subsection titled "Only Practicable Alternative Finding." When there is a regulatory floodway affected by the proposed action, the final EIS should contain a discussion of the consistency of the project with the regulatory floodway.

Coastal Zone Impacts

Where the proposed action is within, or may affect land or water uses within, the area covered by a State Coastal Zone Management Program (CZMP) approved by the Department of Commerce, the environmental document should briefly describe the CZMP plan, identify the potential impacts, and include evidence of coordination with the State Coastal Zone Management agency or appropriate local agency. For FHWA assisted activities, the EIS should include the State Coastal Zone Management agency's determination as to whether the project is consistent with the State CZMP plan. For direct Federal actions, the EIS should include the lead agency's consistency determination. If it is determined that the proposed action is inconsistent with the State's approved CZMP, FHWA will not approve the action except upon a finding by the Secretary of Commerce that the proposed action is consistent with the purposes or objectives of the Coastal Zone Management Act or is necessary in the interest of national security. The final environmental document for the proposed action will document all findings.

Wetlands Impacts

a. All draft EIS's for projects involving new construction in wetlands should include sufficient information to: (1) identify the type of wetlands involved, (2) describe the impacts to the wetlands, (3) evaluate alternatives which would avoid these wetlands, and (4) identify practicable measures to minimize harm to the wetlands. Exhibits showing the wetlands in relation to the alternatives, including the alternatives to avoid construction in the wetlands, should be provided.

b. Executive Order 11990, Protection of Wetlands, requires Federal agencies ". . . to avoid to the extent possible the long and short term adverse impacts associated with the destruction or modification of wetlands and to avoid direct or indirect support of new construction in wetlands wherever there is a practicable alternative . . . ." In evaluating the impact of the proposed project on wetlands, the following two questions should be addressed: (1) what is the importance of the impacted wetlands! and (2) what is the significance of this impact on the wetlands? Merely listing the number of acres taken by the various alternatives of a highway proposal does not provide sufficient information upon which to determine the degree of impact on the wetland's ecosystem. The wetlands analysis should be sufficiently detailed to allow a meaningful discussion of these two questions.

c. In evaluating the importance of the impacted wetlands, the analysis should consider such factors as: (1) the primary functions of the wetlands (e.g., flood control, wildlife habitat, erosion control, etc.), (2) the relative importance of these functions to the total wetlands resource of the area, and (3) other factors such as uniqueness that may contribute to the wetlands importance.

d. In determining the significance of the highway impact, the analysis should focus on how the project affects the stability and quality of the wetlands. This analysis should consider the short- and long-term effects on the wetlands and the significance of any loss such as: (1) flood control capacity, (2) erosion control potential, (3) water pollution abatement capacity, and (4) wildlife habitat value. Knowing the importance of the wetlands involved and the significance of the impact, the SHA and FHWA will be in a better position to determine what mitigation efforts are necessary to minimize harm to these wetlands.

e. For purposes of analyzing alternatives and the wetlands finding, "located in wetlands" means that the proposed right-of-way or easement limits of the highway are located wholly or partially in wetlands or that the highway is located in the vicinity of the wetlands and there is evidence that the new construction will directly cause long-term damage or destruction of the wetlands.

f. Mitigation measures which should be considered include enhancement of existing wetlands, creation of new wetlands, and erosion control. It should be noted that any mitigation measure should be related to the actual adverse impact caused by the project and that acquisition of privately owned wetlands for purposes of protection should only be considered as a last resort.

g. When there is no practicable alternative to an action which involves new construction located in wetlands, the final EIS should contain the finding required by Executive Order 11990 and by DOT Order 5660.1A, entitled Preservation of the Nation's Wetlands, August 24, 1978, in a separate section or exhibit titled "Wetlands Finding." Approval of the final EIS containing this finding will document compliance with the requirements of Executive Order 11990. The finding should contain in summary form and with reference to the detailed discussions contained elsewhere in the final EIS:

    (1) a reference to Executive Order 11990;

    (2) a discussion of the basis for the determination that there are no practicable alternatives to the proposed action;

(3) a discussion of the basis for the determination that the proposed action includes all practicable measures to minimize harm to wetlands; and

(4) a concluding statement as follows: "Based upon the above considerations, it is determined that there is no practicable alternative to the proposed new construction in wetlands and that the proposed action includes all practicable measures to minimize harm to wetlands which may result from such use."

h. A formal wetlands finding is required for all projects processed with EIS's or FONSI's that involve new construction in wetlands. In the case of a project processed as a categorical exclusion, the division office's administrative record should document evaluations of alternatives and measures to minimize harm for these actions.

Land Use Impacts

This discussion should begin with a description of current development trends and the State and/or local government plans and policies with regard to land use and growth in the area. These plans and policies will be reflected in the area's comprehensive development plan, including land use, transportation, public facilities, housing, community services, and other areas.

The land use impact analysis should assess the consistency of the alternatives with the comprehensive development plans adopted for the area. The secondary social, economic, and environmental impacts of significant induced development should be presented.

The EIS should note any proposed alternatives which will stimulate low density, energy intensive development in outlying areas and will have a significant adverse effect on existing communities. Throughout this discussion, the distinction between planned and unplanned growth should be clearly identified.

Joint Development

When applicable, the EIS should discuss how the implementation of joint development projects will preserve or enhance the community's social, economic, environmental, and visual values. This discussion should be included as part of the land use impact presentation.

Historic and Archeological Preservation

The draft EIS should contain a discussion demonstrating that a survey meeting the requirements of 36 CFR Part 800.4 has been performed for each alternative under consideration. The discussion should begin by describing the resources and summarizing the impacts that each alternative will have on these resources that might meet the criteria for inclusion on the National Register of Historic Places. There should be a record of coordination with the State Historic Preservation Officer concerning the significance of the identified resources, the likelihood of eligibility for the National Register, and an evaluation of the effect of the project on the resources.

The draft EIS can serve as a preliminary case report for Section 106 requirements if the document indicates this and it contains the necessary information (36 CFR 800.13). The transmittal memorandum to the Advisory Council on Historic Preservation should specifically request consultation.

The final EIS should demonstrate that all the requirements of 36 CFR Part 800 have been met. If the selected alternative has an effect on a resource that is on or eligible for inclusion on the National Register, the final EIS should contain (a) a determination of no adverse effect concurred in by the Executive Director of the Advisory Council on Historic Preservation or (b) an executed memorandum of agreement or (c) in the case of a unique situation where FHWA is unable to conclude the memorandum of agreement (MOA), a copy of comments transmitted from the Advisory Council to the Secretary of Transportation. When necessary, the discussion should indicate that archeological recovery will be performed. The proposed use of land from a site on or eligible for inclusion on the National Register will normally require a determination pursuant to Section 4(f) of the DOT Act. The treatment of archeological sites is discussed in 23 CFR 771.135(f). Additional details regarding the type of information needed at the draft EIS and final EIS stages are contained in the May 14, 1980, memorandum from the Office of Environmental Policy to all regional offices.

Water Quality Impacts

This discussion should include summaries of analyses and consultations with the State and/or local agency responsible for water quality. Coordination with the Environmental Protection Agency (EPA) under the Federal Clean Water Act may provide assistance in this area. The EIS should discuss any locations where roadway runoff may have a significant affect on downstream water uses, including existing wells. A 1981 FHWA research report entitled "Constituents of Highway Runoff" contains procedures for estimating pollutant loading from highway runoff.

Section 1424(e) of the Safe Drinking Water Act requires that proposed actions which may impact those areas that have been designated as principal or sole-source aquifers be coordinated with EPA. The EPA will furnish information on whether any of the alternatives affect the aquifer. If none of the alternatives affect the aquifer, the requirements of the Safe Drinking Water Act are satisfied. If an alternative is selected which affects the aquifer, a design must be developed to assure, to the satisfaction of EPA, that it will not contaminate the aquifer.

If a rest area is involved, a Section 402 permit is required for point source discharge. Any potential Section 402 permits should be identified in the EIS. Also, for both the Section 402 and Section 404 permits, a water quality certification from the State agency responsible for water quality is necessary.

The MOA with the Corps of Engineers allows for application for permit as soon as the preferred alternative is identified (i.e., final EIS stage). Use of the procedures in the MOA is encouraged to minimize possible delays in the processing of Section 404 permits later in project development. The final EIS should indicate the general location of the fill or dredged activity, approximate quantities of fill or dredged material, general construction grades, and proposed mitigation measures, and should include evidence of coordination with the Corps.

Threatened or Endangered Species

The HA shall request from the Departments of the Interior (DOI) and/or Commerce (DOC) information on whether any species listed or proposed as endangered or threatened may be present in the area of the proposed construction project. If those Departments advise that there are no such species in the area, the requirements of the Endangered Species Act have been met. If those Departments advise that such a species may be present, the FHWA/HA shall undertake a biological assessment to identify any threatened or endangered species which are likely to be affected by the proposed action. This biological assessment should include:

a. An onsite inspection of the area affected by the proposed project.

b. Interviews with recognized experts on the species at issue.

c. A literature review to determine the species distribution, habitat needs, and other biological requirements.

d. An analysis of possible impacts to the species.

e. An analysis of measures to minimize impacts. This biological assessment should be forwarded to DOI/DOC for a biological opinion. The Fish and Wildlife Service (F&WS) is responsible for the protection of terrestrial and fresh-water species and the National Marine Fisheries Service (NMFS) is responsible for the protection of marine species.

Upon completing their review of the biological assessment, the F&WS/NMFS may request additional information and/or a meeting to discuss the project or issue a biological opinion stating that the project: (a) is not likely to jeopardize, or (b) will promote the conservation of or (c) is likely to jeopardize the threatened or endangered species. In selecting a preferred alternative, jeopardy to an endangered or threatened species must be avoided. If either a finding of (a) or (b) is given, the requirements of the Endangered Species Act are met. If a detrimental finding is presented, the proposed action may be modified so that the species is no longer jeopardized. In unique circumstances, an exemption may be requested. If an exemption is denied, the action must be halted or modified. The final EIS should document the results of the coordination of the biological assessment with the appropriate agencies.

Prime and Unique Agricultural Lands

Information on prime and unique agricultural lands should be solicited through early consultation with the Department of Agriculture (USDA), and the EIS should identify the direct and indirect impacts of the proposed action on these lands, including:

a. An estimate of the number of acres that might be directly affected by right-of-way acquisition.

b. Areas where agricultural operations might be disrupted.

c. Potential indirect effects such as those related to project-induced changes in land use.

The EIS should contain a map showing the location of prime and unique agricultural lands in relation to the project alternatives, summarize the results of consultations with the USDA, and include copies of correspondence with USDA regarding the project. Specific actions to avoid or, if that is not possible, to reduce direct and indirect effects on these lands should be identified.

Construction Impacts

The EIS should discuss significant impacts (particularly air, noise, water, detours, safety, visual, etc.) associated with construction of each of the alternatives. Also, where applicable, the impacts of disposal and borrow areas should be discussed along with any proposed measures to minimize these impacts.

Considerations Relating to Pedestrians and Bicyclists

Section 682 of the National Energy Policy Act of 1978 recognizes that bicycles are an efficient means of transportation, represent a viable commuting alternative to many people, and deserve consideration in a comprehensive national energy plan. The FHWA recognizes that bicyclists are legitimate highway users and that FHWA has a responsibility to provide for their transportation needs. Section 109(n) of 23 U.S.C. provides that "the Secretary shall not approve any project under this title that will result in the severance or destruction of an existing major route for nonmotorized transportation traffic and light motorcycles, unless such project provides a reasonable alternate route or such a route exists. The FHWA policy regarding Bicycle Program Activities is further defined in an August 20, 1981, memorandum from Administrator Barnhart to all regional administrators.

Where appropriate, the EIS should consider pedestrian and bicycle use as an integral feature of the project and include a discussion of the relationship of the proposed project to local plans for bicycles and pedestrian facilities and evidence that the project is consistent with 23 U.S.C. 109(n).

Stream Modification and Wildlife Impacts

Title 16 U.S.C. 662(a) requires consultation with the Fish and Wildlife Service and the appropriate State agency regarding any Federal action which involves impoundment (surface area of 10 acres or more), diversion, channel deepening, or other modification of a stream or body of water. Exhibits should be used to identify stream modifications. The use of the stream or body of water for recreation or other purposes should be identified. It should also discuss any significant impacts on fish and wildlife resources, including direct impact to fish and wildlife, loss or modification of habitat, and degradation of water quality.

Visual Impacts

This discussion should include an assessment of the visual impacts of the proposed action, including the "view from the road" and the "view of the road." Where relevant, the EIS should document the consideration given to design quality, art, and architecture in the project planning. These values may be particularly important for facilities located in sensitive urban settings. Where relevant, the draft EIS should be circulated to officially designated State and local arts councils and, as appropriate, other organizations with an interest in design, art, and architecture.

List of Preparers

This section will include lists of :

a. State (and local agency) personnel, including consultants, who were primarily responsible for preparing the EIS or performing environmental studies, and their qualifications, including educational background or experience.

b. The FHWA personnel primarily responsible for preparation or review of the EIS, and their qualifications.

c. The areas of EIS responsibility for each preparer.

List of Agencies, Organizations, and Persons to Whom Copies of the Statement are Sent

List all entities from which comments are being requested (draft EIS) and identify those that submitted comments (final EIS).

Comments and Coordination

a. The draft EIS should summarize the early coordination process, including scoping, meetings with community groups and individuals, and the key issues and pertinent information received from the public and government agencies through these efforts.

b. The final EIS should include a copy of all substantive comments received (or summaries thereof, where the response has been exceptionally voluminous), along with a response to each substantive comment. When the EIS is revised as a result of the comments received, a copy of the comments should contain marginal references indicating where revisions were made, or the discussion of the comments should contain such references. The FHWA comment(s) on the draft EIS should not be included in the final EIS. However, the document should include adequate information for the FHWA reviewer to ascertain the disposition of the comment(s). Formal comments by the Department of Transportation should be included in the final EIS along with an appropriate response to each comment.

c. The final EIS should document compliance with requirements of all applicable environmental laws, Executive Orders, and other related requirements. To the extent possible, all environmental issues should be resolved prior to the submission of the final EIS. Where this is not possible, the final EIS should clearly identify any remaining unresolved issues, the change taken to resolve the issues, and the positions of the respective parties.

d. The final EIS should contain a summary and disposition of substantive comments on social, economic, and environmental issues made at any public hearing or other public involvement activity or which were otherwise considered.

Index

The index should include major subjects and areas of significant impacts so that a reviewer need not read the entire EIS to obtain information on a specific subject or impact.

23 CFR 771 requires compliance to the extent possible with other applicable environmental laws, Executive Orders, and other related requirements. This includes the certifications and reports required by 23 U.S.C. 128 relating to public hearings, considerations of social, economic, and environmental (SEE) effects and consistency of the project with urban planning goals promulgated by the community. The certifications normally are made at the time the final EIS or FONSI is submitted to the FHWA Division Administrator. The report of SEE effects required by 23 U.S.C. 128 will normally be satisfied by the final EIS, FONSI, or identification of the project as a categorical exclusion.

Appendices

Material prepared as appendices to the EIS should:

a. consist of material prepared in connection with the EIS (is distinct from material which is not so prepared and which is incorporated by reference);

b. consist of material which substantiates an analysis which is fundamental to the EIS;

c. be analytic and relevant to the decision to be made; and

d. be circulated with the EIS or be readily available on request. Other reports and studies referred to in the EIS should be readily available for review or for copying at a convenient location.

Alternate Process for Final EIS's

Paragraph 1503.4 of the CEQ regulation (40 CFR 1500, et seq.) provides the opportunity for expediting final EIS preparation in those instances when, after receipt of comments resulting from circulation of the draft EIS, it is apparent that the changes in the proposal or in the EIS in response to the comments received are minor and that:

a. all reasonable alternatives were studied and discussed in the draft EIS, and

b. the analyses in the draft EIS adequately identified and quantified the environmental impacts of all reasonable alternatives.

When these two points can be established, the final EIS can consist of the draft EIS and an attachment containing the following:

a. Errata sheets making corrections to the draft EIS, if applicable,

b. A section identifying the preferred alternative and a discussion of the reasons it was selected. The following should also be included in this section, if applicable:

   (1) final Section 4(f) evaluations containing the information described in Section 6 of these guidelines,

   (2) wetlands finding(s),

   (3) floodplain finding(s), and

   (4) a list of commitments for mitigation measures for the preferred alternative.

c. Copies (or summaries) of comments received from circulation of the draft EIS and public hearing and responses thereto.

4. DISTRIBUTION OF EIS'S AND SECTION 4(f) EVALUATIONS

   Environmental Impact Statements

   a. Copies of all draft EIS's should be circulated for comments to all public officials, private interest groups, and members of the public having or expressing an interest in the proposed action or the draft EIS, and to all Government agencies expected to have jurisdiction, responsibility, interest, or expertise in the proposed action. Internal FHWA distribution of draft and final EIS's is subject to change and is noted in memorandums to the Regional Administrators as requirements change. The FHWA transmittal letter to the Washington Headquarters should include a recommendation regarding the need for the prior concurrence of the Washington Headquarters in accordance with 23 CFR 771(e).

   b. Copies of all approved final EIS's should be distributed to all cooperating agencies, to all Federal, State, and local agencies and private organizations, and members of the public who commented substantively on the draft EIS. A copy of all approved delegated EIS's should be forwarded to the FHWA Washington Headquarters (HEV-10) for recordkeeping purposes.

   Copies of all draft and final EIS's in the categories listed in 23 CFR 771(e) should be provided to the Regional Representative of the Secretary of Transportation at the same time as they are forwarded to the FHWA Washington Headquarters.

   c. Copies of all EIS's should normally be distributed as follows, unless the agency has indicated to the FHWA offices the need for a different number of copies:

(1) The EPA Headquarters: five copies of the draft EIS and five copies of the final EIS (this is the "filing requirement" in Section 1506.9 of the CEQ regulation; the correct address is listed therein).

(2) The appropriate EPA regional office responsible for EPA's review pursuant to Section 309 of the Clean Air Act: five copies of the draft EIS and five copies of the final EIS.

(3) The DOI Headquarters:

   (a) All States in FHWA Regions 1, 3, 4, and 5, plus Hawaii, Guam, American Samoa, Arkansas, Iowa, Louisiana, Missouri, and Puerto Rico: 12 copies of the draft EIS and 7 copies of the final EIS.

   (b) Kansas, Nebraska, North Dakota, Oklahoma, South Dakota, and Texas: 13 copies of the draft EIS and 8 copies of the final EIS.

   (c) New Mexico and all States in FHWA Regions 8, 9, and 10, except Hawaii, North Dakota, and South Dakota: 14 copies of the draft EIS and 9 copies of the final EIS.

Section 4(f) Evaluation

If the Section 4(f) evaluation is included in an EIS, DOI Headquarters should receive the same number of copies listed above for EIS's for consultation in accordance with the requirements of 23 U.S.C. 138. If the Section 4(f) evaluation is processed as a separate document or as part of an EA, the DOI should receive seven copies of the draft Section 4(f) evaluation for coordination and seven copies of the final Section 4(f) statement for information.

In addition, draft Section 4(f) evaluations, whether in a draft EIS, an EA, or a separate document, are required to be coordinated where appropriate with HUD and USDA.

5. RECORD OF DECISION--FORMAT AND CONTENT

The record of decision (ROD) must set forth the reasons for the project decision, based on the material contained in the environmental documents. While cross referencing and incorporation by reference of other documents is appropriate, the ROD should explain the basis for the project decision as completely as possible.

a. **Decision**. Identify the selected alternative. Reference to the final EIS may be used to reduce detail and repetition.

b. **Alternatives Considered**. This information can be most clearly organized by briefly describing each alternative (with reference to the final EIS, as above), then explaining and discussing the balancing of values underlying the decision. This discussion must identify the alternative or alternatives which were considered preferable from a strictly environmental point of view. If the selected alternative is other than the environmentally preferable alternative, the ROD should clearly state the reasons for that decision. In addition, if use of Section 4(f) land is involved, the required Section 4(f) approval should be summarized.

For each individual decision (final EIS), the values (economic, environmental, safety, traffic service, community planning, etc.) which are significant factors in the decisionmaking process may be different and may be given different levels of relative importance. Accordingly, it is essential that this discussion clearly identifies each significant value and the reasons some values were considered more important than others. While any decision represents a balancing of the values, the ROD should reflect the manner in which these values were considered in arriving at the decision.

It is also essential that legislation requirements in 23 U.S.C. be given appropriate weight in this decisionmaking process. The mission of FHWA is to implement the Federal-aid highway program to provide safe and efficient transportation. While this mission must be accomplished within the context of all other Federal requirements, the beneficial impacts of transportation improvements must be given proper consideration and documentation in this ROD.

c. **Measures to Minimize Harm**. Describe all measures to minimize environmental harm which have been adopted for the proposed action. State whether all practicable measures to minimize environmental harm have been incorporated into the decision and, if not, why.

d. **Monitoring or Enforcement Program**. Describe any monitoring or enforcement program which has been adopted for specific mitigation measures, as outlined in the final EIS.

6. SECTION 4(f) EVALUATIONS--FORMAT AND CONTENT

Draft Evaluation--Format

a. Describe proposed action (if separate document).

b. Describe Section 4(f) resource.

c. Impacts on resource (by alternative).

d. Avoidance alternatives and their impacts.

e. Measures to minimize harm.

f. Coordination with appropriate agencies.

g. Concluding statement (final document only).

In the case of a complex Section 4(f) involvement, it is desirable to include the analysis in a separate section of the draft EIS, EA, or for projects processed as categorical exclusions, in a separate document. A Section 4(f) evaluation should be prepared for each location within the project where the use of Section 4(f) land is being considered.

Draft Evaluation--Content

The following information should be included in the Section 4(f) evaluation, as appropriate:

a. A brief description of the project and the need for the project (when the Section 4(f) evaluation is circulated separately).

b. A detailed map or drawing of sufficient scale to identify essential elements of the highway/Section 4(f) land involvement.

c. Size (acres or square feet) and location (maps or other exhibits such as photographs, sketches, etc.) of involvement.

d. Type of property (recreation, historic, etc.).

e. Available activities at the property (fishing, swimming, golfing, etc.).

f. Description and location of all existing and planned facilities (ball diamonds, tennis courts, etc.).

g. Usage (approximate number of users/visitors, etc.).

h. Relationship to other similarly used lands in the vicinity.

i. Access (pedestrian and vehicular).

j. Ownership (city, county, State, etc.).

k. Applicable clauses affecting the title, such as covenants, restrictions, or conditions, including forfeiture.

l. Unusual characteristics of the Section 4(f) land (flooding problems, terrain conditions, or other features that either reduce or enhance the value of portions of the area).

m. The location (using maps or other exhibits such as photographs or sketches) and the amount of land (acres or square feet) to be used by the proposed project including permanent and temporary easements.

n. The probable increase or decrease in environmental impacts (noise, air pollution, visual, etc.) of the alternative locations and designs considered on the Section 4(f) land users.

o. A description of all reasonable and practicable measures which are available to minimize the impacts of the proposed action on the Section 4(f) property. Discussions of alternatives in the draft EIS or EA may be referenced rather than repeated.

p. Sufficient information to evaluate all alternatives which would avoid the Section 4(f) property. Discussions of alternatives in the draft EIS or EA may be referenced rather than repeated. However, this section should include discussions of design alternatives (to avoid Section 4(f) use) in the immediate area of the Section 4(f) property.

q. The determination that there are no feasible and prudent alternatives is not normally addressed at the draft EIS, EA, or preliminary document stage until the results of the formal coordination have been completed.

r. The results of preliminary coordination with the public official having jurisdiction over the Section 4(f) property and with regional (or local) offices of DOI and, as appropriate, the regional (or local office of USDA and HUD.

Section 4(f) Discussion in Final Document

When the selected alternative involves the use of Section 4(f) land, a Section 4(f) evaluation may be included as a separate section in the final EIS or FONSI or for projects processed as categorical exclusions, in a separate final Section 4(f) evaluation. The final evaluation should contain:

a. All information required above for a draft evaluation.

b. A discussion of the basis for the determination that there are no feasible and prudent alternatives to the use of the Section 4(f) land. The supporting information must demonstrate that there are unique problems or unusual factors involved in the use of alternatives and that the cost, environmental impact, or community disruption resulting from such alternatives reaches extraordinary magnitudes.

c. A discussion of the basis for the determination that the proposed action includes all possible planning to minimize harm to the Section 4(f) property.

d. A summary of the appropriate formal coordination with the Headquarters Offices of DOI, and as appropriate, the Headquarters Offices of USDA and HUD.

e. Copies of all formal coordination comments received and an analysis and response to any questions raised.

f. Concluding statement as follows: "Based upon the above considerations, it is determined that there is no feasible and prudent alternative to the use of land from the (Section 4(f) property) and that the proposed action includes all possible planning to minimize harm to the (Section 4(f) property) resulting from such use."

A Section 4(f) approval is the written administrative record which documents the approval required by 23 U.S.C. 138. The Section 4(f) approval will be incorporated into either the final EIS or the ROD. When the Section 4(f) approval is contained in the ROD, the information noted in items (a) through (e) above may be incorporated by reference to the EIS. For a project processed as a categorical exclusion, any required Section 4(f) approval will normally be prepared as a separate document.

7. PREDECISION REFERRALS TO CEQ

   a. Any FHWA office receiving a notice of intent of referral from another agency should provide a copy of that intent of referral to the FHWA Washington Headquarters, Office of Environmental Policy (HEV-10), and the involved Regional Office, Division Office, and HA. This notice of intent of referral would generally be received as part of an agency's comments on the draft EIS. The exception would be when an agency indicates that the draft EIS did not contain adequate information to permit an assessment of the proposal's environmental acceptability. Every reasonable effort should be made to reach agreement with the agency prior to filing of the final EIS. If agreement cannot be reached, the final EIS should document the attempts to resolve the issues and summarize the remaining differences. Prior concurrence of the Washington Headquarters is necessary in the case of Government opposition on environmental grounds.

   b. The response to the notice of referral will be prepared by the Washington Headquarters with input from the Regional, Division, and State offices. The FHWA Washington Headquarters will obtain the concurrence of the Department of Transportation prior to the response to CEQ.

   c. Upon reviewing the draft EIS from another Federal Agency, if the FHWA Regional or Division Office believes a referral will be necessary, it should so advise HEV-1. The Office of Environmental Policy (HEV-1) will review the proposed referral and, if appropriate, will advise the Departmental Office of Environment and Safety (P-20), which will coordinate DOT comments on the draft EIS, including the notice of intended referral. Every reasonable effort should be made to resolve the issues after providing notice of intent to refer and prior to the lead agency's filing of the final EIS with EPA. In the event that the issues have not been resolved, the appropriate field office should prepare a referral to CEQ to be submitted through HEV to P-20 for a determination as to whether a referral to CEQ is appropriate.

8. OTHER AGENCY STATEMENTS

   a. The FHWA review of statements prepared by other agencies will consider the environmental impact of the proposal on areas within FHWA's functional area of responsibility or special expertise.

b. Agencies requesting comments on highway impacts usually forward the draft EIS to the FHWA Washington Headquarters for comment. The FHWA Washington Headquarters will normally distribute these EIS's to the appropriate regional office and will indicate where the comments should be sent. The regional office may elect to forward the draft statement to the division office for response.

c. When a field office has received a draft EIS directly from another agency, it may comment directly to that agency if the proposal does not fall within the types indicated in item (d) of this section. If more than one DOT Administration is commenting at the regional level, the comments should be coordinated by the DOT Regional Representative to the Secretary or designee. Copies of the FHWA comments should be distributed as follows:

   (1) Requesting agency--original and one copy.

   (2) P-20--one copy.

   (3) DOT Secretarial Representative--one copy.

   (4) HEV-10--one copy.

d. The following types of actions contained in the draft EIS require FHWA Washington Headquarters review and such EIS's should be forwarded to the Associate Administrator for Right-of-Way and Environment (HRE-01), along with regional comments, for processing:

   (1) actions with national implications, and

   (2) legislation or regulations having national impacts or national program proposals.

9. PROPOSALS FOR LEGISLATION OR REGULATIONS

Proposals for regulations and legislation will be evaluated by the initiating Washington Headquarters office for compliance with the appropriate NEPA requirements. The proposal may require the development of an EA and FONSI, or an EIS which will be the responsibility of the initiating office in consultation with HEV-10. When a draft EIS for proposed legislation is appropriate, it will be submitted to OST for transmittal to the Office of Management and Budget for circulation in the normal legislative clearance process. Any comments received on the EIS will be transmitted to Congress. Except as provided in 40 CFR Part 1506(b)(2), there need not be a final EIS.

APPENDIX C

THE DELPHI METHOD OF CONSENSUS BUILDING

Developed as a method for structuring the group communication process so that a group of indviduals can deal with a complex problem as a single unit, the Delphi technique has proved to be an effective method of building a consensus within a single group with divergent interests.[1] The characteristics of the method which make the achievement of a consensus more likely include provisions for assessments of the overall group judgment, feedback of individual contributions to the process, an opportunity for individuals to revise their views, and some degree of anonymity.[2]

The conventional Delphi process typically involves the distribution of a questionnaire to a set of participants so that they can individually rank problems or measures according to a perceived order of priority. The results of the survey are then summarized; response means, medians, and variances are computed and redistributed to the respondents along with another questionnaire. This feedback of results encourages the participants to either reinforce their beliefs and stand by their initial response or reconsider and modify their rankings. The process can go through several rounds of voting, collation, and feedback; and with each iteration the distribution of individual responses narrows. The Delphi method tends to either move the opinions of participants toward a fairly strong consensus or to polarize them, thereby identifying areas of disagreement on which open discussion would be desirable.

---

[1] N. Dalkey and O. Helmer, "An Experimental Application of the Delphi Method to the Use of Experts," *Management Science*, vol. 9, no. 3, April 1963.

[2] A. Linstone and M. Turoff (eds.), *The Delphi Method: Techniques and Applications*, Addison-Wesley, Reading, Mass., 1975.

In the Chicago case discussed in Chap. 10, the technique was used to ensure that all members of the subcommittee would have an equal opportunity to influence the outcome in terms of the priorities to be considered in project selection.[3] Mail-back questionnaires were used over three rounds. In the second and third rounds, each respondent was provided with a summary of the group's voting in the previous round and a reminder of how he/she had voted, giving each one an opportunity to modify the rankings (Fig. C-1). Close contact was maintained between the technical staff and decision makers throughout the process so that any confusion over procedures or measures could be dealt with.

The results of the process in the Chicago case are outlined in Table C-1. It shows a general trend toward convergence on a mean value for most of the measures. Note that participants generally value project effectiveness in 1985 more than effectiveness at the

[3] D. Wilson and J. Schofer, "Decision-Maker-Defined Cost-Effectiveness Framework for Highway Programming," *Transportation Research Record 677*, Transportation Research Board, Washington, D.C., 1978.

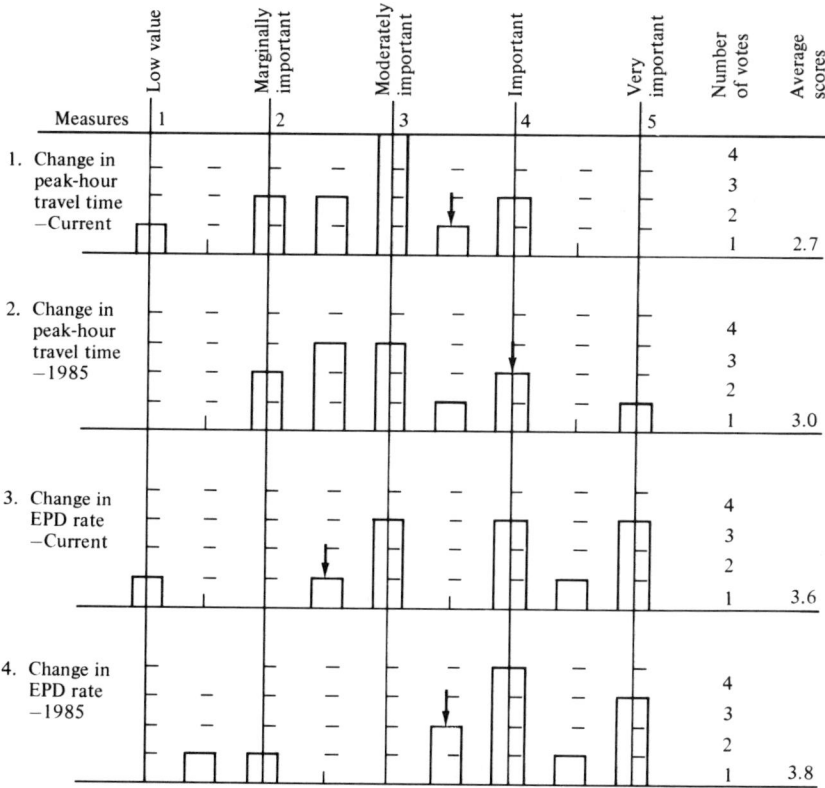

Figure C-1 Example of Delphi measure weighting response form. (D. Wilson and J. Schofer, "Decision-Maker-Defined Cost-Effectiveness Framework for Highway Programming," *Transportation Research Record 677*, Transportation Research Board, Washington, D.C., 1978.)

Table C-1 Means and variances of measure weights for three rounds of Delphi process

	Round 1		Round 2		Round 3	
Measure	Average	Variance	Average	Variance	Average	Variance
Peak-hour travel time						
1975	2.7	0.84	2.7	0.75	2.9	0.27
1985	3.0	0.61	3.0	0.81	2.9	0.97
Equivalent property damage rate						
1975	3.7	1.79	3.6	1.47	3.8	0.79
1985	4.2	0.78	3.8	1.24	4.1	1.3
Volume/capacity						
1975	3.5	0.91	3.5	1.2	3.7	0.46
1985	3.9	0.04	3.8	0.95	3.9	0.32
Off-peak daily travel time						
1975	2.5	1.0	2.6	0.65	2.6	0.28
1985	3.2	1.31	2.8	1.19	2.8	0.62
Environment, 1975						
Noise pollution	2.7	0.39	2.7	0.61	2.6	0.45
Air pollution	2.5	0.79	2.5	0.94	2.5	0.8
Dwellings	3.4	2.17	2.8	1.86	3.1	0.95

Note: 1985 environmental variables have the same value as 1975 variables.

time the decisions were to be made. The simple weighting system used in this case grouped the relevant measures into traffic- and environment-related sets, both of which carried measure-specific weights created by the Delphi process.

INDEX

INDEX

Access facilities:
  controlled, 321–326
  uncontrolled, 326–329
Accessibility factor in location choice, 180
Advocacy planning, 83
Aggregation:
  and data collection, 113–115
  in demand analysis, 230
  in logit demand model, 265–268
Air quality, 53–55
Air quality impact, 338–342
  Denver example, 211
  dispersion models, 339
  emission models, 339
  nomographs for estimating, 338
Altshuler, A., 81, 85
Analysis:
  definition of, 159
  identification of alternatives for, 162
  relationship of, to decision making, 161
  trend, 233–235
  use of models for, 165
  (See also Demand analysis; Supply analysis)
Annual cost assessment method, 404
Arc elasticity demand model, 237
"Arthur Andersen model," 357–359
Assessment methods:
  multiobjective, 406–409
  single objective: annual cost, 404
    benefit/cost, 403–406
    present worth, 403
    rate of return, 405
Attractiveness factor in location choice, 180

Automobile:
  costs to user of, 355, 360–361
  role of, 3–4

Baltimore Corridor study, 419–426
BART impact study, 35, 60, 66
Benefits and costs in evaluation:
  characteristics within, 384–387
  and consumer surplus, 387
  determination of, 392–394
  measurement of, 387
  ratio, 403–407
  and user benefit measures, 387–394
Biemiller, A., 355
Boulding, K., 7
Braybrooke, D., 83

Campbell, D., 427
Capacity, 38, 318
Chicago Area Transportation Study, 78–80
Chicago "futures" conference, 399
Choice theory:
  application of, 269–273
  basis of, in utility theory, 257–259
  probit and logit models in (see Logit demand model)
Cochran, W., 115
Community analysis model (CAM), 196–201
Congestion, 24
Consumer travel behavior:
  demand functions in, 168
  and generalized cost of travel, 169–170
  utility maximization in, 168

Consumer travel behavior *(Cont.)*:
  and value of time, 170
Contingency planning, 59
Cost effectiveness:
  and evaluation, 375
  and priority setting, 450
Cost models:
  automobile use, 355, 360
  basic concepts of, 351–361
  transit, 355–360
Costs (*see* Transportation system costs; Travel costs)
Critical lane method, 327

Data collection:
  classification schemes for, 113–115
  and demand analysis, 227, 276
  and logit demand model, 268
  management plan for, 130–136
  sampling methods in, 115–122
  techniques for, 122–130
  transit applications, 126, 128, 129
  use of, in problem and opportunity identification, 145–152
Decision makers, 8
Decision making:
  and analysis, 161
  characteristics of, 96–98
  conceptual models of, 87–95
    incrementalist approach, 90–91
    organizational process approach, 91–92
    political bargaining approach, 92–93
    rational actor approach, 81, 88–89
    satisficing approach, 89–90
  and demand, 226
  and evaluation, 373–378
  political nature of, 84–87
  and project programming, 437
  and supply, 294–299

Decision-oriented transportation planning, 98–102, 105
Decision variables, 315, 331
Demand analysis:
  choice of technique in, 275
  data collection in, 227, 276
  definitions and basic concepts of, 228–232
  forecasting in, 283
  manual techniques in, 242–244
  and planning process, 225–227
  problem identification in, 274
  tasks within, 273
  and types of aggregation, 230
Denver transportation control plan, 211–217
Derived demand, 228
Diagnostic measures (*see* Performance measures)
Direct demand elasticity model, 235
Disadvantaged, provision of mobility for, 45–51
Discounting:
  and capital recovery factor, 396, 404
  and present value, 395
  rate of, 395–398
  and rate of return, 395, 405
  and real value of money, 395
DRAM land use model, 192

Ecology, 52–53
Economic concepts, 168–173
  consumer travel behavior and, 168–170
  equilibrium, 171–172
  supply curve, 170–172
  welfare measures, 172–173
Economic development, 59–60
Effectiveness, measures of (MOEs):
  characteristics of, 378–383

Effectiveness, measures of (MOEs) *(Cont.)*:
  in cost-effectiveness evaluation, 375
  definition of, 138
  and demand analysis, 275
  and impact-incidence matrix, 382
  and supply analysis, 322
Elasticity-based demand models, 235–242
EMPIRIC land use model, 185–188
Employment forecasting, 184
Energy (*see* Fuel consumption)
Equilibrium:
  economic definition of, 171–172
  and trip assignment, 255–256
Evaluation:
  a priori, 372
  characteristics of, 166–167
  definition of, 159, 373
  measurement of effectiveness in, 378–383
  process of, 372–378
  uncertainty in, 398–403
  (*See also* Benefits and costs in evaluation; Ex post evaluation)
Evaluation framework:
  characteristics implicit in, 373–375
  and cost effectiveness, 406
  types of approaches, 375–378
Ex post evaluation:
  basis of, 372–373, 426
  comparison strategies in, 426–427
  experimental design considerations in, 427–429
  relation of, to implementation strategies, 429–431

Fiscal austerity, 2
Fleet size, 318
Florian, M., 282

Fluid-flow approximations, 310–314
Forecasting:
  and demand analysis, 283
  employment, 184
  of funds, 450–455
  land use, 183–210
  population, 184
Freight (*see* Urban goods movement)
Fuel consumption:
  estimation techniques for, 348–351
  impacts of, 56–59, 348
Funding, availability of, 450–455

Garin, R., 188
Goals-achievement matrix, 408
Goals and objectives:
  definition of, 138–141
  public involvement in, 136
  and transportation planning, 8, 443
Guideways, 37–40

Hamer, A., 84
Headway, 318
Household characteristics, 4

Impact models:
  air quality, 338–342
  fuel consumption, 348–351
  noise, 342–348
Impacts of transportation systems:
  economic, 59–61
  physical, 51–59
  social, 61–62
Innovation, 85
Inventories, 126–127

Joint development, 67

Kain, J., 35
Keeler, T., 35

Land use:
   forecasting, 183–210
      data base requirements, 183
      econometric methods, 185–188
      heuristic methods, 188–192
      limitations of, 203–204
      scenario methods, 201, 203
      simulation methods, 192–201
      types of, 184
   inventory, 127
   and transportation, 62–68, 178–184
   (*See also* Urban activity system)
Lee, D., 182
Lindblom, C., 83
Location choice, 180
Logit demand model:
   and aggregation, 265–268
   data requirements of, 268
   decision structure in, 262–264
   and independence of irrelevant alternatives, 260–262
   and model transferability, 268
   and utility function specification, 264–265
Lowry land use model, 188–192

Maintenance system, 6
Manual demand techniques, 242–244
Market research:
   and Likert scale, 141
   and market segmentation, 141
   and scaling, 143–144
   use of attitudes and preferences in, 144
Massachusetts Bay Transportation Authority (MBTA), 92–93
Mathematical programming, 315–317

Measures of effectiveness (*see* Effectiveness, measures of)
Metropolitan Atlanta Regional Transit Authority (MARTA), 462–466
Metropolitan Toronto Transportation Plan Review, 84
Metropolitan Transportation Commission (MTC), San Francisco, 272
Meyer, J., 35
Microcomputers:
   and comparative assessment, 409
   and demand analysis, 226
Minimum path algorithms, 331
Mobility, provision of, 44–51
Modal split, 251–252
   freeway simulation example, 322–326
   trends in, 27–31
   and trip-end models, 252
   and trip-interchange models, 252–254
Model calibration, 277–279
Model validation, 280–283
Munro, S., 355

NBER land use model, 193–196
Networks:
   analysis problems in, 329–332
   centroids in, 301
   computer packages for, 301
   definition of, 13, 301
   links and nodes in, 301
   routes in, 301
Nguyen, S., 282
Noise:
   decibel measurement of, 55, 57, 342
   equivalent levels of, 344
   impacts of, 56, 342–348
   models of, 342–348

Nomographs in air quality
 estimations, 338

Office of Technology Assessment
 (OTA), 84
Origin-destination analysis:
 and boundary types, 125
 definition of, 229
 survey techniques for, 125

Performance, 299–303
Performance analysis applications:
 exclusive right-of-way operations,
  318–321
 out-of-vehicle measures, 334–338
 shared right-of-way operations,
  321–334
Performance analysis techniques:
 fluid-flow approximation, 310–314
 mathematical programming,
  315–317
 queuing theory, 308–310
 simulation, 314–315
 time-distance diagrams, 304–308
Performance index (PI), 322, 331
Performance measures:
 characteristics of, 145–150
 standards of, 145
Pill, J., 84
Pivot-point demand elasticity
 analysis, 237
Planner, role of, 11, 87, 373
Planning:
 advocacy, 83
 analysis and evaluation in, 161
 and community involvement, 102,
  136, 150
 contingency, 59
 and decision-making process,
  77–105
 and demand analysis, 225–227

Planning *(Cont.)*:
 political factors in, 85–86
 purpose of, 1
 sketch, 162–164, 226
 (*See also* Transportation planning)
Poisson distribution, 309
Political factors:
 in decision making, 84–87, 92–93
 in evolution of transportation
  planning, 81
 and ex post evaluation, 373
 and innovations, 85
Present worth assessment method,
 403
Priority setting, 443, 446–450
Problem identification:
 and data collection, 145–152
 and decision-oriented planning
  process, 97, 99, 103
 and demand analysis, 274
 and public involvement, 150–152
Project priorities, 446–450, 457–462
Project programming process:
 characteristics of effective, 443–
  446
 and decision making, 101, 438
 definition of, 437
 and document design, 455–457
 and related analytical techniques,
  439
Public involvement:
 in decision-oriented planning
  process, 102
 in evaluation process, 377
 in goals and objectives, 138
 in problem identification, 150–152

Queuing theory, 308–310

Rate of return assessment method,
 405

Rate of traffic flow, 38, 305
Rehabilitation, system, 6

Sampling:
  methods of: cluster, 116
    sequential, 116
    simple random, 115
    stratified random, 116
  size determination factors in: data
      item proportion, 115–122
    level of confidence, 116–117
    margin of error, 116
    normal distribution, 117
    t distribution, 118
  steps involved in, 115
Sargent, Francis W., 88
Scale of analysis, 99
Scenarios, 201, 203
Scheduling:
  problems of, 332–334
  of transportation services, 299
Service, level of, 38
Shortest path tree, 332
Signal optimization, 329, 331
Simulation methods:
  freeway flow example, 322–326
  in land use forecasting, 192–201
  in system performance, 314–315
Sketch planning, 162–164, 226
Southeastern Wisconsin Regional
    Planning Commission
    (SEWRPC):
  and Milwaukee area transit study,
      410–419
  and transportation improvement
      program preparation, 457–462
Speed, 37, 303, 320
Stanley, J., 427
Suburbanization, 5–6
Supply analysis:
  components of, 294
  decision-maker involvement, 295

Supply analysis *(Cont.)*:
  planning contexts of, 298
  relation of, to other planning
      functions, 296–297
  types of, 294–295
Supply curve, 170–172

Terminals, 40–44
Time-distance diagrams, 304
Traffic analysis zones, 113
Traffic counts, 127–128
Traffic flow density, 38, 303
Traffic volume, 38, 303
Transfer time, 337–338
Transportation:
  and the elderly, 45–47
  and the handicapped, 47–48
  impact of, on land values, 65–66,
      179
  and the poor, 48–51
  roles for, 4–5
  technologies of, 13–15
  (*See also* Land use, and
      transportation)
Transportation improvement
    program (TIP), 442, 455–462
Transportation planning:
  and a priori evaluation, 372
  characteristics of, 9–11, 82
  data base for, 110–111, 136–138
  and decision making, 83–87, 96–98,
      373
  decision-oriented, 98–102, 105
  definition of, 8
  and demand analysis, 225–227
  evolution of, 77–87
  and ex post evaluation, 426
  and institutional environment, 15,
      81, 181
  and land use planning, 178
  long-range, 8–9
  and programming, 438, 443

Transportation planning *(Cont.)*:
  rational model, 77–81
  short-range, 8–9
  steps in, 102–105
  and supply analysis, 294–299
Transportation system costs:
  capital, 353
  cost models, 355–361
  and evaluation, 392, 394–398
  operating, 38, 353
Travel, urban:
  characteristics of, 21–23
  flows, 20
  peaking, 23–25
Travel costs:
  generalized, 228
  by mode, 32–37
  social, 35
Travel time:
  and exclusive right-of-way operations, 320
  savings, benefit from, 389
  value of, 36
Trend analysis, 233–235
Trip assignment:
  capacity restraint method, 255
  minimum path method, 254
  stochastic method, 256
  system optimization, 254
  user equilibrium, 255–256
Trip chain, 229
Trip distribution:
  gravity model, 250–251
  types of models, 250
Trip generation:
  category analysis, 248–250
  and end classification, 246
  regression model, 247–248
Trips:
  decision process in making, 21, 230
  definition of, 21, 229
  length of, 22
  modal distribution of, 27–31

Trips *(Cont.)*:
  purpose of, 21–23, 229
  spatial distribution of, 27
  temporal distribution of, 23–27

Uncertainty:
  in evaluation process, 398–403
    and program/plan flexibility method, 402
    and scenario building method, 399
  in transportation planning, 3
Urban activity system:
  a priori evaluation, 211
  bid rent, 179
  concepts related to, 178
  and demand analysis, 226
  ex post evaluation, 210
  (*See also* Land use, and transportation)
Urban goods movement, 21
Urban sprawl:
  evolution of, 63
  factors that influence, 67
Urban transportation modeling system (UTMS):
  function of, 182, 244–246, 256
  modal split, 251–253
  role of, in planning, 225–227
  trip assignment, 254
  trip distribution, 250–251
  trip generation, 246–250
User benefit measures:
  accident reductions, 391
  reduced operating costs, 391–392
  travel time savings, 389–391
Utility:
  and consumer travel behavior, 168–170
  multiattribute method in evaluation of, 408–409
  random, concept of, 258

Utility *(Cont.)*:
   specification in logit model,
      258–260

Validity, internal and external:
   definitions of, 427
   threats to, 428–429
Variable work-hour programs, 25
Vuchic, V., 36

Wachs, M., 45
Wait time, 336
Walk time, 335
Welfare measures:
   compensating variation in, 172–173
   and consumer surplus, 172–173,
      387–389
   equivalent variation in, 172
Williams, W., 429
Wohl, M., 35